X 6570

Register Your Book

at ibmpressbooks.com/ibmregister

Upon registration, we will send you electronic sample chapters from two of our popular IBM Press books. In addition, you will be automatically entered into a monthly drawing for a free IBM Press book.

Registration also entitles you to:

- Notices and reminders about author appearances, conferences, and online chats with special guests

- Access to supplemental material that may be available

- Advance notice of forthcoming editions

- Related book recommendations

- Information about special contests and promotions throughout the year

- Chapter excerpts and supplements of forthcoming books

Contact us

If you are interested in writing a book or reviewing manuscripts prior to publication, please write to us at:

Editorial Director, IBM Press
c/o Pearson Education
800 East 96th Street
Indianapolis, IN 46240

e-mail: IBMPress@pearsoned.com

Visit us on the Web: ibmpressbooks.com

Lotus® Notes® Developer's Toolbox

IBM Press

The developerWorks® Series

T he IBM Press developerWorks Series represents a unique undertaking in which print books and the Web are mutually supportive. The publications in this series are complemented by their association with resources available at the developerWorks Web site on ibm.com. These resources include articles, tutorials, forums, software, and much more.

Through the use of icons, readers will be able to immediately identify a resource on developerWorks which relates to that point of the text. A summary of links appears at the end of each chapter. Additionally, you will be able to access an electronic guide of the developerWorks links and resources through ibm.com/developerworks/dwbooks that reference developerWorks Series publications, deepening the reader's experiences.

A developerWorks book offers readers the ability to quickly extend their information base beyond the book by using the deep resources of developerWorks and at the same time enables developerWorks readers to deepen their technical knowledge and skills.

For a full listing of developerWorks Series publications, please visit: **ibmpressbooks.com/dwseries**.

Lotus® Notes®
Developer's Toolbox

Tips for Rapid and Successful Deployment

developerWorks® Series

Mark Elliott

IBM Press
Pearson plc
Upper Saddle River, NJ • Boston • Indianapolis • San Francisco
New York • Toronto • Montreal • London • Munich • Paris • Madrid
Capetown • Sydney • Tokyo • Singapore • Mexico City
ibmpressbooks.com

IBM Press Program Managers: Tara Woodman, Ellice Uffer
Cover design: IBM Corporation

Published by Pearson plc
Publishing as IBM Press

IBM Press offers excellent discounts on this book when ordered in quantity for bulk purchases or special sales, which may include electronic versions and/or custom covers and content particular to your business, training goals, marketing focus, and branding interests. For more information, please contact:

U.S. Corporate and Government Sales
1-800-382-3419
corpsales@pearsontechgroup.com

For sales outside the United States, please contact:

International Sales
international@pearsoned.com

This Book Is Safari Enabled

The Safari® Enabled icon on the cover of your favorite technology book means the book is available through Safari Bookshelf. When you buy this book, you get free access to the online edition for 45 days. Safari Bookshelf is an electronic reference library that lets you easily search thousands of technical books, find code samples, download chapters, and access technical information whenever and wherever you need it.

To gain 45-day Safari Enabled access to this book:

- Go to http://www.awprofessional.com/safarienabled
- Complete the brief registration form
- Enter the coupon code 3ND6-RHZD-FJA5-3GEV-BW57

If you have difficulty registering on Safari Bookshelf or accessing the online edition, please e-mail customer-service@safaribooksonline.com.

Library of Congress Cataloging-in-Publication Data

Elliott, Mark, 1968-
  Lotus Notes developer's toolbox : tips for rapid and successful deployment / Mark Elliott.
    p. cm.
  ISBN 0-13-221448-2 (pbk. : alk. paper)
  1. Lotus Notes. 2. Computer software--Development. 3. Computer security. 4. Business--Computer programs.   I. Title.
  HF5548.4.L692E45 2006
  005.5'7--dc22

                                                        2006023492

Pearson Education, Inc.
Rights and Contracts Department
75 Arlington Street, Suite 300
Boston, MA 02116
Fax: (617) 848-7047
ISBN 0-13-221448-2

Text printed in the United States on recycled paper at RR Donnelly in Crawfordsville, Indiana.

First printing, October 2006

This book is dedicated to my wonderful sons
Ryan and Alex.

Contents

Chapter 3   Navigating the Domino Designer Workspace   21

Chapter 4   Domino Design Elements   33

Chapter 11   Workflow Applications   303

Chapter 15   View Enhancements   487

Chapter 16   Sample Agents   503

Preface

A Vision

Welcome to the *Lotus® Notes® Developer's Toolbox*. Let me start by saying ... I've been in your shoes. I've stood in a local bookstore skimming through publications and wondering how this book is any different from the others on the shelf. Does this book cover the information I need? Will it give me the answers I need? Will it show me step-by-step what to do? These are legitimate questions that deserve a forthright answer.

Having spent the last 20 years developing applications that span the spectrum of technology—from mainframe software to those hosted and accessed from Web servers—I've purchased numerous "how to" books. Most of them taught language syntax, explained rules, and provided abbreviated code examples intended to illustrate a particular programming technique or structure. Although these books had benefits, in my experience they tended to leave me "holding the bag," so to speak, when it came time to develop and implement an application. So what was missing?

Applied knowledge. In other words, most books provided the ingredients but left out the most important part ... the recipe. It's with this thought in mind that I set out to write this book for you. The approach is simple—to provide you with both the ingredients and the recipes to build the most common types of Lotus® Notes® applications and to provide an approach whereby you can learn, through example, to build and customize any Lotus Notes application. With this approach, you will find the explanations you need to successfully build and deploy Lotus Domino® solutions.

If you're under pressure to develop, enhance, and deploy Domino applications, then this book is for you.

Target Audience

Corporate management often has an overly simplistic view and understanding of Lotus Notes development. It's not uncommon for a manager to ask a programmer who has little to no exposure to Notes to develop an application. They assume anyone with a technology degree or programming experience is instantly a Notes development expert.

Although the "any programmer can do it" mentality bears merit, there are still many concepts that must be understood in order to obtain a fundamental proficiency in Lotus development. This book provides the fundamental building blocks and common enhancements that will enable you to successfully develop and support Lotus Notes application development. Unlike any other publication on the market, this book streamlines the learning process from the perspective of an experienced application developer.

This book is intended for any reader who supports a Lotus Notes database application. Readers should have a general understanding of and exposure to application development. However, based on the unique delivery approach, this publication is beneficial to novice and experienced Lotus Notes developers alike. It provides everything needed to streamline the design, development, customization, and support of Lotus Notes applications.

A Tour of the Book

This book features a unique delivery approach that will enable you to rapidly and successfully develop and deploy Lotus Notes applications, which can be classified into one of five categories:

1. Calendar
2. Collaboration
3. Reference Library
4. Workflow
5. Web Site

This book explains how to develop each of these application types and will enable readers to understand and quickly build rock-solid applications.

The publication also includes a wide variety of ready-to-use customizations that can be applied to one of the templates or virtually any database.

Chapter 1, "An Introduction to the Lotus Domino Tool Suite," provides a general overview of the Lotus tool suite. The chapter briefly describes and illustrates the various client and server applications required for a Lotus Notes database.

Chapter 2, "Getting Started with Designer," describes how to install and launch the Lotus Domino Designer client. The chapter also briefly introduces the concept of using templates to create a new Notes database.

Chapter 3, "Navigating the Domino Designer Workspace," presents concise information for navigating the Lotus Domino Designer client. It examines the client layout and general development "panes" used to manage the design and development of a Notes database application.

Chapter 4, "Domino Design Elements," continues to describe the Domino Designer client and explains each of the design elements including framesets, pages, forms, fields, layout regions, sections, buttons, views, folders, shared objects, and libraries. This chapter explains each design element and ways to implement them.

Chapter 5, "An Introduction to Formula Language," deals with the rules and syntax of the Lotus Formula Language. The chapter includes a synopsis of the most common functions and commands.

Chapter 6, "An Introduction to LotusScript," presents the foundations for developing LotusScript routines. LotusScript is a structured, object-oriented programming (OOP) language that's similar to Visual Basic®. Using LotusScript, you can create robust, cross-platform applications. This chapter provides an introduction to the programming language and reviews the basic concepts of object-oriented application development.

Chapter 7, "Fundamentals of a Notes Application," introduces a general roadmap for developing a Lotus Notes database. It explains each of the primary database types and includes a step-by-step project specifically designed to teach how to integrate the various design elements into working database applications. As part of the development process, it also includes sample project plans, schedules, and considerations for managing the project.

Chapter 8, "Calendar Applications," describes the step-by-step procedure for creating a calendar application. The chapter includes two projects that illustrate both a simple and a complex recurrent calendar event. The completed project can be used to schedule conference rooms, reserve equipment, and track vacation plans among other uses.

Chapter 9, "Collaborative Applications," contains the process for building a collaborative database application. Using a collaborative database, team members can collaborate and share information. The chapter includes a discussion forum project and a project control notebook. These projects illustrate how to distribute information through email, response documents, and categorized view columns.

Chapter 10, "Reference Library Applications," further explains how to create a Lotus Notes database to store historical information and includes two projects. The first project illustrates the concept of a reference library by creating a database to manage connection documents. Connection documents are often used to correct the error "Unable to connect to server" typically encountered by users. The second project explains how to generate a Microsoft Excel® spreadsheet for a Notes database.

Chapter 11, "Workflow Applications," details the process for creating a workflow application. A workflow can be defined as a series of activities or steps required to perform a specific business goal. Using a workflow application, you can electronically route documents for action or approval. This type of application allows business users to electronically monitor and track the movement of documents. Workflow applications are ideal for documents that require multiple approvals or actions.

Chapter 12, "Web Applications," discusses how to create a database that can be accessed both from the Lotus Notes client and from a supported Internet browser. This chapter includes a project to build a general-purpose Web application that is accessible from a browser. For illustrative purposes, the database tracks corporate assets; however, the content and form can be customized to meet your individual needs.

Chapter 13, "Design Enhancements Using LotusScript," provides common LotusScript customizations that can be incorporated into most Lotus Notes database applications. Each customization module is self-contained and ready to run. This enables you to copy the code into any existing application with little to no modification.

Chapter 14, "Design Enhancements Using Formula Language," continues to describe customizations that can be applied to virtually any Notes database. This chapter is focused specifically on the Lotus Formula Language. Each customization includes a description of the code, an explanation of how the code works, and instructions for implementing it.

Chapter 15, "View Enhancements," describes several enhancements that can be added to a Lotus Notes view. Readers will learn how to add icons, double-click on a calendar date to create a new document, sort and categorize documents, and several techniques to retrieve view design properties associated with a database application.

Chapter 16, "Sample Agents," provides several sample agents used to automate repeatable tasks. The chapter explains how to create an agent to email weekly status reports or modify all documents that have a field with a particular data value.

Chapter 17, "Miscellaneous Enhancements and Tips for Domino Databases," presents a number of general customizations that can be incorporated into almost any Lotus Notes database application. In this chapter, readers will learn how to add field hints to a form, use a static popup to display text messages (or help), inherit fields between forms, add an icon to an action button, create a custom application interface, set the field tab order, and disable database replication.

Chapter 18, "Data Management," provides tools and techniques that can be used to manage application data. This chapter explains how to import data, export data, copy documents, create agents to manipulate data, and archive application documents.

Chapter 19, "Security," provides information pertaining to database security, access permissions, and roles.

Chapter 20, "Application Deployment and Maintenance," explains how to set up a Lotus Notes development environment and deploy an application. Chapter topics include database templates, replacing/refreshing a database design, creating an application install button, and backup considerations.

Chapter 21, "Troubleshooting," provides some tips and strategies for troubleshooting Formula Language, LotusScript, agents, and general application development problems and errors.

Append A, "Online Project Files and Sample Applications," describes the developer's toolbox. It details the project files, development tools, example graphics, and ready-to-use sample databases provided with the publication.

Appendix B, "Lotus Notes/Domino: What's Next?," outlines the future direction of Lotus Notes. Here you will learn about the "Hannover" release, composite applications, Workplace™ tools, and the Websphere Portlet Factory.

Book Layout

This publication is divided into three primary areas: introduction to Domino architecture and development, building projects, and application support. Chapters 1 through 7 provide an introduction to the Domino software as well as the general programming syntax for LotusScript and Formula Language. Chapters 8 through 12 teach Domino application development through step-by-step procedures. Here you learn how to develop Lotus Notes databases through hands-on experience. Readers who prefer to learn through experience and exposure to the software may want to start with the projects and refer back to the earlier chapters for additional information. Chapters 13 through 21 focus on application enhancements and support. These chapters provide ready-to-run database enhancements, information on database security, and troubleshooting. Throughout the book you'll find a wealth of illustrations, tips, and notes. These items are intended to help navigate the software, point out potential pitfalls, and help with the learning process. As terminology is introduced, the first reference will be highlighted in italic. This will signify a new term.

Readers should have a general familiarity with the Lotus Notes client and terminology, such as forms, views, and agents. Although not required, readers should have a general understanding of application development concepts and techniques.

Companion Web Site

The companion Web site provides online access to the developer's toolbox. Through the companion Web site, you can retrieve

- A working version of each project described in the publication
- An enhanced version of each project that includes additional functionality, features, and graphics
- Supplemental graphic files
- Sample project plans and project schedules
- Example data import files
- Other development tools

The developer's toolbox and companion Web site supplement the publication and learning experience. All source code required to build one of the five common database models has been provided. This enables you, the reader, to focus on "how to build" an application without having to research language syntax or re-type lines of code. After you have registered your book, you can instantly download the developer's toolbox from the companion Web site. Refer to Appendix A for additional information.

Supported Software

The projects and code provided in this publication are designed to run on Release 7 of the Lotus Notes and Domino Designer clients. However, with only a very few exceptions, these projects and enhancements can be utilized on recent versions from 5.0 through 7.0, and beyond.

Comments

As the author of this publication, I would welcome all comments, suggestions, tips, hints, corrections, best practices, likes, dislikes or general feedback on the book. Please send all correspondence or suggestions for improving the publication to the following email address:

LotusNotesAuthor@yahoo.com

Acknowledgments

It took a great many people to produce and publish this book. A special thanks to my family and all the professionals at Pearson Education and IBM who supported and helped make this book a reality. Without the understanding, contributions, and hard work of these people, this book would not have been possible:

Paul Petralia, Michelle Housley, Jessica D'Amico, Chris Guzikowski, Lori Lyons, Ben Lawson, Fadi Abu-Shaaban, David Elliott, Joan Elliott, Kathleen Elliott, Edward Elliott, Kevin Elliott, John Collinsworth, Martin Rabinowitz, Kourtnaye Sturgeon, John Wait, Peter Orbeton, Michelle Housley, Lynn Gordon Curtis, Ronnie Maffa, Jake McFarland, Michael Thurston, Christopher Brown, Thomas Duff, Mark Jourdain, Joe Litton, Karen Origlio, Michael Sobczak, Keith Strickland...

About the Author

Mark Elliott has been employed by the IBM Corporation since the early 1990s as a software engineer and project manager. As a Lotus® Notes® professional, he has been designing, developing, and implementing commercial Notes and Domino applications for industry clients such as IBM, Eastman Kodak, Qualex, Invensys, and Vanity Fair. Prior to joining IBM, he worked as an Application Programmer for the U.S. Department of Defense and as a Quality Assurance Software Engineer for the McDonnell Douglas (Boeing) Corporation.

Mark is a graduate of the University of Missouri–Columbia, where he received an interdisciplinary bachelor of arts degree in computer science. He also has a Master's Certificate from George Washington University in Project Management. Mark has been certified as a Project Management Professional by the Project Management Institute (PMI).

In addition to application development and project management, Mark has authored and been issued numerous patents for the IBM corporation. One of those patents pertains to distribution of Lotus Domino connection documents across multiple network domains.

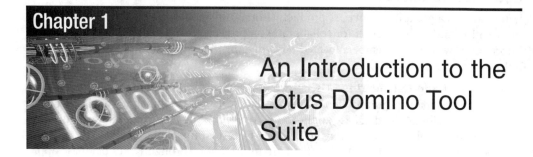

Chapter 1

An Introduction to the Lotus Domino Tool Suite

Chapter Overview

Welcome to IBM Lotus Notes and Domino, the de facto standard for collaborative applications. The Lotus family encompasses many products; this chapter provides an introduction to Lotus tool suite. Although the majority of this publication is focused on the Domino Designer client to develop Lotus Notes and Domino applications, it's important to have a general understanding of each product and how they integrate together.

By the end of the chapter you will have learned

- The main products used to develop and support Domino applications
- About the Lotus Notes client
- About the Domino Designer client
- About the Domino Administrator client
- About the Domino server

Product Overview

There are four products that comprise the Lotus Domino tool suite. Each product is intended for a specific audience. The seamless integration of these products enables applications to be designed, developed, managed, and used. They include

Lotus® Notes® client	Allows end-users to access applications
Domino Designer®	Allows developers to create applications
Domino® Administrator	Allows administrators to manage servers
Domino® server	Manages applications and processes transactions

Additional information on Lotus Notes, Lotus Domino, and the Lotus Workplace family can be found in Appendix B.

1

Lotus Notes Client

Lotus Notes is a groupware software product. Groupware applications allow people to share information and work together (or collaborate) on projects. Using Notes, you can exchange information with team members located anywhere in the world. Its strengths include the following:

- **Email and Calendaring**—Users can send and receive mail, manage personal calendars, manage group calendars, schedule meetings, and much more. As you learn to develop Notes database applications, you'll find the ability to manage and integrate email into applications to be a key feature of the Notes client.
- **Shared Information**—Users can share information through Notes database applications. Information can be accessed from client applications, Web browsers, and various mobile devices.
- **Workflow Management**—Workflow applications allow documents to be automatically processed and routed via email to users. Users can track the status of requests and utilize electronic signatures to manage paperwork.

In addition to robust features, the product incorporates rock-solid security that's unmatched by any other email and groupware products. The client can be run on virtually all Microsoft® Windows® and Apple® Macintosh® operating system platforms and supports all key Internet standards and protocols. Figure 1.1 illustrates the default startup window, which may vary slightly based on your software version and platform.

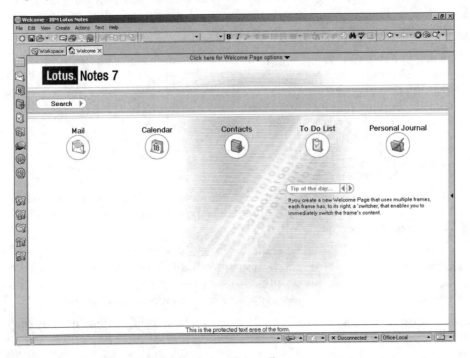

Figure 1.1   Welcome page for the Lotus Notes client

Domino Designer

The Domino Designer client is used to create, edit, and manage Lotus Notes database applications. You'll find that most application development revolves around this client. It provides a means for rapid application development and solution deployment. Its robust features enable developers to create applications that can be accessed from both Lotus Notes clients as well as most Web browsers.

Domino Designer supports and incorporates a wide array of technologies including LotusScript, Formula Language, HTML, XML, SOAP, Java, and JavaScript™, among others. Applications can be developed to interface with application servers, such as Websphere®, and to integrate with databases, such as DB2.

A.1

Many features and technologies are associated with the Designer client. However, you'll soon find that the applications can be classified into one of five categories independent of the language being used.

1. Calendar

2. Collaboration

3. Reference Library (or Data Repository)

4. Workflow

5. Web site

The majority of this book will focus on the use of Domino Designer to create each of these Notes applications. This book explains how to develop each of these application types and will enable any new Lotus Notes developer to understand and quickly build rock-solid applications.

This book is specifically intended for readers who need to design, develop, and deploy Domino applications using the Designer client. Although many languages are available, we'll focus primarily on the LotusScript, Formula, and HTML languages to build applications. Figure 1.2 illustrates the default startup window, which may vary slightly based on your software version and platform.

TIP

Did you know Lotus Notes applications can reside on either the local workstation or a Domino server?

Applications that reside "On Local" are typically for personal use and cannot be accessed by other users, whereas applications that reside "On Server" can be accessed by many other people concurrently.

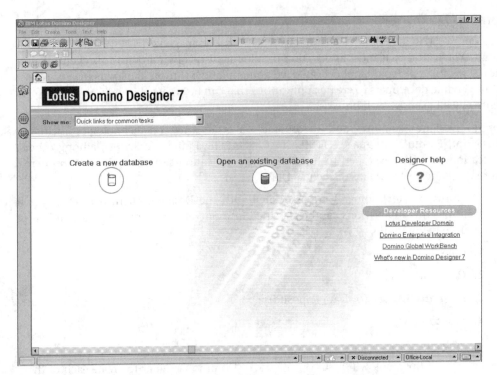

Figure 1.2   Welcome page for the Domino Designer client

Domino Administrator

The Domino Administrator client is used to manage Domino servers and Notes applications that reside on the server. Features of the Domino Administrator client include

- Server management
- Remote server console
- Roaming user support
- Smart upgrades used to deploy Lotus Notes clients
- Server analysis, monitoring, and statistics
- Policy-based management used to automate tasks
- Active directory synchronization
- License tracking
- Server activity logging
- LZ1 data compression support
- Management of spam filters
- Management of mail file quotas

- Management of Web sites
- Management of Web users
- Automatic fault and recovery monitoring of Domino servers
- Database file and Access Control management

Figure 1.3 illustrates a typical Lotus Domino Administrator client display. You'll notice the screen is divided into multiple sections and navigation panes. Across the top of the window there are a number of "tabs" used to display and configure server information. Along the left side of the display are selection options to display information. In this example, Server Tasks has been selected. In the middle of the screen are the actual server tasks associated with the server. Finally, on the right side of the screen are additional tools used to configure and manage the server.

The server administrator may be a single person or a group of people. Many larger companies have a dedicated team of people that manage and monitor multiple Domino servers, whereas smaller companies may only have a single server with one person dedicated to both server administration and application development.

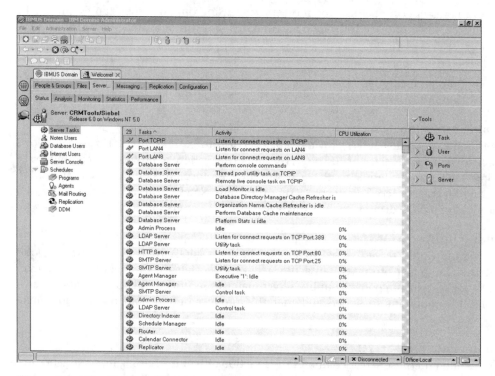

Figure 1.3   The Domino Administrator client

> **TIP**
>
> A good working relationship with your Domino server administrator can help with application deployment, implementation, and debugging.
>
> Administrators manage the server and applications that reside on the server. Administrators have authority to run specialized tools to troubleshoot or analyze databases, set security permissions, "sign" agents, and view the server logs. The server log often contains clues that are helpful in debugging application errors and resolving user access.

Domino Server

A.1.4

The Lotus Domino server is used to process transaction requests associated with security, messaging, Notes, Web applications, and email routing. Lotus offers a variety of configuration packages that enable customers to tailor the Domino server functionality to manage specific business needs.

IBM and Lotus offer numerous Domino Server licensing options—they can essentially be divided into three primary software configurations and can be installed on virtually any operating system platform.

- Domino Messaging server
- Domino Utility server
- Domino Enterprise server

Domino Messaging Server

The Domino Messaging server provides email services to business users. This server allows people to send and receive email. The server supports a variety of protocols including SMTP (Simple Mail Transfer Protocol), POP3 (Post Office Protocol version 3), MAPI, and IMAP (Internet Messaging Access Protocol). Using the Lotus Notes client, a Web browser, and a wide array of mobile devices, such as the Blackberry PDA, users can access mail.

Domino Utility Server

The Domino Utility server is used to support business applications also known as Notes databases. The server processes transaction requests associated with applications. In addition to applications support, the utility server manages security and logs application transactions. It's important to understand that this product option does not include email support.

Domino Enterprise Server

The Domino Enterprise server combines the functionality of the messaging server and utility server. The enterprise server supports both email and Notes applications.

Figure 1.4 illustrates the Domino server console running on a Windows 2000 platform and shows the typical messages displayed during server startup. For most readers, the messages and information displayed in the figure are not something to be concerned about. It is simply included to give you a feel of what a server looks like.

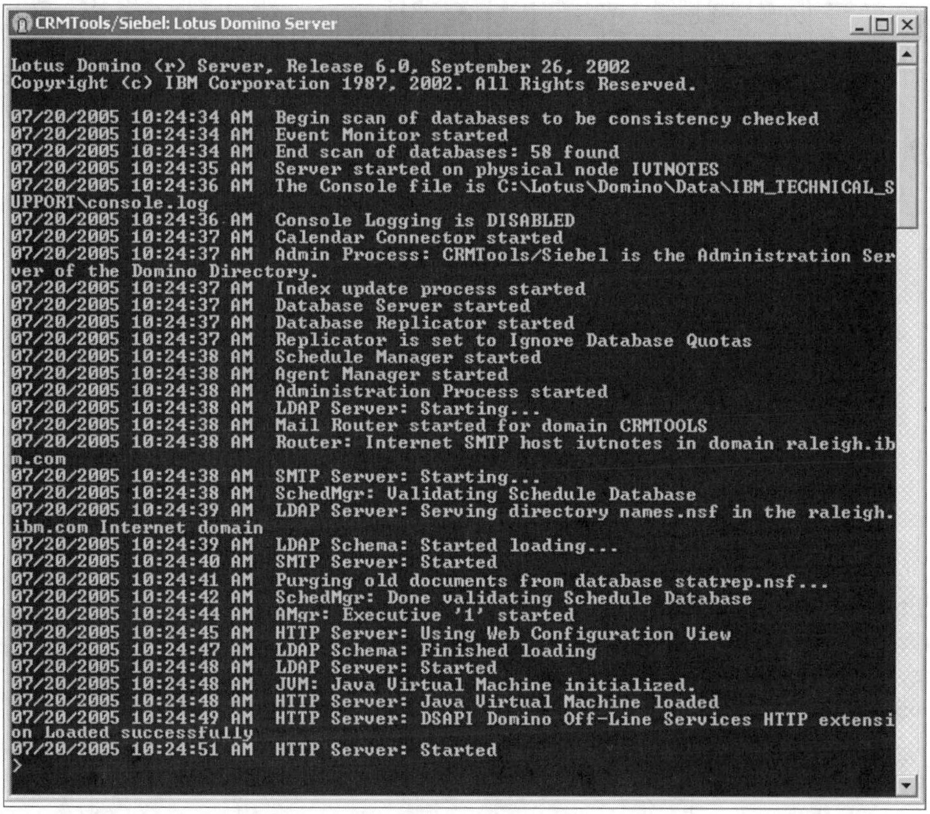

```
CRMTools/Siebel: Lotus Domino Server                          _ □ ×

Lotus Domino (r) Server, Release 6.0, September 26, 2002
Copyright (c) IBM Corporation 1987, 2002. All Rights Reserved.

07/20/2005 10:24:34 AM   Begin scan of databases to be consistency checked
07/20/2005 10:24:34 AM   Event Monitor started
07/20/2005 10:24:34 AM   End scan of databases: 58 found
07/20/2005 10:24:35 AM   Server started on physical node IVTNOTES
07/20/2005 10:24:36 AM   The Console file is C:\Lotus\Domino\Data\IBM_TECHNICAL_S
UPPORT\console.log
07/20/2005 10:24:36 AM   Console Logging is DISABLED
07/20/2005 10:24:37 AM   Calendar Connector started
07/20/2005 10:24:37 AM   Admin Process: CRMTools/Siebel is the Administration Ser
ver of the Domino Directory.
07/20/2005 10:24:37 AM   Index update process started
07/20/2005 10:24:37 AM   Database Server started
07/20/2005 10:24:37 AM   Database Replicator started
07/20/2005 10:24:37 AM   Replicator is set to Ignore Database Quotas
07/20/2005 10:24:38 AM   Schedule Manager started
07/20/2005 10:24:38 AM   Agent Manager started
07/20/2005 10:24:38 AM   Administration Process started
07/20/2005 10:24:38 AM   LDAP Server: Starting...
07/20/2005 10:24:38 AM   Mail Router started for domain CRMTOOLS
07/20/2005 10:24:38 AM   Router: Internet SMTP host ivtnotes in domain raleigh.ib
m.com
07/20/2005 10:24:38 AM   SMTP Server: Starting...
07/20/2005 10:24:38 AM   SchedMgr: Validating Schedule Database
07/20/2005 10:24:39 AM   LDAP Server: Serving directory names.nsf in the raleigh.
ibm.com Internet domain
07/20/2005 10:24:39 AM   LDAP Schema: Started loading...
07/20/2005 10:24:40 AM   SMTP Server: Started
07/20/2005 10:24:41 AM   Purging old documents from database statrep.nsf...
07/20/2005 10:24:42 AM   SchedMgr: Done validating Schedule Database
07/20/2005 10:24:44 AM   AMgr: Executive '1' started
07/20/2005 10:24:45 AM   HTTP Server: Using Web Configuration View
07/20/2005 10:24:47 AM   LDAP Schema: Finished loading
07/20/2005 10:24:48 AM   LDAP Server: Started
07/20/2005 10:24:48 AM   JVM: Java Virtual Machine initialized.
07/20/2005 10:24:48 AM   HTTP Server: Java Virtual Machine loaded
07/20/2005 10:24:49 AM   HTTP Server: DSAPI Domino Off-Line Services HTTP extensi
on Loaded successfully
07/20/2005 10:24:51 AM   HTTP Server: Started
>
```

Figure 1.4   Console window for a Domino server

Depending on the size of your organization, support team, and computing infrastructure, you may have one or more Domino servers. Larger companies typically run multiple servers, with the messaging and application management services hosted on separate servers. Smaller organizations may combine messaging and application management services to utilize a single Domino Enterprise server (see Figure 1.5).

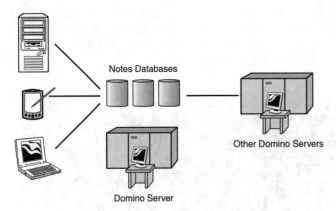

Notes Databases

Other Domino Servers

Domino Server

Figure 1.5 Interaction of workstations, mobile devices, and servers

NOTE

Domino servers are sometimes referred to as "Notes servers." The renaming of the Notes server to Domino server occurred with release 4.6.

Links to developerWorks

A.1.1 Web team. *The History of Notes and Domino.* IBM developerWorks, December 2005. http://www.ibm.com/developerworks/lotus/library/ls-NDHistory/index.html.

A.1.2 McCarrick, Dick. *New features in Lotus Domino 7.0.* IBM developerWorks, August 2005. http://www.ibm.com/developerworks/lotus/library/nd7features/index.html.

A.1.3 Branco, Debbie, McGray, Tom, and Yip, Wai-ki. *Exploiting IBM DB2 in your Lotus Domino 7 application.* IBM developerWorks, January 2006. http://www.ibm.com/developerworks/lotus/library/domino7-db2/index.html.

A.1.4 Stephen, Razeyah, and Davidson, Lori. *Choosing a platform for Domino 6.0: Hardware platform vendors.* IBM developerWorks, August 2002. http://www.ibm.com/developerworks/lotus/library/ls-HWPlatform/index.html.

Chapter 2

Getting Started with Designer

Chapter Overview

In this chapter, you'll learn how to install the Domino Designer client, navigate the application startup, and create a database using an existing application template.

By the end of the chapter you will have learned

- How to install the Domino Designer client
- How to launch the Domino Designer client
- How to create a database based on a template

Installing the Designer Client

Installing the Designer client is simple and can usually be completed in minutes. This section will summarize the installation process for Designer on a Microsoft Windows PC.

> **NOTE**
>
> You can download a free trial version of the Domino Designer client from the Lotus Web site. See the developerWorks Web link information at the end of this chapter.

dW

A.2.

These instructions are intended to be a brief summary for version 7.0 of the Designer client for Microsoft Windows®. Although the instructions, for the most part, are the same across versions, users should follow the instructions provided by Lotus when working with other versions or operating systems. Let's briefly review the system setup requirements.

Supported Microsoft Windows Platforms

- Microsoft® Windows® 98
- Microsoft® Windows® NT, Version 4.0
- Microsoft® Windows 2000® Professional
- Microsoft® Windows XP® Professional

Memory Requirements

- For Windows 98—Minimum of 64MB RAM (128MB recommended)
- For Windows NT—Minimum of 64MB RAM (128MB recommended)
- For Windows 2000—Minimum of 128MB RAM (256MB recommended)
- For Windows XP—Minimum of 128MB RAM (256MB recommended)

Disk Space Requirements

- 2MB for the Designer client
- 39MB for the Designer client help files
- Space for general application development

Before starting the installation process, you'll want to close all applications running on the Desktop. This is especially important if any Lotus products are running. Many Lotus products share files and could affect the installation process if they are running while installing the Designer application.

If you already have the Lotus Notes client installed, you'll want to back up a couple files. Make a copy of these files and store them in a different directory (or change the extension of the copied file to .BAK to store in the same directory). These files contain configuration information and could be overwritten during the installation process.

- **NOTES.INI**—This file contains preferences for the Notes client application and is typically stored either in the `C:\WinNT` or the `C:\Lotus\Notes` directory.
- **NAMES.NSF**—This file contains contact names, addresses, certificates, connection and location information and is typically stored in the `C:\Lotus\Notes\Data` directory.
- **DESKTOP.DSK**—This file contains preferences for the look and feel of your Lotus Notes workspace. This file is typically stored in the `C:\Lotus\Notes\Data` directory. Note: Depending on the version installed, this file may be named **desktop5.dsk** or **desktop6.dsk**.
- *USER*.ID File—This file identifies each person using Lotus Notes (where *user* represents a person's name). It contains your certificate keys, name, and password information. This file is typically stored in the `c:\Lotus\Notes\Data` directory.

To install the Lotus Domino Designer, follow these steps. Readers should install the Lotus Notes client and obtain a valid user ID file and password prior to performing these steps.

1. Insert the Lotus Designer CD-ROM into the computer. If your computer is set up to auto-launch, the installation routine will start automatically. If the installation program does not start, click the **Start** button and choose **Run** from the Windows

Desktop. Then enter the command **drive:\setup.exe** (for example, **d:\setup.exe**) and press **Enter**.

After the installation program starts, the Extracting Files dialog box will appear (see Figure 2.1). This process will copy a number of temporary files to your hard drive. If prompted to select a target directory, accept the default.

2. A general welcome and installation wizard startup window will be displayed (see Figure 2.2). Click **Next** to continue the installation.

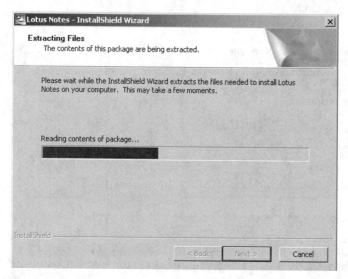

Figure 2.1 Domino Designer InstallShield startup

Figure 2.2 Domino Designer Install Wizard

3. Carefully read the license agreement (see Figure 2.3). If you agree to the terms, click the **I accept the terms in the license agreement** radio button and click **Next** to continue.

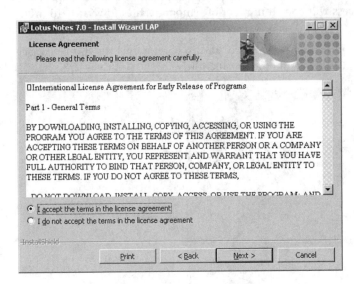

Figure 2.3   Domino Designer License Agreement

4. Specify your name and organization; for example, *Joe User* and *IBM* (see Figure 2.4). These fields can contain any text string and will not affect the installation of the Lotus products. Click **Next** to continue.

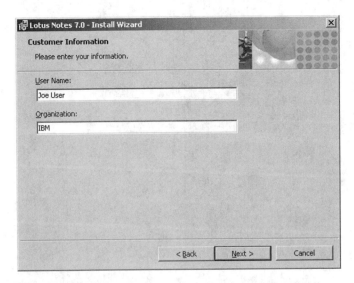

Figure 2.4   Domino Designer Customer Information

5. Accept the default installation directory (which should be C:\Lotus\Notes) and click **Next** to continue.

> **TIP**
>
> Multiple versions of Lotus Notes, Designer, and Administrator can be installed on a workstation. Simply change the default installation location to have multiple software levels installed. Installing in an alternate directory will enable you to run two separate versions of the Lotus software. Refer to the installation manual provided with the Lotus products for additional information.

6. At the installation options dialog, make sure the **Domino Designer** option is enabled. Options marked with an X *will not* be installed. Verify that the installation screen is similar to Figure 2.5.

If these items are not selected, click on the triangle to the left of the **Domino Designer** and **Designer Help** options. Select **This feature will be installed on the local hard drive** to install each of these features.

Click **Next** to continue.

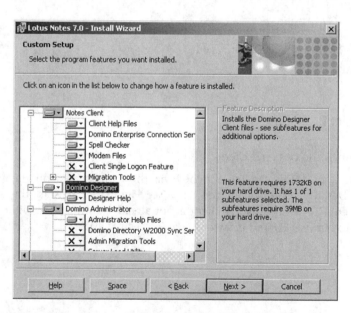

Figure 2.5   Domino Designer Install Options

7. The Ready to Install the Program dialog will display (see Figure 2.6). Click **Install**.

8. When the installation is complete, Lotus displays the Installation Complete dialog box. Click **Finish** to return to the Microsoft Windows Desktop. Congratulations, setup is now complete!

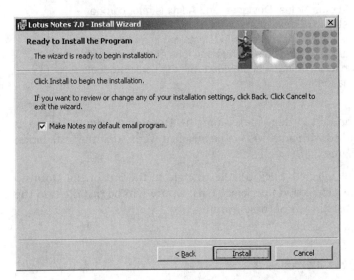

Figure 2.6   Domino Designer Ready to Install Confirmation

Launching the Designer Client

There are four methods to launch the Designer client.

1. **Windows Icon**—The application can be launched via the icon located on the Microsoft Windows Desktop. Double-click the icon (see Figure 2.7) to start the Domino Designer client. If the Lotus Notes client is not already running, you will be prompted to enter your user ID and password.

Figure 2.7   Domino Designer Desktop icon

2. **Notes Toolbar**—To launch the Designer client from the Notes toolbar, simply click the icon (see Figure 2.8). The triangle, located on the icon, signifies the Designer client application. If the icon is not displayed, then either the Designer client has not been installed or the icon has been removed from the toolbar.

Figure 2.8   Lotus Notes client left-side menu bar icon

3. **Start Menu**—Designer can be started from the Microsoft Windows operating system. Select the **Start** > **Programs** > **Lotus Applications** > **Lotus Domino Designer** menu options to start the client (see Figure 2.9).

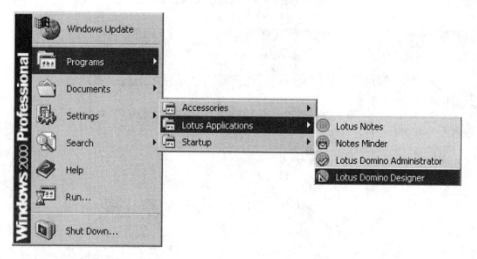

Figure 2.9   Domino Designer access from the Windows Start menu

4. **Notes Database**—The Designer client can be launched from the Notes workspace by right-clicking on the application icon and selecting **Open In Designer** from the popup menu (see Figure 2.10). You'll probably find this option to be the preferred method for opening an application in the Designer client. However, this option will not display if you do not have "Designer" or "Manager" level access to the database. See Chapter 19, "Security," for additional information.

If you launch the Designer client using Option 1, 2, or 3, you should see a display similar to Figure 2.11. Here you can create a new database, open an existing database, or display help information for the Designer client.

Figure 2.10 Starting Domino Designer from the Desktop popup menu

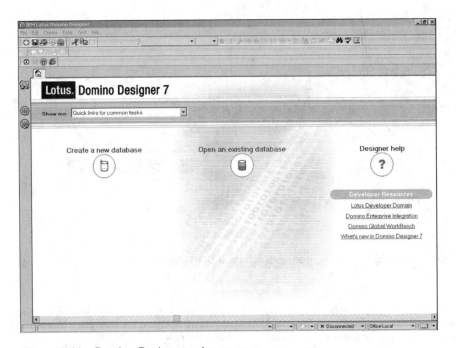

Figure 2.11 Domino Designer welcome page

However, if you elected to open an existing database using Option 4, then design elements for the database will be displayed (see Figure 2.12) instead of the default start-up window.

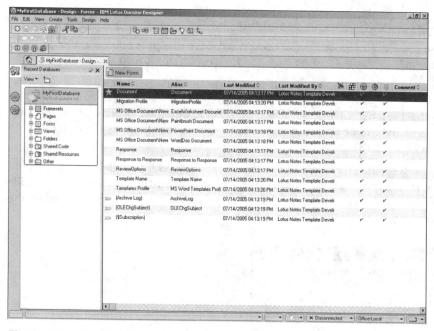

Figure 2.12 Domino Designer workspace

Using the Designer Client for the First Time

Looking back, we've discussed some of the products that encompass the Lotus Domino family and have successfully installed the Domino Designer client. Next we'll create a database and begin to explore the Designer client interface. Although Chapter 3, "Navigating the Domino Designer Workspace," provides an in-depth explanation of the navigation elements, we'll complete this chapter by gaining some hands-on experience with creating a simple database and looking at the design elements.

A.2.

Creating My First Notes Database

Let's start by creating a database using a database *template*. A template is an existing Notes database that's used as the starting point to create a new database. In other words, the template contains all the design information for an existing Notes database application and can be used as the basis for a new database.

A.2.

In this section we'll create a database using a template and open the database in the Design client. The intent of this exercise is to gain some exposure to creating a database and to provide the opportunity to look at a working database design.

First, launch the Designer client and select the **File > Database > New** menu options. Alternatively, click the **Create a new database** button from the Designer client startup welcome page (see Figure 2.13).

For this exercise, keep the server location set to **Local** and specify an application title and file name. The title is the descriptive name that will appear on the database icon. The file name will be the actual name of the database file, which by default will be created in the C:\Lotus\Notes\Data\ directory on your local workstation.

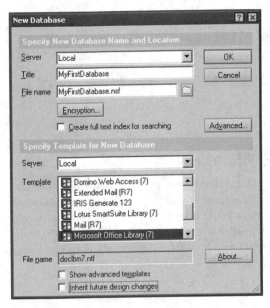

Figure 2.13 New Database property window

For example, you may want to change the title and file name to **MyFirstDatabase** to denote that this is a temporary database. Scroll through the list of templates and select **Microsoft Office Library** as the template type. Be sure to uncheck the **Inherit future design changes** option at the bottom of the window. This separates the design of the new database from the template and prevents changes to the template from automatically applying to the new database you are creating.

> **NOTE**
>
> When you become proficient with Notes application development, you can create your own database design templates. After you've created a template, you'll need to click **Show advanced templates** to display additional templates that reside on your workstation.

Click **OK** to create the database.

> **TIP**
>
> Applications can be created on either a local workstation or a Domino server. You don't need a Domino server to create a new database or to start application development. You only need the Domino server if the application will be accessed and shared by multiple people.

Congratulations, you just created your first database application! The design will automatically be displayed in the Designer client workspace. The display should look similar to Figure 2.12, shown earlier.

In the next chapter we will review the navigation of the Designer client. You may want to keep this database open in the Designer and use this application as a playground to learn the tool. Feel free to open various design elements.

Links to developerWorks

A.2.1 Lotus. *Trials and betas*. IBM developerWorks. http://www14.software.ibm.com/webapp/download/home.jsp?b=LOTUS.

A.2.2 McCarrick, Dick. *New features in Lotus Notes and Domino Designer 7.0*. IBM developerWorks, August 2005. http://www.ibm.com/developerworks/lotus/library/notes-designer7-features/index.html.

A.2.3 Russell, Donald. *Create your own Lotus Notes template storage database with revision history*. IBM developerWorks, June 2005. http://www.ibm.com/developerworks/lotus/library/nd-template/index.html.

Chapter 3

Navigating the Domino Designer Workspace

Chapter Overview

The Domino Designer client (or Designer) is used to develop collaborative Lotus Notes, Web, and mobile device applications. Understanding how to navigate the Designer workspace and various design elements will be the first hurdle to overcome. We'll start by getting acclimated to the main components of the Designer interface. With a little experience you'll find the navigation to be second nature and even intuitive.

By the end of the chapter you will have learned

- The purpose for using the Domino Designer client
- The five primary navigation panes
- How to navigate the Domino Designer client
- How to select the programming language
- How to view the status bar
- How to use the properties dialog window

An Introduction to Designer

Like other software development tools, the Designer client is divided into a series of development sections called *panes*. These panes are used to design, configure, and program applications. Depending on the object being edited, there can be up to five primary design panes. They include the following:

1. Design pane
2. Object pane
3. Programmer's pane
4. Work pane
5. Action pane

It's important to understand the relationship between the development panes and design elements. These development panes are selectively displayed based on the design element being edited.

For example, all five panes are available when editing a *form*. Fewer development panes are presented when editing an *agent* or *view*. We'll talk more about the design elements in the next chapter. In the meantime, understand that the panes displayed will vary based on the design element. In Figure 3.1, you'll notice that all five development panes are displayed.

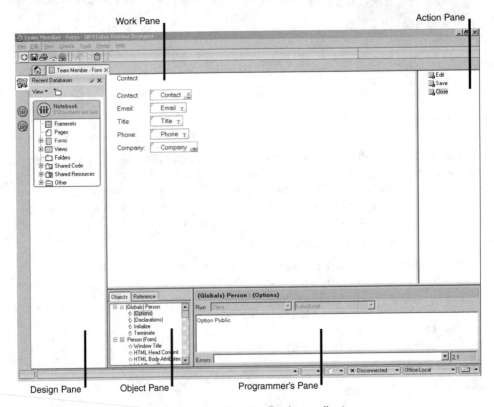

Figure 3.1   Development panes of the Domino Designer client

TIP

To change the size of the pane, hold down the left mouse button while adjusting the dividing line that separates the design sections.

The Design Pane

This pane is used to display the design elements of one or more database applications. This allows developers to select a recently opened database and design element within that database to edit.

> **TIP**
>
> Clicking the **Recent Databases** icon, located on the toolbar on the left, will open the Design pane if it's hidden (see Figure 3.2).

Figure 3.2　Recent Databases icon

You'll notice that the top section of each database (shown in gray) is a header that contains the application name and file location. Below the database header are the construction elements associated with the application. All databases can include these design elements—*Framesets, Pages, Forms, Views, Folders, Shared Code, Shared Resources,* and *Other* (see Figure 3.3). We'll talk more about these elements in the next chapter.

Figure 3.3　Design pane elements

The Work Pane

The Work pane is used to create and edit design elements associated with the application. These are design elements that help the end-user navigate and use the application and include forms, subforms, folders, views, pages, and framesets.

This section works on the WYSIWYG principle—"What You See Is What You Get"—and enables developers to select fonts, add graphics, and generally arrange objects as desired. Using this concept, a single application can be developed to support both the Lotus Notes and Web browser environments. However, it's important to understand that there may be visual differences between the two environments when the application is displayed. These differences can be attributed to a variety of reasons including the database design, access level, working state of the document, or inherent rendering differences between the environments.

Figure 3.4 depicts the Design pane for a form called Contact Information. The form includes a title at the top and several text descriptions along the edge with text fields. Absent from the illustration are the Action, Object, and Programmer's panes, which are hidden. From time to time, you may find the need to hide these panes while designing the form. These panes can be displayed or hidden by selecting the **View** > **Programmer's Pane** or **Action Pane** menu options. Alternatively, you can grab and drag the edge of the pane to display or hide the associated design pane.

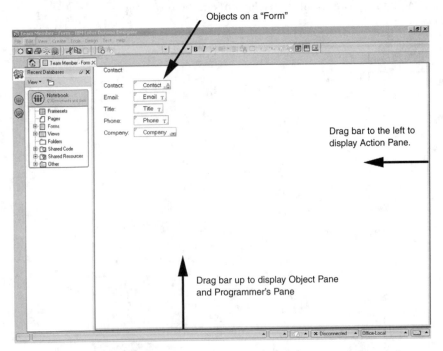

Figure 3.4   Working with design panes

The Object Pane

The Object pane is used to display and configure programmable attributes associated with objects, fields, and events for the design element that is currently open in the Work pane—such as a form or view. As illustrated in Figure 3.5, this section contains two tabs—Objects and Reference.

In the first tab, Objects, you can define the default value for a field, add error checking, or define specific code to be run when an event occurs (e.g., display the message "Document Saved" when the document is saved).

The second tab, as the name implies, contains reference information (see Figure 3.6). It provides the option to display all fields in the database or, more importantly, quick reference information. Depending on the object or event selected, the reference tab will display information pertaining to the functions, commands, LotusScript Language, Domino classes, subroutines, functions, variables, Java, or OLE classes.

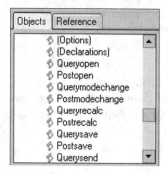

Figure 3.5 Design objects

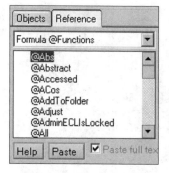

Figure 3.6 Quick Reference for fields, functions, and commands

You'll notice the Object pane contains a code indicator to the left of each object. Diamonds are used to indicate that the object can hold a single data value or set of code instructions. If the diamond is filled in, then the object contains a value or code, whereas the outlined (or "open") diamonds do not contain a value or programming code.

Circles indicate that the object may be used in the development of both Lotus Notes client and Web browser applications. As such, circle elements provide the ability to insert different values or code to accommodate both the Notes and browser environments. The top half of the circle represents the Notes client. The bottom half represents the Web browser. Although there are objects that work in both environments, there are also a few elements that only work in one environment.

The last symbol, a "script" icon, represents work areas for LotusScript (or JavaScript) programming (see Figure 3.7). Similar to the previous symbols, the script symbol changes to a solid color whenever script content has been added to the design.

> **TIP**
>
> Use the quick-reference code indicator to locate objects that contain code. The circles and diamonds will be partially or completely filled in when code is present.

The Object pane has several components. The top section always contains the *Global* objects. These are objects that can be defined once and utilized throughout the design element. Beneath the Global section are events, objects, and actions associated with the design element (e.g., the form or view).

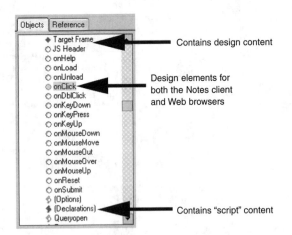

Figure 3.7 Content or code indicators

The Programmer's Pane

The Programmer's pane is used to develop and store source code associated with a form, field, action button, or other design element. Depending on the object, this section allows you to write code using LotusScript, Formula Language, JavaScript, or Java. Based on the design element, the Domino Designer will automatically display the software languages available for the specific element.

You can use this section to set an object to a specific data value or to add programming to be executed when an event occurs. Figure 3.8 illustrates several lines of LotusScript code in the Programmer's pane. More specifically, this figure shows several global objects being defined in the Options section. We'll talk more about how to write LotusScript programs later in the book. For now, you should understand where to add programming code.

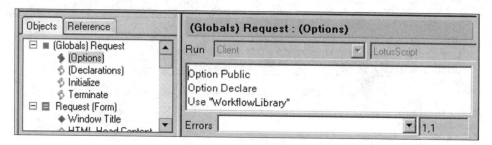

Figure 3.8   Sample LotusScript code in the Programmer's pane

---

TIP

If the Programmer's pane is hidden, select **View** > **Programmer's Pane** to display this section. Alternatively, you can use your mouse to manually open the pane. To do this, locate the horizontal bar at the bottom of the screen and use the left mouse button to drag open the pane.

The Action Pane

The Action pane is used to create and modify actions associated with a particular design element. When created, an action can be displayed as a button or in the Actions menu bar for the application. The Action pane is available in the form, folder, subform, and view constructs.

In Figure 3.9, two action buttons have been created—Save and Close. These buttons will appear at the top of the form when opened in the Lotus Notes client. When selected (or clicked) by the user, the document will either be saved or closed. The Formula Language code, associated with the Save button, can be seen in the Programmer's pane.

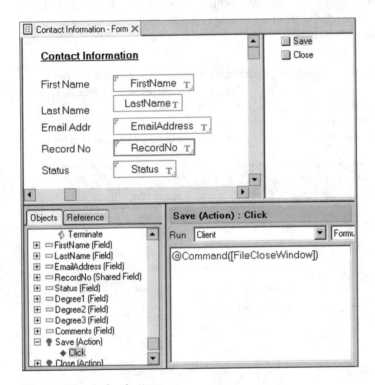

Figure 3.9   Action buttons

Some of the more common buttons added to applications include Create, Save, and Close a document.

> **TIP**
>
> If the Action pane is hidden, select **View > Action Pane** to display this section. Alternatively, you can use your mouse to manually open the pane. To do this, locate the vertical bar at rightmost border of the screen and use the left mouse button to drag open the pane.

Design Tabs

In the previous sections, we talked about the various design panes used to develop applications. In addition to these panes, there are several other features of the Designer client to review and understand.

Multiple design elements can be opened in edit mode simultaneously. Each opened design element will have a separate tab. As a programmer, you can switch between the design elements by clicking on the tabs located at the top of the designer client (see Figure 3.10).

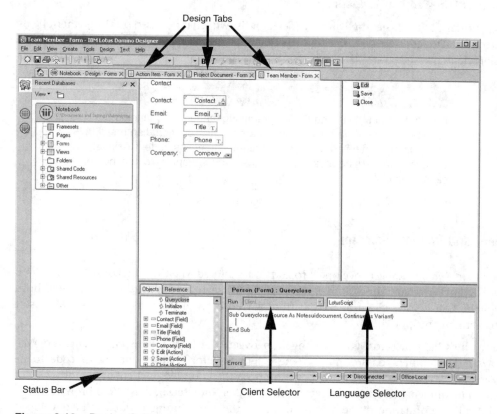

Figure 3.10   Design Selectors

Language Selector

Depending on the element, the Designer client gives you a choice of languages in the Programmer's pane. A dropdown list allows you to select between available languages including Simple Actions, Formula, LotusScript, JavaScript, and Java.

When building an application, you'll find that in some cases it's easier to write some code in Formula Language and other code in LotusScript. Using the *Language Selector* gives you flexibility in how you design the application. Some developers prefer using Formulas; others prefer LotusScript or JavaScript.

It's important to note that the Language Selector list will change based on the element being edited. The Designer client will only display languages that are applicable for the selected design element.

> **NOTE**
>
> Be careful when changing the programming language. Changing the language after you've added code to a particular element can result in the code being deleted! If the object already contains code, Designer will display a warning message that gives you the option to continue or cancel the change.

Client and Browser Selector

The *Client Selector* enables developers to add code tailored to either the Lotus Notes or Web browser environment. For example, it's possible to create an application that is used both from the Lotus Notes client as well as from a Web browser (such as Netscape®, Microsoft Internet Explorer®, or Firefox®).

Using the Client Selector, you can toggle between the Lotus Notes client and the Web browser development environments. The Client Selector enables one set of code to be implemented when accessing the application from the Lotus Notes client and another set of code to be implemented when accessing from a Web browser. Because Web browsers work and display information differently from that of the client, unique code can be developed to accommodate either the Lotus Notes client or Web browser environments.

Status Bar

Located at the bottom of the Lotus Notes and Designer client is an event history area. This area displays the most current event message. In addition to the most recent message, you can click on the *Status bar* to display the last 20 event messages. Messages are displayed from oldest (at the top) to most current (at the bottom).

> **TIP**
>
> The Status bar can be very helpful in debugging applications. Using the `Print` method in LotusScript or `@StatusBar` within a formula, you can display data values at various execution points to determine what code has been executed. See Chapter 21, "Troubleshooting," for additional tips and tricks for debugging a Notes database.

Properties Dialog

The properties dialog is one of the most important aspects of Lotus Domino application development. It's used to set properties for practically every design element, field, object, action, or component of the database. It's important to understand that the options displayed in the properties dialog will change for each design element.

> **NOTE**
>
> You'll need to become proficient with the use of the properties dialog in order to develop Lotus Notes database applications. The properties dialog is a key aspect to all application development and maintenance. There are many configuration options for each design element. Configuration options will change with each form, view, field, agent, action button, etc.

Figure 3.11 illustrates a properties dialog for a form. It's important to note that multiple tabs are displayed across the top of the dialog. Each tab has different properties. The tabs listed will also change depending on the design element being modified.

> **NOTE**
>
> The configuration options displayed in the properties dialog will vary based on design element. In other words, the options displayed for a form will differ from the options displayed for a field, folder, agent, view, etc.

There are several methods to display the properties dialog. Using the menu bar, you can select **File > Database > Properties**. You can also display the dialog by right-clicking on the object (such as a field on a form) and selecting **Properties** from the popup menu. The dialog can also be displayed using the shortcut keys **Alt+Enter**. In some cases, double-clicking on the object will automatically cause the dialog to display. For example, double-clicking on a column in a view will display the properties for the selected column.

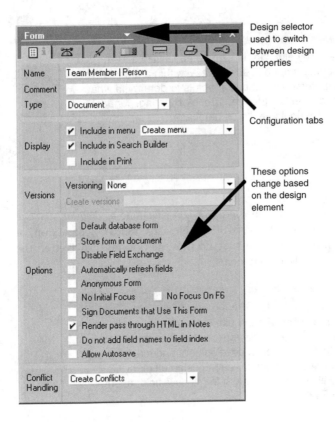

Design selector used to switch between design properties

Configuration tabs

These options change based on the design element

Figure 3.11 Properties dialog

Finally, the very top of the properties dialog indicates what properties are currently displayed. To switch between design elements, click on the triangle (or dropdown indicator) to change the selected design element. This option allows you to switch between the properties for the database, design element (such as a form, view, or folder), or individual object (such as a field or view column).

Links to developerWorks

A.3.1 Savir, Raphael. *Lotus Notes/Domino 7 application performance: Part 1: Database properties and document collections.* IBM developerWorks, January 2006. http://www.ibm.com/developerworks/lotus/library/notes7-application-performance1/index.html.

Chapter 4

Domino Design Elements

Chapter Overview

B y now you should understand how to launch the Domino Designer client and be able to navigate through the design panes. Next, we'll build on this knowledge and take a closer look at the building blocks of a Notes database. We'll explore the various design elements, their related objects, and the basic instructions for building these items.

By the end of the chapter you will have learned

- The basic building blocks of a Notes database
- How to create each design element
- How to set object attributes using the properties dialog
- How to name design elements
- How to create a form to enter and store data
- How to present data using views
- How to customize the user interface using outlines, framesets, pages, and navigators
- How to automate tasks using buttons and agents
- How to automate tasks based on event triggers

As you read through the chapter, you'll notice that the presentation order of the design elements varies slightly from the order displayed in the Designer client. As you develop applications, you'll find that forms and views are the most common design elements in most Lotus Notes database applications. As such, these design elements have been moved to the front of the chapter.

Given the size and detail level provided in this chapter, you might find it easier to skim through the chapter and refer back to it on a regular basis as you work through the projects and enhancements later in the book.

Building Blocks of a Notes Database

Let's start by talking about the unique architecture of a Notes database and the terminology used by Notes developers. Lotus Notes is an event-driven language that stores information in a database called a Notes Storage Facility, or *NSF* file. This file holds both application design information and data. It's important to understand that a Notes application may consist of one or more NSF database files.

Lotus Notes, unlike a relational database management system (RDBMS), stores information in data structures called *documents*. *Forms* are used to enter data and display documents. Documents can contain text, tables, images, and file attachments and can support complex formatting (such as bold, underline, subscript, colors, and fonts) similarly to word-processing documents. This information is stored in one or more *fields* on each document. Forms display and capture information associated with a single document and often contain embedded controls to help the user navigate them. It is the combination of the form, controls, and data that ultimately comprises a "document."

Pages are associated most typically with Web sites and are used to display information. They cannot be used to capture data from or enter data into the database.

Using *views,* you can display multiple documents in a series of rows and columns—like a spreadsheet. The information displayed in the view is determined by a view selection formula, or query. All documents that meet that query are automatically displayed in the view. *Folders*, on the other hand, allow users to move (or group) documents of a common interest to one place. Folders also display data using rows and columns. However, unlike views, documents are typically added to the folder by the application users (either manually or programmatically).

> **NOTE**
>
> Even though Notes data is presented in views in rows and columns, it's important to understand that Lotus Notes is not a relational database. This is a common misconception about Notes databases and is one of the most difficult concepts for new developers to grasp. For example, because the design and data are separate, deleting a column from a view will have no impact on the data already stored in the database. In other words, the view no longer shows the data, but the data still resides in the database.

You can also add *action buttons* and *agents* to improve the usability of the Notes database. Buttons contain automated actions that can be manually triggered by users. Agents are automated tasks. An agent can be called from a button or hotspot, called manually from a menu list, or scheduled to run based on a specific date and time interval. Agents can be created using "simple actions," Formula Language, LotusScript, Java, and Imported Java code. For example, a scheduled agent could be used to send a weekly or monthly status report to everyone in the department.

Finally, to enhance the presentation and navigation of the user interface, we use *framesets, outlines,* and *navigators*. These design elements allow you to give a custom look and feel to the Notes database. Although there are other design components, these are the most commonly used in the development process. Figure 4.1 illustrates just a few of the elements that comprise a Notes database application. Notice that data can be displayed in and utilized by a variety of design elements. This illustration shows that views contain documents and documents contain fields, all of which can access data.

> **NOTE**
>
> It's important to understand that the design (forms, fields, views) and data (documents) are stored separately within a database. In short, the design elements are used to present and modify information and to navigate the application. However, the data that resides within the database is completely isolated from the design elements. This means the design can be changed (and even deleted) without affecting the documents already stored in the database. This can be one of the most difficult concepts to grasp as a Notes developer.

The remainder of this chapter details naming conventions, design elements, and events used to manage applications. First, we'll describe naming conventions and options. Next, we'll review each design element in the sequential order displayed in the Design pane of the Domino Designer client. Finally, at the conclusion of the chapter, we'll briefly discuss how automation can be added to events to manage application functionality. These items are the basic building blocks of any Notes database. As a Notes developer, you will work with any number of these elements to build and maintain applications.

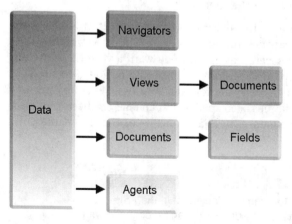

Figure 4.1   Relationship between common design elements and data

Naming Design Elements

Anyone familiar with application development probably understands the importance of naming design elements (such as forms, views, and pages) and objects (such as fields or text paragraphs). Naming conventions not only affect users but also impact code development and maintenance for an application developer. Careful consideration should be given when naming both design elements and objects.

All of the design elements, as discussed later in this chapter, must have a primary element name and optionally an alias name. The primary name, in most cases, will appear in the Notes application and will be visible to the application end-users. Although most design elements have an alias, some do not, such as script libraries and shared fields.

For example, forms are used to capture and display database information. By default, when a form is created and saved, the form name is automatically added to the Create menu in the application. This allows the user to add data to the database via the application menu options. Let's say, for instance, you have an application used to track customer service requests. Naming the form "Service Request," as opposed to "Form A," would be more meaningful and better understood from the user's perspective. To submit a request, the user would simply select the **Create > Service Request** menu options (which makes more sense than **Create > Form A**).

In addition to the primary element name, you can optionally specify an alias name. The alias is a synonym used to reference the same design element. Best practices suggest that you should always provide and reference the alias name when developing a Notes database application. This provides greater flexibility to accommodate changes without impacting code, views, agents, or other aspects of the application. Unlike the primary name, the alias name typically does not appear to the users in the client.

Using the same example of a Service Request, the alias name could be "SR." This alias name would be referenced in other Notes database design elements. For example, let's say the service request application (or database) has several forms, and you want a view that only displays service requests. To create this view, a selection formula would be added to the view to display only service request documents. Now, the formula could reference the primary name, "Service Request," or "SR" if an alias has been specified. If an alias has been provided, the selection formula for the view must reference the alias name. Using the alias name is the recommended development approach.

> **NOTE**
>
> The alias name for a form is stored in the document in the `Form` variable. By storing the alias name, the visual name can be changed without affecting the application. However, be aware that adding an alias after the application has been implemented will most likely affect the display of information in the database. For this reason, it's a good idea to implement an alias name at the start of the project.

As an application developer, you will find that design changes are common when building and supporting applications. So, if the customer suddenly decides the form name should be changed from "Service Request" to "Request For Service," you could accommodate the change with minimal impact to the overall application design, provided that the code referenced the alias name. Otherwise, changing the name to "Request For Service" affects not only the form name but also the view formula and any other design element where the primary name was referenced.

> **NOTE**
>
> Always provide a primary and alias name for a design element. To specify the alias name, type the primary name, a vertical bar "|", and then the alias name (e.g., Request For Service | RFS).

The first time you save a design element, you will be prompted to specify a design element name (see Figure 4.2). With the exception of views (which have a dedicated property for the alias), you should specify a primary name, a vertical bar "|" separator, and then the alias name.

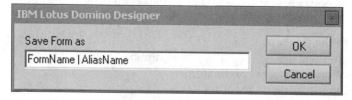

Figure 4.2 How to specify the primary and alias name when saving a design element

> **NOTE**
>
> Be aware that you can save multiple design elements with the same primary and alias name. Although some advanced application designs may implement multiple forms with the same name, in general you should ensure that the primary and alias names are unique and have not already been used in the database design. This will eliminate potential problems. One way to address this issue is to preface the alias name with an abbreviation designating the element type. So the Service Request form could have an alias of formSR, and the Service Request view could have an alias of viewSR.

Working with Forms

Forms are widely considered to be the most important building block for practically every application and are usually the best place to start when creating a new application. A successful application requires a balance between the collection and presentation of information to the end-user. In other words, fields should be created based on functional requirements and placed on the form in a manner that's easily understood by the user community.

Forms organize and provide structure to data records, or documents, in a Notes database. Using forms, you can display information in an organized fashion on the screen. Forms are also used to add new data or modify existing data. Virtually all Notes databases have one or more forms that are used to view and manipulate data records. In short, forms are the most important building block of a Notes database application.

Let's say, for example, that you have a Human Resource application used to manage employee information. For each employee in the company, there is a corresponding document in the database. Each document contains the employee name, Social Security number, birth date, hire date, employee number, department, and phone number (see Figure 4.3). This information is all related to one person and is stored in a single document. Using forms, you can

- Add new employees to the database
- Change existing data in the database (i.e., new phone number)
- Manage what information is displayed on the form
- Manage the layout of information on the form
- Limit who can edit or see the information

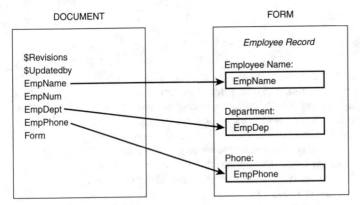

Figure 4.3   Forms display information for a given document.

> **NOTE**
>
> Forms manage data content for a single document. Forms can be designed to display any number of fields associated with the document or none at all.

Many design objects are associated with a form. These objects define the look and feel of the form as well as how the form operates. The following table provides a summary of some of the objects that can be placed on a form. We'll review each of these objects in greater detail later in this chapter.

Object	Object Description
Action button	An action is performed when the user manually clicks a button. Action buttons display either in the action bar (located at the top of the application screen) or in the "Action" menu.
Event	The occurrence of a specific action and the ability to perform a task when that action, or event, occurs (e.g., display the message "Document Saved" when the user clicks the Save button).
Field	An object on a form or subform. Fields are used to enter, store, and display data.
Shared field	A special type of field that can be embedded or used on multiple forms. Enables developers to maintain code or field properties from a single location or instance.
Text	Static text displayed on the form, subform, page, etc. For example, a descriptive label next to a field or the title on a form.
Image	An image, picture, or graphic artwork (e.g., company logo).
Section	A group or collection of related information, which can be text, fields, graphics, buttons, etc. Sections can be expanded to view all information or collapsed under a single section title.
Layout region	A special region that allows fields, images, text, and other objects to overlap. Enables developers to manage multiple layers of information with precise control.
Subform	A special type of form that can be embedded in another form. Enables developers to maintain a common set of fields across multiple forms.
Table	A table that contains rows and columns. Tables can hold static text, fields, buttons, or other design elements.

Now that we've discussed how forms are used and the components that comprise them, let's look at two illustrations—one from the Designer's perspective, the other from the user's perspective. Figure 4.4 shows a form called Contact Information that includes descriptive text, fields, one shared field (RecordNo), two action buttons (Save and Close), a collapsible section for employee education, and a layout region with an edit control or text field.

Now that you have seen a form in the Domino Designer client, let's take a look at the same form from the end-user's perspective using the Lotus Notes client (see Figure 4.5). Notice that the Save and Close buttons display at the top of the form and that the fields are framed with a box corner to show the start and end of each field. The layout region appears at the bottom of the form and includes a text area with a scroll bar.

Designer provides two methods to create forms in a database. Forms can be created from scratch or copied from a preexisting database. As a general rule of thumb, a form should be copied only when the form functionality and layout meets the needs of the new database. Otherwise, you'll probably find it easier to create a new form. This will limit potential problems of integrating a form from one database into another.

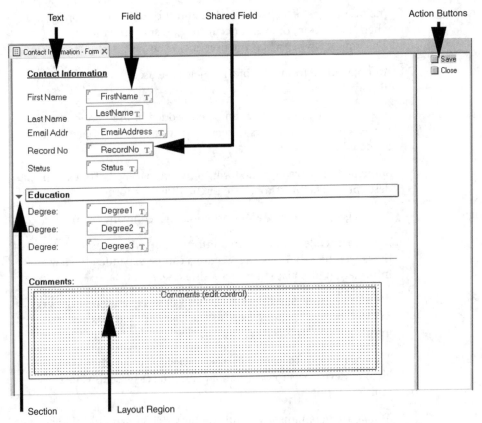

Figure 4.4   Example form with design elements in Domino Designer

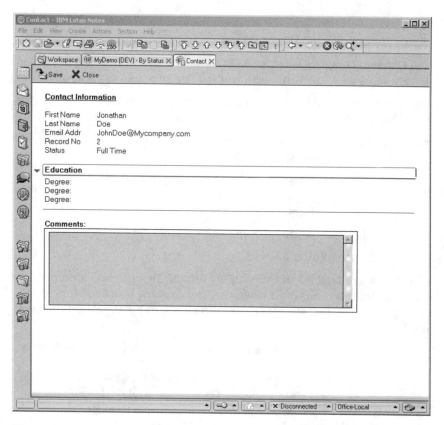

Figure 4.5   Example form as displayed in the Lotus Notes client

---

NOTE

When copying a form, all fields and property settings are duplicated in the new database. However, forms may contain references to other design objects stored external to the form. For example, an action button may reference a subroutine stored in a LotusScript library. These external objects are linked to each other. In other words, when copying a form into a new database, you may need to either copy other design objects from the source database or remove references that do not reside in the new database. There are several indicators that a form contains external references. Most notable is when a form cannot be opened in Lotus Notes and a message, such as "Illegal circular reference," is displayed. If this happens, you'll need to determine the conflicting or missing elements or delete the form. You may be able to determine what is causing the problem by deleting fields or source segments one by one and reopening the form (or database). You've identified the cause of the problem when the error no longer displays.

Creating a Form

Follow these steps to create a new form from scratch.

1. Select the **Create > Design > Form** menu options, and a new form will be created. Alternatively, navigate to the Form section of the Design pane and click **New Form**.

2. Next, define the layout of the form by adding fields, text, buttons, images, sections, and other design elements (described later in this chapter).

3. The first time you save the form, you'll be prompted to specify a form name. Be sure to specify a meaningful primary name and alias name.

Copying a Form

Follow these instructions to copy a form.

1. Open the source database, locate the form, and select it.

2. To copy the form, select **Edit > Copy**.

3. Now open the target database in Designer. By default, Designer will automatically display the application forms pane when the new database is opened (or created). If another design pane is displayed, be sure to navigate to the forms section before continuing.

4. Finally, select menu options **Edit > Paste** to copy the form into the target database.

NOTE

A warning message will display when copying a form from a template database. A template is a special type of Notes database.

"The source database, 'MyProjects,' is a Design Template named 'Project Template.' After being pasted, would you like these forms to be automatically updated when those in the design template change?"

In other words, Designer is asking if you want to synchronize updates when the template changes. In most cases, you will want to select **NO**. This will ensure that any changes you make to the form are not lost when the template changes. Only select **YES** if you want the copied form to continue to match the form in the template database when the template is modified.

Hidden Forms

A *hidden form* is a form that does not display in the Create menu and is typically presented to the user through the implementation of application source code. In other words, hidden form does not mean the form cannot be displayed; it simply means the form is displayed using a method other than the menu options. A hidden form is created the same way as a regular form and contains the same elements: text, fields, layout regions, etc.

Forms are generally hidden when creating a dialog box, which is really just a form that's displayed differently. For example, using hidden forms, you can create custom popup dialog box windows that help the user perform a task or navigate the application.

For example, Figure 4.6 illustrates a hidden form. This hidden form is displayed in a dialog box and allows the user to specify the criteria for scheduling a recurring calendar appointment.

To hide a form, enclose the form name in open and close parentheses, "( )". Only the primary name needs to be enclosed. However, for consistency, it's recommended that you also enclose the alias name as well, such as "(RepeatReservation) | (Repeat)" (see Figure 4.7).

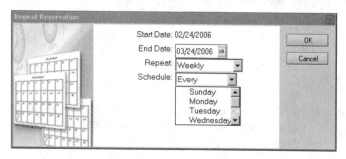

Figure 4.6   Example dialog box using a hidden form

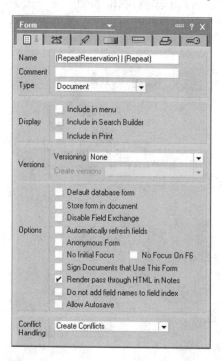

Figure 4.7   Property settings to hide a form

NOTE

Hidden forms do not appear in the application menu even if the **Include in menu** option is selected in the form properties dialog.

TIP

Consider unchecking the **Include in Search Builder** option from the form properties dialog. More often than not, hidden forms are used to aid data entry and can be removed from a database text search. This will help make the search more efficient.

Working with Fields

Fields are used to store data on a form. There are many different types of fields. The field type defines the values that can be stored in the field and, in some cases, the presentation of the field on the form. This section describes each of the field types.

As you work with the various fields in the Designer client, you'll notice that a unique quick-reference icon is embedded in each field. These serve as an indicator of the field type, which is specified in the properties dialog. The following table provides an overview of each field type along with the quick-reference field symbol.

Field Type	Description Summary	Field Symbol
Authors	Refines who can edit a document	Authors
Checkbox	Creates checkboxes on the form (keyword field)	Checkbox
Color	Allows users to pick colors	Color
Combobox	Creates a dropdown on the form (keyword field)	Combobox
Date/Time	Defines format for dates and times	DateTime
Dialog List	Displays a dialog with selectable values (keyword field)	Dialog

Field Type	Description Summary	Field Symbol
Formula	Contains a formula	Formula @
Listbox	Creates a scrollable list of values (keyword field)	Listbox
Names	Used to capture and store user names	Names
Number	Stores and formats numeric values	Number #
Password	Stores an encrypted password value	Password ★
Radio Button	Creates radio buttons on the form (keyword field)	○ Radiobutton
Readers	Defines who can read the document	Readers
Rich Text	Allow users to specify font, color, and size	Richtext T
Rich Text Lite	Similar to a Rich Text field, but developers can limit what types of objects can be stored in the field	RichtextLite T
Text	Used to store plain text	Text T
Time Zone	Allows users to select a time zone	Timezone

TIP

These field types are based on Lotus Notes release 6. Some field types are not available in release 5, and additional field types may be available when using release 7.

Working with Keyword Fields

Before we talk about each field type, let's spend a moment talking about a group of fields that contain predefined values. These fields are classified as "keyword fields" and contain predetermined values that can be selected by users. Using keyword fields, you can enforce a consistent nomenclature for data values and help steer the user as he or she completes the form. There are five field types that are considered to be keyword fields—Checkbox, Combobox, Dialog List, Listbox, and Radio Button.

These field types can be configured to accept only the data values in the field or to allow users to specify new values. These two options, which are set on the second properties tab, offer enormous flexibility in the management of the field content. Some keyword fields also provide the option to select multiple data values. This option is set on the first tab in the properties dialog (see Figure 4.8).

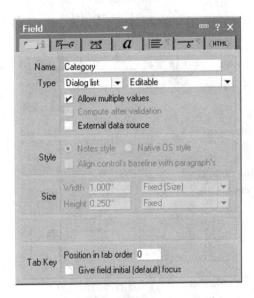

Figure 4.8 Allow multiple values setting

There are several ways to define the data values for this field type. The data values can be based on hard-coded values or a computed formula specified on the second tab of the properties dialog. There are up to five unique methods for defining the data values for keyword fields (see Figure 4.9). Not all of these options appear for every field type. Design options include the following:

- **Enter choices (one per line)**—Used to specify hard-coded values for the field. In general, this field should be used when values will not be added or changed (e.g. male and female, or the months of the year).
- **Use formula for choices**—Used to dynamically define values for a field. Using formulas, you can pull information from documents, fields, or views to populate the

keyword list. This option offers the flexibility to add or remove values from the list without having to modify the Notes database design.

- **Use Address dialog for choices**—Used to display the Personal or Notes address book. This option enables users to select people or servers from a dialog list to populate the field and is often used to define a list of people to receive an email.
- **Use Access Control List for choices**—Used to populate the field with user names from the Access Control List (ACL).
- **Use View dialog for choices**—Used to populate the field with values from a view. Alternatively, you could utilize the "Use Formula" option to achieve the same result.

> **TIP**
>
> See "Working with @DBColumn" and "Working with @DBLookup" in Chapter 14, "Design Enhancements Using Formula Language," to learn how to dynamically build a list of values (and avoid hard-coded values) for checkbox, combobox, dialog list, listbox, and radio button fields. This allows the list of values to change without having to modify the application.

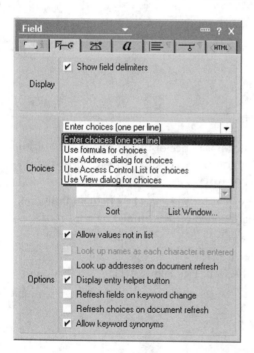

Figure 4.9 Choice types for keyword fields

Authors Field

This is a special field used to manage who can edit a document. The authors field works in conjunction with the ACL and refines who can modify a document. The field affects users with **Author** and **Editor** database access. Only users who are specified in this field can make document updates. The users specified in the field could be computed based on a formula or editable from the document. Users with **Reader** access cannot gain edit authority by including their name in the field. Users with **Author** access are able to modify the document only if their name is included in the field. Users with **Editor** access by default have the ability to edit the document and are unaffected by the authors field. In short, the authors field allows you to refine who can modify a particular document.

Checkbox Field

As the name implies, this field will display a series of checkboxes on a form (see Figure 4.10). Values for the checkbox field are specified in the field properties dialog and can be hard-coded or computed. The field properties dialog also allows you to specify the number of columns and the display presentation. This type of field enables users to select all applicable values associated with the field.

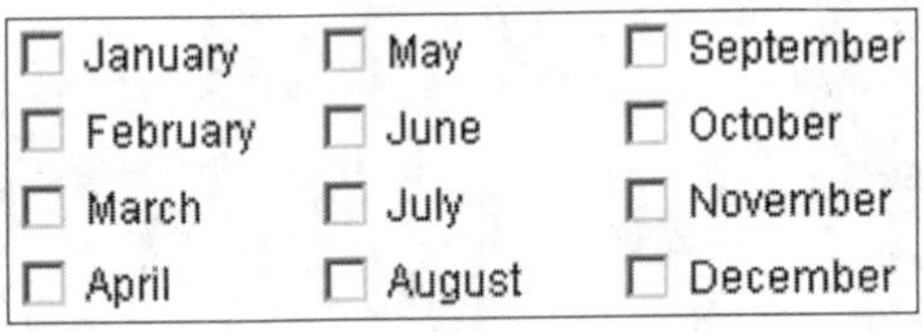

☐ January	☐ May	☐ September
☐ February	☐ June	☐ October
☐ March	☐ July	☐ November
☐ April	☐ August	☐ December

Figure 4.10   Example checkbox field

The properties dialog also allows you to define the appearance of the checkbox field on the form. This is called the border style, and it resides on the second tab of the properties dialog. The border style can be set to **None, Single,** or **Inset.**

The second tab is also used to define the various values for the checkbox field and the number of columns to be displayed. Values can be hard-coded or determined by a formula.

Color Field

Adding a color field displays a color picker on the form (see Figure 4.11). This field allows the user to select a color.

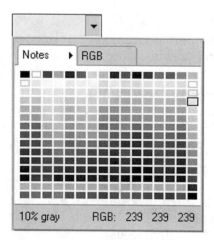

Figure 4.11 Example color field

Combobox Field

The combobox field provides a list of values available for a field. When the user clicks on the field, a dropdown list is displayed and allows the user to select the appropriate value. If the combobox contains a large number of options, the field automatically inserts a scroll box that allows users to move up and down within the field (see Figure 4.12).

As with other keyword fields, a combobox can be configured to accept values not in the list or to only permit users to select from the existing list. The combobox field is commonly used in both Lotus Notes client applications and Web applications.

Figure 4.12 Example combobox field

> **NOTE**
>
> The height and width properties of a combobox field are not supported in Web applications. By default, the field width will be set to the width of the longest text value.

Date/Time Field

Date/Time fields are used to store and display dates and times in various formats. This field supports both the 12-hour and 24-hour time format and dates that range from 1/1/0001 to 12/31/9999.

With Date/Time fields, you can specify to display only the date, only the time, or both. This gives you great flexibility as to the format of the field. As with other fields, the format for the Date/Time field is configured in the properties dialog. The format settings are defined in the second property tab for the field. The following table shows some of the supported date and time formats.

Date/Time Configuration Options	Settings	Example
Month, day, and year	Date	07/28/2005
Weekday, month, day, and year	Date	Thu 07/28/2005
Month and year	Date	07/2005
Month and day	Date	07/28
Year	Date	2005
Month	Date	07
Day	Date	28
Weekday	Date	Thu
Hours, minutes, and seconds	Time	09:28:55 AM
Hours	Time	09
Minutes	Time	28
Seconds	Time	55
Month, day, year, and time	Date and Time	07/28/2005 09:28:55 AM
Weekday, month, day, year, and time	Date and Time	Thu 07/28/2005 09:28:55 AM

> **NOTE**
>
> Using Formula Language, you can create dates with the month spelled out (e.g., January 01, 2005). See "Create a Formatted Date String" in Chapter 14 for additional information.

Dialog List Field

A dialog list field displays a list of valid field choices in a dialog box window. This field can be identified by a "down arrow" located to the right of the field. Clicking on the arrow displays the dialog box. This field can be configured to allow any value or only those currently listed. The values can be hard-coded or determined by a formula. Note that Figure 4.13 illustrates a dialog list where only one value in the list can be selected.

In this second example, users have the ability to select one or more values from the list as well as to enter new keyword values in the field at the bottom of the dialog box (see Figure 4.14).

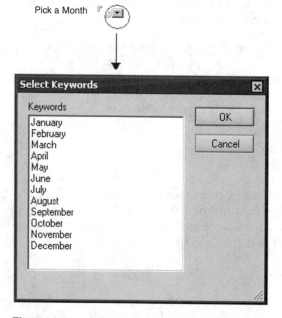

Figure 4.13   Example dialog list field with static values

Figure 4.14   Example dialog list field with dynamic values

Formula Field

The formula field is a special field type used to create a "headline" application. This is a very specialized field that automatically notifies people of changes to the database. The field works in conjunction with a special database called Headlines.nsf.

> **NOTE**
>
> To implement this function, you will need to create a form called $Subscription and include a formula field called $HLFormula. For additional information, see the Domino Designer help for exact setup instructions.

Listbox Field

The listbox field is used to create a scrollable list of data values (see Figure 4.15). Using this properties dialog, you can specify the height and width of the field (which are defined in the first tab). The border style and data values can be defined in the second tab of the properties dialog. The values can be hard-coded or determined by a formula.

Figure 4.15 Example listbox field

> **NOTE**
>
> The listbox height and width properties are not supported in Web appli-
> cations. By default, the field width will be set to the width of the longest
> text value.

Names Field

A names field is used to capture and store user names. This field also has a down arrow, located to the right of field, which displays an address book. The address book allows the application user to select user names from a public or personal address book. More importantly, however, this field stores values based on the Lotus Notes name hierarchy and can be used to generate emails.

> **TIP**
>
> A names field allows users to select names from the address book and
> ensures correct spelling.

For example, you may have an application that tracks project meeting agendas and minutes. The form could be divided into two sections—agenda information and meeting minutes. Each section could have a names field. The first would allow the author to select all the users that have been invited to the meeting. The second names field would be used to track all the users that actually attended the meeting. Because these fields contain names based on the Notes user ID hierarchy, a button could be added that sends meeting minutes to everyone that was invited to the meeting.

> **TIP**
>
> Use the @Name function to change the data format of a names field.
> See Chapter 5, "An Introduction to Formula Language," and the
> Chapter 14 section, "Format a user's name" for additional information
> and examples.

> **NOTE**
>
> You must select the **Allow multiple values** checkbox on the field properties dialog in order to store more than one user name.

Number Field

The number field is used to store numeric values including mathematical symbols (e.g., plus, minus, decimal, percent, dollar, etc.). Using the properties dialog box, you can define the format of the number field, such as the following:

- Number format (Decimal, Percent, Scientific, or Currency)
- Decimal places (Fixed or Varying)
- Thousands separator
- Decimal symbol

Numeric fields accept numbers that range from $2.225E\text{-}308$ to $1.798E308$ with fourteen-digit accuracy.

Password Field

The password field is a plain-text field that replaces letters on the screen with asterisks as characters are entered in the field. It's important to understand that the contents of this field are not encrypted. In other words, this is not a secure field. The information stored in this field is still visible from the document properties dialog box.

Radio Button Field

This type of field displays a series of radio buttons on a form. Radio button values are specified in the properties window and can be hard-coded or computed. The properties window also allows you to specify the number of columns and the display presentation.

Unlike checkbox fields that allow multiple values to be checked, only one radio button value can be selected. For example, you could add a field called "gender" on a form. This field would allow users to select either Male or Female.

The properties dialog also allows you to define the appearance of the radio buttons on the form. This is called the radio button border style, and it resides on the second tab of the properties dialog.

The second tab is also used to define the various values for the radio buttons and the number of columns to be displayed. Values can be hard-coded or based on a formula.

Description	Example	
None	No border is displayed.	○ male ○ female
Single	A single-line box frames the radio button options.	○ male ○ female
Inset	The radio buttons are framed inside a gray box window.	○ male ○ female

Readers Field

The readers field is used to refine who can access or view a particular document in the Notes databases. With this field, only the people listed in the field will have the ability to view the document provided that they have been granted accessed to the database in the ACL.

Another very important aspect of this field is that Lotus Notes will only copy or replicate documents for which the user is included in the reader field. Those documents where a person's name is not included in the list will not be copied when performing a database copy or replicated during the database replication process. In fact, the document will not even appear in a view.

> **TIP**
>
> A readers field is a great way to manage access to content in a database. For example, this field could be implemented such that people will only see documents they create. In other words, John can see only his documents, and Susan can see only her documents.

> **NOTE**
>
> A readers field is an extremely powerful feature. Be sure to thoroughly test the application to ensure that the design is working as intended before deploying the database. If you're not careful, you could easily lock access to documents from everyone including developers and administrators.

Rich Text Field

Notes manages text in several different ways—Rich Text, Rich Text Lite, and plain text. Rich Text fields store the text along with the font, size, color, and other text properties (e.g., underline, bold, subscript, strikethrough, etc.). In addition to robust text features, Rich Text fields enable users to create tables, embed graphics, attach files, add Web links, create buttons, and create OLE objects and sections among other things.

> **NOTE**
>
> The content of a Rich Text field cannot be displayed in a view column. Consider using a text field to display data in a view. However, you can use @Abstract in a separate field and display a subset of the Rich Text contents.

Rich Text Lite Field

This field supports the same formats described in the previous section, "Rich Text Field." However, developers can limit the types of objects that can be stored in the field. For example, developers can set the properties for this field to only allow text or a file attachment.

Text Field

Text fields store data in a plain-text format, accepting only alphanumeric characters (letters A–Z, numbers 0–9, and punctuation characters). A text field, unlike the Rich Text field, does not allow users to set the font, size, or color. This field also does not support tables, graphics, sections, or other robust text formatting. This type of field is strictly intended to capture text.

> **NOTE**
>
> Information stored in a text field can be displayed in a view, whereas the contents of a Rich Text field cannot be displayed in a view.

> **NOTE**
>
> Numerical values stored in a text field cannot be used in a mathematical calculation. However, provided the field only contains numbers, the @TextToNumber function can be used to convert the value.

Time Zone Field

A time zone field is used to display a list of all available time zones in the world (see Figure 4.16). In addition to the time zone, the field includes a representative list of cities associated with the time region.

Figure 4.16 Example time zone field

Setting the Field Mode (Editable versus Computed)

By now you should understand that there are many different types of fields. In addition to defining the type of field, you can also specify how data values are stored in the field. Using the properties dialog, each field can be set to one of four modes—editable, computed, computed for display, or computed when composed (see Figure 4.17). All computed fields must contain a valid formula used to calculate the result. Computed fields cannot be directly modified by the end-user community.

- **Computed**—The data value is automatically computed. Computed fields are often used to calculate one field value based on another field value (e.g., calculate the day of the week given a specified month, day, and year). Computed fields are calculated when a document is created or saved.
- **Computed for display**—The data value is automatically computed when the form is displayed. The value, however, is not actually stored in the document. It's important to note that this mode is not supported with Rich Text fields.
- **Computed when composed**—The data value is automatically computed when the document is first created and cannot be modified. After this value is set, it will not be automatically computed again. For example, this field mode is often used to track the document creation date and author. Because the creation date is a fixed point in time, you can use this option to automatically capture and store the date. However, this type of field can be programmatically changed.
- **Editable**—This field mode allows anyone with appropriate access to edit or modify field content.

Most forms have a combination of these fields, where most are editable fields and perhaps a few are computed fields.

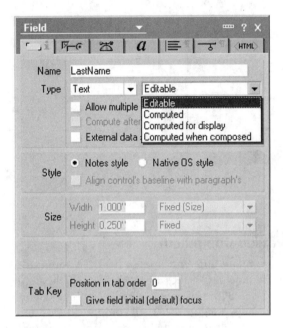

Figure 4.17   Setting the field display mode

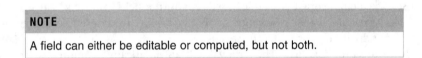

NOTE

A field can either be editable or computed, but not both.

Hiding Objects

Using the "Hide When" property tab, you can define when an object is visible to users. The "Hide When" tab is usually the second to last tab in the properties dialog and is represented by a window shade in the tab (see Figure 4.18). Here you can hide the object

- Based on the client type
- In read-only mode
- In edit mode
- When printing
- When copied to the Clipboard
- Based on a custom formula

This robust set of configuration options can be applied to text strings, fields, sections, buttons, and practically any other object that's displayed to the user. As you develop applications, you'll find that the "Hide When" settings are used to manage the display of buttons as well as sensitive field and text information.

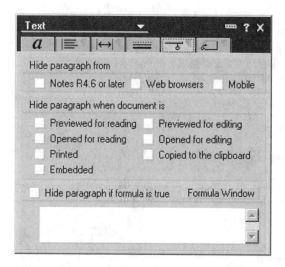

Figure 4.18   Setting the "Hide When" formula

For example, if you currently have a document opened in edit mode, it doesn't make sense to have the Edit button displayed. So, in this case, you'd want to display the button when **Previewed for reading** and **Opened for reading** and hide the button when **Previewed for editing** and **Opened for editing**.

Other times you'll want to hide text paragraphs and fields to limit the display of information to specific groups. For example, unless you're a member of the "Helpdesk," you could hide the employee's workstation specifications—operating system, fix pack level, machine type, and so on. In other words, you can target the display of information based on the person viewing the information.

> **NOTE**
>
> Roles are assigned to a group of people and generally grant the group authority to perform tasks that people outside of the group cannot. See Chapter 19, "Security," for additional information pertaining to application security.

> **NOTE**
>
> A valid formula must be specified if the **Hide paragraph if formula is true** option is selected. Often the formula is set to display information based on a person's access role. See "Managing Access to Forms and Documents" in Chapter 19 for additional information.

TIP

A quick way to completely hide a field is to select **Hide paragraph if formula is true** and set the formula to **1**. Alternatively, if you're looking to hide a field but to retain a hide formula that has already been entered, select all checkboxes under the **Hide paragraph from** section.

NOTE

The "hide" feature should not be used as a means to secure data. Even though the field or paragraph is hidden, it can still be viewed in the document properties dialog box.

Field Processing Order

All fields on a form are calculated in a specific sequence—from left to right, top to bottom. This is most important with regards to placement of computed fields and "Hide When" formulas on the form. Figure 4.19 illustrates a form that contains a number of fields and the processing order sequence.

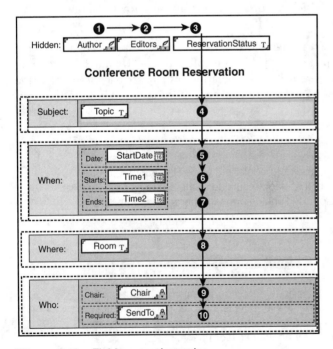

Figure 4.19   Field processing order

So why is the field processing order important? Because the field order can affect other field values for the form. Let's say there are two computed fields on a form. The formula for one field (Time2) is based on the result of another field (Time1). In this situation, placement of the field affects the ability to calculate the data value. If "end time" is placed before "start time" on the form, Lotus Notes will most likely display an error message when the form is initially created.

> **NOTE**
>
> The Designer client will not flag errors in the sequencing of fields. If a computed field is placed on the form ahead of a dependent field, an error message will mostly likely be displayed in the Lotus Notes client when the user attempts to open the form. When this occurs, an error message is presented and the form does *not* display. Whether an error is displayed will depend on the design of the database and the formula stored in the design element.

Setting the Form Type

As a groupware product, Lotus Notes is often used to collaborate, discuss, and share information. To help facilitate this process, Designer allows you to create a hierarchical structure of documents stored within the database. This hierarchy is often called a Main document and Response document.

These form types help facilitate discussion and enable related documents to be grouped together when displayed in a view. There are currently three form types that can be implemented in a Notes database:

- **Document**—This is the default form type for all forms created in the database and is considered to be the main, or parent, document. A main document can have one or more related response documents.
- **Response**—Response documents are tied to a Main document and are often referred to as child documents. When displayed in a view, Response documents appear indented under the parent document.
- **Response to Response**—Finally, as the name implies, this document type is tied to response documents. These documents are often considered to be grandchild documents. In a view, these documents are indented beneath the response document.

> **NOTE**
>
> Although form type can be used to determine whether a document is a child or grandchild document, Notes actually identifies these response documents by the presence of the $REF field on the form. In other words, it's possible to create a child document without specifically setting the form type to "Response." This can be accomplished through the use of the MakeResponse method in LotusScript or the MakeResponse method of the Document class in Java.

Working with Layout Regions

Layout regions are used in forms and subforms. They allow precise control of the placement of the fields, text, and graphics. What makes layout regions special is the ability to place objects on top of one another. Layout regions are generally used to create dialog box displays. This feature was introduced in release 4.

> **NOTE**
>
> Layout regions are *not* supported in Web or mobile applications. However, starting with Lotus Notes release 6, you can utilize *layers* as an alternative to layout regions.

For example, Figure 4.20 shows a layout region in Designer for a repeating calendar reservation. Because the design of the repeating calendar entry allows for many different options, the fields are overlapped. These fields are then selectively displayed in the database and therefore do not appear as jumbled text. In other words, depending on the option selected, fields are either displayed or hidden from the user. This allows the developer to steer the user through the various configuration settings. In this example, there are 16 fields within the layout region, many of which are stacked on top of each other.

Figure 4.21 illustrates the same repeating calendar reservation as displayed in the Notes client. You'll notice that four fields are displayed. However, additional fields will be displayed or hidden based on the option selected in the Repeat field.

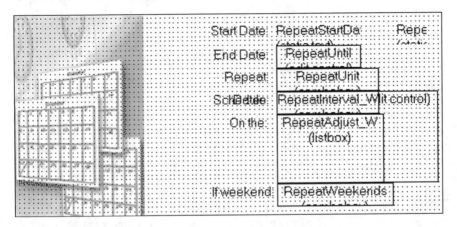

Figure 4.20   Example layout region in Designer

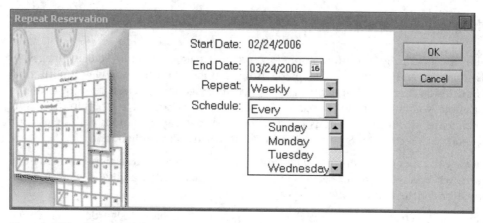

Figure 4.21   Example layout region in Lotus Notes

Creating a Layout Region

The following describes how to create a layout region on a form or subform.

1. Either open an existing form or create a new form, and then position the cursor on the form where the layout region should be created.

2. Select menu options **Create** > **Layout Region** > **New Layout Region**. This will add the object to the form. A rectangular box will frame the area that comprises the region.

3. Like a form, add other design elements—such as fields, text, or graphics—to manage the display and capture of information.

> **TIP**
>
> Use the properties dialog to display a grid and to snap objects to the grid. By default these display options are disabled.

> **NOTE**
>
> Layout regions can also be used to create background graphics or graphic buttons for a form or subform.

> **NOTE**
>
> Although you can cut and paste a field into a layout region in the Designer client, you cannot cut and paste from a layout region to the rest of the form.

Working with Sections

Sections are used to group information—such as text paragraphs, files, tables, images, or fields—that can be expanded or collapsed. Using sections, you can visually group information or fields on a form to simplify the appearance or navigation experience for the end-user. For example, you may want to use sections to separate the various help topics in the "Using This Database" document. Sections can also be used to organize various data fields on a form—such as a section for Software, Hardware, and Network Configuration.

There are two types of sections—*Standard* and *Controlled*. A Standard section is accessible to all users, whereas a Controlled section enables you to manage the ability to view and edit information for the entire grouping.

Sections can be created on forms, subforms, pages, and database design documents such as "About This Database" and "Using This Database." Each section is composed of two elements—the section title and section content.

> **TIP**
>
> In addition to creating sections in Notes applications, Standard sections can be created in the Lotus Notes client. Sections can be created in emails and calendar entries or within any Rich Text field.

When a section is created, the title and related content are grouped together. Sections can easily be identified by the triangle that appears to the left of the title. This is called a *twistie*. Clicking on the twistie will expand and collapse the section. The twistie also serves as a visual status indicator for the section. The twistie will point to the right when the section is collapsed and down when fully expanded.

For example, Figure 4.22 illustrates a standard section used to separate various help topics. It depicts three sections—two collapsed and one expanded.

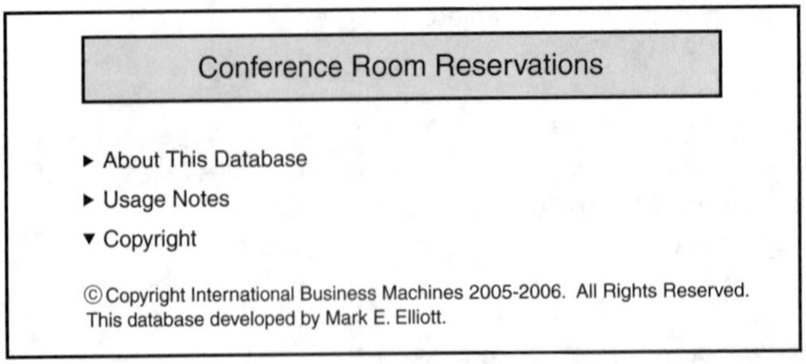

Figure 4.22   Illustrates sections on a form

> **TIP**
>
> Sections are a good way to organize information presented in the "Using This Database" help document or to group related fields on a form.

Creating a Standard Section

The following describes how to create a standard section.

1. First specify a title for the section (e.g., **How to Search the Database**). Underneath the section title, add text paragraphs, tables, images, files, and other information.

2. Select all information, starting with the section title and including all associated information.

3. Select the menu options **Create > Section > Standard**.

> **TIP**
>
> Specifying a meaningful section name will help the user navigate the application.

Editing a Section

Using the properties dialog box, you can also change the default display and appearance settings. Sections can be set to automatically expand or collapse when the document is first opened, edited, or printed. You can also change the colors, fonts, and border graphics.

To edit the section, select or highlight the section. Then select the **Section > Section Properties...** menu options. This will display the properties dialog for the section, which includes four configuration tabs. The first tab enables you to modify the section title, color, and border style (see Figure 4.23). Using the border style, you can customize the appearance of the section.

The second properties tab is used to set the expand and collapse rules for the section. Here you set the section to automatically expand or collapse when the document is previewed, read, edited, or printed. For example, you may want to collapse all sections when the document is previewed and expand all sections when the document is printed.

Three configuration options are available for each of the document modes: previewed, opened for reading, opened for editing, and printed.

Figure 4.23   Setting the border style

> **Don't auto expand or collapse**—Any time the document is accessed, the section will return to the prior state—either expanded or collapsed. This is the default setting.
> **Auto expand section**—Select this option to have the section automatically expanded when the document is accessed.
> **Auto collapse section**—Select this option to have the section automatically collapsed when the document is accessed.

Finally, the remaining two property tabs enable developers to manage the font and permissions associated with the section. These tabs are standard across virtually all Domino object property windows.

> **TIP**
>
> Did you know that you can nest sections within sections? In other words, a single section may contain multiple subsections. This option allows you to further subdivide information and group content.

Sections, by default, are represented by the ▼ symbol located at the top left of the section.

Controlled Sections

Controlled sections work identically to standard sections with one exception. They enable the developer to manage access to the section content within an application. Take, for example, a Notes database used to submit and track workstation service requests. Using controlled sections, you can create a set of fields and instructions for the request information and a second set of fields and instructions for the solution information.

Based on this model, the author completes one section while the technician completes the other section. This approach manages who can edit the content and when. As a result, the technician can add information pertaining to the solution but cannot change the scope of the request. To further illustrate the power of controlled sections, the ability to edit the sections can also be tied to other fields on the form—such as the document status. By adding the status to the controlled section rules, you can then prevent all updates after the status changes. For example, rules could be established to

- Allow the author to edit the request when in a DRAFT status
- Allow the technician to edit the solution when in a SUBMITTED status
- Disable editing for both author and technician when in a COMPLETE status

> **NOTE**
>
> The title of a controlled section cannot be computed, unlike a standard section.

Creating a Controlled Section

Follow these instructions to create a controlled section using the Domino Designer client.

1. First specify a section title (e.g., **How to Search the Database**) followed by text paragraphs, tables, images, files, and other information.

2. Select all section content.

3. Select the menu options **Create > Section > Controlled Access**.

> **NOTE**
>
> Controlled sections are specific to application development using the Domino Designer. Controlled sections cannot be created in documents (such as emails or calendar appointments) in the Lotus Notes client.

4. Immediately after the controlled section is created, the properties dialog window will be displayed in order to configure the controlled section. You'll notice that this property window varies slightly from that of the standard section, and it should really be considered more like an application design element rather than a method to format content. In other words, a controlled section is really a special type of

field that resides on a form, page, or document. For this reason, the first properties tab now includes a Section Field Name field that is used to assign an object name to the design element (see Figure 4.24).

A second notable difference is the Formula tab (or tab number three) in the properties window. This tab, which contains the Access Formula field, defines who can edit the section content (see Figure 4.25). This field must contain a valid formula or rule before you can save the newly created controlled section.

5. Click the **Formula** tab and specify a valid access formula. Access formulas determine who is permitted to edit the section content. Although you could hard-code a user's name (e.g., Mark Elliott/Raleigh/IBM), a more robust method would be to compute the editors based on a field value (such as Status = "DRAFT"), user role (e.g., person is a member of the "AdminGroup" role), or a combination of both. These options provide greater flexibility to manage access to the section via programmatic means. Refer to Chapter 19 for additional information pertaining to security settings and roles.

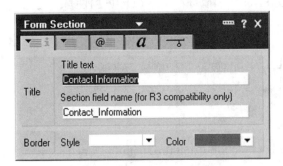

Figure 4.24   Controlled section field name

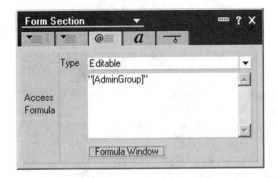

Figure 4.25   Access formula for a controlled section

> **NOTE**
>
> The rules associated with a controlled section only apply to the content of the section. Objects, text, and fields outside the controlled section will not be affected by controlled section rules.

Working with Buttons

Buttons are used to automate tasks and can be added to forms, subforms, pages, views, folders, navigators, layout regions, and layers. There are essentially two types of buttons that can be implemented in a Notes database—*action* buttons and *hotspot* buttons. Both functionally can perform the same task; however, they are distinguished by the location of the button within the application.

Action buttons are created and stored in the Action pane on the right side of the Designer client. By default, this type of button resides at the top of the design element and immediately below the Lotus Notes menu options. By default, the action buttons also appear under the Actions menu. This enables the buttons to be clicked from the graphical interface or selected from the menu bar. For example, many forms include Save and Close buttons to help with application usability.

> **NOTE**
>
> If the Action pane is not displayed in the Designer client, select the **View > Action Pane** menu items to have it displayed. Alternatively, you can drag open the frame using your mouse and left mouse button.

Hotspot buttons, on the other hand, are embedded within the design element and typically help the user to manipulate data or perform a task on the form or subform. For example, let's say you have a form that enables the user to attach three separate files—an Offer Letter, Acceptance Letter, and Resignation Letter (see Figure 4.26). Using buttons, users could locate and select the appropriate file and have it automatically attached in the correct field.

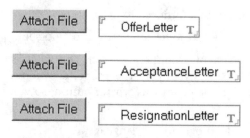

Figure 4.26 Example hotspot buttons

Finally, an embedded button can be displayed as a hotspot or as a button. From a functional perspective, they are equivalent. Visually, however, the graphic representation of a hotspot is slightly different from what most consider a button to look like. From an application development perspective, you'll probably find that most users prefer the traditional button to a hotspot.

Creating an Action Bar Button

Follow these instructions to create an action button for a form, subform, page, view, or folder.

1. Open a form, subform, page, view, or folder and select **Create > Action > Action** from the menu bar. This will create an untitled action button and automatically display the property window.

2. In the Action properties dialog, give the button a name and close the window.

3. Next, select the client (either **Notes** or **Web**) where the button will run and a programming language.

4. Finally, add the source code or use the simple action wizard to define the task that the button will perform.

Creating a Hotspot Button

Follow these instructions to embed a hotspot button in a form, subform, or page.

1. Open a form, subform, or page and click on the area where you want the button to be placed. Then select **Create > Hotspot > Button** from the menu bar. This will create an untitled action button and automatically display the property window.

2. In the properties dialog, give the button a label and close the window.

3. Next, select the client (either **Notes** or **Web**) where the button will run and a programming language.

4. Finally, add the source code or use the simple action wizard to define the task that the button will perform.

Creating an Action Hotspot

Follow these instructions to embed an action hotspot in a form, subform, or page.

1. Open a form, subform, or page and select the text to be converted into a hotspot.

2. Next, select **Create > Hotspot > Action Hotspot** from the menu bar. This will create an untitled action button and automatically display the property window. Unlike an action button, there is no label or name for this type of button, so you can close the property window.

3. Next, select where the button will run and a programming language.

4. Finally, add the source code or use the simple action wizard to define the task that the button will perform. After the hotspot is created, the user can click on the text area, and the action will be performed.

Commonly Implemented Buttons

Buttons can be created for just about any purpose. However, as a developer, you will come to find that some buttons are common to most Notes databases. The following are a few of the more commonly implemented action buttons.

Button	Formula
1. Save	`@Command([FileSave])`
2. Close	`@Command([FileCloseWindow])`
3. Edit	`@Command([EditDocument])`
4. New Document	`@Command([Compose]; "FormName")`
5. Attach File	`@Command([EditGotoField]; "FieldName");` `@Command([EditInsertFileAttachment])`
6. New Response	`@Command([Compose]; "FormName")`
Note: Be sure to select "Response" or "Response to response" as the form type in the properties dialog.	
7. Help	`@Command([HelpUsingDatabase])`
8. Today	`@Command([CalendarGoTo]; @Date(@Now))`
9. Open a database	`Server := "ServerName";` `DBName := "NotesName";` `@If (@Command([FileOpenDatabase];` `Server : DBName; ""; ""; "1");` `@Success; @Prompt([Ok]; "Warning.";` `"An error was encountered. Please` `contact the system administrator.") )`
10. Forward document	`@Command([MailForward])`
Note: Items in **bold** should be replaced with design element, field, database, or server name specific to your Notes database and environment.	

Working with Views

Views are used to organize and display a collection of related data records in a series of rows and columns similar to a spreadsheet. Using a selection formula, Lotus Notes determines which documents are displayed in the view. All documents that meet the selection criteria rule or rules are subsequently included when the view is opened. Every Notes database must have at least one view.

There are two methods for specifying a selection formula—*simple action* and *Formula Language*. Using simple actions, you can build a selection formula using a wizard. Alternatively, you can use Formula Language to create more advanced or complex rules for the view.

Let's say, for instance, that you have a database with multiple forms. Using views, you could create a separate view for each form. To ensure that each view only displays the related documents, a unique selection formula is specified for each view. In this case, the selection criteria for one of the views would look something like

```
SELECT Form = "Reservation";
```

where "Reservation" is one of the forms in the database.

> **NOTE**
>
> Use a selection formula or simple action to refine the information displayed in the view. If no formula is specified, all documents will be returned for the view.

In addition to selecting the content for a view, Designer allows you to specify the sort order, column content, and display appearance. Again, using the properties dialog, you can define a sort sequence for each column in the view. Information can be sorted in ascending order, descending order, or not at all.

From an appearance perspective, there are two types of displays—*Standard Outline* and *Calendar*. The Standard Outline view displays information in rows and columns. A Calendar view, on the other hand, changes the user interface into a calendar where the documents display based on a specific date and time. Both display documents based on a selection formula.

For example, Figure 4.27 illustrates three different Standard Outline views. Each view contains the same information, simply sorted differently. The views could also be modified to include or exclude fields by changing what's displayed in the columns. In the first example, all of the documents are sorted by First Name and Lastname.

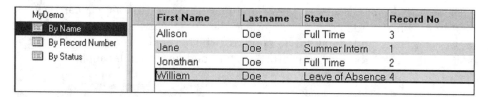

Figure 4.27 Example view sorted by Name

In Figure 4.28, all of the documents are sorted by the Record Number. In many applications, a unique document number is assigned to each record in the database. This view permits users to quickly locate a document based on the document identifier.

In Figure 4.29, information is grouped based on a particular field—the document Status. This is called a "categorized" view. In this view, all documents that have the same status are grouped together and displayed under the green triangle—called a twistie, as mentioned earlier.

MyDemo	Record No	First Name	Lastname	Status
By Name	1	Jane	Doe	Summer Intern
By Record Number	2	Jonathan	Doe	Full Time
By Status	3	Allison	Doe	Full Time
	4	William	Doe	Leave of Absence

Figure 4.28 Example view sorted by Record Number

MyDemo	Status	Record No	First Name	Lastname
By Name	▼Full Time			
By Record Number		2	Jonathan	Doe
By Status		3	Allison	Doe
	▼Leave of Absence			
		4	William	Doe
	▼Summer Intern			
		1	Jane	Doe

Figure 4.29 Example view categorized by Status

> **TIP**
>
> The small green triangle, located to the left of each of the three status values (refer to Figure 4.29), is called a *twistie*. The twistie can be displayed or hidden by setting a checkbox in the view properties dialog.

Finally, Figure 4.30 depicts a Calendar view. To display documents on a Calendar view, the document must contain a date and duration, and the first two columns in the view must contain the start date and duration in minutes (which can be zero). See Chapter 8, "Calendar Applications," for detailed instructions for building a calendar application.

> **TIP**
>
> Designer allows you to sort multiple data columns in a view. Columns are sorted from left to right in the view with the data being displayed in either ascending or descending order.

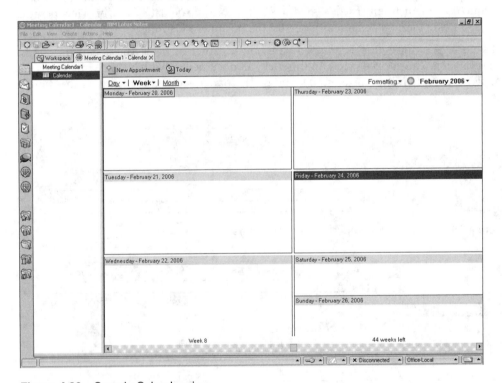

Figure 4.30   Sample Calendar view

Hidden Views

Views are typically used to display information to the users. However, views can also be used to manage the application. In many cases, programming-related views are hidden from the end-user to simplify the overall navigation of the Notes database. In many cases, hidden views are used to provide values for keyword fields or for calculations.

For example, let's say you want to assign a unique, sequential tracking number for each new document added to the database. Any time a user creates a new document, Lotus Notes increments the current tracking number by one and assigns it to the document.

This could be achieved by using a view that contains one column, "Tracking Number," sorted in descending order. As new documents are created, the application retrieves the first record in the view (e.g., the top-most number) and increments the number. As soon as the document is saved, the new document becomes the top-most record in the view. Functionally, the view could be displayed or hidden. However, because users probably will find little benefit from a view that only contains numbers, you could hide it and reduce the number of views displayed to the end-user.

> **TIP**
>
> Hidden views can be displayed in the application by holding down both the **Control** and **Shift** keys while opening (or double-clicking on) the database icon. If navigators or outlines are used, then select the **View > Go to** menu options to display the view.

To hide a view, add the open and close parentheses "( )" when specifying the view name. For example, "TrackingNo" would be visible to the user, whereas "(TrackingNo)" would be hidden.

Creating a Standard Outline View

Follow these instructions to create a standard outline view.

1. From the menu bar, select **Create > Design > View** to create a new view. Alternatively, navigate to the View section of the Design pane and click **New View**. A Create View dialog box window will now appear.

2. Specify a view name. To hide the view, enclose the view name in parentheses. In most cases, you'll want to keep the View type as **Shared**. This will enable the general user community to access the view. To create a view that only you can access, change this value to **Private**.

3. Next, you can elect to create a blank view or base the design on an existing view in the database. If you have specified a default view, this view will be displayed in the **Copy style from view** field (see Figure 4.31). Otherwise, the field value will be set to -**Blank**-. To change this value, click the **Copy From** button and select a new option.

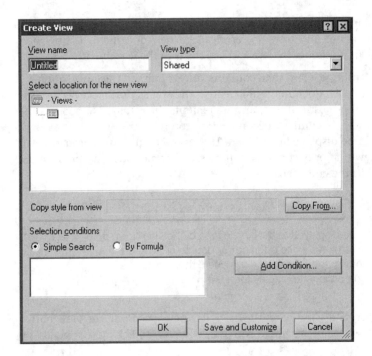

Figure 4.31   Create View dialog

4. Now specify the selection conditions for the view. At this point, you have three
options available to you—use the wizard, specify a formula, or leave the field blank.
To add a query or set of rules using the wizard, click the **Add Condition** button and
complete the form. Alternatively, click the **By Formula** radio button to create rules
using *Formula Language*. If no conditions are specified, the view will automatically
display all documents stored in the database.

> **TIP**
>
> The selection conditions for the view can be changed at any time. If
> you're not sure what the formula should be when creating the view, you
> can omit the conditions and specify them later. To set or change the
> conditions, select the **View Selection** object in the Object pane in the
> Designer client.

5. Click **Save and Customize** to create the view and open it in the Domino Designer
Work pane.

6. To add columns to the view, select **Create > Insert New Column** or **Append New Column**. This will add a column to the view. To define the value of the column, locate the Column Value pane and specify a value. Here you can select a **simple function** (which contains a list of predefined formula values), change the display type to **Field** and select a field from the list of values, or use a **Formula** to determine the column contents.

7. Finally, to set the sort order, click on the column header and select **Edit > Properties**. Click on the second tab to change the sort preferences or to create a categorized view.

Creating a Calendar View

Follow these instructions to create a calendar view.

1. From the menu bar, select **Create > Design > View** to create a new view. Alternatively, navigate to the View section of the Design pane and click **New View**. A Create View dialog box window will now display.

2. Specify a view name.

3. Next, click the **Copy style from view** button and set the value to -Blank- if not already set to this option.

4. Now specify the selection conditions for the view. At this point, you have three options available to you—use the wizard, specify a formula, or leave the field blank. To create a rule or set of rules using the Designer wizard, click the **Add Condition** button and complete the form. Alternatively, click the **By Formula** checkbox to create rules using *Formula Language*. If no conditions are specified, the view will automatically display all documents stored in the database.

5. Click **OK** to build the view.

6. Locate the view in the Design pane and open the view. Select **Edit > Properties** and change the Style from **Standard Outline** to **Calendar**. By default, Designer will display a warning message "Changing to a calendar view may change the attributes of this view. Continue?" Click **Yes** and close the properties window.

7. The first column in the view *must* contain a date/time field value. Change the sort order to ascending. Depending on the application, you may want to hide this column using the properties dialog.

8. The second column in the view *must* contain the duration field value or a hard-coded value of zero. In most cases, you will want to hide this column using the properties dialog.

> **NOTE**
>
> The calendar view will not display if the first and second columns do not respectively contain a date/time and duration value.

Working with Application Menus

In the previous section we discussed how to name design elements and the fact that newly created forms automatically display in the application menu. By default, the form name will be displayed under the Create menu. However, to provide additional structure to the menu, you can implement a cascading menu. A cascading menu is a submenu that appears in the Create menu and can help group related forms together.

For example, let's say you have a Notes database to manage end-user service requests. Using this database, users can request workstation assistance, ask for help with moving furniture, request a name change, schedule an office move, and request a password reset. These could be grouped together into a submenu called Service Request (see Figure 4.32).

Cascading menus are created by inserting the submenu path and a backslash "\" before the primary name of the form (see Figure 4.33). This can be done when the form is first saved or by modifying the form name in the properties dialog.

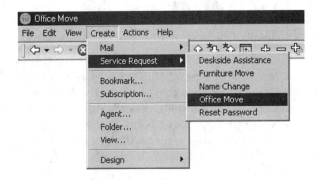

Figure 4.32   Cascading menu of database forms

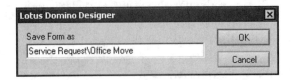

Figure 4.33   Creating a cascading menu for a form

To create a cascading menu after the form has been saved, open the form properties dialog and change the form name.

Similar to cascading forms being displayed in the application menu, cascading views can be used to group related views. To create a submenu of views, specify the main view name, a backslash, and the name of the view.

Working with Folders

Folders are used to store documents and look exactly like views. However, views display or contain documents based on a selection formula or query. Folders, on the other hand, enable users to move documents into them as a storage location for related information.

> **TIP**
>
> Use folders to group related documents. Let's say you have three projects currently being managed. Using folders, you could create a separate folder for each project—Project A, B, and C.

> **NOTE**
>
> It's important to understand that documents placed in a folder are not "moved" out of the view and into the folder. There is only one copy of the document, and the folder stores a reference to that document. If you delete the document from the view, it's deleted from all folders as well.

Creating a Folder

Follow these instructions to create a folder.

1. Select the **Create > Design > Folder** menu options, and a new folder will be created. Alternatively, navigate to the Folder section of the Design pane and click **New Folder**. Be sure to specify a meaningful primary name and alias name.

2. Specify a folder name. In most cases, you'll want to keep the Folder type as **Shared**. This will enable the general user community to access the folder. To create a folder that only you can access, change this value to **Private**.

3. Next, you can elect to create a blank folder or base the design on an existing folder in the database. If you have specified a default folder, it will be displayed in the **Copy style from view** field. Otherwise, the field value will be set to **-Blank-**. To change this value, click the **Copy From** button and select a new option.

4. Click **OK** to create the folder.

Working with Framesets

Framesets allow the application to be divided into multiple sections—like the design panes used to navigate the Designer client. Frames allow you to add structure to a Notes client or Web browser application interface. Each pane can then be set to display unique information—such as form, view, page, etc.

Two Frames	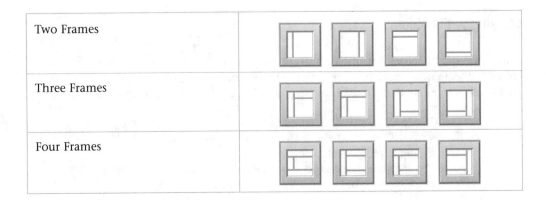
Three Frames	
Four Frames	

For example, your Lotus Notes mail calendar utilizes a two-pane frameset. The left pane displays a monthly snapshot and "To Do" list. Users can also scroll through the calendar months and click on a date to jump directly to the corresponding calendar date entry. The right pane, as illustrated in Figure 4.34, displays the daily, weekly, monthly, and meeting views. The combination of these left and right panes comprises this frameset.

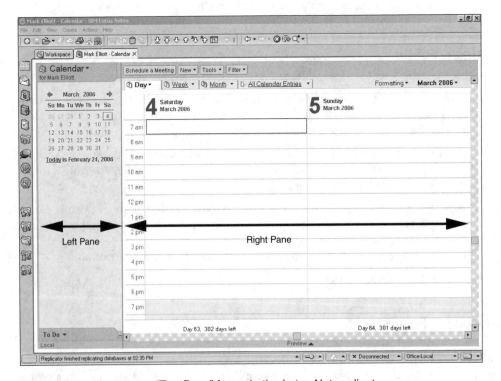

Figure 4.34 Illustrates a "Two Pane" frame in the Lotus Notes client

> **NOTE**
>
> Framesets are used to define the application appearance by dividing the window into multiple frames and are dependent on other design elements. Content is then embedded in each frame section.

Framesets are dependent on other design elements within the Domino Designer. They can be configured in many different ways. See Chapter 12, "Web Applications," for additional information on how to create a frameset for a Notes database or Web application.

Working with Pages

Pages are used to display information in a way that is similar to how Web pages look. However, pages can be used in both a Notes and Web application. Pages can be used to display company information or graphics or to provide links to other applications or Web sites. Using this design element, you can create sophisticated Web pages without having to write HTML source code.

> **NOTE**
>
> As with most application development tools, there are many ways to build a Web page using the Lotus Domino Designer. In addition to pages, you can also use forms, HTML, JavaScript, and other related technologies to build a Web application or Web page.

Creating a Page

Follow these instructions to create a page.

1. Select the **Create > Design > Page** menu options, and a new page will be created. Alternatively, navigate to the Page section of the Design pane and click **New Page**.

2. Next, define the layout of the page by adding text, buttons, images, sections, and other design elements (described later in this chapter).

3. The first time you save the page, you'll be prompted to specify a page name. Be sure to specify a meaningful primary name and alias name.

Working with Shared Code

Shared design elements are items that can be created once and used many places within the database. Using shared objects enables you to create and manage resource attributes from a single location. This simplifies application maintenance, reduces the overall code base, and improves application efficiency. Shared code can include agents, Web services, outlines, subforms, fields, columns, actions, and script libraries.

Agents

Agents are standalone programs used to perform a task. They can be called manually or scheduled to run on set intervals. Agents can be configured to perform a simple action from a predefined list of tasks or programmed using Formula Language, LotusScript, Java, or Imported Java code.

> **NOTE**
>
> See Chapter 9, "Collaborative Applications," Chapter 11, "Workflow Applications," and Chapter 16, "Sample Agents," for example agents and step-by-step setup instructions.

Web Services

A Web service is a self-contained application that can be invoked from a Domino Web application. Typical Web services include LotusScript, Java, SOAP, and XML-based services. Web services are invoked much like an agent and support browser-based applications.

Outlines

Outlines provide a means to navigate an application interface. Using outlines, you can create a navigational structure for the entire database application that is maintained from a single location.

> **NOTE**
>
> See "Create a Custom Application Interface" in Chapter 17, "Miscellaneous Enhancements and Tips for Domino Databases," for step-by-step setup instructions for creating an outline.

Subforms

Subforms look and work just like forms with one exception. Subforms can be embedded, or shared, with other forms in the database. For example, let's say you have a Human Resource database that's used to track vacation, leaves of absence, and travel requests. Each form starts with the same six fields—reference number, first name, last name, employee number, start-date, and end-date. Instead of creating these fields on each of the forms, you could create one subform and embed it into each of the main forms.

> **TIP**
>
> To keep a consistent group of buttons—such as Edit, Save, and Close—across multiple forms, create a subform that only contains action buttons. Embed the subform at the top of each form or use shared action buttons. Be sure to give the subform a meaningful name, such as **Shared Form Buttons** or **Common Buttons**.

Fields

Similar to subforms, shared fields can be defined once and embedded in one or more forms and subforms. The primary benefit of a shared field is to allow the programming behind the field to be shared across multiple design elements.

Columns

A shared column is a column created once and used across multiple views. Changes to the column are automatically applied across all views containing the particular column.

Actions

An action is a self-contained module that performs a task when the user manually clicks a button. Action buttons display either in the action bar (located at the top of the application screen) or in the Action menu. Buttons can also be configured to run an agent. Shared actions provide the ability to maintain programming code from a single location and implement the functionality across the database application.

Script Libraries

Script libraries are used to store a collection of LotusScript, JavaScript, or Java subroutines and functions shared throughout the application. Using a script library, developers can write and maintain code from a single location.

A script library should be created and used anytime you identify reusable code for an application. This simplifies application maintenance (e.g., you only have to modify code in one place), reduces the complexity of the application, and makes the application more efficient.

For example, let's say you have three unique forms, and each form has a Save button that checks to see if the document has a record number (see Figure 4.35). Using a script library, you can maintain a single subroutine that all of the buttons utilize.

Thus, if the code needs to change, you update the source code in one location (as opposed to each of the buttons individually).

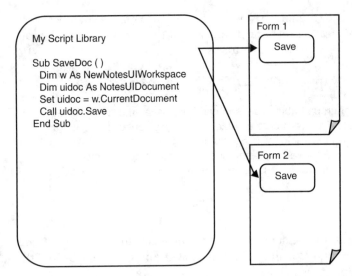

Figure 4.35   LotusScript libraries can be used across the database design elements.

> **NOTE**
>
> In order to utilize a LotusScript library, you must add the statement USE
> LIBRARY where LIBRARY is the name of the LotusScript library. Add
> this to the GLOBAL section of each design element (e.g., form, view,
> agent, etc.).

Working with Shared Resources

Shared resources are objects, typically files, that are not Lotus Domino files or design elements but that can be used and referenced from within the application. Like shared objects,
shared resources enable you to maintain application resource files from a single location.

Images

Shared images are graphics files that can be used throughout the application—such as a
company logo. Valid image file formats include JPEG, GIF, and BMP. These files can be used
on forms, subforms, pages, action buttons, and outlines. Image resources can also be used
as watermark or background images throughout the application.

Files

This section is used to store file attachments including HTML, PDF, word processing files,
spreadsheets, or general presentations.

Applets

Applets are generally used to enhance Web applications but can be used in Lotus Notes applications as well. Through the use of applets, you can enhance the user interface and perform specialized tasks. Applets are created externally to the Notes Designer interface using the Java programming language and are imported into the Notes database design.

Style Sheets

Style sheets, also known as Cascading Style Sheets (CSS), are used to apply a consistent format to a Web page, form, or view. Using style sheets, you can control the look and feel of all related design elements from a common location. For example, style sheets allow you to specify the font, size, and color to be used for all text, buttons, and Web links. This ensures a common presentation across all Web pages and enables the designer to change all attributes from one location.

Data Connections

Starting in release 6, Lotus introduced the Data Connection Resource. This design element enables the Notes database to connect to a relational database. Using this design element, a Notes database can link and store (or retrieve) data external to the NSF file.

> **NOTE**
>
> Implementation of this feature requires the Domino Enterprise Connector Services (DECS) software to be installed on your Domino server.

A.4.

Working with "Other" Design Elements

Finally, the remaining design elements can be found in the "Other" section of the Design pane. For the most part, this section contains design components that apply to the overall database application. This Other section contains the following design elements.

Design Element	Description Overview
Database Resources	Contains special database objects
Icon	Allows the designer to modify the database icon that is shown in the Lotus Notes client
Using This Database	Stores help information on how to use the database
About This Database	Stores help information on the purpose for the database
Database Script	Stores LotusScript code that applies to the overall database

continues

Design Element	Description Overview
Navigators	Enables designers to customize the application graphical user interface
Synopsis	Enables designers to create reports that detail the design of the database

Icon

This special design element stores the image that's displayed on the database from the Lotus Notes client. When a new database is created, Designer creates a default icon. Using this design element, you can customize the appearance of the icon (see Figure 4.36). This helps the user visually recognize the database. A well-designed icon can also act as a visual cue to the purpose of the database.

Figure 4.36   Database icons help users identify databases.

Follow these instructions to edit the database icon.

1. In the Design pane, navigate to **Other > Database Resources**. This will display four special database objects.

2. Select **Icon** to edit the database icon.

3. Using the paintbrush, pencil, eraser, and color, click on the bitmap to modify the icon. When finished, click **OK** to save the database icon image.

Using This Database

Each Lotus Notes database has the option to include two types of help files—*Using This Database* and *About This Database*. The "Using This Database" document generally explains how to use the database. This document is intended to help users navigate the tool. The "Using" document is accessed from the Help menu. The following are some considerations to include in the document.

- Provide a database overview
- Describe the forms
- Describe access groups
- Describe various roles
- List the database administrator

> **TIP**
>
> You may want to keep the "Using This Database" content generic. This way, the help context will always match the actual design of the database. This is a frequent problem when the database design changes but the help content does not, resulting in discrepancies between the help document and the implemented database design.

Follow these instructions to create the "Using This Database" document.

1. In the Design pane, navigate to **Other > Database Resources**. This will display four special database objects.

2. Double-click **Using This Database** to open the document in edit mode.

3. Add information to the document, such as text, images, copyright, attachments, or related information.

4. Select **File > Save** (or **Ctrl+S**) to save the document. You will not be prompted to specify a name when saving this special database object.

About This Database

The "About This Database" document is a special database object. By default, this document is displayed the first time any user opens the database, provided the document exists. This document should provide a general introduction to the database.

Follow these instructions to create the "About This Database" document.

1. In the Design pane, navigate to **Other > Database Resources**. This will display four special database objects.

2. Double-click **About This Database** to open the document in edit mode.

3. Add information to the document, such as text, copyright, release level, primary database contact, or other related information.

4. Select **File > Save** (or **Ctrl+S**) to save the document. You will not be prompted to specify a name when saving this special database object.

The "About" document is an optional design element. The default is to automatically display the document the first time each user accesses the database. However, in the database properties dialog, you can also (1) display the "About" document every time the database is opened, (2) only display it when the document is modified, or (3) never display it when the database is opened.

You may want to display the document every time it is opened to relay important updates or present reminders. Conversely, you can disable the display if desired. To change the options, open the database properties by selecting the **File > Database > Properties** menu options (see Figure 4.37).

> **TIP**
>
> Add text in the "About This Database" and "Using This Database"
> design elements to help users navigate the application. The "About"
> page usually provides a summary of what the database does, whereas
> the "Using" page generally describes how to use or navigate the
> application.

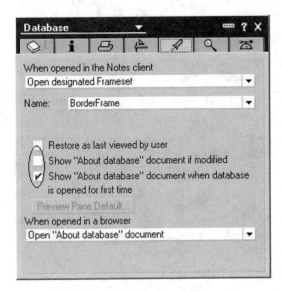

Figure 4.37   Set display properties for the "About" document

> **NOTE**
>
> The "About This Database" document only displays if the document
> exists. Based on the default properties for the database, this document
> is only displayed to users the first time the application is opened.

Database Script

The Database Script is a special design element that contains LotusScript or Formula
Language code that applies to the overall database. The Database Script is similar to the
LotusScript library, except the code applies specifically to the Notes database.

Navigators

Navigators are used to display a graphical user interface in the Notes database. As the name implies, they help the user navigate the application through a series of buttons, hotspots, graphics, and text. Using this interface, the user can click buttons to display information or even jump to another database.

> **NOTE**
>
> Starting with release 5, navigators were replaced with framesets, outlines, and pages, which offer more robust features. However, this function is still supported.

Synopsis

The Synopsis creates a detailed report for various design elements in the Notes database (see Figure 4.38). Using this design feature, you can gather information on the entire database or select design elements. Each report displays the object name, type, property attributes, and associated source code (where applicable).

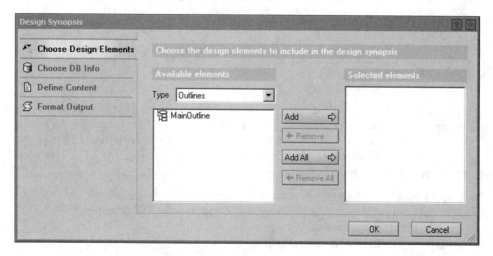

Figure 4.38   Synopsis dialog box

> **NOTE**
>
> The Synopsis is not a design element. Using this feature, you can create design reports to help debug the application or to locate all instances of a text phrase or subroutine call.

Follow these instructions to create a synopsis report.

1. Select **File** > **Database** > **Design Synopsis**. Alternatively, navigate to the Other section in the Design pane and choose **Synopsis**. This will display the Synopsis dialog box that's used to build reports.

2. From the Choose Design Elements tab, select a design type.

3. Next, select one or more design elements and click **Add**. Alternatively, click **Add All** to include all elements in the report. Continue to select design types and elements until the report includes all desired database elements.

4. Click **OK** to generate the report.

> **NOTE**
>
> In most cases, you can include all design types and objects in the synopsis report. However, Designer may encounter problems generating reports if the database contains a significant number of design elements or source code. When this occurs, you will receive an error "Document has too many paragraphs—it must be split into several documents." Reducing the number of design elements selected when building the report request can rectify this problem.

Working with Events

Finally, it is important to understand that a Lotus Notes database is event driven. Every action performed by the user can actually be considered an event. Events can also be scheduled to run based on a date and time via agents. Events are very important to the management of Notes database applications. They are used to control the execution of specific code whenever an event trigger occurs. Using these event triggers, you can

- Display error, warning, or informational messages
- Perform field validation before allowing the user to save a document
- Calculate and set field values on a form
- Prompt for additional information from the user
- Modify data stored anywhere in the current or another database
- Create and send reports
- Set time and date stamps
- Prevent users from copying and pasting documents
- Recalculate fields on a form
- Create a new form or document
- Automatically create a new calendar entry when the user double-clicks on a calendar date

All design elements and objects in the Domino Designer client contain one or more events. Different triggers are associated with each event. For example, the following are some typical event triggers:

- Opening a database
- Opening a document
- Clicking a button
- Saving a document
- Copying a document

For example, let's say you want to force the user to describe changes to a document every time the document is changed and saved. This could be accomplished by adding code to the QuerySave event. The code stored in the event is subsequently run every time the document is saved. Additional information and working examples of event triggers can be found in each of the projects in this book.

Links to developerWorks

A.4.1 Morris, Scott and Sencer, Ethan. *Simplify your DECS DB2 environment.* IBM developerWorks, March 2004. http://www.ibm.com/developerworks/lotus/library/decs-db2/index.html.

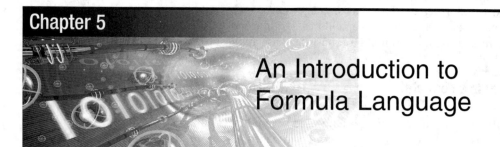

Chapter 5

An Introduction to Formula Language

Chapter Overview

This chapter will introduce you to the Lotus Formula Language. There are many books on the market that teach syntax and how to program. However, this chapter is intended to be a general introduction to facilitate learning and to help you understand the projects provided in this book. Additional information can be found in the Domino Designer help database that is included with the Designer software.

By the end of the chapter you will have learned

- What Formula Language is
- What @Functions are
- What @Commands are
- The basic syntax structure
- How to assign values to variables
- How to construct multi-line formulas
- How to use formulas to calculate a field value
- Frequently used @Functions
- Frequently used @Commands

What Is Formula Language?

Formula Language is a simple, easy-to-use programming language that can be found in many Lotus products—such as Lotus 1-2-3 and Lotus Notes. Formula Language has been integrated into Lotus Notes since its inception in 1989 and has included numerous enhancements over the years.

Then, in 2002, Lotus decided to completely rewrite the underlying processor (or engine) used to interpret the formula language source code. This significantly improved its performance and expanded its capabilities. Using a few simple Formula Language commands and functions, you can build a robust database application.

What Is a Formula?

In the simplest terms, formulas are used to produce a data value or action. This value or action is derived by using one or more commands, functions, or statements to create a *main expression*. All formulas must have a main expression that equates to a result. If the formula does not produce a value or action, the Designer client will not allow you to save the formula.

For example, the following illustrates an invalid formula. Here, the text value "Happy New Year" is assigned to a temporary variable called message. Although the formula does perform a calculation, there is no main expression. This formula does not produce a result.

```
message := "Happy New Year";
```

For this example to be valid, the formula must do something to produce a result. This second example illustrates a valid formula. Looking at this formula, you'll notice that the first line performs a computation by assigning a text value to a temporary variable. The statement is terminated with a semicolon, which separates the first statement from the second. The formula then ends with the main expression, which defines the value for the field.

```
message := "Happy New Year";
message
```

In this case, the main expression is assigned the contents of the variable message. Alternatively, the same result could have been achieved by setting the text string to be the main expression, as illustrated next.

```
"Happy New Year"
```

> **TIP**
>
> When writing a formula containing multiple statements, each statement must be separated by a semicolon, and the last line in the formula must be the "main expression."

Working with Variables

Now let's take a look at the basic syntax rules for working with variables. There are two types of variables that can be utilized in formulas—temporary variables and field name variables.

Temporary variables, as the name implies, are used to temporarily store a value associated with the formula. Temporary variables cannot be referenced outside of the formula and only contain a value for the duration of the formula's execution. In other words, the value stored in a temporary variable is not saved when the document or form is saved and cannot be referenced by other formulas.

The syntax for creating a temporary variable is `VariableName` and the assignment operator `:=` followed by the data value and semicolon. For example, the following assigns `"January"` to the temporary variable called `month`.

```
month := "January";
```

Conversely, field name variables reference actual fields on a document or form. When used in a formula, you can reference or change the value stored in the field name. In other words, by using formulas, you can use field names to calculate the main expression or modify the value already stored in the field.

There are three ways to reference an existing field. The `FIELD` keyword is used to assign a value to an existing field. Using this keyword, the contents of the field are permanently changed and will be stored in the field when the document is saved. The syntax for setting a field value in a form or document is `FIELD FieldName` and the assignment operator `:=` followed by the new value and a semicolon. For example:

```
FIELD Month := "January";
```

It's important to note that if the field exists on the form, the new value will replace the existing data value. If the field does not exist on the form, Notes will create the field and assign the value. Alternatively, you can also use the `@SetField` function. This function works just like `FIELD` with one exception: `@SetField` can be imbedded within other Formula Language functions.

```
@SetField ("Month"; "January");
```

Finally, to acquire the value of an existing field, you can use the `@GetField` function. Using this function, you can use the value stored in field inside another formula. For example, the following will create the text string `"Your project is due in: January"`, assuming the `Month` field contains a value of `"January"`.

```
"Your project is due in: " + @GetField ( "Month" );
```

> **NOTE**
>
> Lotus Notes will recognize a variable name regardless of the letter case. Variable names can be uppercase, lowercase, or mixed case and will still be understood. For example, the following are equivalent variable names: `firstname`, `FIRSTNAME`, `FirstName`, and `FIRSTname`.

Formula Language Keywords

As with any programming language, Formula Language includes a number of reserved keywords that have special meanings. These keywords are used to perform special functions and cannot be used as variables. For example, the following table describes the current list of Formula Language reserved keywords.

Keyword	Meaning
DEFAULT	Used to define the initial or default value for a field. For example, let's say you have a field called Status. Using the following formula, the field will be set to a value of "New Request" when the document is created. This field will continue to hold this value until either the user or the Notes application changes the value. After the stored value is changed and the document is saved, the new value will be stored in the field. `DEFAULT Status := "New Request"; Status`
ENVIRONMENT	Used to assign a value to an environment setting in the user's NOTES.INI file. For example, let's say you have a database to request helpdesk support. Using the environment keyword, you could capture and store the employee's serial number in the NOTES.INI file the first time an employee submits a service request. As new requests are submitted, the database could query for the existence of the field and automatically fill in the EmpNum field with the employee's serial number. If the environment variable does not already exist in the INI file, Notes will create the variable and assign it a value. Otherwise, if the variable already exists, Notes will assign the new value. `ENVIRONMENT EmpNum := "123456";` Note: The @Environment function can also be used to retrieve (or set) an environment variable setting.
FIELD	Used to assign a value to a field on a document or form. If the field exists, the new value will be assigned. If the field does not exist, the field will be created and assigned the value. For example, the following assigns the current date to a field called theDate. `FIELD theDate := @Today;`

REM	Used to add comments to a formula. Comments must be enclosed in quotes or braces and terminated with a semicolon (if part of a multi-line formula). For example:
	`REM "This is a comment.";`
	`REM {This is a comment};`

Keyword	Meaning
SELECT	Used to determine the selection criteria for a view, agent, or replication formula. All documents that match the selection formula will be included in the view, agent, or replication formula. For example, let's say you have a Notes database with multiple forms. To create a view that only displays one of the forms, you would define a selection formula similar to the following: `SELECT form = "ServiceRequest";`

By default, reserved words are always the first word in a statement. Reserved words may be entered in lower, upper, or mixed case. However, Designer will automatically convert lower or mixed case words to uppercase when the formula is saved.

Working with Operators

Operators are used to compare or equate values and for mathematic calculations. The following table lists the primary operators used in formulas.

Operator	Operator Usage or Description
-	Used in subtraction or to represent a negative number
!	Represents a logical NOT
!=	Represents not equal
&	Represents a logical AND
*	Used in multiplication
/	Used in division
:	Used to separate a list of values
:=	Used to assign a value to a variable
|	Represents a logical OR
+	Used in addition or to represent a positive number
<	Represents less than
<=	Represents less than or equal to

continues

Operator	Operator Usage or Description
<>	Represents not equal
=	Represents equal
=!	Represents not equal
>	Represents greater than
><	Represents not equal
>=	Represents greater than or equal to

General Syntax Rules

The Formula Language syntax rules are quite simple. All formulas must adhere to the following five rules.

Rule 1: A semicolon must separate all formulas that contain more than one statement. It's important to understand that multiple statements can reside on a single line, provided that a semicolon delineates each statement. For example, the following are valid multi-statement formulas.

Example 1
```
DEFAULT status := "New Request"; status
```

Example 2
```
DEFAULT status := "New Request";
status
```

Rule 2: At least one space must follow all reserved keywords. Otherwise, any number of spaces—from none to many—may be used to separate operators, punctuation, and values. For example, the following are valid and equivalent statements (with regard to spacing):
```
output := "Today's date is: " + @Today;
output:="Today's date is: " + @Today;
FIELD output:= "Today's date is: " + @Today;
```

Rule 3: Two values, variables, or strings must be separated by at least one operator. For example, the following are valid statements. In the first example, the plus sign is used to sum the two numbers and divide the result by 2. In the second example, the plus sign is used to concatenate two values together. Finally, the third example shows three @Functions separated by the plus operator.
```
output := (100 + 200)/2;
output := "The sum of the two numbers is: " + total;
output := @Month+@Day+@Year;
```

Rule 4: You must use the `:=` assignment operator to assign a value to a variable, whereas the equal sign `=` is used to compare two values when used in a conditional statement (such as the `@IF`, `@WHILE`, or `@FOR` functions).

```
myVariable := "This is a valid assignment";
```

Rule 5: All formulas must contain a main expression that either produces a value or performs an action. For example, the following are valid main expressions.
The following returns today's date.

```
@Today
```

The following checks if the value stored in the `result` variable is equal to one. If the condition is true, then the formula returns the text string `"Yes"`. Otherwise, the formula is set to a text string `"No"`.

```
@If ( result = 1; "Yes"; "No")
```

What Are Functions and Commands?

Formula Language can be divided into two groupings—`@Functions` and `@Commands`. These groupings comprise Formula Language and are used to create formulas.

Functions are used to return a value and can be placed anywhere within a formula. Although most functions simply return a value, some functions interact with users or trigger other actions to occur. For example, the `@Prompt` and `@PickList` functions can be used to request input from the user.

As you gain experience with Formula Language, you'll find that most formulas are built using functions. However, some functions can only be used in specific design objects. The following table lists some of the restricted functions and describes where they can be used.

Restricted Function	Design Objects That Can Use This Function
`@All`	Replication formulas, agents, and view selection formulas
`@AllChildren`	Replication formulas and view selection formulas
`@AllDescendants`	Replication formulas and view selection formulas
`@Command`	Toolbar buttons, manual agents, and action hotspots
`@DBColumn`	Toolbar buttons, actions, hotspots, fields, and agent (except mail)
`@DBLookup`	Toolbar buttons, actions, hotspots, fields, and agent (except mail)

continues

Restricted Function	Design Objects That Can Use This Function
@DeleteDocument	Agents
@DeleteField	Agents and fields
@DocChildren	Column formulas and window title formulas
@DocDescendants	Column formulas and window title formulas
@DocLevel	Column formulas and window title formulas
@DocMark	Agents
@DocNumber	Column formulas and window title formulas
@DocParentNumber	Column formulas and window title formulas
@DocSiblings	Column formulas and window title formulas
@Failure	Field validation formulas
ENVIRONMENT	All formulas with the exception of popup hotspots
@Environment	All formulas with the exception of popup hotspots
FIELD	Toolbar buttons, agents, action hotspots, and fields
@IsCategory	Column formulas
@IsDocBeingLoaded	Forms and fields
@IsDocBeingMailed	Buttons, hotspots, and fields
@IsDocBeingRecalculated	Buttons, hotspots, and fields
@IsDocBeingSaved	Buttons, hotspots, and fields
@IsExpandable	Column formulas
@IsNewDoc	Toolbar buttons, window title formulas, forms, and fields
@MailSend	Toolbar buttons, agents, action hotspots, and fields
@PickList	Toolbar buttons, manual agents, action hotspots, and fields
@Platform	Toolbar buttons, manual agents, hotspots, view design (with the exception of selection and column formulas), forms, and fields

Restricted Function	Design Objects That Can Use This Function
@Prompt	Toolbar buttons, manual agents, action hotspots, and fields
@Responses	Window title formulas and fields
@Return	Toolbar buttons, agents, hotspots, and fields
SELECT	Replication formulas, agents, and view selection formulas
@SetDocField	Toolbar buttons, agents, action hotspots, and fields
@SetEnvironment	All formulas with the exception of popup hotspots
@SetField	Toolbar buttons, agents, action hotspots, and fields
@Success	Validation formulas
@Unavailable	Agents, views, and action buttons
@ViewTitle	Agents, action hotspots, and buttons

NOTE

A select number of functions can be called from LotusScript or have equivalents in LotusScript. Functions are sometimes called from LotusScript to simplify the code instructions. In other words, a single @Function can often replace multiple LotusScript code. In other cases, there are equivalent functions already included in the LotusScript language.

What Are Commands?

Commands are used to perform an action related to the application interface. For the most part, commands mimic menu options and tend to be used primarily in action buttons, hotspots, agents, and events. For example, commands can be used to

- Compose a new form
- Edit, save, or close a form
- Jump to a field and insert text
- Attach a file
- Send an email
- Open the database help document

> **NOTE**
>
> @Commands cannot be called from LotusScript and, with few exceptions, cannot be implemented in Web-based applications.

The following table represents some of the most frequently used commands. In most cases, these commands would be placed in an action button for a given form.

Command	Description	Example
FileSave	Saves the document currently displayed in the Lotus Notes client. Syntax: **@Command ([FileSave]);**	@Command ([FileSave]);
EditDocument	Toggles between edit and read mode for the currently opened document. Optionally, if you set the edit mode to 1, the document only goes to edit mode. If the mode is set to 0, the document goes to read mode. Syntax: **@Command([EditDocument];** **mode; pane)** mode—Set to 1 for edit, 0 for readonly. pane—Set to 1 to display in preview pane.	@Command ([EditDocument]; 1)
CloseWindow	Closes the document currently open in the Lotus Notes client. Syntax: **@Command ([CloseWindow]);**	@Command ([CloseWindow]);
Compose	Creates a new document based on the specified form. Syntax: **@Command ([Compose]; form);** form—An existing form in the database.	@Command([Compose]; "NewEmployee");
EditGoto-Field	Places the cursor in the specified field on the document. Syntax: **@Command ([EditGotoField];** **fieldname);** fieldname—Name of a field on a form.	@Command ([EditGotoField]; "Title");

Working with Text Strings

Many formulas are used to manage and manipulate text strings. Using functions, you can parse information, implement data validation, and enforce consistency across data values. For example, the following are some of the more common functions used to manage text strings.

Function	Description	Example
@UpperCase	Converts a string to uppercase. Syntax: **@UpperCase (_string_);** _string_—Any text string.	@Uppercase ("january"); Result: "JANUARY"
@LowerCase	Converts a string to lowercase. Syntax: **@LowerCase (_string_);** _string_—Any text string.	@Lowercase ("JANUARY"); Result: "january"
@ProperCase	Converts the first letter of each word to a capital. Syntax: **@ProperCase (_string_);** _string_—Any text string.	@Propercase ("john doe"); Result: "John Doe"
@Trim	Removes leading and trailing spaces from a text string and removes duplicate spaces between text words. Syntax: **@Trim (_string_);** _string_—Any text string.	@Trim (" today is Monday "); Result: "today is Monday"
@Text	Converts a number, date, or time to a text string. Syntax: **@Text (_value_);** _value_—The value to be converted into a string.	@Text (100); Result: "100" @Text (@Today); Result: "01/01/2005"
@LeftBack	Searches a string from left to right and returns a substring.	This example returns "Mark". @LeftBack ("Mark Elliott"; " "); This example returns "Mark Ellio". @LeftBack ("Mark Elliott"; 2);
@RightBack	Searches a string from right to left and returns a substring.	This example returns "Elliott". @RightBack ("Mark Elliott"; " "); This example returns "rk Elliott". @RightBack ("Mark Elliott"; 2);

Working with Conditional Branching

The primary method to manage conditional branching is the @IF function. As with most programming languages, this function tests an equation and then branches to the appropriate action. The following describes the syntax for this function.

```
@IF ( condition; action1; action2 );
```

If the `condition` equates to true, then `action1` is performed. Otherwise, if the condition equates to false, then `action2` is performed. It's important to note that you can also nest @IF statements inside @IF statements. For example:

```
@If (@Created = @Today; "Document created today.";
   @If (@Created = @Yesterday; "Document created yesterday."; "Document created in
past."));
```

In this example, the first condition compares the document creation date with today's date. If the two values match, then the formula executes `action1` and returns the text string `"Document created today."` If the values do not match, then the formula executes `action2`, which is the nested @IF statement. Here, the creation date is compared with yesterday's date. If the values match, then the formula returns the string `"Document created yesterday."` Finally, if the document was not created yesterday, the string is set to `"Document created in the past."`

Working with Iterative Loops

The following are functions that can be used to manage loops. To implement these functions, you must be running Lotus Notes release 6 or greater.

Function	Description	Example

@For	Executes one or more statements while the specified condition remains true. After each execution, the condition is rechecked to verify that the statement remains true. Syntax:
	@For (*initialize; condition; increment; statement)*;
	initialize—The starting value for the loop counter.
	condition—A true or false condition.
	increment—A statement that changes the counter.
	statement—A formula language statement to execute. Up to 254 statements can be specified.
		The following loops through the elements of a keyword field called Options. With each iteration, a counter called cntr is incremented and the keyword element is displayed to the user.
		@For(cntr := 1;
		cntr <=
		  @Elements(Options);
		cntr := cntr + 1;
		@Prompt([OK]; "Item "
		  + @Text(cntr) " is ";
		  Options[cntr]))

Function	Description	Example
@While	Executes one or more statements while the specified condition remains true. Syntax: **@While** (*condition*; *statement*); *condition*—A true or false condition. *statement*—A formula language statement to execute. Up to 254 statements can be specified. Note: There is also a @DoWhile statement, which was introduced in release 6.	The following loops through the elements of a keyword field called Options. Each element is displayed and a counter is incremented with each loop. `cntr := 1;` `@While(cntr <=` `  @Elements(Options);` `@Prompt([OK]; "Item "` `  + @Text(cntr) " is ";` `  Options [cntr]);` `cntr := cntr + 1)`

Working with Lookup Functions

A.5.1

Lookup functions are used to retrieve one or more data values from a Notes database. The data values can be retrieved from the current or another database. The database can reside on the current or a different Domino server. Lookup functions are quite frequently used to populate keyword fields or to default computed fields to a specific value.

Function	Description	Example
@DBColumn	Returns a list of values from a view or folder column. Syntax: **@DBColumn(*class : cache ; server : database ; view ; columnNumber*)** *class*—The type of database being accessed. *cache*—Specifies if the results should be cached. *server*—Server name. Defaults to current server if set to " " in the statement. *database*—Database name. Defaults to current database if set to " " in the statement. *view*—The view name or alias name. *columnNumber*—The column number to return values.	The following returns a list of values from column number one for the "By Category" view. `class := "";` `cache := "NoCache";` `server := "";` `db := "";` `view := "By Category";` `colnum := 1;` `@DBColumn (class:cache;` `  server:db; view;` `  colnum);`

continues

Function	Description	Example
@DBLookup	Returns a field value from a specified document in a view or folder. Syntax: **@DBLookup**(*class* : *cache*; *server* : *database*; *view*; *key*; *fieldName*; *keywords*) -or- **@DBLookup**(*class* : *cache*; *server* : *database*; *view*; *key*; *columnNumber*; *keywords*) *class*—The type of database being accessed. *cache*—Specifies if the results should be cached. *server*—Server name. Defaults to current server if set to " " in the statement. *database*—Database name. Defaults to current database if set to " " in the statement. *view*—The view name. *key*—Unique key. *fieldname*—Value to return. *columnNumber*—The column number to return values.	The following searches the view "By Last Name" for the key value. If found, it returns the first name for the document. class := ""; cache := "NoCache"; server := ""; db := ""; view := "By Last Name"; key := "Elliott"; fieldName := "firstname"; @DBLookup (class:cache; server:db; view; key; fieldName);

> **TIP**
>
> Best practices suggest that you should create temporary variables for functions that require multiple parameters. This helps with formula readability and helps ensure that you change the correct parameter if the formula needs updates. Otherwise, you'll need to remember (or look up) what each parameter means and count semicolons to find the parameter.

Where possible, you should limit the number of lookup functions included on a form. Multiple lookup functions can affect the overall performance of the form.

However, if you need to retrieve multiple field values, consider creating a hidden view. Set the first column to a unique key (such as a document number). In the second column, create a formula that contains all data fields separated by a delimiter (such as the tilde ~). Then using @DBLookup in conjunction with @Word, you retrieve multiple field values for a single document using a single lookup.

For example, let's say you have a service request form that requires the user to select their immediate manager. Then, after the user selects a name, the manager's email address, department name, and phone fields automatically populate with the correct information. In this scenario, you would do the following:

1. Create a form that contains manager name, email, department, and phone number.

2. Create a hidden view, such as **(MgrLookup)**.

3. Set the view formula for column1 to MgrName.

4. Set the view formula for column2 to MgrEmail+"~"+MgrDept+"~"+ MgrPhone.

5. Next, add a hidden, computed field (such as MgrData) to the service request form. Set the field formula to the following @DBLookup formula. This field will store a "~"delimited list of values based on the selected manager name.

```
Class :=""
Cache:=""
Host := "";
View := "(MgrLookup)";
Key := MgrName;
Colnum := 2;
output := @DbLookup( class : cache ; host ; view ; key ; colnum );
@If(@IsError(output);"";@If (MgrName=""; ""; output ))
```

6. Finally, create the Email, Department, and Phone fields on the service request form. Make each field computed. Using the @Word function, set the field formula for each respective field. Be sure the form property is set to **Automatically refresh fields**.

```
@Word ( MgrData; "~"; 1);
@Word ( MgrData; "~"; 2);
@Word ( MgrData; "~"; 3);
```

Using this approach, three individual field lookups were replaced with one @DBLookup function call. Note that **Automatically refresh fields** can also affect performance if there is a significant number of computed fields on the form.

Working with Dates

The following table summarizes the common functions used to manage dates.

Function	Description	Example
@Date	Translates a series of numbers into a date value. This function requires a year, month, and day value to be specified. Syntax: **@Date;**	@Date (2005; 12; 31); Result: 12/31/2005

continues

Function	Description	Example
@Day	Returns the day of the month from the specified date. Syntax: **@Day** (*date*); *date*—Any specified date.	@Day ("07/10/2005"); @Day (@Today); Result: 10
@Month	Returns the month from the specified date. Syntax: **@Month** (*date*); *date*—Any specified date.	@Month ("07/10/2005"); @Month (@Today); Result: 07
@Now	Returns the current date and time. Syntax: **@Now;**	@Now; Result: 07/10/2005 9:31:45 AM
@Today	Returns the current date. Syntax: **@Today;**	@Today; Result: 07/10/2005
@Tomorrow	Returns tomorrow's date. Syntax: **@Tomorrow;**	@Tomorrow; Result: 07/11/2005
@Weekday	Returns the day of the week based on the specified date. Returns a number corresponding to the weekday where Sunday=1, Monday=2, and so on through Saturday=7. Syntax: **@Weekday** (*date*); *date*—Any specified date.	@Weekday ("07/10/2005"); @Weekday (@Today); Result: 1
@Year	Returns the current year from the specified date. Syntax: **@Year** (*date*); *date*—Any specified date.	@Year ("07/10/2005"); @Year (@Today); Result: 2005
@Yesterday	Returns yesterday's date. Syntax: **@Yesterday;**	@Yesterday; Result: 07/09/2005

Working with Lists

The following are common functions used to manage a list of values.

Function	Description	Example

@Elements	Counts the number of items in a list and returns a number. Syntax:
	@Elements (*list*);
	list—A list of elements.
		`@Elements`
		`("April":"May":"June");`
		Result: 3

@Explode	Converts a text string into a list of elements. You can optionally specify a string delimiter. If a string delimiter is not specified, the function will default to a space, semicolon, or comma. Syntax:
	@Explode (*string*);
	@Explode (*string*; *delimiter*);
	string—A string of text values.
	delimiter—An optional text string separator.
		`Data:="April May June";`
		`@Explode (Data; " ");`
		Result: `"April" : "May" :`
		`"June"`

@Implode	Converts a list of elements into a single text string. Optionally, you can specify a string delimiter. Syntax:
	@Implode (*list*);
	@Implode (*list*; *delimiter*);
	list—a list of elements.
	delimiter—an optional text string separator.
		`Data:= "April" : "May" :`
		`"June";`
		`@Implode (Data; " ");`
		Result: `"April May June"`

@IsMember	Searches for a value within a text string. Returns a numeric 1 if found and 0 if not found. Syntax:
	@IsMember (*string*; *list*);
	string—The search string.
	list—A list of elements.
		`Data:= "April" : "May" :`
		`"June";`
		`@IsMember ("April"; Data);`
		Result: 1

@Replace	Searches a list for an element. If the element is found, it is replaced with the new element.
	@Replace (*searchlist*; *oldlist*; *newlist*);
	searchlist—The list of elements to be searched.
	oldlist—The list of value(s) to be replaced.
	newlist—The new list of replacement value(s).
		`Data:= "April" : "Dec" :`
		`"June";`
		`@Replace (Data; "Dec";`
		`"May");`
		Result: `"April": "May":`
		`"June"`

continues

Function	Description	Example
@Select	Returns the value specified in the n-th number position. If the number specified is greater than the total values, then the last value is returned. Syntax: @Select (number; value1; value2; valueN); number—Item number to select. value1—First value. value2—Second value. valueN—Last value.	@Select(3; "April"; "May"; "June") Result: "June"
@Word	Selects the word specified in the n-th number position. Words are determined based on the string delimiter. Syntax: @Word (string; delimiter; number); string—The string to be searched. delimiter—The value used to separate "words." number—The word to select from the search string.	Data:="April~May~June"; @Word (Data; "~"; 3); Result: "June"

Working with User Prompts

The following describes several functions that can be used to display information to the user. These functions will display a dialog box window. In some cases, information is static. In other cases, the user can interact with the dialog box, and data values are returned to the underlying form.

Function	Description	Example
@Dialogbox	Displays a user-defined dialog box. Results from the dialog box are subsequently returned to the underlying form. @DialogBox(form ; style : title) form—The name of the form to display in a dialog box. style—Optional keyword that indicates what the dialog box should look like. If multiple options are specified, a colon should separate them.	In the following example, a form called RepeatOptions is displayed. @Dialog box ("RepeatOptions"; [AUTOHORZFIT] : [AUTOVERTFIT]; "Recurring calendar event");

Function	Description	Example
	[AUTOHORZFIT]—Auto-set horizontal size. **[AUTOVERTFIT]**—Auto-set vertical size. **[NOCANCEL]**—Do not display Cancel button. **[NONEWFIELDS]**—Do not create new fields on underlying form if the field does not already exist. **[NOFIELDUPDATE]**—Do not update fields on underlying form. **[READONLY]**—Disable the ability to edit content in the dialog box. **[SIZETOTABLE]**—Auto-set size based on the table. **[NOOKCANCEL]**—Do not display the OK and Cancel buttons on the dialog box. **[OKCANCELATBOTTOM]**—Place the OK and Cancel buttons at the bottom of the form. If parameter is omitted, buttons will display on right side of window. *title*—The title of the dialog box window.	
@Prompt	Displays a popup dialog box to the user. This function can be used to capture data values or to capture the result of a clicked button (i.e., OK or Cancel). Syntax: **@Prompt([*style*] : [NOSORT] ;** *title* ; *prompt* ; *defaultChoice* ; *choiceList* ; *filetype*) *style*—A keyword that indicates what the dialog box should look like. Valid keywords include the following: **[CHOOSEDATABASE]** **[LOCALBROWSE]** **[OK]** **[OKCANCELCOMBO]** **[OKCANCELEDIT]** **[OKCANCELEDITCOMBO]** **[OKCANCELLIST]**	The following are several examples. @Prompt ([OK]; "Warning"; "You must specify a request date"); @Prompt ([YESNO]; "Continue?"; "Do you want to save this form?"); @Prompt ([OKCANCELEDIT]; "Input"; "What is your name?";); FIELD filename := @Prompt([LOCALBROWSE]; "Select a file.";"");1

continues

Function	Description	Example
	[OKCANCELLISTMULT] [PASSWORD] [YESNO] [YESNOCANCEL] NOSORT—An optional keyword. Values are sorted if this parameter is omitted. *title*—The title of the dialog box window. *prompt*—The text to be displayed within the dialog box. *defaultchoice*—The default button or choice in the dialog box. *filetype*—The type of files to be displayed. This parameter is only required for the [LOCALBROWSE] style.	

Debugging Formula Language

Formula Language unfortunately does not provide a user interface that allows developers to debug or examine variables as a formula executes. However, the Designer client does automatically check the formula syntax, which in many cases resolves problems with the formula.

So the question then becomes, how do you debug a formula that meets the language syntax requirements but that fails to produce the correct result? There are several approaches to consider—periodically display values as the formula executes (using @Prompt) or periodically check results as the formula executes (using @IfError or @IsError).

Function	Description	Example

@IfError	Returns a null string if the statement is invalid. Optionally, you can specify an alternate result if the result of *statement1* is invalid. Syntax:
	@IfError (*statement1*);
	@IfError (*statement1*;
	  statement2);
	statement1—The statement to be checked.
	statement2—Optional result to be returned if the first statement is invalid. Note that @IfError has been deprecated in release 7 and is obsolete.
		This example produces a divide-by-zero error. When the formula executes, the IF statement checks the value stored in output. If the value is invalid, the formula returns "Math Error". Otherwise, if the value is valid, the formula returns the output.
		`output := 1/0;`
		`@IfError ( output;`
		`  "Math Error");`

Function	Description	Example

@IsError	Checks the statement to determine if the result is valid. Function returns a 1 if valid and 0 if invalid. Syntax:
	@IsError (*statement*);
	statement—Any formula language statement.
		This is another example of the divide-by-zero error.
		`output := 1/0;`
		`@If( @IsError (output);`
		`  ""; output);`
		Alternatively, instead of returning a null value, you could return a message or use the @Prompt function to display an error message.
		`@If( @IsError (output);`
		`"Divide by Zero"; output);`

@Prompt	See "Working with User Prompts" previously.	See the previous.

> **NOTE**
>
> The @IfError function has been deprecated in release 7 and is obsolete.

 ## Links to developerWorks

A.5.1 Polly, Mark. *Keyword magic for the Web.* IBM developerWorks, October 2003. http://www.ibm.com/developerworks/lotus/library/ls-keyword_pt1/index.html.

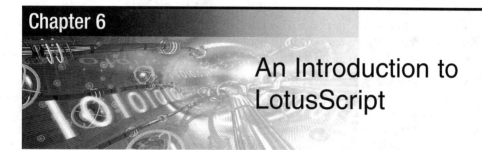

Chapter 6

An Introduction to LotusScript

Chapter Overview

L otusScript is a structured, object-oriented programming (OOP) language that's similar to Visual Basic. Using LotusScript, you can create robust, cross-platform applications. This chapter provides an introduction to the programming language and reviews the basic concepts of object-oriented application development.

By the end of the chapter you will have learned

- Basic terminology of object-oriented programming
- Basic elements of the LotusScript language
- How to create variables and constants
- How to add comments to code
- How to create conditional branching and iterative loops
- How to create arrays
- How to create date and time variables
- How to display messages and dialog boxes
- How and when to compile LotusScript code
- How to create subroutines and functions

Introduction to Object-Oriented Programming

The first step to understanding the LotusScript language is to review OOP terminology. Object-oriented programming sounds complex. However, it's really just another way to organize and develop software code. This organization revolves around objects, classes, properties, and methods.

Objects are considered to be the basic building blocks of a software application. Objects have specific attributes and a distinct set of related capabilities. Let's take, for example, an airplane. It's composed of many parts such as engines, tires, navigational instruments, windows, seats, passenger radio, and so on. Each part, or object, has a distinct set of attributes such as color, size, shape, movement, and so on (see Figure 6.1).

Attributes, also known as *properties*, describe an object. All objects have a unique set of attributes that describe characteristics of that object. For instance, the properties of the "tire" object may include brand name, size, recommended PSI, and performance rating, whereas the properties for the "engine" will be entirely different and may include thrust, weight, size, or similar properties.

Methods, on the other hand, are used to manipulate the object attributes. Like properties, each object has a finite set of commands, or methods, that are used to modify the object. For example, the pilot could set the landing gear to be up or down. This could equate to two separate methods—one to raise the landing gear and another to lower the landing gear.

The combination of these objects (or in this case, airplane parts) comprises a *class* (in this case, a working plane), where each object has a unique set of properties and methods.

Figure 6.1 A plane contains many parts that have specific attributes and functions. Similarly, a class is comprised of many objects that have specific properties and methods.

LotusScript Classes

LotusScript can be divided into two classes—front-end and back-end. The *front-end* class enables you to access an object via the Lotus Notes client interface. The *back-end* class, on the other hand, enables you to manipulate an object independently of the user interface. Using this class, you can manipulate objects stored in the database. For example, a Notes document that LotusScript accesses from the front-end is often called *uidoc* (or user interface doc), whereas the same document accessed from the back-end is often called simply *doc*.

With this important distinction in place, next I'll discuss the primary terminology, constructs, and general syntax that comprise the LotusScript language. As with all programming languages, LotusScript includes keywords, variables, constants, operators, comments, subroutines, and functions.

Keywords

Keywords are reserved words in the LotusScript language that have special meaning or that perform a specific task. These reserved words cannot be used as variables or outside their intended use. For example, TRUE and FALSE are two common keywords that denote success and failure. You could not name a variable either of these keywords.

Variables

Variables are used to store data and can be classified into two primary categories—regular variables and object reference variables. A *regular variable* is used to store a literal string as the program executes. This type of variable can be subdivided into scalar and variant variables.

A *scalar variable* is used to store data based on a specific data type. In other words, the variable type and data value must be compatible. A variable that's defined as an integer could store a number but could not store a text string. The following describes the various scalar data types.

Scalar Type	Keyword	Symbol	Description
Integer	INTEGER	%	Used to store whole numbers between −32,768 and +32,767.
Long	LONG	&	Used to store large numbers between −2,147,483,648 and +2,147,483,647.
Single	SINGLE	!	Used to store floating-point numbers that range between + or − 7 floating point digits.

continues

Scalar Type	Keyword	Symbol	Description
Double	DOUBLE	#	Used to store double-precision floating-point numbers that range between + or – 17 floating point digits.
Currency	CURRENCY	@	Used to store currency values.
String	STRING	$	Used to store alphanumeric text string values.

The symbols are suffix characters that can be used as variable identifiers as well as to implicitly declare the variable. An implicitly defined variable does not require a DIM statement. However, best practices suggest that you should always declare all variables.

Variant variables, on the other hand, are considered to be general purpose and can accept data regardless of the data value. These variables can store any type of value including numbers, strings, arrays, and built-in constant values such as NULL and EMPTY. Although this variable type provides the flexibility to store varying types of data, it's important to understand that it requires more memory and is processed more slowly than scalar variables. Where possible, the use of variant variables should be minimized.

Object reference variables, as the name implies, are used to associate an object with a LotusScript variable. After a variable has been associated with an object, you can obtain its properties or manipulate its content. Figure 6.2 illustrates the relationship between each of the variables.

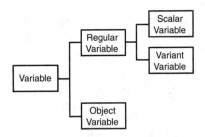

Figure 6.2   Types of variables

Constants

Constants are used to store a data value that never changes. The valued stored in this data type remains fixed and cannot be changed after it is declared. For instance, you could use a constant to store the number of months in a year, days of the week, or a text string such as "Monday".

Operators

As with other programming languages, LotusScript employs a number of operators. These operators are used in mathematical equations and to compare data expressions. Some of the more common operators include the following.

Operator	Symbol	Description
Add	+	Used to sum numbers.
Subtract	–	Used to subtract numbers.
Multiplication	*	Used to multiply numbers.
Division	/	Used to divide numbers.
Concatenate	+	Used to merge string values together.
Concatenate	&	Used to merge values together. All values are automatically converted to string and then merged.
Line Continuation	_	The underscore character indicates that a statement continues, or spans, to the next line.
Equal	=	Used to compare two values. For example, if today equals "Tuesday" then perform an action.
Assignment Operator	=	Used to assign a value to a variable. For example, set a text string to a specific value—such as "Your document has been saved."
Less Than	<	Used to compare two values.
Greater Than	>	Used to compare two values.
Not Equal	<>	Used to compare two values.
Not Equal	><	Used to compare two values.

> **NOTE**
>
> In LotusScript, the equal sign = is used as the assignment operator. This differs from the Formula Language syntax, which uses the colon and equal sign := to assign values to variables.

Comments

Comments are non-executable statements that document or describe LotusScript code. A well-documented application can help other Domino developers understand why code was implemented as well as the results to expect. As a developer, it's good practice to include comments throughout the software code. For example, comments can be used to describe

- A subroutine, function, or major block of code
- Parameters passed between subroutines
- Variables, constants, or objects
- Code changes to resolve problems
- General warnings or things to watch out for

There are two types of comments in LotusScript—single line and multiple line. The apostrophe (') is used to denote a single-line comment. With a single-line comment, all text to the right of the apostrophe is ignored when the code is executed. A single-line comment can reside on a line by itself or can be appended to the end of an executable statement. It's important to understand that single-line comments cannot reside in the middle of an executable statement. The following code includes three single-line comments. Each comment line starts with an apostrophe.

```
'----------------------------
' The following displays a message
'----------------------------
Messagebox ( "Good morning." )
```

With multiple-line comments, all text between the start and end statements is skipped when the program executes. Multi-line statements are helpful when adding a large block of text or to comment out a block of code. All multi-line comments must start with %REM and end with %END REM. All text information, including code instructions, between these two statements will be ignored.

```
%REM
Comment line 1
Comment line 2
Comment line 3
%END REM
```

Defining Variables and Constants

With the terminology and object-oriented programming concepts out of the way, we are ready to discuss the general syntax and structure of the LotusScript language starting with variables. There are essentially two steps required to utilize a variable—declare and set. The DIM statement is used to declare variables in LotusScript. The syntax for declaring a variable is

```
DIM variablename AS declarationType
```

After the variable has been declared, you can the set the variable to a literal string, built-in data value, or object. For example, the following shows several variables being declared.

```
'--- Declare Regular Variables
Dim TotalHolidays As Integer
Dim ThisMonth As String
Dim AuthorName As String

'--- Declare Object Reference Variables
Dim theDate As New NotesDateTime

'--- Set the variables
TotalHolidays = 5
ThisMonth = "January"
theDate.LSLocalTime = Now
```

The following represents some of the built-in values that can be assigned to variables.

Constant	Description
NULL	A special value that indicates "missing" or "unknown" data. It's important to understand that a NULL value does equate to an actual value.
EMPTY	Indicates that the variable does not contain a value.
PI	Sets the variable to the value of pi (which is the ratio between a circle's circumference and its diameter).
TRUE	Sets the value of the variable to 1.
FALSE	Sets the value of the variable to 0.
NOW	The current date and time.
TODAY	The current date.

Alternatively, you can declare regular variables by using the associated symbol. Using this method, the variable is automatically declared and set to the specified variable type. However, best practices suggest that you should always declare the variable.

```
CurrentDirectory$ = "C:\"
TotalHolidays% = 5
```

Constants hold a static value and are typically defined in LotusScript libraries. Constants can be defined throughout the application including in forms and subroutines. The syntax for declaring a constant is as follows.

```
[ Public | Private ] Const ConstName = expression
```

Public—Indicates that the constant can be used outside the current module. This is an optional parameter.

Private—Indicates that the constant is only visible within the current module. This is the default setting and is an optional parameter.

ConstName—The name of the constant to be referenced throughout the LotusScript code. This value must be unique—it cannot be the same name as another variable or constant.

expression—The value to be assigned to the constant.

For example, the following illustrates several constants. As a best practice, consider using all caps or a unique prefix identifier such as "const" to denote a constant variable.

```
'--- Declare Constants
Const MonthsInYear = 12
Const DaysInWeek = 7
Public Const PiValue = PI
```

Defining Object Reference Variables

Object reference variables are used to manage and manipulate objects contained within the Notes applications. There are essentially three steps required to manage an object—declare a variable for the object, associate the variable with the object, and utilize methods and properties to manage the object.

For example, in most cases when working with LotusScript, you'll need to define an object variable that refers to the current database. First, declare the variable using the DIM statement. In Notes development, the database object variable is often named db.

Next, use the SET statement to assign a value to the database variable (e.g., associate mydemo.nsf with the object db). Now you can use the methods and properties associated with the NotesDatabase class to manage the database. In this case, the title property returns the name of the database. When used with the Messagebox statement, this example will display a popup message with the database name.

```
' ---Declare the variable "db"
Dim db As NotesDatabase

' --- Associate "mydemo.nsf" with "db" for the current
' --- computer. The "" signifies the current computer which
' --- could be local or on the server.
Set db = New NotesDatabase( "", "mydemo.nsf" )

' --- Display the database name using the "Title" property
Messagebox( db.Title )
```

Besides working with database objects, you may need to work with document objects (e.g., fields). These objects can be referenced from both the front-end and back-end. To access document objects, you again have to declare a variable and associate an object with the variable before you can manage the object.

This second example illustrates the general process for referencing fields. In many cases, you'll need to use the following statements to reference and work with objects from within the document. These statements are often added to action buttons and document events. Although the process is similar to the database object example, the path to referencing the object is more complex because you have to reference other objects before you get to the form objects.

First, you must declare a variable that refers to the current workspace (w), a variable that refers to the front-end object (uidoc), and one that refers to the back-end object (doc). Next, you must set the front-end variable before setting the back-end variable. Finally, you can manage the document or field objects using methods and properties.

```
Dim w As New NotesUIWorkspace      ' Declare workspace variable
Dim uidoc As NotesUIDocument       ' Declare front-end document
Dim doc As NotesDocument           ' Declare back-end document
Set uidoc = w.CurrentDocument      ' Access front-end object
Set doc = uidoc.Document           ' Access back-end object
doc.Status = "New"                 ' Set field value
doc.Save (True, True)              ' Save document
Call uidoc.Refresh                 ' Refresh display
```

Working with Conditional Branching

Conditional statements are used to execute one or more statements based on the result of an expression. The two most commonly used branching statements include the IF and SELECT CASE statements.

The IF statement is used to conditionally execute code based on an expression. If the resulting expression equates to true, then the action or actions are executed. Alternatively, if the resulting expression equates to false, then a secondary set of instructions is executed (when specified using the keyword ELSE). It's important to note that the ELSE clause is optional. There are two formats for the IF statement—single line and multiple line. The format for the single-line IF statement is as follows:

IF *expression* **THEN** *action1* **ELSE** *action2*

Alternatively, the multiple-line IF statement is used to execute a block of statements depending on the expression result. All multi-line statements must start with the keyword IF and end with the keyword END IF. Optionally, you can also include an ELSE statement with a secondary block of actions to be run. The following shows the syntax for a multi-line statement.

IF *expression* **THEN**
        action1a
        action1b
        action1c
        . . .

```
ELSE
        action2a
        action2b
        action2c
        ...
END IF
```

In both cases, the ELSE statement is optional and can be omitted. This means that if the expression equates to false and the statement does not have an ELSE clause, then no statements will be executed. For example, if the value of the status variable equals "New", then the message "This is a new service request" is displayed. Otherwise, if the values do not equate, the alternate message is displayed. Finally, you can nest multiple IF statements by using the ELSEIF statement.

```
IF status = "New" THEN
    messagebox "This is a new service request"
ELSE
    messagebox "This is an existing service request"
END IF
```

Like the IF statement, the SELECT statement is used to execute one or more instructions based on an expression result. The following shows the syntax for this statement.

```
SELECT CASE variable
CASE value1 :
        action(s)
CASE value2 :
        action(s)
CASE value3 :
        action(s)
CASE ELSE
        action(s)
END SELECT
```

You'll notice that with this statement, an expression or variable is defined at the start of the SELECT statement and subsequently compared with each CASE statement value. After the first match is identified, the action (or actions) for the specific case is executed, and LotusScript exits the SELECT statement. If no match is found, an optional set of actions can be specified in the ELSE clause.

For example, the following code asks the user how many items should be ordered and stores the response in the variant variable called result. This value is then compared with each case statement, and an appropriate message is displayed if a match is found. If no match is found, a warning message along with the user's response is displayed instead.

```
Dim result As String
result = Inputbox$("Do you want 1, 2 or 3 items?")

Select Case result
Case "1" :
    Messagebox "One item ordered"
Case "2" :
    Messagebox "Two items ordered"
Case "3" :
```

```
   Messagebox "Three items ordered"
Case Else
   Messagebox "Incorrect value: " + result
End Select
```

Working with Iterative Loops

LotusScript offers numerous iterative looping constructs including the DO, FOR, and WHILE statements. Each of these statements continuously loops through one or more executable statements based on an expression, value, or computed result.

There are two variations of the DO statement. This statement be can set up to loop either WHILE an expression is true or UNTIL an expression equates to true. In both cases, the condition can be evaluated at the start or end of the loop. The syntax is as follows:

A.6.1

```
DO [ WHILE | UNTIL ] condition
      action(s)
LOOP
```

Alternatively, you can check the expression at the end of the loop by utilizing the following syntax:

```
DO
      action(s)
LOOP [ WHILE | UNTIL ] condition
```

For example, the following code initializes a variable called counter to zero. Next, the LotusScript tests the condition to see if counter is less than five. For each loop, counter is incremented and a message is displayed to the user. The loop terminates when counter reaches the value of five.

```
Dim counter As Integer
counter = 0
Do While counter < 5
   counter = counter + 1
   Messagebox counter
Loop
```

The FOR statement is used to loop a specific number of times through a series of LotusScript statements. With this loop statement, a variable is set and incremented. The loop continues to execute until the desired number of iterations is reached. Optionally, you can specify an incremental value. If the STEP value is omitted, it defaults to an incremental value of one.

For example, an incremental step value of two means the loop will count by twos. The syntax for this statement is as follows:

```
FOR counter = startnum TO endnum [STEP increment]
      action(s)
NEXT counter
```

For example, the following displays the counter number to the user. This counter value starts at one and loops five times. When the counter value equals six, the looping stops.

```
For counter = 1 To 5
   Messagebox counter
Next
```

Finally, the WHILE statement loops continuously, provided that the specified condition equates to a true value. When the condition returns a false value, LotusScript immediately exits the loop.

```
WHILE condition
        action(s)
WEND
```

For example, this code asks the user if they would like to continue. If the user specifies either "Y" or "y", then the input box is redisplayed. The looping stops if any other value is returned.

```
Dim result As String
result = Inputbox$("Do you want to continue (Y / N)?")

While result = "Y" Or result = "y"
   result = Inputbox$("Do you want to continue (Y / N)?")
Wend
```

> **NOTE**
>
> Best practices in software programming suggest that you should always create iterative loops that exit by default. This will prevent the possibility of an endless loop. An endless loop has the potential to lock up the application and client workstation and possibly to consume a significant amount of memory or CPU on the server. The EXIT statement can be used to conditionally exit an iterative loop. The following shows the syntax for this statement:
>
> **EXIT** LoopType
>
> where LoopType represents the current iterative loop such as DO, FOR, or FORALL. This statement can also be used to exit from a FUNCTION, SUB, or PROPERTY.

Communicating with Users

There are many different ways to communicate and interact with the user. Virtually all applications communicate with the user by displaying information, prompting for information, or displaying a custom dialog window. These interactions control the flow of information into the software application as well as force the user to make decisions that affect the database information. For example, you can display a message—"Document Saved"—or confirm an action—"Are you sure you want to delete these documents?"

This section will describe some of the more common commands—Messagebox, Dialogbox, Inputbox, and Print. You'll find that these statements are frequently used in the LotusScript programming language.

Messagebox Statement

The Messagebox statement is probably the most commonly used statement for communicating with users. This command offers many robust options that can be used to interface with the end-user community. The following describes the syntax for this command.

MessageBox *message , options , title*

> *message*—Any text string (including variables, constants, or reference objects).
> *options*—Used to configure the button, icon, display mode, and default "selected" button.
> These parameters are optional.
> *title*—Used to set the popup window title. This parameter is optional.

In the simplest form, this statement is used to display a popup message to the user (see Figure 6.3). For example, the following displays a text string along with the current date and time.

```
Messagebox "The current date and time is: " + Now
```

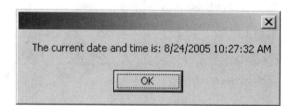

Figure 6.3 Sample *Messagebox*

However, the statement also has many additional parameters that enable you to customize the display of the popup message window. Before we get to the display options, you can add a title to the popup message window. The window title is the third parameter and must be a text string value that does not exceed 128 characters. You'll notice that in Figure 6.4, the second parameter is omitted, which is the reason for the two commas in the sample code.

```
Messagebox "The date and time is: " + Now ,, "Today's Date"
```

Next, you can add graphics, modify the buttons, and set a default button for the message window. This is accomplished via the second parameter, which must equate to a valid value. Adding one or more values together determines the values for the Messagebox statement to display.

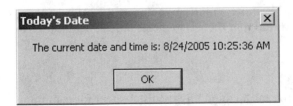

Figure 6.4   Sample *Messagebox* with optional parameters

Value	Constant	Description of Button to Be Displayed
0	MB_OK	OK
1	MB_OKCANCEL	OK and Cancel
2	MB_ABORTRETRYIGNORE	Abort, Retry, and Ignore
3	MB_YESNOCANCEL	Yes, No, and Cancel
4	MB_YESNO	Yes and No
5	MB_RETRYCANCEL	Retry and Cancel

Value	Constant	Description of Icon to Be Displayed
16	MB_ICONSTOP	Stop sign icon
32	MB_ICONQUESTION	Question mark icon
48	MB_ICONEXCLAMATION	Exclamation point icon
64	MB_ICONINFORMATION	Information icon

Value	Constant	Description
0	MB_DEFBUTTON1	Set button 1 as the default button
256	MB_DEFBUTTON2	Set button 2 as the default button
512	MB_DEFBUTTON3	Set button 3 as the default button

Value	Constant	Description
0	MB_APPLMODAL	This options stops the current application until the end-user responds to the message.
4,096	MB_SYSTEMMODAL	This options stops all applications until the end-user responds to the message.

For example, the following illustrates four example Messagebox statements. The first illustrates a message with no parameters. The second prompts the user to select Yes or No and includes the question mark icon. This message also includes a window title—"Caution". The third example includes the Abort, Retry, and Cancel buttons. Using the 256 value, the Retry button is set to the default button. Finally, the last example illustrates the use of the LotusScript constant library, which references MB_OKCANCEL, or a value of 1.

```
' Display an informational message
Messagebox "Document saved."

' Display  YES/NO buttons and Question mark icon
Messagebox "Do you want to continue?", 4 + 32, "Caution"

' Display Abort/Retry/Cancel buttons, stop sign icon and
' make the second button (abort) the default
Messagebox "Unable to open file", 2 + 16 + 256, "Warning"

' Display the OK/Cancel Button.  Must add %Include "LSCONST.LSS"
' in the (Options) section of the Globals values.
Messagebox "Unable to open file", MB_OKCANCEL, "Warning"
```

> **NOTE**
>
> To utilize constant strings (such as MB_OKCANCEL) to manage the messagebox display settings, you must add the following statement to the (Options) section:
>
> ```
> %include "LSCONST.LSS"
> ```
>
> This statement is used to reference a LotusScript file that contains default constants. Refer to the Domino Designer help for a complete listing of constant files and their uses.

Finally, messagebox can be called as a function that returns a value that corresponds to the selected button. The following shows the syntax for a messagebox function call.

MessageBox (*message* , *options* , *title*)

When called in this fashion, the function will return one of the following values.

Value	Constant	Description
1	IDOK	Return value when the OK button is clicked.
2	IDCANCEL	Return value when the Cancel button is clicked.
3	IDABORT	Return value when the Abort button is clicked.
4	IDRETRY	Return value when the Retry button is clicked.
5	IDIGNORE	Return value when the Ignore button is clicked.
6	IDYES	Return value when the Yes button is clicked.
7	IDNO	Return value when the No button is clicked.

For example, the following illustrates how to capture the result of the `messagebox` window.

```
answer% = Messagebox( "Are you sure?", 36, "Continue?" )
If answer% = 6 Then
   Messagebox ( "Update complete.")
 Else
   Messagebox ( "Transaction canceled." )
   Exit Sub
End If
```

> **TIP**
>
> There are two ways to call this statement—Messagebox or Msgbox. Both are valid and equivalent statements.

Print Statement

The `Print` statement is another way to communicate with the user. However, instead of displaying messages in a popup window, the text string is displayed in the Status Bar located at the bottom of the Lotus Notes client. The syntax for this command is

Print *string*

> *string*—Any text string, variable, date, time, or list of values separated by semicolons, colons, or spaces.

```
Print "The current date and time is: " + Now
```

The `Print` and `Messagebox` statements can help debug or track the execution of a LotusScript routine. You can periodically add `Print` statements to determine variable values or track conditional branches as the program executes. For example, the following illustrates how the value of the variable could be displayed. By periodically inserting a print or messagebox statement, you can view the object value as the program executes.

```
Print "The current value is: " + doc.Status(0)
Msgbox "The current value is: " + doc.Status(0)
```

In this second example, you can track the path that the user selects.

```
answer% = Messagebox( "Are you sure?", 36, "Continue?" )
If answer% = 6 Then
    Print "The user selected YES"
Else
    Print "The user selected NO"
End If
```

Inputbox Statement

The `Inputbox` is used to display a popup window where the end-user can specify a value. This value is subsequently returned to the LotusScript routine where it can be processed or stored. The syntax for this function is as follows.

Inputbox (*prompt, title, default, position*)

> *prompt*—A text string expression that describes the input box.
> *title*—Optional. Used to describe the title of the window.
> *default*—Optional. The default to be displayed in the input field.
> *position*—Optional. The x and y coordinates for the window separated by a comma.

For example, the following prompts the user to provide his or her name. When the input box window is displayed, the input field defaults to `"John Doe"` and the title displays at the top of the window (see Figure 6.5). The answer is subsequently displayed in the Status Bar at the bottom of the Lotus Notes client.

```
Dim result As String
result = Inputbox("What is your name?","Question","John Doe")
Print "Your name is: " + result
```

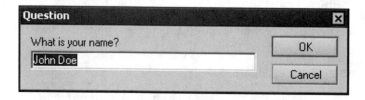

Figure 6.5 Sample *Inputbox*

Dialogbox Statement

The `Dialogbox` method is used to display the current document or a specified form in a popup dialog window. Using this method, you can pass field values between the popup and the underlying form. The following describes the syntax for this method.

```
flag = notesUIWorkspace.Dialogbox ( form , options )
Call notesUIWorkspace.Dialogbox ( form , options )
```

The following describes the various options associated with this method, which are listed in chronological order. To use the default value, simply insert a comma as a placeholder for the parameter. All of the following are optional parameters.

Option	Description
1. `AutoHorzFit`	Automatically size the dialog box horizontally to fit the first layout region or table on the form. This value must be a boolean value of either TRUE or FALSE.
2. `AutoVertFit`	Automatically size the dialog box vertically to fit the first lay out region or table on the form. This value must be a boolean value of either TRUE or FALSE.
3. `NoCancel`	Do not display the Cancel button. This value must be a boolean value of either TRUE or FALSE.
4. `NoNewFields`	By default, any field that contains a value on the dialog form but that does not exist in the underlying document is automatically created. This optional parameter enables or disables the creation of new fields on the underlying document. This value must be a boolean value of either TRUE or FALSE.
5. `NoFieldUpdate`	Used to disable field updates between the dialog window and the underlying document. This value must be a boolean value of either TRUE or FALSE.
6. `ReadOnly`	This value displays the dialog box in "readonly" mode when set to TRUE. Otherwise, by default, the window is displayed in read-write mode. This value must be a boolean value of either TRUE or FALSE.
7. `Title`	The title for the dialog window.
8. `NotesDocument`	Used to display an alternate document instead of the currently selected document.
9. `SizeToTable`	Used to automatically size the dialog based on the first table in the form. This value must be a boolean value of either TRUE or FALSE.

Option	Description
10. `NoOkCancel`	Removes the OK button from the dialog window. This value must be a boolean value of either `TRUE` or `FALSE`.
11. `OkCancelAtBottom`	By default, the OK and Cancel buttons are displayed to the right of the window. When set to `TRUE`, this option displays the button along the bottom of the window. This value must be a boolean value of either `TRUE` or `FALSE`.

For example, let's say you have a conference room form that includes a button called Recurring Event. This button contains the following code that, when clicked, displays a form named (RepeatReservation) in a dialog window. Using this dialog, the user can enter the parameters of the recurring conference room reservation.

When the user clicks OK, the field values are passed from the dialog window back to the corresponding fields on the underlying document. In this scenario, the form in the dialog must contain the same field names as the main form in order for the values to be passed from the DialogBox to the document. If the fields do not exist on the underlying document, they are automatically created.

```
Dim w As New NotesUIWorkspace
Dim uidoc As NotesUIDocument
Dim doc As NotesDocument
Set uidoc = w.CurrentDocument
Set doc = uidoc.Document
Call w.DialogBox("(RepeatReservation)",True,True,,,,,"Repeat")
```

Working with Arrays

Using the DIM statement (which is short for dimension), you can store one or more values in a single variable. This is called an *array* of values. In its simplest form, the DIM statement is used to create a one-dimensional array that contains one to many fixed values. After the array has been declared, you can assign a value to each element in the array (up to the maximum array size specified) using the element index number. For example:

```
Dim theMonth (1 to 12) as String
theMonth (1) = "January"
theMonth (2) = "February"
theMonth (3) = "March"
theMonth (4) = "April"
theMonth (5) = "May"
theMonth (6) = "June"
theMonth (7) = "July"
theMonth (8) = "August"
theMonth (9) = "September"
theMonth (10) = "October"
theMonth (11) = "November"
theMonth (12) = "December"
```

> **NOTE**
>
> `Month` is a keyword and cannot be used as an object identifier. Thus, like the previous example, consider appending "the" as an alternative (e.g., `theMonth`).

A multi-dimensional array is used to store a complex set of values in a single variable. LotusScript currently allows up to eight dimensions. To create a multi-dimensional array, comma-separate each additional array size to the statement. For example:

```
Dim holiday (1 to 12, 1 to 31) as String
holiday (1,1)    = "New Years Day"
holiday (2, 14)  = "Valentines Day"
holiday (4, 1)   = "April Fools Day"
```

Alternatively, you can use the re-dimension (`REDIM`) statement to resize an array of elements. Using this approach, you can change or redefine the total number of elements that can be stored in the array. However, this approach requires a bit more coding to implement. First, you'll need to create a counter to track the total number of elements in the array (or utilize the `Ubound()` statement).

Next, you can manage the contents of the array using an `IF` statement to determine if the array contains any elements. If the counter is set to zero, you'll need to declare the array before you assign a value to the first element in the array. If the counter is greater than zero, the array already contains a value, and you'll need to re-dimension the array. This is accomplished by preserving the current array contents and appending the new value to element list.

```
For x = 1 To 5
    Redim Preserve myList(x) As String
    myList(x) = "This is record number " + x
    Messagebox myList(x)
Next
```

Using Formula Language in LotusScript Code

A.6.3

A subset of Formula Language commands and functions can be run in LotusScript via the `Evaluate` command. This command will interpret a Formula Language statement from a LotusScript program. The statements that are permitted to run are limited. Consult the Lotus Domino Designer help for additional information.

Compiling LotusScript Code

LotusScript is an interpretive language that checks each statement line as it's being entered for syntax errors. During this same check, reserved keywords are changed to the color blue and indented to align nested statements. Syntax errors are subsequently displayed in the "Errors" section of the Programmer's pane. A full source code compile is automatically performed each time the LotusScript code is saved.

> **NOTE**
>
> You can also force a compile by selecting the **Tools** > **Recomplile All LotusScript** menu options from a form, view, library, etc. However, be aware that this option will recompile all LotusScript stored in the database. As a result, this option can affect other functionality in the database. For example, scheduled agents are sometimes "signed" with a special ID that enables them to be run on the server. When using the "recompile all" feature, the scheduled agent will now be signed with the current user's ID, which may affect the ability of the agent to run. See Chapter 19, "Security," for additional information pertaining to application security.

 Links to developerWorks

A.6.1 Gordon, Mark. *Simplifying your LotusScript with the Evaluate statement*. IBM developerWorks, November 1998. http://www.ibm.com/developerworks/lotus/library/ls-The_Evaluate_statement/index.html.

A.6.2 Guirard, Andre. *Debugging LotusScript: Domino Applications Part 2*. IBM developerWorks, August 2003. http://www.ibm.com/developerworks/lotus/library/ls-DebugLS2/index.html.

A.6.3 Steele, Gary. *Combining complex @formulas with LotusScript*. IBM developerWorks, November 1998. http://www.ibm.com/developerworks/lotus/library/ls-Combining_complex_formulas/index.html.

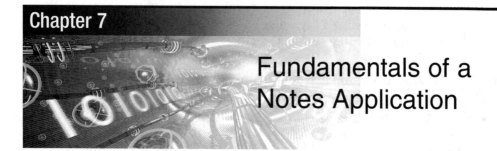

Chapter 7

Fundamentals of a Notes Application

Chapter Overview

This chapter provides a roadmap for building a Notes database. By now you should be able to navigate the development environment and have a fundamental understanding of the various constructs used to build a Notes database.

In this chapter, you will learn the five primary types of Lotus Notes applications. Almost all Notes databases can be separated into one of five different software designs. We'll discuss each type and when to use each of them.

We'll demonstrate a sample software development life cycle and provide pointers to manage the development of a Notes database from start to completion.

Finally, you'll have an opportunity for hands-on experience with developing a database from scratch so that you can understand the importance of forms, fields, and views for managing content. Although other design elements exist, most users will find that these are some of the primary components used in application development. After you've mastered these, you will find that the other design elements can be created in a similar manner. This project will illustrate how to

- Create forms
- Create views
- Create script libraries
- Create action buttons
- Create shared action buttons
- Customize the navigation using an outline, page, and frameset
- Create a welcome screen
- Create a help document
- Customize the database icon

- Restrict access to documents using a Readers field
- Create a hard-coded keyword field
- Use a formula to populate a keyword field
- Update the Access Control List (ACL)
- Hide a field

By the end of the chapter you will have learned

- The five primary Notes application designs
- The basic framework of a development life cycle
- Questions to ask when designing software
- Elements of a project plan and schedule
- How to design a Notes database
- Steps to build a Notes application

The Five Primary Application Types

Each year, corporations spend countless hours and dollars designing, building, and deploying Lotus Notes applications. However, if you spend some time assessing the core functionality of these applications, you'll find that virtually all can be classified into one of five categories:

1. Calendar

2. Collaborative

3. Reference Library

4. Workflow

5. Web Site

Although most books focus on programming language syntax, the remainder of *this* book will focus on the design and implementation of applications based on these five classifications. Later chapters in this book will also provide step-by-step, fast-track instructions for building each application type—allowing you to streamline the development process. Before we get there, let's first review the application types.

- **Calendar Application**—Calendars are perhaps one of the most popular and easy to use components of Lotus Notes. This type of application enables users to add and track events using an online calendar. The calendar can be formatted to display a single day, a week, or an entire month. This type of application is typically used to schedule conference rooms, manage vacation schedules, or display a timetable for events.
- **Collaborative Application**—Collaborative applications are used to gather feedback from a group of people. There are many types of collaborative applications, such as a "discussion forum." This type of application often displays information in tiers and includes three elements—a main document, a response, and (optionally) a response to a response. The top-level document is called the *main topic*. This is

followed by *response documents*, which are indented and appear directly underneath the main topic. Finally, some applications also implement a third level of information and permit a *response to response*. This type of application is used to discuss subjects. For example, a discussion forum is often used for online help. A person could request help on a particular subject (this would be the main topic), and members of the forum could then respond with possible solutions (these would be the responses).

- **Reference Library Application**—As the name implies, a reference library stores information related to a particular subject. This type of application is sometimes used to track project status or to archive important information. For example, many companies utilize a structured project management methodology that includes project tracking. Using a reference library, you could track meeting agendas, minutes, attendees, and reference materials associated with the project. Another example is a quality assurance database that tracks test results and performance metrics.
- **Workflow Application**—Workflow applications are used to electronically route documents to people. Using this application, you can eliminate the hassles associated with the delivery of paper documents. Workflow applications electronically manage document delivery, online approvals, and timestamps, and they provide real-time status of documents. For example, let's say your company has a specific process for procurement of new assets (e.g., computers, office supplies, business cards, etc.). The process enables anyone to submit a procurement request. However, all requests must first be approved by the requester's immediate manager and then be approved by the finance manager. Using a workflow, the appropriate manager is notified at each step in the process, and approvals are obtained online. After being approved, the document automatically goes to the next approver for review. This provides the real-time status of the request without having to track down a document. Workflow applications are truly one of the most powerful features of Lotus Notes.
- **Web Site Application**—Finally, Web-based applications enable the user to view or enter information through a series of Web pages. This type of application can be accessed from both the Notes client and a Web browser, such as Netscape Navigator, Microsoft Internet Explorer, or Mozilla Firefox.

Although virtually all Lotus Notes applications can be classified into one of these categories, it's also possible to build an application that encompasses several of these elements. For example, you may have a Web-enabled workflow application that also includes a calendar with project due dates.

The Application Development Life Cycle

This section is intended to be a primer or a basic roadmap that could be used as a development life cycle. As with any process, this is intended to be a starting point and is only one of many that could be utilized to manage a project. In fact, most companies do implement and utilize a structured approach to application development. Be sure to check with your software organization to see if there are specific processes and procedures you should be following. Otherwise, if no such processes exist, this section can be used as a guide or possibly even as a starting point in implementing a formal process in your organization.

A solid, structured application development life cycle is a key aspect to the development of any software application, regardless of the software language, operating system platform, or underlying technology. The development life cycle is the foundation for capturing requirements, managing design changes, developing the software, deploying the application, and providing support after the software is in production. In short, it's a disciplined approach to the development and support of an application. It defines the overall processes, phases, activities, tasks, and milestones required to implement the project.

Having a documented process is the first and most important step to developing an application. Everyone involved with the project should know and understand the development life cycle. This sets expectations and, essentially, lets everyone know the rules of the game. The purpose of the development life cycle is to identify and describe the generally accepted processes used to manage the development of applications. Furthermore, having these processes and procedures documented helps to significantly reduce the risk of ambiguity or confusion about the process.

For example, a development life cycle typically has several key components (see Figure 7.1). First, someone, usually the project sponsor, initiates the project based on a business need. Second, team members and application stakeholders gather information and begin planning for the project. After the project's objectives, plan, and schedule are in place, you execute the project plan and manage the project deliverables. Finally, the product is built, delivered, and implemented.

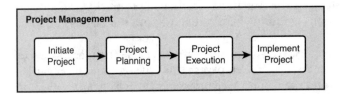

Figure 7.1   Typical project phases

By definition, a project has a definite beginning and end. However, it's the steps in between that are usually more fluid. The development life cycle often contains processes that overlap and interact as the project progresses. This is normal and should not be a deterrent for the project. Moreover, understanding what to expect will help with the design, development, and management of the application. Figure 7.2 illustrates how some of the process may occur for any particular project.

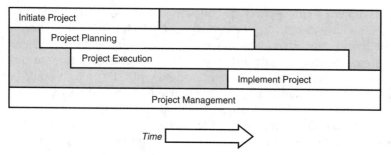

Figure 7.2   Overlap in project phases

Elements of a Project Plan

In addition to understanding the development life cycle, it's equally important to have a plan that defines how the project will be managed and a schedule that defines activities, duration, and target delivery dates. The combination of these two items will help keep the project on schedule and within specifications. A good project plan incorporates many different considerations. The following are some items to consider when building a project plan.

- **Project Overview**—The project overview provides a short summary of the scope of the project. This section is typically intended for management and briefly describes the mission, stakeholders, departments, and milestones associated with the project.
- **Project Objectives**—This section contains a detailed statement of work to be achieved by the project. The statement should include both technical and non-technical goals.
- **General Approach**—The general approach should describe the managerial and technical aspects of the project. It may include the deployment approach (straight cutover or phased implementation) and management structure for the project.
- **Contractual Obligations**—This section should provide specific, measurable deliverables including a list of all project obligations.
- **Scope Management**—Scope management is probably the most important section in the project plan. This section should spell out exactly how to manage changes to the project. This is the process for recording scope changes, approvals, and acceptance criteria. All scope changes should also be assessed to determine their cost and impact to the schedule.
- **Cost Management**—This section describes the process to manage project costs. Costs may be in terms of dollars or number of labor hours required to implement the project. The projected cost of the project is usually based on the "approved" requirement document. It's important to understand that changes to the scope can and usually do affect the cost for the project.

- **Schedule Management**—This section describes in detail the phases, activities, tasks, and milestones associated with the entire project. Each item in the schedule should include a projected start date and duration. The schedule should also include task interdependencies (e.g., task five must be completed before starting task six). Every stakeholder and team member associated with the project should be allowed to participate in the development of the schedule. The project sponsor and key managers should approve, or sign off on, the final schedule. This helps ensure that everyone has agreed to the timeline for the project. In many cases, the project plan includes key milestone dates followed by a detailed project schedule after the requirements are finalized.
- **Project Resources**—The resource section defines the requirements for the project. It should include the staffing resources, skill requirements, system resources, or other material resource requirements.
- **Roles and Responsibilities**—This section describes all project roles and responsibilities. It should clearly spell out what organizations (or individuals) are responsible for specific activities, tasks, or deliverables. This section helps ensure accountability for the project.
- **Quality Assurance**—The quality assurance section, often called application "testing," details the test approach. It specifies the type of tests to be performed, test completion criteria, a method to report and track defects, defect severity levels, and detailed test scenarios.
- **Project Communication**—The communication section describes how information will be distributed to the project team. This section should include a method for communication (email, conference calls, status meetings), frequency of communication, and a list of all project participants.
- **Issue Management**—This section should describe how project conflicts will be managed. It should list contact names, define the escalation path, and specify who makes the final ruling on conflicts.
- **Project Completion Criteria**—The project completion criteria specify the specific tasks or product specifications that must be met in order to consider the project complete. This list should contain specific, measurable items.

TIP

The project sponsor and key project managers should contribute to the project plan. The project plan should be approved by management at the start of the project to ensure that everyone is in agreement with the project scope, schedule, and cost.

NOTE

Sample project plans and schedules are included on the companion Web site.

Elements of a Project Schedule

Schedules are used to manage and track the delivery of project components. At the most fundamental level, virtually all schedules include a Startup Phase, Design Phase, Development Phase, Implementation Phase, and Closeout Phase.

The project schedule is typically created after the scope of the project has been clearly defined and agreed to by key stakeholders. The schedule includes a detailed work breakdown structure—or a detailed list of activities, tasks, and milestones—associated with the project. As the project progresses, it is used to track projected versus actual completion of deliverables and to communicate status to both team members and management. The project schedule should be reviewed on a regular basis, such as at weekly status meetings.

Although many companies use Microsoft Project to manage the schedule, you could also use a spreadsheet or word processor to track this information. The following is a sample project schedule that could be used as the basis for your project.

PHASE I: PROJECT STARTUP

Activity: Project Kickoff

Task: Meet Project Sponsor and Project Team Members

Task: Confirm Project Scope

Task: Determine Project Contingencies, Constraints, Costs, and Dates

Activity: Start Project - Develop Project Plan

Task: Schedule Project Checkpoint Meetings

Task: Gather Initial Requirements

Task: Document and Refine Requirements

Task: Finalize Requirements

Task: Review Requirements with Stakeholders

Task: Validate Engagement Objectives and Goals

Task: Create a Project Plan and Schedule

Milestone: Obtain Approval from the Project Sponsor

PHASE II: SOLUTION DESIGN

Activity: Design the Application

Task: Determine the Overall Application Type

Task: Determine Layout of User Interface

Task: Design the Forms and Fields

Task: Design the Views

Task: Determine Authority Levels for the Database

Task: Determine Agents Required to Support the Database

Task: Document the Database Design

Task: Determine Authority Levels for All User Groups

Task: Design Reporting and Email (where applicable)

Activity: Review Architecture Design

Task: Confirm Design with Stakeholders

Task: Create Non-Functional Prototype—Include Forms, Views, and Buttons

Task: Incorporate Feedback into Overall Database Design
Task: Confirm That Server Backup Procedures Will Include the New Database
Task: Confirm That Disaster Recovery Plan Will Include the New Database
Task: Confirm SMTP Email Routing and Firewall Settings (where applicable)
Activity: Finalize Requirements and Design
Task: Refine and Update Design
Task: Review Design with Stakeholders
Task: Finalize Project Plan and Schedule
Milestone: Freeze Design Requirements (For Initial Release)—Project Baseline

PHASE III: SOLUTION DEVELOPMENT
Activity: Develop the Solution
Task: Create the Database
Task: Create the Forms
Task: Create the Views
Task: Create the User Interface
Task: Create the Action Buttons
Task: Create the Script Libraries
Task: Create the Access Control List Groups
Task: Create the Welcome Screen
Task: Create the Help Information
Task: Customize the Database Icon
Task: Manage Changes to Scope, Schedule, and Cost
Activity: Verify Solution (Quality Assurance)
Task: Conduct Unit Tests (e.g., Verify Fields)
Task: Conduct Functional Tests (e.g., Verify Functionality)
Task: Conduct System Tests (e.g., Verify End-to-End System Operations)
Task: Conduct User Acceptance Test (e.g., Customer Validation)
Milestone: Obtain UAT Approval from the Project Sponsor

PHASE IV: SOLUTION IMPLEMENTATION
Activity: Conduct Training
Task: Create Training Materials
Task: Schedule Training Sessions
Task: Conduct Training
Activity: Load Data
Task: Import Existing Data into Database (where applicable)
Task: Verify That Data Was Imported Correctly
Activity: Prepare for Deployment
Task: Activate Application/Enable Access in ACL
Task: Notify Users That System Is Up and Running
Task: Notify Support Team
Milestone: Solution Deployed

PHASE V: PROJECT CLOSEOUT
Activity: Obtain Project Signoff from Sponsor
Activity: Gather Customer Feedback
Activity: Document Lessons Learned
Activity: Transition Application to Support Team

Questions to Ask When Designing a Database

The following are some questions to consider when designing a Notes database. These questions are intended to be a starting point to help facilitate communication and ultimately start the design process. After the project has been initiated, you'll want to have a meeting to discuss or review the project requirements.

Project Questions

1. What's the purpose of the application?
2. Who are the stakeholders, or users, of the application?
3. How much will the application cost to develop?
4. How much funding is available?
5. What are the project requirements?
6. What is the timeline for implementation?
7. How will project success be defined?
8. Where will the application reside (e.g., on which server)?
9. How will the application be implemented (phased approach or straight cutover)?
10. What tools will be used to manage the project?
11. What is the backup and restore procedure?
12. What is the backup frequency?
13. Are there any country- (or culture-) specific requirements (such as date, phone, and postal code format)?
14. Who will support the application after it is deployed?
15. What are the application support hours?

General Application Questions

1. How many forms will be created?
2. Are there sample forms?
3. What information needs to be captured and stored?
4. Who will use the forms?

5. Will some users have more authority than other users?

6. Will some information be visible to some users and not to others?

7. Will the document need approvals? If so, what's the approval process?

8. Will the application be accessed from Lotus Notes, a Web browser, or both?

9. Who will have access to the database application?

10. What type of reports can be generated?

11. Is there a feedback or problem-reporting mechanism for the tool?

12. Who will have "Admin" authority?

13. Is this an internal or external customer application?

14. Are there additional implications if this is an external application?

15. Are there confidential fields that are visible internally but hidden to external customers?

16. Are there corporate business or security guidelines that must be met?

Workflow Application Questions

1. Are there fields that need to be locked based on the status of the document?

2. What is the workflow process?

3. Who can create documents?

4. Who can approve documents?

5. Is there a process to "reset" the status of a document?

6. If workflow includes a "cancel" status, can the document be reopened?

7. Does the application require a history or log file to track status changes and approvals?

8. Are there multiple levels of approvals?

9. What are the roles, or levels of authority, for the tool?

10. Does the administrator have the authority to override changes?

11. What happens if an approver is out of town—can you specify a backup approver? Can the administrator approve?

Web Application Questions

1. How will users log in to the application (Windows Active Directory or Domino login)?

2. Is there a default browser for the company?

3. Will this be purely a Web-based application, or will the application be accessed from both Web browsers and Lotus Notes clients?

4. Can the customer attach documents via a Web browser?

5. Who will manage the creation of user IDs and passwords?

Designing a Notes Application

Although there's no single approach to building a database, this section provides a general roadmap to building a database from scratch. Included are step-by-step instructions for creating a database using most of the design element constructs. At the completion of the project, you should understand the logical progression of the database design and be familiar with many of the design elements. Now, let's review the sequential steps we'll follow to build the application.

Step 1: Create the Database
Step 2: Create the Form and Fields
Step 3: Create the View
Step 4: Create the Script Library
Step 5: Add Buttons to the Form
Step 6: Add Buttons to the View
Step 7: Add Navigation
Step 8: Create Welcome and Help Documents
Step 9: Customize the Database Icon
Step 10: Set the Database Security

Using this approach, you'll gradually incorporate more and more functionality into the database. Because virtually all database applications contain forms and views, you'll start with these two elements. From here, you'll add code to manage task automation, create buttons, build a script library, and finally customize the appearance and navigation.

Project: Build a Database to Track Web Sites

Difficulty Level:	Moderate
Completion Time:	Approximately 2 hours
Project Materials:	1 Form, 9 Fields, 1 View, 1 Library, 1 Page,
	1 Outline, 1 Frameset, 1 Navigator, 6 Action Buttons
Languages Used:	LotusScript and Formula
Database Type:	Reference Library

Upon completion of this project, you'll have a working database that can be used to store and track Web site links, user IDs, and passwords. The database form will include a Readers field, which, if you recall from Chapter 4, "Domino Design Elements," will limit the ability to view data records created by other users. In others words, a unique set of Web sites will be displayed for each end-user. We'll also add buttons to automatically launch the Web site in the user's specified browser, and finally, we'll customize the navigation by creating a frameset, page, and outline.

Step 1: Create the Database

Okay, let's get started by launching the Designer client. Next, to create the database, select the **File > Database > New** menu options, and a dialog box will be displayed (see Figure 7.3). Select the server location for the database (or alternatively leave the field set to **Local** to create the database on your workstation). In the application title field, specify **Websites**. Verify that the template type is set to **-Blank-** and click **OK** to create the database.

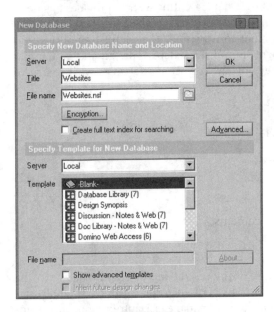

Figure 7.3 New Database dialog

> **NOTE**
>
> You may need to request authority to create a database on the server. The system administrator sometimes has this authority and decides who can create a Notes database on the server. Some companies allow anyone to create a database, while other companies restrict this ability to the system administrators. By default, if you create the database, you'll have "Manager" authority. This is the highest permission level, and it provides the ability to manage the application design and security. Conversely, when the database is created for you by an administrator, they typically give you the second highest authority level, "Designer," which enables you to modify the design of the database, but you cannot change the database access control settings. So, you can see that a good working relationship with the system administrator can be beneficial to the design and development of Notes database applications. See Chapter 19, "Security," for additional information on database security.

After it is created, the database (with no design elements) will be added to the Designer client Design pane. You've now cleared the first hurdle in the development of the Notes database. Next, you'll start to build and shape the forms used to manage data records, or documents.

Step 2: Create the Form and Fields

The Web Site form will be used to capture and display information regarding a specific Internet site. After it is created, this form will only allow the author of the document to view the Web site information. This enables each user to store and manage his or her own Web URL links.

To create a form, select the **Create > Design > Form** menu options. After the form has been created, add a descriptive title such as **Web Site** at the top of the form and the following field descriptions down the left side of the form.

- Title:
- Link:
- Category:
- Rank:
- UserID:
- Password:
- Last Update:
- Description:

Next, add the fields as specified in the following table. To create a field, select the **Create > Field** menu options. Be sure to set the data type, formula, and other attributes for each field on the form using the properties dialog box and/or Programmer's pane. To view the properties dialog, click on the object and select the **Design > Field Properties** menu option.

Field Name	Type	Formula/Value	Remarks
Title	Text,		
Link	Text, Editable		

Category	Dialog List, Editable	`Class :="";`
		`Cache := "NoCache";`
		`Host := "";`
		`View := "Category";`
		`Column := 1;`
		`output := @Trim(@Unique`
		`  (@DbColumn( Class :`
		`  Cache; Host; view ;`
		`  Column )));`
		`@If (output = ""; "";`
		`  output)`
			Select the **Allow multiple values** setting for the field in tab 1 of the properties dialog. Select **Allow values not in list** on tab 2. Change the choice type to **Use formula for choices** and add the formula to the associated field.

continues

Field Name	Type	Formula/Value	Remarks
Rank	Combobox, Editable	1-Star 2-Star 3-Star 4-Star 5-Star	Set the **Choices** in tab 2 of the properties dialog box.
UserID	Text, Editable		
Password	Text, Editable		
LastUpdate	Time/Date; Computed	@If (@IsDocBeingSaved; @Now; LastUpdate);	Set the field to display both the date and time in tab 2 of the properties dialog box.
Description	Rich Text, Editable		

This form will contain a hidden field called Readers. This field determines who can view the document. Insert a blank line above the form title. Select the **Create > Field** menu options and create the field on the first line of the form.

Field Name	Type	Default Value Formula	Remarks
Readers	Readers, Computed when Composed, Hidden	@UserName	Select **Design > Field Properties**. Switch to tab 6. Check the **Hide paragraph if formula is true** checkbox and set the formula to 1. Change the font color of the field to **RED** to indicate that this is a hidden field. Make this the first and top-most field on the form.

Your form should now look similar to Figure 7.4.

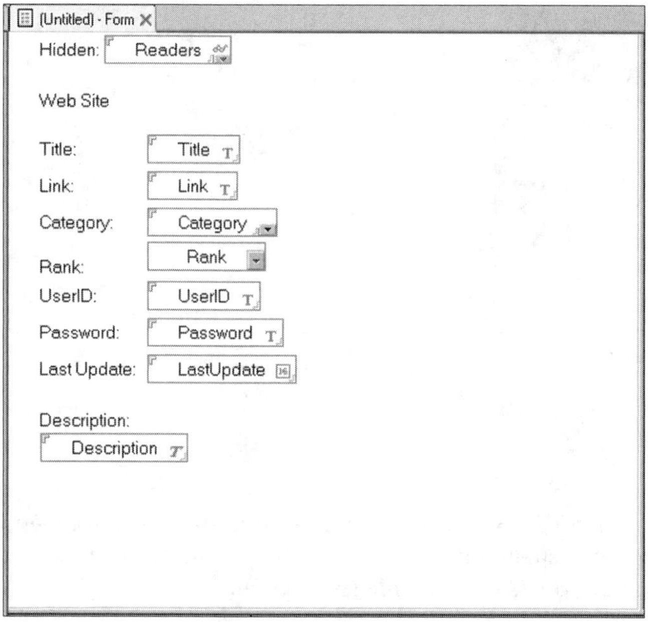

Figure 7.4 Completed Web Site form

Finally, save the form by selecting the **File** > **Save** menu options. You'll be prompted to specify the form name. Set the form name to **Web Site|Website** and click **OK** to save the form design.

Congratulations, you've successfully created your first form! Give it a try. Switch to your Lotus Notes client, open the database, and select the **Create** > **Web Site** menu options to play with the newly created form.

NOTE

The Category field will display a warning message. This is a temporary message. The warning message will be resolved by the time the project is completed.

Step 3: Create the View

Every database must contain at least one view. By default, a view called "(untitled)" is automatically created when the database is first created. To configure this view, navigate to **Views** in the Design pane and double-click on the default view.

After the view is opened, the Designer client will immediately display the properties dialog for the view (see Figure 7.5). Specify **By Category** in the Name field and **Category** in the Alias field.

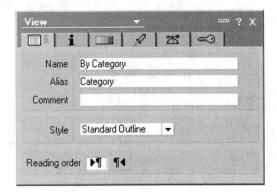

Figure 7.5   View property dialog

Column 1

This column will display the Category field. Select the **Design > Column Properties** menu options. In the properties dialog, set the column title to **Cat.** and column width to **2** and select the option **Show twistie when row is expandable** (see Figure 7.6).

To illustrate groupings, you will make this a "categorized" view. Switch to tab 2 to set the sort type to **Ascending** and type to **Categorized**. Finally, switch to tab 3 to change the text color to **blue** and style to **bold**. After these properties are set, close the properties dialog.

Next select **Field** as the display type in the Programmer's pane and select the **Category** field. You have just assigned the "category" field to display in the column.

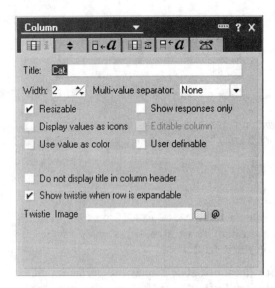

Figure 7.6   Column property dialog

Column 2

This column will display the Web site name. Select the **Create > Append New Column** menu options to create the column. Then select the **Design > Column Properties** menu options to define the characteristics. On tab 1, set the column title to **Title**. Switch to tab 2 and set the column to display in **Ascending** order. Next, select **Field** as the display type in the Programmer's pane and select the **Title** field.

Column 3

This column will display the userID. Append a new column. In the properties dialog, set the column title to **UserID** and close the properties dialog. Next, set Display to **Field** in the Programmer's pane and click on **UserID**.

Column 4

This column will display the password. Append a new column. In the properties dialog, set the column title to **Password** and close the properties dialog. Next, set Display to **Field** in the Programmer's pane and click on **Password**.

> **TIP**
>
> By default, all categories will be automatically expanded when the view is opened. To set the view to automatically collapse all categories, select **View > Properties** (see Figure 7.7). If the property window is set to **COLUMN**, click on the triangle and switch to **VIEW**. Finally, on tab 2, select the **Collapse all when database is first opened** checkbox.

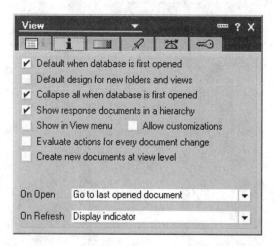

Figure 7.7   Collapse categories property for the view

Now, it's important to note that this view does not include a selection formula (see Figure 7.8). So, by default, all documents in the database will be displayed in the view. If the view were to include a selection formula, it would have been placed in Programmer's pane for the View Selection object.

Congratulations, you've successfully created your first view! Select the **File** > **Save** menu options to save the updates. Your view should look like Figure 7.9.

Close the view.

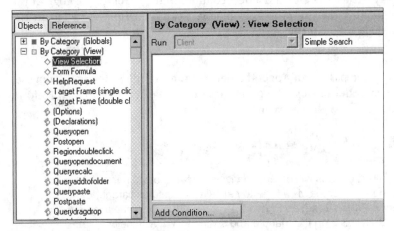

Figure 7.8   View Selection section for the view

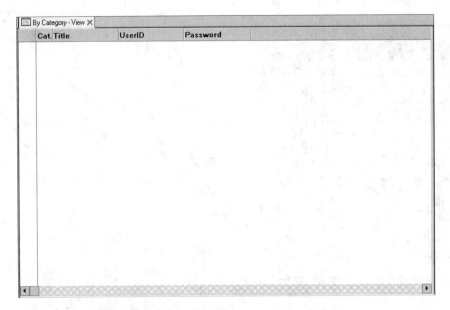

Figure 7.9   Completed By Category view

Step 4: Create the Script Library

To illustrate the concept of shared programming, next you'll create a LotusScript library. Here, as with all projects in the book, working source code has been provided that can be manually typed or copied from the text file included on the companion Web site.

At first glance, the LotusScript code may appear intimidating. However, the routines provided here are intended to introduce you to the concept of shared code, script libraries, and the LotusScript language without having to worry about the programming syntax. As you work through this section, the intent is to learn how to build and use a LotusScript library. The library will store source code for several of the application action buttons as well as a function that checks to ensure that required fields on the form contain a value. To create the library, select **Create** > **Design** > **Script Library** > **LotusScript Library** menu options.

> **TIP**
>
> The following code is available in the developer's toolbox. Simply open the "Project Library" database in your Lotus Notes client and navigate to the "Script Library" section for the appropriate project. After you locate the project, copy and paste the code into the Designer client for the current project. Be sure the programmer's pane has focus before pasting the code. Alternatively, you can elect to manually type the code

The library contains two subroutines and one function. The subroutines—`LaunchSiteFromDoc` and `LaunchSiteFromView`—will launch the Web site when a user clicks a button either from within the document or from the By Category view. The function—`CheckFieldValues`—will perform field validation as users add new documents to the database.

This subroutine retrieves the Web site link value from the currently opened document and launches the Web site in the user's default browser. To create the subroutine, add the following to the Programmer's pane, which is the lower-right-most pane of the Designer client. Note that if you start typing (or paste the code) in the Options section, Designer will automatically create the new section for the subroutine.

```
Sub LaunchSiteFromDoc ( )

    '---------------------------
    ' Launch the Web site from the document.
    ' Display a warning message if there's a
    ' problem with the browser configuration.
    '---------------------------
    On Error Goto oops
    Dim w As New NotesUIWorkspace
    Dim uidoc As NotesUIDocument
    Dim doc As NotesDocument
    Dim siteName As String
```

```
Set uidoc = w.CurrentDocument
Set doc = uidoc.Document
siteName = doc.Link(0)
Print "Launch website: " siteName
Call w.URLOpen ( siteName )
Exit Sub

oops:
Msgbox "Browser error.  The Internet browser "+_
"may not be configured " +Chr$(13)+ " correctly.   "+_
"Check your location document in your address "+_
" book "+Chr$(13)+"or contact the help desk for "+_
"additional assistance."
Resume

End Sub
```

The second subroutine is used to launch the Web site from a view. This code works slightly differently from the previous subroutine. In the previous routine, the link was retrieved from the currently opened document. With this subroutine, the Web site link information is pulled from the selected document in the view. This routine verifies that the selected row is actually a document and not a categorized group name. It also verifies that only one Web site document is selected. Add the following in the Programmer's pane of the LotusScript library.

```
Sub LaunchSiteFromView

    '---------------------------
    ' Launch the Web site from the view.
    ' Display a warning message if there's a
    ' problem with the browser configuration.
    '---------------------------
    On Error Goto oops
    Dim s As notessession
    Dim db As notesDatabase
    Dim collection As NotesDocumentCollection
    Dim doc As NotesDocument
    Dim w As New NotesUIWorkspace
    Dim siteName As String

    Set s = New NotesSession
    Set db = s.CurrentDatabase
    Set collection = db.UnprocessedDocuments

    If collection.count = 0 Then
        Msgbox ("Please select a Web site.  "+_
        "The current selection is a category.")
    Elseif collection.count > 1 Then
        Msgbox ("Please select only one document.")
    Else
        Set doc = collection.GetFirstDocument
        siteName = doc.Link(0)
        Print "Launch website: " siteName
```

```
      Call w.URLOpen ( siteName )
   End If
   Exit Sub

oops:
   Msgbox "Browser error.  The Internet browser "+_
   "may not be configured " +Chr$(13)+ " correctly.  "+_
   "Check your location document in your address "+_
   " book "+Chr$(13)+"or contact the help desk for "+_
   "additional assistance."
   Resume

End Sub
```

This function checks three fields on the Web Site form to ensure that they contain a value. The Title, Link, and Category fields must contain a non-blank value in order to save the document. If any of these fields do not contain a value, an error message will be displayed. The function returns a TRUE value if all fields are valid so that processing can continue. It returns a FALSE value if invalid fields are identified in order to halt processing.

```
Function CheckFieldValues ( DocRef As NotesDocument )

   '----------------------------
   ' Declare fields.
   '----------------------------
   Dim MsgText As String
   CheckFieldValues = True
   MsgText = ""

   '----------------------------
   ' Validate each field
   '----------------------------
   If Trim(DocRef.Title(0)) = "" Then
      MsgText = MsgText + "Specify a Site Name." + Chr$(13)
   End If

   If Trim(DocRef.Link(0)) = "" Then
      MsgText = MsgText + "Specify a Web Link." + Chr$(13)
   End If

   If Trim(DocRef.Category(0)) = "" Then
      MsgText = MsgText + "Specify a Category." + Chr$(13)
   End If

   '----------------------------
   ' Display message if fields are invalid.
   '----------------------------
   If MsgText <> "" Then
      Msgbox MsgText,16,"Required Fields."
      CheckFieldValues = False
   End If

End Function
```

> **NOTE**
>
> All functions must return a value. The return value is set by creating a variable within the function and setting it to a string, number, or value. The return variable name must match the name of the function. In this case, the return variable (and function name) is called `CheckFieldValues`. The function returns `TRUE` if all fields pass validation and `FALSE` if one or more fields do not pass validation.

To save the library, select **File > Save**. When prompted, name the library **Website**.

Step 5: Add Buttons to the Form

With the LotusScript library in place, the action buttons and field validation can be added to the form. You will create four action buttons—Edit, Save, Close, and Launch Site. Field validation will be added to the `QuerySave` event. Both the buttons and field validation will reference the LotusScript library created in the previous step.

Return to the Web Site form and open the design element. In the Objects pane (the lower section of the screen), locate the (Globals) section (see Figure 7.10). This section will be located at the very top of the list of objects. You may need to scroll up to locate this section. Next, click on **Options** and add the following statement in the Programmer's pane:

```
Option Public
USE "Website"
```

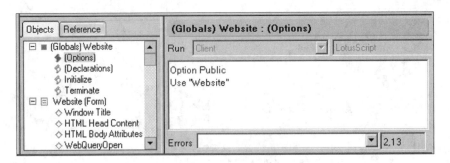

Figure 7.10   (Globals) section for the Web Site form

The USE statement ties the form and LotusScript library together. Without this statement, Lotus Notes is unable to locate the subroutines and functions.

Create the Edit Button

To create an Edit button, select **Create > Action > Action**. In the properties dialog, title the button **Edit** in tab 1. Switch to tab 2. Select the **Previewed for editing** and **Opened for editing** options. Close the properties dialog and add the following in the Programmer's pane:

```
@Command([EditDocument]);
```

Create the Save Button

To create a Save button, select **Create** > **Action** > **Action**. In the properties dialog, title the button **Save** in tab 1. Switch to tab 2. Select the **Previewed for reading** and **Opened for reading** options. Close the properties dialog and add the following in the Programmer's pane:

```
@Command([FileSave]);
```

Create the Close Button

To create a Close button, select **Create** > **Action** > **Action**. In the properties dialog, title the button **Close** in tab 1. Close the properties dialog and add the following in the Programmer's pane:

```
@Command([FileCloseWindow]);
```

Create the Launch Site Button

To create a Launch Site button, select **Create** > **Action** > **Action**. In the properties dialog, title the button **Launch Site** in tab 1 and close the properties dialog. Next, change the Language Selector from **Formula** to **LotusScript** and add the following in the Programmer's pane:

```
Sub Click(Source As Button)
      Dim ws As New NotesUIWorkspace
      Dim uidoc As NotesUIDocument
      Dim doc As NotesDocument
      Set uidoc = ws.CurrentDocument
      Set doc = uidoc.Document
      Call LaunchSiteFromDoc ( )
End Sub
```

The updated form should now look like Figure 7.11.

> **TIP**
>
> Designer allows you to add a graphic icon to each action button. This is set on tab 1 of the properties dialog for each action. To add a graphic, double-click on the action and locate the **Icon** section of the properties dialog. Change the radio button from **None** to **Notes** and select a graphic from the dropdown (see Figure 7.12).

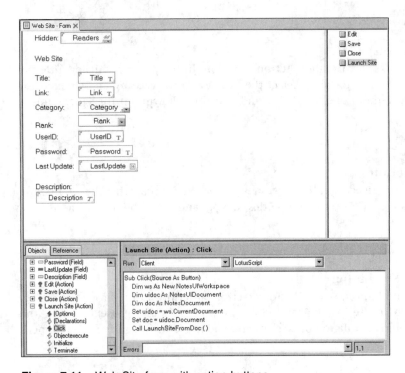

Figure 7.11   Web Site form with action buttons

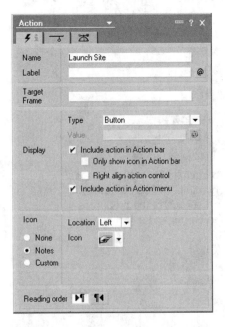

Figure 7.12   Setting the icon for an action button

Add Field Validation to the Form

To add field validation to the form, locate the QuerySave event in the Objects pane. This event will be found within the section entitled "Website (Form)". Add the following in the Programmer's pane.

```
Sub Querysave(Source As Notesuidocument, Continue As Variant)
    Dim w As New NotesUIWorkspace
    Dim uidoc As NotesUIDocument
    Dim doc As NotesDocument
    Set uidoc = w.CurrentDocument
    Set doc = uidoc.Document
    Continue = CheckFieldValues ( doc )
End Sub
```

Updates to the form are complete. Save and close the form.

Step 6: Add Buttons to the View

Two buttons will be added to the view—New Site and Launch Site. Return to the By Category view and open the design element. This view, similar to the form, will require the USE statement to be added in order to utilize the LotusScript library.

In the Objects pane (the lower section of the screen), locate the "By Category (Globals)" section. This section will be located at the very top of the list of objects. You may need to scroll up to locate this section. Next, click on **Options** and add the following statement in the Programmer's pane:

```
Option Public
USE "Website"
```

Create the New Site Button

This button will allow users to create new Web site documents. When clicked, a new document will be created. To create the button, select **Create > Action > Action**. In the properties dialog, title the button **New Site** in tab 1. Close the properties dialog and add the following in the Programmer's pane:

```
@Command([Compose]; "Website")
```

Create the Launch Site Button

This button will launch the selected Web site in the designated default browser. To create the button, select **Create > Action > Action**. In the properties dialog, title the button **Launch Site** in tab 1 and close the properties dialog. Next, change the Language Selector from **Formula** to **LotusScript** and add the following in the Programmer's pane:

```
Sub Click(Source As Button)

    Call LaunchSiteFromView ()

End Sub
```

Step 7: Add Navigation

To enrich the overall appearance of the tool, you'll create a custom application interface by creating an outline, page, and frameset. The combination of these three elements will be used to display and navigate the application.

Create the Outline

The first step is to create the outline. The outline defines the navigational elements and is displayed in the left pane of the frameset. To create the outline, select the **Create** > **Design** > **Outline** menu options. After the outline is created, the next step will be to define the elements to be included or listed in the display.

Select the **New Entry** button, located at the top of the display, to add an entry to the outline. This first entry will display the outline title. In the properties dialog, label the entry **My Websites**. In this case, the user interface will display the application name. This is an arbitrary title and can be set to any text value.

Next, you will create a spacer or blank line to separate the outline title from the remaining outline entries. Select the **New Entry** button but do not specify a label.

To create the navigational items for the outline, click the **New Entry** button a third time. In the properties dialog (see Figure 7.13), label the entry **By Category**. Next, set the type field to **Named Element** and **View**. In the Value field, enter **By Category** as the view name.

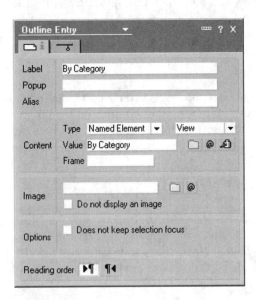

Figure 7.13 Setting an outline element to display a view

We've now completed the design of the outline: Select the **Save Outline** button and specify **MainOutline** for the design element name.

> **NOTE**
>
> As a general practice, you should always use the alias name when working with design elements. However, outlines automatically default to the primary name and do not allow the alias name to be specified. This means that if the view name is changed, you'll also need to update the outline to reflect the name change.

Create the Page

To utilize the outline, you'll embed the design element on a page. To create the page, select the **Create > Design > Page** menu options. Using the properties dialog, open the second tab and select a color, such as light blue. Next, select **Create > Embedded Element > Outline** to add the navigation outline (named MainOutline) to the page. Save the page and name the element **MainPage**.

Create the Frameset

To complete the navigation setup, a two-pane frameset must be created. The left pane will contain the outline, and the right pane will display data. To create the frameset, select the **Create > Design > Frameset** menu options. When prompted to select a design, click **OK** to accept the default settings.

The frameset is configured in two steps. First you will configure the left pane and then the right pane. To start, click on the left pane and select the **Frame > Frame Properties** menu options (see Figure 7.14). Set the name to **Main**, set the **Type** to **Named Element** and **Page**, enter **MainPage** as the value, and set **Default target for links in frame** to **Right**.

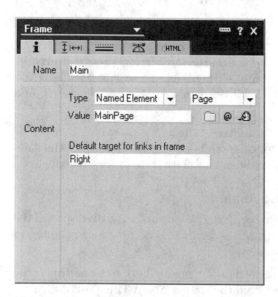

Figure 7.14 Left frame property settings

With the property window still displayed, click on the right pane (see Figure 7.15). Set the name to **Right**, set the **Type** to **Named Element** and **View**, enter **By Category** as the value, and set **Default target for links in frame** to **Right**.

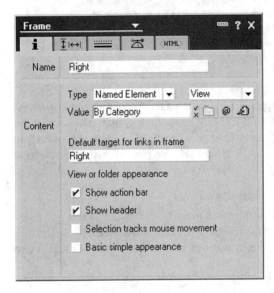

Figure 7.15   Right frame property settings

Configuration for the frameset is now complete. Select **File > Save**, name the design element **MainFrame**, and close the design element.

Enable the Frameset

To enable the frameset, the default settings for the database must be modified to display the newly created frameset. To change the default settings, select the **File > Database > Properties** menu options. Switch to tab 5. Select **Open designated Frameset** and **MainFrame** to complete the setup.

Congratulations, you've just added a custom interface to the application. You can view the new addition by switching to the Lotus Notes client and opening the database. If the database is already open, you may need to close and reopen the database to see the changes.

Step 8: Create Welcome and Help Documents

The "About This Database" document, also known as the "Welcome" screen, is displayed the first time the database is opened in the Lotus Notes client. This document can be used to display information pertaining to the database.

The "About This Database" document is a special design element. It can be set to display the first time the database is opened or accessed from the **Help > About This Database** menu options.

To edit this design element, navigate to the Other section and select **Database Resources** from the Design pane. Double-click on the "About database" document to edit the item (see Figure 7.16). Add a title to the document and provide a description of the database.

Also in the "Database Resources" section is the "Using This Database" document. This document should be used to describe the functionality of the database. After content has been added to the document, it can be accessed by selecting the **Help > Using this database** menu options in the Lotus Notes client.

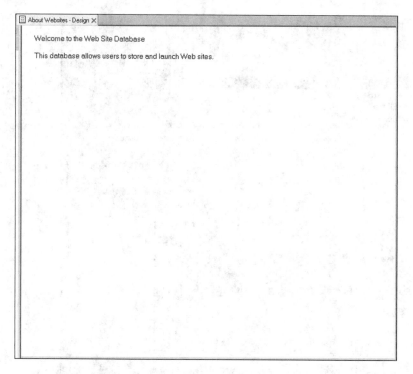

Figure 7.16 About This Database document

Step 9: Customize the Database Icon

Database icons are used as visual indicators for the database. They help users more rapidly locate a database from the Lotus Notes workspace. To customize the database icon, navigate to the Other section and select **Database Resources** from the Design pane. Edit the Icon design element. This will display the special pixel editor where you create a custom graphic to represent the database.

A.7.1

Step 10: Set the Database Security

Application security is the last step in the project. To adjust the Access Control List (ACL) settings, select the **File** > **Database** > **Access Control** menu options.

By default, the Basics tab should be active. Click on the -**Default**- user in the center of the screen. Then change the Access field (right side) to **Author** and select both the **Create documents** and **Delete documents** checkboxes (see Figure 7.17). These options will allow only the author to modify or delete the Web site document.

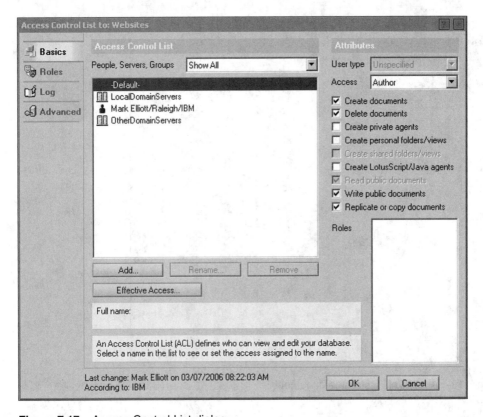

Figure 7.17   Access Control List dialog

Congratulations, you've just created your first Lotus Notes database! When opened in the Lotus Notes client, you will see the By Category calendar view. When you click on the **New Site** button, a new document will be created. Give it a try by adding a popular Web site (such as www.cnn.com or www.yahoo.com). Note that the Category field will be empty until you add your first document.

Figure 7.18 illustrates the completed project with several example Web site documents added.

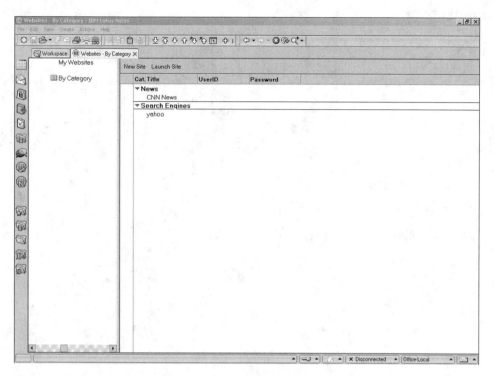

Figure 7.18 Completed project with sample Web sites

If would you like to further customize the application, refer to Chapters 13 through 17 for additional enhancements.

Links to developerWorks

A.7.1 Lotus Notes Sandbox. *Sample Database Icons*. IBM developerWorks. http://www. lotus.com/ldd/sandbox.nsf/Search?SearchView&Query=icons&SearchOrder=0&Start= 1&Count=100.

Chapter 8

Calendar Applications

Chapter Overview

This chapter will cover the nuts and bolts of a calendar application. The Lotus Notes calendar is perhaps one of the most popular and easy to use components of Notes. It's a great collaborative tool that's simple to develop.

Calendars can be used for many different purposes. Some of the more popular uses include

- Vacation planner
- Conference room reservations
- Equipment reservations
- Shared business or department calendar
- Resource or event planner

By the end of the chapter you will have learned

- The elements of a calendar
- The elements of a recurring event
- How to create a calendar application
- How to manage simple recurring events
- How to manage complex recurring events
- How to create a custom dialog box
- How to create and use layout regions

This chapter includes step-by-step instructions for building two distinctly different calendar applications. The first project illustrates how to create a simple recurring event calendar. The second illustrates an alternative design approach that permits complex repeating calendar events.

Application Architecture

There are two primary components that make up a calendar application—a form and a view. The form is used to capture information such as the appointment date, time, and subject. The view simply displays the subject, based on the specified date and time provided in the form. Believe it or not, using these two elements, you will be able to build a calendar application that can manage recurring events.

Before you start programming, you need to understand the rules for building a calendar application and the process used to manage recurring events.

RULE 1—The appointment *form* must have a start date field. This field determines where to display the event on the calendar. The start date is the anchor for the calendar application.

RULE 2—The appointment *form* must contain a duration. This field must be numeric and represents the number of sequential minutes for the event. This can be computed by including a start and end time on the form.

> **NOTE**
>
> The duration is used in column 2 of the calendar view. This value can be omitted from the form if the calendar view column contains a value or formula.

RULE 3—Column 1 of the calendar *view* must contain a "date/time" value sorted in ascending order. This column should be hidden from the user.

> **NOTE**
>
> You must sort the first column in ascending order for the calendar view to display correctly.

RULE 4—Column 2 of the calendar *view* must contain the "duration" for the calendar event. This value specifies the duration in minutes for the event. The duration can be a field, value, or formula.

> **NOTE**
>
> The duration value can be positive or negative. Positive numbers will display calendar events to the right (or future) of the start date. Negative numbers will display calendar events to the left (or prior) to the start date. Note that zero is a valid value.

RULE 5—The Style of the *view* must be set to Calendar. This setting changes the appearance of the view from the traditional look to an actual calendar.

Now let's delve deeper into the architecture and design options for managing recurring calendar events. The complexity of the application will revolve around the process required to
manage repeating events. As with any software language, there are many ways to design,
develop, and implement a solution. The next sections will discuss two possible solutions.

Managing Recurring Events Using Single Documents

We have already discussed the primary elements of the calendar application—a form and a
view. The next step is to discuss options for managing recurring events. This first approach
is a simple and efficient method to manage sequential calendar events.

A sequential event is an appointment that continues beyond the initial date. In other words,
you can create a single appointment that is displayed on numerous calendar dates. However,
all calendar dates must be in sequence, such as April 4 through 7.

The "Single Document" approach creates one document and displays the appointment
across the calendar date range. This approach is simple to implement. If you're looking to
quickly build a calendar application or add a calendar to an existing application, this is a
good starting point (see Figure 8.1).

This architecture is quick and simple to implement.

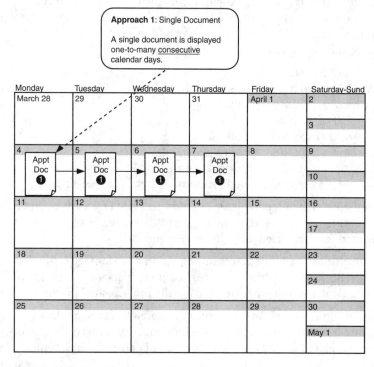

Figure 8.1   Single Document recurring event

Single Document Recurring Event

The primary advantage to this approach is the simplicity of implementing it. You can generate a new application (or enhance an existing application by adding a couple of fields and creating a calendar view) with minimal effort.

Also, because all calendar dates reference the same (or single) document, users only need to update one document, and changes will be reflected across each calendar date. For example, let's say the author wants to include a conference phone number in the body of the appointment. The author can make one update, and the change is immediately available across all calendar dates. With this design, other team members can open any of the documents and see the same information.

The disadvantage to this approach is the inability to manage complex recurring events. If you're looking for the ability to schedule events for the second Friday or third day of each month, then the single document approach will require the user to manually create an entry for each date.

The next section will cover a more robust, comprehensive architecture for repeating events.

Managing Recurring Events Using Multiple Documents

The "Multiple Document" approach creates a separate document based on the recurring event parameters specified in the initial appointment. This second approach provides much greater flexibility to manage recurring events but is considerably more complex to implement. Using this architecture allows you to create repeating events

- **By date**—April 4 (one-day event).
- **Daily by date**—April 4 through April 7 (sequential).
- **Weekly by day**—Monday, Wednesday, and Friday.
- **Monthly by date**—First of each month.
- **Monthly by day**—Third Friday of each month.
- **Custom dates**—A comma-delimited list of calendar dates.
- **Skip weekends**—Do not create if event is on a Saturday or Sunday.
- **Next business day**—Move event to Monday if computed day is a weekend.

With the multiple document approach, a separate document is generated for each calendar date. When the initial appointment is saved, all recurring event dates are calculated, and a separate document is generated for each calendar date (see Figure 8.2).

This architecture offers much greater flexibility in scheduling. Another advantage is the ability to move and delete events. Because each event is stored as a unique document, users can move, delete, or update one calendar event without affecting the other related events.

The disadvantage to this approach is the complex algorithm required to calculate the event dates. Also, because a separate document is created for each calendar date, each document will need to be independently updated should the author need to update the subject or body for all related appointments.

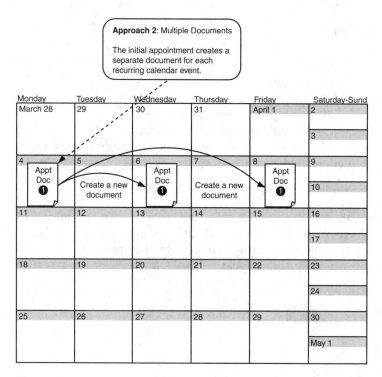

Figure 8.2   Multiple Document recurring event

Additional challenges are associated with deleting, or removing, a scheduled appointment. Because there are multiple documents, each document will need to be manually deleted, or a subroutine will need to be developed to automate the deletion process.

Implementing this second approach requires additional information to be captured in the initial appointment form. This is managed via a separate dialog window that prompts the user to specify the recurring event parameters—weekly, daily, day of the week, skip weekends, monthly, custom dates, and so on. This information is added to the initial appointment document. Each recurring appointment document is generated after the document is saved for the first time.

> **NOTE**
>
> This publication includes all subroutines and sample code required to build the simple and complex calendar projects. The code is also available in the developer's toolbox. Simply open the "Project Library" database in your Lotus Notes client and navigate to the appropriate project. After you locate the project, copy and paste the code into the Designer client for the current project.

Project A: Build an Event Calendar

Difficulty Level:	Easy
Completion Time:	1 to 2 hours
Project Materials:	1 Form, 6 Fields, 1 View, 2 Action Buttons
Languages Used:	LotusScript and Formula
Recurring Events:	Yes, "Single Document" Approach
Possible Usages:	Conference room reservations, equipment rentals, vacation planner

Create the Database

Let's start building the calendar application by launching the Lotus Domino Designer client and creating a blank database. When the Designer client is running, select the **File > Database > New** menu options. Specify **Meeting Calendar** as the application title and **MtgCalendar.nsf** as the file name. Be sure to select **-Blank-** as the template type (see Figure 8.3).

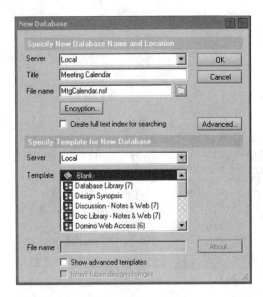

Figure 8.3   New database dialog

> **TIP**
>
> It's a good idea to remove all spaces from the File Name field. Spaces can cause problems when working with web applications. For example, replace **Meeting Calendar.nsf** with **MtgCalendar.nsf**.

Create the Appointment Form

The appointment form captures the event start and end dates, total number of recurring appointment days, author, subject, and details. The number of appointment days will be automatically computed based on the start and end dates. Most of the work associated with calendar applications resides in the appointment form, including management of recurrent events.

To create a form, click the **New Form** button or select the **Create > Design > Form...** menu options. After the form has been created, add a descriptive text title such as **Appointment** at the top of the form and the following field descriptions down the left side of the form.

- Start Date:
- End Date:
- Total Days:
- Person:
- Subject:
- Details:

Your form should now look similar to Figure 8.4.

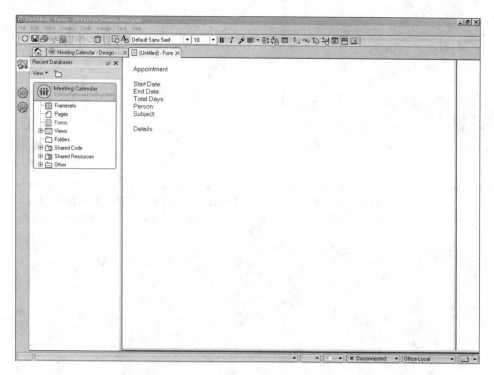

Figure 8.4 Appointment form with field titles

Define the Fields

Next, add the fields beside each field title as specified in the following table. To create a field, select the **Create > Field** menu options (see Figure 8.5). Be sure to set the data type, formula, and other properties in the properties dialog window for each field. The field name, type, and style will be defined in the properties dialog.

By default, the properties dialog window will be displayed when the first field is created. Select **Edit > Properties** if the properties dialog window is not visible.

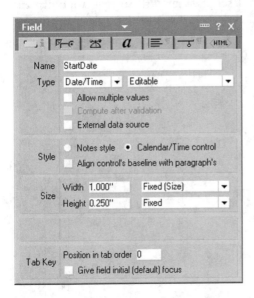

Figure 8.5   Field property dialog

The field Formula will be placed in the Value or Default Value section of the Programmer's pane, located in the lower section of the Designer client. Select **View > Programmer's Pane** if the pane is not visible. Figure 8.6 shows the Programmer's pane for the StartDate field.

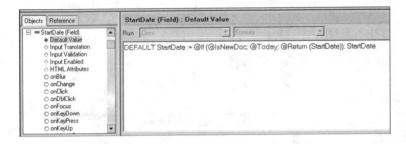

Figure 8.6   Default value formula for StartDate field

Field Name	Type	Formula	Remarks
StartDate	Date/Time, Editable	`DEFAULT StartDate:= @If(@IsNewDoc; @Today; @Return(StartDate)); StartDate`	In tab 1 of the properties dialog, set the Style to **Calendar/Time control.**
EndDate	Date/Time, Editable		In tab 1 of the properties dialog, set the Style to **Calendar/Time control.**
TotalDays	Number, Computed	`@If(StartDate = ""; 0; EndDate = ""; 0; @BusinessDays( StartDate; EndDate ));`	This formula will automatically compute the total number of days associated with the calendar event based on the start and end dates.
Person	Names, Computed when Composed	`@UserName;`	This formula will automatically compute the author's name.
Subject	Text, Editable		
Body	Rich Text, Editable		

Your calendar appointment form should now look like Figure 8.7.

Set the Form Objects and Properties

The Window Title displays in a tab at the top of the Lotus Notes client whenever a document is opened. The title helps make the application more user-friendly and can be set to any arbitrary value or text string. However, because the display space on the tab is limited, you should limit the text value. To set the window title, locate the Window Title section and add the following in the Programmer's pane (see Figure 8.8):

```
"Appointment"
```

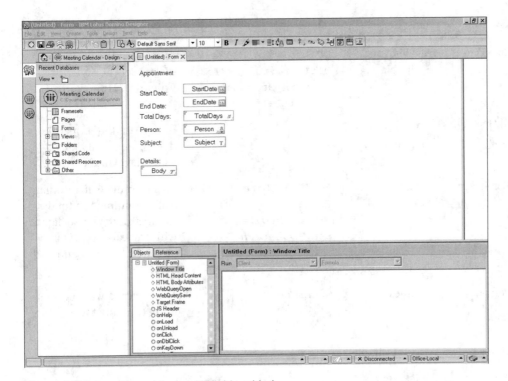

Figure 8.7 Appointment form with fields added

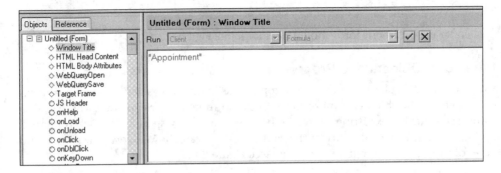

Figure 8.8 Window Title for Appointment form

QuerySave Event

The QuerySave event will be used to refresh the current document any time the document
is saved. This will ensure that the most current data is displayed to the user any time the
form is saved (e.g., when the user selects the **File > Save** menu options). Add the following
to the QuerySave event located in the Objects section of the Programmer's pane.

```
Sub Querysave(Source As Notesuidocument, Continue As Variant)
    Source.Refresh
End Sub
```

Form Property

Finally, select the **Design > Form Properties** menu options. This will display the properties dialog window for the form. On tab 1, check the **Automatically refresh fields** setting in the Options section (see Figure 8.9). This option will refresh computed fields as you change the data on the appointment form. For example, when the start and end dates are changed, the total number of days value will automatically update.

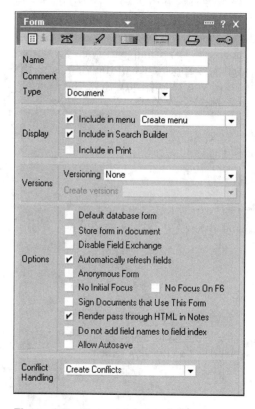

Figure 8.9   Form database dialog

To complete the form, specify **Appointment | Appt** in the Name field of the form properties dialog. The vertical bar indicates the alias name for the form. This completes the setup of the appointment form. Save and close the form.

> **TIP**
>
> Always provide a form name and alias name. All code should then refer to the alias name. This provides greater flexibility to change the form name without impacting existing code and/or view formulas.

Create the Calendar View

The majority of the project is now complete. The only step remaining is the creation of the calendar view used to display the appointments. Whenever a database is created, a default view—called "(untitled)"—is automatically generated. Select **Views** in the Design pane and double-click on it to open in edit mode.

The next step is to define the properties for the view. Select the **Design > View Properties** menu options. Set the name to **Calendar** and alias name to **Cal**. Change the view Style from **Standard Outline** to **Calendar**. This setting changes the appearance of the view from the traditional look to a graphical calendar display. After you change the view, the Domino Designer client will display a warning message similar to Figure 8.10.

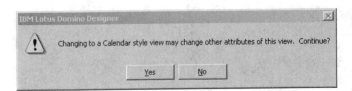

Figure 8.10   Warning message when selecting calendar view

Click **Yes** to continue.

> **NOTE**
>
> The calendar graphical display only appears in the Lotus Notes client and is not what you will see in the Designer client as the view is being developed.

Define the Columns

For this project, the view will include three columns. As mentioned in the architecture section, the first two columns are required for the calendar views. These columns will be hidden. The third column will display information associated with the appointment.

Column 1

Column 1 is a hidden column and must contain the start date/time value sorted in ascending order. To set the properties for this column, click on the column header and select the **Design > Column Properties** menu options.

In tab 1, set the Title to **Date**. In tab 2, set the Sort type to **Ascending** and select **Show multiple values as separate entries**. This is the option used to show one document across multiple calendar dates. Now switch to tab 6 and select the **Hide column** checkbox (see Figure 8.11).

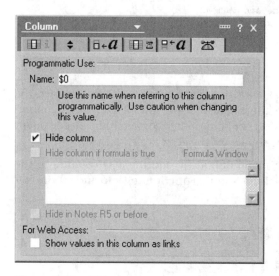

Figure 8.11   Hide column on tab 6 of the view property dialog

> **NOTE**
>
> Column titles are not displayed in the calendar view. However, providing a column header name will help you and other developers understand the view design and column content.

With the column properties defined, next set the column value. In the Programmer's pane, change the display type from **Simple Function** to **Formula** and set the column formula to the following:

```
REM "Column1 contains the list of start dates";
REM "as defined in the appointment form";
DateList := @Explode(@TextToTime(@Text(StartDate)
+ "-" + @Text(EndDate)));
@TextToTime(DateList)
```

Column 2

The second column must contain the duration in order for the calendar to display correctly. This column will also be hidden. Select the **Create > Append New Column** menu options to add the new column. Select the **Design > Column Properties** menu options to display the column properties dialog window. In tab 1, set the Title to **Duration**. Then switch to tab 6 and select the **Hide column** checkbox.

With the column properties defined, next set the column value. For this project, the duration will be set to zero. In the Programmer's pane, change the display type from **Simple Function** to **Formula** and set the column formula to the following:

```
REM "Column2 contains the duration for the appointment";
REM "Set this column to zero, unless you set a start and";
REM "stop time for each appointment";
0
```

Column 3

The third column simply displays a text value for the calendar event. For this project, the appointment subject will be displayed on the calendar view. Alternatively, this column could contain the person, person and subject, or some other combination of document fields and text. This is the value that will be shown on the actual calendar view.

Select the **Create > Append New Column** menu options to add the new column. In the Programmer's pane, change the display type from **Simple Function** to **Field** and set the column formula to the following:

```
Subject
```

> **TIP**
>
> You may want to set the background color for the column to enhance the application usability. This will highlight the entry and help users locate calendar events on the view. To set the background color, select the third tab in the View properties dialog. The Background setting is located in the Entry section.

Set the View Objects and Properties

This project includes three methods for creating new appointments—the menu bar, an action button, and clickable calendar events. This will allow users to select the **Create > Appointment** menu options, click the **New Appointment** button (described later in this section), or double-click on a calendar date.

The `RegionDoubleClick` event allows users to double-click on a calendar date and automatically launch the new appointment form. When the form is displayed, the start date is populated with the date selected on the calendar.

This event also contains a data validation check to see if the selected date is before the current date. If the date is in the past, the user receives the prompt, "Date in past. Do you want to continue?" If the user selects Yes, the `answer` variable is set to 6 (which is a default value automatically set by the Lotus Notes application).

To configure this functionality, locate the `RegionDoubleClick` event in the Objects section of the Programmer's pane and then add the following LotusScript code. This code will create a new appointment if the date is today, in the future, or if the user answered Yes to create the record in the past. This routine is only executed if the user double-clicks on a calendar date.

```
Sub Regiondoubleclick(Source As Notesuiview)

    Dim doc As NotesDocument
    Dim workspace As New NotesUIWorkspace
    Dim uidoc As NotesUIDocument
    Dim view As NotesView
    Dim dateTime As New NotesDateTime( "" )
    Dim answer As Integer

    ' Display warning if selected date is in the past.
    Call dateTime.SetNow
    If Source.CalendarDateTime < dateTime.LSLocalTime Then
        answer%=Msgbox("Date in past. Do you want to continue?", _
        292, "Continue?")
    End If

    ' Create the appointment if date is in the past and user
    ' clicked, YES or create the appointment if date is in
    ' the future.
    If (answer% = 6) Or _
    (Source.CalendarDateTime >= Cdat (dateTime.DateOnly)) Then
        Set view = Source.View
        Set uidoc = workspace.ComposeDocument ( "", "", "Appt" )
        Set doc = uidoc.Document
        doc.StartDate = Source.CalendarDateTime
    End If

End Sub
```

> **TIP**
>
> This code can be added to the `RegionDoubleClick` event for any calendar view. This code checks to see if the date is in the past and prompts the user if they want to continue. To incorporate this feature into an existing database application, simply change `Appt` to the appropriate form name and add the code. This will make the application more user-friendly and enhance general usability.

Create Action Buttons for the View

Two action buttons will be created for the view. One button will be used to create new appointments. The other button will jump the calendar view to the current date.

To create the first button, select the **Create > Action > Action** menu options and name the button **New Appointment**. Close the properties dialog and add the following to the Programmer's pane.

```
@Command([Compose];"":"Appt")
```

To create the second button, select the **Create > Action > Action** menu options and name the button **Today**. Close the properties dialog and add the following to the Programmer's pane.

```
@Command([CalendarGoTo];@Date(@Now))
```

> **TIP**
>
> Optionally, you can add an icon to the action button. To add an icon, click on the action button and select the **Design > Action Properties** menu options. Then select an icon in the lower section of the properties dialog window.

Save and close the view. Congratulations, you have completed the project! If would you like to further customize the application, refer to Chapters 13 through 17 for additional enhancements. When you open the Lotus Notes client, your project should look similar to Figure 8.12.

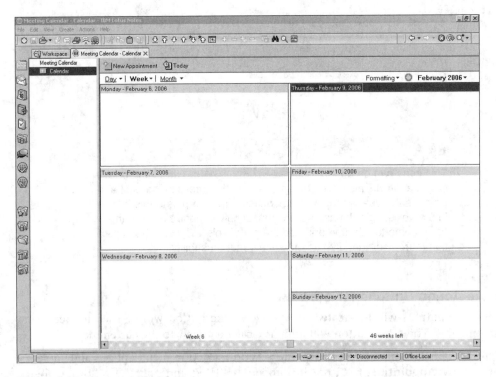

Figure 8.12   Completed project

Project B: Build a Conference Room Reservation System

Difficulty Level:	Advanced
Completion Time:	3 to 5 hours
Project Materials:	2 Forms, 22 Fields, 1 View, 2 Libraries, 4 Action Buttons
Languages Used:	LotusScript and Formula
Recurring Events:	Yes, "Multiple Document" Approach
Possible Usages:	Conference room reservations, equipment rentals, vacation planner

This project will explore the intricacies associated with complex recurring calendar events using the "Multiple Document" approach. The overall complexity level of this project is significantly greater than the simple recurring calendar project. You will need to pay particular attention to the property settings for fields because most will require changes on multiple property configuration tabs.

At the completion of this project, you'll understand how to build a Notes calendar that includes complex recurring calendar events. This project can be used as-is, utilized as the starting point for a custom application, or copied into an entirely different application.

Create the Database

Similar to the first calendar project, the appointment form will be used to capture and schedule events on the meeting calendar. This form will include start and end dates, duration, author, and subject. However, the primary difference from the previous application will be the ability to create complex recurring events using a custom dialog box. The custom dialog box will be used to select the recurring event parameters. Let's look at some of the key fields associated with the project.

Three primary variables are used to control the creation of calendar appointments.

- **StartDate**—This value represents the calendar date of the first appointment. The appointment document created on this date is the anchor point for recurring events. This document will be used to generate the recurring calendar documents.
- **ReservationStatus**—This variable controls the creation of appointments through various status flags. When a new appointment form is created (e.g., when a user clicks the **New Reservation** button), this field defaults to the value of "New". This signifies that the document has not been processed and that no calendar entry has been created.

  The "New" state allows a user to open and cancel the appointment request without creating a calendar document. However, when the user saves the document or clicks the **Submit** button, the ReservationStatus field is changed to the value "Submit". This value is set in the QuerySave event.

  At this point the anchor document is saved to the calendar. If the user decides to make the appointment a recurring event, the application creates the additional entries when the document is closed. The creation of the recurring appointments will be managed in the `QueryClose` event when the appointment is initially closed. In other words, recurring appointments are not generated each time the document is opened and closed—only on the first time the document is closed.

- **`RepeatUnit`**—This stores the type of recurring calendar event. There are five types of recurring events. These values will be used to call the appropriate LotusScript library subroutine and create the specific type of recurring appointment in the database. Based on the user selection, this field will contain one of the following values.

  D—Signifies repeat daily

  W—Signifies repeat weekly

  MP—Signifies repeat monthly by day

  MD—Signifies repeat monthly by date

  C—Signifies custom specified dates

Start by launching the Domino Designer client and creating a new database. When the client is open, select the **File > Database > New** menu options. Specify **Meeting Calendar2** as the application title and **MtgCalendar2.nsf** as the file name. Be sure to select **-Blank-** as the template type (see Figure 8.13).

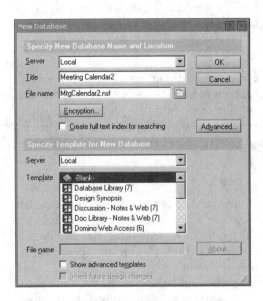

Figure 8.13   New Database dialog

Create the Appointment Form

Next, create the appointment form. To create the form, click the **New Form** button or select the **Create > Design > Form** menu options. After the form has been created, add a descriptive text title such as **Appointment** at the top of the form and the following field descriptions down the left side of the form.

- Topic:*
- Start Date:*
- Start Time:*
- End Time:*
- Location:
- Created By:
- Chairperson:
- Description:
- Appointment Editors:

> **NOTE**
>
> Topic, Start Date, Start Time, and End Time will be required fields in this project. To denote this on the form, consider placing an asterisk next to these fields to signify that they are required.

Next, add the fields beside each field title as specified in the following table. To create a field, select the **Create** > **Field** menu options. By default, the properties dialog window will be displayed when the first field is created. Select **Edit** > **Properties** if the properties dialog window is not visible. Be sure to set the data type, formula, and other properties in the properties dialog window for each field. The field name, type, and style will be defined in the properties dialog (refer to Figure 8.5).

After setting the field properties, the field Formula will be placed in the Value or Default Value section of the Programmer's pane, located in the lower section of the Designer client. Select **View** > **Programmer's Pane** if the pane is not visible (refer to Figure 8.6).

Using the following table, create the following fields in sequential order on the appointment form. To create a field, select the **Create** > **Field** menu options. Be sure to correctly set the data type, formula, and other properties values for each field on the form. These fields will be visible and editable on the form.

Field Name	Type	Default Value Formula	Remarks
Topic	Text, Editable		
StartDate	Date/Time, Editable		On tab 1 of the properties dialog, set the Style to **Calendar/Time control.**
Time1	Date/Time, Editable		On tab 1 of the properties dialog, set the Style to **Calendar/Time control.**

continues

Field Name	Type	Default Value Formula	Remarks
			On tab 2, select the **Display Time** setting. Make sure the **Display Date** option is *not* selected.
Time2	Date/Time, Editable		On tab 1, select the **Calendar/Time control** option. On tab 2, select the **Display Time** setting. Make sure the **Display Date** option is *not* selected.
Room	Text, Computed when Composed	Room	
Author	Authors, Computed when Composed	@UserName	
Chair	Names, Editable	@UserName	On tab 2, set **Choices** to **Use Address dialog for choices**.
Body	Rich Text, Editable		
Editors	Authors, Editable	" "	On tab 1, select the **Allow multiple values** checkbox. On tab 2, set **Choices** to **Use Address dialog for choices**.

Your form should now look similar to Figure 8.14.

Next, create the following hidden, computed fields at the top of the form in one continuous row. These fields will drive the overall application functionality. To signify that these are hidden fields, consider setting the text color to **RED** for these fields in tab 4 of the field properties dialog. You can optionally add a text description **Hidden:** just prior to the fields.

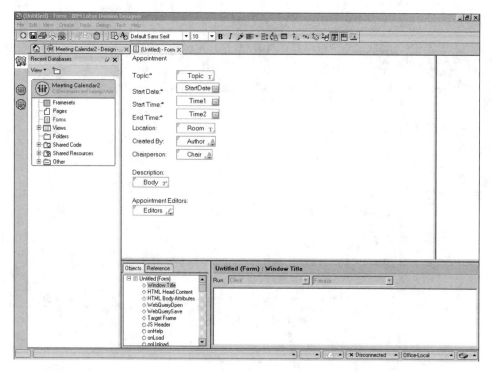

Figure 8.14 Appointment form with fields and field labels

Insert the following fields on the first line of the form (just above the **Appointment** title).

Field Name	Type	Default Value Formula	Remarks

ReservationStatus	Text, Computed	`DEFAULT Reservation-`
		`  Status := "NEW";`
		`ReservationStatus`	

TimeRange	Date/Time, Computed	`value := @Text(Time1)`
		`  + " - " +`
		`  @Text(Time2);`
		`@TextToTime (value)`
			On tab 2, select the **Display Time** option and *uncheck* the **Display Date** option.

RepeatInstance-Dates	Date/Time, Computed	`RepeatInstanceDates`	On tab 1, select the **Allow multiple values** checkbox. On tab 6, check the **Hide paragraph if formula is true** checkbox and set the formula to 1. This will make the entire line hidden.

The form should now look like Figure 8.15.

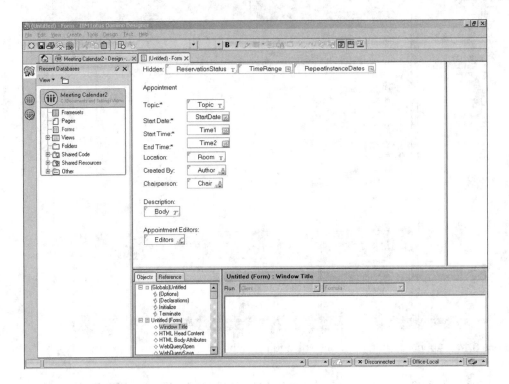

Figure 8.15   Appointment form with hidden fields at top

Window Title

Locate the Window Title section in the Programmer's pane and add the following. This will be the descriptive title that will appear in the Lotus Notes client "window tab" (as opposed to the title of the form, which appears directly on the document). Refer to Figure 8.15, at the bottom of the figure.

```
"Appointment"
```

At this point we've completed the basic framework for the form.

Select the **File** > **Save** menu options and specify **Appointment | Appt** as the form name when prompted. The vertical bar indicates the alias name for the form. After the form has been saved, close the form.

We'll return to this form later in the project to add programming to various form events and to add action buttons. These steps have to be performed after the LotusScript library and Repeat Entry form are created.

Create the Repeat Entry Form

The Repeat form is used to manage the recurring calendar events. This will be a custom dialog box that is created using the form and layout region design elements.

First, select the **Create > Design > Form** menu options. Next, select the **Create > Layout Region > New Layout Region** menu options. Select the **Design > Layout Region Properties** menu options. Set the form width to **4.800"** and height to **2.177"**.

> **TIP**
>
> You can set the display options for the layout region in the properties dialog such as **Show Grid**.

Next, create the following fields. Click inside the layout region and select the **Create > Field** menu options. After the field is created, be sure to select the correct field type, formula, field position, and size values in the properties dialog.

Field Name	Type	Default Value Formula	Position

RepeatStartDate	Date/Time, Computed	`@If (StartDate = "";`
		`    @Date(@Today);`
		`    @Date(StartDate))`
		Note: Be sure to make this a "computed" field, not editable.
			Width = 0.950"
			Height = 0.200"
			Left = 3.950"
			Top = 0.100"

RepeatUntil	Date/Time, Editable	`DEFAULT RepeatUntil :=`
		`    @Adjust( RepeatStartDate`
		`; 0; 0; 28; 0; 0; 0);`
		`    RepeatUntil`
			Width = 0.950"
			Height = 0.229"
			Left = 3.950"
			Top = 0.350"

RepeatUnit	Combobox, Editable, Refresh on keyword change (tab 2)	`@If(RepeatUnit = "";` `    "W"; RepeatUnit)`	Width = 1.250" Left = 3.950" Top = 0.600"

RepeatInterval_W	Combobox, Editable, Refresh on keyword change (tab 2)	`@If(RepeatUnit = "W" &`
		`    RepeatInterval != "";`
		`    RepeatInterval;`
		`    RepeatInterval_W = "";`
		`    "1"; RepeatInverval_W)`
			Width = 1.150"
			Left = 3.950"
			Top = 0.850"

continues

Field Name	Type	Default Value Formula	Position

RepeatAdjust_W	Listbox, Editable, Allow multiple values	`@If(RepeatUnit = "W" &`
		`  RepeatAdjust != "";`
		`  RepeatAdjust;`
		`  @Text(@Weekday`
		`  (StartDateTime)-1))`
			Width = 1.200"
			Height = 0.750"
			Left = 3.950"
			Top = 1.100"

RepeatDates	Date/Time, Editable, Allow multiple values, On tab 3, set **Separate Value when user enters** field to **Comma, Semi-colon and New line**. Also set **Display separate values** to **New Line**.	`@If(RepeatUnit = "C";`
		`  RepeatDates; "")`
		
		Top = 0.850"
			Width = 1.800"
			Height = 1.000"
			Left = 3.950"

RepeatAdjust_MP	Listbox, Editable, Allow multiple values	`@If(RepeatUnit = "MP" &`
		`  RepeatAdjust != "";`
		`  RepeatAdjust;`
		`  RepeatAdjust_MP)`
			Width = 1.350"
			Height = 0.750"
			Left = 3.950"
			Top = 1.100"

RepeatAdjust_MD	Listbox, Editable, Allow multiple values	`@If(RepeatUnit = "MD" &`
		`  RepeatAdjust != "";`
		`  RepeatAdjust;`
		`  RepeatAdjust_MD)`
			Height = 0.750"
			Left = 3.950"
			Top = 1.100"

RepeatAdjust_ MDMP	Combobox, Editable, Refresh on keyword change (tab 2)	`@If(RepeatUnit = "MD" :`
		`  "MP" & RepeatInterval`
		`  != ""; RepeatInterval;`
		`  RepeatInterval_MDMP =`
		`  ""; "1"; RepeatInterval`
		`  _MDMP)`
			Width = 1.150"
			Left = 3.950"
			Top = 0.850"

RepeatWeekends	Combobox, Editable	`@If(RepeatWeekends = "";` `  "X"; RepeatWeekends)`	Width = 1.300" Left = 3.950" Top = 1.850"

RepeatDateDiff	Number, Computed	`dt1 := RepeatStartDate;`
		`dt2 := RepeatUntil;`
		`seconds:= dt2 - dt1;`
		`days:= @Integer`
		`(seconds/86400); days`
		Note: Be sure to make this a "computed" field, not editable.
			Width = 0.500"
			Height = 0.250"
			Left = 5.100"
			Top = 0.100"

At this point, you have created the fields and placed them at specific geographic coordinates on the form. The next step will be to add the descriptive text titles next to each field. To create field titles, select the **Create > Layout Region > Text** menu options for each item in the following table. Be sure to set the alignment and field position in the properties dialog window for each title.

Text Value	Alignment	Position	"Hide When" Formula (Tab 5)
Start Date:	Right	Left = 3.200" Width = 0.700" Top = 0.100" Height = 0.200"	
End Date:	Right	Left = 3.200" Width = 0.700" Top = 0.350" Height = 0.200"	Select **Hide paragraph when formula is true** and add the formula: `RepeatUnit = "C"`
Repeat:	Right	Left = 3.100" Width = 0.800" Top = 0.600" Height = 0.200"	
Schedule:	Right	Left = 3.100" Width = 0.800" Top = 0.850" Height = 0.200"	Select **Hide paragraph when formula is true** and add the formula: `RepeatUnit = "YD": "C" : "D"`
Dates:	Right	Left = 3.450" Width = 0.450" Top = 0.850" Height = 0.200"	Select **Hide paragraph when formula is true** and add the formula: `RepeatUnit != "C"`
On the:	Right	Left = 3.400" Width = 0.450" Top = 1.100" Height = 0.200"	Select **Hide paragraph when formula is true** and add the formula: `!(RepeatUnit = "MP" : "MD")`

If weekend:	Right	Left = 3.150"
		Width = 0.800"
		Top = 1.850"
		Height = 0.200"
			Select **Hide paragraph when formula is true** and add the formula:
			`!(RepeatUnit = "D" |`
			`RepeatUnit = "Daily" |`
			`RepeatUnit = "MD" |`
			`RepeatUnit = "Monthly by Date")`

At this point, you've created the fields and field titles for the custom dialog box. You've also placed the design elements in the correct position on the layout region.

You'll notice that many of the fields overlap. However, when the form is displayed to the user, only select fields will be visible. The form will automatically display the correct fields using the value stored in the RepeatUnit field and the Hide When formulas. Your form should now look like Figure 8.16.

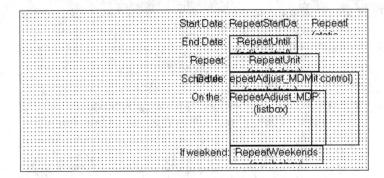

Figure 8.16   Repeat Calendar Entry layout region

The companion Web site includes additional graphics that you can optionally insert on the layout region to enhance the appearance. Follow the instructions provided in the appendix to download and extract the files. To add a graphic, click anywhere inside the layout region and select the **Create > Picture** menu options.

When prompted, change the file type to "GIF Image" and locate the companion Web site file called "CalendarArt.gif" on your computer and click **OK**. A second popup window will prompt you to specify the "Paste As" type, select **Graphic**. The form should now look like the following diagram.

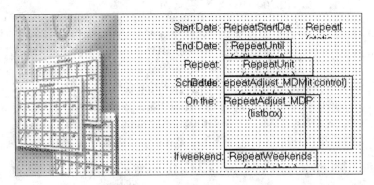

Figure 8.17   Repeat calendar entry with graphic

To complete the recurring event custom dialog box, default field choices and Hide When formulas need to be added in the properties dialog for each field. The field choices are set on tab 2 and the hide formula on tab 5 of the field properties dialog. As a reminder, be sure to click the checkbox **Hide paragraph when formula is true** as well as add the formula.

> **TIP**
>
> Use the Object pane to locate and select the various fields. When the field is selected in the Object pane, open the properties dialog, switch to the appropriate tab, and set the field choices or hide formulas.

> **NOTE**
>
> See the text file **RepeatChoices.txt** provided with the developer's toolbox. You can cut and paste these values directly into the Choices section of the properties dialog.

Field Name	Choices (Tab 2)	Hide Formula (Tab 5)
RepeatAdjust_MP	1st Sunday|1.0 1st Monday|1.1 1st Tuesday|1.2 1st Wednesday|1.3 1st Thursday|1.4 1st Friday|1.5 1st Saturday|1.6 2nd Sunday|2.0 2nd Monday|2.1 2nd Tuesday|2.2 2nd Wednesday|2.3 2nd Thursday|2.4 2nd Friday|2.5 2nd Saturday|2.6 3rd Sunday|3.0 3rd Monday|3.1 3rd Tuesday|3.2 3rd Wednesday|3.3 3rd Thursday|3.4 3rd Friday|3.5 3rd Saturday|3.6 4th Sunday|4.0 4th Monday|4.1 4th Tuesday|4.2	Select **Hide paragraph when formula is true** and add the formula: `RepeatUnit != "MP"`

continues

Field Name	Choices (Tab 2)	Hide Formula (Tab 5)
	4th Wednesday|4.3 4th Thursday|4.4 4th Friday|4.5 4th Saturday|4.6 Last Sunday|5.0 Last Monday|5.1 Last Tuesday|5.2 Last Wednesday|5.3 Last Thursday|5.4 Last Friday|5.5 Last Saturday|5.6	
RepeatAdjust_MD	1st day|1 2nd day|2 3rd day|3 4th day|4 5th day|5 6th day|6 7th day|7 8th day|8 9th day|9 10th day|10 11th day|11 12th day|12 13th day|13 14th day|14 15th day|15 16th day|16 17th day|17 18th day|18 19th day|19 20th day|20 21st day|21 22nd day|22 23rd day|23 24th day|24 25th day|25 26th day|26 27th day|27 28th day|28 29th day|29 30th day|30 31st day|31	Select **Hide paragraph when formula is true** and add the formula: `RepeatUnit != "MD"`

Field Name	Choices (Tab 2)	Hide Formula (Tab 5)

RepeatAdjust_MDMP	Every month |1
	Note: Also check **Refresh fields on keyword change.**
		Select **Hide paragraph when formula is true** and add the formula:
		`!(RepeatUnit = "MP" :`
		`  "MD")`

RepeatDates		Select **Hide paragraph when formula is true** and add the formula: `RepeatUnit != "C"`
RepeatUntil		On tab 5, select **Hide paragraph when formula is true** and add the formula. `RepeatUnit = "C"`
RepeatUnit	Daily|D Weekly|W Monthly by Date|MD Monthly by Day|MP Custom Dates|C Note: Also check **Refresh fields on keyword change.**	
RepeatInterval_W	Every|1 Note: Also check **Refresh fields on keyword change.**	Select **Hide paragraph when formula is true** and add the formula: `RepeatUnit != "W"`
RepeatDateDiff		Select **Hide paragraph when formula is true** and add the formula: `1`
RepeatAdjust_W	Sunday|0 Monday|1 Tuesday|2 Wednesday|3 Thursday|4 Friday|5 Saturday|6	Select **Hide paragraph when formula is true** and add the formula: `RepeatUnit != "W"`

continues

Field Name	Choices (Tab 2)	Hide Formula (Tab 5)

RepeatWeekends	Do not schedule|X
	Keep reservation|D
	Change to Friday|F
	Change to Monday|M
		Select **Hide paragraph when formula is true** and add the formula:
		`!(RepeatUnit = "D" |`
		`RepeatUnit = "Daily" |`
		`RepeatUnit = "MD" |`
		`RepeatUnit = "Monthly by`
		`Date")`

Lastly, select the **Design > Form Properties** menu options and uncheck the option **Include in menu**. This will remove the form from the application menu bar because we do not want users to be able to create documents in the database based on this form. This form will be used to capture recurring event settings and to add the settings to an open appointment form (described later in the project).

Save and close the form. When prompted to specify a form name, specify **(RepeatReservation) | (Res)**. The custom dialog that will be used to specify the recurring event parameters is now complete.

> **NOTE**
>
> Be sure the Hide When formulas are entered correctly because they will be used to determine what fields are displayed to the user. This is a critical step in the development of the project.

Create the Repeat Calendar Event Script Library

The LotusScript library will hold a number of common subroutines used to process recurring calendar events. Specifically, the library will have a separate subroutine to process each recurring event type—daily, weekly, monthly, monthly by day, monthly by date, and custom. To create the library, select the **Create > Design > Script Library > LotusScript Library** menu options.

> **TIP**
>
> The following code is available in the developer's toolbox. Simply open the "Project Library" database in your Lotus Notes client and navigate to the "Script Library" section for the appropriate project. After you locate the project, copy and paste the code into the Designer client for the current project. Be sure the programmer's pane has focus before pasting the code. Alternatively, you can elect to manually type the code.

Declarations

Add the following global statements to the LotusScript library in the "(Declarations)" section. These items will be used throughout the script library.

```
Dim session As NotesSession
Dim db As NotesDatabase
Dim uidoc As NotesUIDocument
Dim doc As NotesDocument
Dim docA As NotesDocument
Dim docB As NotesDocument
Dim x As Integer
Dim y As Integer
Dim i As Integer
```

> **TIP**
>
> Add **Option Explicit** or **Option Declare** to the "(Options)" section. This forces you to declare (e.g., DIM) all variables and will help you with debugging. If the variable is not defined, the statement referencing it will be flagged as a syntax error. This makes it much easier to find problems in the code (e.g., mistyped variable names).

> **TIP**
>
> The properties dialog for the Programmer's pane includes an option to **Automatically add "Option Declare"** to the LotusScript code (see Figure 8.18).

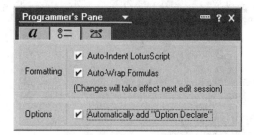

Figure 8.18 Repeat calendar entry layout region

Initialize

Add the following to the initialize section. This section will initialize the various global objects.

```
Sub Initialize
   Dim workspace As New NotesUIWorkspace
   Set session = New NotesSession
   Set db = session.CurrentDatabase
End Sub
```

Repeat Daily

The "Repeat Daily" subroutine creates a recurring calendar entry for every day between the start date and end date. For example, if the start date is set to January 1 and end date is set to January 31, then a calendar entry would be created for every date in the month of January (provided the user selected to save the document) even if the date falls on a weekend.

This routine also includes a date check to see if the day of the week falls on a weekend. When the date falls on a weekend, the routine keeps the date (D), shifts the date to the previous Friday (F), shifts the date to the following Monday (M), or skips the reservation (X). This course of action depends on the options selected by the user in the repeat dialog window.

```
Sub RepeatDaily (DocRef As NotesDocument)

    Dim workspace As New NotesUIWorkspace
    Dim dtWeekend As Integer
    Set uidoc = workspace.CurrentDocument
    Set docA = uidoc.Document

    ' Msgbox "Repeat on daily basis."
    Dim dtValue As New NotesDateTime( docA.StartDate(0) )
    x% = docA.RepeatDateDiff(0)

For i = 1 To x
    Call dtValue.AdjustDay( i )
    dtWeekend = Weekday ( dtValue.DateOnly )
    If dtWeekend = 1 Or dtWeekend = 7 Then
        Select Case docA.RepeatWeekends(0)
        Case "X"   : REM "place holder for future use"
        Case "D"
            Call CreateRepeatEntry ( dtValue.DateOnly,DocRef)
        Case "F"   : REM "place holder for future use"
        Case "M"
            If dtWeekend = 7 Then
                If x < i+2 Then
                    Call dtValue.AdjustDay( 2 )
                    Call CreateRepeatEntry(dtValue.DateOnly,DocRef)
                    Call dtValue.AdjustDay( -2 )
                End If
            End If
        Case Else : Msgbox "Should not be here. (RepeatDaily)"
        End Select
    Else
        Call CreateRepeatEntry ( dtValue.DateOnly, DocRef )
    End If
    Print "Creating appointment "& i & " of " & x &  "."
    Call dtValue.AdjustDay( -i )
    Next

End Sub
```

Repeat Weekly

The "Repeat Weekly" subroutine calculates reservation dates on a week-by-week basis. For example, you could create a reservation on Mondays for five consecutive weeks. The number of repeating calendar events is based on the computed field `RepeatDateDiff`. This field contains the difference between the start date and end date in terms of days. Next, the routine loops through each date. Each time the weekday of the current date matches a loop date, a new calendar entry is created.

```
Sub RepeatWeekly (DocRef As NotesDocument)

   Dim workspace As New NotesUIWorkspace
   Dim dtWeekday As Integer
   Set uidoc = workspace.CurrentDocument
   Set docA = uidoc.Document


   ' Msgbox "Repeat on weekly basis."
   Dim dtValue As New NotesDateTime( docA.StartDate(0) )
   x% = docA.RepeatDateDiff(0)
   For i = 1 To x
      Call dtValue.AdjustDay( i )
      dtWeekday = Weekday ( dtValue.DateOnly )
      Forall d In docA.RepeatAdjust_W
         If d = Cstr( dtWeekday - 1) Then
            Call CreateRepeatEntry ( dtValue.DateOnly, DocRef)
         End If
      End Forall
      Call dtValue.AdjustDay( -i )
   Next

End Sub
```

Repeat Monthly by Day

The "Repeat Monthly by Day" routine creates a monthly calendar entry based on the day. For example, you could create a reservation on the second and fourth Friday for 6 consecutive months. Like the previous routine, this routine loops through the total number of days (from start date to end date) and compares the days. A record is created when the values match.

```
Sub RepeatMonthlyDay (DocRef As NotesDocument)

   Dim workspace As New NotesUIWorkspace
   Dim dtWeek As Integer
   Dim dtWeekday As Integer
   Dim dtDay As Integer
   Dim tmpDate As String
   Dim indicator As String
   Dim category As NotesItem

   Set uidoc = workspace.CurrentDocument
   Set docA = uidoc.Document
   Set category = docA.GetFirstItem ("RepeatAdjust_MP")
   tmpDate$ = Month(docA.StartDate(0)) & "/01/" & Year(docA.StartDate(0))
   Dim dtValue As New NotesDateTime( tmpDate$ )
```

```
' Msgbox "Repeat on monthly by day basis."
dtWeek = 1
Do Until Cdat (dtValue.DateOnly) > Cdat (docA.RepeatUntil(0))
    dtWeekday = Weekday ( dtValue.DateOnly )
    For dtDay = 0 To 6
        indicator = dtWeek & "." & (Weekday(dtValue.DateOnly) -1)
        If category.Contains( indicator ) Then
            If Datevalue(dtValue.DateOnly) >
            ➥Datevalue(docA.StartDate(0)) Then
            Call CreateRepeatEntry ( dtValue.DateOnly, DocRef )
            End If
        End If
        Call dtValue.AdjustDay( 1 )
        If Day (dtValue.DateOnly) = 1 Then
            dtWeek = 0
            Exit For
        End If
        Next
    dtWeek = dtWeek + 1
Loop

End Sub
```

Repeat Monthly by Date

The "Repeat Monthly by Date" routine compares day of the month values and creates a calendar entry when they match. For example, you could create a reservation on the 15th of each month for twelve consecutive months.

This routine also includes a date check to see if the day of the week falls on a weekend. When the date falls on a weekend, the routine keeps the date (D), shifts the date to the previous Friday (F), shifts the date to the following Monday (M), or skips the reservation (X). This course of action depends on the options selected by the user in the repeat dialog window.

```
Sub RepeatMonthlyDate    (DocRef As NotesDocument)

    Dim workspace As New NotesUIWorkspace
    Dim dtWeek As Integer
    Dim dtWeekday As Integer
    Dim dtWeekend As Integer
    Dim dtDay As Integer
    Dim ddd As String
    Dim tmpDate As String
    Dim Indicator As String
    Dim dtRange As Variant
    Dim category As NotesItem

    Set uidoc = workspace.CurrentDocument
    Set docA = uidoc.Document

    ' Msgbox "Repeat on monthly by date basis."
    Dim dtValue As New NotesDateTime( docA.StartDate(0) )
    x% = docA.RepeatDateDiff(0)
    For i = 1 To x
```

```
      Call dtValue.AdjustDay( i )
      Forall d In docA.RepeatAdjust_MD
         dtDay = Day ( dtValue.DateOnly )
         If Cint(d) = dtDay Then
            dtWeekend = Weekday ( dtValue.DateOnly )
            If dtWeekend = 1 Or dtWeekend = 7 Then
               Select Case docA.RepeatWeekends(0)
               Case "X"   : REM "place holder for future use"
               Case "D"
                  Call CreateRepeatEntry(dtValue.DateOnly,DocRef)
               Case "F"
               Set dtRange = docA.GetFirstItem("RepeatAdjust_MD")
                  If dtWeekend = 1 Then
                     Call dtValue.AdjustDay( -2 )
                     ddd$ = Day ( dtValue.DateOnly )
                     If Not dtRange.Contains( ddd$ ) Then
                     Call CreateRepeatEntry(dtValue.DateOnly,DocRef)
                     End If
                     Call dtValue.AdjustDay( 2 )
                  Else
                     Call dtValue.AdjustDay( -1 )
                     ddd$ = Day ( dtValue.DateOnly )
                     If Not dtRange.Contains( ddd$ ) Then
                     Call CreateRepeatEntry ( dtValue.DateOnly, DocRef)
                     End If
                     Call dtValue.AdjustDay( 1 )
                  End If
               Case "M"
                  Set dtRange = docA.GetFirstItem("RepeatAdjust_MD")
                  If dtWeekend = 1 Then
                     Call dtValue.AdjustDay( 1 )
                     ddd$ = Day ( dtValue.DateOnly )
                     If Not dtRange.Contains( ddd$ ) Then
                        Call CreateRepeatEntry ( dtValue.DateOnly, DocRef)
                     End If
                     Call dtValue.AdjustDay( -1 )
                  Else
                     Call dtValue.AdjustDay( 2 )
                     ddd$ = Day ( dtValue.DateOnly )
                     If Not dtRange.Contains( ddd$ ) Then
                        Call CreateRepeatEntry ( dtValue.DateOnly, DocRef)
                     End If
                     Call dtValue.AdjustDay( -2 )
                  End If
               Case Else : Msgbox "Error in RepeatMonthlyDate"
               End Select
            Else
               Call CreateRepeatEntry ( dtValue.DateOnly, DocRef)
            End If
            Exit Forall
         End If
      End Forall
   Call dtValue.AdjustDay( -i )
   Next

End Sub
```

Repeat Custom Dates

The "Repeat Custom Dates" subroutine creates calendar reservations based on the user-pro-
vided dates. This routine is the simplest of the LotusScript library subroutines. Here, the program loops to the total number elements in the `RepeatDates` array and creates a calendar
entry for each user-specified date.

```
Sub RepeatCustom (DocRef As NotesDocument)

    Dim workspace As New NotesUIWorkspace
    Set uidoc = workspace.CurrentDocument
    Set docA = uidoc.Document

    ' Msgbox "Repeat on custom basis."
    x = 1
    y = Ubound(docA.RepeatDates) + 1
    Forall i In docA.RepeatDates
        Print "Creating appointment " & x & " of " & y & "."
        Call CreateRepeatEntry ( i, DocRef)
        x = x + 1
    End Forall

End Sub
```

Process Repeating Calendar Event

The "Process Repeat Type" routine is the entry point for processing recurring calendar
events. This routine calls the appropriate subroutine and subsequently generates the recurring calendar documents.

```
Sub ProcessRepeatType (DocRef As NotesDocument)

    Dim workspace As New NotesUIWorkspace
    Set uidoc = workspace.CurrentDocument
    Set docA = uidoc.Document

    If docA.RepeatUnit(0) <> "" Then
        Select Case docA.RepeatUnit(0)
        Case "D"  : Call RepeatDaily (DocRef)
        Case "W"  : Call RepeatWeekly (DocRef)
        Case "MP"  : Call RepeatMonthlyDay  (DocRef)
        Case "MD" : Call RepeatMonthlyDate  (DocRef)
        Case "C" : Call RepeatCustom  (DocRef)
        Case Else: Msgbox "Repeat Unit error in ScriptLibrary"
        End Select
        Print "Repeat reservations complete"
    End If

End Sub
```

Display Repeat Dialog Window

The following routine controls the display of the custom dialog called "(Res)." This is a hidden form, as indicated by the "( )" in the form name, and it allows the user to specify the

parameters for the recurring calendar entries. Values from this dialog will automatically pass through to the underlying appointment form.

```
Sub DisplayRepeatDialog

    Dim w As New NotesUIWorkspace
    Set uidoc = w.CurrentDocument
    Set doc = uidoc.Document
    Call w.DialogBox("(Res)",True,True,,,,,"Repeat Reservation")

End Sub
```

Create Repeating Calendar Entries

The "Create Repeat Entry" subroutine actually generates the calendar entry based on the date passed to the subroutine. This routine utilizes the `CopyAllItems` method to duplicate the initial appointment form document. The date is subsequently changed to the value stored in the `RepeatDateValue` field. Finally, the date of the newly created recurring event is added to the initial appointment for reference purposes.

```
Sub CreateRepeatEntry ( RepeatDateValue As Variant , DocRef As NotesDocument)

    Dim workspace As New NotesUIWorkspace
    Dim dateRange As NotesDateRange
    Dim sdate As String
    Dim repeatDate As String
    Dim date1 As NotesDateTime
    Dim theRepeatDate As NotesDateTime
    Dim theStartDate As NotesDateTime
    Dim rStartDate As String

    Set uidoc = workspace.CurrentDocument
    Set docA = uidoc.Document
    Set docB = New NotesDocument( db )
    Set dateRange = session.CreateDateRange()


    '-----------------------------------------------------
    ' Make copy of original reservation
    '-----------------------------------------------------
    Call docA.CopyAllItems( docB, True )


    '-----------------------------------------------------
    ' Change the date on the new repeat entry
    '-----------------------------------------------------
    dateRange.Text = uidoc.FieldGetText( "TimeRange" )
    sdate$ = Datevalue( RepeatDateValue ) & " " & dateRange.StartDateTime.LocalTime
    Set date1 = New NotesDateTime( sdate$ )
    docB.StartDateTime = date1.LSLocalTime
    docB.StartDate = date1.LSLocalTime


    '-----------------------------------------------------
    ' Cleanup/Reset various data fields
    '-----------------------------------------------------
    docB.RemoveItem("Invite")
```

```
docB.ReservationStatus = "CLOSED"
Call docB.Save( True, True, True )

'----------------------------------------------------
' Set the "repeat date instances" in the main record.
' Required to process repeat appt in LN email client.
'----------------------------------------------------
Dim oldArray
Dim newArray() As Variant
rStartDate$ = Datevalue (DocRef.StartDate(0)) & " " & docRef.Time1(0)
Set theStartDate = New NotesDateTime ( rStartDate$ )
repeatDate$ = Datevalue (RepeatDateValue)  & " " & docRef.Time1(0)
Set theRepeatDate = New NotesDateTime ( repeatDate$ )
If DocRef.RepeatInstanceDates(0) = "" Then
    DocRef.RepeatInstanceDates = theStartDate.LSLocalTime
End If
oldArray = docRef.RepeatInstanceDates
Redim Preserve newArray(Ubound(oldArray)+1)
newArray(0) = theRepeatDate.LSLocalTime
For x = 1 To Ubound(newArray)
    newArray(x) = oldArray(x-1)
Next
docRef.RepeatInstanceDates = newArray

End Sub
```

Create the *CheckFields* Subroutine

The CheckFieldValues function will manage field validation for the form. This routine
verifies that each of the four fields contains a value. If the field is blank, then an error message is appended to the MsgText field. After all fields have been checked, the user is notified of all invalid fields. Using this approach, a single error message is presented to the user
that outlines all problems (as opposed to a separate message for each error). Add the following to the LotusScript library.

```
Function CheckFieldValues ( DocRef As NotesDocument )

    Dim MsgText As String
    CheckFieldValues = True
    MsgText = ""
    If DocRef.Topic(0) = "" Then
        MsgText = MsgText + "Specify a topic." + Chr$(13)
    End If

    If DocRef.StartDate(0) = "" Then
        MsgText = MsgText + "Specify a start date." + Chr$(13)
    End If

    If DocRef.Time1(0) = "" Then
        MsgText = MsgText + "Specify a start time." + Chr$(13)
    End If

    If DocRef.Time2(0) = "" Then
```

```
        MsgText = MsgText + "Specify an end time." + Chr$(13)
    End If

    If MsgText <> "" Then
        Msgbox MsgText,16,"Required Fields."
        CheckFieldValues = False
    End If

End Function
```

Save and close the library. When prompted, specify **RepeatCalendarLib** as the LotusScript library name.

Set the Appointment Form Objects and Properties

Next, define global objects associated with the form in the "(Globals)" section. The global section allows you to define an object once and refer to the same object throughout the form. This simplifies your code and also makes the application code more efficient and easier to maintain. In this case, the global section will reference the LotusScript library routines.

Locate and reopen the Appointment form in the Forms section of the Design pane. Scroll to the "(Globals)Reservation" section in the Programmer's pane. This section will be at the very top of the pane. Add the following line to the "(Options)" item (see Figure 8.19). The Use statement incorporates code in a LotusScript library called RepeatCalendarLib into the form.

```
Option Public
Use "RepeatCalendarLib"
```

Figure 8.19 (Globals) section of the Appointment form objects

QuerySave

If you recall, the QuerySave event is called every time the form is saved. In this case, a LotusScript subroutine will check the status of the object reference variable called ReservationStatus on the form to determine if the form has been processed.

The default value for this field will be "NEW", which indicates that the appointment has not been processed. Setting the status to "SUBMIT" indicates that the form is ready for processing in the QueryClose event. After the appointment form has been processed, the field will be set to "CLOSED".

This will enable the calendar appointment to be opened without creating new repeating appointments. In other words, we only want to process the appointment form one time, not each time the document is closed. Add the following code to the QuerySave event on the form.

```
Sub Querysave(Source As Notesuidocument, Continue As Variant)

    Dim doc As notesdocument
    Set doc=Source.document
    Continue = CheckFieldValues ( doc )
    If Continue Then
        If doc.ReservationStatus(0)= "NEW" Then
            doc.ReservationStatus= "SUBMIT"
        End If
        doc.save True,True
    End If

End Sub
```

QueryClose

This event, which is called as the document is about to close, will manage two primary transactions—creation of the recurring calendar events and a refresh of the underlying calendar view. Again, similar to the QuerySave event, if the ReservationStatus field exists and contains the value of "SUBMIT", then a call is made to the ProcessRepeatType subroutine.

This will create the recurring calendar reservations and set the value to "CLOSED". This way, the application only processes the recurring calendar events one time, not each time the document is opened and closed.

```
Sub Queryclose(Source As Notesuidocument, Continue As Variant)

    Dim s As New NotesSession
    Dim db As NotesDatabase
    Set db =s.CurrentDatabase
    Dim doc As notesdocument
    Set doc=Source.document

    ' Create Recurring Records if new appointment
    If doc.ReservationStatus(0) = "SUBMIT" Then
        Call ProcessRepeatType ( doc )
        doc.ReservationStatus= "CLOSED"
        doc.save True,True
    End If

    ' Refresh the conf room view if a view exists.
    If doc.Room(0) <> "" Then
        Dim view As NotesView
        Set view = db.GetView( doc.Room(0) )
        Call view.Refresh
    End If

End Sub
```

Save the form before continuing to the next section.

> **NOTE**
>
> Designer sometimes encounters problems recognizing LotusScript libraries immediately after the library is created. When attempting to save the form, you may receive the following error with the `Use` statement highlighted in red: **Data not saved due to script error(s)**. To correct this, you should close all open design elements (including the appointment form) and close the database application if it is open in the Lotus Notes client. Next, select the **Tools** > **Recompile all LotusScript** menu options. This usually fixes the problem and enables you to save the form. Be aware that this option will recompile all LotusScript stored in the database, which could affect other database design elements. For example, any scheduled agents signed with a special ID will be signed with the current user's ID. As a result, this may affect the scheduled agent's capability to run. Although this project does not include any scheduled agents, this is just something to remember when recompiling all code in other database applications.

Create Action Buttons for the Appointment Form

This project includes two action buttons. The first one, Repeat, will be used to display the custom dialog box that allows users to define the recurring event parameters. The second button, Submit, will be used to create the appointment in the database.

Repeat Button

To create the Repeat button, select the **Create** > **Action** > **Actions** menu options. On tab 1 of the properties dialog, title the button **Repeat**. On tab 2, hide the button by checking the **Previewed for reading**, **Opened for reading**, and **Hide action if formula is true** options, and insert the following in the formula section.

```
ReservationStatus = "CLOSED"
```

Next, change the language **Simple Action(s)** to **LotusScript**. Add the following in the `Click` event in the Programmer's pane.

```
Sub Click(Source As Button)
   Call DisplayRepeatDialog
End Sub
```

Submit Button

To create a button, select the **Create** > **Action** > **Actions** menu options. On tab 1 of the properties dialog, title the button **Submit**. On tab 2, hide the button by checking the **Previewed for reading**, **Opened for reading**, and **Hide action if formula is true** options, and insert the following in the formula section (see Figure 8.20).

```
ReservationStatus = "CLOSED"
```

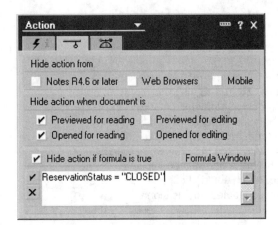

Figure 8.20   Hide property settings for the Submit action button

Next, change the language **Simple Action(s)** to **LotusScript**. Add the following in the `Click` event in the Programmer's pane.

```
Sub Click(Source As Button)

   Dim workspace As New NotesUIWorkspace
   Dim uidoc As NotesUIDocument
   Dim doc As NotesDocument
   Dim continue as Integer

   Set uidoc = workspace.CurrentDocument
   Set doc = uidoc.Document
   Continue = CheckFieldValues ( doc )
   If Continue Then
      doc.ReservationStatus = "SUBMIT"
      uidoc.Refresh
      uidoc.Save
      uidoc.close
   End If

End Sub
```

Save the changes to the appointment form and close it.

To summarize, we've created the appointment form, custom dialog form, and a LotusScript library that processes recurring calendar events. All that remains is the setup and customization of the application calendar view.

Create the Calendar View

The calendar view will consist of four columns—two hidden and two displayed. As outlined in the application architecture, the first two columns must respectively contain the date/time and duration. The last two columns will display the appointment time and title on the calendar.

Whenever a database is created, a default view—called "(untitled)"—is automatically generated. To configure the calendar view, select **Views** in the Design pane and double-click on it to open in edit mode.

To set the view properties, select the **Design > View Properties** menu options. Set the name to **MainRoom** and alias name to **MainRoom**.

> **NOTE**
>
> The view name and alias can be changed to any value. For this project it's been named **MainRoom**, but it could also be called anything such as **Room123**. Be sure to specify both the view name and an alias for the view. The alias will be used to automatically populate the room field on the appointment form. These values are especially important if multiple calendar views are created in the database. The combination of the view alias and room field will ensure that documents appear on the correct calendar view. To add multiple calendar views, simply copy the completed calendar view and rename both the view name and alias name.

Next, change the view Style from **Standard Outline** to **Calendar** in the properties dialog. This setting changes the appearance of the view from the traditional look to a graphical calendar display.

When changed, the Domino Designer client will display a warning message (refer to Figure 8.10). Click **Yes** to continue. The view property settings are now complete.

Define the Columns

The next step is to create and define the view columns. By default, the view already includes a predefined column. You'll need to modify the existing column and add three additional columns.

Column 1

The first column must contain the date and time for the calendar event. To get these values, we'll parse the `TimeRange` and append it to the `StartDate`. To set the properties for this column, click on the column header and select **Design > Column Properties** menu options.

Set the column title to **Date** in tab 1 and the Sort type to **Ascending** in tab 2. Now switch to tab 6 and select the **Hide column** checkbox (refer to Figure 8.11).

In the Programmer's pane, change the display type from **Simple Function** to **Formula** and set the column formula to the following.

```
REM "Column 1 contains the start date/time for the appointment";
value := @Word (@Text(TimeRange); "-"; 1);
@TextToTime(@Text(StartDate) + " " + value)
```

Column 2

The second column must contain the duration in order for the calendar to display correctly. This column will also be hidden. Select the **Create > Append New Column** menu options to add the new column. Select the **Design > Column Properties** menu options to display the column properties dialog window. In tab 1, set the Title to **Duration**. Then switch to tab 6 and select the **Hide column** checkbox.

In the Programmer's pane, change the display type from **Simple Function** to **Formula** and set the column formula to the following.

```
REM "Column 2 contains the duration for each appointment";
0
```

Column 3

Column three will display the time range for the appointment. Select the **Create > Append New Column** menu options to add the new column. Select the **Design > Column Properties** menu options to display the column properties dialog window.

Set the column title to **Time** in tab 1 and column width to **11**. Switch to tab 2 and set the Sort type to **Ascending**. Switch to tab 4 and change the display type to **Date/Time**. Uncheck the **Display Date** option and change **Show Time** to **Hours and minutes**.

In the Programmer's pane, change the display type from **Simple Function** to **Formula** and set the column formula to the following.

```
REM "Column 3 represents the time range for the appointment";
TimeRange;
```

Column 4

The last column will display the title or subject line in the calendar. Select the **Create > Append New Column** menu options to add the new column. Select the **Design > Column Properties** menu options to display the column properties dialog window. Set the column title to **Topic** in tab 1.

In the Programmer's pane, change the display type from **Simple Function** to **Formula** and set the column formula to the following.

```
REM "Column 4 contains the appointment topic";
Topic;
```

Set View Objects and Properties

With the columns in place, add the view selection criteria and code to manage various trigger events. To set the view selection formula, click inside the view (as opposed to a column header) to give the view focus.

Locate and click on **View Selection** in the Objects section of the Programmer's pane. Change the programming language from **Simple Search** to **Formula** and insert the following code.

```
theRoom := @Subset(@ViewTitle; -1);
SELECT Form = "Appt" & Room=theRoom
```

RegionDoubleClick Event

This event allows users to add an appointment by double-clicking on a calendar date. When the appointment form is displayed, the selected calendar date is automatically populated on the form. This event also inserts the view name into the room location field.

Locate and click on Regiondoubleclick in the Objects section of the Programmer's pane and insert the following code.

```
Sub Regiondoubleclick(Source As Notesuiview)

    Dim doc As NotesDocument
    Dim workspace As New NotesUIWorkspace
    Dim uidoc As NotesUIDocument
    Dim view As NotesView
    Dim dateTime As New NotesDateTime( "" )
    Dim answer As Integer
    Call dateTime.SetNow

    ' --- Check to see if date is in the past ---
    If Source.CalendarDateTime < Cdat (dateTime.DateOnly) Then
        answer=Msgbox("Date in past... Do you want to continue?",_
        292, "Continue?")
    End If
    If (answer = 6) Or (Source.CalendarDateTime >= Cdat _
        (dateTime.DateOnly)) Then
        ' --- Create reservation ---
        Set view = Source.View
        Set uidoc = workspace.ComposeDocument ( "", "", "Appt" )
        Set doc = uidoc.Document
        doc.Room = view.Aliases
        doc.StartDate = Source.CalendarDateTime
    End If

End Sub
```

QueryPaste Event

The QueryPaste event will be programmed to prevent users from copying and pasting documents into the view. Users will receive a warning message every time they attempt to paste a document into the view. Insert the following into the QueryPaste event.

```
Sub Querypaste(Source As Notesuiview, Continue As Variant)
    Msgbox "Sorry, users are not permitted" + _
    "to copy and paste.", 48, "Warning"
    Continue = False
End Sub
```

Create Action Button for the View

In addition to creating a new appointment using the regiondoubleclick event, this view will include a button. However, because a start date is not known, this code causes the appointment start date to default to today's date.

Select **Create > Action > Action** to create a button. Title the button **New Appointment**. Switch the programming language to **LotusScript** and insert the following code.

```
Sub Click(Source As Button)

    Dim ws As NotesUIWorkspace
    Dim session As NotesSession
    Dim db As NotesDatabase
    Dim doc As NotesDocument
    Dim uidoc As NotesUIDocument
    Set ws = New NotesUIWorkspace
    Set session = New NotesSession
    Set db = session.CurrentDatabase
    Dim newdoc As New NotesDocument(db)
    Dim uiview As NotesUIView
    Set uiview = ws.CurrentView
    Dim dateTime As New NotesDateTime( "" )
    Dim EventDate As New NotesDateTime( "" )
    Set EventDate= New NotesDateTime(ws.CurrentCalendarDateTime)
    Call dateTime.SetNow
    Dim answer as Integer
    Dim viewalias as String

    ' --- Check to see if date is in the past ---
    If ws.CurrentCalendarDateTime < Cdat (dateTime.DateOnly) Then
        answer = Msgbox("Date in past... Do you want to continue?",_
        292, "Continue?")
    End If
    If (answer = 6) Or (ws.CurrentCalendarDateTime >= Cdat _
        (dateTime.DateOnly)) Then
        ' --- Create reservation ---
        Set uidoc = ws.ComposeDocument ( "", "", "Appt" )
        Set doc = uidoc.Document
        viewalias = uiview.ViewAlias
        doc.Room = viewalias
        Call uidoc.GotoField( "StartDate" )
        Call uidoc.Clear
        Call uidoc.InsertText ( EventDate.DateOnly )
    End If

End Sub
```

Save and close the view.

Security

Application security is the last step in the project. To adjust the Access Control List (ACL) settings, select the **File > Database > Access Control** menu options.

By default, the Basics tab should be active. Click on the **-Default-** user in the center of the screen. Then change the Access field (right side) to **Author** and select both the **Create documents** and **Delete documents** checkboxes (see Figure 8.21). These options will allow only the author of the appointment and anyone listed in the "editors" field to modify or delete the appointment.

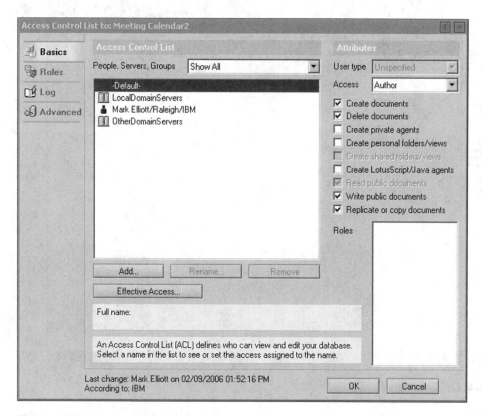

Figure 8.21 Access Control List dialog

Congratulations, you've just created a multi-document recurring appointment calendar application! When opened in the Lotus Notes client, you will see the "Weekly" calendar view. When you click on the **New Appointment** button, you should see a form similar to Figure 8.22.

If would you like to further customize the application, refer to Chapters 13 through 17 for additional enhancements.

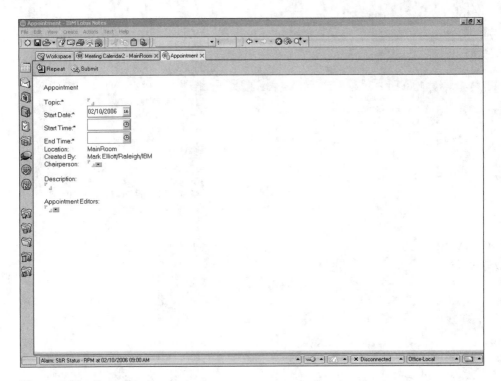

Figure 8.22   Completed project

Links to developerWorks

A.8.1 Kahn, Bruce. *A technical overview of the IBM Lotus Notes/Domino busytime system.* IBM developerWorks, April 2005. http://www.ibm.com/developerworks/lotus/library/busytime/index.html.

Chapter 9

Collaborative Applications

Chapter Overview

This chapter will focus on two types of collaborative applications—discussion forums and newsletters. Technically speaking, virtually all Lotus Notes applications are considered collaborative in nature because they enable users—often separated geographically—to work together, share information, and achieve a common goal.

Some of the common types of collaborative applications include

- Discussion forum
- Newsletter forum
- For Sale forum
- Q&A forum
- Project notebook

By the end of the chapter you will have learned

- Elements of a discussion forum
- How to create and manage Response documents
- How to trigger client-side emails
- How to trigger server-side emails
- How to create scheduled agents
- How to create a button to attach files
- How to automatically populate fields on a form based on another form
- How to create a cascading menu
- How to create subforms
- How to create shared fields
- How to create shared agents

This chapter includes step-by-step instructions for two Lotus Notes applications.

Collaborative Applications

There are many types of collaborative applications, and the ones you implement will vary based on the business needs of your company. But for all their variety, they share a common purpose—to facilitate sharing, dissemination, and discussion of information. However, for purposes of this chapter, we'll look at two applications used to share information—a discussion forum and a project control notebook.

For this chapter, we'll review the architecture and design elements with each project because the rules are project specific. At the most fundamental level, both of these applications allow users to capture and share information.

Project A: Build a Discussion Forum

Difficulty Level: Moderate
Completion Time: 5 to 8 hours
Project Materials: 4 Forms, 1 Subform, 1 Library, 5 Action Buttons, 3 Shared
                      Fields, 6 Views, 1 Access Control List Role, 1 Scheduled Agent
Languages Used: Formula Language, LotusScript
Possible Usages: Online help, questions & answers, items for sale

Application Architecture

Discussion forums, as the name implies, allow users to discuss and respond to forum topics. Traditionally, this type of architecture includes a multi-tiered methodology to organize information, beginning with a *Main document*, a *Response document* and *Response to Response document.*

This architecture might be used in an online "help" or "for sale" database in which a person posts a main discussion topic that becomes the focal point for subsequent discussion. This type of application might be compared to the classified section of a newspaper in which a person places, or posts, an item for sale and potential buyers ask questions regarding the item.

In this example, the initial posting is the main document, also known as the parent document. Any person who responds to the parent document generates a Response document, also called a child document. In addition to the parent and child document, Lotus Notes also provides the ability to create a Response to Response or grandchild document.

Figure 9.1 depicts the parent, child, and grandchild relationship and illustrates how a main discussion topic can have multiple related sub-documents.

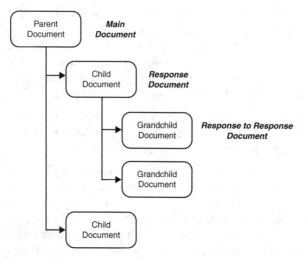

Figure 9.1   Parent, child, grandchild relationship

Continuing the analogy of a classified section, this project allows each main document to be grouped or categorized through the use of a dropdown menu with related postings. For this example, "for sale" categories might include

- Appliances
- Boats
- Electronics
- Employment opportunities
- Miscellaneous
- Real estate
- Vehicles

There are essentially two ways that a category can be implemented—it can be hard-coded or created dynamically. With hard-coding, values are stored with the programming code. Although this may require less time up front, it is more difficult and costly to make changes later. Creating a category dynamically may require more time up front but makes it easier to manage information later.

> **NOTE**
>
> Dynamic categories can be created such that either the administrator manages the valid list of categories or users are given the flexibility to create categories as needed. This project will illustrate how to create an application where an administrator controls the category names. This enforces a strict nomenclature for document classifications. The next project in this chapter will illustrate an alternative method for dynamic creation of categories.

Implementing dynamic categories requires three additional design elements—a form, a view, and program logic. The Category form will be used to create new category names. The view will be used to populate values in the dropdown menu. Items can simply be removed by deleting the appropriate category document from the view. Programming logic, as opposed to hard-coded values, is then added to the dropdown design element. This allows for easier management of information with no additional coding required in the future.

This application will include three different views—By Topic, By Author, and By Category. Each view will contain the same information, simply sorted and displayed differently. This provides the user with several different options when searching for information.

In addition to the discussion topic views, three administrative views will be created— Categories, Subscriptions, and Email Queue. These views manage the overall usage of the application. The Category view is used to manage the classification of documents and will populate the Category field on the parent document. The Subscription view lists all individuals that have registered with the discussion forum. This view will be used to send email notifications as new postings are created. The Email Queue is used by the server to send notifications. This view will list new postings that have not been emailed to registered users.

Finally, the architecture for this project includes two methods to send email notifications— client based and server based. Using the client-based method, emails are automatically triggered each time a document is posted to the discussion forum. When these emails are sent, the person posting the article will be listed in the "From" field of the email. The second method shifts the notification process to the server. Using a scheduled agent, email notifications are sent from the server based on a specified interval (say every five minutes). With this method, the server name will be listed in the email "From" field. This method also shifts the processing from the client to the server. If you have a significant number of registered users, you'll probably want to implement the server-based methodology.

NOTE

This project includes both methods for sending email notices to registered users—client based and server based. Both options have been included in the project to illustrate methods for generating and sending email notifications. From an implementation perspective, we recommend the server approach, but either can be implemented. If you elect to implement both, users will receive two email notifications as topics are posted to the database.

NOTE

The Lotus Notes client includes a discussion template that essentially does the same thing as this project. With that in mind, the intent of this project is to teach how to create an application that utilizes a "Response Document" hierarchy.

Create the Database

To start this project, launch the Lotus Domino Designer client. When the Designer client is running, select the **File** > **Database** > **New** menu options to create a new database. Specify **Forum** as the application title and **Forum.nsf** as the file name (see Figure 9.2). Be sure to select **-Blank-** as the template type.

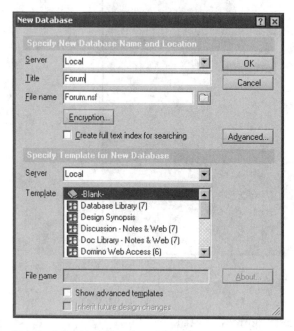

Figure 9.2   New Database dialog

Set the Database Roles

After the database is created, start by establishing the roles associated with the database. Roles enable specific people to perform actions that others cannot. In this case, the "Admin" role will enable the application administrator to create new categories for the discussion forum. Anyone that does not have this role will have this authority.

To create the role, select the **File** > **Database** > **Access Control** menu options. By default, the Basics tab should be active. Switch to the Roles tab and select the **Add** button (located at the bottom of the dialog window).

This will display a new popup window called Add Role (see Figure 9.3). Type **Admin** and click the **OK** button to add the role.

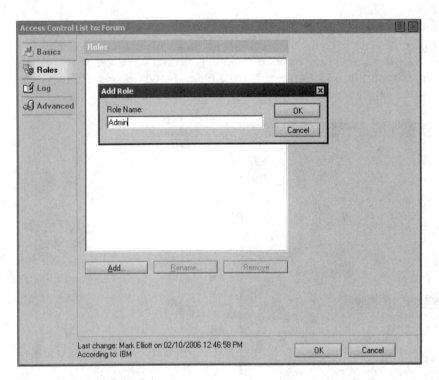

Figure 9.3   Add Role dialog

Click **OK** a second time to close the Access Control List (ACL) window.

Create the Discussion Forum Script Library

The next step will be to create the LotusScript library because virtually all of the design elements will utilize shared subroutines. To create the library, select the **Create > Design > Script Library > LotusScript Library** menu options.

> **TIP**
>
> The following code is available in the developer's toolbox. Simply open the "Project Library" database in your Lotus Notes client and navigate to the "Script Library" section for the appropriate project. After you locate the project, copy and paste the code into the Designer client for the current project. Be sure the programmer's pane has focus before pasting the code. Alternatively, you can elect to manually type the code.

CheckFieldValues Function

The `CheckFieldValues` function checks two fields, Topic and Category, to make sure they contain a value on the form. This function is called from the Topic form. An error message is displayed and returns a `False` value if one of the fields is null. A `True` value must be returned before the user can save the document in the database.

```
Function CheckFieldValues ( DocRef As NotesDocument )

    CheckFieldValues = True
    MsgText = ""
    If DocRef.Topic(0) = "" Then
        MsgText = MsgText + "Specify a topic description." + Chr$(13)
    End If

    If DocRef.Category(0) = "" Then
        MsgText = MsgText + "Specify a discussion category" + Chr$(13)
    End If

    If MsgText <> "" Then
        Msgbox MsgText, 16, "Required Fields."
        CheckFieldValues = False
    End If

End Function
```

SendNotice Subroutine

The `SendNotice` subroutine is used to send client-based emails to registered users. The routine is called the first time a new posting is saved and closed. Using this option, emails are triggered by the user that submitted the posting.

Emails will be sent to all registered users that have subscribed to the forum and have requested emails on the posted category (e.g., Compact Cars). Later in the project we'll discuss how to implement or disable this email delivery option.

```
Sub SendNotice ( uidoc As NotesUIDocument )

    '-------------------------------
    ' Initialize primary objects
    '-------------------------------
    Dim ws As NotesUIWorkspace
    Dim s As NotesSession
    Dim db As NotesDatabase
    Dim doc As NotesDocument
    Dim viewA As NotesView
    Dim docA As NotesDocument

    Set ws = New NotesUIWorkspace
    Set s = New NotesSession
    Set db = s.CurrentDatabase
    Set doc = uidoc.Document
    Set viewA = db.GetView( "Subscriptions" )
    Set docA = viewA.GetFirstDocument
```

```
'--------------------------------
   ' Build the email document
'--------------------------------
Dim docMemo As NotesDocument
Set docMemo = New NotesDocument (db)
docMemo.Form = "Memo"
docMemo.Subject = doc.Topic
Set rtitem = New NotesRichTextItem(docMemo, "Body")
Call rtitem.AddNewLine( 2 )
Call rtitem.AppendText ("Open Document --> " )
Call rtitem.AppendDocLink( Doc, "Discussion Topic" )
Call rtitem.AddNewLine( 1 )
Call rtitem.AppendText ("Open Database --> " )
Call rtitem.AppendDocLink( db, db.Title )


   '--------------------------------
   ' Loop through subscriptions.  Send email to interested parties.
   '--------------------------------
While Not ( docA Is Nothing )
    'Msgbox "Sending email to: " + docA.InternetMail(0)
    If docA.AllowEmails(0) = True Then
        If ( foundElement (docA.Category, doc.Category(0) )) Then
            Print "--- Sending email to: " + docA.InternetMail(0)
            docMemo.SendTo = docA.InternetMail(0)
            docMemo.Send False
        End If
    End If
    Set docA = viewA.GetNextDocument( docA )
Wend

End Sub
```

SendNewPostings Subroutine

The `SendNewPostings` subroutine is the second email delivery option and is used for server-based email notifications. This subroutine is called from a scheduled agent. Using this option, emails will originate from the server, as opposed to the user that submitted the discussion topic. Later in the project we'll cover how to enable or disable this delivery option.

```
Sub SendNewPostings

    Dim s As NotesSession
    Dim db As NotesDatabase
    Dim viewA As NotesView
    Dim viewB As NotesView
    Dim docA As NotesDocument
    Dim docB As NotesDocument
    Dim docC As NotesDocument
    Set s = New NotesSession
    Set db = s.CurrentDatabase
    Set viewA = db.GetView( "EmailQue" )
    Set docA = viewA.GetFirstDocument
    Set viewB = db.GetView( "Subscriptions" )


    '--------------------------------
    ' Loop through email queue.
```

```
'--------------------------------
While Not ( docA Is Nothing )
    Print "Processing topic: " + docA.Topic(0)

        '--------------------------------
        ' Build the email document
        '--------------------------------
    Dim docMemo As NotesDocument
    Set docMemo = New NotesDocument (db)
    docMemo.Form = "Memo"
    docMemo.Subject = docA.Topic
    Set rtitem = New NotesRichTextItem(docMemo, "Body")
    Call rtitem.AddNewLine( 1 )
    Dim rtitemB As Variant
    Set rtitemB = docA.GetFirstItem( "Body" )
    Call rtitem.AppendRTItem( rtitemB )
    Call rtitem.AddNewLine( 2 )
    Call rtitem.AppendText ("Open Document --> " )
    Call rtitem.AppendDocLink( DocA, "Discussion Topic" )
    Call rtitem.AddNewLine( 1 )
    Call rtitem.AppendText ("Open Database --> " )
    Call rtitem.AppendDocLink( db, db.Title )

        '--------------------------------
        ' Send email to interested parties
        '--------------------------------
    Set docB = viewB.GetFirstDocument
    While Not ( docB Is Nothing )
        If docB.AllowEmails(0) = "-1" Then
            If ( foundElement (docB.Category, docA.Category(0) )) Then
                Print "-- Sending email to: " + docB.InternetMail(0)
                docMemo.SendTo = docB.InternetMail(0)
                docMemo.Send False
            End If
        End If
        Set docB = viewB.GetNextDocument ( docB )
    Wend

        '--------------------------------
        ' Get next document before updating current status.
        '--------------------------------
    Set docC = viewA.GetNextDocument( docA )
    docA.Status = "COMPLETE"
    docA.Save True, True
    Set docA = docC
  Wend

End Sub
```

FoundElement Function

The FoundElement function is used to search for a specified element in a list array. The function returns True if the element is found and False if the element is not found. In this case, the function checks to see if the registered user is interested in the posted discussion topic category.

```
Function foundElement (varFromList As Variant, varTarget As Variant) As Variant

    '-------------------------------
    ' Check for the existence of an element in an array.
    '-------------------------------
    foundElement = False
    Forall varElement In varFromList
       If varElement = "All" Then
           foundElement = True
           Exit Forall
       Elseif varElement = varTarget Then
           foundElement = True
           Exit Forall
       End If
    End Forall

End Function
```

SaveForm Function

The SaveForm function is called from the QuerySave event each time the main document or Response document is saved. This routine will call the CheckFieldValues function to verify that the fields are not empty. If all fields are valid, the message "Are you ready to post this topic?" will be displayed prior to saving the topic to the discussion forum.

If the user selects "Yes", then the Status field is set to "SUBMIT", and the form is closed. Setting the status to "SUBMIT" indicates that the form has been submitted and will trigger email notifications in the QueryClose event.

```
Function SaveForm As Integer

    Dim ws As New NotesUIWorkspace
    Dim uidoc As NotesUIDocument
    Dim doc As NotesDocument
    Dim answer As Integer
    Dim Continue As Integer
    Set uidoc = ws.CurrentDocument
    Set doc = uidoc.Document

    Continue = CheckFieldValues ( doc )
    If Continue Then
       If doc.IsNewNote Then
           answer% = Msgbox("Are you ready to post this topic?", _
           292, "Continue?")
           If answer% = 6 Then
              doc.Status = "SUBMIT"
              uidoc.Close
           Else
              continue = False
           End If
       End If
    End If
    SaveForm = Continue

End Function
```

CloseForm Subfunction

The `CloseForm` subroutine is called from the `QueryClose` event each time the main or Response document is closed. When called, this routine will check the value in the Status field. If this is the first time the document is being closed, the status will be set to `"SUBMIT"` and will trigger client-based email notifications.

After the email notifications are sent, the status is set to `"POSTED"` to signify that the topic has been sent to all interested subscribers via the client-based method. If the server-based method is implemented, the scheduled agent will trigger emails based on a status of `"POSTED"`.

> **NOTE**
>
> As implemented here, client-based notifications will be enabled. To disable client-based notifications, comment out the statement `"Call SendNotice ( uidoc )"` in the following code. To implement server-based notifications, a scheduled agent (discussed later in the project) will need to be created to send out the notifications.

```
Sub CloseForm
    Dim w As New NotesUIWorkspace
    Dim uidoc As NotesUIDocument
    Dim doc As NotesDocument
    Set uidoc = w.CurrentDocument
    Set doc = uidoc.Document
    If doc.Status(0) = "SUBMIT" Then

        ' Comment out the "SendNotice" statement to
        ' implement the server-based email notifications
        Call SendNotice ( uidoc )

        doc.Status = "POSTED"
        doc.Save True, True
    End If
End Sub
```

Save and close the LotusScript library. When prompted, name the library **DiscussionForum**.

Create the Shared Action Buttons

This project includes five action buttons—New Topic, Reply, New Category, Subscribe, and Submit. These buttons will be used throughout the application on multiple forms and views.

New Topic Button

This button is used to post new discussion topics, or parent documents, in the forum. Select the **Create > Design > Shared Action** menu options and name the button **New Topic** in the properties dialog. Add the following in the Programmer's pane. Save and close the design element.

```
@Command([Compose]; "Topic")
```

Reply Button

The Reply button will allow users to post either a Response or Response to Response document. Depending on the document that is currently selected, the button will create either a child or grandchild document. This is accomplished by checking the form name of the selected document.

If the current document in the view is a Response, then we know to create a Response to Response document. Otherwise, we know the current document is a parent, and therefore we create a child document. In other words, users will be able to use a single button for both types of Response documents. This button will only display if the document has already been posted.

Select the **Create > Design > Shared Action** menu options and name the button **Reply** in the properties dialog. Next, switch to tab 2. Check the **Hide action if formula is true** option and add the following to the formula window of the properties dialog.

```
@IsNewDoc
```

Add the following in the Programmer's pane. Save and close the design element.

```
Form := @If (@IsResponseDoc; "ResToRes"; "Res" );
@PostedCommand([Compose]; Form)
```

New Category Button

This button allows the application administrator to dynamically create discussion topic categories. Only select users will have authority to see this button and create new categories. This ability is managed through the ACL. Only users with the "Admin" role in the ACL will be permitted to create a new category or access the related view.

To create the button, select the **Create > Design > Shared Action** menu options and name the button **New Category**. Next, switch to tab 2. Check the **Hide action if formula is true** option and add the following to the hide formula window within the properties dialog.

```
!@IsMember("[Admin]";@UserRoles)
```

Next, close the property window and add the following in the Programmer's pane. Afterward, save and close the design element.

```
@Command([Compose]; "Cat")
```

Subscribe Button

The Subscribe button allows users to manage email notifications for the discussion forum. This button will create a new subscription document in the database for the user. Select the **Create > Design > Shared Action** menu and name the button **Subscribe**.

```
@Command([Compose]; "Subscribe")
```

Submit Button

The Submit button is used to post new discussion topics and trigger the email notifications to registered users. This button also calls a subroutine that ensures that all required fields on the document have been completed before saving the document. The Submit button only appears for new documents. After the document has been submitted, the button is hidden.

Select the **Create > Design > Shared Action** menu and name the button **Submit** in the properties dialog. Next, switch to tab 2. Check the **Hide action if formula is true** option and add the following to the formula window of the properties dialog.

```
!@IsNewDoc
```

Close the property window and add the following in the Programmer's pane. Change the language type from **Formula** to **LotusScript**. Now, in the Programmer's pane, select the **(Options)** section and add the following statement.

```
Use "DiscussionForum"
```

Next add the following in the `Click` event section of the Programmer's pane. This subroutine calls the front-end `save` function and includes an `On Error` call. In some cases, Lotus Notes may throw an exception error when trying to synchronize the front-end and back-end documents when the document is just being created. However, because this error will not affect the overall processing and functionality of the application, we'll use the `On Error` branch to catch the error and continue. Afterward, save and close the design element.

```
Sub Click(Source As Button)

    On Error Goto oops
    Dim w As New NotesUIWorkspace
    Dim uidoc As NotesUIDocument
    Set uidoc = w.CurrentDocument
    uidoc.save
oops:
    Exit Sub

End Sub
```

> **NOTE**
>
> The email notifications are triggered after the document is saved using both the `QuerySave` and `QueryClose` events. Using this approach, notifications can be triggered by using the Submit button or through the Esc key to close the document.

Create the Forum Fields Subform

The Main Topic, Response, and Response to Response forms each have several fields in common. Instead of creating separate fields on each form, this project will utilize a subform. These objects can be maintained from a single location if changes are needed. After the subform is created, it will be added to each of the three forms—Main Topic, Response, and Response to Response (created later in the project).

To create the subform, select the **Create > Design > Subform** menu options. After the subform has been created, add the following field descriptions down the left side of the form.

- Author:
- Created:
- Details:

Next, select the **Create > Field** menu options for each of the following fields. Be sure to set the data type in the field properties dialog and set the default value formula for each field in the Programmer's pane.

Field Name	Type	Default Value Formula	Remarks
Authors	Authors, Computed when Composed	@UserName	
Created	Date/Time, Computed when Composed	@Now	On tab 2 select the **Display Time** setting. Make sure both the date and time options are selected.
Body	Rich Text, Editable		Add the **Body** field below the "Details" text label.

To complete the subform, two shared action buttons need to be added—Reply and Submit. These buttons will be used on all three documents. Select the **Create > Action > Insert Shared Action** menu options, choose both buttons, and click **Insert** to add them to the subform. Click **Done** to close the Insert Shared Action dialog window. The subform should now look like Figure 9.4.

Save and close the design element. Title the subform **ForumFields** when prompted.

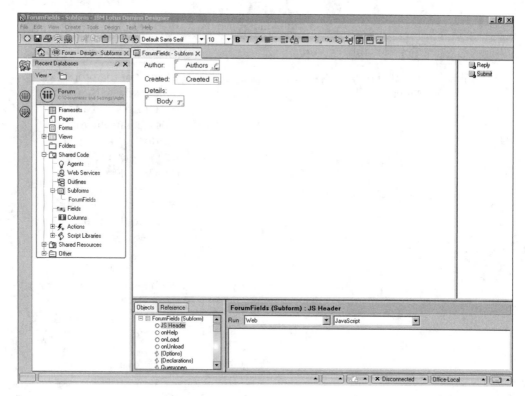

Figure 9.4   ForumFields subform

Create the New Topic Form

With the script library, subform, and shared actions in place, the next step is to create the main discussion topic form. This form will be used to post new discussion topics (or parent documents) to the forum. To create the form, click the **New Form** button or select the **Create > Design > Form** menu options.

After the form has been created, add a descriptive text title such as **Discussion Topic** at the top of the form and the following field descriptions down the left side of the form.

- Topic:
- Category:

Next, add the fields as specified in the following table. To create a field, select the **Create > Field** menu options. Be sure to set the data type, formula, and other attributes for each field on the form using the properties dialog box and/or Programmer's pane.

Field Name	Type	Default Value Formula	Remarks
Topic	Text, Editable	Topic	

Category	Combobox, Editable	Category	In tab 2 of the properties dialog, select **Use formula for choices** and add the following in the formula window:
			`REM {Set a default`
			`  value if no`
			`    categories setup};`
			`REM {Otherwise, display`
			`  the selected`
			`    category};`
			`DefaultCat := "General";`
			`Class :="";`
			`Cache := "NoCache";`
			`Host := "";`
			`View := "Category";`
			`Column := 1;`
			`output := @Unique(`
			`  @DbColumn( Class :`
			`  Cache; Host; view ;`
			`  Column ));`
			`@If (output = "";`
			`  DefaultCat; output)`

Set the Form Objects and Properties

Next, locate the "(Globals)Untitled" section in the Objects tab of the Programmer's pane. This section is located at the very top of the Objects pane. You many need to scroll up to locate this section. Click on **(Options)** and add the following statement in the Programmer's pane:

```
USE "DiscussionForum"
```

This statement ties the form and script library together. Without this statement, Lotus Notes will not be able to locate the subroutines and functions.

QuerySave Event

Insert the following in the QuerySave event of the Programmer's pane. This will call the LotusScript library function (described earlier in the project).

```
Sub Querysave(Source As Notesuidocument, Continue As Variant)

   Continue = SaveForm( )

End Sub
```

QueryClose Event

Insert the following in the QueryClose event of the Programmer's pane. This will call the LotusScript library subroutine (described earlier in the project).

```
Sub Queryclose(Source As Notesuidocument, Continue As Variant)

   Call CloseForm

End Sub
```

To complete the form, insert the ForumFields subform. Place the text cursor just below the Category field and select the **Create > Resource > Insert Subform** menu options. When prompted, select the ForumFields subform and add it to the form.

Select the **File > Save** menu options. When prompted, title the form **New Topic | Topic**. The form should now look like Figure 9.5.

Close the form when complete.

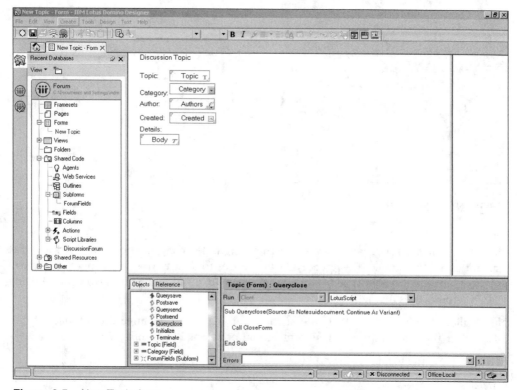

Figure 9.5   New Topic form

Create the Response Form

The Topic form will be used as the basis for the Response form. From the Design pane, highlight the Topic design element form and select the **Edit > Copy** menu options. Now select the **Edit > Paste** menu options and open the form in the Designer client.

Next, select **Design > Form Properties** to display the Form properties dialog. Change the form name to **Response | Res** and the form type to **Response**. Now switch to tab 2 and select the **Formulas inherit values from selected document** option located at the top of the properties dialog (see Figure 9.6).

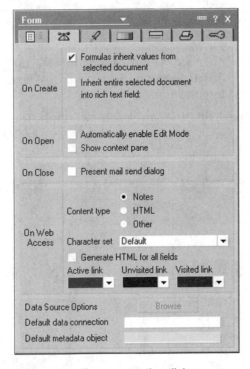

Figure 9.6   Form properties dialog

Next, you will need to change several of the design elements on the form. Click on the Categories field and select **Design > Field Properties** to display the field properties dialog. On tab 1, change the field type from **Combobox** to **Text** and make this a **Computed** field. Close the properties dialog.

Now replace the descriptive text title at the top of the form. Change the text label from **Discussion Topic** to **Response**. The form should now look like Figure 9.7.

Save and close the form.

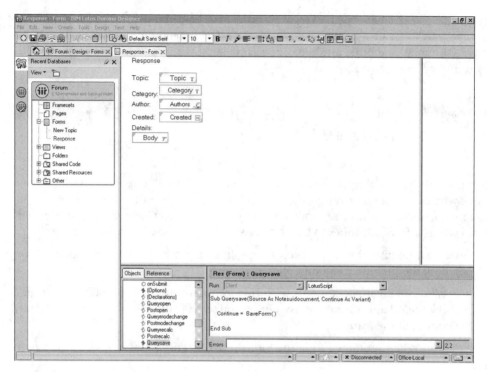

Figure 9.7 Response form

Create the Response to Response Form

This form will be based on the Response form. From the Design pane, highlight the Response form and select the **Edit > Copy** menu options. Now select the **Edit > Paste** menu options and open the form in the Designer client.

Next, select **Design > Form Properties** to display the form properties dialog. Change the form name to **Response To Response | ResToRes** and set the form type to **Response to response**. Close the properties dialog.

Next, replace the descriptive text title at the top of the form. Change the text label to **Response to Response**. Save and close the form.

Create the Category Form

This category form will be used to create new discussion topic categories or classifications. The values stored in this form will be used to populate the Category combobox field on the parent or main document. To create the form, select the **Create > Design > Form** menu options.

Next, create a text label called **Category** and a new field immediately below the label
Category field. To create a field, select the **Create > Field** menu options. Be sure to set the
data type, formula, and other attributes for each field on the form using the properties dialog box and/or Programmer's pane.

Field Name	Type	Default Value Formula	Remarks
Category	Text, Editable		

This form will only be accessible to users assigned the "Admin" role in the ACL. To help
manage who can create new categories, you will need to remove the form from the application menu, update the access permissions for the form, and create a button on the view
that selectively allows categories to be created (which is performed later in the project).

To remove the form from the menu, select the **Design > Form Properties** menu options. On
tab 1, uncheck the **Include in menu** option.

To set the **Who can create documents with this form** property, switch to tab 7 (see Figure
9.8). Uncheck the **All authors and above** option and select **[Admin]** (which will most likely
be at the bottom of the listbox).

Save the form. When prompted, title the form **New Category | Cat** and close the design
element.

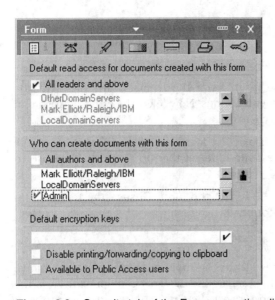

Figure 9.8   Security tab of the Form properties dialog

Create the Subscription Form

This form is used to register discussion forum users. Here, users can set email notification preferences based on discussion forum categories. Users can elect to receive email notices for all discussion forum topics or only a select few. This form also allows users to enable or disable notices altogether. To create the form, select the **Create** > **Design** > **Form** menu options.

Next, label the form **Forum Subscription** at the top of the form and add the following text labels down the left side.

- Name:
- Notes Email:
- Internet Email:
- Notifications:
- Categories of Interest:

Select the **Create** > **Field** menu options and create fields based on the following table. Be sure to set the data type, formula, and other attributes for each field on the form using the properties dialog box and/or Programmer's pane.

Field Name	Type	Default Value Formula	Remarks
Name	Text, Editable	@Name([CN];@UserName)	
NotesMail	Text, Editable	@Name([Abbreviate]; @UserName)	
InternetMail	Text, Editable	@LeftBack(@NameLookup([NoUpdate]; @UserName; "Shortname"); ";")	
AllowEmails	RadioButton, Editable		Select **Enter choices one per line** in tab 2. Insert the default choices in the choices field. Yes, send me notifications | -1 No, do not send me notifications | 0

continues

Field Name	Type	Default Value Formula	Remarks

Category	Checkbox, Editable	`Category`	Select **Use Formula for choices** in tab 2. Add the following formula.
			`REM {Set default`
			`  category};`
			`DefaultCat :=`
			`  "General";`
			`REM {Retrieve select`
			`  if specified};`
			`Class :="";`
			`Cache := "NoCache";`
			`Host := "";`
			`View := "Category";`
			`Column := 1;`
			`output := @Unique(`
			`  @DbColumn( Class :`
			`  Cache; Host; view ;`
			`  Column ));`
			`@If (output = "";`
			`DefaultCat; "All":`
			`  output)`

Define Who Can Update the Forum Subscription

Only the person that subscribes to the forum should have the ability to modify notification preferences. To define who can update the subscription, an Authors field needs to be added to the form. This will ensure that only the author of the document can change the document.

Insert a blank line at the top of the form above the Forum Subscription title. Next, select the **Create > Field** menu options and create the following field. Be sure to set the data type, formula, and other attributes for each field on the form using the properties dialog box and default value in the Programmer's pane.

Field Name	Type	Default Value Formula	Remarks
Author	Authors, Computed when composed	`@UserName`	On tab 6, select **Hide paragraph when formula is true** and add the formula: 1

Save the form. When prompted, name the form **Subscribe | Subscribe**. The form should now look similar to Figure 9.9.

Close the form after all updates are complete.

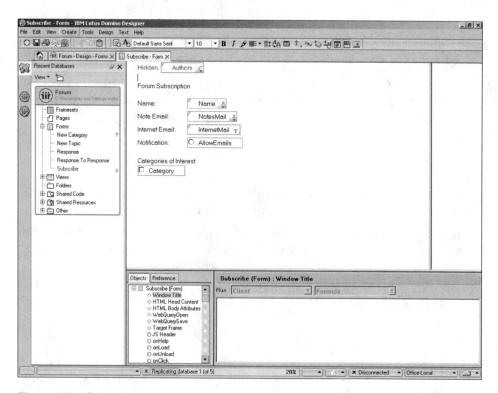

Figure 9.9 Subscribe form

Create the By Topic View

By default, a view called *(untitled)* was automatically created when the database was first created. To configure this view, navigate to Views in the Design pane and double-click on the view called "(untitled)".

When the view is displayed, the Designer client will immediately display the properties dialog for the view. Specify **1. By Topic** in the name field and **Topic** in the alias field. The view has been named, so you can close the dialog window.

Column 1

This column will display the number of Response documents associated with the parent document. To configure this column, click on the predefined column header (#) and select the **Design > Column Properties** menu options. Set the column width to 2.

A.9.1

Next, change the Language Selector from **Simple Function** to **Formula** and add the following in the Programmer's pane.

```
@If( !@IsResponseDoc; @DocDescendants( "0"; "%"; "%"); "")
```

Column 2
The second column will be used to sort the documents in the view. This will be a hidden column. Select the **Create > Append new column** menu options to add a new column.

In the properties dialog, set the column width to **1** on tab 1, set the sort type to **Ascending** in tab 2, and select the **Hide column** option in tab 6.

Next, select **Creation Date** as the simple function in the Programmer's pane.

```
Creation Date
```

Column 3
This column will display all child and grandchild documents. This will be a hidden column. Select the **Create > Append new column** menu options to add a new column.

In the properties dialog, set the column width to **1** and select the **Show twistie when row is expandable** and **Show Responses Only** options in tab 1. *Make sure these options are selected. Without these options selected, the view will not work properly.*

Then change the Language Selector from **Simple Function** to **Fields** and select the following in the Programmer's pane.

```
Topic
```

Column 4
This column will display all parent documents. Select the **Create > Append new column** menu options to add a new column.

In the properties dialog, set the column title to **Topic**, set the width to **45**, and select **Show twistie when row is expandable** on tab 1. Set the font style to **Bold** and text color to **Blue** on tab 3.

Then change the Language Selector from **Simple Function** to **Fields** and select the following in the Programmer's pane.

```
Topic
```

View Selection Formula
The view selection formula determines what documents are selected and displayed in the view. To set the selection formula, click inside the view (as opposed to a column header) to give the view focus. Then locate the View Selection section in the Programmer's pane. Change the Language Selector from **Simple Search** to **Formula** and add the following in the Programmer's pane.

```
SELECT Form = "Topic" | Form = "Res" | Form = "ResToRes"
```

Action Buttons

To complete the view, two action buttons need to be added—New Topic and Reply. These buttons will allow the user to click on a button to add a new parent, child, or grandchild topic to the discussion forum. Select **Create > Insert Shared Action** to add these buttons. When the popup dialog box displays, insert first the **New Topic** button followed by the **Reply** button. Click **Done** after the buttons have been added. Your view should look like Figure 9.10.

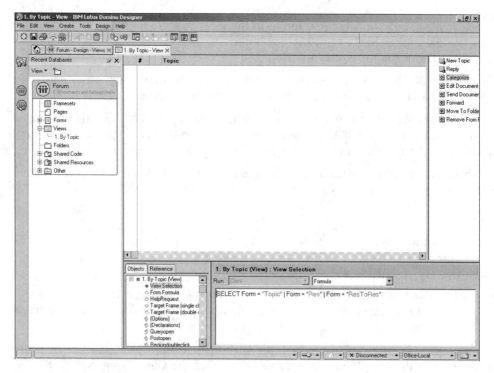

Figure 9.10   By Topic view

Save and close the view.

Create the By Category View

With one view already in place, you'll use this as the basis for the By Category view. This is achieved by making a copy of the By Topic view and then modifying it.

In the Design pane, highlight the **1. By Topic** view design element and select the **Edit > Copy** menu options. Now select the **Edit > Paste** menu options. Double-click on the **Copy of By Topic** view to open it in design mode.

Select the **Design > View Properties** menu options. In the properties dialog, change the view title to **2. By Category** and the view alias to **By Category**.

> **NOTE**
>
> Be sure to specify **By Category** for the alias. Another view in the database will be named **Category**. These alias names must be unique.

The next step will be to update the columns in the view. You will need to insert a new column as the first column in the view. This column will be used to sort and display documents based on the discussion topic category name.

To insert the column, select the **Create > Insert New Column** menu options. This action will insert a new column and shift all existing columns to the right.

In the properties dialog, set the column width to **1** and select the **Show twistie when row is expandable** option. On tab 2, set the sort order to **Ascending** and type to **Categorized**. Last, set the font text color to **Blue** and **Bold** on tab 3.

Then change the Language Selector from **Simple Function** to **Fields** and select the following in the Programmer's pane.

```
Category
```

Save and close the view.

Create the By Author View

The By Author view will display documents grouped by author. Using this view, users will be able to find documents based on the person that posted the discussion topic. To create the view, select the **Create > Design > View** menu options.

When prompted, set the view name to **3. By Author|By Author**. Next, change the **Copy style from view** field to **-Blank-**. To set this value, click the **Copy From** button. Finally, change the selection conditions to **By Formula** and insert the following in the dialog box.

```
SELECT Form = "Topic" | Form = "Res" | Form = "ResToRes"
```

The dialog box should look like Figure 9.11.

Click **Save and Customize** to create the view and open it in edit mode.

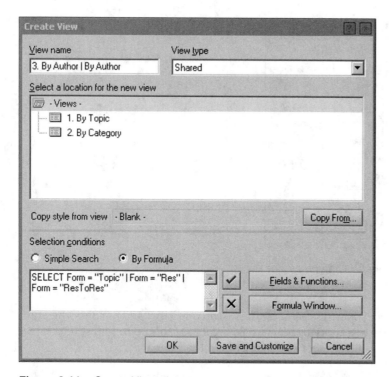

Figure 9.11 Create View dialog

Column 1

This column will display the total number of documents posted by an author. In this view, both the parent and Response documents will be grouped together based on the author's name. To compute the total number of documents, you'll use a built-in function that counts documents by category.

To configure this column, click on the predefined column header (#) and select the **Design > Column Properties** menu options. Set the column width to **2** on tab 1. Then switch to tab 2 and change the **Totals** field from **None** to **Total**. Also select the **Hide detail rows** option (see Figure 9.12).

Next, change the Language Selector from **Simple Function** to **Formula** and add the following in the Programmer's pane.

1

At this point, you've configured the column to count the documents associated with an author. However, for the count to be accurate, the view properties will also need to be modified. Otherwise, the count total will be incorrect.

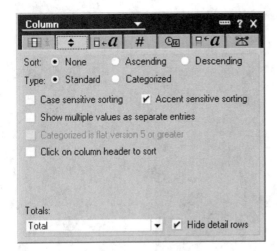

Figure 9.12   Sort tab of the Column properties dialog

Select the **Design > View Properties** menu options. Switch to tab 2 and uncheck the **Show response documents in a hierarchy** option (see Figure 9.13). This option must be disabled in order to correctly count the number of documents in the category.

Figure 9.13   Information tab of the View properties dialog

Column 2
This column will display the author's name. Select the **Create > Append New Column** menu options.

In the properties dialog, set the column width to **1** and select the **Show twistie when row is expandable** option. On tab 2, set the sort order to **Ascending** and **Categorized**. Next, switch to tab 3 and set the font text color to **Blue** and **Bold**.

Next, change the Language Selector from **Simple Function** to **Formula** and add the following in the Programmer's pane.

```
@Name([CN]; Authors)
```

Column 3

This column is used to sort documents in the view and will be hidden. Select the **Create > Append New Column** menu options.

In the properties dialog, set the column width to **1**, set the sort type to **Ascending** in tab 2, and select the **Hide column** option in tab 6.

Next, select **Creation Date** as the simple function in the Programmer's pane.

```
Creation Date
```

Column 4

This column will display all parent documents. Select the **Create > Append new column** menu options to add a new column.

In the properties dialog, set the column title to **Topic**, set the width to **45** on tab 1, and close the properties dialog.

Then change the Language Selector from **Simple Function** to **Fields** and select the following in the Programmer's pane.

```
Topic
```

Action Buttons

To complete the view, two action buttons need to be added—New Topic and Reply. These buttons will allow the user to click on a button to add a new parent, child, or grandchild topic to the discussion forum. Select **Create > Insert Shared Action** to add these buttons. When the popup dialog box displays, insert first the **New Topic** button followed by the **Reply** button. Click **Done** after the buttons have been added.

Save and close the view.

Create the Subscriptions Administration View

The Subscription view, along with the next three views, will be used to manage the discussion forum settings. This first view will allow users to register or subscribe to the discussion forum. Here, users can enable and disable notifications, select categories of interest, or remove themselves altogether.

The By Author view will display documents grouped by author. Using this view, users will be able to find documents based on the person that posted the discussion topic. To create the view, select the **Create > Design > View** menu options.

When prompted, set the view name to **4. Admin\a. Subscriptions|Subscriptions**. Next, change the **Copy style from view** field to **-Blank-**. To set this value, click the **Copy From** button. Finally, change the selection conditions to **By Formula** and insert the following in the dialog box.

```
SELECT Form = "Subscribe"
```

> **NOTE**
>
> The backslash in the view name is used to create a cascaded view menu. This allows you to group related views together.

Click **Save and Customize** to create the view.

Column 1

This column will display all users that have subscribed to the forum. To configure this column, click on the predefined column header (#) and select the **Design > Column Properties** menu options. Set the column name to **Name** on tab 1. Switch to tab 2 and set the sort preference to **Ascending**.

Then change the Language Selector from **Simple Function** to **Fields** and select the following in the Programmer's pane.

```
Name
```

Column 2

This column will display the Lotus Notes email address setting for the user. Select the **Create > Append new column** menu options. In the properties dialog, set the column title to **Email** and width to **20**.

Then change the Language Selector from **Simple Function** to **Fields** and select the following in the Programmer's pane.

```
NotesMail
```

Action Buttons

To complete the view, you will need to add the Subscribe action button to the view. To add the button, select **Create > Insert Shared Action**. When the popup dialog box displays, select and insert the Subscribe button.

Save and close the view.

Create the Categories Administration View

This view will display all discussion forum categories. The contents of this view will also be used to populate the Category combobox on the Topic forum. To create the view, select the **Create > Design > View** menu options.

When prompted, set the view name to **4. Admin\b. Categories|Category**. Next, change the **Copy style from view** field to **-Blank-**. To set this value, click the **Copy From** button. Finally, change the selection conditions to **By Formula** and insert the following in the dialog box.

```
SELECT Form = "Cat"
```

Click **Save and Customize** to create the view.

Column 1

This column will display all categories for the forum. To configure this column, click on the predefined column header (#) and select the **Design > Column Properties** menu options. Set the column name to **Category** on tab 1 and column width to **20** on tab 1. Switch to tab 2 and set the sort preference to **Ascending**.

Then change the Language Selector from **Simple Function** to **Fields** and select the following in the Programmer's pane.

```
Category
```

Action Button

To complete the view, we'll add the New Category action button to the view. To add the button, select **Create > Insert Shared Action**. When the popup dialog box displays, select and insert this button.

> **NOTE**
>
> The New Category button will not display when running the database in Local mode. This button will only display when the application is running on the server and the user has been assigned the "Admin" role. We'll explain how to create a role later in the project.
>
> However, by selecting the **Enforce consistent ACL** option on the Advanced tab of the ACL properties, the users with the "Admin" role will be able to see the button.

Save and close the view.

Create the Email Queue Administration View

This view will be used for server-based email notifications. This view will contain a list of all newly posted topics that have yet to be sent to the list of forum subscribers. Specifically, the view will contain all documents whose status flag is set to "POSTED".

A scheduled agent will then query this view on a regular interval (say every five minutes). If documents are found in the view, the agent will notify all forum subscribers, change the status flag to "COMPLETE", and remove the document from the view. To create the view, select the **Create > Design > View** menu options.

When prompted, set the view name to **4. Admin\c. Email Queue|EmailQue**. Next, change the **Copy style from view** field to **-Blank-**. To set this value, click the **Copy From** button. Finally, change the selection conditions to **By Formula** and insert the following in the dialog box.

```
SELECT Form = "Topic" | Form = "Res" | Form = "ResToRes"
```

Click **Save and Customize** to create the view.

After the view is created, select the **Design > View Properties** menu options. Switch to tab 2 and uncheck the **Show response documents in hierarchy** option. This step is very important. If you miss this step, all child and grandchild documents will be omitted from the email queue.

Column 1

This column will display the author of the discussion topic. In the properties dialog, set the column title to **Author**.

Make sure the Language Selector is set to **Simple Function** and select the following value in the Programmer's pane.

```
Author(s)  (Simple Name)
```

Column 2

This column will display the creation date for the discussion forum topic. Select the **Create > Append New Column** menu options to add the column. In the properties dialog, set the column title to **Created On** and width to **14**.

Make sure the Language Selector is set to **Simple Function** and select the following value.

```
Creation Date
```

Column 3

The last column for the view will display the title of the discussion topic. Select the **Create > Append New Column** menu options to add the column. In the properties dialog, set the column title to **Topic** and width to **40**. In the Programmer's pane, change the display type to **Field** and select the following value.

```
Topic
```

Save and close the view.

Create an Email Scheduled Agent

This section describes how to create a scheduled agent used to manage server-based email notifications for new discussion topics. This agent can be implemented in lieu of the `SendNotication` subroutine call in the `QueryClose` event for parent, child, and grand-child forms. To create the agent, select the **Create > Design > Agent** menu options.

After the agent is created, the properties dialog will display. Set the agent name to **SendNewPostings** and select **On schedule** as the trigger type (see Figure 9.14).

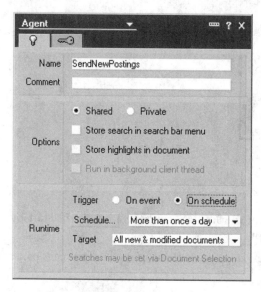

Figure 9.14 Agent properties dialog

Next, click the Schedule to set the run frequency. This will display a secondary dialog window. Set the agent to run on five-minute intervals and also change the field **Run on** to **-Any Server-**.

> **NOTE**
>
> It's very important to use the correct setting in the **Run on** field. This value must be set to **-Any Server-** or to a specific server name for the scheduled agent to run (see Figure 9.15).

Click **OK** to accept the schedule settings and close the agent properties dialog window.

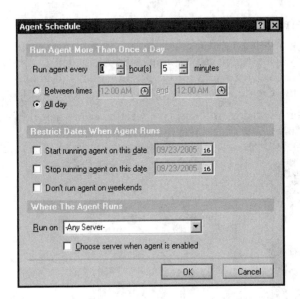

Figure 9.15   Schedule settings for an agent

Agent LotusScript Routine

The next step will be to create the LotusScript routines for the scheduled agent. Start by changing the Language Selector to **LotusScript**.

Next, insert the following LotusScript code in the **(Options)** section of the Programmer's pane.

```
Option Public
USE "DiscussionForum"
```

Add the following code in the `Initialize` section.

```
Sub Initialize

   Call SendNewPostings

End Sub
```

Save and close the agent.

> **NOTE**
>
> For this agent to run correctly on the server, you will need to "sign" the agent using either the server root certificate or an ID that has sufficient rights to run restricted agents on the server. If the agent is not signed or the last person to edit the agent has insufficient authority to run agents on the server, then the scheduled agent will not run. Contact your Domino server administrator to ensure that the agent is signed with an authorized ID. See Chapter 19, "Security," for additional information regarding application security.

Security

Now that the database design is complete, the last step is to configure the database security settings in the ACL. As mentioned at the start of this project, this application applies some granularity to the security using "roles" to manage who can create categories.

Select the **File** > **Database** > **Access Control** menu options. By default, the Basics tab should be active. Click on the **-Default-** user in the center of the screen. Change the access field (right side) to **Author**. Also select the **Create Documents** and **Delete Documents** checkboxes. These options will allow only the author of the appointment and anyone listed in the editors field to modify or delete the appointment.

Next, identify the person who will manage the application. Click the **Add** button (located at the bottom of the ACL dialog window) to add a user. After the user has been added, give the person **Editor** access and select the **[Admin]** role.

Congratulations, the project is now complete (see Figure 9.16)!

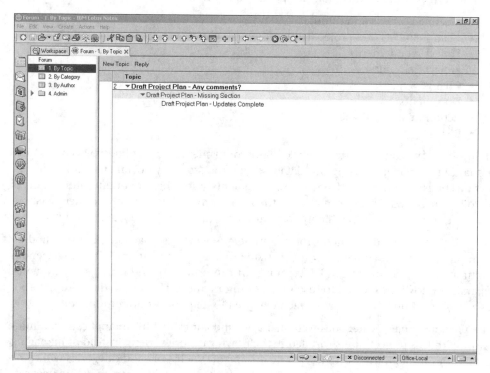

Figure 9.16   Completed project

Project B: Build a Project Control Notebook

Difficulty Level:	Easy
Completion Time:	3 hours
Project Materials:	4 Forms, 5 Action Buttons, 4 Shared Fields, 9 Views
Languages Used:	Formula Language, LotusScript
Possible Usages:	Project management, department meetings, audit readiness

Application Architecture

Another type of collaborative tool is a project control notebook—an electronic file cabinet for project materials. Managers and team members can use this tool to track and share project information. It provides a central location to store and retrieve information associated with a project. Features of this tool include the ability to track

- Meeting agendas and minutes
- Team members and project contacts (email, phone, etc.)
- Project requirements
- Project deliverables
- Change requests
- Documents
- Action items and issues
- Risks

Such information is often critical to track. Many companies implement business control and compliance requirements. Using this database, you can store key documents and track customer meetings, action items, deliverables, agreements, and other important information as the project progresses. This information is then readily available as new team members join the project or in the event that a corporate auditor requires project documentation.

This project includes four unique forms, numerous views, and an alternate method to dynamically manage document categories. Using this tool, users can track meeting agendas and minutes, store documents, track team member information, and manage action items. A separate form will be created for each type of information. The application also incorporates a significant number of views—each designed to help users find information.

In the previous project, categories were managed and controlled by an application administrator. With this project, users can define their own categories. Here, instead of managing the categories through the use of a separate document, the list of valid categories will come directly from existing documents in the database. We'll also enable users to define new categories that will automatically display on forms.

The ability to find information is key to the successful implementation and use of any software application. As such, this project includes a considerable number of views. These views allow users to quickly search for documents based on different criteria or keywords.

Like the previous project, the project control notebook implements a main document and Response document architecture. In this case, the Meeting form will be the main or parent document, and the Action Item form will be the response or child document. This will enable action items to be grouped with meetings.

Create the Database

To start this project, launch the Lotus Domino Designer client. When the Designer client is running, select the **File** > **Database** > **New** menu options. Specify an application title and file name (see Figure 9.17). Be sure to select **-Blank-** as the template type.

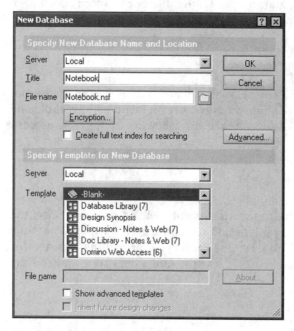

Figure 9.17 New Database dialog

Create the Shared Action Buttons

This project will include five shared action buttons—Edit, Save, Close, Attach File, and Action Item. These buttons will be used throughout the application to help the user manage the various transactions within the application.

Edit Button

The Edit button will change the document from read mode to edit mode. Select the **Create** > **Design** > **Shared Action** menu options and name the button **Edit**. Now switch to tab 2 in the properties dialog and select both the **Previewed for editing** and **Opened for editing** checkboxes. Close the properties dialog and add the following to the Programmer's pane. After the code has been added, save and close the action.

```
@Command([EditDocument])
```

Save Button

The Save button will cause the document to be saved to the database. This button will only display if the document is in edit mode. Select the **Create > Design > Shared Action** menu options and name the button **Save**. Now switch to tab 2 in the properties dialog and select both the **Previewed for reading** and **Opened for reading** checkboxes. Close the properties dialog and add the following to the Programmer's pane. After the code has been added, save and close the action.

```
@Command([FileSave])
```

Close Button

The Close button, as the name implies, closes the document and returns the user to the previously opened view. Select the **Create > Design > Shared Action** menu options and name the button **Close**. Close the properties dialog and add the following to the Programmer's pane.

```
@Command([FileCloseWindow])
```

Attach File Button

The Attach File button is used to add a file to the Attachments field on the form. Select the **Create > Design > Shared Action** menu options and name the button **Attach File**. Now switch to tab 2 in the properties dialog and select the **Previewed for reading, Opened for reading,** and **Previewed for editing** checkboxes. Close the properties dialog and add the following to the Programmer's pane.

```
@Command ([EditGotoField]; "Attachments");
@Command ([EditInsertFileAttachment])
```

Action Item Button

The Action Item button is used to create a new project task. The Action Item form is configured as a "response" document so that tasks can be associated and displayed with meetings. Select the **Create > Design > Shared Action** menu options and name the button **Action Item**. Close the properties dialog and add the following to the Programmer's pane.

```
@PostedCommand([Compose]; "Action")
```

Create the Shared Fields

This project utilizes four shared fields—Authors, Subject, Attachments, and Body. These fields are used throughout the application. To create the shared field, select the **Create > Design > Shared Field** menu options for each of the following fields. Be sure to set the data type and default value formula for each shared field. After the shared field is created, you may close the window and create the next shared field.

Field Name	Type	Default Value Formula	Remarks
Authors	Authors, Computed when composed	`@Name ([Abbreviate]; @UserName)`	
Subject	Text, Editable		
Body	Rich Text, Editable		
Attachments	Rich Text, Editable		
Created	Date/Time, Computed when composed	`@Now`	On tab 2, select the **Display Time** setting. Make sure both the date and time options are selected.
Updated	Date/Time, Computed	`value := @If (@IsDocBeingEdited; @Now; Updated); value`	On tab 2, select the **Display Time** setting. Make sure both the date and time options are selected.

Create the Meeting Form

This form will be used to track meeting agendas and minutes. To create the form, select the **Create > Design > Form** menu options. After the form has been created, add a descriptive text title such as **Meeting** at the top of the form and the following field labels down the left side of the form.

- Subject:
- Location:
- Date:
- Time:
- Chair:
- Agenda:
- Minutes:

Next, add the fields as specified in the following table. To create a field, select the **Create > Field** menu options. Be sure to set the data type, formula, and other attributes for each field on the form using the properties dialog box and/or Programmer's pane.

Field Name	Type	Default Value Formula	Remarks
Subject	Text, Editable		
Location	Text, Editable		
MtgDate	Date/Time, Editable	`@Today`	On tab 1, select the **Calendar/Time control** option.
MtgTime	Date/Time, Editable		On tab 1, select the **Calendar/Time control** option. On Tab 2 select the **Display Time** setting and *uncheck* the **Display Date** option.
Chair	Text, Editable	`@Name ([Abbreviate]; @UserName)`	
Agenda	Rich Text, Editable		Add the field just below the text label.
Minutes	Rich Text, Editable		Add the field just below the text label.
Key	Text, Computed	`@Text(MtgDate)+" - "+Subject`	Make this the very last field on the form. Ensure that no other fields are on the same row. Set this field to be hidden in tab 6 of the properties dialog. Check the **Hide paragraph if formula is true** checkbox and set the formula to 1. Change the font color of the field to **RED** to indicate that this is a hidden field.

Select the **Design > Form Properties** menu options to display the properties dialog for the form. Set the form name to **Project Meeting|Meeting** and select the **Automatically refresh fields** option on tab 1.

Next, select the **Create > Action > Insert Shared Action** menu options and insert the shared action buttons. This form will include the **Edit, Save, Close**, and **Action Item** buttons. The subform should now look like Figure 9.18.

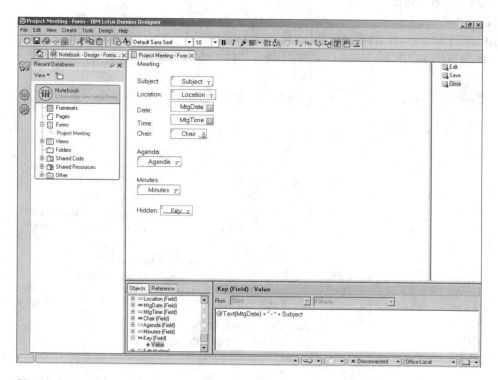

Figure 9.18   Project Meeting form

Save and close the form.

Create the Project Document Form

This form will be used to store project-related documents. This form allows text or file attachments to be stored in the document. This offers the flexibility to accommodate a variety of project materials. To create the form, click the **New Form** button or select the **Create > Design > Form** menu options. After the form has been created, add a descriptive title such as **Project Document** at the top of the form and the following field labels down the left side of the form.

- Title:
- Category:
- Company:
- Created:
- Updated:
- Details:
- Attachments:

Next, add the fields as specified in the following table. To create a field, select the **Create >
Field** menu options. Be sure to set the data type, formula, and other attributes for each field
on the form using the properties dialog box and/or Programmer's pane.

Field Name	Type	Default Value Formula	Remarks
Subject	Text, Editable		

Category	Dialog List, Editable	Class :="";
		Cache := "NoCache";
		Host := "";
		View := "Category";
		Column := 1;
		  output := @Unique(
		  @DbColumn(Class :
		  Cache; Host; view ;
		  Column));
		  @If (output = "";
		  "General"; output)
		Add this formula to the properties dialog as outlined in the remarks.
			Select **Allow multiple values** on tab 1. Select **Allow values not in list** on tab 2. Change the choice type to **Use formula for choices** and add the formula to the associated field.

Company	Dialog List, Editable	Class :="";
		Cache := "NoCache";
		Host := "";
		View := "Team";
		Column := 1;
		  output := @Unique(
		  @DbColumn(Class :
		  Cache; Host; view ;
		  Column));
		@If (output = "";
		  ""; output)
		Add this formula to the properties dialog as outlined in the remarks.
			Select **Allow multiple values** on tab 1. Select **Allow values not in list** on tab 2. Change the choice type to **Use formula for choices** and add the formula to the associated field.

The remaining fields on the form will be shared fields. Select the **Create > Resource > Insert shared field** menu options. Add the Created, Updated, Body, and Attachments fields.

Shared Actions

To complete the form, add the **Edit**, **Save**, **Close**, and **Attach File** shared action buttons. Select the **Create > Action > Insert Shared Action** menu options and insert the buttons. The form should now look similar to Figure 9.19.

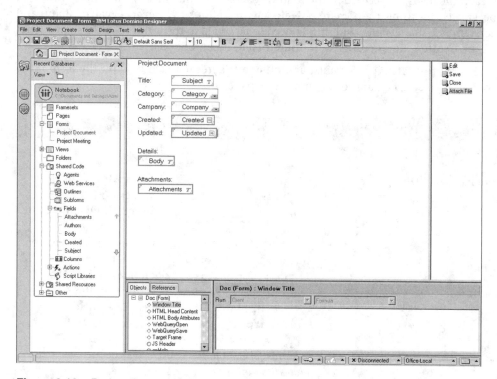

Figure 9.19 Project Document form

Save and close the form. When prompted, name the form **Project Document|Doc**.

Create the Action Item Form

This form is used to assign and track project action items. To create the form, click the **New Form** button or select the **Create > Design > Form** menu options. After the form has been created, add a descriptive title such as **Action Item** at the top of the form and the following field descriptions down the left side of the form.

- Subject:
- Owner:

- Status:
- Open Date:
- Due Date:
- Close Date:
- Details:
- Attachments:

Next, add the fields as specified in the following table. The majority of these fields will need to be created by using the **Create > Field** menu options. However, Created, Body, and Attachment are shared fields and simply need to be added to the form. To add a shared field, select the **Create > Resource > Insert Shared Field** menu options.

Be sure to set the data type, formula, and other attributes for each field on the form using the properties dialog box and/or Programmer's pane.

Field Name	Type	Default Value Formula	Remarks
Subject	Text, Editable		

Contact	Dialog List, Editable	Class := "";
		Cache := "NoCache";
		Host := "";
		View := "Team";
		Column := 2;
		output := @Unique(
		  @DbColumn(Class :
		  Cache; Host; view ;
		  Column));
		@If (output = "";
		  ""; output)
		Add this formula to the properties dialog as outlined in the remarks.
			Select **Allow multiple values** on tab 1. Select **Allow values not in list** on tab 2. Change the choice type to **Use formula for choices** and add the formula to the associated field.

Status	Combobox	Open In Progress Closed *Add these choices to the Field properties dialog on tab 2.*	On tab 2, add the choices to the Field properties dialog.
Created			This is a shared field. Add this field to the form.

Field Name	Type	Default Value Formula	Remarks
DueDate	Date/Time, Editable		On tab 1, select **Calendar/Time control** for the style.
CloseDate	Date/Time, Editable		On tab 1, select **Calendar/Time control** for the style.
Body			This is a shared field. Add this field to the form.
Attachments			This is a shared field. Add this field to the form.
Key	Text, Computed, Hidden Field	@If (@IsResponseDoc ; ""; Key)	Make this the very last field on the form. Ensure that no other fields are on the same row. Set this field to be hidden in tab 6 of the properties dialog. Check the **Hide paragraph if formula is true** checkbox and set the formula to 1. Change the font color of the field to **RED** to indicate that this is a hidden field.

Next, add the **Edit, Save, Close,** and **Attach File** shared action buttons to the form. Select the **Create > Action > Insert Shared Action** menu options and insert the buttons. The form should now look similar to Figure 9.20.

Action items can be created from the application menu, from the action item view, or from within a meeting document. When called from the meeting document, action items will be associated with the meeting and appear in the Meetings view. For this to work, the Key field will need to be set. This can be achieved through inheritance.

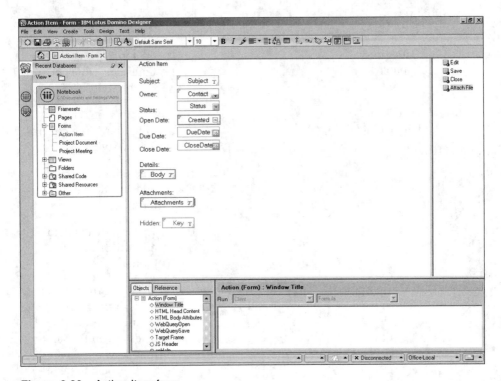

Figure 9.20   Action Item form

To inherit field values, select the **Design > Form Properties** menu options. On tab 1, name the form **Action Item|Action**. Switch to tab 2 and select the **Formulas inherit values from selected form** option. Save and close the form.

Create the Team Member Form

This form is used to document all team members associated with the project. To create the form, select the **Create > Design > Form** menu options. After the form has been created, add a descriptive title such as **Team Member** at the top of the form and the following field descriptions down the left side of the form.

- Contact:
- Email:
- Title:
- Phone:
- Company:

Next, add the fields as specified in the following table. To create the fields, select the **Create** > **Field** menu options. Be sure to set the data type, formula, and other attributes for each field on the form using the properties dialog box and/or Programmer's pane.

Field Name	Type	Default Value Formula	Remarks
Contact	Names, Editable		Select **Use address dialog for choices** on tab 2.
Email	Text, Editable		
Title	Text, Editable		
Phone	Text, Editable		

Company	Dialog List, Editable	`Class :="";`
		`Cache := "NoCache";`
		`Host := "";`
		`View := "Team";`
		`Column := 1;`
		`output := @Unique(`
		`  @DbColumn( Class :`
		`  Cache; Host; view ;`
		`  Column ));`
		`@If (output = ""; "";`
		`  output)`
			Select **Allow values not in list** on tab 2. Change the choice type to **Use formula for choices** and add the formula to the associated field.

Next, add the **Edit**, **Save**, and **Close** shared action buttons. Select the **Create** > **Action** > **Insert Shared Action** menu options and insert the buttons. The form should now look similar to Figure 9.21.

Save and close the form. When prompted, name the form **Team Member|Person**.

Create the Meeting View

By default, a view called *(untitled)* was automatically created when the database was first created. To configure this view, navigate to Views in the Design pane and double-click on the view called "(untitled)".

When the view is displayed, the Designer client will immediately display the properties dialog for the view. Specify **1. Meetings** in the name field and **Meeting** in the alias field. The view has been named, so you can close the dialog window.

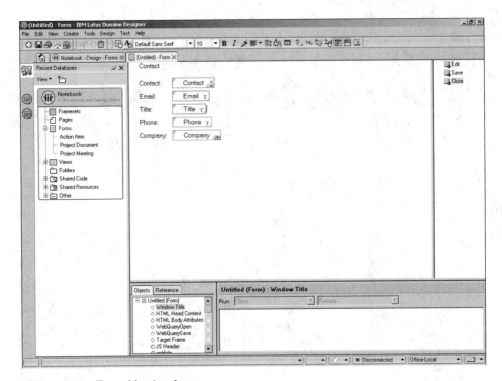

Figure 9.21   Team Member form

Column 1

This first column displays the meeting date and subject. This is a categorized column in which the meeting and related action items will be grouped together. In order to group the related documents, both documents will use the Key field because both documents have this field in common.

To configure this column, click on the predefined column header (#) and select the **Design > Column Properties** menu options. Set the column name to **Document** and column width to **2** and select **Show twistie when row is expandable**. Switch to tab 2. Set the sort order to **Descending** and the sort type as **Categorized** in tab 2. Set the text type as **Bold** and text color as **Blue** on tab 3.

Next, change the Language Selector from **Simple Function** to **Field** and select the following in the Programmer's pane.

```
Key
```

Column 2

This column will display either the Meeting or Action Item documents. Select the **Create >
Append New Column** menu options to add the column. Change the display type from
Simple Function to **Formula** and add the following value.

```
Form
```

Column 3

This column will display the subject line for the meeting or action item. Because both forms
contain this field, you can use the Subject field to populate the column. Select the **Create >
Append New Column** menu options to add the column. In the properties dialog, set the
column name to **Subject** and column width to **40**. Then change the Language Selector from
Simple Function to **Field** and select the following value.

```
Subject
```

View Selection Formula

To complete the view, add the view selection criteria. To set the view selection formula, click
inside the view (as opposed to a column header) to give the view focus. Locate the View
Selection section of the Programmer's pane. Change the Language Selector from **Simple
Search** to **Function** and add the following.

```
SELECT (Form = "Action" | Form = "Meeting") & Key != ""
```

Save and close the view.

Create the Documents By Category View

This view will display documents based on the document category such as design requirements, schedules, and test plans or similar category. After it is created, this view will be used
as a basis for the next—By Person. Both views contain the same information, simply sorted
and presented differently. To expedite the application development process, you will copy
the view and make minor adjustments to build the remaining "document" views. To create
the By Category view, select the **Create > Design > View** menu options.

When prompted, set the view name to **2. Documents\By Category**. Next, change the **Copy
style from view** field to **-Blank-**. To set this value, click the **Copy From** button. Finally,
change the selection conditions to **By Formula** and insert the following in the dialog box.

```
SELECT Form = "Doc"
```

Click **Save and Customize** to create the view and open it in edit mode.

Column 1

This column will display the various document categories. Click on the column header and
select the **Design > Column Properties** menu options. Set the column width to **2** and select
Show twistie when row is expandable in tab 1. Switch to tab 2. Set the sort order to

Descending and the sort type as **Categorized**. Switch to tab 3. Set the text type as **Bold** and text color as **Blue** on tab 3. Change the Language Selector to **Field** and select the following in the Programmer's pane.

```
Category
```

Column 2

The second column will display the document title. Select the **Create > Append New Column** menu options to add the column. In the properties dialog, set the column name to **Title** and the column width to **30**. Change the Language Selector to **Field** and select the following in the Programmer's pane.

```
Subject
```

Column 3

The last column will display the company responsible for the document. Select the **Create > Append New Column** menu options to add the column. In the properties dialog, set the column name to **Company** and set the field value to the following.

```
Company
```

Save and close the view.

Create the Documents By Date View

This view will display documents based on the creation date. You will use the previously created view as the basis for this view. This is achieved by making a copy of the By Topic view and then modifying it.

In the Design pane, highlight the **2. Documents\By Category** view design element and select the **Edit > Copy** menu options. Now select the **Edit > Paste** menu options. Double-click on the copy to open it in design mode. In the properties dialog, change the view title to **2. Documents\By Date** and the view alias to **Date**.

Column 1

The first column will contain the creation date for the document. This will be a new column. Select **Create > Insert New Column** to add the column. Next, edit the column properties. Set the column name to **Date** in the properties dialog. Switch to tab 2 and set the sort order to **Descending**. Then change the Language Selector to **Formula** and add the following in the Programmer's pane.

```
@Date ( @Created )
```

Column 2

This column currently contains the document category. Click on the column to make it the active design element. In the properties dialog, set the column name to **Category** and width to **10** on tab 1. Switch to tab 2 and set the sort type to **None**.

Save and close the view.

Create the Action Items By Date View

This view will be included in the project notebook to track action items by person, date, and past due. To create the By Category view, select the **Create > Design > View** menu options.

When prompted, set the view name to **3. Action Items\By Date**. Next, change the **Copy style from view** field to **-Blank-**. To set this value, click the **Copy From** button. Finally, change the selection conditions to **By Formula** and insert the following in the dialog box.

```
SELECT Form = "Action"
```

Click **Save and Customize** to create the view and open it in edit mode. After the view is created, uncheck the option **Show response documents in hierarchy** in tab 2 of the properties dialog for the view.

Column 1

This column will display the action items by target due date. Click on the default column and select the **Design > Column Properties** menu options. In the properties dialog, name the column **Due Date** and set the column width to **7** in tab 1 and sort order to **Descending** in tab 2. To set the column value, change the Language Selector to **Field** and select the following in the Programmer's pane.

```
DueDate
```

Column 2

This column displays the contact name for the action item. Select the **Create > Append New Column** menu options to add the column. In the properties dialog, name the column **Contact**. To set the column value, change the Language Selector to **Field** and select the following in the Programmer's pane.

```
Contact
```

Column 3

Column three contains the action item status. Select the **Create > Append New Column** menu options to add the column. In the properties dialog, name the column **Status** and set the column width to **6**. To set the column value, change the Language Selector to **Field** and select the following in the Programmer's pane.

```
Status
```

Column 4

The last column in the view displays the descriptive title for the action item. Select the **Create > Append New Column** menu options to add the column. In the properties dialog, set the column name to **Subject** and width to **40**. To set the column value, change the Language Selector to **Field** and select the following in the Programmer's pane.

```
Subject
```

Save and close the view.

Create the Action Items By Person View

The second action item view will display all action items by the task owner. This will allow team members to track and monitor tasks that are assigned to them. To create this view, highlight the **3. Action Items\By Date** view and select the **Edit > Copy** menu options. Now select the **Edit > Paste** menu options. Double-click on the design element to open the view in design mode. When the view is open, rename the view title to **3. Action Items\By Person** in the properties dialog.

Using your mouse, click on the **Contact** header (column 2) and drag the column in front of column 1. This will make the **Contact** column the first column and **Due Date** the second column. Click on the header for column 1 to make it the active column.

Next, select the **Design > Column Properties** menu options. On tab 1, remove the column title, set the column width to **2**, and select the **Show twistie when row is expandable** option. Switch to tab 2. Set the sort order to **Ascending** and sort type as **Categorized**. Set the text type as **Bold** and text color as **Blue** on tab 3.

Save and close the view.

Create the Late Action Items View

The third action item view will show only those action items that are past due. This view will help project managers monitor past due tasks. From the Design pane, highlight the **3. Action Items\By Date** view design element and select the **Edit > Copy** menu options. Now select the **Edit > Paste** menu options. Double-click on the design element to open the view in design mode. In the properties dialog, rename name the view to **3. Action Items\Past Due**.

To complete the view, locate the View Selection section and add the following formula in the Programmer's pane.

```
SELECT form = "Action" & (@Today > DueDate) & (Status != "Closed")
```

Save and close the view.

Create the Team Member View

The Team Member view will show all people associated with the project. Team members will be grouped by company. This view will also include a button that enables users to create a memo to all team members selected in the view.

To create the view, select the **Create > Design > View** menu options. When prompted, set the view name to **4. Team Members|Team**. Next, change the **Copy style from view** field to **-Blank-**. To set this value, click the **Copy From** button. Finally, change the selection conditions to **By Formula** and insert the following in the dialog box.

```
SELECT Form = "Person"
```

Click **Save and Customize** to create the view and open it in edit mode.

Column 1

This column will display the company name. The column will be categorized and sorted in ascending order. This will enable all team members associated with a company to be grouped together. Click on the default column and select the **Design > Column Properties** menu options.

Next, remove the column title, set the width to **2**, and select the **Show twistie when row is expandable** option. Switch to tab 2. Set the sort order to **Ascending** and column type to **Categorized**. Switch to tab 3. Set the font style to **Bold** and select **Blue** as the color.

To set the column value, change the Language Selector to **Field** and select the following in the Programmer's pane.

```
Company
```

Column 2

This column will contain the team member's name. Select the **Create > Append New Column** menu options to add the column. In the properties dialog, set the column title to **Contact** on tab 1 and sort type to **Ascending** on tab 2. Close the properties dialog and set the column formula to the following.

```
Contact
```

Column 3

This column will contain the team member's email address. Select the **Create > Append New Column** menu options to add the column. In the properties dialog, name the column **Email** and set the width to **15** on the first property tab. Close the properties dialog and set the column formula to the following.

```
Email
```

Column 4

This column will contain the office phone number for the team member. Select the **Create > Append New Column** menu options to add the column. In the properties dialog, name the column **Phone**. Close the properties dialog and set the column formula to the following.

```
Phone
```

Action Button

The Create Email button, when clicked, will create an email and populate the Send To field with the email addresses for all selected team members in the view. This subroutine uses the `DocumentCollection` object to store all selected documents from the team member view. Using an iterative process, the email address from each team member is retrieved and then inserted into a memo.

A.9.2

To create the button, select the **Create > Action > Action** menu options and title the button **Create Email**. Close the properties dialog.

Change the programming language to **LotusScript** and add the following in the `Click` event of the Programmer's pane.

```
Sub Click(Source As Button)
    Dim s As NotesSession
    Dim db As NotesDatabase
    Dim Maildb As NotesDatabase
    Dim collection As NotesDocumentCollection
    Dim w As New NotesUIWorkspace
    Dim doc As NotesDocument
    Dim uidoc As NotesUIDocument
    Dim theList As Variant
    Dim MailServer As String
    Dim MailFile As String
    Set s = New NotesSession
    Set db = s.CurrentDatabase
    Set collection = db.UnprocessedDocuments
    If collection.count = 0 Then
        Messagebox("Please select at least one team member. ")
        Exit Sub
    Else
        theList = ""
        Set doc = collection.GetFirstDocument
        While Not( doc Is Nothing )
            theList = doc.Email(0) & ", " & theList
            Set doc = collection.GetNextDocument( doc )
        Wend
        MailServer$ = s.GetEnvironmentString ( "MailServer" , True )
        MailFile$ = s.GetEnvironmentString ( "MailFile" , True )
        Set mailDB = s.GetDatabase ( MailServer$ , MailFile$ )
        Call mailDB.OpenMail
        Set uidoc = w.ComposeDocument ( "", mailDB.FilePath, "Memo" )
        Call uidoc.FieldSetText( "EnterSendTo", theList )
        Call uidoc.Refresh
    End If
End Sub
```

Save and close the view.

Security

The project is complete after the ACL is defined for the project. To set the ACL settings, select the **File > Database > Access Control** menu options. By default, the Basics tab should be active. Click on the -**Default**- user in the center of the screen.

Next, change the Access field (right side) to **Author** and select both the **Create Documents** and **Delete Documents** checkboxes. These options will allow only the author of the appointment and anyone listed in the editors field to modify or delete the appointment.

Congratulations, the project is now complete (see Figure 9.22)!

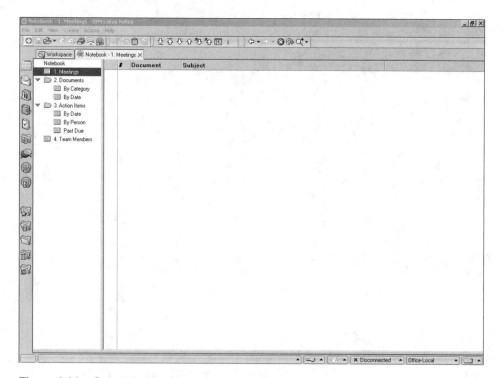

Figure 9.22   Completed project

Links to developerWorks

A.9.1 Green, Brian. Finding the Top-level document. IBM developerWorks, October 1998. http://www.ibm.com/developerworks/lotus/library/ls-Finding_the_ Top-level_Document/index.html.

A.9.2 Savir, Raphael. Lotus Notes/Domino 7 application performance: Part 1: Database properties and document collections. IBM developerWorks, January 2006. http://www.ibm.com/developerworks/lotus/library/notes7-application-performance1/index.html.

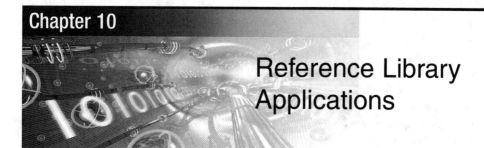

Chapter 10

Reference Library Applications

Chapter Overview

This chapter will focus on Reference Library applications. These applications are used to store information and tend to be used for reference purposes. This chapter includes two projects—a connection document manager and a spreadsheet report generator.

Reference Library applications can be used for a variety of purposes, such as to

- Store documents or files
- Store Web links
- Store lessons learned from projects
- Store labor hours
- Store postal codes
- Store names, addresses, and phone numbers
- Store and track company assets

By the end of the chapter you will have learned

- How to import and send connection documents
- How to send a connection document to a coworker
- How to send a form through email
- How to build a button to query a Domino server
- How to generate spreadsheets from a database view
- How to attach a file to an email
- How to remove a character from a string
- How to store a form in the document

Reference Library Applications

In general, Reference Library applications can be quickly and easily built. This type of application typically stores static or historical information and tends to be used for reference purposes. In many cases, the application simply contains a form and view and can be built in a few hours.

This chapter includes two projects. The first project is designed to manage server connection documents. Connection documents are used by the Lotus Notes client and typically correct the error "Unable to find path to server." This is a common problem encountered by users when multiple Domino servers are implemented.

The second project builds Microsoft Excel spreadsheets from any Lotus Notes view. This project supplements Reference Library applications. Here, users select a default view to be used to build the spreadsheet. The routine then calculates the number of columns, column names, and column widths to build a spreadsheet report. All columns that contain a field value are then added to the spreadsheet. When complete, this LotusScript library can be added to any new or existing Notes application.

> **NOTE**
>
> You must have the Microsoft Office and Excel applications installed in order to generate spreadsheets from Lotus Notes database applications.

Project A: Build a Connection Document Database

Difficulty Level:	Easy
Completion Time:	2 hours
Project Materials:	2 Forms, 1 View, 10 Action Buttons, 1 Role
Languages Used:	Formula Language, LotusScript
Possible Usages:	Management of server connection documents

Architecture

This Reference Library application is designed to manage Lotus Notes connections to company-wide Domino servers. In many cases, companies utilize multiple Domino servers to host Lotus Notes applications. However, unless each server is located in the same Lotus Notes domain, users often receive the error "Unable to find path to server" when trying to open a database link.

Lotus Notes users typically receive this message because the client is unable to resolve, or figure out, the server address. In technical terms, the server address is referred to as either the Fully Qualified Domain Name (e.g., server01.raleigh.ibm.com) or the Internet Protocol Address (e.g., 9.1.67.100). In most cases, the creation of a server connection document will correct this error message and enable the user to connect to the server application.

Connection documents are stored in the user's Personal Address Book (PAB) in the Lotus Notes client. Here's how they work. When the user attempts to access a server, or an application on a server, the client checks the PAB for the server address. If the server information is found, then the Lotus Notes client uses this information to connect to the server. If the server information is not stored in the PAB, then a general query (also known as a network broadcast) is sent across the network to try to find the server address. If the server address cannot be determined, then the "Unable to find path to server" message is displayed.

This application offers one solution to manage Domino server connection documents. The purpose of this application is to provide a simple method to create, manage, and distribute IP addresses to the Lotus Notes client. Features of this application include

- A central repository of server connection information
- The ability for administrators to add and update server connections
- The ability for anyone to send a connection document to a coworker
- The ability for anyone to import or refresh existing server connections

Using this program, users can send or retrieve the most current connection documents and have them stored in their PAB. In most cases, this will ensure that users can access a server or a database on that server.

There are three primary features for this application—managing connection documents, sending a single connection document, and importing all connection documents. First, this application restricts the ability to create or edit connection document information. Only application administrators will have this authority. Second, anyone will have the authority to select a connection document and email it to a coworker. Finally, the application will include a feature to update or refresh all server connection documents that are stored in the user's PAB.

Create the Database

To start this project, launch the Lotus Domino Designer client. When the Designer client is running, select the **File > Database > New** menu options. Specify an application title and file name (see Figure 10.1). Be sure to select **-Blank-** as the template type.

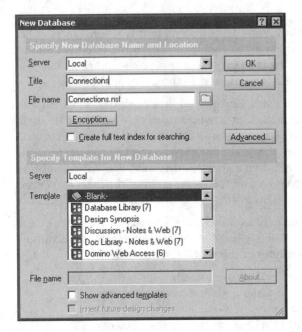

Figure 10.1   New Database dialog

Set the Database Roles

After the database is created, start by establishing the roles associated with the database. Roles enable specific people to perform actions that others cannot. In this case, the "Admin" role will enable the application administrator to create new server connection documents. Anyone who does not have this role will not have this authority.

To create the role, select the **File > Database > Access Control** menu options. By default, the Basics tab should be active. Switch to the **Roles** tab and select the **Add** button (located at the bottom of the dialog window).

This will display a new popup window called Add Role (see Figure 10.2). Type **Admin** and click the **OK** button to add the role.

Click **OK** a second time to close the Access Control List (ACL) window.

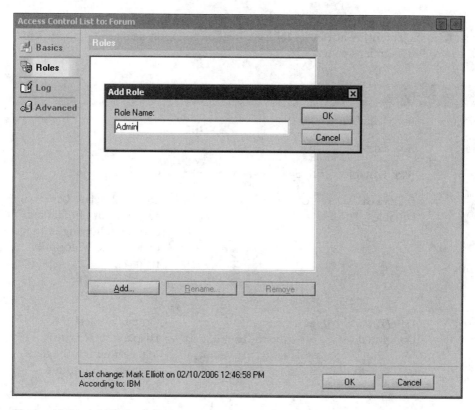

Figure 10.2 Add Role dialog

Create the Connection Form

This form is used to store Domino server connection information and includes five fields—server name, Internet Protocol (or fully qualified domain) address, port, connect type, and updates. These fields will be used to build or update server connection documents in the user's PAB. All fields on the form are required. The general public will be able to open the documents. Only users assigned the "Admin" role will be permitted to create or update connection information in the database.

To create the form, select the **Create > Design > Form** menu options. Give the form a descriptive title at the top of the form—such as **Domino Server Connection**—and add the following text field descriptions down the left side of the form.

- Server Name:*
- Server IP:*
- Connect Type:*
- Connect Port:*
- Last Updated:

Next, create the following fields using the **Create > Field** menu options. Be sure to set the data type, formula, and other attributes for each field on the form using the properties dialog box and/or Programmer's pane.

Field Name	Type	Default Value Formula	Remarks
ServerName	Text, Editable		
ServerIP	Text, Editable		
Type	Text, Editable	`"Local Area Network"`	
Port	DialogList, Editable	`"TCPIP"`	On tab 2, select **Use formula for choices** and add the following in the dialog window formula field. `@GetPortsList ([Enabled])`
Updated	Date/Time, Computed	`value := @If (@IsDocBeingEdited; @Now; @ThisValue); value`	On tab 2, select the **Display Time** setting. Make sure both the date and time options are selected.

QuerySave Event

The `QuerySave` event will be used to verify that all required fields contain a valid value. In this case, the subroutine verifies that none of the fields are blank. Using the `Continue` built-in design flag, the document can only be saved if this variable contains a `True` value at the completion of the subroutine. If any field contains an invalid value—blank in this case—the `Continue` variable is set to `False`, and the document is not saved. Locate the `QuerySave` event found in the Objects pane for the form and insert the following code.

```
Sub Querysave(Source As Notesuidocument, Continue As Variant)

    Dim doc As NotesDocument
    Dim MsgText As String
    Set doc = source.Document
    Continue = True
    MsgText = ""

    If Trim(Doc.ServerName(0)) = "" Then
        MsgText = MsgText + "Specify a Server Name." + Chr$(13)
    End If

    If Trim(Doc.ServerIP(0)) = "" Then
```

```
      MsgText = MsgText + "Specify an IP Address." + Chr$(13)
   End If

   If Trim(Doc.Type(0)) = "" Then
      MsgText = MsgText + "Specify a Connect Type." + Chr$(13)
   End If

   If Trim(Doc.Port(0)) = "" Then
      MsgText = MsgText + "Specify a Connect Port." + Chr$(13)
   End If

   If MsgText <> "" Then
      Msgbox MsgText,16,"Required Fields."
      Continue = False
   End If

End Sub
```

The next step will be to create the action buttons for the form—Edit, Save, Close, and Query Server. These buttons will manage the various document transactions within the application.

Edit Button

The Edit button will change the document from read mode to edit mode. Select the **Create > Action > Action** menu options and name the button **Edit**. Now switch to tab 2 in the properties dialog and select both the **Previewed for editing** and **Opened for editing** checkboxes. Close the properties dialog and add the following to the Programmer's pane. After the code has been added, save and close the action.

```
@Command([EditDocument])
```

Save Button

The Save button will cause the document to be saved to the database. This button will only display if the document is in edit mode. Select the **Create > Action > Action** menu options and name the button **Save**. Now switch to tab 2 in the properties dialog and select both the **Previewed for reading** and **Opened for reading** checkboxes. Close the properties dialog and add the following to the Programmer's pane. After the code has been added, save and close the action.

```
@Command([FileSave])
```

Close Button

The Close button, as the name implies, closes the document and returns the user to the previously opened view. Select the **Create > Action > Action** menu options and name the button **Close**. Close the properties dialog and add the following to the Programmer's pane.

```
@Command([FileCloseWindow])
```

Query Server Button

The Query Server button will issue the Ping command to query whether the server is connected to the network. The result of the query is displayed to the user in a text message.

Select the **Create > Action > Action** menu options. In the properties dialog, name the button **Query Server** and close the dialog window. Then, change the Language Selector from **Formula** to **LotusScript** and add the following in the Click event.

```
Sub Click(Source As Button)


    Dim w As New NotesUIWorkspace
    Dim uidoc As NotesUIDocument
    Dim doc As NotesDocument
    Dim statement As String
    Dim fileName As String
    Dim fileNum As Integer
    Dim result As String
    Dim text As String

    Set uidoc = w.CurrentDocument
    Set doc = uidoc.Document
    fileName$ = "c:\pingtext.txt"
    statement$ = "command.com /c ping " + _
        doc.ServerIP(0) + " > " + fileName$
    result = Shell ( statement, 6)
    Sleep( 10 )
    result = ""

    fileNum% = Freefile()
    Open fileName$ For Input As fileNum%
    Do While Not Eof( fileNum% )
        Line Input #fileNum%, text$
        result = result + text$ + Chr$(13 )
    Loop
    Close fileNum%
    Msgbox result , , "Result From Server Query"
    Kill fileName$

End Sub
```

The form should look like Figure 10.3 in the Lotus Domino Designer client.

To complete the form configuration, you will need to define who can create documents with this form. For this project, only those users assigned the "Admin" role will be able to create or modify documents. Select the **Design > Form Properties** menu options (see Figure 10.4).

Set the form name to **Connection|ConDoc** on tab 1 and then switch to tab 6. In the "**Who can create documents with this form**" section, uncheck the "**All authors and above**" option and select only the **[Admin]** option.

Save and close the form.

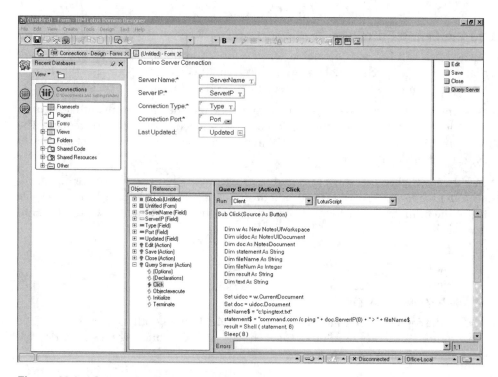

Figure 10.3 Connection Document form

Figure 10.4 Security tab of the Form properties dialog

Create the Memo Form

The Memo form will be used to email a server connection document to another person. When the server connection document is received, the recipient can use the Import Connection button to add or update the server connection document in their PAB.

All design information associated with the form will be included in the email that's sent to the user. The user will have the option to import the connection or cancel the request. The design information must be sent in the email in order for the Import and Cancel buttons to display in the user's mail database.

To create the form, click the **New Form** button or select the **Create > Design > Form** menu options. After the form has been created, add the following field label descriptions down the left side of the form, leaving a couple blank lines after the **Subject** and the **Instructions to recipient** label.

- Send To:
- Copy To:
- Subject:
- Instructions to recipient:

Next, create the following fields using the **Create > Field** menu options. Be sure to set the data type, formula, and other attributes for each field on the form using the properties dialog box and/or Programmer's pane.

Field Name	Type	Default Value Formula	Remarks
SendTo	Names, Editable	@UserName *By default, the email will be sent to the person sending the connection. If you do not want the "SendTo" field to have a default, remove this formula.*	Select **Allow multiple values** in tab 1 and Use **Address Dialog for choices** in tab 2.
CopyTo	Names, Editable		Select **Allow multiple values** in tab 1 and Use **Address Dialog for choices** in tab 2.
Subject	Text, Editable		

Body	Rich Text, Editable	`"This note contains a`
		`   Domino Server`
		`   Connection Document.`
		`   Select the 'Import`
		`   Connection Doc'" +`
		`@NewLine +`	

Field Name	Type	Default Value Formula	Remarks

		`"button in the action`
		`bar to import the`
		`document into your`
		`personal address book.`
		`In most cases," +`
		`@NewLine +`
		`"importing the`
		`connection document`
		`will resolve network`
		`connectivity problems`
		`associated with the`
		`" + @NewLine +`
		`"specified Lotus Notes`
		`server. " + @NewLine`
		`+ @NewLine`	

Sign	Text, Computed	`"1"`	Signs the memo email with the user ID credentials of the person sending the connection document. Create this field at the very bottom of the form. Change the font color of the field to **RED** to indicate that this is a hidden field.
SaveOptions	Text, Computed	`"0"`	Prevents the memo from being saved in the database. Add this field next to the Sign field. In tab 6, check the **Hide paragraph if formula is true** checkbox and set the formula to 1. Change the font color of the field to **RED** to indicate that this is a hidden field.

Create the Send Button

The Send button will transmit the server connection document to all people listed in the SendTo and CopyTo fields. This button will only be visible to the person sending the connection document and will not be visible to the email recipients. Select the **Create > Action > Action** menu options to create the button.

In the properties dialog, name the action button **Send**. Then switch to tab 2, check the **Hide paragraph if formula is true** checkbox, and set the formula to the following in the properties dialog. When complete, close the properties dialog.

```
!@IsNewDoc
```

Next, change the Language Selector from **Formula** to **LotusScript** and add the following in the Click event.

```
Sub Click(Source As Button)

   Dim w As New NotesUIWorkspace
   Dim uidoc As NotesUIDocument
   Set uidoc = w.CurrentDocument
   Call uidoc.Send
   Call uidoc.Close

End Sub
```

Create the Cancel Button

The Cancel button will cancel the current transaction. This button closes the current memo and also cancels the connection document import for the user who will eventually receive the memo. Select the **Create > Action > Action** menu options. In the properties dialog, name the action button **Cancel** and close the properties dialog. Next, add the following formula in the Programmer's pane.

```
@Command([FileCloseWindow])
```

Create the Import Connection Button

The Import Connection button updates the connection document information in the user's PAB. Select the **Create > Action > Action** menu options. In the properties dialog, name the action button **Import Connection**. Then switch to tab 2, check the **Hide paragraph if formula is true** checkbox, and set the formula to the following in the properties dialog. When complete, close the properties dialog.

```
@IsNewDoc
```

Next, change the Language Selector from **Formula** to **LotusScript** and add the following in the Click event.

```
Sub Click(Source As Button)

   Dim s As NotesSession
```

```
    Dim w As New NotesUIWorkspace
    Dim db As NotesDatabase
    Dim view As NotesView
    Dim uidoc As NotesUIDocument
    Dim docA As NotesDocument
    Dim docB As NotesDocument
    Dim answer as Integer
    Set uidoc = w.CurrentDocument
    Set docB = uidoc.Document
    Set s = New NotesSession
    Set db = New NotesDatabase ("", "Names.nsf")
    Set view = db.GetView ( "Connections" )
    Set docA = view.GetDocumentByKey ( docB.ServerName(0), True)


    '------------------------------
    ' Create document if none exist
    '------------------------------
    Dim docC As New NotesDocument( db )
    If docA Is Nothing Then
        docC.Form = "local"
        docC.Destination = docB.ServerName(0)
        docC.LanPortName = docB.Port(0)
        docC.PortName = docB.Port(0)
        docC.OptionalNetworkAddress = docB.ServerIP(0)
        docC.PhoneNumber= docB.ServerIP(0)
        docC.Type = "Connection"
        docC.ConnectionType = "0"
        docC.Source = "*"
        docC.ConnectionLocation = "*"
        docC.Save True, True
        Msgbox "Connection document created." , , "Success"
    Else
        '------------------------------
        ' Ask to replace document if one exists
        '------------------------------
        answer% = Msgbox ("An existing connection was found."+_
        "Replace the existing document?", 36, "Continue?")
        If answer% = 6 Then
            docA.Remove ( True )
            docC.Form = "local"
            docC.Destination = docB.ServerName(0)
            docC.LanPortName = docB.Port(0)
            docC.PortName = docB.Port(0)
            docC.OptionalNetworkAddress = docB.ServerIP(0)
            docC.PhoneNumber= docB.ServerIP(0)
            docC.Type = "Connection"
            docC.ConnectionType = "0"
            docC.Source = "*"
            docC.ConnectionLocation = "*"
            docC.Save True, True
            Msgbox "Connection document created." , , "Success"
        End If
    End If

End Sub
```

Update Form Properties

In order for the Import Connection and Cancel buttons to display in the user's memo, the design information for this form must be included in the email notification. This is accomplished through the properties dialog for the form.

Select the **Design > Form Properties** menu options (see Figure 10.5). Name the form **Memo|Memo**. Next, uncheck the **Include in menu** and **Include in Search Builder** options and select the **Store form in document** option.

Figure 10.5 Form properties dialog

The form should look similar to Figure 10.6.

Save and close the form.

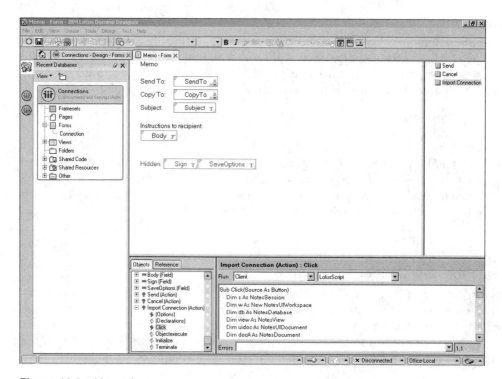

Figure 10.6 Memo form

Create the Servers View

By default, a view called *(untitled)* is automatically created when the database is first created. To configure this view, navigate to Views in the Design pane and double-click on the view called "(untitled)". When the view is displayed, the Designer client will immediately display the properties dialog for the view. Specify **Servers** as the view name and alias name. Close the properties dialog.

Column 1

This column will list the server name for all documents stored in the application database. Double-click on the default column and rename the column title to **Server** in the properties dialog. Switch to tab 2 and set the sort order to **Ascending**.

To set the column value, change the display type from **Simple Function** to **Field** and select the following field.

```
ServerName
```

Column 2

The second column will list the associated IP address or fully qualified domain name for the server. Select the **Create > Append New Column** menu options to add the column. In the properties dialog, set the column name to **Address** and column width to **20** on tab 1. Change the display type from **Simple Function** to **Field** and select the following field.

```
ServerIP
```

Column 3

The last column displays the last modification date of the connection document. Select the **Create > Append New Column** menu options to add the column. In the properties dialog, set the column name to **Updated** and width to **15** on tab 1. Change the display type from **Simple Function** to **Field** and select the following field.

```
Updated
```

Create the New Connection Button

The application administrator will use the New Connection button to create new server connection documents in the database. This button will not be available to the general public. Select the **Create > Action > Action** menu options. In the properties dialog, set the button name to **New Connection** in tab 1. Next, switch to tab 2 to select the **Hide action if formula is true** option and add the following to the formula window of the properties dialog.

```
!@IsMember("[Admin]";@UserRoles)
```

Close the properties dialog and add the following in the Programmer's pane.

```
@Command([Compose]; "ConDoc")
```

> **NOTE**
>
> This button will not be visible when accessing the database in "local" mode. Administrators must access the application on the server in order for the button to appear. However, by selecting the **Enforce consistent ACL** option on the **Advanced** tab of the ACL properties, the users with the "Admin" role will be able to see the button.

Create the Send Connection Button

This action button will allow users to send a single connection document to one or more coworkers. Select the **Create > Action > Action** menu options. In the properties dialog, set the button name to **Send Connection** in tab 1.

Next, change the Language Selector from **Formula** to **LotusScript** and add the following in the Programmer's pane in the Click event.

```
Sub Click(Source As Button)

    Dim s As NotesSession
    Dim w As New NotesUIWorkspace
    Dim db As NotesDatabase
    Dim dc As NotesDocumentCollection
    Dim uidoc As NotesUIDocument
    Dim docA As NotesDocument
    Dim docB As NotesDocument
    Dim text As String
    Set s = New NotesSession
    Set db = s.CurrentDatabase
    Set dc = db.UnprocessedDocuments
    Set docA = dc.GetFirstDocument

    If dc.Count <> 1 Then
        Msgbox "Please select only one connection document."
    Else
        Call w.ComposeDocument ( "", "", "Memo" )
        Set uidoc = w.CurrentDocument
        Set docB = uidoc.Document
        Call docA.CopyAllItems( docB, True )
        Call docB.RemoveItem("Authors")
        docB.SignOnSend = True
        Call uidoc.Reload
        text$ = " Server Connection for " + docA.ServerName(0)
        Call uidoc.FieldSetText( "Subject", text$ )
    End If

End Sub
```

Create the Refresh Connections Button

This button allows users to add or update all server connection documents stored in their PAB. When clicked, the application will compare the documents stored in the database with that of the address book. If the document does not exist, a new connection document will be created in the PAB. If the document already exists, the information will be replaced.

Select the **Create > Action > Action** menu options. In the properties dialog, set the button name to **Refresh Connections** in tab 1. Next, change the Language Selector from **Formula** to **LotusScript** and add the following in the Programmer's pane in the Click event.

```
Sub Click(Source As Button)

    Dim s As NotesSession
    Dim w As New NotesUIWorkspace
    Dim db As NotesDatabase
    Dim view As NotesView
    Dim viewA As NotesView
    Dim viewB As NotesView
    Dim docA As NotesDocument
    Dim docB As NotesDocument
    Dim dc As NotesDocumentCollection
```

```
'------------------------------
' Get list of connections in application
'------------------------------
Set s = New NotesSession
Set db = s.CurrentDatabase
Set viewA = db.GetView( "Servers" )
Set docA = viewA.GetFirstDocument


'------------------------------
' Locate the connections view in the PAB
'------------------------------
Set db = New Notesdatabase ("", "Names.nsf")
Set view = db.GetView ( "Connections" )


'------------------------------
' Loop through the list of connections
'------------------------------
While Not ( docA Is Nothing )
    Print "Checking: " + docA.ServerName(0)
    Set docB = view.GetDocumentByKey(docA.ServerName(0),True)
    If docB Is Nothing Then
        Dim docC As New NotesDocument( db )
        docC.Form = "local"
        docC.Destination = docA.ServerName(0)
        docC.LanPortName = docA.Port(0)
        docC.PortName = docA.Port(0)
        docC.OptionalNetworkAddress = docA.ServerIP(0)
        docC.PhoneNumber= docA.ServerIP(0)
        docC.Type = "Connection"
        docC.ConnectionType = "0"
        docC.Source = "*"
        docC.ConnectionLocation = "*"
        docC.Save True, True
            Print "Creating connection: " + docA.ServerName(0)
    Else
        If docA.ServerIP(0)<>docB.OptionalNetworkAddress(0) Then
            docB.Form = "local"
            docB.LanPortName = docA.Port(0)
            docB.PortName = docA.Port(0)
            docB.OptionalNetworkAddress = docA.ServerIP(0)
            docB.PhoneNumber= docA.ServerIP(0)
            docB.Type = "Connection"
            docB.ConnectionType = "0"
            docB.Source = "*"
            docB.ConnectionLocation = "*"
            docB.Save True, True
            Print "Updating connection: " + docA.ServerName(0)
        End If
    End If
    Set docA = viewA.GetNextDocument( docA )
Wend
Print "Updates complete."

End Sub
```

The view should look similar to Figure 10.7.

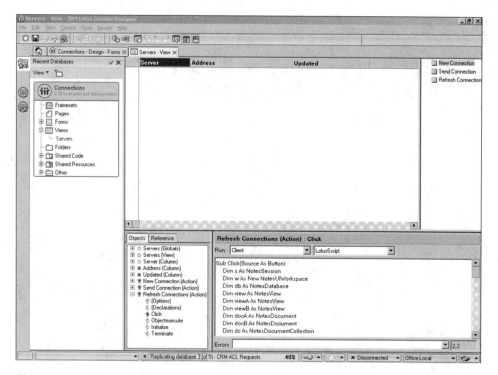

Figure 10.7   Server view

Save and close the view design element.

Application Security

Application security is managed through the ACL and "roles." Roles are used to give specific people the ability to view information or perform actions that others cannot. For this project, only users assigned the "Admin" role will have the authority to create and modify server connection documents.

To set the ACL settings, select the **File** > **Database** > **Access Control** menu options. By default, the Basics tab should be active. Click on the **-Default-** user in the center of the screen. Change the access level (right side) to **Author**.

Next, identify the person who will manage the application. Click the **Add** button (located at the bottom of the ACL dialog window) to add a user. After the user has been added, give the person **Editor** access and select the **[Admin]** role. Click **OK** to save the ACL settings (see Figure 10.8).

Congratulations, you've completed the project!

Figure 10.8 Completed project

Project B: Build a Spreadsheet Generator

Difficulty Level:	Easy
Completion Time:	1 hour
Project Materials:	1 Form, 1 View, 1 Shared Action Button, 1 LotusScript Library
Languages Used:	LotusScript
Possible Usages:	Add to any Lotus Notes database to create reports

Architecture

This project contains two Domino design elements—a shared action button and a LotusScript library. When built, these two design elements can be added to any Lotus Notes database to generate Microsoft Excel spreadsheets. Although this project is not a "Reference Library" application, you may want to include it in a reference or any database.

The first design element is a shared action button. This button triggers the PromptUser sub-routine and asks the user to select a view to be used as the basis for the spreadsheet. Users have the option to select a view from the dropdown list or to cancel the transaction.

The second design element, the LotusScript library, contains all subroutines and functions required to produce a spreadsheet. This library consists of four subroutines and one function. The combination of these design elements performs the following tasks.

1. Scan the database and build a list of views

2. Prompt the user to select the view to be used as the basis for the spreadsheet

3. Scan the selected view to retrieve the view name, column titles, field values, and column widths

4. Use the view parameters to the build the spreadsheet

5. Generate a unique file name based on the date and time stamp

6. Create the spreadsheet object

7. Format the cells of the spreadsheet by setting the font type and style

8. Parse the documents displayed in the view and add them to the spreadsheet

9. Close the spreadsheet

10. Email the spreadsheet to the user

> **NOTE**
>
> This script library is designed to work with columns that are set to a field value. All columns that contain a formula or simple action are ignored. It's important to note that the spreadsheet could include columns containing a formula and could also build graphs. However, this requires more advanced programming to generate. The point of this exercise is to generate a simple spreadsheet and to illustrate how the code can be applied to a database.

> **NOTE**
>
> This script library requires the Microsoft Excel product to be installed on the user's workstation. The user will receive an error if Microsoft Excel is not installed.

Create the Database

To start this project, launch the Lotus Domino Designer client and create a blank database. When the Designer client is running, select the **File > Database > New** menu options (see Figure 10.9). Specify an application title and file name. Be sure to select **-Blank-** as the template type.

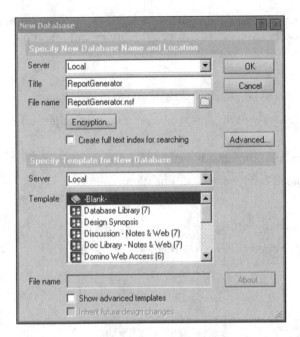

Figure 10.9   New Database dialog

Create the Spreadsheet Script Library

The LotusScript library will hold a number of common subroutines used to generate a
Microsoft Excel spreadsheet based on a view in the Lotus Notes database.

> **TIP**
>
> The following code is available in the developer's toolbox. Simply open
> the "Project Library" database in your Lotus Notes client and navigate
> to the "Script Library" section for the appropriate project. After you
> locate the project, copy and paste the code into the Designer client for
> the current project. Be sure the programmer's pane has focus before
> pasting the code. Alternatively, you can elect to manually type the
> code. You can then save and close the library. When prompted for a
> name, specify **ReportLibrary**.

To create the library, select the **Create > Design > Script Library > LotusScript Library**
menu options.

Declarations

Locate the "(Declarations)" section and add the following global statements in the Programmer's pane. These objects will be used throughout the library subroutines and functions.

```
Dim s As NotesSession
Dim db As NotesDatabase
Dim view As NotesView
```

Initialize Subroutine

The following statements are used to initialize the session and database objects. Add these statements in the `Initialize` section of the Programmer's pane.

```
Sub Initialize

   Set s = New NotesSession
   Set db = s.CurrentDatabase

End Sub
```

PromptUser Subroutine

The `PromptUser` subroutine displays a list of views in the Notes application database to the user. The user then selects a view to be used as the basis for the spreadsheet. Type the following in the Programmer's pane.

```
Sub PromptUser

   Dim w As New NotesUiWorkspace
   Dim view As NotesView
   Dim x As Integer
   Dim result as String

   '-----------------------------
   ' Build an array of views in the database
   '-----------------------------
   x=0
   If Not Isempty (db.Views) Then
      Forall v In db.Views
         Redim Preserve myList(x) As String
         myList(x) = v.Name
         x = x + 1
      End Forall
   End If

   '-----------------------------
   ' Ask the user to select a view to generate the spreadsheet
   '-----------------------------
   result$ = w.Prompt( PROMPT_OKCANCELCOMBO, +_
   "Make your choice","Select a view to build the spreadsheet",+_
   "Select View", myList)
   If result$ <> "" Then
      Print "Found view: " + result$
```

```
    Call GenerateReport ( result$ )
  End If
  Print "Complete"

End Sub
```

GenerateReport Subroutine

This subroutine will parse the design elements in the selected view into arrays. This subroutine builds an array of column titles, column widths, and field values. It also counts the total number of columns and identifies the view name. These arrays and data values are then passed to another subroutine—CreateSpreadsheet—to build the spreadsheet file. Insert the following in the Programmer's pane.

```
Sub GenerateReport ( result As String )

    '-----------------------------
    '---- Build data arrays for the selected view
    '-----------------------------
    Dim x As Integer
    Set view = db.GetView( result$ )
    x=0
    Forall c In view.Columns
       If c.IsField Then

            ' Build an array of column names
            Redim Preserve ColumnName(x) As String
            ColumnName(x) = c.Title

            ' Build an array of column Widths
            Redim Preserve ColumnWidth(x) As Variant
            ColumnWidth(x) = c.width

            ' Build an array of column field names
            Redim Preserve FieldName(x) As String
            FieldName(x) = c.ItemName

            x = x + 1
       End If
    End Forall


    '-----------------------------
    '---- Create spreadsheet based on the selected view.
    '---- Parm1 - array of all valid fields in the view
    '---- Parm2 - array of the column titles
    '---- Parm3 - array of the column widths
    '---- Parm4 - the name of the view
    '---- Parm5 - total number of columns in the view
    '-----------------------------
    Call CreateSpreadsheet ( FieldName , ColumnName, _
    ColumnWidth,  view.Name, x-1 )


End Sub
```

CreateSpreadsheet Subroutine

The `CreateSpreadsheet` subroutine is used to build the Microsoft Excel spreadsheet. This subroutine requires five parameters—an array of field names, an array of column titles, an array of column widths, a view name, and the total number columns in the view. These parameters define the content and layout of the spreadsheet. Type the following in the Programmer's pane.

```
Sub CreateSpreadsheet ( field As Variant, column As Variant, ColWidth As Variant,
Sheetname As String, cntr As Integer)

    On Error Goto oops
    Dim file As Variant
    Dim wksSheet As Variant
    Dim filename As String
    Dim alphabet(25) As String
    Dim cell As String
    Dim value As String
    Dim doc As NotesDocument
    Dim row As Long
    Dim x As Integer
    Dim n As Integer


    '-----------------------------
    '---- Build the filename for the spreadsheet
    '-----------------------------
    Dim theDate As String
    Dim theTime As String
    theDate = removeString ( Format(Date$, "Medium Date"), "-")
    theTime = removeString ( Format(Time$, "Long Time"), ":")
    theTime = removeString ( theTime, " ")
    Filename = "C:\Report" + "_" + theDate + "_" + theTime
    Print "Building file: " + Filename


    '-----------------------------
    '---- Build an array of the alphabet
    '-----------------------------
    For n = 65 To 90
        'Print "Letter" + Cstr(n-65) + " = " + Chr$(n)
        alphabet(n-65) = Chr$(n)
    Next


    '-----------------------------
    '---- Create the spreadsheet file object
    '-----------------------------
    Set file = CreateObject("Excel.Application")
    file.Visible = False
    file.DisplayAlerts = False
    file.Workbooks.Add
    Set wksSheet = file.Worksheets.Add
    wksSheet.name = Sheetname
    file.Worksheets("Sheet1").Delete
    file.Worksheets("Sheet2").Delete
    file.Worksheets("Sheet3").Delete
```

```
Set wksSheet = file.Worksheets( Sheetname )
wksSheet.Select

'-----------------------------
'---- Set the column width for first 26 columns
'-----------------------------
For x=0 To cntr
wksSheet.columns(Alphabet(x)).Columnwidth=Cint(colWidth(x)+5)
Next
Print "Set the default column width complete."

'-----------------------------
'---- Set font style for spreadsheet
'-----------------------------
With file.Range("A:Z")
    .WrapText = True
    .Font.Name = "Arial"
    .Font.FontStyle = "Regular"
    .Font.Size = 8
End With
Print "Set the font style complete."

'-----------------------------
'---- Set font style for header row
'-----------------------------
With file.Range("A1:Z1")
    .WrapText = True
    .Font.Name = "Arial"
    .Font.FontStyle = "Bold"
    .Font.Size = 8
End With
Print "Spreadsheet initialized."

'-----------------------------
'---- Load the spreadsheet with data
'-----------------------------
Print "Starting data load into spreadsheet. Please be patient"
Set view = db.GetView( SheetName )
Set doc = view.GetFirstDocument
row = 1

' Create the column title row
Set wksSheet = file.Worksheets( Sheetname )
wksSheet.Select
For x=0 To cntr
    cell$ = Alphabet(x) + Cstr( row )
    file.Range( cell$ ).Select
    file.Activecell.FormulaR1C1 = Column(x)
Next
row = 2

' Create the data rows
While Not(doc Is Nothing)
    Set wksSheet = file.Worksheets( Sheetname )
    wksSheet.Select
```

```
        'Loop through each column and add data to the row
        For x=0 To cntr
            cell$ = Alphabet(x) + Cstr( row )
            file.Range( cell$ ).Select
            file.Activecell.FormulaR1C1 =doc.GetItemValue(field(x))
        Next
        Set doc = view.GetNextDocument( doc )
        row = row + 1
    Wend
    Print "Data load complete."

    '-----------------------------
    '---- Save, close and email file to the person
    '-----------------------------
    file.activeworkbook.saveas Filename
    file.activeworkbook.close

    ' Comment out the following line to skip sending the email
    SendReport ( Filename )
    Print "Report sent."

    ' Comment out the following line to save file to the harddrive
    Kill Filename+".xls"

    Set file = Nothing
    Exit Sub

oops:
    Msgbox "Error" & Str(Err) & ": " & Error$
    file.activeworkbook.close
    Kill Filename+".xls"

End Sub
```

> **NOTE**
>
> By default, this subroutine will email the spreadsheet to the user.
> However, if you prefer that the files be saved to the user's hard
> drive, comment out the following three statements: `SendReport`
> `( Filename )`, `Print "Report sent."`, and `Kill`
> `Filename+".xls"`. This will cause the files to be saved to the
> user's hard drive in the `C:\` directory.

RemoveString Function

This function removes all instances of a specific character from the target object string. This function checks each character in the string. If the current character does not match the search string, then the character is added to a temporary variable. If the character does match, then the character is skipped. The result is a rebuilt string that is returned to the calling subroutine. Insert the following in the Programmer's pane.

```
Function RemoveString ( object As String, SearchString As String) As Variant

   Dim tempString As String
   Dim j as Integer
   tempString = ""
   For j% = 1 To Len( object )
      If Mid$(object, j%, 1) <> SearchString Then
         tempString = tempString + Mid$(object, j%, 1)
      End If
   Next
   RemoveString = tempString

End Function
```

SendReport Subroutine

The SendReport subroutine is used to create an email, attach the spreadsheet file, and send it to the person who generated the report. Type the following in the Programmer's pane.

```
Sub SendReport ( filename As String )

   Dim PersonName As New NotesName(s.UserName)
   Dim rtitem As NotesRichTextItem
   Dim object As NotesEmbeddedObject
   Dim doc As NotesDocument
   Set doc = New NotesDocument( db )
   doc.Form = "Memo"
   doc.SendTo = PersonName.Abbreviated
   doc.Subject = "Report — " + filename
   Set rtitem = New NotesRichTextItem( doc, "Body" )
   Call rtitem.AddNewline(1)
   Call rtitem.AppendText("Attached below is the requested report. ")
   Call rtitem.AddNewline(2)
   Set object = rtitem.EmbedObject ( EMBED_ATTACHMENT, "", Filename+".xls")
   doc.Send False
   Msgbox "The requested report has been sent to you.", 0, "Success"

End Sub
```

Save and close the LotusScript library. When prompted, name the library **ReportLibrary**.

Create the Generate Report Shared Action

The shared action button prompts the user to select the view to be used to build the spreadsheet. To create the button, select the **Create > Design > Shared Action** menu options and name the button **Generate Report**. Close the properties dialog.

Next, change the Language Selector from **Formula** to **LotusScript**. Locate the **(Options)** section and insert the following in the Programmer's pane.

```
Use "ReportLibrary"
```

Add the following in the Click event.

```
Sub Click(Source As Button)
```

```
   Call PromptUser
End Sub
```

Save and close the button when complete.

Create the Contact Form

This form is being created for illustration purposes to demonstrate the `GenerateReport` subroutine. However, this form is not required to actually implement the spreadsheet script library. This form includes four fields—name, address, phone, and email.

To create the form, select the **Create > Design > Form** menu options. Give the form a descriptive title at the top of the form—such as **Contact**—and add the following text field descriptions down the left side of the form.

- Name:
- Address:
- Phone:
- Email:

Next, create the following fields using the **Create > Field** menu options. Be sure to set the data type, formula, and other attributes for each field on the form using the properties dialog box and/or Programmer's pane.

Field Name	Type	Default Value Formula	Remarks
Name	Text, Editable		
Address	Text, Editable		
Phone	Text, Editable		
Email	Text, Editable		

Select the **File > Save** menu options to save the file. When prompted, name the form **Contact | Contact**. Close the form after the file has been saved.

Create the Contact View

This view will be used as the basis to demonstrate the `GenerateReport` functionality and is included for illustration purposes.

By default, a view called *(untitled)* is automatically created when the database is first created. To configure this view, navigate to Views in the Design pane and double-click on the view called "(untitled)". When the view is displayed, the Designer client will immediately display the properties dialog for the view. Specify **Contacts** as the view name and alias in tab 1. Close the properties dialog.

Next, click on the header for the predefined column and delete the column. To build the view, select the **Create > Append New Column** menu options to add four columns to the view. For each column, switch the Language Selector to **Field**. Set column one through four to the following field values:

- Name
- Address
- Phone
- Email

After the column value is specified, select **Design > Column Properties**. Click on the column header and specify a title in the properties dialog for each column.

Finally, select the **Create > Action > Insert Shared Action** menu options and insert the Generate Report shared action button. Save and close the view.

Congratulations! You have completed the project.

Add a couple contact documents and give the button a try. Note: You must have Microsoft Excel installed on your workstation in order for the report generator to work.

Chapter 11

Workflow Applications

Chapter Overview

Workflow applications are used to electronically route documents to people for review or online approvals. With this type of application you can eliminate the hassles associated with the delivery of paper documents. Workflow applications electronically manage delivery of documents, online approvals, and timestamps and provide the real-time status of documents. Workflow applications can be used for a variety of purposes, such as

- Procurement requests
- Defect management
- Request for service
- Action item tracking
- Activity assignment and management
- Help desk service request

By the end of the chapter you will have learned

- How to create a workflow application
- How to automatically number documents
- How to automatically record activities in a "history" field
- How to create an email message repository
- How to build a system profile document to manage database settings
- How to utilize action buttons to control document status

This chapter includes step-by-step instructions for building a Lotus Notes workflow application to manage procurement requests. However, with minor modifications, the application could easily be modified to be used for action items, service requests, or other business processes that require document routing and approval.

Defining a Workflow Application

A workflow can be defined as a series of activities or steps required to perform a specific business goal. Using a workflow application, you can electronically route documents for action or approval. This type of application allows users to electronically monitor and track the movement of documents. Workflow applications are ideal for documents that require multiple approvals or actions.

Let's take, for example, a procurement application where employees place orders for office supplies or equipment. To initiate the process, an employee completes a "procurement order" form and lists all items to be requisitioned. When complete, the order is electronically routed to an authorized person for review.

At this point, the approver can "approve" or "decline" the order. Similarly, the employee can withdraw the request. With each action, one or more emails are triggered to let everyone know the status of the requests and/or what actions are needed.

Approved orders are subsequently sent to a person in the procurement department. To keep track of their status, the person processing the order changes the status to "in process" after the order is placed and "complete" after the items arrive.

From a software perspective, the workflow application includes a form and emails. There are at least three people who are required to perform an action for each document. As the document is electronically routed, the status of the document changes and unique emails are sent with specific instructions to follow.

Figure 11.1 depicts the various paths the procurement order form can follow. The text in quotes represents the status of the document, with the person responsible for the workflow step in parentheses.

The design of a workflow application can range from very simple to complex. However, in general, there are several elements that tend to be common across all workflow applications. These items should be considered when building any workflow application.

- **Workflow Stages**—Understanding the stages, or steps, that a document can take is critical to the overall development of a workflow application. To define the workflow, it's important to have input and participation from each person (or group) that will own a particular workflow step. As illustrated in Figure 11.1, you need to be able to map where a document can be routed and who specifically owns that step. Although this requirements gathering process is often time consuming, it's well worth your time to complete this early in the design of the application.
- **User Roles**—The second most important aspect deals with roles and responsibilities. To build the application, you have to know who the key people are and what actions they can take. This will be used to build the application security (who can edit the document and when) and display formulas for action buttons (what actions can be performed). In the procurement example, there are three primary roles—employee, approver, and procurement people. However, many workflow

applications also include a person, or role, that has overall authority for the application, such as a system administrator. The administrator is typically responsible for the application configuration and in many cases has "super user" authority to perform any action or modify the application at any time.

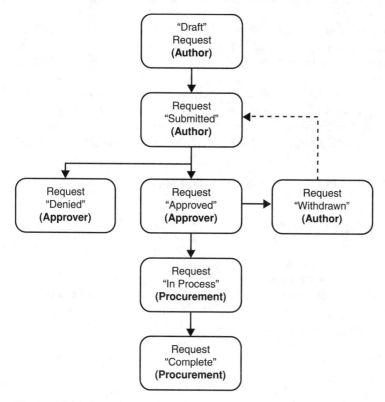

Figure 11.1 Process workflow

- **Document Routing**—Virtually all workflow applications are dependent on email routing. An action button typically triggers emails. However, scheduled agents can also trigger them. For example, if a particular person has not responded to (e.g., approved or declined) a document within a specified time, the system can automatically send a reminder notice. Emails are usually tailored to a particular status and person. In the following project, the emails are configurable and do not require programming intervention to change. All emails include a document link that allows the user to jump back to the document in the database (as opposed to sending a copy of the actual document).

A.11.1

- **Security**—Application security determines who can edit or take action on a document at any given point in time. For example, after the procurement form is submitted, it is locked. This prevents an employee from modifying the procurement request downstream. Security also prevents the employee from approving his or her own procurement order. Security is typically implemented at both the application layer and document layer.
- **Action Buttons**—In most cases, actions buttons are used to manage or control the document workflow. As a document is routed through the various workflow stages, the buttons that are available will depend on the user's role, security, and "Hide When" formulas.
- **Application Views**—Workflow applications tend to have many views. This provides users multiple ways to locate and track a document. For example, you could have a view such as "orders pending approval" and "orders in process". These views would be considered "work queues" for the "Approver" and the "Procurement" people.

In this chapter you will build a procurement order workflow application.

Project: Building a Workflow Database

Difficulty Level:	Advanced
Completion Time:	4 to 6 hours
Project Materials:	3 Forms, 8 Views, 1 Script Library, 7 Action Buttons
Languages Used:	Formula Language, LotusScript
Possible Usages:	Procurement, Service requests, Issue tracking

Architecture

The architecture for this application can be divided into several distinct areas—forms, roles, email notifications, views, and configuration.

Forms

This project will include three forms—the procurement form, email message form, and system configuration form. The procurement form will contain information pertaining to the request. This document will be routed from person to person. The email message form will be created and maintained by the system administrator. A separate email message will be created for each stage or step in the workflow process. The system configuration document will be used to configure the application and will be created and maintained by the system administrator.

Roles and Responsibilities

As previously described, there will be four roles associated with the application. The following table describes each role, responsibility, and overall authority granted with the project.

Role	Responsibility	Submit	With-draw	Approve	Deny	In Process	Com-plete
Employee	Creates and submits the initial procurement order.	X	X				
Approver	Reviews all order requests.			X	X		
Procurement	Places and tracks the procurement order.					X	X
Admin	Configures the application. Can perform any action. Manages email message content and the overall application configuration.	X	X	X	X	X	X

Roles are created and managed via the Access Control List (ACL) for the application. The definition and setup of the user roles will be the first step in the project after the new database has been created (see Figure 11.2).

Email Notifications

Several components are required to trigger and manage email notifications. First, a document that includes the following fields must be created for each mail message.

- A unique message identifier
- Send To
- Copy To
- Blind Copy To
- Email Subject
- Email Body

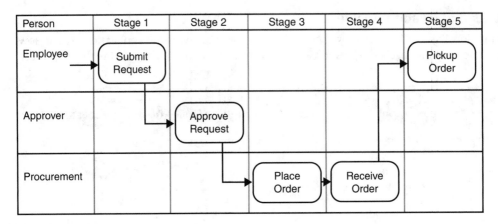

Figure 11.2   Process workflow by role

A separate action button will be created for each workflow stage—Submit, Approve, Deny, Withdraw, In Process, and Complete. Each button will update the document status flag and make a call to the SendNotice LotusScript library subroutine.

The subroutine then opens the system configuration document to determine which messages should be sent (e.g., whenever a person submits a document, send message number 100). After the message numbers are determined, the subroutine then locates the message(s), creates the email, and sends it to the recipient list (see Figure 11.3). For each workflow stage, one or more messages can be triggered.

In many cases, the recipient of the email can be added directly to the message document. However, because the author of the procurement request can be any employee, there needs to be a way to send mail notifications to the author of the request. In this project, the message document can accept any valid email address or the keyword "AUTHOR" (in uppercase). Any time this value is found in the SendTo, CopyTo, or BlindCopyTo field, it will be replaced with the author of the procurement request prior to transmitting the email.

Views

The project will include a number of views tailored for the user community. However, it will also include three views specifically designed to manage the application. One view will be used to create a unique procurement request number for each order. The second view will be used to create a unique message identifier for each message document. The last administrative view will show the "system profile" document for the application.

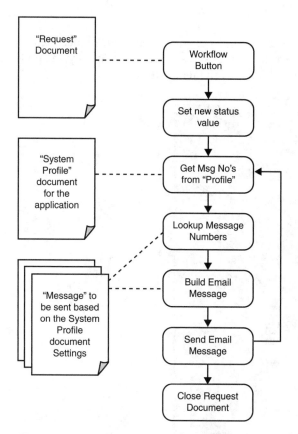

Figure 11.3   Message lookup architecture

Configuration

The System Profile form will be used to manage overall settings for the application. This form will be restricted to people assigned the "Admin" role. The form will specify which messages should be transmitted for each workflow stage. The form will also include a feature to turn on and turn off email notifications. This feature has been included for testing purposes and will allow the administrator to implement or disable messages as the application is being developed or enhanced.

Finally, you should consider event logging. In other words, does the application track changes to the document? For this project, the date, timestamp, person, and transaction will be logged in the History field. Any time the status changes, the event will be logged for audit purposes.

Create the Database

To start this project, launch the Lotus Domino Designer client. When the Designer client is running, select the **File > Database > New** menu options (see Figure 11.4). Specify an application title and file name. Be sure to select **-Blank-** as the template type.

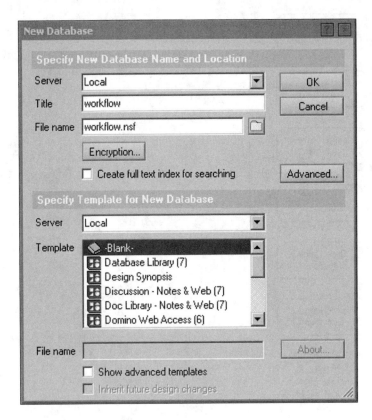

Figure 11.4   New Database dialog

Set the Database Roles

After the database is created, start by establishing the roles associated with the database. Roles enable specific people to perform actions that others cannot. This database will include three roles—Admin, Approver, and Procurement.

To create the roles, select the **File > Database > Access Control** menu options. By default, the Basics tab should be active. Switch to the **Roles** tab and select the **Add** button, located at the bottom of the dialog window (see Figure 11.5). This will display a new popup window called Add Role. Add the following roles.

- Admin
- Approver
- Procurement

Click **OK** a second time to close the ACL window.

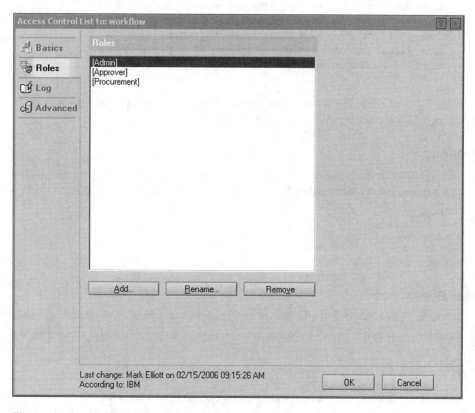

Figure 11.5 Add Role dialog from the Access Control List

Create the Workflow Script Library

The LotusScript library will include a number of common subroutines and functions used to manage document routing, status, and field validation for the workflow database.

> **TIP**
>
> The following code is available in the developer's toolbox. Simply open the "Project Library" database in your Lotus Notes client and navigate to the "Script Library" section for the appropriate project. After you locate the project, copy and paste the code into the Designer client for the current project. Be sure the programmer's pane has focus before pasting the code. Alternatively, you can elect to manually type the code. You can then save and close the library. When prompted for a name, specify **WorkflowLibrary**.

To create the library, click the **New LotusScript Library** button or select the **Create > Design > Script Library > LotusScript Library** menu options.

Declarations

Locate the "(Declarations)" section and add the following global statements in the Programmer's pane. These statements will be used throughout the LotusScript library.

```
Dim s As NotesSession
Dim db As NotesDatabase
Dim profileView As NotesView
Dim systemprofileDoc As NotesDocument
Dim MsgText As String
```

Initialize Subroutine

Locate the `Initialize` event and add the following statements in the Programmer's pane.

```
Sub Initialize

    Set s = New NotesSession
    Set db = s.CurrentDatabase
    Set profileView = db.GetView("Profile")
    Set systemprofileDoc = profileView.GetDocumentByKey("Profile",True)

End Sub
```

ChangeStatus Subroutine

The `ChangeStatus` subroutine updates the Status field with a new value. This value subsequently determines how the application functions—meaning who can update the form and click the various workflow buttons.

This subroutine requires three parameters—new status, person, and timestamp. The first parameter defines the value of the Statusfield. The next two values are used to record the person and timestamp for the transaction. These two values are field names on the form. If you decide not to utilize this feature—meaning you do not want to record the person and timestamp—simply pass double-quotes (" ") as parameters.

Add the following to the LotusScript library.

```
Sub ChangeStatus ( StatusValue As String, PersonField As String, DateField As String )

    Dim w As New NotesUIWorkspace
    Dim uidoc As NotesUIDocument
    Dim doc As NotesDocument
    Dim item As NotesItem
    Dim timestamp As New NotesDateTime( "" )
    Dim LogEntry As String
    Set uidoc = w.CurrentDocument
    Set doc = uidoc.Document
    Dim person As New NotesName(s.UserName)

    '-----------------------------------------------------------
    ' Set the status field to the new value
    '-----------------------------------------------------------
    Call CheckEditMode
    doc.Status = StatusValue

    '-----------------------------------------------------------
    ' Update any additional fields, do nothing if field ""
    '-----------------------------------------------------------
    Call timestamp.SetNow
    Set item=doc.ReplaceItemValue(PersonField,person.Abbreviated)
    Set item=doc.ReplaceItemValue(DateField,timestamp.LocalTime)

    '-----------------------------------------------------------
    ' Append a log entry to the history field
    '-----------------------------------------------------------
    LogEntry="("+Cstr(Now)+") - " + person.Common + " - " + _
    "Status changed to " + StatusValue
    Set item = doc.GetFirstItem("History")
    Call item.AppendToTextList( LogEntry )

End Sub
```

CheckFieldValues Function

The CheckFieldValues function checks the RequestTitle field to make sure it contains a valid value in the Request document. An error message is displayed and False is returned if the field is empty. A True value must be returned before the user can save the document in the database.

```
Function CheckFieldValues ( DocRef As NotesDocument )

    CheckFieldValues = True
    MsgText = ""

    If Trim(DocRef.RequestTitle(0)) = "" Then
        MsgText = MsgText + "Specify a request title." + Chr$(13)
    End If

    If MsgText <> "" Then
        Msgbox MsgText, 16, "Required Fields."
```

```
         CheckFieldValues = False
   End If

End Function
```

CheckMsgFieldValues Function

The CheckFieldValues function checks two fields, SendTo and Subject, to make sure they contain valid values in the Message document. An error message is displayed and False is returned if the field is empty. A True value must be returned before the user can save the document in the database.

```
Function CheckMsgFieldValues ( DocRef As NotesDocument )

   CheckMsgFieldValues = True
   MsgText = ""

   If Trim(DocRef.SendTo(0)) = "" Then
      MsgText=MsgText+"Specify an email in the SendTo field" + _
      Chr$(13)
   End If

   If Trim(DocRef.Subject(0)) = "" Then
      MsgText = MsgText + "Specify an email Subject." + Chr$(13)
   End If

   If MsgText <> "" Then
      Msgbox MsgText, 16, "Required Fields."
      CheckMsgFieldValues = False
   End If

End Function
```

CheckEditMode Subroutine

This subroutine checks the edit mode for the current document. If the document is in read-only mode, then the document is changed to edit mode. Add the following to the Programmer's pane.

```
Sub CheckEditMode

   Dim w As New NotesUIWorkspace
   Dim uidoc As NotesUIDocument
   Set uidoc = w.CurrentDocument
   If uidoc.EditMode = False Then
      Call w.EditDocument( True )
   End If

End Sub
```

SendNotice Subroutine

The `SendNotice` routine generates and sends workflow notification messages. First, the routine checks to see if emails should be generated based on the system profile setting. If the AllowNotifications field is set to `"Yes"`, then the emails are generated.

Next, six standard statements are defined in the subroutine. These statements describe the request and include

1. Procurement request title

2. Author of the request

3. Creation date of the request

4. Current status

5. A document link to the request

6. A database link to the application

The routine then queries the system profile to obtain the message ID numbers to be sent. Because one or more messages may be sent with each workflow step, the routine loops through each message number in the list. Each email message is subsequently built and sent. Add the following in the Programmer's pane.

```
Sub SendNotice ( NotifyMsg As String, DocRef As NotesDocument )

    Dim rtitem As NotesRichTextItem
    Dim rtitemB As NotesRichTextItem
    Dim doc As NotesDocument
    Dim msgDoc As NotesDocument
    Dim view As NotesView
    Dim key As Variant
    Dim Line1 As String
    Dim Line2 As String
    Dim Line3 As String
    Dim Line4 As String
    Dim Line5 As String
    Dim Line6 As String


    '------------------------------------------------------------
    ' Check to see if emails are permitted
    '------------------------------------------------------------
    If systemprofileDoc.AllowNotification(0) = "Yes" Then

        ' Set the default line statements for body of email
        line1 = "Request Title:    " + DocRef.RequestTitle(0)
        line2 = "Request By:       " + DocRef.RequestBy(0)
        line3 = "Request Date:     " + DocRef.CreateDate(0)
        line4 = "Request Status: " + DocRef.Status(0)
        line5 = "Click here to open the document --> "
        line6 = "Click here to open the database   --> "


    '------------------------------------------------------------
    'Lookup up which message to send out
```

```
'----------------------------------------------------------
    key = systemprofileDoc.GetItemValue( NotifyMsg )

    Forall x In key
        '---------------------------------------------------
        ' Get the message text information
        '---------------------------------------------------
        Set View = db.GetView("(MsgID)")
        Set MsgDoc = View.GetDocumentByKey( Cint( x ) ,True)


        '---------------------------------------------------
        'Generate email and send notice
        '---------------------------------------------------
        Set doc = New NotesDocument( db )
        doc.Form = "Memo"
        doc.SendTo=ReplaceElement (msgDoc.SendTo, "AUTHOR", DocRef)
        doc.CopyTo=ReplaceElement (msgDoc.SendCC, "AUTHOR", DocRef)
        doc.BlindCopyTo=ReplaceElement(msgDoc.SendBCC,"AUTHOR",DocRef)
        doc.Subject = msgDoc.Subject(0)
        Set rtitem = New NotesRichTextItem( doc, "Body" )
        Call rtitem.AddNewline(1)
        Set rtitemB = msgDoc.GetFirstItem( "Body" )
        Call rtitem.AppendRTItem( rtitemB )
        Call rtitem.AddNewline(2)
        Call rtitem.AppendText( line1 )
        Call rtitem.AddNewline(1)
        Call rtitem.AppendText( line2 )
        Call rtitem.AddNewline(1)
        Call rtitem.AppendText( line3 )
        Call rtitem.AddNewline(1)
        Call rtitem.AppendText( line4 )
        Call rtitem.AddNewline(2)
        Call rtitem.AppendText( line5 )
        Call rtitem.AppendDocLink( DocRef,  db.Title )
        Call rtitem.AddNewline(1)
        Call rtitem.AppendText( line6 )
        Call rtitem.AppendDocLink( db,  db.Title )
        Call rtitem.AddNewline(2)
        Call rtitem.AppendText(  "MessageID: " + x )
        doc.Send False
    End Forall
  End If

End Sub
```

ReplaceElement

The ReplaceElement routine checks all elements in an array and replaces the element if found. In this case, the routine will check the SendTo, CopyTo, and BlindCopyTo fields for the keyword "AUTHOR". If found, the value is replaced with the email address of the person that submitted the form.

```
Function ReplaceElement ( varFromList As Variant, varTarget As Variant, DocRef As
NotesDocument) As Variant

    Redim ReturnArray(0) As String
    Dim i As Integer
    i = 0
    Forall varElement In varFromList
        Redim Preserve ReturnArray (i) As String
        If varElement = varTarget Then
            ReturnArray(i) = DocRef.RequestBy(0)
        Else
            ReturnArray(i) = varElement
        End If
        i = i + 1
    End Forall
    ReplaceElement = ReturnArray

End Function
```

Save and close the LotusScript library. When prompted, name the library **WorkflowLibrary**.

Create the Request Form

The Request form is the primary document associated with the workflow application. This document captures the user's information and is sent to an authorized person for review and approval. There are several key elements on this form.

First, it's important to capture the email address of the person who created the request as well as the date and time. This information is needed to know where to send email updates. It's also helpful to track when the request was created to know how long the request takes to be processed.

Next, it's equally important to track the status and document identifier. The Status field is the heart of the workflow application. Buttons are displayed and hidden based on the value of this field.

Finally, the history field keeps a running log of all status changes. This field shows the date, time, person, and type of update each time the document changes.

To create the form, select the **Create > Design > Form** menu options. At the top of the form, add a descriptive form title such as **Procurement Request**.

Create the Labels

Next, insert a couple blank lines and create a table in the form. To create the table, select the **Create > Table** menu options. When prompted, select 5 rows, 4 columns, and **Fixed Width**. Select **OK** to create the table. Add the labels in columns 1 and 3 and create the associated fields (as described in the next section) in columns 2 and 4.

Request No:	*RequestNo*	Request Status:	*Status*
Request By:	*RequestBy*	Created Date:	*CreateDate*
Modified By:	*ModifyBy*	Modified Date:	*ModifyDate*
Approved By:	*ApprovedBy*	Approved Date:	*ApprovedDate*
Completed By:	*CompletedBy*	Completed Date:	*CompletedDate*

Below the table, add the following additional text labels.

- Request Title
- Request Details
- Comments
- History

Your form should now look like Figure 11.6.

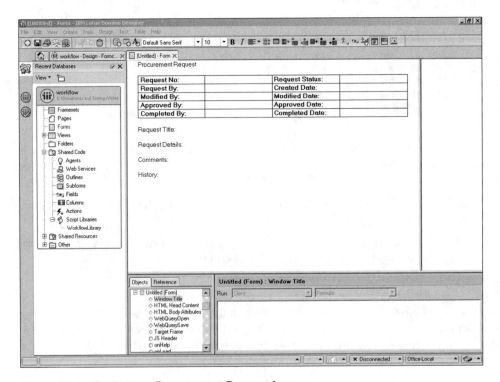

Figure 11.6   Preliminary Procurement Request form

Create the Fields

Now create the following fields using the **Create > Field** menu options. Be sure to set the data type, formula, and other attributes for each field on the form using the properties dialog box and/or Programmer's pane.

Field Name	Type	Default Value Formula	Remarks
RequestNo	Number, Computed	`RequestNo`	
RequestBy	Names, Computed when Composed	`@UserName`	

ModifyBy	Names, Computed	`value := @If`
		`(@IsDocBeingSaved;`
		`@Name([Abbreviate];`
		`@UserName);`
		`@Thisvalue); value`	

ApprovedBy	Names, Computed	`@ThisValue`	
CompletedBy	Names, Computed	`@ThisValue`	
Status	Text, Computed	`DEFAULT Status:=` `"Draft"; Status`	
CreateDate	Date/Time, Computed when Composed	`@Now`	On tab 2, select the **Display Time** setting. Make sure both the date and time options are selected.

ModifyDate	Date/Time, Computed	`value := @If`
		`(@IsDocBeingSaved;`
		`@Now; @ThisValue);`
		`value`
			On tab 2, select the **Display Time** setting. Make sure both the date and time options are selected.

continues

Field Name	Type	Default Value Formula	Remarks
ApprovedDate	Date/Time, Computed	`ApprovedDate`	On tab 2, select the **Display Time** setting. Make sure both the date and time options are selected.
Completed Date	Date/Time, Computed	`CompletedDate`	On tab 2, select the **Display Time** setting. Make sure both the date and time options are selected.
RequestTitle	Text, Editable		
RequestDetails	RichText, Editable		
Comments	RichText, Editable		
History	Text, Computed	`History`	On tab 1, select **Allow multiple values** of the properties dialog. On tab 3, set the **Display separate values with** field to **New Line**.

The form should now look like Figure 11.7.

Create the Controlled Section

Controlled sections are just one of several ways to manage who can edit content. In this case, only the person that created the request can modify the request title and details. However, the author can only modify the content while the document is in "draft" status. After the document has been submitted, the author can no longer change the information.

To create the controlled section, highlight the label and field for both Request Title and Request Detail, as in Figure 11.8.

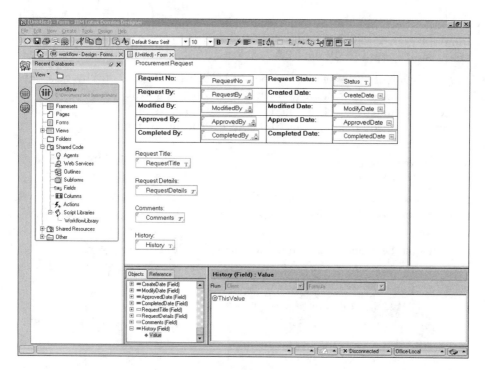

Figure 11.7 Updated Procurement Request form

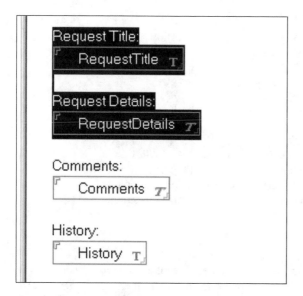

Figure 11.8 Highlighted area for the controlled section

Select the **Create > Section > Controlled Access** menu options. This creates the controlled section and displays the properties dialog. On tab 1, remove the text title. Switch to tab 2. Select **Auto-expand section** for all modes.

The ability to edit content in this section will be managed using a formula. In this case, only the author of the request (or the name of the person in the RequestedBy field) can edit the content while the document is in Draft mode. Switch to tab 3. Change the Access Formula Type to **Computed** and add the following in the **Access Formula** window of the properties dialog.

```
@If (Status = "Draft"; RequestBy;
     Status = "Submitted"; "[Admin]";
     Status = "Approved"; "[Admin]";
     Status = "In Process"; "[Admin]";
     Status = "Withdrawn"; RequestBy;
     "None")
```

After the formula has been added, the properties dialog should look like Figure 11.9.

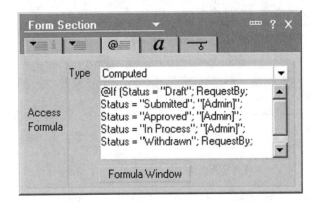

Figure 11.9   Access formula for the controlled section

TIP

The system administrator (or the person assigned the "Admin" role) will have the authority to modify the request at any time as long as the pro-curement request status has not changed to a "Completed" status.

Options

In order to utilize the LotusScript library, a Use statement needs to be added to the form. The Use statement includes the script library with the form. Without this statement, Lotus Notes is unable to locate the subroutines and functions. If you omit this statement, users will receive an error message when opening the form. Locate the **(Options)** section and add the following statements in the Programmer's pane.

```
Option Public
Use "WorkflowLibrary"
```

Window Title

The window title displays at the top of the screen whenever this form is opened in the Lotus Notes client. The title helps make the application more user friendly. The window title is not used anywhere else in the application and can be changed to any value you prefer—such as **Request**. Locate the Window Title object and add the following in the Programmer's pane.

```
"Request " + @Text(RequestNo)
```

Set the *QuerySave* Event

The QuerySave event is called every time the document is saved. In this event, the application will verify that all required fields contain valid values and will assign a unique document number (if one has not already been assigned). The document cannot be saved until it passes the validation check.

```
Sub Querysave(Source As Notesuidocument, Continue As Variant)

    Dim s As New NotesSession
    Dim w As New NotesUIWorkspace
    Dim uidoc As NotesUIDocument
    Dim doc As NotesDocument
    Dim db As NotesDatabase
    Dim numView As NotesView
    Set w = New NotesUIWorkspace
    Set db = s.CurrentDatabase
    Set s = New NotesSession
    Set uidoc = w.CurrentDocument
    Set doc = uidoc.Document
    Continue = CheckFieldValues ( doc )

    If Continue Then
       If doc.RequestNo(0) = "" Then
          Dim view As NotesView
          Dim DocRef As NotesDocument
          Set numView = db.GetView ("(RequestNo)")
          Set DocRef = numView.GetFirstDocument
          If (DocRef Is Nothing) Then
             doc.RequestNo = 1000
          Else
             doc.RequestNo = DocRef.RequestNo(0) + 1
       End If
       End If
    End If

End Sub
```

Create the Close Button

This button closes the document and returns the user to the previously opened view. Select the **Create > Action > Action** menu options and name the button **Close**. Close the properties dialog and insert the following in the Programmer's pane.

```
@Command([FileCloseWindow])
```

Create the Submit Button

The Submit button initiates the workflow and is clicked by the author of the request. This button triggers an email message to the person that needs to approve the request. The routine first changes the Status field to "Submitted" and then sends the email messages listed in the system profile.

Select the **Create > Action > Action** menu options and name the button **Submit** in tab 1. Switch to tab 2. Select the **Hide paragraph if formula is true** checkbox and set the formula to the following.

```
(Status != "Draft" & Status != "Withdrawn") &
!@IsMember("[Admin]";@UserRoles)
```

Close the properties dialog window. Change the language type from **Formula** to **LotusScript** and add the following in the `Click` event of the Programmer's pane.

```
Sub Click(Source As Button)

    Dim w As New NotesUIWorkspace
    Dim uidoc As NotesUIDocument
    Dim doc As NotesDocument
    Set uidoc = w.CurrentDocument
    Set doc = uidoc.Document
    Call ChangeStatus ( "Submitted", "", "" )
    Call SendNotice ( "NotifyMsg1", doc )
    doc.Save True, True
    uidoc.Save
    uidoc.Close

End Sub
```

Create the Approved Button

This button triggers an email message to the person that needs to approve the request. The routine first changes the Status field to "Approved" and then sends the email messages listed in the system profile. Only people assigned the role "Approver" will have the ability to see this button.

Select the **Create > Action > Action** menu options and name the button **Approved** on tab 1. Switch to tab 2. Select the **Hide paragraph if formula is true** checkbox and set the formula to the following.

```
(!@IsMember("[Approver]";@UserRoles) |
Status != "Submitted") &
!@IsMember("[Admin]";@UserRoles)
```

Close the properties dialog window. Change the language type from **Formula** to **LotusScript** and add the following in the `Click` event of the Programmer's pane.

```
Sub Click(Source As Button)

    Dim w As New NotesUIWorkspace
    Dim uidoc As NotesUIDocument
    Dim doc As NotesDocument
    Dim continue As Integer
    Set uidoc = w.CurrentDocument
    Set doc = uidoc.Document

    Continue = CheckFieldValues ( doc )
    If Continue Then
        Call ChangeStatus("Approved","ApprovedBy","ApprovedDate")
        Call SendNotice ( "NotifyMsg1", doc )
        doc.Save True, True
        uidoc.Save
        uidoc.Close
    End If

End Sub
```

Create the Denied Button

This button changes the Status field to `"Denied"` and then sends the email messages listed in the system profile. Only people assigned the role "Approver" will have the ability to see this button.

Select the **Create > Action > Action** menu options and name the button **Denied** in tab 1. Switch to tab 2. Select the **Hide paragraph if formula is true** checkbox and set the formula to the following.

```
(!@IsMember("[Approver]";@UserRoles) |
Status != "Submitted") &
!@IsMember("[Admin]"; @UserRoles)
```

Close the properties dialog window. Next, change the language type from **Formula** to **LotusScript** and add the following in the `Click` event of the Programmer's pane.

```
Sub Click(Source As Button)

    Dim w As New NotesUIWorkspace
    Dim uidoc As NotesUIDocument
    Dim doc As NotesDocument
    Dim continue As Integer
    Set uidoc = w.CurrentDocument
    Set doc = uidoc.Document

    Continue = CheckFieldValues ( doc )
    If Continue Then
        Call ChangeStatus ( "Denied", "", "" )
        Call SendNotice ( "NotifyMsg3", doc )
        doc.Save True, True
        uidoc.Save
```

```
     uidoc.Close
   End If

End Sub
```

Create the In Process Button

The person authorized to manage all approved requests uses this button. This person will place (or order) the actual procurement request. This button first changes the status field to "In Process" and then sends the email messages listed in the system profile. Only people assigned to the "Procurement" role will have the ability to see this button.

Select the **Create > Action > Action** menu options and name the button **In Process** in tab 1. Switch to tab 2. Select the **Hide paragraph if formula is true** checkbox and insert the following formula.

```
(!@IsMember("[Procurement]";@UserRoles) |
Status != "Approved") &
!@IsMember("[Admin]";@UserRoles)
```

Close the properties dialog window. Change the language type from **Formula** to **LotusScript** and add the following in the Click event of the Programmer's pane.

```
Sub Click(Source As Button)

   Dim w As New NotesUIWorkspace
   Dim uidoc As NotesUIDocument
   Dim doc As NotesDocument
   Dim continue As Integer
   Set uidoc = w.CurrentDocument
   Set doc = uidoc.Document

   Continue = CheckFieldValues ( doc )
   If Continue Then
      Call ChangeStatus ( "In Process", "", "" )
      Call SendNotice ( "NotifyMsg4", doc )
      doc.Save True, True
      uidoc.Save
      uidoc.Close
   End If

End Sub
```

Create the Complete Button

Similar to the In Process button, this button is clicked by a person who will fulfill the procurement order. This is the last step in the workflow, and it notifies the author that the procurement order has arrived. This button first changes the Status field to "Complete" and then sends the email messages listed in the system profile. Only people assigned the role "Procurement" will have the ability to see this button.

Select the **Create > Action > Action** menu options and name the button **Complete** in tab 1. Switch to tab 2. Select the **Hide paragraph if formula is true** checkbox and set the formula to the following.

```
(!@IsMember("[Procurement]";@UserRoles) |
Status != "In Process") &
!@IsMember("[Admin]";@UserRoles)
```

Close the properties dialog window. Next, change the language type from **Formula** to **LotusScript** and add the following in the `Click` event of the Programmer's pane.

```
Sub Click(Source As Button)

    Dim w As New NotesUIWorkspace
    Dim uidoc As NotesUIDocument
    Dim doc As NotesDocument
    Dim continue As Integer
    Set uidoc = w.CurrentDocument
    Set doc = uidoc.Document

    Continue = CheckFieldValues ( doc )
    If Continue Then
        Call ChangeStatus("Complete","CompletedBy","CompletedDate")
        Call SendNotice ( "NotifyMsg5", doc )
        doc.Save True, True
        uidoc.Save
        uidoc.Close
    End If

End Sub
```

Create the Withdraw Button

Finally, this button provides the option for the author to withdraw the procurement request. This button is only available to the author of the request. Requests can be withdrawn any time before the order has been placed and the status has changed to `"In Process"`. This button first changes the status field to `"Withdrawn"` and then sends the email messages listed in the system profile.

Select the **Create > Action > Action** menu options and name the button **Withdraw** in tab 1. Switch to tab 2. Select the **Hide paragraph if formula is true** checkbox and set the formula to the following.

```
(!@IsMember( @UserName;  RequestBy ) |
Status = "Draft" |
Status = "Withdrawn" |
Status = "In Process" |
Status = "Denied" |
Status = "Complete") &
!@IsMember("[Admin]";@UserRoles)
```

Close the properties dialog window. Change the language type from **Formula** to **LotusScript** and add the following in the `Click` event of the Programmer's pane.

```
Sub Click(Source As Button)

    Dim w As New NotesUIWorkspace
    Dim uidoc As NotesUIDocument
    Dim doc As NotesDocument
    Dim continue As Integer
    Set uidoc = w.CurrentDocument
    Set doc = uidoc.Document

    Continue = CheckFieldValues ( doc )
    If Continue Then
        Call ChangeStatus ( "Withdrawn", "", "" )
        Call SendNotice ( "NotifyMsg6", doc )
        doc.Save True, True
        uidoc.Save
        uidoc.Close
    End If

End Sub
```

The Request form should now look similar to Figure 11.10.

Save and close the form. When prompted, name the form **Request | Request**.

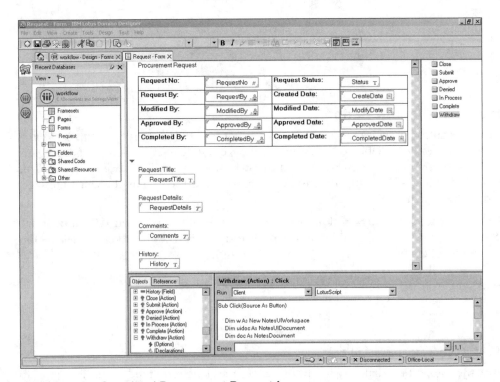

Figure 11.10   Completed Procurement Request form

Create the Message Form

To create the form, select the **Create > Design > Form** menu options. Give the form a descriptive title at the top of the form—such as **Workflow Message**—and add the following text field descriptions down the left side of the form.

- Msg ID:
- Send To:
- Send CC:
- Send BCC:
- Subject:
- Body:

Next, create the following fields using the **Create > Field** menu options. Be sure to set the data type, formula, and other attributes for each field on the form using the properties dialog box and/or Programmer's pane.

Field Name	Type	Default Value Formula	Remarks
MsgID	Number, Computed	`MsgID`	
SendTo	Names, Editable	`@Name([Abbreviate]; SendTo)`	Select **Allow multiple values** in tab 1 and **Use Address Dialog for choices** in tab 2.
SendCC	Names, Editable	`@Name([Abbreviate]; SendCC)`	Select **Allow multiple values** in tab 1 and **Use Address Dialog for choices** in tab 2.
SendBCC	Names, Editable	`@Name([Abbreviate]; SendBCC)`	Select **Allow multiple values** in tab 1 and **Use Address Dialog for choices** in tab 2.
Subject	Text, Editable		
Body	Rich Text, Editable		

At the very bottom, append the following usage notes on the form. These notes will serve as a reminder for anyone that needs to create a new message or modify an existing message.

> **NOTE**
>
> (1) To send the email to the person who submitted the request, add the keyword AUTHOR (in all capitals) to any of the send to fields. Be sure to separate multiple values with a comma or semicolon. (2) Remember to update the ACL settings and role assignments if the recipient needs to perform an action. Otherwise, they will receive an email, but will not see any of the workflow buttons.

The form should now look like Figure 11.11.

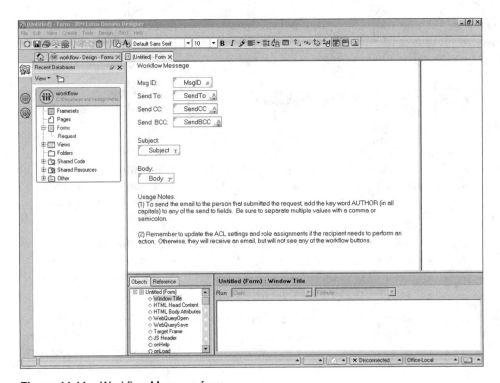

Figure 11.11   Workflow Message form

Create the Controlled Section

Controlled sections are used to refine access to specific sections on the form. In this case, only those people assigned the "Admin" role will have the authority to create or change the application message notifications.

To create the controlled section, select the **Edit > Select All** menu options. This will high-light all text and fields on the form. Now select the **Create > Section > Controlled Access** menu options. This creates the controlled section and displays the properties dialog (see Figure 11.12). Switch to tab 2 and select **Auto-expand section** for all modes.

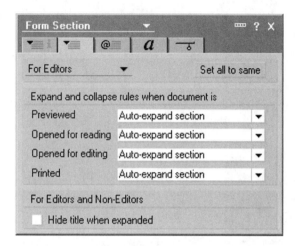

Figure 11.12   Expand and collapse settings for the controlled section

The ability to edit content in this section will be determined by a formula. Switch to tab 3. Set the access formula type to **Computed**. Next, add the following in the Access Formula window of the properties dialog (see Figure 11.13).

```
"[Admin]"
```

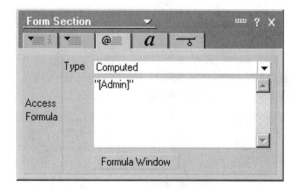

Figure 11.13   Access Formula for the controlled section

The last step is to disable the form from displaying in the menu and to set the permissions for creating application messages. Select the **Design > Form Properties** menu options. On tab 1, uncheck the **Include in menu** option. To restrict who can create documents, switch to tab 7. Uncheck the **All authors and above** checkbox and select only the **[Admin]** option (see Figure 11.14).

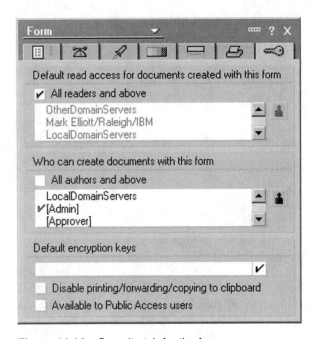

Figure 11.14   Security tab for the form

Your form should now look like Figure 11.15.

Options

Locate the **(Options)** section of the form and insert the following in the Programmer's pane. The Use statement will include the LotusScript library in the form.

```
Option Public
Use "WorkflowLibrary"
```

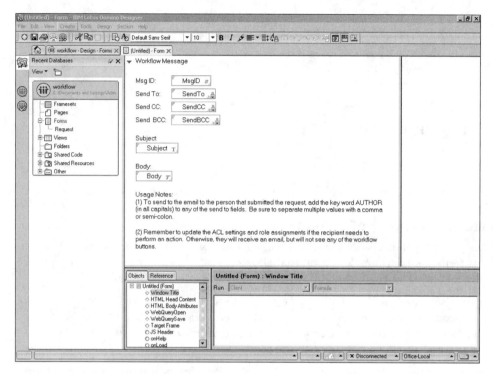

Figure 11.15 Completed Workflow Message form

Set the *QuerySave* Event

To complete the form, you will add a field validation check and message number generator to the QuerySave event. Locate the QuerySave event in the Objects pane and add the following LotusScript code in the Programmer's pane.

```
Sub Querysave(Source As Notesuidocument, Continue As Variant)

    Dim s As New NotesSession
    Dim w As New NotesUIWorkspace
    Dim uidoc As NotesUIDocument
    Dim doc As NotesDocument
    Dim db As NotesDatabase
    Dim numView As NotesView
    Set db = s.CurrentDatabase
    Set s = New NotesSession
    Set uidoc = w.CurrentDocument
    Set doc = uidoc.Document

    Continue = CheckMsgFieldValues ( doc )
    If Continue Then
        If doc.MsgID(0) = "" Then
```

```
        Dim view As NotesView
        Dim DocRef As NotesDocument
        Set numView = db.GetView ("(MsgID)")
        Set DocRef = numView.GetFirstDocument
        If (DocRef Is Nothing) Then
            doc.MsgID = 1000
        Else
            doc.MsgID = DocRef.MsgID(0) + 1
        End If
    End If
  End If

End Sub
```

Save and close the form. When prompted, name the form **Message | Message**.

Create the System Profile Form

The System Profile form is used to set general application configuration settings. In particular, this form will have a radio button that allows the administrator to turn email notifications on and off. This can be helpful when testing application enhancements.

The form also contains a list of all messages to be sent based on a specific step in the workflow. For example, the form can be configured to send one or more messages every time a new request is submitted. An acknowledgement email may be sent to the author and a "please process" email could be sent to the approver(s).

To create the form, select the **Create > Design > Form** menu options. Give the form a descriptive title at the top of the form—such as **System Profile**—and add the following field labels down the left side of the form.

- Notifications:
- Workflow Messages:

Below the Notifications label, create the following field using the **Create > Field** menu options.

Field Name	Type	Default Value Formula	Remarks
AllowNotification	Radio Button, Editable	"Yes"	On tab 2, select **Enter choices one per line** and insert the following in the choices field. Yes No

Next, create a table below the Workflow Messages label. To create the table, select the **Create > Table** menu options. When prompted, select 7 rows, 2 columns, and **Fixed Width**. Select **OK** to create the table.

On the first row of the table, insert the column labels **When document is:** and **Send Message(s)**. Then, starting on the second row and continuing through the end of the table, add the following labels in column 1 (see Figure 11.16 in the next section).

1. Submitted

2. Approved

3. Denied

4. In Process

5. Complete

6. Withdrawn

Create the following fields in column 2 using the **Create > Field** menu options. Be sure to set the data type, formula, and other attributes for each field on the form using the properties dialog box and/or Programmer's pane. Place the AllowNotification field below the Notification label and all other fields in column 2 of the table (see Figure 11.16).

Field Name	Type	Default Value Formula	Remarks
NotifyMsg1	Text, Editable		Select **Allow multiple values** on tab 1.
NotifyMsg2	Text, Editable		Select **Allow multiple values** on tab 1.
NotifyMsg3	Text, Editable		Select **Allow multiple values** on tab 1.
NotifyMsg4	Text, Editable		Select **Allow multiple values** on tab 1.
NotifyMsg5	Text, Editable		Select **Allow multiple values** on tab 1.
NotifyMsg6	Text, Editable		Select **Allow multiple values** on tab 1.

Created the Controlled Section

Only those people assigned the "Admin" role will have the authority to create or change the system configuration profile for the application.

To create the controlled section, select the **File > Select All** menu options. This will highlight all text and design elements on the screen. Now select the **Create > Section > Controlled Access** menu options. This creates the controlled section and displays the properties dialog. Switch to tab 2 and select **Auto-expand section** for all modes.

The ability to edit content in this section will be determined using a formula. In this case, everyone that has been assigned the "Admin" role can edit the content. Switch to tab 3. Set the access formula type to **Computed** and insert the following formula.

```
"[Admin]"
```

The last step for the form is to set the permissions for creating application messages. To restrict who can create documents using this form, select the **Design > Form Properties** menu options. Switch to tab 7. Uncheck the **All authors and above** checkbox and select only the **[Admin]** option. Your form should now look like Figure 11.16.

Save and close the form. When prompted, name the form **System Profile | Profile**.

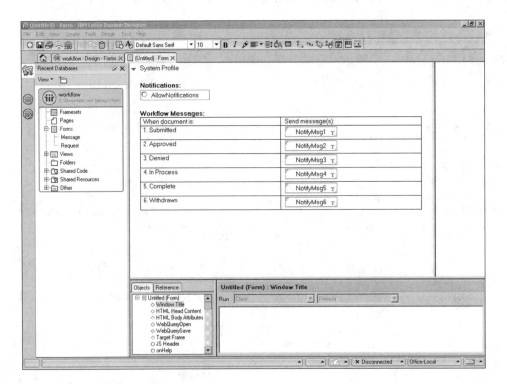

Figure 11.16   System Profile form

Create the By Number View

The By Number view will display all procurement documents sorted by request number. By default, a view called *(untitled)* is automatically created when the database is first created. To configure this view, navigate to Views in the Design pane and double-click on the view called "(untitled)".

When the view is displayed, the Designer client will immediately display the properties dialog for the view. Specify **1. By Number** as the view name and **Number** as the alias name. Close the properties dialog.

Column 1

This column will list the request number for each document stored in the application database. Double-click on the default column. Change the column title to **No.** and the column width to **4** on tab 1.

To set the column value, change the display type from **Simple Function** to **Formula** and insert the following formula.

```
@Text(RequestNo)
```

Column 2

The second column will be used to sort the documents in the view. It's important to note that the first column could have included a sort order. However, a second column has been added to provide some flexibility in the design of the view.

Select the **Create > Append New Column** menu options to add the column. In the properties dialog, set the column width to **1** on tab 1, select **Descending** as the sort order on tab 2, and select **Hide column** on tab 7.

In the Programmer's pane, change the display type from **Simple Function** to **Field** and select the following value.

```
RequestNo
```

Column 3

Column three displays the author of the request. Select the **Create > Append New Column** menu options to add the column. In the properties dialog, set the column name to **Created By** and width to **15** on tab 1. Change the display type from **Simple Function** to **Formula** and add the following value.

```
@Name([CN]; RequestBy)
```

Column 4

Column four displays the status of the request. Select the **Create > Append New Column** menu options to add the column. In the properties dialog, set the column name to **Status** and width to **6** on tab 1. Change the display type from **Simple Function** to **Field** and select the following value.

```
Status
```

Column 5

The last column displays the title of the request. Select the **Create > Append New Column** menu options to add the column. In the properties dialog, set the column name to **Request Title** and width to **40** on tab 1. Change the display type from **Simple Function** to **Field** and select the following value.

```
RequestTitle
```

Set the View Selection Criteria

Click inside the view (instead of a column header) to give the view focus. Next, change the programming language from **Simple Search** to **Formula** and enter the following in the View Selection section of the Programmer's pane.

```
SELECT Form = "Request"
```

Set the *QueryPaste* Event

The `QueryPaste` event will prevent users from copying and pasting documents into the view. Users will receive a warning message anytime someone attempts to paste a document in the view. This will force the user to create new documents using the application forms. It will also prevent duplicate document numbers in the application.

Click inside the view (as opposed to a column header) to give the view focus. Locate the `QueryPaste` event in the Object pane and enter the following in the Programmer's pane.

```
Sub Querypaste(Source As Notesuiview, Continue As Variant)

   Msgbox "Sorry, users are not permitted to copy and paste.",_
   48, "Warning"
   Continue = False

End Sub
```

> **NOTE**
>
> This project requires the option **Default when database is first opened** to be selected in the View properties dialog. By default, this option will already be enabled. Any view in the database can be selected as the "Default" just as long as one view is selected as the default for the database. The database will not function correctly if no view has been designated as the default.

Save and close the view.

Create the By Status View

With the one view already in place, you will use this as the basis for the status view. From the Design pane, highlight the **1. By Number** view design element and select the **Edit > Copy** menu options. Now select the **Edit > Paste** menu options. Double-click on the **Copy Of 1. By Number** view to open it in design mode.

When the view is opened, the properties dialog should automatically appear. Change the view title to **2. By Status** and the alias name to **Status**.

Next, click on the **Status** column and drag it to the first column. This will make the status column the first column in the view followed by the document number. In the properties dialog, select the **Show twistie when row is expandable** option on tab 1. Switch to tab 2. Set the sort order to **Ascending** and type to **Categorized**. Switch to tab 3. Set the font text color to **Blue** and **Bold** on tab 3.

Save and close the view.

Create the By Author View

Similar to the previous view, highlight the **1. By Number** view design element and select the **Edit > Copy** menu options. Now select the **Edit > Paste** menu options. Double-click on the **Copy Of 1. By Number** view to open it in design mode.

When the view is opened, the properties dialog should automatically appear. Change the view title to **3. By Author** and the view alias to **Author**.

Next, click on the **Created By** column and drag it to the first column. This will make the author of the request the first column in the view followed by the document number. In the properties dialog, set the column width to **8** and select the **Show twistie when row is expandable** option on tab 1. Switch to tab 2. Set the sort order to **Ascending** and type to **Categorized**. Switch to tab 3. Set the font text color to **Blue** and **Bold** on tab 3.

Save and close the view.

Create the Work Queues\Approvers View

This view will only display documents when the Status field contains `"Submitted"`. This is achieved through the View Selection formula. Similar to the previous view, highlight the **1. By Number** view design element and select the **Edit > Copy** menu options. Now select the **Edit > Paste** menu options. Double-click on the **Copy Of 1. By Number** view to open it in design mode.

When the view is opened, the properties dialog should automatically appear. Change the view title to **4. Work Queue\Pending Approval** and the view alias to **ApproveQue**.

To set this view selection formula, click inside the view to make it the active design element. Locate the View Selection section and change the formula to the following in the Programmer's pane.

```
SELECT Status = "Submitted"
```

Create the Work Queues\Procurement View

This view will only display documents when the status field contains "Submitted". This is achieved through the View Selection formula. Similar to the previous view, highlight the **1. By Number** view design element and select the **Edit > Copy** menu options. Now select the **Edit > Paste** menu options. Double-click on the **Copy Of 1. By Number** view to open it in design mode.

When the view is opened, the properties dialog should automatically appear. Change the view title to **4. Work Queue\Pending Procure** and the view alias to **ProcureQue**.

To set this formula, click inside the view to make it the active design element. Locate the View Selection section and change the formula to the following in the Programmer's pane.

```
SELECT Status = "Approved"
```

Create the Admin\Messages View

The Messages view will list all email messages that can be generated by the application. Each message is given a unique number. Messages are sorted in descending order. This way, when new messages are added, the top number in the view is incremented by one and assigned to the new document. To create the view, select the **Create > Design > View** menu options.

When prompted, set the view name to **Admin\Messages|(MsgID)**. Next, change the **Copy style from view** field to **-Blank-**. To set this value, click the **Copy From** button. Finally, change the selection conditions to **By Formula** and insert the following in the dialog box.

```
SELECT Form = "Message"
```

The dialog box should look like Figure 11.17.

Click **Save and Customize** to create the view and open it in edit mode.

Column 1

The first column will display the sequential list of message numbers sorted in descending order. This column is used as the basis for numbering new messages. Click on the default column to give the design element focus and select the **Design > Column Properties** menu options.

In the properties dialog, change the column name to **No.** and width to **4**. Switch to tab 2 and set the sort order to **Descending**.

To set the column value, change the display type from **Simple Function** to **Field** and select the following in the Programmer's pane.

```
MsgID
```

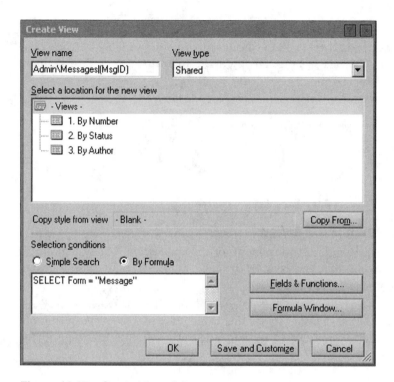

Figure 11.17 Create View dialog

Column 2

Column two displays the recipient of the message. Select the **Create > Append New Column** menu options to add the column. In the properties dialog, set the column name to **Recipient** and width to **15** on tab 1. Change the display type from **Simple Function** to **Formula** and insert the following value.

```
@Name([Abbreviate]; SendTo)
```

Column 3

Column three displays the title of the message. Select the **Create > Append New Column** menu options to add the column. In the properties dialog, set the column name to **Subject** and width to **40** on tab 1. Change the display type from **Simple Function** to **Field** and select the following value.

```
Subject
```

Set the *QueryPaste* Event

Click inside the view (as opposed to a column header) to give the view focus. Locate the QueryPaste event in the Objects section and insert the following in the Programmer's pane.

```
Sub Querypaste(Source As Notesuiview, Continue As Variant)

    Msgbox "Sorry, users are not permitted to copy and paste.",_
    48, "Warning"
    Continue = False

End Sub
```

Save and close the view.

Create the Admin\System Profile View

This view will display the system profile document for the application. The system profile contains configuration settings that manage how the application works. To create the view, select the **Create > Design > View** menu options.

When prompted, set the view name to **Admin\System Profile|Profile**. Next, change the **Copy style from view** field to **-Blank-**. To set this value, click the **Copy From** button. Finally, change the selection conditions to **By Formula** and insert the following in the dialog box.

```
SELECT Form = "Profile"
```

Click **Save and Customize** to create the view and open it in edit mode.

Column 1

This column will display the form name. Click on the default column and select the **Design > Column Properties** menu options.

In the properties dialog, set the column name to **Form** and width to **20**. Switch to tab 2 and set the sort order to **Ascending**. To set the column value, change the display type from **Simple Function** to **Formula** and insert the following in the Programmer's pane.

```
Form
```

Set the *QueryPaste* Event

Click inside the view (as opposed to a column header) to give the view focus. Locate the QueryPaste event in the Objects section and enter the following in the Programmer's pane.

```
Sub Querypaste(Source As Notesuiview, Continue As Variant)

    Msgbox "Sorry, users are not permitted to copy and paste.",_
    48, "Warning"
    Continue = False

End Sub
```

Save and close the view.

Create the Request Number View

The Request Number view, similar to the Message view, is used to determine the current document number. As new requests are submitted, the top-most number is incremented by one and assigned to the new request. This view will be hidden from the users. To hide a view, simply enclose the view name in parentheses. To create the view, select the **Create > Design > View** menu options.

When prompted, set the view name to **(RequestNo)|RequestNo**. Next, change the **Copy style from view** field to **-Blank-**. To set this value, click the **Copy From** button. Finally, change the selection conditions to **By Formula** and insert the following in the dialog box.

```
SELECT Form = "Request"
```

Click **Save and Customize** to create the view and open it in edit mode.

Column 1

This column will display the form name. Click on the default column and select the **Design > Column Properties** menu options.

In the properties dialog, set the column name to **Request No**. Switch to tab 2. Set the sort order to **Descending**. To set the column value, change the display type from **Simple Function** to **Field** and insert the following in the Programmer's pane.

```
RequestNo
```

Save and close the view.

Application Security

Application security is managed through the ACL and roles. As mentioned at the start of the project, roles give specific people the ability to view information, edit content, or perform certain actions that others cannot. This step has already been completed. To configure the remainder of the database security, select the **File > Database > Access Control** menu options.

By default, the Basics tab should be active. Click on the **-Default-** user in the center of the screen. Change the access field (right side) to **Editor**.

> **NOTE**
>
> Even though **Editor** is the default setting, users will not be able to modify the procurement request after the document has been submitted. This is due to the implementation of the controlled section on the form. Without the controlled section, anyone would be able to edit the document. See Chapter 19, "Security," for additional information pertaining to database security.

Next, identify the person that will manage the application. Click the **Add** button (located at the bottom of the ACL dialog window) to add a user. After the user has been added, give the person **Editor** access and select the [**Admin**] role.

Now identify and add the person that will manage the procurement request approvals. After you have added the person, assign them **Editor** access and select the [**Approver**] role.

Repeat this process for the procurement person. Identify and add the person to the ACL. After the person has been added, assign them **Editor** access and select the [**Procurement**] role.

TIP

It's important to note that users can be assigned more than one role. In general, users with multiple roles have more authority to perform actions in the database.

TIP

The person assigned the "Admin" role will be able to see all action buttons on the document. This enables the administrator to revert the status of the document to any point in the workflow. Only people assigned this role will have this capability. For all other users, they will only be able to see select buttons based on the status of the document.

Configure the Workflow Application

The overall design of the database is now complete. However, you must configure the application in the Lotus Notes client before it can be used. This will be a two-step process. First, the workflow messages need to be created. Then you need to create the system profile. After these steps are complete, the database will be ready for use.

Set the Workflow Messages

To configure the workflow email messages, open the database application and select the **Create > Message** menu options. Create a new message document for each item in the following table. Be sure to create these messages in sequential order to ensure that the correct message numbers are assigned to the documents.

NOTE

Be sure to replace the "approver@company.com" and "procure@company.com" with a valid intranet or Internet email address. These values have been included in the table for illustration purposes and must be customized for your company.

SendTo	Subject	Body
1. approver@company.com (or approver/company/com)	Action Required: New procurement request pending review	The following is a new procurement request. Please review the request. Click the Approve button to accept the request or Denied to cancel the request.
2. AUTHOR	Procurement request approved	This is a courtesy notification. The following procurement request has been approved. You will be notified when the request has been ordered.
3. procure@company.com (or procure/company/com)	Action Required: Procurement request approved, pending processing	The following procurement request has been approved. Please take appropriate action to process the request. Click the In Process button after the order has been placed and the Complete button after the order has arrived.
4. AUTHOR	Procurement request denied	The following request has been declined. Please see the comments section for additional information.
5. AUTHOR	Procurement request ordered	The following request is currently in process. You will be notified when the shipment arrives and the request has been completed.
6. AUTHOR	Procurement request complete	The following request has been completed. The procurement items will be delivered shortly.
7. approver@company.com (or approver/company/com)	Procurement request withdrawn	The following request has been withdrawn. No additional action is required at this time.

The Message view should now look like Figure 11.18.

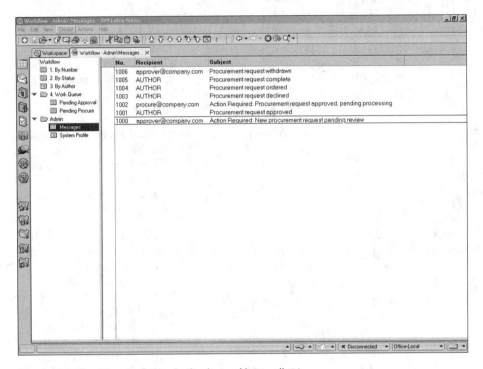

Figure 11.18   Message view in the Lotus Notes client

Create the System Profile

To complete the setup, select the **Create > System Profile** menu options to create the profile document. When created, add the following message numbers in the table.

When Document Is:	Send Message(s):
1. Submitted	1000
2. Approved	1001; 1002
3. Denied	1003
4. In Process	1004
5. Complete	1005
6. Withdrawn	1006

Save and close the document. Congratulations, the project is now complete! Figure 11.19 illustrates the Procurement Request form for the database.

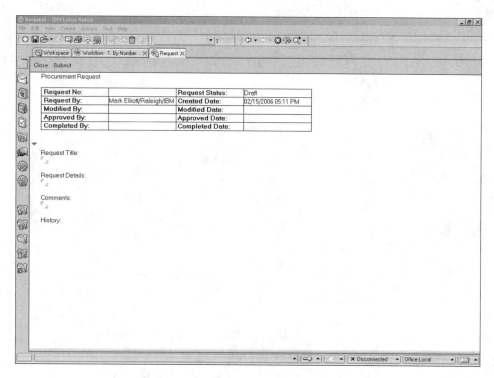

Figure 11.19   Actual Procurement Request in the Lotus Notes client

Optional Configuration

It's important to understand that replica databases (or local copies of the database) can affect the numbering of documents. For example, if several users create local copies of the database and submit new requests, then it's possible that the same request number could be assigned to two or more requests. There are several ways to prevent this. See "Disable Database Replication" in Chapter 17, "Miscellaneous Enhancements and Tips for Domino Databases," for one possible solution.

 ## Links to developerWorks

A.11.1 Robson, Marc. Send Note links through the Internet. IBM developerWorks, January 2000. http://www.ibm.com/developerworks/lotus/library/ls-Send_Notes_Links/index.html.

Chapter 12

Web Applications

Chapter Overview

Web-based applications enable the user to view or enter information through a series of Web pages. This type of application can be accessed both from the Notes client and Web browsers—such as Netscape Navigator, Microsoft Internet Explorer, and Mozilla Firefox.

This chapter includes a project to build a general-purpose Web site application. For illustrative purposes, the database will be used to track corporate or department assets. However, the content of the form can be customized to meet your individual or corporate needs. Web applications can be used for a variety of purposes, such as

- Discussion forum
- Workflow application
- Document library
- Knowledge repository
- Online survey
- Web log (Blog)
- Commerce Web site
- Customer feedback
- Word dictionary

A.12.1

A.12.2

By the end of the chapter you will have learned

- How to create an application accessible from both Lotus Notes and a browser
- How to create Edit, Save, Help, and Home buttons for a Web document
- How to set display messages when working with Web documents
- How to utilize the $$NavigatorTemplate and $$NavigatorView design elements
- How to display an informational message in the Web browser

- How to create a "computed text" field
- How to create "Pass-thru HTML" to be used in a Web browser
- How to create Next and Previous buttons for a Web view
- How to access the "Using This Database" document from a browser

Defining a Web Application

Web applications enable users to view or enter information through the Internet. This enables access from both the Lotus Notes client and Web browsers—such as Netscape Navigator, Microsoft Internet Explorer, and Mozilla Firefox. The ability to implement a single Domino database that is accessible from many clients has many advantages and is one of the most powerful features of Lotus Notes.

The ability to have a common database accessible from both Lotus Notes and a Web browser enables access to information for a much wider set of users. It also offers advantages such that information can be controlled based on the client type (meaning the content or display of information for the Web browser may intentionally vary from that displayed on the Lotus Notes client). For example, say you have a database that is accessed by both your employees and your customers. With this type of database, you can set access permissions such that employees can see all information and customers can only see a subset of information. Alternatively, you could have no restrictions where everyone can view all information in the database.

In many cases, any given Lotus Notes database can be accessed via a Web browser without having to add HTML to the design. This is because the Domino server renders the HTML by default. However, depending on the design and complexity of the database, some design elements of the database may need to be updated to work over the Internet or enhanced to improve the visual appearance in a browser.

This chapter will illustrate how to enhance a database by incorporating additional design elements in the database. These design elements improve the overall usability of the database and help to maintain a consistent appearance between clients. Let's take a moment to review project architecture. When complete, the Lotus Notes client will look like Figure 12.1.

The same database, when accessed from a Web browser, will look like Figure 12.2. You'll notice that the overall appearance is similar, but there are some changes. First, a company logo and Web site name have been added. Second, a welcome page has been included to provide general usage information (but could be tailored to contain anything). Otherwise, the New Document action button is used to create new documents and the views are used to display information sorted as desired.

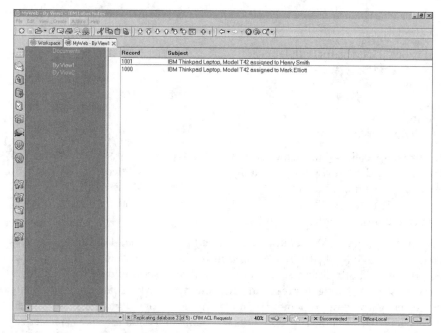

Figure 12.1   Completed Web application in Lotus Notes

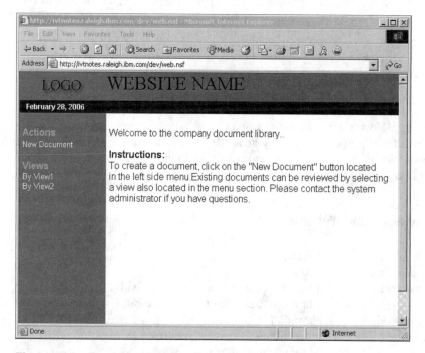

Figure 12.2   Completed Web application in a Web browser

Implementing these changes requires several additional design elements to be incorporated in the database design.

- A form called $$NavigatorTemplate
- A form called $$NavigatorView
- A frameset
- A page
- An outline
- A LotusScript library

A.12.3

Domino uses several special design elements to manage Web content. This includes the $$NavigatorTemplate and $$NavigatorView design elements. These elements are used to associate a particular design element with a Web browser. Both of these items are dependent on other design elements (such as forms, outlines, pages, etc.), and they must follow a specific naming convention in order to be utilized.

For the purpose of this project, $$NavigatorTemplate will point to the MainNav—a navigator for the database—and $$NavigatorView will point to the default view for the database. As mentioned previously, both design elements must follow a specific naming nomenclature. The syntax must be **$$NavigatorTemplate for** *navigator* (where *navigator* represents the name of the navigator design element). Similarly, the second item must be named **$$NavigatorView for** *view* (where *view* represents the name of a database view). This effectively embeds one design element in the other. In other words, these two items will work in conjunction with the navigator. The navigator, which includes a frameset, page, and outline, will give both clients a similar visual appearance.

The last design element for the project includes a LotusScript library. This library will include subroutines that will display information back to the user and that will process transactions initiated via Web browser.

Finally, implementing a Web-based architecture will most likely require coordination with the Domino server administrator. There are a variety of server settings that manage the ability to "Web-enable" a Notes database. For example, some administrators implement "user authentication," which requires users to provide an ID and password in order to access the database through a Web page. The administrator can also disable the ability to render Web pages and control how many documents are displayed in a view.

Project: Building a Domino Web Site

Difficulty Level:	Advanced
Completion Time:	5 to 7 hours
Project Materials:	3 Forms, 4 Subforms, 4 Shared Fields, 3 Views, 1 Script Library, 1 Page, 1 Outline, 1 Navigator, 2 Graphic Images
Languages Used:	Formula Language, LotusScript, JavaScript, and HTML
Special Notes:	Implementation may require coordination with the System Administrator

Create the Database

To start this project, launch the Lotus Domino Designer client. When the Designer client is running, select the **File > Database > New** menu options. Specify an application title and file name such as **MyWeb** (see Figure 12.3). Be sure to select **-Blank-** as the template type.

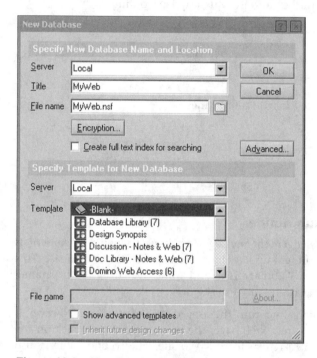

Figure 12.3 New Database dialog

Create the Website LotusScript Library

The LotusScript library will hold a number of common subroutines used to create and manage document updates made from a Web browser.

> **TIP**
>
> The following code is available in the developer's toolbox. Simply open the "Project Library" database in your Lotus Notes client and navigate to the "Script Library" section for the appropriate project. After you locate the project, copy and paste the code into the Designer client for the current project. Be sure the programmer's pane has focus before pasting the code. Alternatively, you can elect to manually type the code. You can then save and close the library. When prompted for a name, specify **WebsiteLibrary**.

To create the library, select the **Create > Design > Script Library > LotusScript Library** menu options.

Declarations

Declare common objects to be used in the various LotusScript subroutines.

```
%INCLUDE "lsconst.lss"
Dim s As NotesSession
Dim db As NotesDatabase
```

Initialize

Establish common objects to be utilized for the subroutines.

```
Sub Initialize

    Set s = New NotesSession
    Set db = s.CurrentDatabase

End Sub
```

Create the *SaveWebOutput* Subroutine

This subroutine displays an acknowledgement message to the user when a document is saved. This lets the user know the document updates have been applied to the database. This subroutine requires two parameters—a Web page URL and a message string. Both parameters are embedded in the message that is presented to the user.

A.12.4

By default, the Web page will automatically return the user to the default view. However, if the browser does not redirect to the correct Web page, the user can manually click on the URL link (embedded in the message) to return to the Web site. The second value is also included in the message. Here you can pass a text string such as `"Your document has been saved."`

```
Sub SaveWebOutput ( urlStr As String, msg As String )

    Print {<META HTTP-EQUIV="refresh" CONTENT="3;URL=}+urlStr+{">}
    Print {<br><br><br><center><FONT FACE="Arial" SIZE=3><b>}+msg+{</b>}
    Print {<br><br><FONT SIZE=2>If page does not return in a couple of seconds, click
    <a href = "}+_
    urlStr+{">Return</a></center></FONT>}

End Sub
```

Create the *AssignTrackingNumber* Subroutine

This subroutine assigns a unique record number to each newly created document when the document is saved for the first time. The subroutine is utilized by both the Lotus Notes and Web browser clients. The record number is assigned by querying the "(RecordNo)" view. This view is sorted in descending order such that the first document in the view contains the most recently created record number. The subroutine retrieves this number, increments it by one, and assigns it to the newly created document.

```
Sub AssignTrackingNumber ( docRef As NotesDocument )

    Dim num As Integer
    If docRef.RecordNo(0) = "" Then
        Dim numView As NotesView
        Set numView = db.GetView ("(RecordNo)")
        Dim numDoc As NotesDocument
        Set numDoc = numView.GetFirstDocument
        If (numDoc Is Nothing) Then
            num = 1000
        Else
            num = numDoc.RecordNo(0) + 1
        End If
        docRef.RecordNo = num
    End If

End Sub
```

Save and close the library. When prompted, name the library **WebsiteLibrary**.

Create the wSaveDocAgent Agent

This agent manages document updates made from the Web site. The agent is called every time a new or existing document is saved. To create the agent, select the **Create > Design > Agent** menu options.

After the agent is created, the properties dialog will display. Name the agent **wSaveDocAgent** and verify that the option type is set to **Shared**. In the Runtime section, select **Agent list selection** and **None** for the target type (see Figure 12.4). Close the properties dialog window.

To build the agent, change the Language Selector from **Simple action(s)** to **LotusScript** and insert the following statements.

> **NOTE**
>
> The following code is available in the developer's toolbox. Simply open the "Project Library" database in your Lotus Notes client and navigate to the "Script Library" section for the appropriate project. After you locate the project, copy and paste the code into the Designer client for the current project. Be sure the programmer's pane has focus before pasting the code. Alternatively, you can elect to manually type the code.

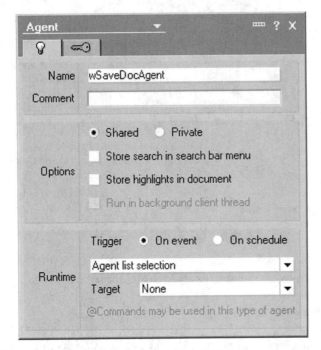

Figure 12.4   Agent properties dialog

(Options)

This agent will utilize the LotusScript library created earlier in the project. In order to utilize the library, a Use statement needs to be inserted in the **(Options)** section. The Use statement ties the agent and script library together. Without this statement, the agent is unable to locate the subroutines and functions in the LotusScript library. If you omit this statement, the agent will not be able to run, and users will not receive messages in their Web browsers. Locate this section and insert the following statements in the Programmer's pane.

```
Option Public
Use "WebsiteLibrary"
```

Initialize

The Initialize section contains the main statement for the agent. First, the agent checks to see if a document number has been assigned and assigns one if the "RecordNo" field is empty. After the document has been saved, a message is displayed to let the user know the updates were successful. These actions are triggered by the value of the "SaveMode" field. These actions occur anytime the document is saved (using a browser) and the "SaveMode" field is set to "save".

The agent also includes the framework for expanding the functionality of the database. For example, should you decide to implement workflow in the database, this field could be used to trigger events based on the field value. By changing the field value and saving the form, additional actions or messages could be displayed. For now, just be aware that this functionality has been included in the agent.

Locate the `Initialize` section and insert the following statements in the Programmer's pane.

```
Sub Initialize
    '----------------------------------------------------------------
    ' Initialize variables
    '----------------------------------------------------------------
    Print "Content-Type:text/html"
    Print {<Body><Form>}
    On Error Goto oops
    Dim urlStr As String
    Dim msg As String
    Dim doc As NotesDocument
    Set doc=s.DocumentContext

    '----------------------------------------------------------------
    ' Create record number if not assigned yet
    '----------------------------------------------------------------
    If doc.RecordNo(0) = "" Then
        Call AssignTrackingNumber(doc)
    End If

    '----------------------------------------------------------------
    ' Set the web browser message
    '----------------------------------------------------------------
    msg = {Document <font color="red">}+_
    Cstr(doc.RecordNo(0))+{</font> has been saved.   }
    doc.Form= "Asset"
    urlStr = doc.URLRedirectTo(0)

    '----------------------------------------------------------------
    ' Perform addition actions based on doc status
    '----------------------------------------------------------------
    Select Case doc.saveMode(0)
    Case "save"
        msg = msg + "<p>Thank you for your update."
    Case "future use"
        msg = msg + "<p>Thank you for your submittal."
    Case Else
        msg = msg + "<p>Thank you."
    End Select

    '----------------------------------------------------------------
    ' Display the message in the web browser
    '----------------------------------------------------------------
    Call SaveWebOutput ( urlStr, msg )
    doc.SaveStatus = "No Errors"
    Print "</Form></Body>"
    Print "</HTML>"
```

```
    Exit Sub

Oops:
    doc.SaveStatus = "Error " & Err() & ": " & Error()
    Print "</Form></Body>"
    Print "</HTML>"
    Resume
End Sub
```

Save and close the agent.

Create the Shared Fields

This project includes a number of shared fields. With shared fields, you can create a field once and use it across multiple design elements in the application. This creates a single design object that, when changes are needed, can be maintained from a single location. For this project, these shared fields will store data values to allow documents to be displayed in a Web browser.

To create the shared fields, select the **Create > Design > Shared Field** menu options for each of the following fields. Be sure to set the data type and default value formula for each shared field. After the shared field is created, close the design element and create the next shared field.

Field Name	Type	Default Value Formula	Remarks
Roles_d	Text, Computed for Display	@UserRoles	Contains the roles assigned to the person and can be used to manage read/write access permissions. This field is used if users are required to log in to the Web site. The field is not used for anonymous login.
SaveMode	Text, Editable	"save"	Contains the status of the document. The value in this field determines the action to be taken in the wSaveDocAgent. This value is case sensitive and must be in lowercase.
Server_Name	Text, Computed for Display	Server_Name	Contains the Domino server name. This field is required to build the URL link.

Field Name	Type	Default Value Formula	Remarks
URLRedirectTo	Text, Computed	REM { Reminder: the following must contain a valid view name }; "/"+@ReplaceSubstring (@Subset(@DbName; -1); "\\"; "/") +"/ View1?OpenView"	Contains the default view to display after saving the document.

Create the wMenuTop Subform

This subform is used to generate the Web page when the database is accessed from a Web browser. This form contains the HTML used to display the company logo, Web site name, and left-side navigation.

A.12.5

The majority of this subform is built using HTML, but it does include several Domino design elements as well. To create the form, select the **Create > Design > Subform** menu options. This will create a blank subform.

> **NOTE**
>
> The design and layout of the Web site has been provided as a basis for the project. If you are familiar with HTML development, the Web site design can be modified or replaced. However, it is strongly recommended that you implement the current design and make changes after the project is completed.

Create the Hidden Fields

This form will contain two hidden fields. Both fields are required to display the document in a Web browser. These fields will contain the direct path to the application on Domino server. Select the **Create > Field** menu options and create both fields on the first line of the subform.

Field Name	Type	Default Value Formula	Remarks
DBPath	Text, Computed for Display	@WebDbName+"/"	
DBPathWeb	Text, Computed for Display	@WebDbName	

These two fields are computed fields and should be hidden. However, because text properties carry over from line to line, it's *very important* to add several blank lines after the first
line before setting the hide formula. This way, the hide formula will not inadvertently carry
over to the next line in the subform, causing all text to be hidden.

After you have added several blank lines, use your mouse to highlight the first line and
select the **Text > Text Properties** menu options. In tab 5, check the **Hide paragraph if formula is true** checkbox and set the formula to **1**. Change the font color of the field to **RED**
to indicate that these are hidden fields.

Build the Web Page

To create the Web page, add the following HTML statements to the form.

```
<STYLE type = "text/css">
  A.nav:link    {color:white;
                      font-size: 10pt;
                      text-decoration:none}
  A.nav:active   {color:white;
                      font-size: 10pt;
                      font-weight:bold;
                      text-decoration:none}
  A.nav:visited {color:white;
                      font-size: 10pt;
                      text-decoration:none}
  A.nav:hover    {color:white;
                      font-size: 10pt;
                      font-weight:bold;
                      text-decoration:none}
  A.act:link      {color:darkblue;
                      font-size: 10pt;
                      text-decoration:none}
  A.act:active   {color:blue;
                      font-size: 10pt;
                      font-weight:bold;
                      text-decoration:none}
  A.act:visited   {color:blue;
                      font-size: 10pt;
                      text-decoration:none}
  A.act:hover    {color:blue;
                      font-size: 10pt;
                      font-weight:bold;
                      text-decoration:none}
  .hidden        {background-color:white;
                      color:white;
                      font-size: 8pt;
                      text-decoration:none}
  .dkgd          { background: #999966;
                      color: #ffffff;
                      font-family: Arial, sans-serif;
                      font-weight: bold;
                      font-size: 12px; }
  .blckbg        { background: #000000;
                      color: #ffffff;
```

```
                        font-family: Arial, sans-serif;
                        font-weight: bold;
                        font-size: 12px; }
    .hdgd          { color: #ffffff;
                        font-family: Arial, sans-serif;
                        font-weight: bold;
                        font-size: 12px;}
    .mdgd          { color: #666633;
                        background: #CCCC99;
                        font-family: Arial, sans-serif;
                        font-weight: bold;
                        font-size: 12px;}
    .flgd           { background: #F7F7E7;}
    .tbgc            { background: #336699;}
    .navbg         { background: #336699 }
    .sth            {font-size: 11px; color: #ffffff;}
    .gbg           { background-color: #cccccc; }
    .dgbg          { background-color: #999999; }
    .lines {background: url(/HERE/lines?OpenImageResource) repeat}
    a.pref:link{ text-decoration: none;
                    color: #ffffff;
                    font-weight: bold;}
    a.pref:visited { text-decoration: none;
                    color: #ffffff;
                    font-weight: bold;}
    a.pref:hover { text-decoration: none;
                    color: #ffffff;
                    font-weight: bold;}
</STYLE>

<BODY Face="Arial" bgcolor="#cccccc" topmargin="2"
bottommargin="2" rightmargin="2" leftmargin="2"
marginheight="0" marginwidth="0">
<! -------------------------------------------------- >
<! --- Create the logo and title for the website    --- >
<! -------------------------------------------------- >
<TABLE width="100%" border="0" cellspacing="0" cellpadding="0">
    <TR VALIGN="Top">
        <TD width="150" height="47" class = "tbgc">
        <img src="/HERE/logo.jpg?OpenImageResource"
        width = "150 height = "47" border="0" ALT="Logo"></TD>
        <TD class="tbgc" width="100%" height="47">
        <FONT size = "6">WEBSITE NAME</FONT></TD>
    </TR>
    <TR>
    <TD width="150" height="21" class="blckbg">   
        <SCRIPT LANGUAGE = "JavaScript1.2">
            var DateString = new Date();
            var month = new Array(13);
            month[0]    = "January";
            month[1]    = "February";
            month[2]    = "March";
            month[3]    = "April";
            month[4]    = "May";
            month[5]    = "June";
```

```
            month[6]   = "July";
            month[7]   = "August";
            month[8]   = "September";
            month[9] = "October";
            month[10] = "November";
            month[11] = "December";
            var theMonth = month[ DateString.getMonth() ];
            var theDay = DateString.getDate();
            var theYear = DateString.getYear();
            document.write( theMonth + " " + theDay  + ", " + theYear);
        </SCRIPT>
        </TD>
        <TD width="100%" height="21" class="blckbg"></TD>
    </TR>
</TABLE>

<! ----------------------------------------------------- >
<! --- Create the left-side navigation menu --- >
<! ----------------------------------------------------- >
<TABLE border ="0" cellspacing = "0" cellpadding = "0">
    <TR VALIGN=top>
        <TD>
        <TABLE border = "0" cellspacing = "0" cellpadding = "5">
            <TR VALIGN = top>
                <TD class="navbg" width = "150" height="400" nowrap><FONT face =
                "Arial">
                <BR><B><FONT SIZE=3 COLOR="999999">Actions</FONT></B>
                <BR><a class="nav" href="/HERE/Asset?OpenForm">New
                Document</A></b>
                <BR>
                <P><B><FONT SIZE=3 COLOR="999999">Views</FONT></B><BR>
                <A class = "nav" href="/HERE/View1?OpenView">By View1</A><BR>
                <A class = "nav" href="/HERE/View2?OpenView">By View2</A><BR>
                <BR>
                <BR>
                </TD>
                <TD bgcolor = "#FFFFFF" width = "100%">
                <FONT face = "Arial">
```

Now, using your mouse, select all HTML statements, but do *not* include the hidden fields at the top of the form. With the HTML statements highlighted, select the **Text > Pass-thru HTML** menu options. This will enable the HTML statements to be processed by the Web browser. After you have completed this step, all statements (with the exception of the hidden fields) will be highlighted in light blue. This will signify that they are considered to be "pass-thru HTML" statements.

To complete the subform, four text values in the HTML must be converted into "computed text" fields. Computed text fields enable the application to be run on any Domino server by computing the server name and directory of the database. There are five instances of the word **HERE** (highlighted in bold previously) in the HTML. Locate each instance and perform the following steps:

1. Locate and highlight the word **HERE**, making sure not to select any other characters.

2. Select the **Create > Computed Text** menu options. After you have completed this step, the word **HERE** will be replaced with **<Computed Value>**. Close the properties dialog if displayed.

3. Locate the Value section and insert the following in the Programmer's pane.

4. Repeat process for all five instances.

```
DBPathWeb
```

Save and close the design element. When prompted, name the subform **wMenuTop**.

Create the wMenuBottom Subform

The HTML used to generate the Web page has been divided into two sections—a top and bottom. Later in the project, these subforms will be embedded in a form. The HTML has been divided into two sections in order to place other Domino design elements in between. To create the form, select the **Create > Design > Subform** menu options. Insert the following HTML statements.

```
            </TD>
         </TR>
       </TABLE>

            </TD>
         </TR>
  </TABLE>
```

Using your mouse, select all statements. With the HTML statements highlighted, select the **Text > Pass-thru HTML** menu options. This will enable the HTML statements to be processed by the Web browser. Save and close the design element. When prompted, name the subform **wMenuBottom**.

Create the wNextPrevTop Subform

The wNextPrevTop and wNextPrevBottom subforms will contain navigation buttons to be displayed in the Web browser. These subforms will include the following functions:

- Ability to scroll forward and backward in the view using Next and Previous links
- Ability to Collapse and Expand the view if it is categorized
- Ability to display "Using This database" document by clicking on the Help button

To create the form, select the **Create > Design > Subform** menu options. Add the following on the first line of the subform. Use the vertical bar "|" to visually separate the various text strings. This is purely for visual purposes to help the users from a readability perspective.

```
     Previous | Next | Expand All | Collapse All | Help <br><br>
```

Using your mouse, select all   statements and select the **Text > Pass-thru HTML** menu options. Repeat the process, selecting the <br> statements to convert them to pass-thru HTML.

> **NOTE**
>
> The   HTML statement forces a "space" to be displayed in the browser. In this case, four spaces are inserted just prior to the action button hotspots.

> **WARNING**
>
> Make sure only the   and <br> statements are converted to pass-thru HTML. Do not convert the action hotspot buttons. This will cause the hotspots not to function in the Web browser.

Five text strings now need to be converted to action hotspots. They include "Previous", "Next", "Expand All", "Collapse All", and "Help". These functions will help the user to navigate the Web page.

Create the Previous Hotspot

The Previous button is used to scroll backward through the documents in the Web view. The number of documents displayed will be determined by a setting in the Domino server configuration. You will need to work with the Domino server administrator to adjust the number of documents displayed to an appropriate amount. Highlight **Previous** and select the **Create > Hotspot > Action Hotspot** menu options. Insert the following statement in the Click event of the Programmer's pane.

```
@DbCommand("Domino";"ViewPreviousPage")
```

Create the Next Hotspot

Then Next button is used to scroll forward through the list of documents in the Web page. Highlight **Next** and select the **Create > Hotspot > Action Hotspot** menu options. Insert the following statement in the Click event of the Programmer's pane.

```
@DbCommand("Domino";"ViewNextPage")
```

Create the Expand All Hotspot

The next two buttons are really intended for future use. For this project, none of the views are categorized. However, if there are views that include categorized sections, this button will expand all sections in the view. Highlight **Expand All** and select the **Create > Hotspot >**

Action Hotspot menu options. Insert the following statement in the Click event of the Programmer's pane.

```
@Command([ViewExpandAll])
```

Create the Collapse All Hotspot

The Collapse All button is used to condense all sections in the view to just the category headings. Highlight **Collapse All** and select the **Create > Hotspot > Action Hotspot** menu options. Insert the following statement in the Click event of the Programmer's pane.

A.12.6

```
@Command([ViewCollapseAll])
```

Create the Help Hotspot

The Help button is used to display information from the "Using This Database" document. However, the "Using This Database" document must be created in order for this button to work. Highlight **Help** and select the **Create > Hotspot > Action Hotspot** menu options. Insert the following statement in the Click event of the Programmer's pane.

```
@Command ( [HelpUsingDatabase] )
```

> **NOTE**
>
> The Help button will only function if the "Using This Database" document is created. An error message will display in the Web browser if this design element is not created. You must create the "Using This Database" document first. This step will be covered later in the project.

Save and close the design element. When prompted, name the subform **wNextPrevTop**.

Create the wNextPrevBottom Subform

This subform will be a copy of the **wNextPrevTop** subform with one minor change. Locate the **wNextPrevTop** subform and select the **Edit > Copy** menu options. Then select the **Edit > Paste** menu options. After the subform has been created, double-click on the design element to edit the subform.

Select the **Design > Subform Properties** menu options to display the properties dialog. Change the subform name to **wNextPrevBottom** and close the properties dialog.

Next cut the

 text string located at the end of the statement and paste it at the beginning of the statement. The
 HTML command forces a new line to be inserted in the Web browser. Because this subform will be displayed at the bottom of the page, the line break will need to occur before the hotspots. The revised statement should look like the following.

```
<br><br>     Previous | Next | Expand All | Collapse All | Help
```

Save and close the design element.

Create the $$NavigatorTemplate for MainNav Form

This form will be used to display the welcome page for the Web site in the Web browser. This is a special Domino design element intended specifically for Web applications. It's important that this form be named exactly as described here because this form works in conjunction with the MainNav navigator (created later in the project). This form includes shared fields, a subform, and a number of additional fields. To create the form, select the **Create > Design > Form** menu options.

The first step is to create the hidden fields for the form. These fields will reside on the first line of the form. Select the **Create > Resource > Insert Shared Field** menu options. Insert the **Server_name** and **Roles_d** shared fields and a couple blank lines.

Next, highlight the first line and select the **Text > Text Properties** menu options. Change the font color of the field to **RED** to indicate that this is a hidden field. In tab 6, check the **Hide paragraph if formula is true** checkbox and set the formula to **1**.

Insert the Top HTML Subform

To continue with the form design, the next step is to insert the HTML subform created previously in the project. Place the cursor on line 2 and select the **Create > Resource > Insert Subform** menu options. When prompted, select the **wMenuTop** subform. The form should now look like Figure 12.5.

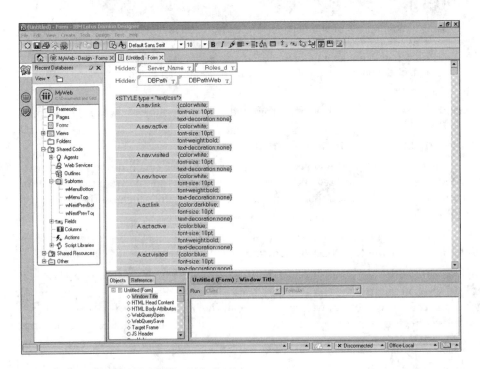

Figure 12.5   Form with HTML added

Add the Welcome Text

To help users become acclimated to the Web site, scroll to the bottom of the form and add the following statements. After the statements have been added, highlight the text and select the **Text > Pass-thru HTML** menu options.

```
<BR>Welcome to the equipment inventory database.<BR>
<BR><B>Instructions:</B>
<BR>To create a document, click on the "New Document"
<BR>button located in the left side menu. Existing documents
<BR>can be reviewed by selecting a view (also located in the
<BR>menu section.) Please contact the system administrator
<BR>if you have questions.
```

Insert the Bottom HTML Subform

At this point, the "top" and "middle" sections of the Web page have been designed. To complete the HTML, you will need to append the "bottom" menu subform to the form. This will complete the HTML for the form.

Place the cursor at the bottom of the form and select the **Create > Resource > Insert Subform** menu options. When prompted, select the **wMenuBottom** subform. This action will append the bottom portion of the HTML to the welcome page form.

HTML Body Attributes

This section is used to configure the attributes for the body of the Web page. Locate the HTML Body Attributes section and insert the following in the Programmer's pane.

```
"topmargin=\"0\"
bottommargin=\"0\"
rightmargin=\"0\"
leftmargin=\"0\"
marginheight=\"0\"
marginwidth=\"0\""
```

Set Form Properties

This form is specifically used to display information in the Web browser. As such, users should not be permitted to create documents using this form, and this form should be excluded when users search the database. To disable these items, you will need to update the form properties.

Select the **File > Document Properties** menu options to display the properties dialog. On tab 1, name the form **$$NavigatorTemplate for MainNav**. Be sure that the name matches exactly. The form name must include "**for MainNav**" in order for the Web page to display properly. Then uncheck the **Include in menu** and **Include in Search Builder** options. Save and close the form.

Create the $$ViewTemplateDefault Form

The $$ViewTemplateDefault is another special design element. This form contains the HTML used to display the view in the Web browser. Because this form is very similar to the previous one, you will copy and modify the $$NavigatorTemplate form.

From the design pane, highlight the **$$NavigatorTemplate for MainNav** form and select the **Edit > Copy** menu options. Select the **Edit > Paste** menu options to create a copy of the form.

After the form has been created, double-click on the design element to open the form in design mode. Starting with the line **
Welcome to the company document library**, select this line and all remaining statements and delete the statements—leaving the **wMenuTop** subform in place. The updated form should now look like Figure 12.6.

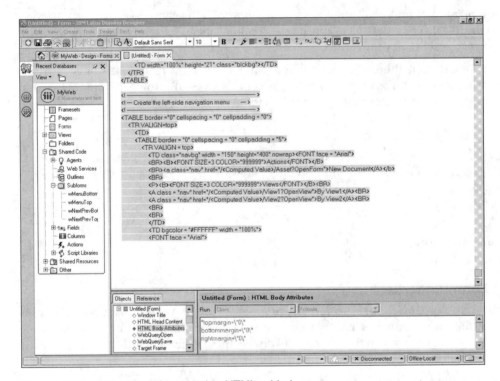

Figure 12.6   Form with left navigation HTML added

Insert the Top Hotspots Subform

Now place the cursor at the bottom of the form and select the **Create > Resource > Insert Subform** menu options. When prompted, select the **wNextPrevTop** subform. This action will append the various Web buttons just below the **wMenuTop** subform. Insert a blank line after this subform.

Create the $$ViewBody Field

The $$ViewBody field is a special field that stores the "view name" to be displayed on the Web browser. Select the **Create > Field** menu options. Configure the field based on the following settings.

Field Name	Type	Default Value Formula	Remarks
$$ViewBody	Text, Editable		A special design element that stores the view to be displayed on the Web browser.

Insert the BottomHotspots Subform

Insert another line and select the **Create > Resource > Insert Subform** menu options. When prompted, select the **wNextPrevBottom** subform. This action will append the various Web buttons just below the newly created field.

Insert the Bottom Menu Subform

To complete the form, the bottom half of the HTML needs to be inserted. Select the **Create > Resource > Insert Subform** menu options. When prompted, select the **wMenuBottom** subform. The bottom half of the form should now look like Figure 12.7.

Select the **Design > Form Properties** menu options. Change the form name from **Copy of $$NavigatorTemplate for MainNav** to **$$ViewTemplateDefault**. Save and close the form.

Create the AssetForm

This form is being created for illustrative purposes to demonstrate the Web site database. For the purposes of this project, this form has arbitrarily been designed to track department or corporate assets. However, the form is generic in nature and can be modified (or renamed) to meet your needs after the project is complete. To create the form, select the **Create > Design > Form** menu options and add a couple blank lines to the form.

Similar to the other forms in the database, the first line in the form will contain hidden, computed fields. These fields will contain data values required for Web browser navigation. At the first line, select the **Create > Resource > Insert Shared Field** menu options. Insert the **Server_name, Roles_d, SaveMode**, and **URLRedirectTo** shared fields.

Next, highlight the first line and select the **Text > Text Properties** menu options. In tab 5, check the **Hide paragraph if formula is true** checkbox and set the formula to **1**. Change the font color of the field to **RED** to indicate that this is a hidden field.

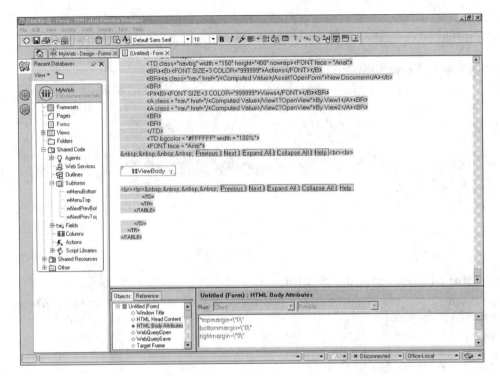

Figure 12.7 Form with bottom navigation added

Create Web Page Buttons

In order to manage the document from a browser, several buttons will need to be added to the form—Edit, Save, Home, and Help. These buttons will only be visible when the document is accessed from a browser. The buttons will be placed on the form in a table. Similar to the Lotus Notes client, "Hide When" formulas will be used to control when the buttons are displayed.

Select **Create > Table** and select 1 row and 4 columns. To set the column widths, select the **Table > Properties** menu options. If the **Table** menu option is not visible, first click on the table. When the properties dialog is displayed, click on each cell and set the width to **1.000"**.

Now highlight all cells in the table and return to the properties dialog. Switch to tab 2 and select the **Set All to 0** button. This will hide the table lines from displaying on the form.

Create the Edit Button

Place the cursor inside cell one and select the **Create > Hotspot > Button** menu options. In the properties dialog, name the button **Edit** and set the width to **Fit Content** on tab 1. On tab 5, select **Notes R4.6 or later** and the **Opened for editing** checkbox. Add the following formula in the Programmer's pane for the button.

```
@Command([EditDocument])
```

Create the Save Button

Place the cursor inside cell two and select the **Create > Hotspot > Button** menu options. In the properties dialog, name the button **Save & Close** and set the width to **Fit Content** on tab 1. On tab 5, select **Notes R4.6 or later** and the **Opened for reading** checkbox. Add the following formula in the Programmer's pane for the button.

```
@Command([FileSave]);
@Command([FileCloseWindow])
```

Create the Home Button

Place the cursor inside cell three and select the **Create > Hotspot > Button** menu options. In the properties dialog, name the button **Home** and set the width to **Fit Content** on tab 1. On tab 5, select the **Notes R4.6 or later** checkbox. Add the following formula in the Programmer's pane for the button.

```
REM { Reminder: the following must contain a valid view name };
webpage := @WebDbName + "/View1?OpenView";
@URLOpen( webpage )
```

Create the HelpButton

Place the cursor inside cell four and select the **Create > Hotspot > Button** menu options. In the properties dialog, name the button **Help** and set the width to **Fit Content** on tab 1. On tab 5, select the **Notes R4.6 or later** checkbox. Add the following formula in the Programmer's pane for the button.

```
@Command( [HelpUsingDatabase] )
```

The form should now look like Figure 12.8.

At this point, the Web-related design elements have been incorporated into the form design. The next step will be to add the fields and labels used to store data. Skip a line below the table and give the form a descriptive title at the top of the form—such as **Asset Record**. Then add the following text field descriptions down the left side of the form.

- Record:
- Author:
- Created:
- Subject:
- Body:

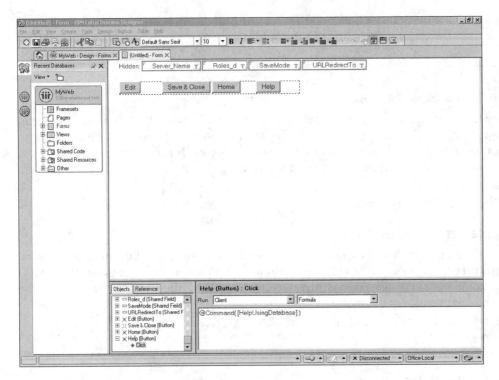

Figure 12.8 Hotspot buttons for Web browser client

Create the following fields using the **Create > Field** menu options. Be sure to set the data type, formula, and other attributes for each field on the form using the properties dialog box and/or Programmer's pane.

Field Name	Type	Default Value Formula	Remarks
RecordNo	Number, Computed	@ThisValue	
RequestBy	Names, Created when Composed	@UserName	
CreateDate	Date/Time, Created when Composed	@Now	On tab 2, select the **Display Time** setting. Make sure both the date and time options are selected.

Field Name	Type	Default Value Formula	Remarks
Subject	Text, Editable		
Body	RichText, Editable		

Set the "Global (Options)" Parameters

This form will utilize the LotusScript library. Locate the "Global (Options)" section and add the following in the Programmer's pane.

```
Option Public
Use "WebsiteLibrary"
```

Update the HTML Head Content Object

The statements in this object are utilized when the application is accessed from a Web browser. They specify the "Meta" tags, server name, and database path information. Locate the HTML Head Content section and add the following statements in the Programmer's pane.

```
nl := @NewLine;
vPath:=@WebDbName;
nl + "<base href=\"http://"+ Server_name + DBPath + "\" />"
+ nl + "<META http-equiv=Content-Type content=\"text/html; charset=iso8859-1\">" + nl
```

Update the *WebQuerySave* Event

This event is triggered every time a document is saved via a Web browser. When a document is saved, the wSaveDocAgent will assign a document number and return an informative message to the user. After the message is displayed for five seconds, the main Web page will be redisplayed.

```
@Command([ToolsRunMacro]; "wSaveDocAgent")
```

Update the *QuerySave* Event

This event is triggered when the document is saved via the Lotus Notes client. When a document is saved, a document number is assigned, if needed, and the user is returned to the previously selected view.

```
Sub Querysave(Source As Notesuidocument, Continue As Variant)

    Dim w As New NotesUIWorkspace
    Dim uidoc As NotesUIDocument
    Dim doc As NotesDocument
    Set uidoc = w.CurrentDocument
    Set doc = uidoc.Document
```

```
Call AssignTrackingNumber ( doc )

End Sub
```

The form should now look similar to Figure 12.9.

Save and close the form. When prompted, name the form **Asset|Asset**.

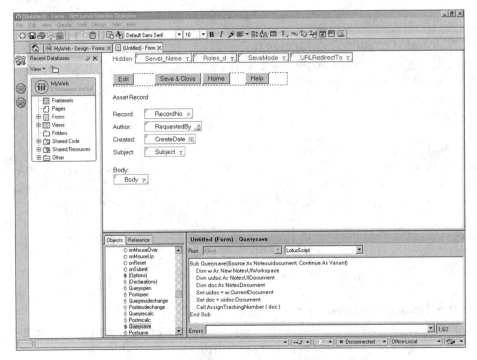

Figure 12.9   Asset Record form with fields, labels, and hotspots

---

TIP

If you decided to rename the form, all references to **Asset** will need to be updated in the database. Updates include the following: (1) change the form name in the Form Properties dialog, (2) edit the **By View1** view and change the View Selection Formula, and (3) edit the **By View2** view and change the View Selection Formula. To ensure that all references have been updated, navigate to the Other section in the Design pane and select the **Synopsis** feature. When prompted, add all design elements. Then use the **Edit > Find** menu options to locate all references to the keyword **Asset**. No references should be found. If you do locate an additional reference, you will need to edit that design element and update the item.

Create View 1

By default, a view called *(untitled)* is automatically created when the database is first created. To configure this view, navigate to Views in the Design pane and double-click on the view called "(untitled)". When the view is displayed, the Designer client will immediately display the properties dialog for the view. Specify **By View1** as the view name and **View1** as the alias name. Close the properties dialog.

Column 1

This column will display the record number for all documents stored in the application database. Double-click on the default column and rename the column title to **Record** in the properties dialog. Switch to tab 2 and set the sort order to **Descending**. Close the properties dialog.

To set the column value, change the display type from **Simple Function** to **Field** and select the following field.

```
RecordNo
```

Column 2

The second column will display the subject for the document. Select the **Create > Append New Column** menu options to add the column. In the properties dialog, set the column name to **Subject** and column width to **40** on tab 1. Change the display type from **Simple Function** to **Field** and select the following value.

```
Subject
```

Set the View Selection Criteria

Click inside the view (as opposed to a column header) to give the view focus. Next, change the programming language from **Simple Search** to **Formula** and add the following to the View Selection section of the Programmer's pane.

```
SELECT Form = "Asset"
```

Save and close the view.

Create View 2

With one view already in place, you will use this as the basis for the second view. From the Design pane, highlight **By View1** and select the **Edit > Copy** menu options. Now select the **Edit > Paste** menu options. Double-click on the **Copy Of By View1** to open it in design mode. When the view is opened, the view properties dialog should automatically appear. Change the view title to **By View2** and alias name to **View2**.

Next, drag the **Subject** column to the first column. This will make the subject column the first column in the view followed by the document number. In the properties dialog for the column, switch to tab 2 and set the sort order to **Ascending**.

Save and close the view.

Create the RecordNo View

The record number view is an administrative view used to compute the record number for documents. As new requests are submitted, the top-most number is incremented by one and assigned to the new request. This view will be hidden from the users.

To create the view, select the **Create > Design > View** menu options. When prompted, set the view name to **(RecordNo)|RecordNo**. Next, change the **Copy style from view** field to **-Blank-**. To set this value, click the **Copy From** button. Finally, change the selection conditions to **By Formula** and insert the following in the dialog box.

```
SELECT RecordNo != ""
```

Click **Save and Customize** to create the view and open it in edit mode.

Column 1

This column will display the record numbers, sorted in descending order, for all existing documents. Click on the column header and select the **Design > Column Properties** menu options. Set the column name to **Record No.** Switch to tab 2 and set the sort order to **Descending**. Close the properties dialog.

> **NOTE**
>
> Be sure the column sort order is set to **Descending** in the properties dialog. The record numbers will not generate correctly if the sort type is not set to **Descending**.

To set the column value, change the display type from **Simple Function** to **Field** and select the following value.

```
RecordNo
```

Save and close the view.

Import Graphics

Sample graphics have been provided for this project, and you can enhance them with your company logo or other design elements after the project is complete. Graphic files are created external to Domino Designer and then imported into the application design. You will need to work with a graphic artist or utilize a graphics application if you want to modify or create new graphics for this project

To import the files, access the files on the companion Web site. Then select the **Create > Design > Image Resource** menu options. Be sure to select the **Image Resource** menu option. This option is used specifically for images and is different from the **File Resource** menu option, which is used to store reference files (such as spreadsheets or PDF files).

Two files will be used in this project. The first graphic will be used as the background navigation image when users access the application from a Lotus Notes client. The second image represents the company logo and will be displayed on the Web site.

Locate the file **background.gif** and click **OK** to import the image. Repeat the process for the **logo.jpg** graphic. You will need to change the file type from **GIF Image** to **JPEG Image** in order to locate the second file on the companion Web site.

Create the MainNav Navigator

The navigator will be used to determine the default view to display when the application is accessed. This design element will be used by several design elements in the database. To create the document, select the **Create > Design > Navigator** menu options.

Next, select the **Design > Navigator Properties** menu options to display the properties dialog window. Set the name to **MainNav** and select **By View1** as the initial view to display (see Figure 12.10).

Save and close the design element.

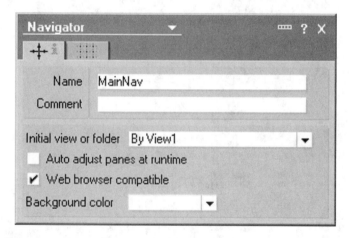

Figure 12.10   Navigator properties dialog

Create the Notes Client Navigation

To enrich the overall appearance of the tool, you will create a custom user interface using an outline, page, and frameset. The combination of these three elements will be used to display and navigate the application interface from both a Lotus Notes client and Web browser.

Create the Outline

The outline will define the navigational elements and will be displayed in the left pane of the frameset. To create the outline, select the **Create > Design > Outline** menu options.

To create a descriptive title for the user interface, click the **New Entry** button located at the top of the display window. In the properties dialog, label the entry **Documents**. This is an arbitrary title and can be set to any text value.

To create a spacer, or a blank line between the outline title and the display options, select the **New Entry** button but do not specify a label.

To add a view to the outline, select the **New Entry** button and label the entry **By View1**. Next, set the type field to **Named Element** and **View** (see Figure 12.11). In the **Value** field, enter **By View1** as the view name. Repeat this process and add **By View2**.

Figure 12.11   Outline Entry properties dialog

> **NOTE**
>
> As a general practice, you should always use the alias name when working with design elements. However, outlines automatically default to the primary name and do not allow the alias name to be specified. This means that if the view name is changed, you'll also need to update the outline to reflect the name change.

> **TIP**
>
> By default, icons are displayed next to the view design element when the application is accessed via the Lotus Notes client. To disable the icon from displaying (or to change the icon), double-click on the **By View1** to display the properties dialog. Then check the **Do not display image** option. To change the icon, import a graphic resource file and then select it from the properties dialog.

Save and close the outline. When prompted, name the design element **MainOutline**.

Create the Page

To create the page, select the **Create > Design > Page** menu options. The page will display the outline created in the previous step. Select the **Create > Embedded Element > Outline** menu options. When prompted, select **MainOutline** to add the design element to the page.

To add some flare to the display, we'll add a background graphic to the interface. Single-click on the outline element and select the **Element > Outline Properties** menu options. The **Element** menu will only display if **MainOutline** is the active design item.

When the outline properties dialog is displayed, switch to tab 2 to set the text colors. Select light gray for the **Normal** setting and white for the **Selected** and **Moused** options (see Figure 12.12). These settings will make the text more visible to the users.

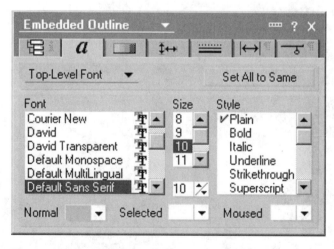

Figure 12.12   Embedded Outline dialog

Next, add the background image to the outline. Select the **Design > Page Properties** menu options. Switch to tab 2. Specify **background.gif** in the Resource field and select **Repeat once** in the Options section (see Figure 12.13).

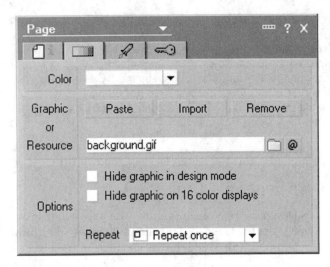

Figure 12.13   Page properties dialog

The page should now look like Figure 12.14.

Save and close the design element. When prompted, name the item **MainPage**.

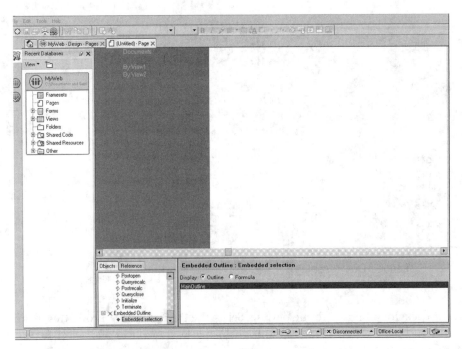

Figure 12.14   Completed page

Create the Frameset

To complete the navigation setup, a two-pane frameset must be created. The left pane will contain the outline, and the right pane will display data. To create the frameset, select the **Create > Design > Frameset** menu options. When prompted to select a design, click **OK** to accept the default settings.

The frameset is configured in two steps. First, you will configure the left pane and then the right pane. To start, click on the left pane and select the **Frame > Frame Properties** menu options. Set the name to **Main**, set the **Type** to **Named Element** and **Page**, enter **MainPage** as the value, and set **Default target for links in frame** to **Right** (see Figure 12.15).

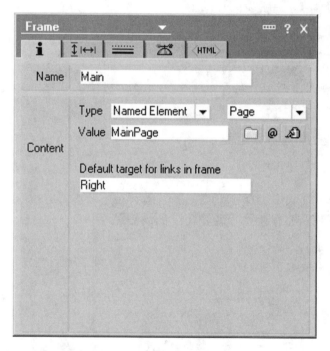

Figure 12.15   Left frame properties dialog settings

With the property window still displayed, click on the right pane. Set the name to **Right**, set the **Type** to **Named Element** and **View**, enter **By View1** as the value, and set **Default target for links in frame** to **Right** (see Figure 12.16).

You have now completed the frameset configuration. Select **File > Save** and name the design element **MainFrame**. The frameset should now look like Figure 12.17.

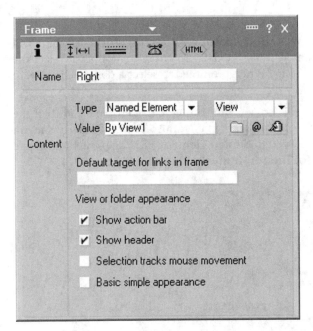

Figure 12.16   Right frame properties dialog settings

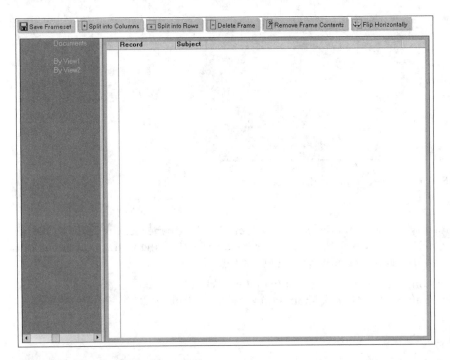

Figure 12.17   Completed frameset

Set the Database Default

To activate the frameset, the database properties must be updated. Select the **File > Database > Properties** menu options and switch to tab 5. Change **When opened in the Notes client** to **Open designated Frameset** and set the name to **MainFrame**.

Then change **When opened in a browser** to **Open designated Navigator in its own window** and set the navigator to **MainNav** (see Figure 12.18).

Figure 12.18 Set default navigator for the database

Update the "Using This Database" Document

In order to use the Help button, the "Using This Database" document must be created. To create this design element, navigate to the Other section and select **Database Resources** from the Design pane. Edit the "Using This Database" document. Add a title to the top of the document and describe the purpose of the database. Save and close the design element when complete.

> **TIP**
>
> You can add files such as word processor documents, spreadsheets, or PDF files in the "Using This Database" design document. When accessed via the Lotus Notes client, the user can save the file to their workstation. When accessed from a Web browser, users can download the file.

> **TIP**
>
> You can selectively display help information by setting the "Hide When" text formulas in the "Using This Database" document. This enables you to customize the help information. Lotus Notes users can view information specific to the Notes client, while Web users can view information suited for Web navigation. To set the "Hide When" formulas, highlight the text and select the **Text > Properties** menu options. Then select the appropriate checkbox to hide the text from either **Web** or from **Notes 4.6 or greater**. However, be sure to select either one option or the other. Selecting both will result in no text being displayed.

Security

Application security is managed through the Access Control List (ACL) and "roles". To define access permissions, select the **File** > **Database** > **Access Control** menu options. By default, the Basics tab should be active. Click on the **-Default-** user in the center of the screen. Change the access field (right side) to **Author**. This will allow anyone to edit documents in the database using the Lotus Notes client.

You will also need to configure the access permission to allow users to access the database from a Web browser. There are three options available—allow anyone to access the Web page, require users to log in using Domino authentication, or require users to log in using Windows NT authentication.

Anonymous Access

To allow any user to access the application from a Web browser, a special user called "Anonymous" must be added to the ACL. It's important to note that some companies might not allow anonymous access to be included in the database ACL. To implement, click the **Add** button and specify **Anonymous** when prompted. Set the access level to **Editor** and click **OK** to save the settings.

Domino Authentication

To force users to log in, you need to implement either Domino or Windows authentication. Domino authentication can be established by creating a "Person" document in the Notes Address Book (NAB) for each person. Be sure to specify a password in the Internet Password field. You will also need to remove the "Anonymous" user from the ACL to force authentication.

Windows NT Authentication

Windows NT authentication can also be used to log in to the Web page. This setup is documented in the Domino Server Administration guide. You will need to work with the

Domino administrator to configure this option. Remember to remove the "Anonymous" user from the ACL to force authentication.

Troubleshooting

There are several areas that may cause problems when building this or other Web applications. The following are several items to consider when trying to troubleshoot a Web application.

Security. In many cases, the Web pages do not display properly because of the ACL settings. Confirm that the ACL is configured (as stated earlier) and that a valid user ID and password is being used for authentication.

Changing the number of documents displayed in the Web browser view. The number of documents displayed in the Web browser view is determined by a setting in the Domino server configuration file. You will need to work with your Domino administrator to change these settings.

Changing the URL link. By default, the first column in the view will be used as the URL link when documents are displayed in the Web browser. To change the default column to be used as the URL link, open the view in edit mode. Click on the column header and select the **View > Column Properties** menu options. Switch to tab 7 and enable the **Show values in this column as links** property located at the bottom of the properties dialog.

Server Settings. The Domino server must be configured to support and host Web applications. Check with your system administrator to ensure that the proper settings are in place.

A.12.7

Web Page Error. Some HTML statements in this project are case and space sensitive. Ensure that all code is typed exactly as illustrated in this publication. For example, this project requires several "computed text" formulas to be added to the HTML. Extra spaces before or after the "computed text" will cause errors. When this occurs, the URL typically includes the characters %20 in the link (see Figure 12.19). To correct this, remove the spaces before and after the computed text formula in the wMenuTop subform.

How to determine the URL link for the application. The URL link for the application, in general, should be as follows:

http://**ServerName**.**Domain**.Com/**Directory**/application.nsf

where **ServerName** represents the name of the Domino server, **Domain** represents the fully qualified Internet domain name, directory path for the application and name of the application. For example,

http://server123.ibm.com/applications/website.nsf

Check with your system administrator to verify the naming convention implemented with your Domino server.

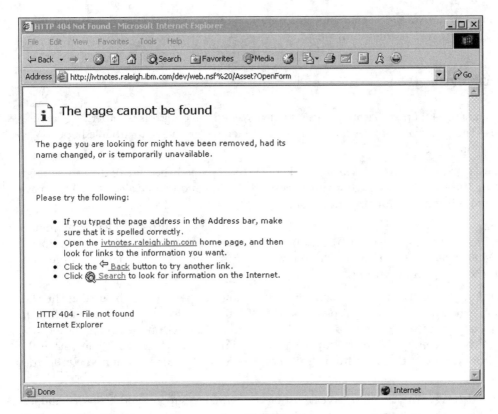

Figure 12.19   Sample error message in a Web browser

Changing the field display properties when accessed from a Web browser. The way a
field displays in a Web browser is slightly different from how it is displayed in the Lotus
Notes client. This is due to the differences between the software applications. To change
the field display for text fields, the following settings need to be added to the HTML
Attributes section (see Figure 12.20) for each text field on the form.

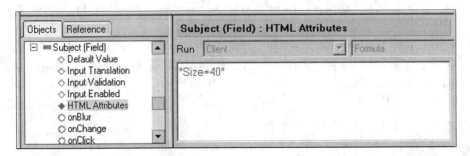

Figure 12.20   HTML field attributes

For example, to set the field width to 40 characters for a Text field, add the following statement in the HTML Attributes section of the Object pane.

```
"Size = 40"
```

You can also specify the number of rows and have text automatically wrap for Rich Text fields. For example, the following statement will set the field with 70 characters, display 8 rows, and wrap text.

```
"Rows=8 Cols=70 wrap=Virtual"
```

Links to developerWorks

A.12.1 DeJean, David. *Domino blogging: Blogs and blogging*. IBM developerWorks, September 2004. http://www.ibm.com/developerworks/lotus/library/blogging/index.html.

A.12.2 Patrick, Michael. *Anatomy of a Domino e-commerce Web site*. IBM developerWorks, October 2002. http://www.ibm.com/developerworks/lotus/library/ls-e-commerce_1/index.html.

A.12.3 Chamberlain, John. *Building Web applications in Domino 6: Web site rules*. IBM developerWorks, October 2002. http://www.ibm.com/developerworks/lotus/library/ls-Web_site_rules/index.html.

A.12.4 Schultz, Dale. *Making Web browsers look smarter with Domino 6*. IBM developerWorks, October 2002. http://www.ibm.com/developerworks/lotus/library/ls-WebPref/index.html.

A.12.5 Kovner, Larry. *Shocking your Domino Web site*. IBM developerWorks, Feb 1998. http://www.ibm.com/developerworks/lotus/library/ls-Shocking_your_Domino_Web_site/index.html.

A.12.6 Gibson, Becky. *Building dynamic collapsible views for Web applications*. IBM developerWorks, November 2002. http://www.ibm.com/developerworks/lotus/library/ls-DynamicCollapsibleViews/index.html.

A.12.7 Chamberlain, John. *Building Web applications in Domino 6: A tutorial on Web site addressing*. IBM developerWorks, October 2002. http://www.ibm.com/developerworks/lotus/library/ls-Web_site_addressing/index.html.

Chapter 13

Design Enhancements Using LotusScript

Chapter Overview

This chapter provides a number of LotusScript functions and subroutines that can be incorporated into a Lotus Notes database. Each module is for the most part self-contained and designed to run with minimal modifications. This enables you to copy the code into any existing application and implement it.

The intent of this chapter is to provide common customizations that can be added to any database application. Each customization includes a functional summary, an explanation regarding how the code works, and detailed instructions for installing the code. This means that each code section will run with no additional code required.

However, when adding code to an existing application, you may need to replace field names, search strings, or remove duplicate code lines—such as declaration (or DIM) statements—when implementing a LotusScript customization. It's also important to note that these functions and subroutines are intended to illustrate one way to solve a particular problem. As with all programming, there may be other ways to achieve the same result. In short, these modules are intended to be framework models to be incorporated into applications. Customizations include the following:

- Compare two dates
- Check for an element in an array
- Replace an element in an array
- Remove a character from a string
- Remove an element from an array
- Compare two arrays
- Define a dynamic array
- Create a custom popup dialog box

- Refresh a document from the user interface
- Search for a document
- Format dates and times
- Compute the day of the week
- Reference "$" variables
- Set the "Return Receipt" for an application generated email
- Add field validation to a form
- Display an "Are you sure?" message
- Disable the ability to create documents in a local database
- Format a user's name
- Automatically update a history field when documents are changed
- Prompt the user to describe changes and log to history field
- Create a unique document identifier
- Pad a text number with zeros
- Add text information to a Rich Text object
- Attach a file to a Rich Text object
- Format text strings in a Rich Text object
- Change a document to edit mode
- Obtain the current roles assigned to a user
- Create a document in another database
- Generate a new document based on an existing document
- Prompt in LotusScript
- Generate and send email to multiple recipients
- Add a view icon and mood stamp to an email
- Update the NOTES.INI file
- Copy one Rich Text object to another Rich Text object
- Add a database and document link to a Rich Text field
- Create a button to add a calendar event

Note to readers: This chapter does not describe the various LotusScript classes (e.g., `NotesDocument`, `NotesSession`, `NotesUIWorkspace`, etc.). Readers should review Chapter 6, "An Introduction to LotusScript," for an introduction to the language and refer to the Designer help manual, which is included with the Lotus Domino Designer install package, for additional information pertaining to classes.

A working example of all customizations can be found in the developer's toolbox in the **BookCodeLibrary.NSF** database. See Appendix A for additional information.

Custom LotusScript Functions and Routines

This chapter provides a number of predeveloped LotusScript functions and subroutines. It provides a general exposure to the language for novice programmers as well as a quick implementation solution for experienced Domino programmers. The chapter includes a wide variety of enhancements and working source code that can be incorporated into the project databases in this book or any other Notes database. All the source code provided in this section is self-contained and designed to work with no additional code. This means the code can be plugged into virtually any application and implemented with little to no additional work.

All code provided in this section is also provided on the companion Web site in a code library database. Where feasible, working buttons can be clicked to illustrate the various solutions. As a result, the code (and in some cases the buttons themselves) can be copied directly into your database. However, before implementing any of the solutions, let's spend a moment discussing how the information for the section will be presented.

- As a general reminder, the Use *LIBRARY* statement must be added to the global section of the design element when utilizing code stored in a LotusScript library. The library and related subroutines and functions must be created prior to adding the Use statement to the form, view, agent, or other Domino element.
- Each module provided in this book is designed to work "as is." However, when integrating into an existing application, you may need to comment out or remove duplicate statements. In LotusScript, an object can only be declared once within the routine. If multiple declaration statements are present, you will receive a compile error when you try to save the Domino design element.

  All duplicate statements will subsequently be highlighted in red. To correct this, we recommend commenting out the duplicate statements using the single quote or REM statement and test the code. For example, the NotesDatabase object is commonly found in LotusScript routines. The following illustrates how to comment out a single statement in LotusScript.

  ```
  REM db as NotesDatabase
  ' DIM db as NotesDatabase
  ```

  You can also use %REM and %ENDREM to comment out a block of test statements.

  ```
  %REM
  Dim w As New NotesUIWorkspace
  Dim s As New NotesSession
  Dim db As NotesDatabase
  %ENDREM
  ```

  After you have verified that the LotusScript code is working as intended, delete the commented statements from the code. If there are a significant number of lines to be deleted, make a copy of the database for historical purposes before removing the extra statements from the design.
- In some cases, integration of code into the Notes database may require a reference to a database object such as a form name, field name, view name, or target search string. All items that must be replaced with actual design elements from your database are illustrated in all bold, capital letters. The following are the replacement keywords used throughout this chapter.

DATABASE.NSF—Substitute with a valid Lotus Notes database file name
EMAIL—Substitute with a valid Internet email address or Notes name

FIELD—Substitute with an actual field name
FORM—Substitute with an actual form name
PATH—Substitute with a valid directory path or folder name
SEARCHSTRING—Substitute with a text string
SERVER—Substitute with a valid Domino server name
VALUE—Substitute with a text string or numerical value
VIEW—Substitute with an actual view name

Finally, where feasible, an alternate implementation of many of the following LotusScript modules can also be found in Chapter 14, "Design Enhancements Using Formula Language."

Compare Two Dates

The purpose of this subroutine is to compare two dates. This code may be useful when performing field validation for a form or to check if the selected date is in the past. For example, you may want to compare today's date with a date on a form. If the date is in the past, you could display a warning message.

How It Works

Two date values are assigned to the DateTime1 and DateTime2 objects. In the first example, DateTime1 holds the current calendar date while DateTime2 references a field on a form. After they are assigned, the dates can be compared using the IF statement. It's important to understand that both date/time values must be strings. When using hard-coded dates, the value must be enclosed in double quotes (in the format mm/dd/yyyy). When using a field, the retrieved field value must also be a string.

Use the TEXT property to ensure that the returned field value is a string. In the following examples, the dateTime2 statement could be replaced with the following to ensure that the returned value equates to a string.

```
Set dateTime2=New NotesDateTime(doc.GetFirstItem("FIELD").text)
```

Implementation—Example 1

Date checks are often implemented in data validation and could be added to a QuerySave event or other event within a form, agent, or view. To implement a date comparison, assign a date value to both date objects.

```
Dim w As New NotesUIWorkspace
Dim s As New NotesSession
Dim db As NotesDatabase
Dim uidoc As NotesUIDocument
Dim doc As NotesDocument
```

```
Set s = New NotesSession
Set db = s.CurrentDatabase
Set uidoc = w.CurrentDocument
Set doc = uidoc.Document
Dim dateTime1 As NotesDateTime
Dim dateTime2 As NotesDateTime

' Both values MUST be a STRING.
Set dateTime1 = New NotesDateTime( "Today" )
Set dateTime2 = New NotesDateTime( doc.FIELD(0) )

If dateTime2.DateOnly < dateTime1.DateOnly Then
   Msgbox "Date1 is greater than Date2"
Elseif dateTime2.DateOnly > dateTime1.DateOnly Then
   Msgbox "Date1 is less than Date2"
Else
   Msgbox "Date1 equals Date2"
End If
```

Implementation—Example 2

Alternatively, you may require a minimum number of days for a user-specified date. Let's say you have a form with a "desired completion date" field and you require 14 days for all service request documents. Using the `AdjustDay` method, you could compare the dates. If the date is less than the adjusted date, a warning message is displayed.

```
Dim w As New NotesUIWorkspace
Dim s As New NotesSession
Dim db As NotesDatabase
Dim uidoc As NotesUIDocument
Dim doc As NotesDocument
Set s = New NotesSession
Set db = s.CurrentDatabase
Set uidoc = w.CurrentDocument
Set doc = uidoc.Document

Dim dateTime1 As NotesDateTime
Dim dateTime2 As NotesDateTime

Set dateTime1 = New NotesDateTime( "Today" )
Call dateTime1.AdjustDay( 14 )
Set dateTime2 = New NotesDateTime( doc.FIELD(0) )

If dateTime2.DateOnly < dateTime1.DateOnly Then
   Msgbox "2 weeks advance notice is required for all requests"
   ' continue = false   ' Uncomment to halt the document save
   ' Exit Sub           ' Uncomment to exit event
Else
   Msgbox "Thank you for advance notice."
End If
```

> **TIP**
>
> To implement this technique as part of data validation for a form, add the previous code to the form's `QuerySave` event and set `Continue` to `false` if the values do not pass the validation check. This will halt execution of the document save. To halt execution of the `QuerySave` code, you could also include an `Exit Sub` statement after displaying the validation error message. See additional information later on data validation. Both statements are included in the code. To implement, uncomment the appropriate statement.

> **TIP**
>
> To compare two date fields on a form, replace the value stored in `DateTime1` with a field reference. For example, change
>
> ```
> Set dateTime1 = New NotesDateTime( "Today" )
> ```
>
> to reference a field on the form
>
> ```
> Set dateTime1 = New NotesDateTime( doc.FIELD(0) )
> ```

Check for an Element in an Array

The `FoundElement` function is used to search for a specified element in an array. For example, the function could be used to check if an email address or person's name is already included in an array of values.

How It Works

The function loops through each element in the array and compares the current element to the target value. It returns Boolean `True` if the element is found and `False` if the element is not found.

Implementation

This code should be added to a LotusScript library so that it can be invoked from multiple design elements without being duplicated. However, it could also be added directly to a form, view, or other design element. Two parameters must be specified to utilize this function—an array of values and a search string.

```
Function foundElement (varFromList As Variant, varTarget As Variant) As Boolean

    '----------------------------------------------------------------------
    ' Check for the existence of an element in an array.
    '----------------------------------------------------------------------
    foundElement = False
```

```
Forall varElement In varFromList
   If varElement = varTarget Then
      foundElement = True
      Exit Forall
   End If
End Forall

End Function
```

The following illustrates how this function could be called from a form, view, or other design element.

```
If (foundElement (doc.FIELD, "SEARCHSTRING" )) Then
   msgbox "Element found in the array."
Else
   msgbox "Element not found in the array."
End If
```

> **NOTE**
>
> The `ArrayGetIndex` function could also be used to achieve a similar result. Refer to the Domino Designer help for additional information pertaining to this function.

Replace an Element in an Array

This function will substitute a single element in an array with a replacement value.

How It Works

The loop counter variable called `i` is initialized to zero. The function then loops through each element in the search array and compares the current element to the target value. If the element is found, the element value is replaced with the new value. All values are stored in a temporary array called `ReturnArray`, which is subsequently returned to the calling code.

Implementation

To implement this technique, add the following to a LotusScript library. Three values must be passed to this function—an array of values, the search value, and the replacement value.

```
Function ReplaceElement ( varFromList As Variant, varTarget As Variant,
varReplacement As Variant) As Variant

   Redim ReturnArray(0) As Variant
   Dim i As Integer
   i = 0

   Forall varElement In varFromList
```

```
      Redim Preserve ReturnArray (i) As Variant
      If varElement = varTarget Then
         ReturnArray(i) = varReplacement
      Else
         ReturnArray(i) = varElement
      End If
      i = i + 1
   End Forall

   ReplaceElement = ReturnArray

End Function
```

The following illustrates how this function could be called from an action button. In this example, team member Tom is replaced with team member Tammy (see Figure 13.1). The updated array is subsequently returned assigned to the newTeam array.

```
Sub Click(Source As Button)

   Dim newTeam As Variant
   Dim theTeam (0 To 2) As String
   theTeam (0) = "Tom"
   theTeam (1) = "Henry"
   theTeam (2) = "Mark"
   Msgbox Implode( theTeam, ", " ), , "Old Team"
   newTeam =  ReplaceElement ( theTeam, "Tom", "Tammy" )
   Msgbox Implode ( newTeam, ", "), , "New Team"

End Sub
```

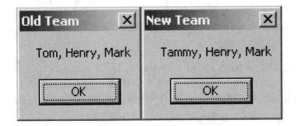

Figure 13.1   Replace an element in an array

Remember to include the Use *LIBRARY* statement in the calling design element if the function is stored in a LotusScript library.

> **NOTE**
>
> The ArrayReplace function could also be used to achieve a similar result. Refer to the Domino Designer help for additional information pertaining to this function.

Remove a Character from a String

This function will search for a specific character in a text string and remove the specified character when it is found.

How It Works

A text string and search string are passed to the function. The function loops through each character in the text string and compares each character with the specified search string. If the two values do not match, the current character is added to a temporary string. The loop is then incremented, and the next character is checked. If the values match, the current character is not added to the temporary array. After all characters are checked, the temporary string is returned to the calling code with all instances of the search string removed.

Implementation

This function requires two parameters—a text string and the target character to be removed by the text search string.

```
Function RemoveString ( TextString As String, SearchString As String )

    Dim tempString As String
    Dim currChar As String
    Dim x As Integer
    tempString = ""

    For x = 1 To Len( TextString )
       currChar = Mid$( textString, x, 1 )
       If currChar <> SearchString Then
          tempString = tempString + currChar
       End If
    Next

    RemoveString = tempString

End Function
```

The following illustrates how this function could be called from an action button. In this example, the character "B" is removed from the text string "ABCD" (see Figure 13.2). The revised text string, "ACD", is subsequently stored in the MyOutput string.

```
Sub Click(Source As Button)

    Dim MyOutput As String
    Msgbox "ABCD", , "Original String"
    MyOutput =  RemoveString ( "ABCD", "B" )
    Msgbox MyOutput, , "Replaced String"

End Sub
```

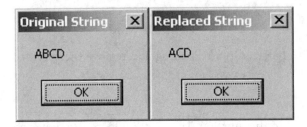

Figure 13.2 Remove a character from a string

Remove an Element from an Array

The `RemoveElement` function checks each element in an array for a target value. If the target value is found, that item is removed from the array.

How It Works

This function requires an array and target search value. The function loops through each element in the array and compares the value to the search string. If the values do not match, the element is added to a temporary array. If the values do match, it is skipped and thus not included in the array. After all elements are checked, the temporary array is returned with all references to the target search value removed.

Implementation

This function requires two parameters—an array of values and the search value.

```
Function RemoveElement ( varFromList As Variant, varTarget As Variant ) As Variant

    '-----------------------------------------------------------------------
    ' Removes an element from an array.
    '-----------------------------------------------------------------------
    Redim ReturnArray(0) As Variant
    Dim i As Integer
    i = 0

    Forall varElement In varFromList
        Redim Preserve ReturnArray (i) As Variant
        If varElement <> varTarget Then
            ReturnArray(i) = varElement
                i = i + 1
        End If
    End Forall

    RemoveElement = ReturnArray

End Function
```

The following illustrates how the function could be called from an action button. In this example, the name "Tom" is removed from the array theTeam (see Figure 13.3). After the function call, the returned array will contain "Henry", "Mark", and "Steve".

```
Sub Click(Source As Button)

    Dim newTeam As Variant
    Dim theTeam (0 To 3) As String
    theTeam (0) = "Tom"
    theTeam (1) = "Henry"
    theTeam (2) = "Mark"
    theTeam (3) = "Steve"
    Msgbox Implode ( theTeam, ", "), ,"Original Team"
    newTeam = removeElement ( theTeam, "Tom" )
    Msgbox Implode (newTeam, ", "), , "New Team"

End Sub
```

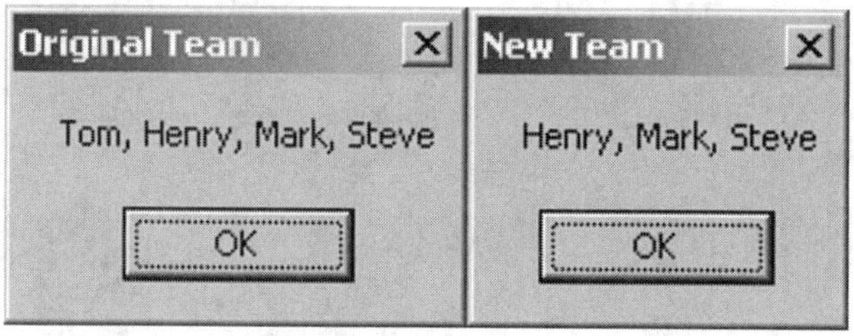

Figure 13.3 Remove an element from an array

Compare Two Arrays

This function compares the values of the first array with the values of the second array. If all values in the first array are present in the second array, regardless of the order of the values, the function returns a Boolean TRUE. Otherwise, the function returns a FALSE value. It's important to understand that the second array could contain additional elements that are not in the first array, and the function would still return a TRUE value as long as all of the elements in the first array are included.

How It Works

The CompareArray object will store the result of the comparison. At the start of the function, this object is set to TRUE. Next, two ForAll loops are established, one for each array. Each element in the first array is then compared to all array elements in the second array. If ElementA is found in ArrayB, then the inner loop stops and the next value in ArrayA is compared. This prevents unnecessary looping in ArrayB when a match is found. If no match is found in `ArrayB`, then the `CompareArrays` object is set to `FALSE`, and the function exits.

Implementation

This function requires two arrays. After the arrays are compared, the function will return either a `TRUE` or `FALSE` value.

```
Function CompareArrays ( ArrayA As Variant, ArrayB As Variant ) As Boolean

    Dim FoundMatch As Boolean
    Dim ArrayMatch As Boolean
    CompareArrays = True

    Forall varElementA In ArrayA
        FoundMatch = False
        Forall varElementB In ArrayB
            If varElementA = varElementB Then
                FoundMatch = True
                Exit Forall
            End If
        End Forall

        If FoundMatch = False Then
            CompareArrays = False
            Exit Forall
        End If
    End Forall

End Function
```

The following code illustrates the `CompareArrays` function. In this example, two arrays are passed to the LotusScript library function. A message box then displays either `"All elements found"` (see Figure 13.4) or `"All elements not found"` based on the result of the array comparison.

```
Sub Click(Source As Button)
    Dim TeamA (0 To 2) As String
    TeamA (0) = "Tom"
    TeamA (1) = "Henry"
    TeamA (2) = "Mark"

    Dim TeamB (0 To 2) As String
    TeamB (0) = "Mark"
    TeamB (1) = "Tom"
    TeamB (2) = "Henry"

    Msgbox Implode (TeamA, ", "),, "Team A"
    Msgbox Implode (TeamB, ", "),, "Team B"
    If CompareArrays( TeamA, TeamB) Then
        Msgbox "All elements found"
    Else
        Msgbox "All elements not found"
    End If

End Sub
```

Figure 13.4   Compare two arrays

The array values passed to the CompareArrays function can also reference fields on a form provided that the arrays are of the same type (e.g., string or numbers). In other words, an array of strings will not compare to an array of numbers. To implement this solution, simply replace the references to TeamA and TeamB with document fields as illustrated next (where **FIELDA** and **FIELDB** represent fields on a form).

```
Dim w As NotesUIWorkspace
Dim s As NotesSession
Dim db As NotesDatabase
Dim uidoc As NotesUIDocument
Dim doc As NotesDocument
Set w = New NotesUIWorkspace
Set s = New NotesSession
Set db = s.CurrentDatabase
Set uidoc = w.CurrentDocument
Set doc = uidoc.Document

If CompareArrays( doc.FIELDA, doc.FIELDB ) Then
    Msgbox "All elements found"
Else
    Msgbox "all elements not found"
End If
```

Working with Dynamic Arrays

Dynamic arrays are used to store a relatively boundless number of array elements. Using dynamic arrays, you can adjust the total number of elements stored in the array (as opposed to a fixed maximum).

How It Works

Using the Redim statement in conjunction with the Preserve parameter, you can dynamically allocate and resize the storage space needed for an array. The Redim statement is used to redefine the number of elements in the array. The Preserve parameter keeps (or preserves) all existing element values as the array size is increased. The Redim statement is often used with loops or the Ubound function (which determines the upperboundary of the array) to increment or decrement the size of the array.

Implementation

To implement this solution, a loop is used to create the initial array of elements. On the first pass, the array is established, and the first value is assigned. During the following passes, the `Preserve` parameter is used to retain previous array element values and append values to the array. Using the `Ubound` function, the upper boundary of the array is identified and incremented (but could also be decremented) and new elements are appended to the array while the previous values are preserved.

```
Sub Click(Source As Button)

    Dim w As New NotesUIWorkspace
    Dim s As New NotesSession
    Dim db As NotesDatabase
    Dim uidoc As NotesUIDocument
    Dim doc As NotesDocument
    Dim counter As Integer

    Set w = New NotesUIWorkspace
    Set s = New NotesSession
    Set db = s.CurrentDatabase
    Set uidoc = w.CurrentDocument
    Set doc = uidoc.Document

    '----------------------------------------------------
    ' Add elements to array for illustration purposes
    '----------------------------------------------------
    For counter = 0 To 3
       If counter = 0 Then
           Redim myList(0) As String
           myList ( counter ) = "Element " & counter
       Else
           Redim Preserve myList( counter ) As String
           myList( counter ) = "Element " & counter
       End If
    Next

    '----------------------------------------------------
    ' Display initial array
    '----------------------------------------------------
    Msgbox Implode(myList, ", "),, "Array 1"

    '----------------------------------------------------
    ' Dynamically add an element to the array
    '----------------------------------------------------
    counter = Ubound ( myList ) +1
    Redim Preserve myList( counter ) As String
    myList( counter ) = "Element " & counter

    '----------------------------------------------------
    ' Display dynamic array
    '----------------------------------------------------
    Msgbox Implode(myList, ", "),, "Array 2"
```

```
'----------------------------------------------------
' Assign array to an arbitrary field for illustration
'----------------------------------------------------
doc.FIELD = myList

End Sub
```

Create a Custom Popup Dialog Box

Custom popup dialogs are often used to control field values or to help the user navigate a database. Using a custom popup, users can select from a predetermined set of values and perform data calculations that are subsequently passed to an underlying document. For example, one of the calendar projects allows users to schedule a recurring calendar event. These values are captured using a custom popup dialog, as illustrated in Figure 13.5, and passed to the calendar appointment.

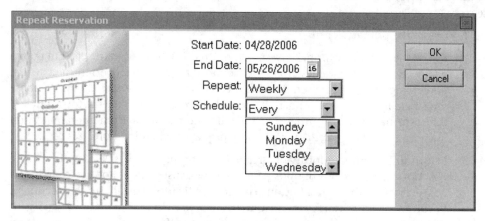

Figure 13.5   Example of a custom dialog box

How It Works

A custom dialog box is really just a form that's displayed using the DialogBox method. A button is used to display the custom popup from a form or from a view. To exchange information between the main document (or the primary form) and custom popup (or secondary form), both forms must have identically named fields. The main document must also be in edit mode in order for values to be returned from the popup when the user clicks the **OK** button. To limit data values on the primary form to those returned from the custom popup, set the fields on the primary form to be computed with the formula set to @ThisValue.

> **NOTE**
>
> There are many parameters associated with the `DialogBox` method. See Chapter 6 for additional information pertaining to this method.

In most cases, you will want to remove the custom popup form from the database menu bar and search criteria. This will prevent users from generating documents using the form. To optimize database queries, you will want to uncheck the **Include in menu** and **Include in Search Builder** options in the form properties. This will help ensure that the form cannot be used to create documents and will only be displayed using the `dialogbox` method. It will also remove the form from database searches.

Implementation

Implementation requires three primary elements—an action button, the primary form, and a custom dialog form. To implement a custom dialog window for an existing form, follow these steps.

Step 1. Create the primary form.

Step 2. Create the secondary form. This is the form that will be used in the custom popup dialog. If you want values from the popup dialog form to be returned to the underlying form, the field names on this dialog form must exactly match those same field names on the primary form. When prompted to save the form, enclose the form name in parentheses. This will hide the form from the application menus and ensure that the form is only displayed when the button is clicked.

Step 3. Return to the primary form and create an action button by selecting the **Create > Action Button** menu options. When created, insert the following code in the `Click` event of the action button. This code will automatically set the document to edit mode and display the custom dialog box. Be sure to replace **(FORM)** with the actual name of the second form and **TITLE** with a description of the custom popup dialog.

```
Sub Click(Source As Button)

    Dim w As NotesUIWorkspace
    Dim uidoc As NotesUIDocument
    Dim doc As NotesDocument
    Dim DocChanged As Boolean


    Set w = new NotesUIWorkspace
    Set uidoc = w.CurrentDocument
    Set doc = uidoc.Document
    Call w.EditDocument( True )
    DocChanged=w.DialogBox("(FORM)", True, True, , , , , "TITLE")
```

```
        If DocChanged Then
            uidoc.Save
        End If

    End Sub
```

Refresh a Document from the User Interface

The Refresh method can be used to refresh all fields on the user interface document. When called, fields on the form are recomputed and field values are updated. Bear in mind that this solution may negatively affect the performance of the database and should only be implemented if absolutely necessary. Overall impact to the database will depend on the design, usage, and size of the database. Where possible, it is better to explicitly update other fields on the form when exiting the current field, as opposed to refreshing all fields on the form.

How It Works

All fields on the form are recomputed when the user exits, or "tabs out," of a particular field. The refresh can also be called from a form event such as the QuerySave event. For example, there may be one or more computed fields on the form. After the user selects a value for a field, you may want to refresh other field values or recompute fields.

Implementation

To implement a form refresh, add the following code to a field or form event.

```
Sub Exiting(Source As Field)
    Dim w As NotesUIWorkspace
    Dim uidoc As NotesUIDocument
            Set w = new NotesUIWorkspace
    Set uidoc = w.CurrentDocument
    Call uidoc.Refresh
End Sub
```

> **NOTE**
>
> Lotus Notes also provides a form property to automatically refresh fields. All fields on the form are recomputed with each field change. This is achieved by selecting the **Automatically refresh fields** option on the Form properties dialog window (see Figure 13.6). However, readers should understand that this option can have a detrimental impact to the form's load time and overall performance. Use of this form property should be limited—it should be used only as a last resort.

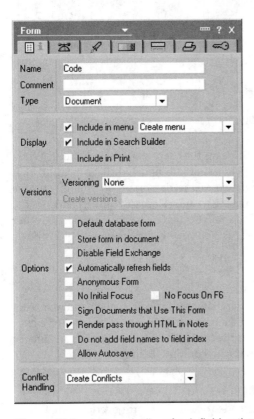

Figure 13.6   Automatically refresh field option on the Form properties dialog

Search for a Document

From time to time, you may find the need to search for a document stored in the current or alternate database. A document search is often used when you need data from one document to populate fields in another document. This section describes several methods to search for a document in a Notes database.

How It Works

A wide variety of solutions can be used to locate a document in a database. This section illustrates how to use `While` loops, the `GetDocumentByKey` method, and the `Search` method to retrieve a particular document.

Implementation—Example 1

In this first example, the GetDocumentByKey method is used to search a particular view for a text string. If the text string key is found, a handle to the document is assigned to the Doc object. After they are assigned, objects on the document can be referenced or updated. In order to use this approach, the search key must reside in the first column, which must be sorted in either ascending or descending order.

To implement this solution, create a view where the first column in the view contains the search key. Sort the first column in either ascending or descending order. To locate the document, add the following code in a button, agent, or event. Be sure to replace **KEY** and **VIEW** with valid values in the following code example.

```
Dim s As NotesSession
Dim db As NotesDatabase
Dim view As NotesView
Dim doc As NotesDocument
Dim key as String
Set s = New NotesSession
Set db = s.CurrentDatabase

key = "John Doe"
Set view = db.GetView( "VIEW" )
Set doc = view.GetDocumentByKey( key ,True)
```

> **NOTE**
>
> The GetDocumentByKey method includes a match parameter. Set the parameter to TRUE to enforce a perfect match or FALSE to allow for a partial string match.

Implementation—Example 2

In this second example, the Search method and a static key are used to locate a document in the database. This approach can be a bit tricky because it requires delimiters, such as the vertical bars or double quotes, to separate the various parameters. This approach also requires a search string key, a DateTime value, a form name, and a field name. If multiple documents are returned, use the GetFirstDocument method to retrieve the first document or the Forall statement to loop through each document.

To implement this solution, add the following code in a button, agent, or event. Be sure to replace **KEY**, **FORM**, and **FIELD** with valid values in the following code example.

```
Dim w As New NotesUIWorkspace
Dim s As New NotesSession
Dim db As NotesDatabase
Dim doc As NotesDocument
Dim collection as NotesDocumentCollection
Dim key As String
```

```
Dim searchformula As String
Dim searchdate As NotesDateTime
Set db = s.CurrentDatabase
Set searchdate = New NotesDateTime("")


'------------------------------------------------------------------
' Set the search key and search formula values
'------------------------------------------------------------------
key = "VALUE"
searchformula = "Form=""FORM"" & FIELD="""+Key+""""

Set collection = db.Search( searchformula, searchdate, 0 )
Set doc = collection.GetFirstDocument
```

Implementation—Example 3

In this third example, the `Search` method and a dynamic key are used to locate a document in the database. As with the previous example, you will need to pay particular attention to enclose parameters in the correct number of delimiters (or quotes). Here, the actual search is a dynamic value and references a text string field on the current form.

```
Dim w As NotesUIWorkspace
Dim s As NotesSession
Dim db As NotesDatabase
Dim uidoc As NotesUIDocument
Dim collection As NotesDocumentCollection
Dim docA As NotesDocument
Dim docB As NotesDocument
Dim searchformula As String
Dim searchdate As NotesDateTime

Set w = New NotesUIWorkspace
Set s = New NotesSession
Set db = s.CurrentDatabase
Set searchdate = New NotesDateTime("")
Set uidoc = w.CurrentDocument
Set docA = uidoc.Document

searchformula = "Form=""FORM"" & FIELD="""+DocA.FIELD(0)+""""
Set collection = db.Search( searchformula, searchdate, 0 )
Set docB = collection.GetFirstDocument
```

Implementation—Example 4

Finally, this last example illustrates how to loop through all documents in a particular view. If a field on each document matches a target value, then an action is taken. For example, using this approach, you could change all documents where the OWNER field equals a person's name such as John Doe.

```
Dim w As NotesUIWorkspace
Dim s As NotesSession
Dim db As NotesDatabase
Dim doc As NotesDocument
Dim view As NotesView
```

```
Set w = new NotesUIWorkspace
Set s = new NotesSession
Set db = s.CurrentDatabase
Set view = db.GetView("VIEW")
Set doc = view.GetFirstDocument

While Not(doc Is Nothing)
   If doc.FIELD(0) = "VALUE" Then
      msgbox "Found a match."
      ' do something here.
   End If
   Set doc = view.GetNextDocument( doc )
Wend
```

Working with Dates and Times

Dates and times are defined and set using the NotesDateTime class. After a value has been assigned to an object, the Format() command can be used to format the value, or a variety of methods (such as AdjustDay and AdjustMonth) can be used to modify the object value. You can also use various object properties to refine the values associated with the date and time.

How It Works

Declare a DateTime object variable and set its value. After it is set, use one of the NoteDateTime properties such as LocalTime, DateOnly, TimeOnly, or TimeZone to extract a particular value. To modify the date or time, use one of the methods to adjust the object value.

Implementation—Example 1

The first example retrieves only the time value associated with a NotesDateTime object (see Figure 13.7).

```
Dim dateStamp As NotesDateTime
Set dateStamp = New NotesDateTime( "08-17-2005 02:00:00 PM ET" )
Msgbox dateStamp.TimeOnly
```

Figure 13.7　Example of the *TimeOnly* property

Implementation—Example 2

This second example returns just the date associated with a `DateTime` object (see Figure 13.8).

```
Dim dateStamp As NotesDateTime
Set dateStamp = New NotesDateTime( "08-17-2005 02:00:00 PM ET" )
Msgbox dateStamp.DateOnly
```

Figure 13.8   Example of the *DateOnly* property

Implementation—Example 3

This third example illustrates the `DateOnly` property and how to retrieve the current date using the `Today` function. In this example, the current date is November 11, 2005.

```
Dim dateStamp As NotesDateTime
Set dateStamp = New NotesDateTime( "Today" )
Msgbox dateStamp.DateOnly
```

Implementation—Example 4

This fourth example illustrates how to use the `AdjustDay` method to change the date 10 days in the future (see Figure 13.9). Be sure the `dateStamp` object contains a valid date prior to using the `AdjustDay` (or any other) method.

```
Dim dateStamp As NotesDateTime
Set dateStamp = New NotesDateTime( "Today" )
Call dateStamp.AdjustDay( 10 )
Msgbox "10 days in future: " & dateStamp.DateOnly
```

Figure 13.9   Example of the *AdjustDay* method

> **NOTE**
>
> You can adjust the date or time backward by passing a negative value to the method. For example, to adjust the date backward by 10 days, replace the `AdjustDay` value above with `-10`.

Compute the Day of the Week

This LotusScript code will determine the day of the week based on the provided date.

How It Works

One way to manage the day of the week is to utilize the `Select Case` statement in conjunction with the `Weekday` function. The `Weekday` function returns a numeric value that represents Sunday (1) through Saturday (7). After the numeric value is returned, the appropriate day of the week string is computed via the `Select` statement.

Implementation

Set a date value for the `dateStamp` object. Use the `Weekday` function to return the day of the week for the specified date value (see Figure 13.10). In the following example, the date is set to the current day. However, this could be any date value, or you could reference a field on a form.

```
Dim theDayofWeek As String
Dim dateStamp As NotesDateTime
Set dateStamp = New NotesDateTime( "Today" )

Select Case Weekday( dateStamp.DateOnly )
Case 1
   theDayofWeek = "Sunday"
Case 2
   theDayofWeek = "Monday"
Case 3
   theDayofWeek = "Tuesday"
Case 4
   theDayofWeek = "Wednesday"
Case 5
   theDayofWeek = "Thursday"
Case 6
   theDayofWeek = "Friday"
Case 7
   theDayofWeek = "Saturday"
End Select

Msgbox "Today is " & theDayofWeek
```

Figure 13.10   Compute the day of the week using the *Weekday* function

The following illustrates a simplified methodology to determine the day of the week (see Figure 13.11). In this example, only the number corresponding to the weekday is returned (e.g., Friday).

```
Msgbox Weekday( Now )
```

Figure 13.11   Example of the *Weekday* function

How to Reference "$" Fields

Fields that start with a dollar sign are special Domino design elements that store values related to the management of the Lotus Notes documents. For example, the following are just a few of the dollar-sign fields that may be referenced.

- **$KeepPrivate**—Disables the ability to copy, print, or forward a document
- **$Moods**—Displays a mood graphic in an email
- **$PublicAccess**—Sets access permissions
- **$Readers**—Determines who can read the document
- **$File**—Displays an entry for all file attachments
- **$Link**—Shows an entry for all links
- **$Revisions**—Shows the date and time for each document update
- **$UpdatedBy**—Shows the list of users that have updated the document

How It Works

The tilde symbol is used to indicate that the following character is a special character.

Implementation—Example 1

This first example illustrates how to reference a dollar field using the tilde character. Without this prefix, you will receive a LotusScript error message at compile time.

```
Dim s As NotesSession
Dim w As NotesUIWorkspace
Dim uidoc As NotesUIDocument
Dim doc As NotesDocument
Dim db As NotesDatabase
Set s = New NotesSession
Set db = s.CurrentDatabase
Set w = New NotesUIWorkspace
Set uidoc = w.CurrentDocument
Set doc = uidoc.Document

'---------------------------------------------
' Example statement using the tilde
' to reference a "$" field
'---------------------------------------------
Msgbox doc.~$UpdatedBy(0)
```

Implementation—Example 2

This second example illustrates how to reference a dollar field using the GetFirstItem method from the NotesItem class to retrieve the item value (see Figure 13.12).

```
Dim s As NotesSession
Dim w As NotesUIWorkspace
Dim uidoc As NotesUIDocument
Dim doc As NotesDocument
Dim db As NotesDatabase
Dim item As NotesItem
Set s = New NotesSession
Set db = s.CurrentDatabase
Set w = New NotesUIWorkspace
Set uidoc = w.CurrentDocument
Set doc = uidoc.Document

'---------------------------------------------
' Example statement using the
' GetFirstItem method to reference
' a "$" field
'---------------------------------------------
Set item = doc.GetFirstItem ( "$UpdatedBy" )
Msgbox item.Text
```

NOTE

Many of the dollar-sign objects are managed by Domino and cannot be modified.

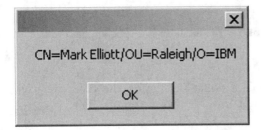

Figure 13.12   Using *GetFirstItem* to return the value of the $UpdatedBy field

How to Set the "ReturnReceipt" for LotusScript-Generated Email

The return receipt feature allows the sender of an email to be notified when the recipient opens the document.

How It Works

The ReturnReceipt field is a default field included in the default Lotus Notes mail template. When this field is set to 1, the sender will be notified when the email has been opened for the first time. After it is opened, the Lotus Notes mail template will automatically set a flag on the email to signify that the return notification has been triggered.

The following illustrates how to implement this feature in LotusScript-generated email. In this example, an email is sent to the person that clicks the button. The return receipt is generated after the email is opened in Lotus Notes. Note that no return receipt is generated if the sender and receiver are the same person.

```
Sub Click(Source As Button)

Dim s As NotesSession
Dim db As NotesDatabase
Dim doc As NotesDocument
Set s = New NotesSession
Set db = s.CurrentDatabase
Set doc = New NotesDocument( db )
'-----------------------------------------------------------------
' Create the memo header
'-----------------------------------------------------------------
Dim Person As NotesName
Dim rtitem as NotesRichTextItem
Set Person = New NotesName(s.UserName)
doc.Form = "Memo"
doc.SendTo = Person.Abbreviated
' doc.SendTo = "john doe/org/company"
doc.Subject = "This is the message subject"
doc.ReturnReceipt = "1"
```

```
'---------------------------------------------------------------
' Create the email message body
'---------------------------------------------------------------
Set rtitem = New NotesRichTextItem(doc, "Body")
Call rtitem.AddNewLine( 1 )
Call rtitem.AppendText("This is the body of the email message.")
Call rtitem.AddNewLine( 1 )


'---------------------------------------------------------------
' Send the email notification
'---------------------------------------------------------------
doc.Send ( False )
msgbox "An email has been sent."

End Sub
```

> **NOTE**
>
> In addition to the SendTo field, you can also set the CopyTo and
> BlindCopyTo fields.

Add Field Validation to a Form

Field validation is often added to forms to enforce consistency of data across the application or as input criteria for other data processing within the database. This can be accomplished by adding data checks in the "Input Validation" event for each individual field or alternatively in the QuerySave event.

Although either approach will produce the same result, you will most likely find that the QuerySave event option provides a consolidated location for all field validation. Using this approach, all data checks are in a common location, which allows all invalid data fields to be displayed in a single message.

A.13.1

How It Works

Form validation occurs when the user attempts to save the document. When this occurs, the validation in the QuerySave event is triggered. A text message field (MsgText) is used to track all warning messages to be displayed. At the start of the routine, this field is set to an empty value. A series of IF statements is then used to compare the field values with a set of validation criteria. If the field does not meet the specified criteria, a warning message is appended to the text string. The Chr$(13) statement is used to separate each warning message by forcing a new line character. After all validation has occurred, the routine checks the state of the text message field. If this field is empty, all validation is successful and the QuerySave continues. Otherwise, a message box is displayed to the user.

Implementation

To implement this solution, insert the following LotusScript code in the QuerySave event of the form. Replace the **FIELDA** and **FIELDB** values with valid field names and set the validation criteria. In the following example, both fields must contain a non-blank value. If either field is blank, a message is appended to a text message field, and the message string is displayed to the user upon completion of the field checks (see Figure 13.13).

```
Sub Querysave(Source As Notesuidocument, Continue As Variant)
    Dim s As NotesSession
    Dim w As NotesUIWorkspace
    Dim uidoc As NotesUIDocument
    Dim doc As NotesDocument
    Dim db As NotesDatabase
    Dim MsgText As String

    Set s = New NotesSession
    Set w = New NotesUIWorkspace
    Set db = s.CurrentDatabase
    Set uidoc = w.CurrentDocument
    Set doc = uidoc.Document

    '-----------------------------------
    ' Begin validation
    '-----------------------------------
    Continue = True
    MsgText = ""
    If doc.FIELDA(0) = "" Then
        MsgText=MsgText + "Specify a value for field A." + Chr$(13)
    End If

    If doc.FIELDB(0) = "" Then
        MsgText=MsgText + "Specify a value for field B." + Chr$(13)
    End If

    If MsgText <> "" Then
        Msgbox MsgText, 16, "Required Fields."
        Continue = False
    End If
End Sub
```

Figure 13.13   Example message produced by a field validation routine

Display an "Are You Sure?" Message

This routine prompts the user before processing continues. Let's say, for example, you have a button on a form that generates an email message. Using this routine, you can verify that the user really wants to proceed before performing an action, such as generating an email.

How It Works

A prompt is displayed by using the Messagebox statement. This command offers a variety of parameters that enable developers to specify the buttons, icons, and message strings to display. After the message is displayed and the end-user clicks a button, the resulting button value (if applicable) is returned to the LotusScript routine. This value allows you to determine how to proceed (e.g., continue or halt processing).

When formatting the Messagebox statement, the first parameter is the message string to be displayed. The second parameter determines the buttons and icon that should be displayed. The last parameter dictates the title of the message window. See Chapter 6 for additional information regarding parameters for the LotusScript Messagebox statement.

Implementation—Example 1

In this first example, the user is asked, "Do you want to continue?" The message box includes both the Yes and No buttons as indicated by the value 4 and is titled "Continue?" (see Figure 13.14). Based on the button clicked, the Messagebox function returns a 6 when the Yes button is clicked and 7 when the No button is clicked. To implement this technique, insert the following code in an action button.

```
Sub Click(Source As Button)

    '-------------------------------------------------------------
    ' Display message
    '-------------------------------------------------------------
    Dim answer As Integer
    answer = Msgbox ("Do you want to continue?", 4, "Continue?")
    If answer = "6" Then
        Msgbox "Yes button"
    Else
        Msgbox "No button"
    End If

End Sub
```

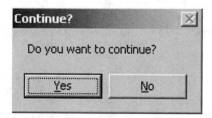

Figure 13.14 Example of the prompt to continue message using Yes and No buttons

Implementation—Example 2

This second code example illustrates functions similar to the previous example but offers a more robust approach to managing actions. Using the `Select` statement, you can manage any of the return values based on the `Messagebox` buttons (see Figure 13.15).

```
Sub Click(Source As Button)
    Dim answer As Integer
    answer = Msgbox ("Do you want to continue?", 2, "Continue?")
    Select Case answer
    Case "1"
        Msgbox "Okay button"
    Case "2"
        Msgbox "Cancel button"
    Case "3"
        Msgbox "Abort button"
    Case "4"
        Msgbox "Retry button"
    Case "5"
        Msgbox "Ignore button"
    Case "6"
        Msgbox "Yes button"
    Case "7"
        Msgbox "No button"
    End Select
End Sub
```

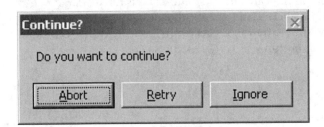

Figure 13.15   Example of the prompt to continue message using Abort, Retry, and Ignore buttons

Format a User's Name

Several properties are associated the `NotesName` class that enable you to return different versions of a user's Lotus Notes name. Several of the more common properties include the `Common`, `Abbreviated` and `Canonical` formats.

How It Works

Simply assign a value to an object and reference one of the property formats.

Implementation—Example 1

This first example displays the user's name in the common format (see Figure 13.16).

```
Dim s As NotesSession
Dim person As NotesName
Set s = New NotesSession
Set person = New NotesName( s.UserName )
Msgbox "This is the COMMON format: " & person.Common
```

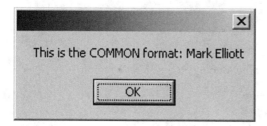

Figure 13.16 Example of the *Common* user name format

Implementation—Example 2

This second example illustrates the user's name in the Abbreviated format (see Figure 13.17). This format as well as the Common format can be used to send emails.

```
Dim s As NotesSession
Dim person As NotesName
Set s = New NotesSession
Set person = New NotesName( s.UserName )
Msgbox "This is the ABBREVIATED format: " & person.Abbreviated
```

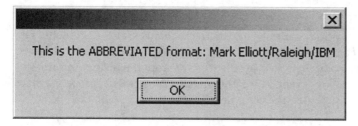

Figure 13.17 Example of the *Abbreviated* user name format

Implementation—Example 3

The third example shows the user's name in the `Canonical` format (see Figure 13.18).

```
Dim s As NotesSession
Dim person As NotesName
Set s = New NotesSession
Set person = New NotesName( s.UserName )
Msgbox "This is the CANONICAL format: " & person.Canonical
```

Figure 13.18   Example of the *Canonical* user name format

Automatically Update a "History" Field When a Document Changes

This routine illustrates how to automatically append an event stamp to the document field every time the document is saved using the Notes client user interface (also known as the "front-end" interface). Each time the document is saved, the date, time, and user name are added to the history field. It's important to recognize that changes are not logged if the document is modified through "back-end" LotusScript programming. The following illustrates event stamps that could be appended to the field each time the document is saved.

    12/10/2005 8:42:10 AM—Mark Elliott—Document changed.
    12/15/2005 5:12:45 PM—Mark Elliott—Document changed.
    12/16/2005 1:29:23 PM—Mark Elliott—Document changed.

How It Works

There are a variety of ways to automatically log or track changes to a document. One method often used to track changes is to log a comment each time the document is saved. This is achieved by creating a computed field on the form to store the history information and adding code in the `QuerySave` event to log the update. Using this approach, a statement is appended to the field each time the document is saved.

Implementation

To implement this solution, complete the following steps.

Step 1. Create a new field on the form. In the properties dialog, set the field name to **History** and field type to **Computed** and select **Allow multiple values**. On tab 2, set the **Display separate values** field to **New Line** and then close the properties dialog. If you elect to use an alternate field name, be sure to adjust the following instruction and statements.

Step 2. In the Programmer's pane, set the "value" formula for this field to **History**.

Step 3. To complete the setup, add the following code to the `QuerySave` event for the form.

```
Sub Querysave(Source As Notesuidocument, Continue As Variant)

    Dim w As New NotesUIWorkspace
    Dim s As New NotesSession
    Dim db As NotesDatabase
    Dim uidoc As NotesUIDocument
    Dim doc As NotesDocument
    Dim statement As String
    Dim person As NotesName
    Dim item As NotesItem


    '-----------------------------------------
    ' Set object values
    '-----------------------------------------
    Set s = New NotesSession
    Set db = s.CurrentDatabase
    Set uidoc = w.CurrentDocument
    Set doc = uidoc.Document


    '-----------------------------------------
    ' Define statement to be added to log
    '-----------------------------------------
    Set person = New NotesName( s.UserName )
    statement = Cstr(Now) + " - " + person.Common +_
    " - " + "Document changed."


    '-----------------------------------------
    ' Append statement to log
    '-----------------------------------------
    Set item = doc.GetFirstItem( "HISTORY" )
    Call item.AppendToTextList( statement )

End Sub
```

Prompt the User to Describe Document Changes and Update the "History" Log

This routine prompts the user to describe changes made to the document each time it's saved. The user must provide a description of the change in order to save the document. Otherwise the document is not saved and the user is returned to the document. When the user provides a non-blank description of the change, the history field is updated, including the date, time, person, and description of the change. The following illustrates event stamps that could be appended to the field each time the document is saved.

12/10/2005 8:42:10 AM—Mark Elliott—Updated document description.
12/15/2005 5:12:45 PM—Mark Elliott—Changed project start date.
12/16/2005 1:29:23 PM—Mark Elliott—Assigned project to John Doe.

How It Works

A computed field is created on the form to store historical updates. Each time the document is saved in the Lotus Notes user interface, the QuerySave event is triggered and the user is prompted to describe the change (see Figure 13.19). When the user provides a non-blank response, the statement is appended to the history field. Using this approach, a unique description of the change is appended to the history field each time the document is modified and saved.

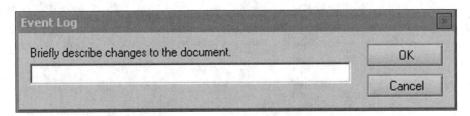

Figure 13.19   Example of the "document changes" prompt

Implementation

To implement this solution, complete the following steps.

Step 1. Create a new field on the form. In the properties dialog, set the field name to **History** and field type to **Computed** and select **Allow multiple values**. On tab 2, set the **Display separate values** field to **New Line** and then close the properties dialog. If you elect to use an alternate field name, be sure to adjust the following instruction and statements.

Step 2. In the Programmer's pane, set the "value" formula for this field to **History**.

Step 3. To complete the setup, insert the following code into the QuerySave event for the form.

```
Sub Querysave(Source As Notesuidocument, Continue As Variant)

    Dim w As NotesUIWorkspace
    Dim s As NotesSession
    Dim db As NotesDatabase
```

```
        Dim uidoc As NotesUIDocument
        Dim doc As NotesDocument
        Dim comment As String
        Dim statement As String
        Dim person As NotesName
        Dim item As NotesItem


        '----------------------------------------
        ' Set object values
        '----------------------------------------
        Set w = New NotesUIWorkspace
        Set s = New NotesSession
        Set db = s.CurrentDatabase
        Set uidoc = w.CurrentDocument
        Set doc = uidoc.Document
        Continue = True


        '----------------------------------------
        ' Prompt user to describe change
        '----------------------------------------
        Comment = w.Prompt (PROMPT_OKCANCELEDIT, _
        "Event Log", "Briefly describe changes to the document.")

        If Trim(Comment) = "" Then
            '----------------------------------------
            ' No comment. Display warning.
            '----------------------------------------
            Msgbox "You must provide a comment to save "+_
            "the document.", 16, "Warning"
            Continue = False
        Else
            '----------------------------------------
            ' Add statement to log
            '----------------------------------------
            Set person = New NotesName( s.UserName )
            statement = Cstr(Now)+" - "+ person.Common+" - "+ comment
            Set item = doc.GetFirstItem( "HISTORY" )
            Call item.AppendToTextList( statement )
        End If

    End Sub
```

Create a Unique Document Record Number

Document numbers are often assigned to work orders, service requests, or similar documents for tracking and reference purposes. Document numbers are usually numeric or alphanumeric. Instructions to implement both options are provided in this section. Although there are many potential programmatic solutions to this problem, this section details how to use the form's QuerySave event to assign document numbers.

How It Works

The document record number is generated the first time the document is saved. LotusScript code is added to the QuerySave event. When the user attempts to save the document for the first time, code in the QuerySave event determines whether the RecordNo field contains a value. If a number has already been assigned, the QuerySave event continues executing.

If the document has not been assigned a record number, the routine queries a view and retrieves the top-most document number. This number is incremented and assigned to the document. If no documents are present in the view, a default starting number is assigned to the document.

Three components are required to implement this solution—a hidden view, a computed field, and code in the QuerySave event. The hidden view is used to compute the record number. The first column in the view must contain the record number sorted in descending order. The field is used to store the computed record number. The QuerySave event is used to compute the record number value. This occurs the very first time the user saves the document.

> **NOTE**
>
> It's important to understand that duplicate document numbers may occur with local or server replicas (e.g., when the database is replicated to multiple servers). Whether a duplicate number is generated will depend on the frequency with which new documents are generated and the frequency with which updates are replicated. Depending on the database usage and replication frequency, this current model may be sufficient. However, if you desire more strict control over the assignment of document numbers, you could (1) disable local replicas, (2) create a scheduled agent to identify and correct duplicate numbers, (3) create a scheduled agent to assign record numbers, or (4) force users to create new documents on the server instance of the database. This last option provides the ability for local replicas but requires that new documents be created on the server instance. See "Limit the Ability to Create Documents on a Local Database" in this chapter for additional information regarding this option.

Implementation

The following steps describe the procedures for implementing a document identifier. After the initial setup is complete, you can elect to implement either the numeric or alphanumeric document identifier by selecting from the following code.

Step 1.　Create a new field on the form. In the properties dialog, set the field name to **RecordNo** and field type to **Number** and **Computed**. After the field type has been set to **Computed**, locate the Value section in the Programmer's pane for this field and insert **RecordNo** as the formula. If you decide to use a different field name, be sure to adjust the following instructions and code accordingly. Finally, make note of the form name. You will need the form name for step 2. Save and close the form.

Step 2. Create a view that contains document record numbers. To create the view, select the **Create > Design > View** menu options. When prompted, set the view name to **(RecordNoView)** and set the **Copy From** style to **-Blank-** (see Figure 13.20). Also check the **By Formula** option and insert `Select Form = "MYFORM" &` `RecordNo <> ""` (where MYFORM represents the form name from step 1) in the formula field.

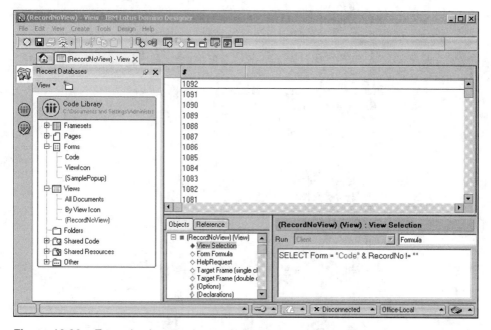

Figure 13.20 Example view used to track document record numbers

Click **Save and Customize** to create the view.

Step 3. Set the column value for the view. Click on column 1. Change the field type to **Field** and select the **RecordNo** field. Next, select the **Design > Column Properties** menu options. Switch to tab 2 and select **Descending** as the sort order. This will ensure that the document with highest RecordNo is displayed at the top of the view. This number will be incremented and assigned to the next document created in the database. Save the view.

Step 4. Add code to compute the document number. Two implementation options have been provided here—numeric (option A) and alphanumeric (option B). The document number is computed using the QuerySave event. Return to the form and complete the instructions based on the selected option as outlined next.

Option A—Numeric Only

This first option illustrates the code to generate a numeric document number. By default, the first document will start with 1000 and will sequentially increment as additional documents are created. To adjust the start number, change the value in the following code.

Step 5a. Insert this code in the QuerySave event of the form.

```
Sub Querysave(Source As Notesuidocument, Continue As Variant)
    Dim s As NotesSession
    Dim w As NotesUIWorkspace
    Dim uidoc As NotesUIDocument
    Dim doc As NotesDocument
    Dim db As NotesDatabase
    Dim num As Integer
    Dim numView As NotesView
    Dim numDoc As NotesDocument


    '----------------------------------------
    ' Set object values
    '----------------------------------------
    Set s = New NotesSession
    Set db = s.CurrentDatabase
    Set w = New NotesUIWorkspace
    Set uidoc = w.CurrentDocument
    Set doc = uidoc.Document


    '----------------------------------------
    ' Increment the document number
    '----------------------------------------
    If doc.RecordNo(0) = "" Then
        Set numView = db.GetView ( "(RecordNoView)" )
        Set numDoc = numView.GetFirstDocument
        If (numDoc Is Nothing) Then
            ' Set the default starting number
            num = 1000
        Else
            num = numDoc.RecordNo(0) + 1
        End If
        doc.RecordNo = num
    End If
End Sub
```

> **TIP**
>
> You can prefix a text string on the form (just prior to the field) to give the appearance that the document has an alphanumeric value. This is a simple method to update the interface without having to make significant code changes. For example, let's say you have a form that tracks customer Requests for Service (RFS) (see Figure 13.21). To prefix the document number with "RFS", insert a text string on the form just prior to the field (as illustrated next). You will also need to update all view columns that display this field. This provides a quick implementation solution to convert from a numeric to pseudo-alphanumeric document tracking number.

Figure 13.21   Appending text to the field on a form

Option B—Alphanumeric

This second option illustrates the code to generate an alphanumeric document number. This option works like the numeric-only option. However, implementation requires two fields—one field to store the numeric value (e.g., RecordNo) and a second field to store the alphanumeric value (e.g., RecordID). By default, the first document will start with 1000 and will sequentially increment as additional documents are created. The RecordNo field will be used to store only the number value—similar to the first option.

After it is computed, this value is then converted to a string and used to create the alphanumeric value. This value is subsequently stored in the RecordID field as a Text value. For example, you could prefix the document identifier with text such as RFS (Request for Service) or SR (Service Request), or you could append the transaction year.

- RFS-1000
- SR-1000-2005
- 2005-SR-1000

Step 5b.   Create a new field on the form. In the properties dialog, set the field name to **RecordID** and the field type to **Number** and **Computed**. After the field type has been set to **Computed**, locate the Value section in the Programmer's pane for this field and insert **RecordID** as the formula.

Step 6b.   Insert the following code in the QuerySave event. To adjust the start number, change the default start value. (Note: The following example will produce a document number in the format RFS-1000-2006, where 1000 represents the unique record number and 2006 represents the year the document was created.)

```
Sub Querysave(Source As Notesuidocument, Continue As Variant)
    Dim s As NotesSession
    Dim w As NotesUIWorkspace
    Dim uidoc As NotesUIDocument
    Dim doc As NotesDocument
    Dim db As NotesDatabase
    Dim num As Integer
    Dim numView As NotesView
    Dim numDoc As NotesDocument


    '-------------------------------------------
    ' Set object values
    '-------------------------------------------
    Set s = New NotesSession
    Set db = s.CurrentDatabase
    Set w = New NotesUIWorkspace
```

```
Set uidoc = w.CurrentDocument
Set doc = uidoc.Document

'----------------------------------------
' Increment the document number
'----------------------------------------
If doc.RecordNo(0) = "" Then
    Set numView = db.GetView ( "(RecordNoView)" )
    Set numDoc = numView.GetFirstDocument

    '----------------------------------------
    ' Set the numeric value
    '----------------------------------------
    If (numDoc Is Nothing) Then
        ' Set the default starting number
        num = 1000
    Else
        num = numDoc.RecordNo(0) + 1
    End If

    '----------------------------------------
    ' Set the alpha-numeric value
    '----------------------------------------
    doc.RecordNo = num
    doc.RecordID = "RFS-" & num & "-" & Year( Today )
End If

End Sub
```

Limit the Ability to Create Documents on a Local Database

As a Domino developer, you may find the need to limit the ability to create documents in a local replica of a database. For example, if the Notes application automatically assigns sequential document numbers as new documents are created and users are permitted to create documents in local replicas, then it's possible that the same document number could be assigned to multiple documents. One solution is to restrict the ability to create new documents on the local database.

How It Works

The QueryOpen event is triggered as documents are about to be displayed in the Lotus Notes user interface. Here, you can check the state of the document (e.g., new or existing document) as well as the location of the database (e.g., local or server). The combination of these two values enables you to limit the creation of documents.

First, the routine determines whether the document is new or preexisting using the IsNewDoc function. If the document already exists in the database, a FALSE value is returned and processing continues. Otherwise, a TRUE value is returned. This indicates that a new document is about to be created via the user interface, and an additional validation check is performed.

To determine whether the document is on the server, the LotusScript code checks the
`Server` property for the database object. If this property is empty, a local database is being
used. When the database is a local instance, a warning message is displayed and processing
stops. Otherwise, the database resides on the server and processing continues.

> **NOTE**
>
> This solution limits the ability to create new documents via the user
> interface. Depending on the database design and user skill level, a
> Notes-savvy person may still be able to create a new document
> through back-end programming.

Implementation

To implement this solution, insert the following code in the `QueryOpen` event for a given
form.

```
Sub Queryopen(Source As Notesuidocument, Mode As Integer, Isnewdoc As Variant,
Continue As Variant)

    Dim s As NotesSession
    Dim db As NotesDatabase
    Set s = New NotesSession
    Set db = s.CurrentDatabase

    Continue = True
    If source.IsNewDoc Then
        If db.Server = "" Then
            '-------------------------------------------
            ' Local instance halt processing
            '-------------------------------------------
            Msgbox "New documents must be created "+_
            "on the server.", 16, "Local Database"
            continue = False
        Else
            '-------------------------------------------
            ' Server instance continue processing
            '-------------------------------------------
            ' Msgbox "Database resides on a server."
        End If
    End If

End Sub
```

How to Zero Pad a Text Number

This routine illustrates how to zero pad a text number. This solution might be used when
creating an alphanumeric document record number (refer to the section entitled "Create a
Unique Document Record Number" for additional information).

How It Works

This solution compares the string length of value (num) with a total number of digits required (requiredDigits). If the difference is less than the required value, zeros are prefixed to the value by using the String function and concatenating it with the original value. To adjust the number of zeros padded to the number, increase or decrease the numeric value assigned to requiredDigits.

Implementation

To implement this solution, set the total number of digits required (see Figure 13.22) and assign a value to the num object. In the example, the prompt statement is used to assign a value to the num object.

```
Dim w As New NotesUIWorkspace
Dim num As String
Dim diff As Integer
Dim requiredDigits As Integer

'--------------------------------------
' Specify total number of digits required.
' A number less than this value will be
' zero padded.
'--------------------------------------
requiredDigits = 4

'--------------------------------------
' Prompt user to specify a value
'--------------------------------------
num = Trim(w.Prompt (3, "Enter a value",+_
"Specify a number to zero pad?"))

'--------------------------------------
' Compare string lengths and pad with zeros
'--------------------------------------
diff = requiredDigits - Len(num)
If Len (num) < requiredDigits Then
    num = String ( diff, "0" ) + num
End If
Msgbox "This is a zero padded number: " + num,, "Padded Value"
```

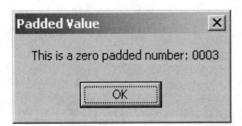

Figure 13.22   Pad a text number with zeros

How to Add Text to a Rich Text Object

Unlike a text field, where you assign a text string to an object, a Rich Text field requires additional statements using the NotesRichTextItem class. The methods and properties associated with this class enable you to insert text strings and format a Rich Text field.

How It Works

In order to reference a Rich Text field, you must instantiate a NotesRichTextItem object. Then using methods such as AddNewLine and AppendText, you can change the text and appearance of the Rich Text object.

Implementation

To insert text in a new Rich Text field, you must obtain a handle to a document (doc) and create a NotesRichTextItem object. The following will insert a single blank line, the statement "This is a test", and another blank line in a field called **ATTACHMENTS**. To implement this code, replace **ATTACHMENTS** with the appropriate Rich Text field name.

```
Dim s As NotesSession
Dim db As NotesDatabase
Dim doc As NotesDocument
Dim rtitem as NotesRichTextItem

Set s = New NotesSession
Set db = s.CurrentDatabase
Set doc = New NotesDocument (db)
Set rtitem = New NotesRichTextItem( doc, "ATTACHMENTS")

Call rtitem.AddNewLine( 1 )
Call rtitem.AppendText("This is a test")
Call rtitem.AddNewLine( 1 )
```

How to Attach a File to a Rich Text Object

This routine illustrates how to attach a file to a Rich Text field using LotusScript. Using this solution, users can click on an action button and select a file, and the selected file is appended to the predefined Rich Text field on the form.

How It Works

Files can be attached to a Rich Text object using the NotesEmbeddedObject class. First, you must instantiate a NotesEmbeddedObject and a NotesRichTextItem object. Then, using the EmbedObject method, a user can select a file to be attached to the specified NotesRichTextItem field.

Implementation

The following code illustrates how to prompt the user to select a file, attach the file to the Rich Text field called "Body", and email the file to yourself. To implement this solution, create an action button on either a form or view, change the Language Selector to **LotusScript**, and insert the following code in the Programmer's pane.

```
Sub Click(Source As Button)

    '---------------------------------------------------------
    ' Define the objects
    '---------------------------------------------------------
    Dim s As New NotesSession
    Dim w As New NotesUIWorkspace
    Dim db As NotesDatabase
    Dim doc As NotesDocument
    Dim rtitem As NotesRichTextItem
    Dim object As NotesEmbeddedObject
    Dim Person As NotesName
    Dim filename as Variant

    Set s = new NotesSession
    Set w = new NotesUIWorkspace
    Set db = s.CurrentDatabase
    Set doc = New NotesDocument (db)

    '---------------------------------------------------------
    ' Prompt user to select a file.
    '---------------------------------------------------------
    filename = w.OpenFileDialog ( True, "Select a file." , , "c:\" )

    '---------------------------------------------------------
    ' Build the email
    '---------------------------------------------------------
    Set Person = New NotesName

    doc.Form = "Memo"
    doc.SendTo = Person.Abbreviated
    doc.Subject = "Requested File"

    '---------------------------------------------------------
    ' Format the Rich Text field and send email
    '---------------------------------------------------------
    Set rtitem = New NotesRichTextItem( doc, "Body" )
    Call rtitem.AddNewline(1)
    Call rtitem.AppendText( "Here is the file you requested." )
    Call rtitem.AddNewline (2)
    Set object = rtitem.EmbedObject ( EMBED_ATTACHMENT, +_
    "", filename(0) )
    doc.Send False
    Msgbox "The requested file has been sent.", 0, "Success"

End Sub
```

How to Format Text in a Rich Text Object

Using the `NotesRichTextStyle` class, you can format the content of a Rich Text object. This routine illustrates how to set the font, change the font size, and apply color to text.

How It Works

To format Rich Text objects, a style property is assigned to a `NotesRichTextStyle` object (such as the font). This style is then applied to the Rich Text object. After it is applied, all subsequent text inserted into the object will contain these applied characteristics. The style changes can be applied prior to any text insertions.

Implementation

Formatting text strings requires a `NotesRichTextItem` and `NotesRichTextStyle` object. After they are defined, set the style properties prior to inserting text. The following illustrates an action button that sends an email with three uniquely formatted text strings. Notice that the style properties are set and applied to the Rich Text object (called `rtitem`) prior to using the `appendtext` method to insert a text string.

```
Sub Click(Source As Button)

    '-----------------------------------------------------------
    ' Define the objects
    '-----------------------------------------------------------
    Dim s As NotesSession
    Dim w As NotesUIWorkspace
    Dim db As NotesDatabase
    Dim doc As NotesDocument
    Dim PersonName As NotesName
    Dim rtitem As NotesRichTextItem
    Dim richStyle As NotesRichTextStyle

    Set s = New NotesSession
    Set w = New NotesUIWorkspace
    Set db = s.CurrentDatabase
    Set doc = New NotesDocument (db)

    '-----------------------------------------------------------
    ' Build the email header
    '-----------------------------------------------------------
    Set Person = New NotesName ( s.UserName )
    doc.Form = "Memo"
    doc.SendTo = Person.Abbreviated
    doc.Subject = "Sample email with formatted Richtext"

    '-----------------------------------------------------------
    ' Create the Rich Text item and style objects
    '-----------------------------------------------------------
```

```
Set richStyle = s.CreateRichTextStyle
Set rtitem = New NotesRichTextItem( doc, "Body" )

'-----------------------------------------------------------
' Set Font=courier, Fontsize=14
'-----------------------------------------------------------
richStyle.NotesFont = FONT_COURIER
richStyle.FontSize = 14
Call rtitem.AppendStyle(richStyle)
Call rtitem.AddNewline(1)
Call rtitem.AppendText( "You are invited to a..." )
Call rtitem.AddNewline (2)


'-----------------------------------------------------------
' Set Fontsize=24, Color = Dark Magenta
' Font is still Courier, Bold and Italic
'-----------------------------------------------------------
richStyle.NotesColor = COLOR_DARK_MAGENTA
richStyle.FontSize = 24
richStyle.Bold = True
richStyle.Italic = True
Call rtitem.AppendStyle(richStyle)
Call rtitem.AppendText("New Years Eve party!")
Call rtitem.AddNewline (2)


'-----------------------------------------------------------
' Set Font=Roman, Fontsize=14, Color=Blue
' Turn off Italic, Bold is still enabled
'-----------------------------------------------------------
richStyle.NotesColor = COLOR_BLUE
richStyle.NotesFont = FONT_ROMAN
richStyle.FontSize = 14
richStyle.Italic = False
Call rtitem.AppendStyle(richStyle)
Call rtitem.AppendText("See you there!")


'-----------------------------------------------------------
' Send the email
'-----------------------------------------------------------
doc.Send False
Msgbox "Sample email has been sent."

End Sub
```

Figure 13.23 illustrates the email generated by this LotusScript code example.

Figure 13.23   Format text in a Rich Text field or object

Change Document to Edit Mode

Using a subroutine, you can change the state of the current document (as displayed in the user interface) to either read-only or edit mode. This solution is handy if you have buttons that update fields using the user interface and the document must be in edit mode, or if you want to change the document state after performing a change. This approach provides a user-friendly implementation. The document is automatically switched to edit mode prior to setting values on the document.

How It Works

The document state is changed based on the Boolean value passed to the SetEditMode subroutine. Passing a TRUE value will open the document in edit mode. Passing a FALSE value will set the document to read-only mode. Using the EditDocument method, the subroutine toggles between document states.

Implementation

This routine can only be implemented when documents are accessed from the front-end. Pass a TRUE or FALSE parameter to the LotusScript subroutine, and the document edit mode will change accordingly. Place the following in a LotusScript library.

```
Sub SetEditMode ( value as Boolean )

   Dim w As NotesUIWorkspace
   Set w = New NotesUIWorkspace
   If (value = True) or (value = False) Then
      Call w.EditDocument( value )
   Else
      msgbox "Invalid parameter passed to SetEditMode subroutine."
   End If

End Sub
```

The following code illustrates how to call the subroutine to change the document into edit mode. When the document is in edit mode, you can insert additional code to continue with application processing.

```
Sub Click(Source As Button)

   Call SetEditMode ( True )
   REM continue with processing

End Sub
```

> **NOTE**
>
> Remember to include the Use *LIBRARY* statement (where *LIBRARY* represents the name of the LotusScript library) if adding this subroutine to a shared library. Otherwise, you will receive an error when attempting to save the design element. No Use statement is required if the subroutine is included in the current design element.

Obtain the Current Roles Assigned to a User

The QueryAccessRoles method of the NotesDatabase class allows you to obtain the user's role prior to performing an action or setting a data value. This approach enables you to customize the subroutine based on the Access Control List (ACL) roles for the user or to inform the user that he or she has insufficient access to perform a particular task, among other uses.

How It Works

This is a built-in Domino function. The roles assigned to the current user are returned by using the `QueryAccessRoles` method of the `NotesDatabase` class. Simply pass a Lotus Notes name to the method, and the roles are returned for a given database.

Implementation—Example 1

First, create one or more roles in the ACL for the Notes database application. Assign roles to users and user groups. Then set a database object and use the `QueryAccessRole` method to retrieve the current roles for the specified user. The following illustrates an action button that displays all roles assigned to the current user.

```
Sub Click(Source As Button)

   Dim s As NotesSession
   Dim db As NotesDatabase
   Dim roles as Variant

   Set s = new NotesSession
   Set db = s.CurrentDatabase
   roles = db.QueryAccessRoles( s.UserName )

   If Roles(0) = "" Then
      Msgbox "No roles assigned or this is a local database."
   Else
      Msgbox "You currently have the following roles:" +_
      Chr$(13) + Implode ( roles, Chr$(13) )
   End If

End Sub
```

Implementation—Example 2

This second example illustrates how to conditionally execute statements based on the role assigned to the user. Here, you perform different tasks or elect not to perform tasks based on the role.

```
Sub Click(Source As Button)

   Dim s As NotesSession
   Dim db As NotesDatabase
   Dim roles as Variant

   Set s = new NotesSession
   Set db = s.CurrentDatabase
   roles = db.QueryAccessRoles( s.UserName )

   Forall role In roles
      If role = "[Developer]" Then Msgbox "Perform a task A"
      If role = "[TeamLead]" Then Msgbox "Perform a task B"
      If role = "[Employee]" Then Msgbox "Perform a task C"
   End Forall

End Sub
```

Generate a Document in Another Database

This routine illustrates how to create a button that, when clicked, composes a document in another database. This approach can be used to

- Create a document in another database using values from the current database document
- Provide a user-friendly method to locate and create a document in another database

The button can then be incorporated in an existing Notes database application or inserted into an email and distributed to users. This solution creates the new document through the user interface (or via front-end objects).

How It Works

To create a document in another database, you will need to gather information pertaining to the database, form, and fields. After this information has been determined, you can instantiate a `NotesDatabase` object that references the secondary database. Then, using the `NotesDocument` class, you can generate the document, preset field values, and display the form via the `ComposeDocument` method.

Implementation

The following outlines the process to create an action button that creates a form in another database.

Step 1.   Verify that users have appropriate access to the target database. Users must have authority to access the target database. If the user that clicks the button does not have at a minimum "Depositor" access, then he or she will not be able to create a document.

Step 2.   Gather design properties for the target database. Determine the Domino server name, directory path, and database name for the target application. This can be achieved by manually opening the database using the Lotus Notes client and selecting the **File > Database > Properties** menu options. This will display a dialog box similar to Figure 13.24. Make note of the server name (e.g., **IBMTOOLS**) and filename information (e.g., **Apps\RFS.nsf**, where **Apps** is the directory path and **RFS.NSF** is the database name).

Step 3.   Determine the default form name. Open the target database and open an existing document. Select the **File > Document Properties** menu option. Switch to tab 2. Make note of the value assigned to the **Form** field (see Figure 13.25).

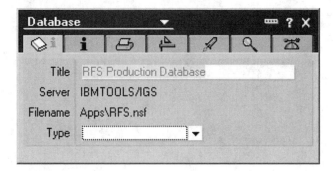

Figure 13.24 Database properties dialog

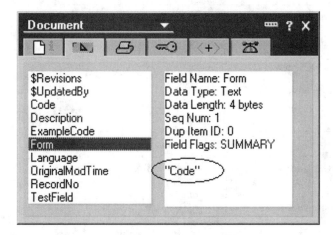

Figure 13.25 Field names and values for a document in a database

Step 4. Create an action button in the current database and insert the following LotusScript code in the Programmer's pane. Then set the database connection field values (located at the top of the code). Replace **SERVER, PATH, DATABASE,** and **FORM** with values that reference the target database.

> **NOTE**
>
> A double back-slash must be used to separate the directory path and the database file name. If the Notes application is stored in the server root directory, then simply omit the directory and back-slash values.

```
Sub Click(Source As Button)

    Dim mydb As NotesDatabase
    Dim w As NotesUIWorkspace
    Dim uidoc As NotesUIDocument
    Dim server As String
    Dim DBPath As String
    Dim DBForm As String

    '------------------------------------------------------------------
    ' Set target database information
    '------------------------------------------------------------------
    Server = "SERVER"
    DBPath = "PATH\\DATABASE.NSF"
    DBForm = "FORM"


    '------------------------------------------------------------------
    ' Attempt connection to target server
    '------------------------------------------------------------------
    Print "Connection established to target database"
    Set mydb = New NotesDatabase( "", "" )
    Call mydb.Open( Server, DBPath )

    If (mydb Is Nothing) Then
        Msgbox "Warning: unable to open target database."
    Else
        '------------------------------------------------------------------
        ' Create new document
        '------------------------------------------------------------------
        Print "Connection established to: " + mydb.FileName
        Set w = New NotesUIWorkspace
        Print "Composing change management record"
        Set uidoc = w.ComposeDocument ( Server, DBPath, DBForm )

        '------------------------------------------------------------------
        ' Set default values on target form (optional)
        '------------------------------------------------------------------
        Print "Setting default values"
        Call uidoc.FieldSetText ( "FIELD1", "VALUE1" )
        Call uidoc.FieldSetText ( "FIELD2", "VALUE2" )
    End If
    Print "Generate document complete."
End Sub
```

Step 5. Next, return to the target database and either open or select a form in the database. Select the **File > Document Properties** menu options. Switch to tab 2 and locate the field called **FORM**. Assign this value to the DBForm variable in the LotusScript routine. (Alternatively, if you have Designer- and Manager-level access to the database, you can look up the form name in the Designer client.)

Step 6. With the document properties dialog still open, identify the target fields to populate with values and update the LotusScript.

> **TIP**
>
> If you are unable to determine the target fields from the document properties dialog, try creating a new "local copy" of the target database (using the "design only" option) and open the form in Designer to determine the target fields to populate. If you are unable to make a new copy, then the database design may be restricted.

Generate a New Document by Duplicating an Existing Document

This routine illustrates how to create a new document using field values from an existing document. Let's say, for example, that you have a database that tracks projects, and a customer has just requested that a project that was previously deployed in St. Louis also be deployed in Atlanta. Using this approach, you can use the content of the existing project document as the basis for the new project document. After the project document is created, the project manager can change all references from St. Louis to Atlanta, update the target delivery dates, and assign project members.

How It Works

The `CopyAllItems` method associated with the `NotesDocument` class is used to obtain all object values and assign them to a new object. Using this method, all object values of one document (`doc`) are assigned to a second document (`newdoc`). If multiple documents are selected in the view, the code uses the first selected document as the basis for the new document. This solution creates the new document through back-end objects and then displays the document in the user interface.

Implementation

To implement, create an action button on a view and insert the following LotusScript code in the Programmer's pane. Optionally, modify or clear field values associated with the form on the new document prior to calling the `Save` method.

```
Sub Click(Source As Button)
    Dim s As NotesSession
    Dim db As NotesDatabase
    Dim collection As NotesDocumentCollection
    Dim w As NotesUIWorkspace
    Dim doc As NotesDocument
    Dim uidoc As NotesUIDocument
    Dim newdoc As NotesDocument


    '-----------------------------------------------------------
    ' Set object values
    '-----------------------------------------------------------
```

```
Set w = New NotesUIWorkspace
Set s = New NotesSession
Set db = s.CurrentDatabase
Set collection = db.UnprocessedDocuments

'----------------------------------------------------------------
' Check if select item is a document
'----------------------------------------------------------------
If collection.count = 0 Then
    Msgbox("Please select a document. " +_
    "The current item is a ""category"". ")
    Exit Sub
Else
    '------------------------------------------------------------
    ' Make a copy of the existing document
    '------------------------------------------------------------
    Set doc = collection.GetFirstDocument
    Set newdoc =New NotesDocument( db )
    Call doc.CopyAllItems( newdoc, True )

    '------------------------------------------------------------
    ' Reset/Update field values
    '------------------------------------------------------------
    newdoc.FIELDA = ""

    '------------------------------------------------------------
    ' Display newly created document
    '------------------------------------------------------------
    Set uidoc = w.EditDocument (True, newdoc )
End If

End Sub
```

Prompt in LotusScript

The LotusScript Prompt function displays a popup window where the user can specify or select a value (see Figure 13.26). This function can be used to interact with the user and manage data content. For example, the function allows users to describe changes to a document as it is being saved or display a dropdown list of values that the user must select from. This latter option allows you to control the content stored in a particular document field.

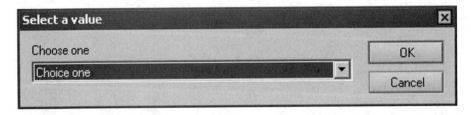

Figure 13.26   Example of the *Prompt* function to display and select values

This routine illustrates how to create a prompt that contains a dropdown list of values. The values can be static (where values are hard coded) or dynamic (where values are created based on other design object values).

How It Works

This is a built-in Domino function. The `Prompt` function includes several parameters—button style, title, caption, default choice, and a list of values. See Chapter 6 for additional information pertaining to the `Prompt` function.

Implementation—Static Example

This first example illustrates how to implement the `Prompt` function with static, or hard-coded, values. After the user selects a value, it is stored in the `Result` object. A confirmation message is displayed to the user if the value is not blank.

```
Sub Click(Source As Button)

    Dim w As NotesUIWorkspace
    Dim s As NotesSession
    Dim db As NotesDatabase
    Dim doc As NotesDocument
    Dim choices (1 To 3) As String
    Dim Buttons as Integer
    Dim Title as String
    Dim Caption as String
    Dim Default as String
    Dim Result as String


    '-----------------------------------------------------
    ' Set object values
    '-----------------------------------------------------
    Set w = New NotesUIWorkspace
    Set s = New NotesSession
    Set db = s.CurrentDatabase


    '-----------------------------------------------------
    ' Set the choices
    '-----------------------------------------------------
    choices(1) = "Choice one"
    choices(2) = "Choice two"
    choices(3) = "Choice three"


    '-----------------------------------------------------
    ' Set prompt title, buttons and default
    '-----------------------------------------------------
    Buttons = PROMPT_OKCANCELCOMBO
    Title = "Select a value"
    Caption = "Choose one"
    Default = choices(1)

    result$ = w.Prompt ( Buttons,Title,Caption,Default,Choices )
    If result$ <> "" Then
```

```
        Msgbox result$,, "You selected:"
    End If

End Sub
```

Implementation—Dynamic Example

In this second example, the code loops through the documents in a particular view and dynamically generates the prompt values by building a list based on a particular field. To implement this solution, insert a valid view name and field name.

```
Sub Click(Source As Button)

    Dim w As NotesUIWorkspace
    Dim s As NotesSession
    Dim db As NotesDatabase
    Dim doc As NotesDocument
    Dim view As NotesView
    Dim choices () As String
    Dim Buttons as Integer
    Dim Title as String
    Dim Caption as String
    Dim Default as String
    Dim Result as String
    Dim I as Integer


    '----------------------------------------------------
    ' Set object values
    '----------------------------------------------------
    Set w = New NotesUIWorkspace
    Set s = New NotesSession
    Set db = s.CurrentDatabase
    Set view = db.GetView("VIEW")


    '----------------------------------------------------
    ' Loop through view to build choice selection
    '----------------------------------------------------
    i=0
    Set doc = view.GetFirstDocument
    While Not( doc Is Nothing )
        Redim Preserve choices( i )
        choices( i ) = doc.FIELD(0)
        i = i + 1
        Set doc = view.GetNextDocument( doc )
    Wend


    '----------------------------------------------------
    ' Set prompt title, buttons and default
    '----------------------------------------------------
    Buttons = PROMPT_OKCANCELCOMBO
    Title = "Select a value"
    Caption = "Choose one"
    Default = choices(1)
    result$ = w.Prompt ( buttons,title,caption,default,choices )
```

```
    If result$ <> "" Then
        Msgbox result$,, "You selected: "
    End If
End Sub
```

> **NOTE**
>
> This routine can produce duplicate values if the field values are not unique. Additional programming logic is required to manage duplicate values.

Sending Email to Multiple Recipients Using LotusScript

Using LotusScript, you can generate and send email messages. When creating the email message, recipient email addresses must be assigned to the SendTo field. To send an email to a single recipient, simply set the object value to a valid email address. For example:

```
doc.SendTo = "someone@ibm.com"
```

However, when sending email to multiple recipients, you must create an array of values and append the values to the SendTo, CopyTo, or BlindCopyTo field(s). This can be achieved by building either a static or dynamic array of values.

> **NOTE**
>
> You must create an array of values in order to assign values to the SendTo field. Assigning a comma-delimited string of email addresses—such as "JohnDoe@company.com, JaneDoe@company.com"—will be interpreted as a string email value and will produce an error when the email is sent.

How It Works

Create an array of email addresses and assign the array to the SendTo, CopyTo, or BlindCopyTo field(s). This can be accomplished through a static array (where addresses are hard-coded in the code) or dynamic array (where values are parsed from a view or other Lotus Notes object). Both implementation options are described in the following.

Implementation—Static Array Example

The following illustrates how to implement the static array approach. In this example, three values are assigned the SendTo field. To implement this solution, insert this code in an action button. Replace **"EMAIL"** with valid email addresses (such as "myname@ company.com"). When clicked, the email will be sent to all recipients.

```
Sub Click(Source As Button)
    Dim s As NotesSession
    Dim db As NotesDatabase
    Dim doc As NotesDocument
    Dim rtitem as NotesRichTextItem
    Set s = New NotesSession
    Set db = s.CurrentDatabase
    Set doc = New NotesDocument( db )

    '----------------------------------------------------------------
    ' Build static list of email addresses
    '----------------------------------------------------------------
    Dim addresses ( 1 to 3 ) as String
    addresses(1) = "EMAIL"
    addresses(2) = "EMAIL"
    addresses(3) = "EMAIL"


    '----------------------------------------------------------------
    ' Create and send email message
    '----------------------------------------------------------------
    doc.Form = "Memo"
    doc.SendTo = addresses
    doc.Subject = "This is the message subject"
    Set rtitem = New NotesRichTextItem(doc, "Body")
    Call rtitem.AddNewLine( 1 )
    Call rtitem.AppendText("The body of the email message.")
    doc.Send ( True )
    Msgbox "Sample email sent"
End Sub
```

Implementation—Dynamic Array Example

The following illustrates how to implement the dynamic array approach. In this example, the array of email addresses is dynamically built by looping through all documents in a particular view. The array is created based on a specific document field for each document in the view. This approach could be used where users create a profile or email subscription for the database. The subscription view is then used to build the array of email recipients. To implement this solution, insert this code in an action button. Replace **FIELD** and **VIEW** with valid database design elements.

```
Sub Click(Source As Button)
    Dim s As NotesSession
    Dim db As NotesDatabase
    Dim doc As NotesDocument
    Dim rtitem As NotesRichTextItem
    Dim i As Integer
    Set db = s.CurrentDatabase
    Dim view As NotesView
    Set view = db.GetView( "VIEW" )

    '----------------------------------------------------------------
    ' Build dynamic list of email addresses
    '----------------------------------------------------------------
    i=0
```

```
    Set doc = view.GetFirstDocument
    While Not( doc Is Nothing )
       Redim Preserve addresses( i )
       addresses( i ) = doc.FIELD(0)
       i = i + 1
       Set doc = view.GetNextDocument( doc )
    Wend

    '--------------------------------------------------------------------
    ' Create and send email message
    '--------------------------------------------------------------------
    Set doc = New NotesDocument( db )
    doc.Form = "Memo"
    doc.SendTo = addresses
    doc.Subject = "This is the message title"
    Set rtitem = New NotesRichTextItem(doc, "Body")
    Call rtitem.AddNewLine( 1 )
    Call rtitem.AppendText("The body of the email message.")
    doc.Send ( True )
    Msgbox "Sample email sent"
End Sub
```

Add a View Icon and Mood Stamp to an Email

The default Lotus Notes mail template includes two special fields that, when defined, will display an image either in the Inbox or in the actual email itself. Mood stamps can be used to convey a message—such as "Urgent," "Newsflash," or "Great Job." When displayed in the Inbox, a relatively small icon is displayed to the side of the mail subject line. When displayed in the message, the graphic displays at the top of the message. It's important to understand that implementation of this feature will depend on the mail template that has been implemented at your facility.

How It Works

Two special fields can be added to LotusScript-generated email—_ViewIcon and $Moods. To utilize one or both of these items, simply set the field value prior to sending the email.

The _ViewIcon field is used to display a graphic icon next to the subject line in the user's Lotus Notes Inbox. This field must be set to a number between 1 and 77. See "Display an Icon in a View" in Chapter 15, "View Enhancements," for additional information pertaining to view icons.

The $Moods field is used to display a graphic at the top of the email itself. To display a mood stamp in the email, two fields must be set to the same value—$Moods and SenderTag—when generating the email message. Both fields must be set to the same text string character. The following are the default values.

$Moods Value	Description	Image
C	Displays the stop or confidential icon.	
F	Displays a flaming or hot email.	
G	Displays a gold star.	
J	Displays for your eyes only icon.	
M	Displays the reminder icon.	
P	Displays the gold stamp	
Q	Displays a question mark.	
R	Displays the secret agent.	
T	Displays a happy face.	
Y	Displays a newsflash.	

This is a Lotus Notes–specific feature designed to work with the default Lotus Notes mail template. This solution has no effect when sending email to an alternate mail client (i.e., Outlook or Yahoo). Actual implementation will depend on the mail template design implemented at your facility.

Implementation

The following code illustrates the implementation of the fields in an action button. It's important to note that both objects start with special characters—a "$" and "_". To reference these fields in LotusScript, you must prefix the field with the tilde "~" character.

```
Sub Click(Source As Button)

    '-----------------------------------------------------------------
    ' Define the objects
    '-----------------------------------------------------------------
    Dim s As NotesSession
    Dim db As NotesDatabase
    Dim doc As NotesDocument
    Dim Person As NotesName
    Dim rtitem As NotesRichTextItem
    Set s = New NotesSession
    Set db = s.CurrentDatabase
    Set doc = New NotesDocument( db )
```

```
    '--------------------------------------------------------------------------
    ' Create the memo
    '--------------------------------------------------------------------------
    Set Person = New NotesName(s.UserName)
    doc.Form = "Memo"
    doc.SendTo = Person.Abbreviated
    doc.Subject = "This is message title"
    Set rtitem = New NotesRichTextItem(doc, "Body")
    Call rtitem.AddNewLine( 1 )
    Call rtitem.AppendText("The body of the email message.")
    Call rtitem.AddNewLine( 1 )


    '--------------------------------------------------------------------------
    ' Set the view icon to a value between 1 and 177)
    '--------------------------------------------------------------------------
    doc.~_ViewIcon = 159


    '--------------------------------------------------------------------------
    ' Set the mood stamp.  Be sure to set both
    ' the $Moods and SenderTag fields.
    '--------------------------------------------------------------------------
    REM "C" Displays the stop or confidential icon.
    REM "F" Displays a flaming or hot email.
    REM "G" Displays a gold star.
    REM "J" Displays for your eyes only icon.
    REM "M" Displays the reminder icon.
    REM "P" Displays the gold stamp
    REM "Q" Displays a question mark.
    REM "R" Displays the secret agent.
    REM "T" Displays a happy face.
    REM "Y" Displays a news flash.
    doc.~$Moods = "G"
    doc.SenderTag = "G"


    '--------------------------------------------------------------------------
    ' Send the email
    '--------------------------------------------------------------------------
    doc.Send ( False )
    Msgbox "Sample email sent."

End Sub
```

Retrieve and Update NOTES.INI Environment Values

The NOTES.INI file contains global environment settings used to manage the Lotus Notes client and associated databases.

How It Works

Using the GetEnvironmentString and SetEnvironmentString methods, you can obtain and set values stored in the NOTES.INI file. Both methods are associated with the NotesSession class. Retrieved values can be assigned, modified, and updated in the file.

New environment names and values can also be created and appended to this file. You may want to do this to track a value that is specific to a particular database.

Implementation

The following example illustrates both the Get and Set methods. To manage values in NOTES.INI, first determine the variable name that you want to retrieve, modify, or insert into the file. The NOTES.INI file is typically stored in the /Notes directory. Next, adjust the following code to reference the variable name and insert the code into an action button (or other LotusScript event). You will need to update the variable name and uncomment the associated statements to try the Set method. You will also need to make a backup of the file prior to implementing code that updates this file.

```
Sub Click(Source As Button)

    Dim s As New NotesSession
    Dim theValue As String

    '--------------------------------------------------------------------
    ' Get an environment value
    '--------------------------------------------------------------------
    Set s = New NotesSession
    theValue = s.GetEnvironmentString( "TimeZone", True )
    Msgbox "The current time zone value is: " & theValue

    '--------------------------------------------------------------------
    ' Set an environment value
    '--------------------------------------------------------------------
    ' theValue = "VALUE"
    ' Call s.SetEnvironmentVar( "FIELD", theValue, True )

End Sub
```

Assign One Rich Text Object to Another Rich Text Object

This section illustrates how to assign one Rich Text object to another. Unlike Text objects, where the object value can be easily set or reassigned, additional steps are required when working with Rich Text objects.

How It Works

One Rich Text object can be assigned to another Rich Text object by using the AppendRTItem method. To utilize this method, both objects must be defined as Rich Text. To assign one Rich Text object to another, call the AppendRTItem method and pass the name of the Rich Text object as a parameter. In the following example, rtItemB is copied into rtItemA.

This approach might be used to copy a Rich Text field from an existing document into a Rich Text field of a new document. This could also be used to copy a Rich Text field into the Body of an email message.

Implementation

The following illustrates how to assign Rich Text values. In this example, the Rich Text field (rtItemB) from a selected view document is appended to another Rich Text field (rtItemA). The result is sent via email to the person that clicked the button. To implement this solution, create an action button on a view and insert the following LotusScript code.

As a reminder, be sure to replace **FIELD** with the name of a Rich Text field that resides on the form. This field will be appended to the Rich Text field called "Body" and subsequently emailed to the person that clicks the button.

```
Sub Click(Source As Button)

    '---------------------------------------------
    ' Define the objects
    '---------------------------------------------
    Dim s As NotesSession
    Dim db As NotesDatabase
    Dim collection As NotesDocumentCollection
    Dim newdoc As NotesDocument
    Dim Person As NotesName
    Dim doc As NotesDocument
    Dim rtitemA As Variant
    Dim rtitemB As Variant
    Set s = New NotesSession
    Set db = s.CurrentDatabase
    Set collection = db.UnprocessedDocuments

    '----------------------------------------------------------
    ' Is a document selected?
    '----------------------------------------------------------
    If collection.count = 0 Then
        Msgbox("Please select a document.")
    Else
        '----------------------------------------------------
        ' Create email header
        '----------------------------------------------------
        Set newdoc = New NotesDocument( db )
        Set Person = New NotesName( s.UserName )
        newdoc.Form = "Memo"
        newdoc.SendTo = Person.Abbreviated
        newdoc.Subject = "This is the message subject"

        '----------------------------------------------------
        ' Copy itemB into itemA
        '----------------------------------------------------
        Set doc = collection.GetFirstDocument
        Set rtitemB = doc.GetFirstItem( "FIELD" )
```

```
    Set rtitemA = New NotesRichTextItem( newdoc, "Body" )
    Call rtitemA.AppendRTItem( rtitemB )

    '--------------------------------------------------
    ' Send email
    '--------------------------------------------------
    newdoc.Send ( False )
    Msgbox "Sample email sent"
  End If

End Sub
```

Add a Document, View, or Database Link to a Rich Text Field

Document, view, and database links offer a quick and easy way to reference database information. Links are often embedded in email messages and allow users to jump directly to a
referenced item when clicked. This routine illustrates how to generate and embed a link in
a Rich Text field.

How It Works

This is a built-in feature of the Lotus Notes client. Document, view, and database links are
generated using the AppendDocLink method. Links can only be inserted in a Rich Text field
or object.

A.13.2

Three parameters are associated with the AppendDocLink method. The first parameter
passed to the AppendDocLink method must be a document, view, or database object. The
second parameter is optional and displays in the bottom of the Lotus Notes client when the
mouse hovers over the link. A third parameter can also be supplied that replaces the icon
with a text link.

Implementation

The following code illustrates how to attach both the document and database links. When
the button is clicked, an email message is sent with the links to the current database and
document. To implement this technique, create an action button and insert the following
LotusScript code in the Programmer's pane.

```
Sub Click(Source As Button)

    Dim w As NotesUIWorkspace
    Dim s As NotesSession
    Dim db As NotesDatabase
    Dim uidoc As NotesUIDocument
    Dim doc As NotesDocument
    Dim newdoc As NotesDocument
    Dim rtitem as NotesRichTextItem
    Dim Person As NotesName
    Set w = New NotesUIWorkspace
```

```
'-----------------------------------------------------------------
' Set object values
'-----------------------------------------------------------------
Set s = New NotesSession
Set db = s.CurrentDatabase
Set uidoc = w.CurrentDocument
Set doc = uidoc.Document
Set newdoc = New NotesDocument( db )
Set Person = New NotesName(s.UserName)


'-----------------------------------------------------------------
' Create the email and richtext object
'-----------------------------------------------------------------
newdoc.Form = "Memo"
newdoc.SendTo = Person.Abbreviated
newdoc.Subject = "Sample document and database link"
Set rtitem = New NotesRichTextItem( newdoc, "Body" )


'-----------------------------------------------------------------
' Append the document link (doc)
'-----------------------------------------------------------------
Call rtitem.AddNewLine( 1 )
Call rtitem.AppendDocLink( doc, db.Title )
Call rtitem.AppendText(" <--- Click to open document.")


'-----------------------------------------------------------------
' Append the database link (db)
'-----------------------------------------------------------------
Call rtitem.AddNewLine( 1 )
Call rtitem.AppendDocLink( db, db.Title )
Call rtitem.AppendText(" <--- Click to open database.")


'-----------------------------------------------------------------
' Send message
'-----------------------------------------------------------------
newdoc.Send ( False )
Msgbox "Sample email sent"

End Sub
```

Troubleshooting

A default view must be associated with the database in order to implement this solution. Although there are no specific references to any view in the LotusScript code, a default view association must exist in order to generate the document link. If a default view has not been established, an error message similar to Figure 13.27 will display.

To assign a default view, select and open the view in the Domino Designer client. Select the **Design > View Properties** menu option to display the properties dialog. Switch to tab 2 and select the option **Default when database is first opened** (see Figure 13.28).

Figure 13.27   No default view specified error message

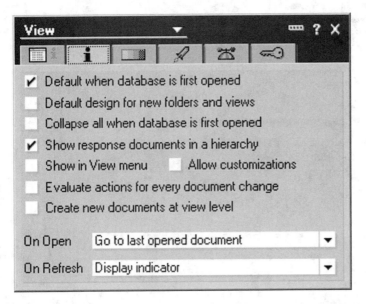

Figure 13.28   "Default when database is first opened" setting in the View properties dialog

Save and close the view.

> **TIP**
>
> If users are unable to open the document or database when clicked,
> you may need to have them create a connection document in order to
> correct the error "Unable to find path to server." See Chapter 21,
> "Troubleshooting," for additional information on troubleshooting and how
> to create a connection document. If the user is still unable to access
> the document or database, the ACL may need to be updated to grant
> access to the database (see Chapter 19, "Security," for additional infor-
> mation on database security settings).

Create a Button to Add a Calendar Event

Using LotusScript, you can create a button that adds a calendar event to the user's personal calendar. After the button is created, it can be added to an email message and distributed to any Lotus Notes user. When the button is clicked, the calendar event is created.

How It Works

In this solution, the calendar event is created by using back-end LotusScript classes. When the user clicks the button, a new document is created with the calendar values specified in the code. Five primary fields must be set in order to generate a calendar event—Form, AppointmentType, StartDateTime, EndDateTime, and Subject.

- **Form**—This field must be set to "Appointment". This value sets the form name to associate with the document.
- **AppointmentType**—This field determines the type of event to be created. Set the value of this field to the string value "0" for appointments or "4" for reminders. Note that appointments require a start and end date/time pair. Reminders only need the starting date and starting time.
- **StartDateTime**—This field must contain the start date and time for the calendar event. The value assigned to this field must be a text string, such as "11/08/2006 3:00pm".
- **EndDateTime**—This field must contain the end date and time for the calendar event. Although the end date can match the start date, the time must be greater than the starting time by at least one minute. The value assigned to this field must be a text string, such as "11/08/2006 4:00pm".
- **Subject**—This field contains the topic of the appointment (and is optional). In general, this value should be a short text string or a couple lines at most. This example illustrates how to include three separate information lines in the subject field.

For this solution, the user will be clicking the button from within their mail client, and the database object will default to the user's mail database. So, there is no need to compute the location of the mail database. After these values are set and saved, the document is added to the current database.

Implementation

This section illustrates how to create a button that adds an event to the user's personal calendar. This example is designed to be used from the Lotus Notes mail database. To implement this solution, complete the following steps.

Step 1.   Create an action button and insert the following LotusScript code.

```
Sub Click(Source As Button)

    Dim StartDateTime As String
    Dim EndDateTime As String
    Dim Line1 As String
```

```
Dim Line2 As String
Dim Line3 As String
Dim Subject As String
Dim Room As String

'-----------------------------------------------------------
' Configure the calendar event properties
' StartDateTime = "11/09/2006 3:00 PM"
' EndDateTime = "11/09/2006 4:00 PM"
'-----------------------------------------------------------
StartDateTime   = Cstr(Today) +  " 3:00 PM"
EndDateTime     = Cstr(Today) +  " 4:00 PM"
Line1      = "Project Status Meeting"
Line2      = "Mandatory Attendance"
Line3      = "Conference line 555-1212"
Subject = Line1 + Chr(10) + Line2 + Chr(10) + Line3
Room    = "Building 100, Room 130"


'-----------------------------------------------------------
' Define the objects
'-----------------------------------------------------------
Dim s As NotesSession
Dim w As NotesUIWorkspace
Dim db As NotesDatabase
Dim docA As NotesDocument
Dim docB As NotesDocument
Dim uidoc As NotesUIDocument
Dim rtitem As NotesRichTextItem
Dim date1 As NotesDateTime
Dim date2 As NotesDateTime
Set s = New NotesSession
Set w = New NotesUIWorkspace
Set db = s.CurrentDatabase


'-----------------------------------------------------------
' Get handle to email memo
'-----------------------------------------------------------
Set uidoc = w.CurrentDocument
Set docA = uidoc.Document


'-----------------------------------------------------------
' Generate the calendar event entry
'-----------------------------------------------------------
Set docB = New NotesDocument( db )
Set date1 = New NotesDateTime( StartDateTime )
Set date2 = New NotesDateTime( EndDateTime )
docB.From = docA.From
docB.Form = "Appointment"
docB.Subject = Subject
docB.StartDateTime = date1.LSLocalTime
docB.EndDateTime = date2.LSLocalTime
docB.CalendarDateTime = date1.LSLocalTime
docB.TimeRange = date1.LSLocalTime & "-" & date2.LSLocalTime
docB.AppointmentType = "0"
docB.CHAIR = s.UserName
```

```
            docB.ExcludefromView = "D"
            docB.BookFreetime = ""
            docB.~$BusyName = s.UserName
            docB.~$BusyPriority = "1"
            docB.~$PublicAccess = "1"
            docB.Location = Room


            '-----------------------------------------------------------
            ' Additional info for the body of the event
            '-----------------------------------------------------------
            Set rtitem = New NotesRichTextItem( docB, "Body" )
            Call rtitem.AddNewLine( 1 )
            Call rtitem.AppendText("This is the body of the calendar event.")


            '-----------------------------------------------------------
            ' Save the event
            '-----------------------------------------------------------
            docB.save True, True


            '-----------------------------------------------------------
            ' Uncomment allow users to update
            '-----------------------------------------------------------
            ' Call w.EditDocument( True, docB )


            '-----------------------------------------------------------
            ' Display completion message
            '-----------------------------------------------------------
            Msgbox "This event has been added to your calendar."+_
            Chr$(13) + Subject +_
            Chr$(13) + "Start time: " + StartDateTime +_
            Chr$(13) + "End time: " + EndDateTime,  64, "Success"

        End Sub
```

Step 2. Set the event parameters, including

- StartDateTime
- EndDateTime
- Subject Line(s)
- Meeting Room

Step 3. (Optional) To have the calendar event display in the Lotus Notes client, uncomment the following statement. This will display the new appointment after it is created.

```
            '-----------------------------------------------------------
            ' Uncomment allow users to update
            '-----------------------------------------------------------
            Call w.EditDocument( True, docB )
```

Step 4. Copy and paste the button into an email message. The button can then be distributed to any Lotus Notes user.

Links to developerWorks

A.13.1 Prasad, Manish K. *Tip: Validating a rich text field in Lotus Notes*. IBM developerWorks, December 2005. http://www.ibm.com/developerworks/lotus/library/rich-text-field-notes/ index.html.

A.13.2 Robson, Marc. *Send Notes links through the Internet*. IBM developerWorks, January 2000. http://www.ibm.com/developerworks/lotus/library/ls-Send_Notes_Links/index.html.

Chapter 14

Design Enhancements Using Formula Language

Chapter Overview

This chapter provides a number of Formula Language customizations that can be incorporated into most Lotus Notes databases. Each customization module is self-contained and designed to run independently. This enables you to copy the code into any existing application and implement it with little to no modification.

The intent of this chapter is to provide common customizations that can be added to any database. Each customization includes a functional summary, an explanation of how the code works, and detailed instructions for installing the code. Each code section will run with no additional code logic required. Customizations include the following:

- Compare two lists
- Create Expand and Collapse buttons
- Get the current day of the week
- Get the current month of the year
- Create a formatted date string
- Create an Attach File button
- Display the Microsoft Windows File Finder dialog
- Create a new document
- Create a "Last Updated By" field
- Create a "Last Modified On" date field
- Format a user's name
- Hide design elements based on a user's role
- Use @DBColumn to set field values
- Use @DBLookup to set field values
- Parse a text string

- Format field values using Input Translation
- Add field validation
- Display an "Are you sure?" warning message
- Generate an email
- Sort a list of values

Formula Language Enhancements

This section is dedicated to Formula Language customizations and includes a wide variety of enhancements and working source code that can be incorporated into the projects in this book or any other Notes database.

All code provided in this section is also provided on the companion Web site in a code library database. In many cases, working examples and buttons can be clicked to illustrate each customization module. The code and buttons can also be copied directly into your database. Before implementing any of the solutions, let's spend a moment discussing the content of this chapter.

In some cases, integrating code into a Lotus Notes database may require a reference to a database object such as a form name, field name, view name, or target search string. All of these references must be replaced with the actual design elements in your database and are illustrated in all bold, capital letters.

The following list contains those references that will need to be replaced throughout this Formula Language chapter.

DATABASE.NSF—Substitute with a valid Lotus Notes database file name
EMAIL—Substitute with a formatted, valid Internet email address
FIELDNAME—Substitute with an actual field name
FORM—Substitute with an actual form name
PATH—Substitute with a valid directory path or folder name
ROLENAME—Substitute with a valid role specified in the Access Control List
SERVER—Substitute with a valid Domino server name
VALUE—Substitute with a text string or numerical value
VIEW—Substitute with an actual view name

A working example of all customizations can be found in the developer's toolbox in the **BookCodeLibrary.NSF** database. See Appendix A for additional information.

Compare Two Lists

This routine illustrates how to compare two fields or lists that contain multiple values. The resulting string or text list subsequently contains the differences between the two arrays.

How It Works

Using the @Replace statement, all elements in List1 that are found in List2 are replaced with a null string. The @Trim() function removes all null strings from the result. The new value is then stored in the Result object. Using the @Prompt statement, the results are displayed to the user.

Implementation—Example 1

This first example illustrates how to sort static values. This example displays the contents of List1, List2, and the difference(s) between the lists. To implement this solution, insert the following statements in an action button formula, column formula, or the default value formula for a field, replacing the list values. The @Prompt statement is used for illustrative purposes and can be removed or updated as desired.

```
List1 := "Mark" : "John" : "Steve";
List2 := "John" : "Mark";
Result := @Trim( @Replace(List1; List2; "") );

@Prompt([Ok]; "Compare Lists";
"List1: " + @Implode(List1) + @NewLine +
"List2: " + @Implode(List2) + @NewLine +
"Delta: " + @Implode(Result))
```

When the button is clicked, the message shown in Figure 14.1 is displayed. Notice that the correct result is produced even when each list contains values sorted in a different order.

Figure 14.1 Example of comparing two arrays

Implementation—Example 2

The second example illustrates how to sort dynamic values. Here, List1 and List2 reference fields on a document, and Delta contains the difference between the two lists. To implement this solution, insert the following statements in an action button formula, column formula, or the default value formula for a field. Replace **FIELDA** and **FIELDB** with valid document field names. The @Prompt statement is used for illustrative purposes and can be removed or updated as desired.

```
List1 := FIELDA;
List2 := FIELDB;
Result := @Trim( @Replace(List1; List2; "") );

@Prompt([Ok]; "Compare Lists";
"List1: " + @Implode(List1) + @NewLine +
"List2: " + @Implode(List2) + @NewLine +
"Delta: " + @Implode(Result))
```

> **TIP**
>
> Select **Allow multiple values** if using this approach to set a field on a form and the result may contain multiple values. This option is located on tab 1 of the field properties dialog.

Expand and Collapse All Document Sections

Expand and Collapse buttons provide a user-friendly method to manage the display of information stored in document sections. These buttons are particularly handy when a document contains numerous sections. When clicked, all sections on the document expand or collapse. Without these buttons, users have to manually adjust each section.

How It Works

Sections are expanded and collapsed using the built-in Formula Language commands SectionCollapseAll and SectionExpandAll. These commands are typically added to action buttons. When users click the button, all sections on the document expand or collapse. If there are no sections on the document, the buttons will have no effect when clicked.

Implementation

To implement this solution, create two action buttons called Expand and Collapse on the form. Insert the following formula to collapse the sections.

```
@Command( [SectionCollapseAll] )
```

Insert this formula to expand all sections on a document.

```
@Command( [SectionExpandAll] )
```

Expand and Collapse All View Categories

Expand and Collapse buttons can be implemented on views to manage categorized documents (see Figure 14.2). When implemented on views, all view categories are expanded or collapsed similarly to sections on a document—as illustrated in the previous section. These buttons provide a user-friendly method to manage the display of information.

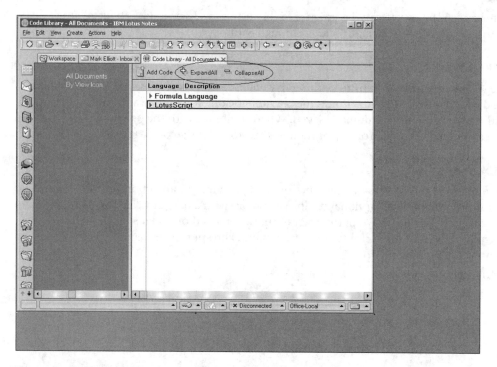

Figure 14.2   Categorized view with Expand and Collapse buttons

How It Works

Sections are expanded and collapsed using the built-in Formula Language commands ViewCollapseAll and ViewExpandAll. These commands are typically added to action buttons. When users click the button, all sections on the document expand or collapse. If there are no sections on the view, the buttons will have no effect when clicked.

Implementation

To implement this solution, create two action buttons called Expand and Collapse on the view. Insert the following formula to collapse the sections.

```
@Command([ViewCollapseAll])
```

Insert this formula to expand all sections on a view.

```
@Command([ViewExpandAll])
```

Get the Current Day of the Week

The day of the week can be calculated by using two Formula Language functions—
@Weekday and @Select (e.g., Sunday through Saturday).

How It Works

The @Weekday function returns a numeric value between one and seven, corresponding to
the day of the week. The function returns a numeric one for Sunday and continues through
Saturday, which returns a numeric seven. When combined with the @Select statement, the
corresponding text value (or day of the week) is stored in the Result.

Implementation

To implement this solution, insert the following formula in an action button, column, or
default value for a field. Optionally, replace @Today with a date or field. The @Prompt statement is used for illustrative purposes and can be removed or updated as desired. However,
if removed, be sure the formula contains a main expression (i.e., Result) as the last statement in the formula.

```
result := @Select( @Weekday ( @Today );
            "Sunday";
            "Monday";
            "Tuesday";
            "Wednesday";
            "Thursday";
            "Friday";
            "Saturday"
            );
@Prompt([Ok];"Day of week";  result )
```

Figure 14.3 depicts the result when the button is pressed on a Tuesday.

Figure 14.3 Example day of the week

Get the Current Month of the Year

The month of the year can be calculated by using two Formula Language functions—@Month and @Select (e.g., January through December).

How It Works

The @Month function returns a numeric value between one and twelve, corresponding to the month of the year. The function returns a numeric one for January and continues through December, which returns a numeric twelve. When combined with the @Select statement, the corresponding text value is stored in the Result.

Implementation

To implement this solution, insert the following formula in an action button, column, or default value for a field. Optionally, replace @Today with a date or field. The @Prompt statement is used for illustrative purposes and can be removed or updated as desired. However, if removed, be sure the formula contains a main expression (i.e., Result) as the last statement in the formula.

```
Result := @Select( @Month( @Today );
                "January";
                "February";
                "March";
                "April";
                "May";
                "June";
                "July";
                "August";
                "September";
                "October";
                "November";
                "December"
                );
@Prompt([Ok];"Current month";  result );
```

Figure 14.4 depicts the result when the button is pressed in the month of April.

Figure 14.4 Example month of the year

Create a Formatted Date String

This routine illustrates how to create a formatted date string that includes the day of the
week, month, day, and year (e.g., Friday April 14, 2006).

How It Works

The formatted date is computed with a combination of the @Today, @Weekday, @Year,
@Month, and @Day functions. The returned values are subsequently used to create the formatted date string, which is stored in the theDate variable.

Implementation

To implement this solution, insert the following formula in an action button, column, or
default value for a field. Optionally, replace @Today with a date or field. The @Prompt statement is used for illustrative purposes and can be removed or updated as desired. However,
if removed, be sure the formula contains a main expression (i.e., Result) as the last statement in the formula.

```
theDate := @Today;

theWeekday := @Select( @Weekday ( theDate );
            "Sunday"; "Monday";
            "Tuesday"; "Wednesday";
            "Thursday"; "Friday";
```

```
                    "Saturday"
                    );

theMonth := @Select( @Month( theDate );
                    "January"; "February"; "March";
                    "April"; "May"; "June";
                    "July"; "August"; "September";
                    "October"; "November"; "December"
                    );

theDay := @Text ( @Day ( @Today ) );

theYear := @Text ( @Year ( theDate ) );

result := "Today is "  +
theWeekday + " " +
theMonth + " " +
theDay + ", " +
theYear;

@Prompt([Ok];"Result";  result );
```

Figure 14.5 depicts the result when implemented in an action button.

Figure 14.5   Example of a formatted date string

Create an Attach File Button

Creating an Attach File button for an application provides the ability to insert files into the intended field. This routine prompts the user to select a file from the file finder and insert the file into the specified field.

How It Works

When the button is clicked, the cursor jumps to the specified field and launches the file finder. If the user selects a file, it is inserted in the specified field. In order to implement this solution, the target field must be set to Rich Text. Also note that the document must be in edit mode in order for the selected file to be applied to the designated field.

> **NOTE**
>
> You can also use Rich Text Lite, which by default will place a button next to the field.

Implementation

To implement this technique, create a Rich Text field on a form and make note of the field name. Next, create an action button and name it **Attach File**. To ensure that the button is only available when the document is in edit mode, set the "Hide When" properties for the button (see Figure 14.6).

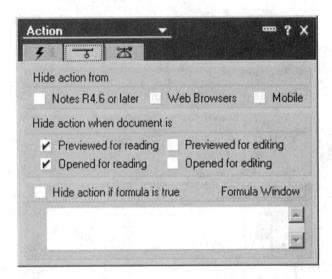

Figure 14.6 Hide property settings for an action button

Finally, insert the following formula in the Programmer's pane. Replace **FIELDNAME** with the name of a Rich Text field on the form.

```
@Command([EditGotoField]; "FIELDNAME");
@Command([EditInsertFileAttachment])
```

> **NOTE**
>
> If the document is not in edit mode or there is no Rich Text field on the form, the error message shown in Figure 14.7 will most likely display.

Figure 14.7   Error when attempting to attach a file to a document in read mode

Display the Windows File Finder Dialog

The file finder dialog allows users to locate and select a workstation file. After a file has been selected, you can attach the file to a field, store the file location, or use the value in a formula. Figure 14.8 depicts the file finder dialog.

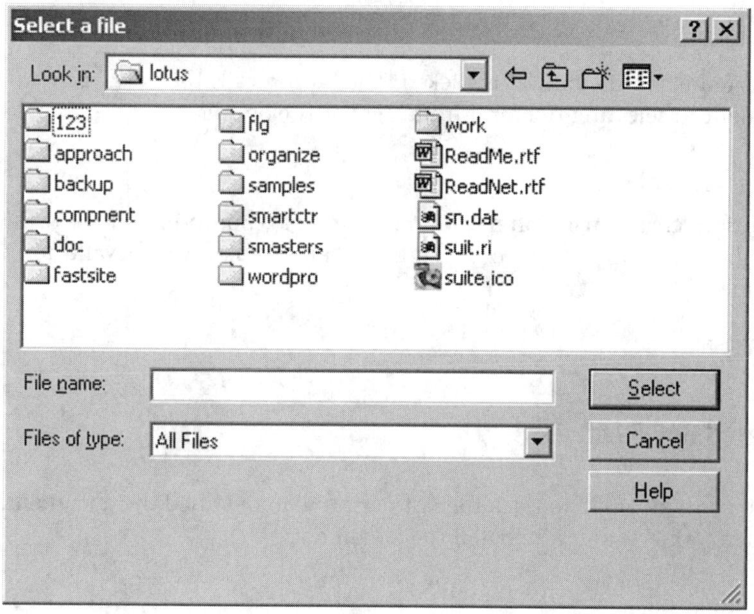

Figure 14.8   Example of the Windows file finder dialog

How It Works

The @Prompt command includes a LocalBrowse parameter that displays the Windows file finder dialog. The fully qualified path and the file name are then stored in the document field specified in the formula.

Implementation

To implement this solution, create a field on a form. Next, create a button on the form and insert the following formula, making sure to replace **FIELDNAME** with the actual name of the field on the form.

```
FIELD FIELDNAME := @Prompt([LocalBrowse];"Select a file";"");
@Prompt([Ok];"Selected file"; FIELDNAME)
```

Create a New Document

The Compose command is one of the most frequently used functions in a Lotus Notes database. This command is used to create a new document in a database. When added to a button, it provides a user-friendly method to generate a new document. A button offers an alternative to creating a new document via the Lotus Notes menu bar.

How It Works

A new document is created when the button is clicked. The button calls the Compose command, which is equivalent to selecting the form from the Lotus Notes menu.

Implementation

To implement this solution, create an action button on a view, page, or form and insert the following formula in the Programmer's pane. Be sure to replace **FORM** with a valid form name or form alias name.

```
@Command([Compose]; "FORM" )
```

Create a "Last Updated By" Field

Often, a document will contain a field to track the last person who modified the document. This enables users to determine who last updated the document.

How It Works

To automatically store the name of the person who last updated the document, create a computed field on the form. Then use the @IsDocBeingSaved function to determine whether the document is being saved from the Lotus Notes user interface. If the document is being saved, store the name of the user who issued the save command. Otherwise, the formula returns the current value for the field.

Implementation

To implement this solution, create a computed field on the form and insert the following formula in the Programmer's pane.

```
result := @If (@IsDocBeingSaved;
          @Name([Abbreviate];
          @UserName); @ThisName);
result
```

> **TIP**
>
> Lotus Notes automatically updates the $UpdatedBy field with a running list of user IDs that have saved the document. This field is automatically generated for documents but is not automatically displayed on the document. You may want to consider adding this field to the form design for supplemental information purposes. Simply create a computed text field called $UpdatedBy. Select **Allow multiple values** in the field properties dialog and set the value formula to @ThisName.

Create a "Last Modified On" Date Stamp

This section describes how to create a field to track the date of the last document modification. When implemented, the current date (and optionally time) is automatically stored in the specified field.

How It Works

A computed field on the document is automatically updated every time the document is saved.

Implementation

To implement this solution, create a computed field on a form. In the properties dialog, set the field type to **Date/Time** and **Computed** on tab 1. By default, the field properties will display only the time, so to display the date *and* time in the field, switch to tab 2 and select both the date and time options (see Figure 14.9).

After the field properties are set, add the following formula in the Programmer's pane.

```
result := @If ( @IsDocBeingSaved;
          @Now;
          @ThisName );
result
```

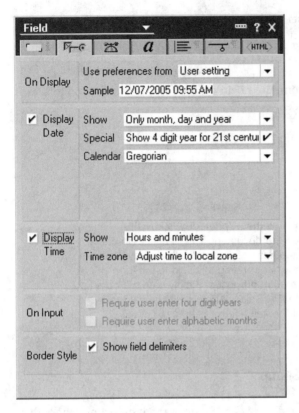

Figure 14.9 Date and time property settings dialog

Format a User's Name

Using several Formula Language functions, you can format a user's name. Formatting a name allows you to change the appearance and content.

How It Works

The @Name function is used to format a name string. The @UserName function is used to return the fully qualified Lotus Notes user name. The combination of these two functions can be used to retrieve and format a user's name. The following examples illustrate the CN, Abbreviate, and Canonical name formats.

Implementation—Example 1

To implement this technique, create an action button or computed field and insert the following formula. The @Prompt statement is used for illustrative purposes and can be removed or updated as desired. However, if removed, be sure the formula contains a main expression (i.e., Result) as the last statement in the formula. In this example, the common name is returned—Mark Elliott (see Figure 14.10).

```
result := @Name([CN]; @UserName);
@Prompt([Ok];"CN Format";  result );
```

Figure 14.10   Example of the CN-formatted user name

Implementation—Example 2

This second example, when added to an action button, illustrates the common, abbreviated, and canonical name formats (see Figure 14.11).

```
@Prompt([Ok]; "Formatted User Name";
"CN Format: " + @Name([CN]; @UserName) + @NewLine +
"Abbreviate: " + @Name([Abbreviate]; @UserName) + @NewLine +
"Canonical: " + @Name([Canonicalize]; @UserName) )
```

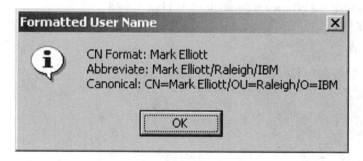

Figure 14.11   A comparison of the user name formats

Hide Text and Design Elements Based on a User's Role

One way to control visibility of text, buttons, fields, forms, views, and other design elements is through the use of roles. Using roles, you can manage the display of information or database functionality. For example, you can custom-tailor instructions for completing a form based on the user's role, where one paragraph is displayed to users assigned the "Employee" role and a different set of instructions is displayed for those assigned the "TeamLead" role. Roles can also be used to manage the display of action buttons, the visibility of database views, or the ability to access a controlled section on a document.

> **NOTE**
>
> Hiding a field based on a user role is not a security feature. Users will still be able to view fields using the Document Properties dialog box. See Chapter 19, "Security," for additional information regarding document security.

How It Works

The @UserRoles function returns the current roles assigned to a given person. When added to the **Hide paragraph when formula is true** property section, you can manage the display of text, a field, or an action button, among others. Roles are created in the Access Control List (ACL) for the database, as illustrated in Figure 14.12.

After the role is created, the role must be assigned to a person, server, or group. This is also accomplished in the Basics tab of the database ACL. See Chapter 19 for additional information pertaining to database security.

> **NOTE**
>
> The @UserRoles function only works on server-based databases or local databases where the **Enforce a consistent ACL across all replicas** property has been enabled.

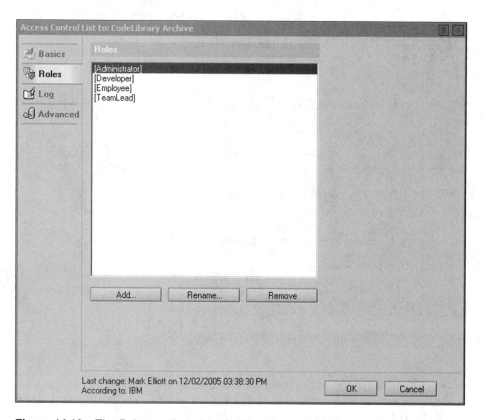

Figure 14.12 The Roles section of the Access Control List

Implementation

The following outlines how to use roles to manage the display of design elements and data.

Step 1. First, create the roles for the database. Select the **File > Database > Access Control** menu options. You must have "Manager" level authority in order to change the ACL settings for the database. When the dialog is displayed, switch to tab 2 (left side). Click the **Add** button to define one or more roles for the database. Then switch to the Basics tab and assign the role(s) to a person, server, or group.

Step 2. Create a design element, such as a button, field, or view. Open the properties dialog for the design element and locate the tab that contains the "Hide When" settings. This tab will contain a "window shade" icon on the tab. The location of this tab will vary based on the design element. Figure 14.13 depicts the property setting for a field, which is located on tab 6.

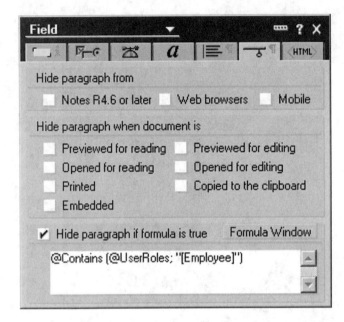

Figure 14.13   Set the "Hide When" formula based on a user's role

Step 3.   Select the **Hide paragraph if formula is true** option and insert the following formula. Be sure to replace the role with a valid role name (as illustrated in Figure
14.13). This first formula will hide the element if the user has the specified role.

```
@Contains (@UserRoles; "[ROLENAME]");
```

Conversely, to implement a formula that checks whether the user does not have
a particular role, simply prefix the formula with an exclamation point "!". The
exclamation point is a logical "Not" character.

```
!@Contains (@UserRoles; "[ROLENAME]");
```

> **NOTE**
>
> Be sure to include the left and right brackets when referencing a role.
> These characters are required in order to reference the role.

Working with *@DBColumn*

The @DBColumn function can be used to dynamically populate a field with values. In other
words, the options displayed in a radio button, checkbox, listbox, prompt, or other design
element can be dynamically managed without having to change the design of the database.

How It Works

When using the @DBColumn function, all values from a particular view column are returned to the routine. For example, let's say you have an action item database, and one view contains a separate document for each person in the department. As each new team member arrives, a person document is created. As team members migrate to other departments or projects, their documents are removed. Using the @DBColumn function, you can dynamically assign new tasks to team members represented by person documents (see Figure 14.14).

Figure 14.14 Using *@DBColumn* to provide values for a checkbox field

Implementation

Step 1. Determine (or create) the view and column that contain the values to be utilized by the field. Make note of the view name and column number. These design elements can be hidden or displayed. If the column is not the first in the view, be sure to accurately count the column number.

Step 2. Create a field and select the field type as desired (such as radio button, combobox, checkbox, or listbox) in tab 1 of the properties dialog. In tab 2, change the **Choices** option to **Use formula for choices** and insert the following formula in the dialog box. Be sure to change the formula to include the actual view name and desired column number. Close the properties dialog when finished.

```
Class :="";
Cache := "NoCache";
Host := "";
Viewname := "VIEW";
Column := 1;
result := @Unique( @DbColumn( Class : Cache; Host; Viewname ; Column ) );
@Sort ( result; [Ascending] );
```

> **TIP**
>
> Use the @Sort function to display results in ascending or descending order. An example of this function is covered later in this chapter.

Working with *@DBLookup*

The @DBLookup function can be used to dynamically populate a field with values. In other words, the options displayed in a radio button, checkbox, listbox, prompt, or other design element can be dynamically managed without having to change the design of the database. Using this function, the values are retrieved from a single document, as opposed to @DBColumn, which retrieves a list of values from a column in a view.

How It Works

The @DBLookup function is used to return a field value from a specific database document. This approach can be used when you need to retrieve values from one document and utilize them in another document.

For instance, say you have a worldwide service request database with one or more project managers assigned to each country (or region, state, district, etc.). A view could be created to store the contact information for each country. As new document service requests are created, the fields on the form (such as the project manager's email address) could automatically populate based on the originating country of the request. In this scenario, the service request document queries the specified view for a document and retrieves the value(s) of a specific field.

Implementation

Step 1.   Create (or determine) the view that contains the target documents to be searched. Also identify the criteria, or key, that will determine which document will be accessed by the @DBLookup formula. In many cases, the "key" will probably be another field on the document, but it could also be a hard-coded value.

For example, in Figure 14.15, the country field is used as the key. This value points to the North America document. The values in the Email field are then returned by the lookup.

Step 2.   Create a field. Using the properties dialog, set the field type (such as radio button, combobox, checkbox, or listbox) in tab 1. In tab 2, change the **Choices** option to **Use formula for choices** and insert the following formula in the dialog box. Be sure to adjust the formula to include the actual view name, key, and field to retrieve. Close the properties dialog when finished.

```
Class :="";
Cache := "NoCache";
Host := "";
Viewname := "VIEW";
Key := "KEY";
Fieldvalue := "FIELDNAME";
@DbLookup( Class : Cache; Host; Viewname; Key; Fieldvalue )
```

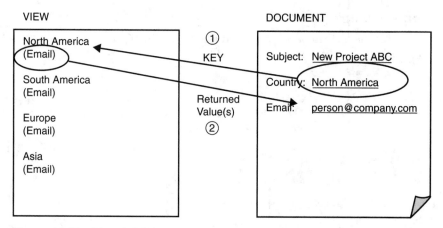

Figure 14.15   Use *@DBLookup* to retrieve a field value from a specific document

> **NOTE**
>
> Use the `cache` parameter to store the values returned in memory. This option is more efficient and should be used when the results from the lookup do not frequently change. Using the `Nocache` parameter forces the data retrieval every time the `@DBLookup` or `@DBColumn` function is called.

Parse a Text String

There are a variety of functions that can be used to parse text strings. This section illustrates the @RightBack, @LeftBack, and @Word functions to retrieve a subset of text from a text string.

How It Works

The following describes a few of the Formula Language functions that can be used to parse text strings.

@Rightback—Returns the right-most characters from a string based on a specified delimiter or starting character position. The delimiter could be a single character, such as a comma, or several characters, such as "Record=".

@Leftback—Returns the left-most characters from a string based on a specified delimiter or starting character position.

@Word—Returns a specific word from a text string based on a specified delimiter and word to return.

Implementation—Example 1

The following illustrates the @Rightback command (see Figure 14.16).

```
myString := "Mark Elliott";
myResult :=  @RightBack( myString; " ");

@Prompt([Ok]; "RightBack with space delimiter";
"Initial string: " + myString + @NewLine +
"Result string: " + myResult)
```

Figure 14.16   Example of the *@Rightback* function

Implementation—Example 2

The following illustrates the @Leftback command (see Figure 14.17).

```
myString := "Mark Elliott";
myResult :=  @LeftBack( myString; " ");

@Prompt([Ok]; "LeftBack with space delimiter";
"Initial string: " + myString + @NewLine +
"Result string: " + myResult)
```

Figure 14.17   Example of the *@Leftback* function

Implementation—Example 3

The following illustrates the @Word command (see Figure 14.18).

```
myString := "Mark Elliott";
word1 := @Word( myString; " "; 1);
word2 := @Word( myString; " "; 2);

@Prompt([Ok]; "Word using a space delimiter";
"Initial string: " + myString + @NewLine +
"Word 1: " + word1 + @NewLine +
"Word 2: " + word2)
```

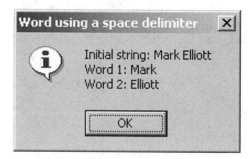

Figure 14.18   Example of the @Word function

How to Format Field Values Using "Input Translation"

Using the "Input Translation" event, you can format the data for a particular field as the form is being created or updated. This event is particularly handy for ensuring a consistent data format or naming nomenclature. For example, this event can be used to ensure that all text is translated to uppercase, that extraneous spaces are removed from text, or that a telephone number is formatted with hyphens.

How It Works

The "Input Translation" event is located in the Programmer's pane for most editable fields. This event is not present for computed fields or Rich Text fields. Field translation occurs based on a specified formula when the document is saved or refreshed. Some of the common Formula Language functions used to translate data values include @Trim, @UpperCase, @LowerCase, and @ProperCase.

Implementation

To implement this solution, insert a formula in the field's Input Translation event. The following illustrate some of the field translation formulas.

Example 1

The @Trim function removes extraneous leading, trailing, and embedded spaces from the string.

```
@Trim ( FIELDNAME )
```

Example 2

The @Uppercase function changes the string to all uppercase.

```
@UpperCase ( FIELDNAME )
```

Example 3

The @ProperCase function changes the string such that the first character of each word is capitalized.

```
@ProperCase ( FIELDNAME )
```

Example 4

The @LowerCase function changes the string to all lowercase letters.

```
@LowerCase ( FIELDNAME )
```

> **TIP**
>
> If you're looking for additional Input Translation samples, check out the Lotus Notes discussion forums at http://www-10.lotus.com/ldd/46dom.nsf/ or http://www-10.lotus.com/ldd/nd6forum.nsf. For example, if you're looking to format a telephone number, you could search these databases. A good example can be found in the 46dom.nsf database. Simply search for "Validation Code for a Phone Number field" or "Phone Number". Be sure to include quotes to narrow down the results.

How to Add Field Validation

Several different approaches can be used to implement field validation. This section illustrates how to add validation to fields on a form. This approach can be utilized on forms designed to run on the Lotus Notes client (as opposed to a Web browser). Field validation allows you to control and validate the information entered in a field.

> **NOTE**
>
> An alternative solution for field validation that utilizes the QuerySave event can be found in Chapter 13, "Design Enhancements Using LotusScript."

How It Works

A formula is added in the "Input Validation" event for a particular field. The "Input Validation" event is located in the Programmer's pane for most editable fields. Most notably, this event is not available for computed or Rich Text fields. Validation occurs when the document is saved or refreshed. If the resulting field value equates to TRUE, then the user can continue with the form. Otherwise, the user must successfully enter or select a value before continuing to the next field.

Implementation—Example 1

To implement this solution, insert a formula that checks the field for validity in the "Input Validation" event of the specific field. This first example ensures that the field contains a non-null value. The user must enter a value in order to continue with the form.

```
@If( @ThisValue = "";
         @Failure("Please specify a value for the field.");
         @Success);
```

Implementation—Example 2

This second example illustrates how to check a number field for a value. First, the formula checks to see whether the field contains a non-null value. If the field is null, the user receives the first error message to specify a value. If a number has been provided, the formula then verifies that the value is between 1 and 99. If the value is outside this range, then the user receives the invalid number error message.

```
myValue := FIELDNAME;
@If( myValue = "";
   @Failure("Please specify a value between 1 and 99.");
   @If( myValue < 1 | myValue > 99;
      @Failure("Invalid Value. Specify a number from 1 to 99);
      @Success)
      );
```

> **NOTE**
>
> Be sure that the validation formulas are placed in the "Input Validation" event and not the "Input Translation" event. If added to the "Input Translation" event, the error text may be embedded in the field, and the popup error message will not display.

Display an "Are You Sure?" Warning Message

In some cases, you may want to prompt the user to confirm that he or she really wants to continue before performing an action. For example, say the application includes a button to change the status of the document or to send an email. This routine illustrates how to prompt the user with a message such as "Are you sure?" before continuing with the transaction.

How It Works

The @Prompt function can be used to return a TRUE or FALSE value. When combined with the @IF statement, you can determine what action (if any) should be taken based on the user's response to the question.

Implementation

To implement this solution, create an action button on a form, view, or page. Insert the following code. Replace the @Prompt statements with commands to be issued based on the Yes or No response (see Figure 14.19). For example, if the user selects Yes, issue the @MailSend command.

```
result := @Prompt([YesNo]; "Continue?"; "Do you want to continue?");
@If (result = @True;
            @Prompt( [Ok]; "Result"; "You selected YES.");
            @Prompt( [Ok]; "Result"; "You selected NO."));
```

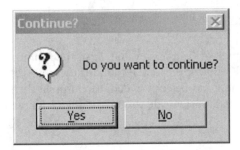

Figure 14.19   Example "Do you want to continue?" prompt

> **NOTE**
>
> A similar implementation can also be achieved using LotusScript. Refer to Chapter 13 for additional information pertaining to this subject.

Generate Email Using Formula Language

There are essentially two methods that can be used to generate an email using Formula Language—@Command([Mailsend]) and @MailSend. The @Command([Mailsend]) statement is used to send the current document to a list of recipients. @MailSend, on the other hand, is used to create and send a custom email message.

How It Works

The `@Command([Mailsend])` command generates an email based on the current document. This statement is typically added to an action button on a form. This approach also requires the form to include a field called SendTo. This field must contain a valid list of one or more email addresses. Optionally, the form can also include Subject, CopyTo, and BlindCopyTo fields.

The `@MailSend` function sends a custom email message based on function call parameters instead of using field values on the document. With this approach, the email is generated by specifying the list of recipients, subject, and body information within the function. When executed, the function sends a message to all recipients listed in the SendTo, CopyTo, and BlindCopyTo fields. Like its counterpart, this function is also typically placed in an action button on the form. When clicked, the message is sent.

> **TIP**
>
> You may want to save and close the document after either button is pressed. This is achieved by appending `@Command( [FileSave] )` to save the document and `@Command( [FileCloseWindow] )` to close the document.

Implementation—Example 1

To implement the `@Command([Mailsend])` approach, create a form that includes the SendTo and Subject fields. Next, create an action button and insert the following formula in the Programmer's pane. When clicked, the `@Mailsend` statement retrieves the field values from the document and sends the email message to the recipient list.

```
@Command ( [MailSend] )
```

Implementation—Example 2

To implement the `@MailSend` approach, create an action button and insert the following formula. Be sure to adjust the SendTo value to reflect all intended email recipients as well as the subject line.

```
SendTo := @UserName;
CopyTo := "";
BlindCopyTo := "";
Subject := "This is a sample email";
Remark := "";
BodyFields := "This is the body of the email.";
Flags := "";
@MailSend( sendTo ; copyTo ; blindCopyTo ; subject ; remark ; bodyFields ; Flags );
@Prompt( [Ok]; "Success"; "Message sent.");
```

How to Sort a List of Values

Using the @Sort function, you can sort a list of values in descending or ascending order.

How It Works

The @Sort function is a built-in Formula Language function. This function requires two parameters—a list of values and the sort order expression(s). There are numerous sort order expressions, including

Ascending—[ASCENDING]
Descending—[DESCENDING]
Accent-Sensitive—[ACCENTSENSITIVE]
Accent-Insensitive—[ACCENTINSENSITIVE]
Case-Sensitive—[CASESENSITIVE]
Case-Insensitive—[CASEINSENSITIVE]
Custom Sort—[CUSTOMSORT]
Pitch-Sensitive—[PITCHSENSITIVE]
Pitch-Insensitive—[PITCHSENSITIVE]

One or more expressions can be specified in the function call. Each expression must be enclosed in brackets and separated by semicolons.

Implementation

To sort the list, simply include the list of values and sort order expression(s). The following illustrates how to sort a list of values in ascending order (see Figure 14.20). Simply replace the list of values or assign a field to the myValues variable. The @Prompt statement is used for illustrative purposes and can be removed or updated as desired.

```
myValues := "Mark" : "Ryan" : "Kyle" : "Alex";
result := @Sort ( myValues; [Ascending] );

@Prompt( [Ok]; "Sample Sort";
"Original List: " + @Implode(myValues; ", ") + @NewLine +
"Sorted List: " + @Implode(result; ", "))
```

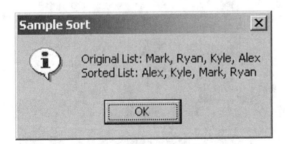

Figure 14.20   Example of the *@Sort* function

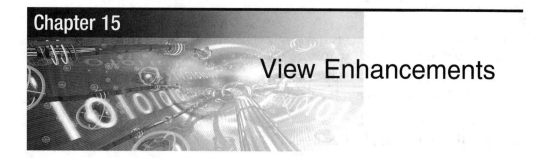

Chapter 15

View Enhancements

Chapter Overview

This chapter provides a number of LotusScript and Formula Language routines associated with views. These enhancements can be incorporated into almost any Lotus Notes database. Each customization is self-contained and designed to run independently. This enables you to copy the code into any existing application and implement it with little to no modification.

The intent of this chapter is to provide common customizations that can be added to any database application. However, when adding a LotusScript enhancement to an existing application, you may need to replace field names or search strings or remove duplicate code lines—such as declaration (DIM) statements.

Customizations include the following:

- Create a new document by double-clicking on a calendar date
- Display documents in a view by year and month
- Display an icon in the view
- Retrieve all views in a database
- Retrieve all columns in a database
- Retrieve all columns for each view in the database
- Manage conflict documents
- Manage applications with multiple forms
- Disable the ability to paste documents into a view

View Enhancements

This section covers enhancements specifically designed for Lotus Notes views. It includes enhancements written in both LotusScript and Formula Language.

A working example of all customizations can be found in the developer's toolbox in the **BookCodeLibrary.NSF** database. See Appendix A for additional information.

Create a New Document by Double-Clicking on a Calendar Date

The `RegionDoubleClick` event for a view can be used to trigger the creation of a new document. When a user double-clicks on a calendar date, a new document is created, and the date field is automatically populated with the selected calendar date.

How It Works

When the user clicks on a calendar date, the current date is retrieved. Then a new document is created, the appropriate field on the form is populated, and the form is displayed to the user. Be sure that the field used to generate the calendar view is also the field on the form that is populated with the calendar date.

Implementation

Create a calendar view and insert the following LotusScript code in the `Regiondoubleclick` event in the Programmer's pane. Be sure to replace **FORM** and **FIELD** with actual design element names. If other fields on the form need to be present, insert the additional statements before calling the "EditDocument" statement.

```
Sub Regiondoubleclick(Source As Notesuiview)

    '-----------------------------------------------------------
    ' Define the objects
    '-----------------------------------------------------------
    Dim s As NotesSession
    Dim db As NotesDatabase
    Dim doc As NotesDocument
    Dim uidoc As NotesUIDocument
    Set ws = New NotesUIWorkspace
    Set s = New NotesSession
    Set db = s.CurrentDatabase
    Dim newdoc As New NotesDocument(db)

    '-----------------------------------------------------------
    ' Set the form name and date field
    ' Replace FORM with a valid form name
    ' Replace FIELD with a valid date field name
    '-----------------------------------------------------------
    newdoc.form  = "FORM"
    newdoc.FIELD = Source.CalendarDateTime
```

```
        REM set other default field values here (as needed)

        '------------------------------------------------------------
        ' Create document
        '------------------------------------------------------------
        Set uidoc = ws.EditDocument (True, newdoc)

End Sub
```

Display Documents in a View by Year and Month

The ability to quickly and easily locate a document is often tied to the design of one or more database views. Many database documents include fields such as Creation Date, Due Date, Invoice Date, etc., that could be used as the basis for a view. This section illustrates an approach that can be used to sort documents first by year and then by month. For example, A.15.1 Figure 15.1 illustrates a view that displays company invoices.

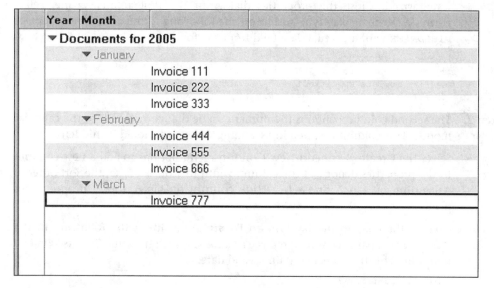

Figure 15.1   Example view with documents sorted by year and month

How It Works

Several Formula Language functions are used to convert numeric year and month values into text strings. Three columns are required to implement this technique. The first column displays the year using the @Year function. The resulting value is subsequently converted to a string by using the @Text function. The second column, which is hidden, contains the numeric month value and is used to sort the months in sequential order. The third column contains the month of the year. This is computed by using the @Select statement to compute the @Month value. The last column displays data from the document.

When implemented, all documents are grouped together (or categorized) based on a specified document date. If unable to determine the date for a given document, the document is displayed in a default category called "No Date Specified". This is an arbitrary message that can be changed as desired.

Implementation

To implement this solution, create a view with four columns. Complete the following steps to configure the view columns.

Step 1.   The first column will contain the year associated with the document. Double-click on the default column to display the properties dialog. On tab 1, set the column name to **Year**, specify a column width and select **Show twistie when row is expandable**. Switch to tab 2. Set the sort order to **Descending** and **Categorized**. Close the properties dialog. In the Programmer's pane, select **Formula** as the display type and insert the following formula. Be sure to replace **FIELDNAME** with an actual date field from the form.

```
myDate := FIELDNAME;
msg1 :=  "Documents for " + @Text(@Year( myDate ));
msg2 := "No Date Specified";
@If (@Text(myDate) = ""; msg2; msg1)
```

Step 2.   The second column contains the numeric value that corresponds to the calendar month. This column is sorted in ascending order and should be hidden.

Select the **Create > Append New Column** menu options to add a new column. In the properties dialog, set the column width to **1** on tab 1, set the sort order to **Ascending** on tab 2, and select **Hide column** on tab 6. Close the properties dialog.

Change the column display type to **Formula** and insert the following in the Programmer's pane. Be sure to replace **FIELDNAME** with the same field used in column one. This field must contain a valid date.

```
myDate := FIELDNAME;
msg1 := @Select(@Month( myDate );
             "1"; "2"; "3"; "4"; "5"; "6";
             "7"; "8"; "9"; "10"; "11"; "12");
msg2 := "0";
@If (@Text(myDate) = ""; msg2; @TextToNumber(msg1))
```

Step 3. The third column converts the numeric month to a text month value. This is a categorized column and is sorted in ascending order.

Select the **Create > Append New Column** menu options to add a new column. In the properties dialog, set the column width to **7** and select **Show twistie when row is expandable** on tab 1. Set the sort order to **Ascending** and **Categorized** on tab 2. Close the properties dialog.

In the Programmer's pane, set the column display type to **Formula** and insert the following formula. Be sure to replace **FIELDNAME** with the same field name value used in column one.

```
myDate := FIELDNAME;
msg1 := @Select(@Month(myDate);
              "January"; "February"; "March";
              "April"; "May"; "June";
              "July"; "August"; "September";
              "October"; "November"; "December");
msg2 := "No Date";
@If (@Text(myDate) = ""; msg2; @Text(msg1))
```

Step 4. Create additional view columns as needed to display the remaining document information in the view.

Display an Icon in a View

In addition to displaying data, columns can also be used to display a small visual icon. This is a built-in feature and is typically used to signify some state associated with a particular document. Icons could be used to indicate the status of a document (such as a green, yellow, or red stoplight icon) or whether the document has an attachment (such as a Word document, spreadsheet, or sound file). This enables users to quickly gather information pertinent to a document.

How It Works

To display a view icon, two items must be set—the column property and the column formula. To display an icon for any given column, you must select **Display values as icons** in the properties dialog. Additionally, the column formula must equate to a corresponding icon value. There are 180 default icons provided with release 7 that can be displayed in a view column (see Figure 15.2). These icons are automatically included with Lotus Notes and cannot be changed.

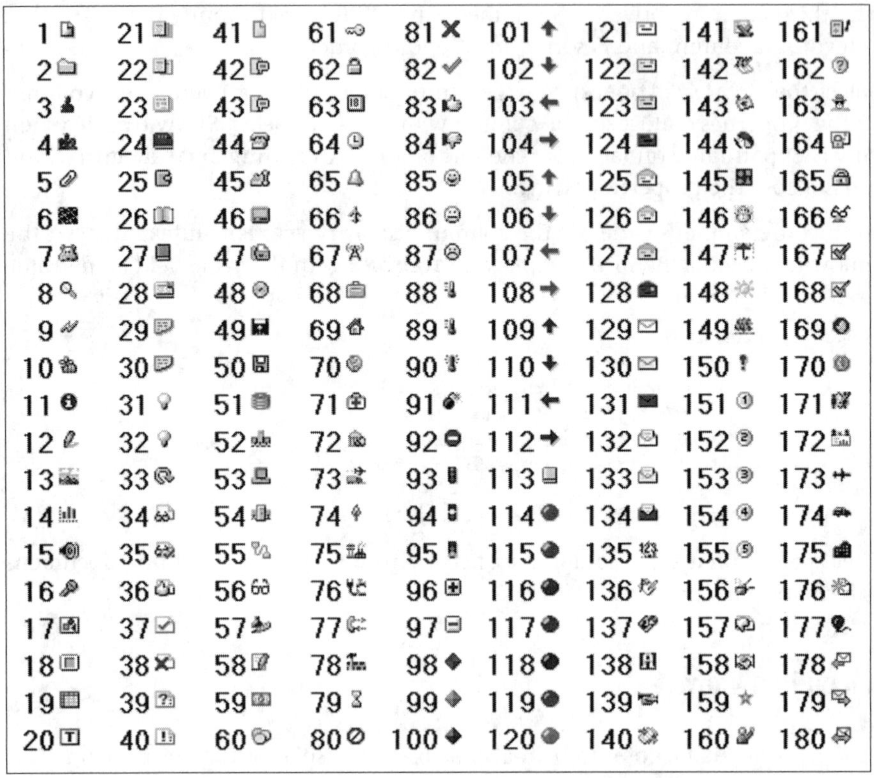

Figure 15.2 All default view icons displayed by reference number

Implementation

This example illustrates how to set the view icon for a document attachment. The unique icon number is computed based on the extension of the attached file. To implement this solution, perform the following steps.

Step 1. Create a view.

Step 2. Create a column. In the column properties dialog, set the column width to **1** and enable the **Display values as icons** configuration option (see Figure 15.3). Close the properties dialog after these values have been set.

Step 3. Set the column display type to **Formula** and insert the following in the Programmer's pane for the column.

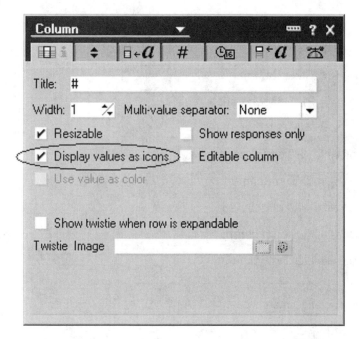

Figure 15.3   "Display values as icons" column property setting

```
REM {Display Lotus Database icon for NSF files};
REM {Display Photo Icon for GIF files};
REM {Display PowerPoint icon for PPT files};
REM {Display Sound icon for WAV and MP3 files};
REM {Display Lotus 123 icon for WK3 or WK4 files};
REM {Display MS Word icon for DOC files};
REM {Display MS Excel icon for XLS files};
REM {Display File Icon for TXT files};

@If (@Attachments = 1;
    @If ( @Contains( @UpperCase (@AttachmentNames); ".NSF"); 4;
        @Contains( @UpperCase (@AttachmentNames); ".GIF"); 13;
        @Contains( @UpperCase (@AttachmentNames); ".PPT"); 14;
        @Contains( @UpperCase (@AttachmentNames); ".WAV"); 15;
        @Contains( @UpperCase (@AttachmentNames); ".MP3"); 15;
        @Contains( @UpperCase (@AttachmentNames); ".TXT"); 21;
        @Contains( @UpperCase (@AttachmentNames); ".WK3"); 135;
        @Contains( @UpperCase (@AttachmentNames); ".WK4"); 135;
        @Contains( @UpperCase (@AttachmentNames); ".XLS"); 141;
        @Contains( @UpperCase (@AttachmentNames); ".DOC"); 142;
        5);
    @Attachments > 1; 5;
    0)
```

Figure 15.4 shows an example view with a column icon that indicates attachment type.

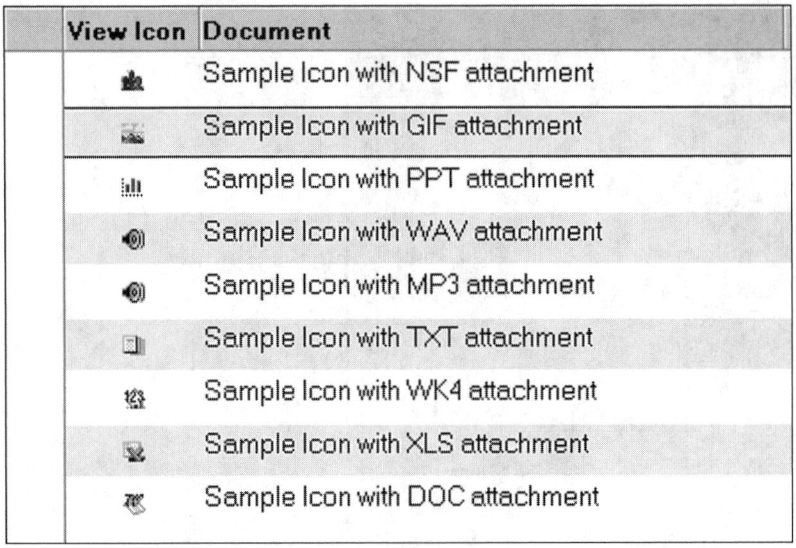

View Icon	Document
🏛	Sample Icon with NSF attachment
🖼	Sample Icon with GIF attachment
📊	Sample Icon with PPT attachment
🔊	Sample Icon with WAV attachment
🔊	Sample Icon with MP3 attachment
📄	Sample Icon with TXT attachment
📋	Sample Icon with WK4 attachment
📉	Sample Icon with XLS attachment
📝	Sample Icon with DOC attachment

Figure 15.4   Column icon indicating attachment type

Retrieve All Views in a Database

This routine illustrates how to retrieve all views associated with a database and could be used to build custom buttons that retrieve data based on a selected view.

How It Works

Using the NotesDatabase and NotesView classes, the routine iterates through all views in a database and displays a message to the user.

Implementation

In the following example, all database views (hidden or otherwise) will be processed with the name of each view appended to a string and displayed in a message window. Alternatively, you may want to store the view names in a dynamic array or perform some other data query for each view. To implement this technique, create an action button. Set the Language Selector to **LotusScript** and insert the following statements in the Programmer's pane.

```
Sub Click(Source As Button)

    '------------------------------------------------------------------
    ' Define the objects
    '------------------------------------------------------------------
    Dim s As NotesSession
    Dim db As NotesDatabase
    Dim view As NotesView
    Dim strViewTitles As String
    Set s = New NotesSession
    Set db = s.CurrentDatabase


    '------------------------------------------------------------------
    ' Display all view names for the database
    '------------------------------------------------------------------
    If Not Isempty (db.Views) Then
       Forall v In db.Views
          strViewTitles = strViewTitles & Chr$(10) & v.Name
       End Forall
       Msgbox (strViewTitles)
    End If

End Sub
```

Retrieve All Columns in a View

This routine iterates through each column in a specified view and displays the column name. When retrieved, the values could be used to produce a spreadsheet or for data manipulation purposes.

How It Works

Using the NotesDatabase and NotesView classes, the routine iterates through a specific view and returns the column names property. Alternatively, you may want to store the column names in a dynamic array or perform some other action with each view column.

Implementation

In the following example, all column names for a given view are processed with the name of each column appended to a string and displayed in a message window. To implement this technique, create an action button. Set the Language Selector to **LotusScript** and insert the following statements in the Programmer's pane.

```
Sub Click(Source As Button)

    '------------------------------------------------------------------
    ' Define the objects
    '------------------------------------------------------------------
    Dim s As NotesSession
    Dim db As NotesDatabase
```

```
Dim strColTitles As String
Dim view As NotesView
Set s = New NotesSession
Set db = s.CurrentDatabase
Set view = db.GetView( "VIEW" )

'----------------------------------------------------------------
' Display all column titles for specified view
'----------------------------------------------------------------
Forall c In view.Columns
    strColTitles = strColTitles & Chr$(10) & c.Title
End Forall
Messagebox( strColTitles )

End Sub
```

Retrieve All Columns for Each View in a Database

This routine displays all columns for all views in the database.

How It Works

Using the `NotesDatabase` and `NotesView` classes, the routine iterates through every view in the database and returns all columns for the view. Alternatively, you may want to store the column names in a dynamic array or perform some other action with each view column.

Implementation

To implement this routine, create an action button. Set the Language Selector to **LotusScript** and insert the following statements in the Programmer's pane.

```
Sub Click(Source As Button)

    '----------------------------------------------------------------
    ' Define the objects
    '----------------------------------------------------------------
    Dim s As NotesSession
    Dim db As NotesDatabase
    Set s = New NotesSession
    Set db = s.CurrentDatabase
    Dim view As NotesView

    '----------------------------------------------------------------
    ' Display all columns for each database view
    '----------------------------------------------------------------
    If Not Isempty (db.Views) Then
        Forall v In db.Views

            Msgbox "Found View: " + v.Name
            Set view = db.GetView( v.Name )
            Forall c In view.Columns
                Msgbox ( "----" + c.Title )
```

```
      End Forall

    End Forall
  End If

End Sub
```

How to Manage Conflict Documents

Conflict documents are created when a document is opened and saved by more than one person at the same time. When this occurs, a secondary document, called a "conflict document," is created. The document is created either when the document is saved or when a local document is replicated to the server. There are three primary approaches that can be used to manage database conflict documents.

1. Monitor and correct conflicts as they occur

2. Have Lotus Notes merge replication conflicts

3. Implement document locking

When managing a large database, conflict documents can be hard to locate. To manage and quickly locate conflict documents, create a view that displays all conflicts in the database. It's a good idea to monitor and periodically clean up conflict documents in the database.

How It Works

Any time a conflict document is created, Domino adds a special field to the document. This variable is called $Conflict. To show all conflicts in the database, create a view and set the selection criteria to only display documents that contain the $Conflict field.

A.15.2

Implementation—Approach 1—Monitor Conflicts

The first approach is to monitor conflict documents in the database. As new conflict documents are created, you monitor conflicts and notify document authors so that the changes can be applied to the main document. This will ensure that the document changes are eventually integrated and applied to the database. To implement this solution, complete the following steps.

Step 1. Create a view.

Step 2. In the properties dialog, give the view a unique name—such as **Conflicts**. Switch to tab 2 and uncheck **Show response documents in hierarchy**. Close the properties dialog after these configuration parameters are set.

Step 3. Insert the following formula in the Selection Criteria section of the Programmer's pane. This will ensure that only conflict documents are displayed in the view.

```
SELECT @IsAvailable($Conflict)
```

Implementation—Approach 2—Merge Replication Conflicts

The second approach is to have Lotus Notes automatically merge replicated changes into a single document. Lotus Notes will automatically merge documents, provided that the fields modified are unique between the two documents. If the same field is modified between the local and server documents, a conflict document will still be generated. Otherwise, the changes will be merged into a single document. To implement this approach, complete the following steps.

Step 1.   Open the form in the Domino Designer client.

Step 2.   Select the **Design > Form Properties** menu options. In the properties dialog, select the **Merge replication conflicts** option.

Implementation—Approach 3—Lock Documents

The third approach locks documents and disables the ability for a single document to be opened in edit mode by multiple users. It's important to note that this approach only works when implemented on the server. You must have "Manager" access to the database in the ACL to utilize this technique. To implement it, complete the following steps.

Step 1.   Select the **File > Database > Access Control** menu options. Switch to the Advanced tab and specify the Domino server to be used as the **Admin Server**. In many cases, this will be the same server that is used to host the database. Save and close the Access Control List window after this value has been specified.

Step 2.   Open the database and select the **File > Database > Properties** menu options. Select the **Allow document locking** option on tab 1 of the database properties dialog.

> **TIP**
>
> Review the Notes Designer help to learn more about the document locking feature. Be aware that some users will mostly encounter problems where documents stay locked. To counter this problem, create a hidden view for documents that contain $Writers and $WritersDate. Then create a scheduled agent to release the lock on these documents based on an established time, for example, for documents that remain in a locked status for longer than one, two, or three days.

> **TIP**
>
> Create a view icon column to indicate when the document is locked. You could also create a computed field on the form that indicates the document lock status at the time the document is opened.

Display All Documents by Form Name

Databases that contain multiple forms can sometimes be cumbersome to manage—making it difficult to locate documents when errors occur. In other words, if the selection criterion for each view is based on the form, it's possible that some documents may never be visible due to the view formula.

One method to manage this problem is to create a view, possibly restricted to just the database administrator or developer, that categorizes documents by the form name. This way, every document in the database will be accessible.

How It Works

By setting the first view column formula to Form, all documents in the database will be grouped together by form name. For example, let's say you have a service request database that includes the following forms:

- Move Offices
- Reset Password
- Revoke UserID
- Workstation Problem
- Manager Lookup
- Employee Lookup
- System Configuration

In this example, the database includes four forms used to manage service requests (Move Offices, Reset Password, Revoke UserID, and Workstation Problem), two forms used to display custom dialog boxes (Manager Lookup and Employee Lookup), and a general form used to manage application settings (System Configuration). By creating a view where the selection formula is set to @All, all documents will be visible from a single view.

Implementation

To implement, select the **Create > Design > View** menu options. When prompted, be sure the **Copy style from view** field is set to -**Blank**-. To change this value, click the **Copy From** button. Also make sure the selection conditions are empty. Give the view a unique name such as **All Documents**. Next, select the **Select by Formula** checkbox and click **OK** to create the view.

When the newly created view is displayed, the Designer client will immediately display the properties dialog for the view. Click on the default column to make this the active design element. Then in the properties dialog, name the column **Form** and switch to tab 2. Set the sort order to **Ascending** and display type to **Categorized** (see Figure 15.5). Close the properties dialog.

Finally, with the column still in focus, change the display type to **Formula** and add the following in the Programmer's pane.

```
Form
```

Save and close the view.

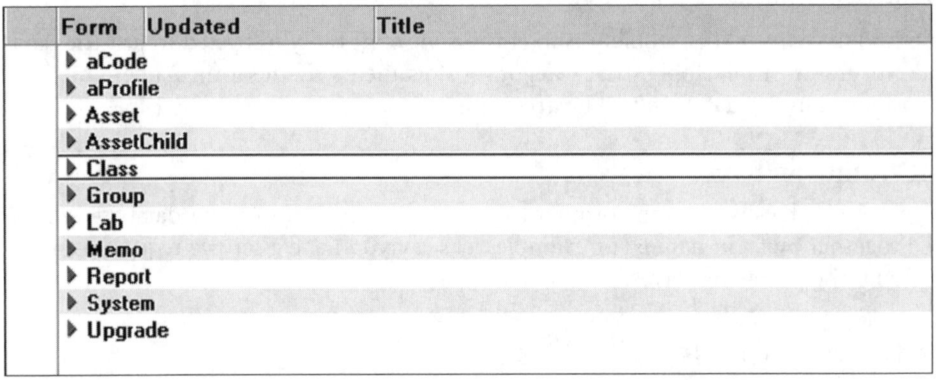

Form	Updated	Title
▶ aCode		
▶ aProfile		
▶ Asset		
▶ AssetChild		
▶ Class		
▶ Group		
▶ Lab		
▶ Memo		
▶ Report		
▶ System		
▶ Upgrade		

Figure 15.5   Example view sorted by all the various database forms

Disable the Ability to Paste Documents into a View

Depending on the database design, you may want to disable the ability to paste copied documents into a database view. This technique forces users to create new documents by using the buttons or menu options in the database. You may want to implement this to manage field content. For example, let's say that you've implemented code to assign a unique reference number for each database document. This assignment occurs during the QuerySave event. By allowing documents to be copied and pasted into a view, two or more documents will have duplicate reference numbers.

How It Works

All views include a QueryPaste event. This event can be used to disable the ability to paste documents into the view. This is achieved by assigning a Boolean value to the Continue variable. A TRUE value enables documents to be pasted. A FALSE value disables the ability to paste documents.

Implementation

To implement this solution, insert the following code in the QueryPaste event for the view. Remember to add this to all views in the database. Otherwise, you only restrict the ability to paste documents in views that include this formula.

```
Sub QueryPaste (Source As Notesuiview, Continue As Variant)

    Continue = False

    Messagebox "Sorry, users are not permitted "+_
    "to paste documents.", 48, "Warning"

End Sub
```

 ## Links to developerWorks

A.15.1 Russell, Donald. *Tip: Overcoming the default alphabetical column sort when sorting by rank*. IBM developerWorks, December 2004. http://www.ibm.com/developerworks/lotus/library/sort-rank/index.html.

A.15.2 DeJean, David. *LotusScript: Programming views in Notes/Domino 6*. IBM developerWorks, August 2003. http://www.ibm.com/developerworks/lotus/library/ls-LS_views/index.html.

Chapter 16

Sample Agents

Chapter Overview

This chapter illustrates a number of sample agents. These agents demonstrate how an agent can be used to create a report or modify data. These agents can be incorporated into almost any Lotus Notes database. Each technique is self-contained and designed to run independently. This enables you to copy the code into any existing application and implement it with little to no modification.

The intent of this chapter is to provide common customizations that can be added to any database. However, when adding a LotusScript enhancement to an existing application, you may need to replace field names or search strings or remove duplicate code lines—such as declaration (DIM) statements.

Customizations include the following:

- Simple action agent to modify all documents
- LotusScript agent to modify all documents containing a specific value
- LotusScript agent to manually generate an email report
- LotusScript scheduled agent to send a daily, weekly, or monthly email report

Agent Enhancements

Agents are used to automate repeatable tasks. This section includes a number of sample agents that can be added to virtually any Lotus Notes database.

A working example of all customizations can be found in the developer's toolbox in the **BookCodeLibrary.NSF** database. See Appendix A for additional information.

Simple Action Agent to Modify All Documents

Simple action agents utilize predefined actions to perform a task in the database. Using simple actions, you can quickly build an agent with little to no programming. A few of the simple actions include the following:

- Copy a Database
- Copy a Folder
- Delete from Database
- Mark Document Read
- Mark Document Unread
- Modify Field
- Modify Fields by Form
- Move to Folder
- Remove from Folder
- Reply to Sender
- Run Agent
- Send Document
- Send Mail Message
- Send Newsletter Summary
- @Function Formula

To illustrate the concept of a simple action agent, this section explains how to create an agent that modifies all documents by appending a value to a specific field value. Let's say you want to append a comment to the History field for all documents in the database. Using a simple agent, you could append a comment to the field.

How It Works

Simple action agents are created primarily through a series of Lotus Notes generated dialog windows. The Modify Field action is used to update documents. The agent iterates through all documents and allows you to either replace or append the value for a specific field. The agent loops through each document and, for this example, appends the specified text string to the selected field.

Implementation

To implement this solution, complete the following steps.

Step 1.   Select the **Create > Design > Agent** menu options to create the agent. When the properties dialog displays, give the agent a name such as **Update History** and close the property window. Note: By default, the agent type will be set to **Simple action(s)**.

Step 2. Click the **Add Actions** button located at the bottom of the screen to configure the action. Set the action to **Modify Field**, set **Modify by** to **Appending**, and select a field to modify (see Figure 16.1).

Step 3. Specify the value to be appended to the selected field.

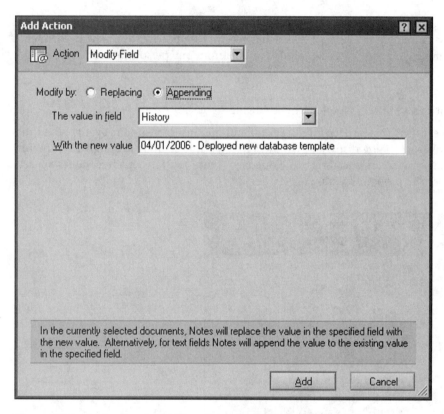

Figure 16.1 Using the Add Action dialog to create a simple agent

Step 4. Select **Add** to insert the action into the agent. Save and close the agent to complete the process. To run the agent, open the database in the Lotus Notes client and select **Update History** from the Actions menu.

LotusScript Agent to Modify All Documents Containing a Specific Field Value

Like simple actions, LotusScript can be used to manage and perform actions in a database. However, LotusScript offers greater flexibility to create more robust agents. This section illustrates how to modify all documents in a database where a field contains a specific value.

A.16.1

How It Works

For this example, LotusScript is used to iterate through database documents in a specific view and compare field values. When a match is found, the new value is assigned to the field, and the document is saved. The looping then continues with the next document in the list.

This example could be used to modify field values for select documents in a database view. Let's say, for example, that a team member has recently transferred to a new department. Using this sample, you could reassign all documents from one person to another person.

Implementation

To implement this solution, complete the following steps.

Step 1. Select the **Create > Design > Agent** menu options to create the agent. When the properties dialog displays, give the agent a name such as **Reassign Documents** and set the Runtime Target to **None** (see Figure 16.2). After these values are set, close the properties dialog.

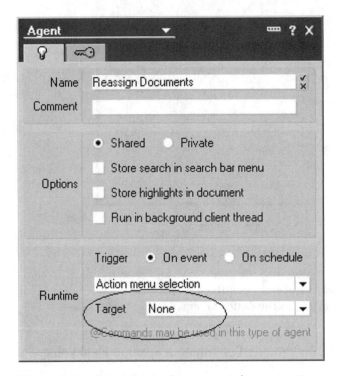

Figure 16.2   Setting the runtime property for an agent

Step 2.   Change the Language Selector from **Simple action(s)** to **LotusScript**.

Step 3.   Insert the following code in the Programmer's pane. Be sure to replace **VIEW** with the name of the view to iterate through, **FIELD** with the field name to check, **VALUE1** with the comparison string, and **VALUE2** with the replacement string. If the search-and-replace objects are numbers, remember to remove the quotes to indicate that the value is a number (and not a string).

```
Sub Initialize

    Dim s As New NotesSession
    Dim db As NotesDatabase
    Dim doc As NotesDocument
    Dim view As NotesView
    Set db = s.CurrentDatabase
    Set view=db.GetView("VIEW")

    Set doc = view.GetFirstDocument
    While Not (doc Is Nothing)

        If doc.FIELD(0) = "VALUE1" Then
            doc.FIELD = "VALUE2"
        End If
        Call doc.Save( True, False )
        Set doc=view.GetNextDocument( doc )

    Wend
    Print "Complete"

End Sub
```

Step 4.   Save and close the agent to complete the configuration. To run the agent, open the database in the Lotus Notes client and select **Reassign Documents** from the Actions menu.

> **NOTE**
>
> Performance for this agent will be affected by a variety of factors—total documents in the database, total fields in the document, runtime location (server versus local), and so on. If performance becomes an issue, consider replacing `If doc.FIELD(0) = "Value1"` with the statement `If doc.GetItemValue ( "FIELD")(0) = "Value1"`. The `GetItemValue` method is more efficient and will improve overall agent performance for large databases.

Agent to Manually Generate an Email Report

This example illustrates how to create an agent that generates a report. The agent is manually triggered by the user through an action button or the database menu. When executed, a report is generated and sent to the person who triggered the agent.

How It Works

After the agent is created, the user manually triggers execution of the agent through an action button or from the Action database menu. The agent iterates through all documents in the specified view and builds an email. After all documents have been processed, the report is emailed to the user who manually triggered the agent. The email message includes a document link and title for all documents processed.

Let's say you have a database with a view that contains open action items. Using this approach, you could generate an email report with document links. The report could then be forwarded to management or team members.

Implementation

To implement this solution, complete the following steps.

Step 1. Create or select a view to be used when generating a report. Make note of the view name.

Step 2. Select the **Create > Design > Agent** menu options to create the agent. When the properties dialog displays, give the agent a name such as **Generate Report** and set the Runtime Target to **None**. After these values are set, close the properties dialog.

Step 3. Change the Language Selector from **Simple action(s)** to **LotusScript**. Add the following in the `Initialize` sections. Be sure to replace **VIEW** with the name of the view to be used to create the report. Also, to display a description next to each document link, replace **FIELD** with a valid text field from the form.

```
Sub Initialize
    Dim s As New NotesSession
    Dim db As NotesDatabase
    Dim view As NotesView
    Dim doc As NotesDocument
    Dim memo As NotesDocument
    Dim rtitem As NotesRichTextItem
    Dim PersonName As New NotesName(s.UserName)


    '----------------------------------------------------
    ' Set object values
    ' Replace VIEW with a valid View name
    '----------------------------------------------------
    Set db = s.CurrentDatabase
    Set memo = New NotesDocument (db)
    Set view = db.GetView( "VIEW" )
    Set doc = view.GetFirstDocument


    '----------------------------------------------------
    ' Begin processing
    '----------------------------------------------------
```

```
If doc Is Nothing Then
   Print "Success: Agent ran, no items found"
Else
   '----------------------------------------------------
   ' Create the newsletter
   '----------------------------------------------------
   memo.Form = "Memo"
   memo.SendTo = PersonName.Abbreviated
   memo.Subject = "Database Report"
   Set rtitem = New NotesRichTextItem(memo, "Body")
   Call rtitem.AddNewLine( 1 )
   Call rtitem.AppendText("Here is the requested report.")
   Call rtitem.AddNewLine( 2 )


   '----------------------------------------------------
   ' Add the newsletter items
   ' Replace FIELD with a valid field on the document
   '----------------------------------------------------
   While Not ( doc Is Nothing )
      Call rtitem.AddNewLine( 1 )
      Call rtitem.AppendDocLink( doc, db.Title )
      Call rtitem.AppendText( " -- " + doc.FIELD(0) )
      Set doc = view.GetNextDocument( doc )
   Wend

   '----------------------------------------------------
   ' Close and send the report
   '----------------------------------------------------
   Call rtitem.AddNewLine( 3 )
   Call rtitem.AppendText("<---- END OF REPORT ---->")
   Call memo.Send ( False )

   Print "Success: Report generated and sent. "
End If

End Sub
```

> **NOTE**
>
> Depending on the database security settings, an Execution Control List (ECL) message may be displayed for some users. Users will need to select an execution option, such as **Run Once**, for the agent to run. See Chapter 19, "Security," for additional information pertaining to database security as well as how to "sign" a database.

Figure 16.3 shows a sample email report.

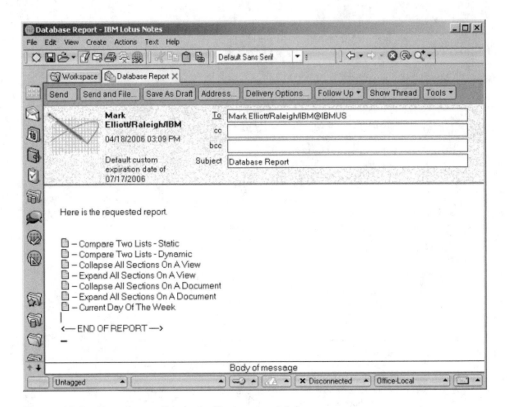

Figure 16.3   Sample email report with document links

Schedule Agent to Send a Daily, Weekly, or Monthly Email Report

Scheduled agents run on the database server and perform tasks on a set interval. Agents can be configured to run daily, weekly, or monthly. They can even be configured to run multiple times a day at intervals such as every 1, 15, 30, or 60 minutes. These options equate to great flexibility in the configuration of scheduled agents.

To illustrate the concept of a scheduled agent, this section describes how to create a scheduled agent that sends a weekly email report to a list of people who have "subscribed" to the database. This example presumes that a database has been established and includes a form where users can sign up (or subscribe) to receive weekly email reports. The report contains all documents listed in a particular view. This approach could be used to receive a report containing new business opportunities.

How It Works

The scheduled agent runs on a set interval. In this case, the agent will be scheduled to run weekly. When the agent executes, three primary activities will occur—the agent will build an array of email addresses, loop through all documents in a particular view to build the email, and send the email after all documents in the view have been processed.

Implementation

To implement this solution, complete the following steps.

Step 1.   Create a form to manage email subscriptions. This form will allow users to create a subscription profile. At a minimum, the form must contain a field for the user's email address, but it may also include fields for their name, phone number, title, and so on (see Figure 16.4).

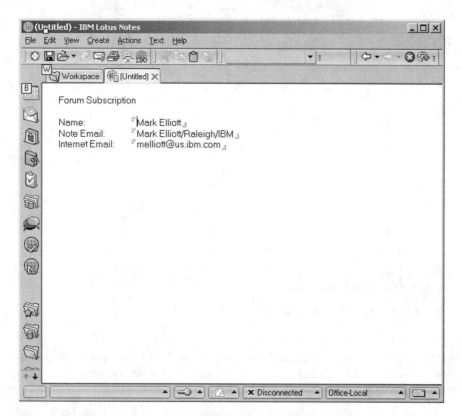

Figure 16.4   Example email subscription form

Step 2. Create a view to display only the email subscription documents. Set column one to display the user's email address (see Figure 16.5). Other columns can be added as desired for name, phone number, title, etc. Be sure that the selection criterion for this view is set to only include the email subscription form. Make note of the view name, then save and close the view. You will need to replace **VIEW1** with this view name in the following code.

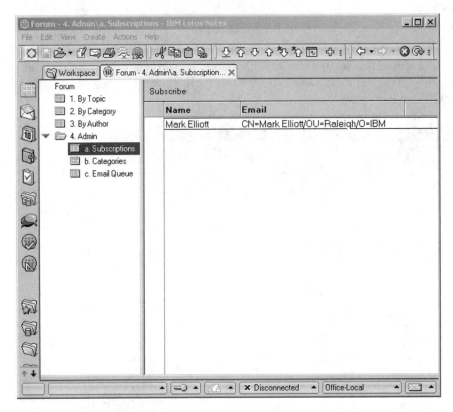

Figure 16.5 Sample view used to display subscription documents

Step 3. Select or create a view that contains documents for the report. Make note of the view name, then save and close the view. You will need to replace **VIEW2** with this view name in the following code.

Step 4. Create the scheduled agent. Select the **Create > Design > Agent** menu options to create the agent. When created, give the agent the name **Weekly Report**. With the properties dialog still displayed, change the trigger type to **On schedule**, select **Weekly** as the runtime frequency, and set the target to **All documents in the database** (see Figure 16.6).

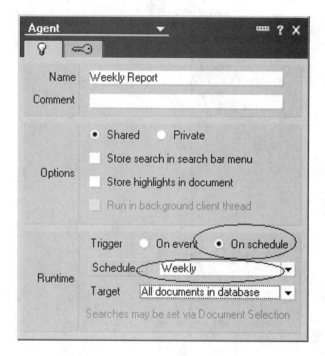

Figure 16.6   Example properties values for a scheduled agent

Step 5.   Configure the interval frequency for the scheduled agent. Click **Schedule**. Set the day and time for this agent to run (see Figure 16.7). Also set the **Run on** value to the server in which the database resides. After these configuration values are set, click **OK** to close the windows.

> **NOTE**
>
> Use caution when setting the **Run on** server to **-Any Server-** when the database is replicated across multiple servers. When set to this value, the agent will run on each server instance. Although this may be valuable in some cases, it may be detrimental in others. In this example, for instance, the user will receive duplicate email reports—one email from each server to which the database is replicated.

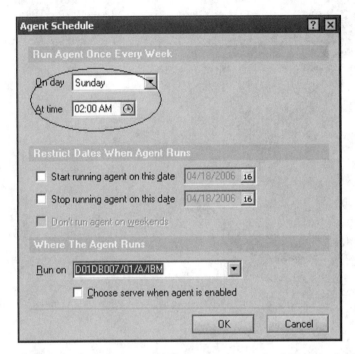

Figure 16.7   Setting the run frequency for a scheduled agent

Step 6.   Insert the LotusScript code used to produce and send the report. In the Programmer's pane, change the Language Selector from **Simple action(s)** to **LotusScript**. Next, insert the following code in the `Initialize` section. Be sure to replace the following to ensure that the agent runs correctly.

- Replace **VIEW1** with the name of the view that contains the distribution email addresses.

- Replace **VIEW2** with the name of the view to be used to create the report.

- Replace **FIELD1** with the text field that contains the email address for the document.

- Replace **FIELD2** with the text field that contains the document subject or description.

```
Sub Initialize
    Dim s As New NotesSession
    Dim db As NotesDatabase
    Dim view1 As NotesView
    Dim view2 As NotesView
    Dim doc As NotesDocument
    Dim memo As NotesDocument
    Dim rtitem As NotesRichTextItem
```

```
Dim Person As NotesName
Dim i As Integer

'--------------------------------------------------------
' Set object values
' Replace VIEW1 with view containing email addresses
' Replace VIEW2 with view containing documents
'--------------------------------------------------------
Set db = s.CurrentDatabase
Set view1 = db.GetView( "VIEW1" )
Set view2 = db.GetView( "VIEW2" )
Set memo = New NotesDocument (db)
Set doc = view2.GetFirstDocument
Set Person = New NotesName( s.UserName )

'--------------------------------------------------------
' Begin processing
'--------------------------------------------------------
If doc Is Nothing Then
   Print "Success: Agent ran, no items found in view"
Else
   '-----------------------------------------------------
   ' Build dynamic list of email addresses
   ' Replace FIELD1 with the email field
   '-----------------------------------------------------
   i = 0
   Set doc = view1.GetFirstDocument
   While Not( doc Is Nothing )
      Redim Preserve addresses( i ) As String
      addresses( i ) = doc.FIELD1(0)
      i = i + 1
      Set doc = view1.GetNextDocument( doc )
   Wend

   '-----------------------------------------------------
   ' Create the newsletter report memo
   '-----------------------------------------------------
   memo.Form = "Memo"
   memo.SendTo = addresses
   memo.Subject = "Database Report"
   memo.Principal = "Report Administrator"
   Set rtitem = New NotesRichTextItem(memo, "Body")
   Call rtitem.AddNewLine( 1 )
   Call rtitem.AppendText("Here is the requested report.")
   Call rtitem.AddNewLine( 2 )

   '-----------------------------------------------------
   ' Add the newsletter items
   ' Replace FIELD2 with a document text field
   '-----------------------------------------------------
   Set doc = view2.GetFirstDocument
   While Not ( doc Is Nothing )
      Call rtitem.AddNewLine( 1 )
      Call rtitem.AppendDocLink( doc, db.Title )
      Call rtitem.AppendText( " -- " + doc.FIELD2(0) )
      Set doc = view2.GetNextDocument( doc )
   Wend
```

```
'----------------------------------------------------
' Close and send the newsletter
'----------------------------------------------------
Call rtitem.AddNewLine( 3 )
Call rtitem.AppendText("<---- END OF REPORT ---->")
Call memo.Send ( False )

    Print "Success: Report generated and sent. "
  End If

End Sub
```

> **NOTE**
>
> Depending on the database security settings, you may need to "sign"
> the agent (or database) for the agent to run. By default, the agent will
> be signed by the person who last saved the agent. If this person has
> insufficient rights in the ACL to run the agent, the scheduled agent will
> not run. In this case, the agent will either need to be signed by a Notes
> ID that is authorized to run scheduled agents, or the ACL will need to
> be modified such that the person has sufficient rights. Although not
> required, it's a good practice to sign all agents with an ID authorized to
> run agents. See Chapter 19 for additional information pertaining to
> database security as well as how to "sign" a database.

> **TIP**
>
> Server-generated emails will appear to be sent by the person who last
> saved (or signed) the agent. If you want to show the email as coming
> from the server (or someone else), add a principal field to the memo
> (e.g., `memo.Principal = "Report Administrator"`).

> **NOTE**
>
> Database, view, and document links can only be sent to Lotus Notes
> email addresses (e.g., John Doe/Company). Be sure that email
> addresses only contain Lotus Notes names if the report will contain
> links.

Links to developerWorks

A.16.1 Russell, Donald. *Tip: Get database agent status with one click!* IBM developerWorks,
November 2004. http://www.ibm.com/developerworks/lotus/library/agent-status/index.
html.

Chapter 17

Miscellaneous Enhancements and Tips for Domino Databases

Chapter Overview

This chapter provides a number of miscellaneous application design techniques that can be applied to virtually any Lotus Notes database. Most of the customizations in this chapter enhance the overall usage of the database. These customizations will help the user navigate the application as well as manage data content.

In this chapter you'll learn how to perform the following:

- Disable the ability to print, copy, cut, and forward documents
- Add field hints to a form
- Use static popups to display text messages (or help)
- Inherit fields between forms
- Add an icon to an action button
- Create a custom application interface
- Set the field tab order on a form
- Disable database replication
- Use Domino shortcut keys

Miscellaneous Enhancements

The following are general configuration tips and enhancements that can be incorporated or applied to Lotus Notes databases.

A working example of all customizations can be found in the developer's toolbox in the **BookCodeLibrary.NSF** database. See Appendix A for additional information.

Disable the Ability to Print, Copy, Cut, and Forward Documents

The **$KeepPrivate** field is a special Lotus Notes field that manages the ability to copy, print, and forward documents in a database. When enabled, the associated menu options and shortcut keys are disabled. This prevents the user from performing any of these actions. This feature is often implemented as a means to manage the dissemination of information.

How It Works

This is a built-in feature of the Lotus Notes client. Users will not be able to copy, print, or forward any document that includes the **$KeepPrivate** field where its value is set to a text string `"1"`.

> **NOTE**
>
> This field does not prevent users from reading the document. To manage who can read a document, consider implementing the **$KeepPrivate** field in conjunction with a **Readers** field. See Chapter 19, "Security," for additional information pertaining to document security.

This feature can be implemented by using static or dynamic field values. When implemented with a static value, the copy, paste, and print functions are disabled for all documents, and the setting cannot be changed. Using a dynamic approach, the setting can be toggled between enabled and disabled by using a checkbox, radio button, action button, and so on.

Implementation—Example 1

This first example illustrates the static approach. To implement this technique, complete the following instructions.

Step 1.   Create a field on the form.

Step 2.   In the field properties dialog, name the field **$KeepPrivate** and set the field type to either **Computed** or **Computed when composed**.

Step 3.   In the Programmer's pane, insert the following formula in the **Value** section for the field.

```
"1"
```

Implementation—Example 2

This second example illustrates the dynamic approach. This approach will allow users to enable or disable the copy, paste, and print features on a document-by-document basis. To implement this technique, complete the following instructions.

Step 1.   Create a field on the form.

Step 2.   In the field properties dialog, name the field **$KeepPrivate** and set the field type
to **Checkbox** and **Computed**. Switch to tab 2. Select the **Enter choices (one per
line)** option and add this formula to the field properties dialog (see Figure 17.1).

```
Prevent copying and printing | 1
```

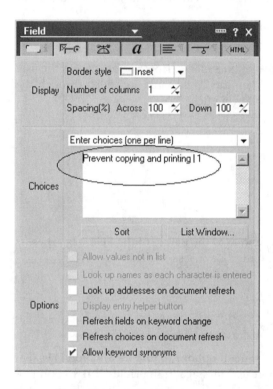

Figure 17.1   Example field choice setting to disable copying and printing

This will produce a field on the form that looks like Figure 17.2.

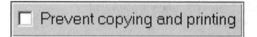

Figure 17.2   Example of the disable copying and printing checkbox

Using Field Hints on a Form

Field hints provide a brief description (or hint) of what can be stored in a field. This feature is often used to illustrate field syntax or the expected value for the field. For example, a field hint for a date field might illustrate the American date format of "mm/dd/yyyy" or the European date format of "dd/mm/yyyy", whereas a text field might illustrate the format for a phone number as "111-222-3333".

How It Works

Field hints display automatically in newly created documents. However, as soon as the user places the cursor in the field, the field hint disappears. Field hints are added through the properties dialog and can only be set for the following field types.

- Text
- Date
- Rich Text
- Rich Text Lite
- Names
- Readers
- Password

Field hints cannot be added to other field types due to the nature of the field (e.g., there is no place for a hint to be displayed in a radio button or checkbox field).

Implementation

To implement this solution, complete the following steps.

Step 1. Create a field that supports field hints (as listed previously).

Step 2. Select the **Design > Field Properties** menu options to display the properties dialog. Switch to tab 3 and type a short text message in the **Field Hint** section (see Figure 17.3).

> **NOTE**
>
> This tab also includes a section called **Help Description**. Any text message added to this property setting will be displayed in the status bar located at the bottom of the form. The help message is displayed when the document is open in edit mode and the cursor is in the given field.

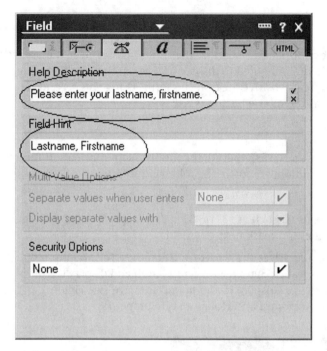

Figure 17.3   Example field hints in the Field properties dialog

Using Static Popups to Display Help Messages

Static text popup messages are used to display additional information to the user. These popup messages can be used to define acronyms, illustrate syntax for a field, or convey general help information. Popup messages can be created on forms or pages. Let's say, for example, that you have a Notes database that includes a number of forms, and each form includes an instructional paragraph for using that particular form. To help the user understand the instructions, you may want to add popup text for acronyms referenced in the paragraph.

The static popup could also be utilized to create field-level help messages. This could be achieved by adding a "?" character next to each field and setting it to display a help message specific to the field. This approach would enable additional or custom information to be presented to the user for each field on the form. Figure 17.4 illustrates a sample popup message.

This is a required field. Enter a valid number between 0 and 100.

Figure 17.4   Example static popup message

How It Works

The popup message can be configured to display "on mouse over" or "on click". When set to "on mouse over", the popup text displays as soon as the mouse passes over the area. Alternatively, the text message could be configured to display only when the user clicks and holds the mouse button on the context-sensitive area on the form. Using this second setting, the popup text closes as soon as the mouse button is released.

Implementation

The following illustrates how to create a static popup that contains help information for a particular field. To implement this solution, complete the following steps.

Step 1.   Create a form.

Step 2.   Add text characters to the form (such as "?" or "Help") to apply the text message to. For example, type a question mark next to a field.

Step 3.   Highlight the text string and select the **Create > Hotspot > Text** popup menu option. This will create the static popup region on the form and display the properties dialog. Type a message to display in the popup message (see Figure 17.5). Optionally, adjust the **Show popup** and **Hotspot style** properties.

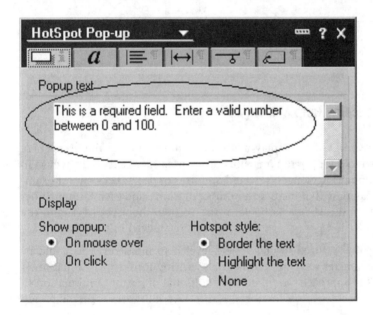

Figure 17.5   Setting the popup text message in the properties dialog

How to Inherit Fields Between Forms

Using the "Inherit" feature, field values in one document automatically transfer to and populate fields on another document. This feature is typically implemented in conjunction with custom dialog windows and "response" and "response to response" documents.

For example, let's say that you are building a database to manage service requests. The database includes two forms—one to track the customer's request and another to track the cost estimate. When building the database, you would like three fields from the "request" to automatically populate the related fields on the "estimate". The three fields are

- RequestTitle
- RequestNumber
- RequestAuthor

Using the Inherit property, these fields transfer to the new form when created. This saves the user some time by avoiding the need to manually create the new "estimate," and it ensures that related information is accurate.

How It Works

This feature works by transferring data between two fields (see Figure 17.6). Both forms must have the exact same fields, and the Inherit property must be set on the secondary form (i.e., the "estimate" document). In many cases, you'll want to set the fields on the secondary form to be computed to prevent users from changing the values.

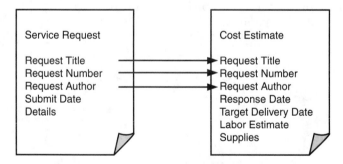

Figure 17.6 Field inheritance between forms

After the forms have been designed, a button to generate the secondary form should be added to the primary form. For example, a button called Create Estimate would reside on the service request form. When the user clicks this button, a new "estimate" document would be created (using the compose command), and field values would be transferred to the new document.

Implementation

To implement this technique, complete the following steps.

Step 1. Create a primary and secondary form. After the primary form and associated fields have been established, create the fields on the secondary form.

Step 2. In order for the inherit function to work, one or more field names on the secondary form must match the field names on the primary form exactly (or fields on the second form must contain formulas that reference fields on the primary form). As an alternative to creating new fields, you could also copy all fields from the primary form to the secondary form. Optionally, you could change the fields to **Computed** to prevent the field values from being changed. If you make the fields computed, set the formula to the field name.

Step 3. To enable the inherit feature, select the **Design > Form Properties** menu option on the secondary form. Switch to the second tab and select the **Formulas inherit values from selected document** option (see Figure 17.7).

Step 4. The final step is to create an action button on the primary form. The action button will compose a new document and should reference the "secondary" form. The following illustrates how to create an action button using Formula Language; however, LotusScript could also be utilized.

```
@Command([Compose]; "FORM" )
```

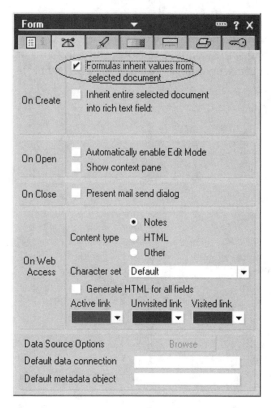

Figure 17.7   Setting the field inheritance property for a form

Add an Icon to an Action Button

The Domino Designer client includes a number of default icons that can be added to an action button. In addition to the default icons, the Designer provides the ability to import custom graphics in JPG or GIF format that can be assigned to a button.

How It Works

The default icons are automatically included with the Domino Designer client and can be utilized by setting the icon value for the button in the properties dialog. It's important to note that the icon feature is available for buttons displayed on a form or view. The feature is not available for hotspot action buttons.

Implementation

To implement this technique, open a form (or view) and select the **Create > Action > Action** menu options. From the properties dialog, change the icon type to **Notes** and select an icon from the dropdown list. Figure 17.8 illustrates the default images that can be assigned to the button.

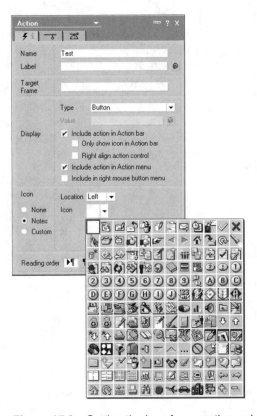

Figure 17.8   Setting the icon for an action or hotspot button

Create a Custom Application Interface

Creating a custom interface for a Notes database can give it a professional look and can also help the user navigate the application. By default, when a database is created, the left pane contains the list of available views. By adding a custom interface, you can incorporate graphics, add buttons, format the font, and customize the view names. For example, Figure 17.9 illustrates a database that includes a custom user interface.

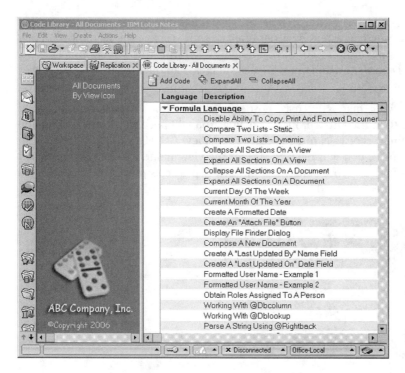

Figure 17.9 Sample custom interface applied to a database

How It Works

Building a custom application interface requires a number of Domino design elements including a frameset, page, and outline. The combination of these elements is used to build and display the interface when the user opens the database.

In this example, the frameset will contain two panes—Left and Right. The interface will be displayed in the left pane of the frameset. This pane will contain a page, and the page will contain an outline. As such, you will start by creating the outline, followed by the page and frameset. Optionally, a navigator can be created for Web navigation. The right pane will display data and will reference database views.

Implementation

To implement this solution, complete the following steps.

Step 1. Create a database with one or more views and forms.

Step 2. Create the outline. The outline defines the navigational elements and will be displayed in the left pane of the frameset. To create the outline, select the **Create** > **Design** > **Outline** menu options.

Step 3.   Add entries to the outline. There are two methods to generate the outline entries—manually create the entries one at a time or have the Domino Designer client generate entries. To have Designer perform this function, click the **Generate Default Outline** button. This will create an outline entry for each view in the database.

Alternatively, to manually create entries, click the **New Entry** button. This will display the Outline Entry properties dialog. You will need to specify a **Label** and set the content type to **Named Element** and **View** (see Figure 17.10). In the content value field, you will need to specify the view name (or click on the folder icon to select a design element from a list). Repeat this process until all desired entries have been applied to the outline.

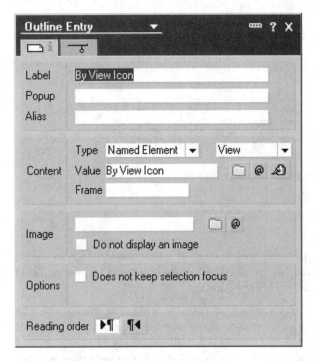

Figure 17.10   Outline Entry settings

TIP

To create a spacer, or a blank link between outline entries, click the **New Entry** button but do not specify a label. A spacer might be used to separate groups of views or entries to improve overall readability.

> **NOTE**
>
> As a general practice, you should always use the alias name when working with design elements. However, outlines automatically default to the primary name and do not allow the alias name to be specified. This means that if the view name is changed, you'll also need to update the outline to reflect the name change.

Step 4. Save the outline. Select the **Save Outline** button and specify **MainOutline** for the design element name. The outline should look similar to Figure 17.11 (except the outline entries reference views that are specific to your database design).

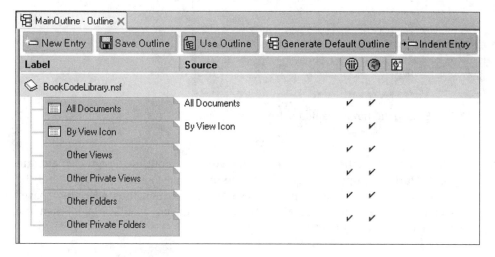

Figure 17.11 Newly created outline

> **TIP**
>
> By default, icons are displayed next to the view design element when the application is accessed via the Lotus Notes client. To disable the icon from displaying (or to change the icon), double-click on the Outline Entry to display the properties dialog. Then check the **Do not display image** option. To change the icon, import a graphic resource file and then select it from the properties dialog.

Step 5. Create a page. The outline must be embedded in a page in order to display the interface. To create the page, select the **Create > Design > Page** menu options.

Step 6.   Add the outline to the page. Select the **Create** > **Embedded Element** > **Outline** menu options. When prompted, select **MainOutline** to add the design element to the page (see Figure 17.12).

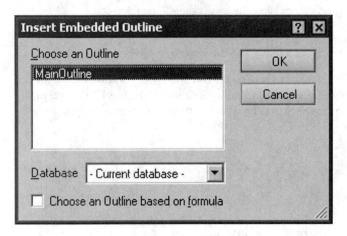

Figure 17.12   Embed the newly created outline in the page.

Step 7.   Set the text properties. Right-click on the embedded outline design element and select **Outline Properties** from the popup menu (see Figure 17.13). (Note: If the "outline properties" menu option does not display, then the underlying "page" element is still in focus. Single-click on the embedded outline, and then the menu should be available.)

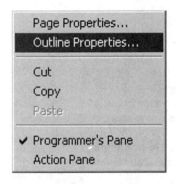

Figure 17.13   Open the outline properties using the popup menu.

To set the text properties, switch to tab 2. Select light gray for the **Normal** setting and white for the **Selected** and **Moused** options (see Figure 17.14). These settings will make the text more visible with the selected background graphics.

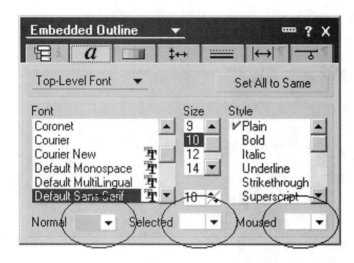

Figure 17.14   Change the text color properties for the outline.

Step 8.   Add a background image to the page. This will add some color to the display and make the outline text more visible. Select the **Design > Properties** menu options. Switch to tab 2 and select the yellow folder icon located to the left of the Resource field (see Figure 17.15).

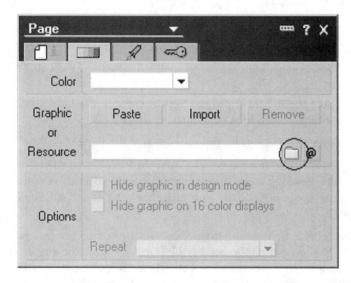

Figure 17.15   Click the folder to select a graphic or resource file.

This will display the Insert Image Resource dialog window (see Figure 17.16). Click the **New** button to add an image resource file.

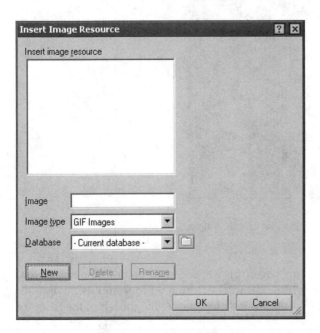

Figure 17.16   Click **New** to insert a new image.

Use the file finder dialog to locate the **SampleBackground.gif** image file in the developer's toolbox folder. Click **Open** to add the image. Then click **OK** to apply the image to the page.

After it is applied, change the **Repeat** setting to **Repeat Once** in the Page properties dialog. The **MainPage** should look similar to Figure 17.17.

Save and close the design element. When prompted, name the item **MainPage**.

Step 9.   Create a two-pane frameset. The left pane will contain the page, and the right pane will display a corresponding view. To create the frameset, select the **Create > Design > Frameset** menu options. When prompted to select a design, click **OK** to accept the default.

Step 10.   Configure the frameset. The frameset configuration will be completed in two parts. First, configure the left pane followed by the right. To configure the left pane, click inside the left pane. Then, using your right mouse button, select **Frame Properties** from the popup menu. Set the values as shown in Figure 17.18.

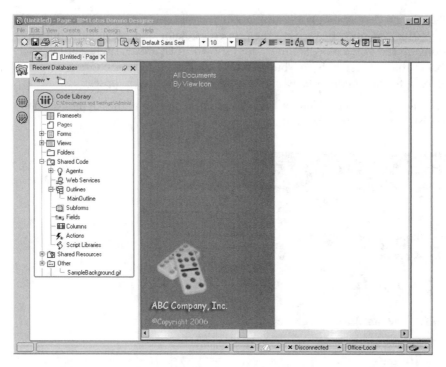

Figure 17.17 Completed Outline Entry settings with a sample background image

Figure 17.18 Setting the right-side frame properties

With the property window still displayed, use your mouse and click on the right pane. This will shift the focus of the properties dialog and provide the option to configure the other pane. Set the values shown in Figure 17.19. Be sure to select a view that corresponds to your database when setting the content value (as opposed to **All Documents**, which is used for illustrative purposes).

Save and close the frameset. When prompted, name the design element **MainFrame**. The frameset should now look like Figure 17.20.

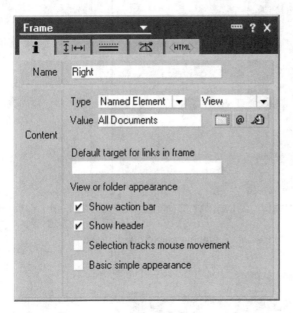

Figure 17.19   Setting the left-side frame properties

Step 11. Enable the user interface. Select the **File** > **Database** > **Properties** menu options and switch to tab 5. Select **Open designated Frameset** and **MainFrame** when opened in Notes client (see Figure 17.21).

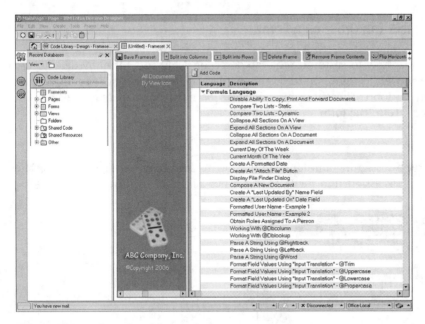

Figure 17.20   Completed frame design

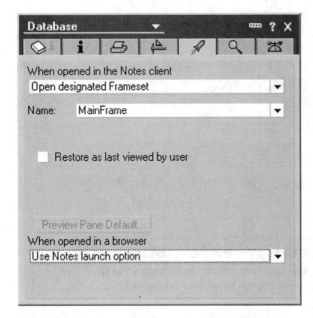

Figure 17.21   Set default frameset for the database

How to Set the Field Tab Order on a Form

This section describes how to customize the tab order for fields on a form. By default, the tab order for a form is left-to-right, top-to-bottom with the default cursor position in the first editable field on the form. However, this order can be changed such that the field tab sequence is customized to the form.

How It Works

The tab order is set by assigning a unique tab number to each field (see Figure 17.22). The tab sequence number is assigned in the Field properties dialog for each field.

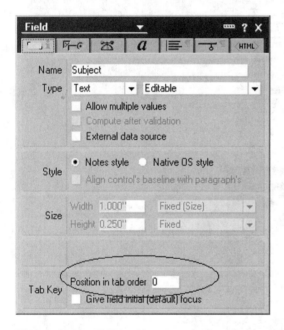

Figure 17.22   Tab position property for a field

> **NOTE**
>
> To set a default starting field on the form, select the **Design > Field Properties** menu options and enable the **Give field initial (default) focus** option at the bottom of the dialog box.

Implementation

To implement this technique, complete the following steps.

Step 1. Open the form and click on the field to be designated as the first tab stop.

Step 2. Select the **Design > Field Properties** menu options to display the properties dialog and specify a numerical value in the **Position in tab order** field (located at the bottom of the dialog). With the properties dialog still open, click the next field and set its tab sequence number. Repeat this process for each field on the form.

Domino Shortcut Keys

Shortcut keys offer an alternative method to performing functions with the mouse or the Lotus Notes menu bar. All of the products in the Domino product family include shortcut keys. The list is rather substantial and varies depending on the state of the application. The following are the more common shortcut keys grouped by application and transaction state.

Function Key Shortcuts for the Lotus Notes Client

Keys	Description
F1	Help
F2	Increase text size
Shift+F2	Decrease text size
F3	Next document
Shift+F3	Previous document
F4	Next unread document
Shift+F4	Previous unread document
Alt+F4	Close application
F5	Log off notes
Alt+F5	Minimize application window size
Ctrl+F6	Step through each window
F7	Indent first line in the paragraph

continues

Keys	Description
Shift+F7	Remove indent to first line in paragraph
F8	Indent entire paragraph
Shift+F8	Remove indent for entire paragraph
F9	Refresh
Shift+F9	Rebuild views
Ctrl+F9	Cascade desktop windows
F10	Menu bar
Ctrl+F10	Maximize all desktop windows
Alt+F10	Maximize Lotus Notes client (OS/2 only)
Alt	Menu bar

General Usage Shortcut Keys

Keys	Description
Esc	Cancel or exit
Alt+Enter	Display or close properties dialog
Shift+Tab	Display previous unread document
Ctrl+A	Select all
Ctrl+C	Copy
Ctrl+F	Find
Ctrl+G	Find next
Ctrl+M	Create an email
Ctrl+N	Create a new database
Ctrl+P	Print
Ctrl+V	Paste
Ctrl+X	Cut

Keys	Description
Shift+Backspace	Display previous parent document in view
Shift+Enter	Display next parent document in view
F4	Display next unread document
Shift+F4	Display previous unread document
Ctrl+F6	Cycle through all open window panes
Shift+F9	Rebuild the current view. Sometimes corrects problems when data is displaying incorrectly in the view.
Shift+Ctrl+F9	Rebuild all views in the database. Sometimes corrects problems when data is displaying incorrectly in the view.
Insert	Mark document read or unread from a view
Shift+Delete	Immediately delete the document from database
Tab	Display next unread document
Ctrl+Tab	Cycle through all open window panes

Shortcut Keys for Editing a Document

Keys	Description
Alt+Enter	Display or close properties dialog
Ctrl+A	Select all
Ctrl+B	Bold
Ctrl+C	Copy
Ctrl+E	Edit
Ctrl+F	Find/replace
Ctrl+G	Find next/replace
Ctrl+I	Italic

continues

Keys	Description
Ctrl+J	Format paragraph
Ctrl+K	Format text
Ctrl+M	Create an email
Ctrl+N	Create a new database
Ctrl+P	Print
Ctrl+R	Ruler
Ctrl+T	Normal text
Ctrl+U	Underline
Ctrl+V	Paste
Ctrl+W	Close document
Ctrl+X	Cut
Ctrl+Z	Undo
F2	Increase text size
Shift+F2	Decrease text size
F7	Indent first line in the paragraph
Shift+F7	Remove indent to first line in paragraph
F8	Indent entire paragraph
Shift+F8	Remove indent for entire paragraph
Insert	Toggle between read and edit mode for the open document

Workspace Shortcut Keys for the Lotus Notes Client

Keys	Description
Alt	Menu bar
F1	Help
Alt+F4	Close application
F5	Log off notes
Alt+F5	Minimize application window size
F9	Show unread document counter
Ctrl+F9	Shrink application to task bar
Alt+F10	Maximize application window size
Ctrl+M	Create an email
Ctrl+N	Create a new database
Ctrl+O	Open a database
Ctrl+Break	Stop or halt current transaction
Shift+Ctrl	Display hidden views in the database (from the workspace, hold down the keys while double-clicking on the database icon)
Esc	Cancel or exit

Chapter 18

Data Management

Chapter Overview

Data management is an important aspect of any database, especially when you consider that the primary purpose for most databases is to manage and distribute business-critical information. This chapter provides a number of tools and techniques that can be used to manage data.

By the end of the chapter you will have learned how to

- Import data
- Export data
- Copy data
- Modify data using simple agents
- Modify data using LotusScript agents
- Refresh all data records
- Automatically archive data

Importing Data

Lotus Notes provides a variety of methods to import data into databases—migrating existing documents between databases, and importing from an ASCII text file or spreadsheet.

This section details how to load information into a database from a spreadsheet. When you understand the process to import from a spreadsheet, a similar process can be applied to ASCII text files. Later in this chapter, you'll also learn how to transfer documents between databases, including how to automatically archive documents.

Importing data from a spreadsheet is relatively straightforward but does require some planning to ensure that the information maps to the overall design of the database.

How It Works

Importing data into a Lotus Notes database requires a properly formatted spreadsheet where each row equates to a document and each column maps to a field on the document. A separate column must be created for each field on the form. The first row in the spreadsheet must contain the corresponding Lotus Domino field name. This is called a *"Title Row,"* and all data in each column will be mapped to the corresponding field name in this row (see Figure 18.1).

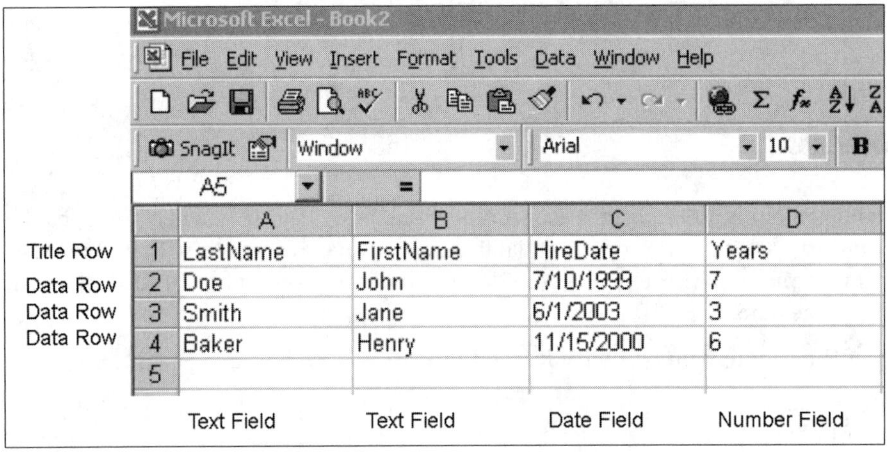

Figure 18.1   Example spreadsheet used to load data into a Domino database

Using this approach, the data columns can be listed in any order because the information is mapped to the associated field name on the document. In other words, the sequence of the columns does not need to match the field tab order of the actual Domino design form.

However, the cell properties associated with each column in the spreadsheet should be set to match the field type defined on the form. For example, in Figure 18.1, the first and last name columns are set to "text", the employee hire date is set to "date", and the total number of years of experience is set to a number.

> **NOTE**
>
> If the field name in the spreadsheet does not match a field name in the form, the import process will create a new field (even if the field is not actually displayed on the form). In other words, the data will be present on the document but not visible via the form. To view the data, you can add the field to the form or locate the field using the document properties dialog.

In most cases, creating, formatting, and mapping the spreadsheet to the Notes database design will be the most time-consuming aspect of the import. After it is properly formatted, the data can be imported in a few short steps.

Implementation

Follow these steps to import data into a Lotus Notes database application. This process illustrates how to import "main" documents into a database as opposed to "response" documents.

Step 1. Create the database, including forms and views, into which data will be imported. Identify all key fields on the form that will be used during the data import.

Step 2. Generate the spreadsheet. Create a separate column for each data field. Put the field name in the first row for each column that contains data. This is the "Title Row" that specifies the target field to hold all data in each column. Put the data in all subsequent rows.

Step 3. Format each column in the spreadsheet. For each column in the spreadsheet, select the column and set the column properties to match that of the corresponding field—text, date, time, or number.

This is a critical step in the import process. If the cell type in the spreadsheet and field type in the form do not match, strange results may occur in the database. Information may not display properly in the fields, and computed fields may not generate the correct results.

Step 4. Save the spreadsheet. Lotus Notes expects the spreadsheet to be in the Lotus 1-2-3 format (e.g., **DataLoad.wk4**). If using Microsoft Excel, be sure to utilize the **Save As** function to make a copy of the spreadsheet in the Lotus 1-2-3 format before importing the file.

Step 5. Import the data. Launch the Lotus Notes client and open the target database. Select the **File > Import** menu options. This will display the configuration dialog window that defines the data import specifications.

> **TIP**
>
> You may want to use a copy of the database when testing the data import. This can be especially beneficial when loading data into a database that already contains documents. This way you can verify the data imports without affecting existing data or having to search through the database to sort out the old and new documents.

Change the file type to **Lotus 1-2-3**. Then locate and select the spreadsheet file (see Figure 18.2). Click the **Import** button to continue with the import configuration process.

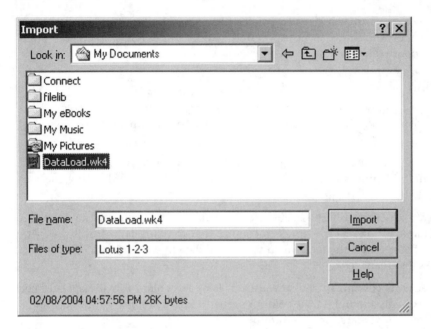

Figure 18.2   Sample dialog used to select a file for import

Select **Main Document(s)** as the document import type and select the form to be used. Also change the **Column Format** value to **Defined by the WKS title** (see Figure 18.3). This signifies that the first row in the spreadsheet will be used to determine the destination field for each column in the imported file.

Step 6.   Optionally, select **Calculate fields on form during document import** if the form contains computed fields, Input Translation, or Input Validation formulas. When selected, all computed fields on the form are calculated after the database has been added to the form prior to saving the document.

> **TIP**
>
> Be sure that the spreadsheet includes all required fields and that they are in the correct format if the form includes validation. Otherwise, documents may not be created during the data import when the **Calculate fields on form during document import** option is checked. If this option is not selected and data is imported, the data validation will not be triggered until the document is saved by a user in the Lotus Notes client, and depending on the design of the database, this could force the user to enter data in order to close the document. Either way, be sure that the spreadsheet contains all required data fields and that the information is formatted correctly based on the design of the database application, forms, and views.

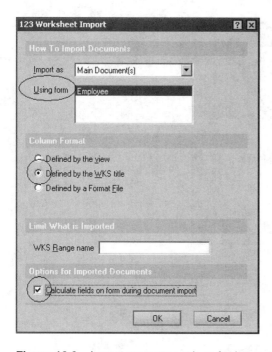

Figure 18.3   Import property settings for Lotus 1-2-3 data files

Step 7.   Select **OK** to begin the data import process. Afterward, verify that the data imported correctly by checking the data in the various views and by inspecting the document data with the form you selected during the import process.

You may also want to open the document properties dialog and check the field value for each field on the form. This will ensure that the data types are correct. To inspect the field properties, select the **File > Document Properties** menu options from a view or a document. Switch to the second tab and scroll through each field to verify that the **Data Type** value is correct (see Figure 18.4).

TIP

Try the sample database and data import file provided on the companion Web site. Create a new copy of the **Dataload.nsf** database on the local workstation. Then use the **DataLoad.wk4** file to try the import process.

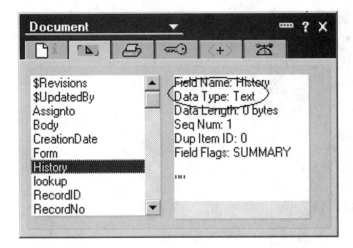

Figure 18.4   Data Type associated with a particular field

Exporting Data

Exporting data allows you to extract information to a variety of formats. There are currently four export formats. Although the exported information is the same for each type, the structure changes for each export format type. The formats include the following:

- **Comma-Separated Value**—Commas separate all data fields with one document per row in the export file. The resulting file can be opened with any ASCII text editor application. Some spreadsheet applications can also import the file, using each tab stop as the column delimiter. It's important to note, however, that commas in the data will also be exported to the data file and may make it difficult to parse the export file.
- **Lotus 1-2-3**—All data fields are separated by columns with one document per row stored in a Lotus 1-2-3 spreadsheet. The resulting file can be opened with most spreadsheet applications.
- **Structured Text**—All data fields are exported in basically the same structured format that's displayed when the document is opened in the Lotus Notes client. This format varies from the remaining formats, which export information in rows. This format exports information by documents. The resulting file can be opened with any ASCII text editor application.
- **Tabular Text**—Tabs separate all data fields with one document per row in the export file. The resulting file can be opened with any ASCII text editor application. Some spreadsheet applications can also import the file, using each tab stop as the column delimiter.

How It Works

The process for exporting data is essentially the same irrespective of the output format. All information from each selected document will be exported to a specified file on the local workstation and formatted based on the selected export type.

> **NOTE**
>
> When exporting data, you can only access data visible to your user ID. This means that the data export is tied to the Access Control List (ACL) and roles assigned to you. If you select to export all documents in the view, only those documents that match your authority level will be exported, even if there are more documents in the view than you can see or access.

Implementation

Follow these steps to export information from a Lotus Notes database to a file or spreadsheet. The steps are basically the same regardless of the output file format.

Step 1. Select one or more documents by placing a checkmark next to each one in the view or open a specific document.

Step 2. Select the **File > Export** menu options to display the Export dialog window. Specify the destination folder in the **Save in** field, enter the output file name, and pick the export format type (see Figure 18.5).

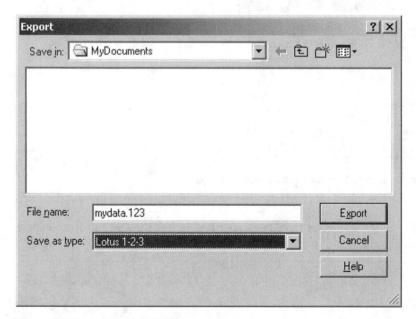

Figure 18.5   Export data dialog

> **NOTE**
>
> Be sure to specify a file extension in the file name. Lotus Notes does not automatically append the extension to the file name. Consider using **.TXT** for text files and **.WK4** for Microsoft Excel spreadsheets.

Step 3.   Click the **Export** button to continue with the export configuration process. At this point, an additional export dialog window will be displayed that will enable you to further refine the format and content to be exported.

However, the export options presented on the dialog will vary depending on the export format. In other words, the options presented when exporting to Lotus 1-2-3 will be different from those displayed when exporting to Structured Text, Comma-Separated Text, or Tabular Text.

Step 4.   From the secondary export configuration dialog, select either **All documents** to export all documents from the view or **Selected documents** to only export those checked in the view. To include the column titles from the view, select the **Include View titles** option. This option will add the view column titles when exporting in Lotus 1-2-3, Comma-Separated Text, or Tabular Text.

Other options will also be available depending on the selected export file format. Figure 18.6 illustrates the secondary export configuration dialog for the Lotus 1-2-3 format.

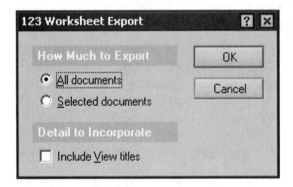

Figure 18.6   Settings used to determine which values to export

Step 5.   After all export parameters have been specified, select the **OK** button to export the selected data to the specified file.

Migrating Data

One of the easiest methods for moving information from one database to another is through the use of the copy, cut, and paste commands. These commands enable information such as the following to be moved between documents or databases:

- Text information
- File attachments
- Images or graphics
- Document links
- Database links
- Documents

Using this approach, data is temporarily stored in the "clipboard" and then inserted into the target database or document. The clipboard, incorporated in most operating systems, provides storage in memory for the information and acts as the gateway between the databases or documents. Be aware that the total number of documents that can be copied at a time is limited.

More importantly, this approach provides a quick and easy method to manage a moderate amount of information. Most users are familiar with this concept and can usually perform it with very little training. Now, in most cases, data can be copied from document to document with little to no training required.

The most notable impact will probably be associated with Rich Text fields. When copying data from a Rich Text field, the target field should also be a Rich Text field. Otherwise, text formatting will be lost. If the item being copied is a file or graphic, these items can only be moved (or pasted) into another Rich Text field.

How It Works

The function works by temporarily storing information, documents, files, or graphics in memory. Then, by using the standard editing commands, the data can be inserted into a target database or document. As documents are copied to the clipboard, a status bar will display to indicate progress (see Figure 18.7).

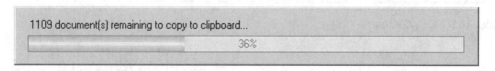

Figure 18.7 Progress bar

Implementation

Open a database and select one or more documents in a view by placing a checkmark next to each document to be copied or moved. Then select the **Edit > Copy** menu options to copy the documents to the clipboard. To migrate the documents without keeping a copy in the current database, select the **Edit > Cut** menu options. Next, open the destination database and select the **Edit > Paste** menu options. This will create a new instance of the documents in the destination database.

Be aware that when copying documents from one database to another, documents may not display in views or be displayed when opened. In some cases, you may need to copy the Domino design form and also modify the view selection formulas. One method to ensure that documents are compatible between databases is to make a copy of the destination database and try pasting documents into it.

To make a copy of the destination database, select the database from the Lotus Notes client workspace and select the **File > Database > New copy** menu option (see Figure 18.8).

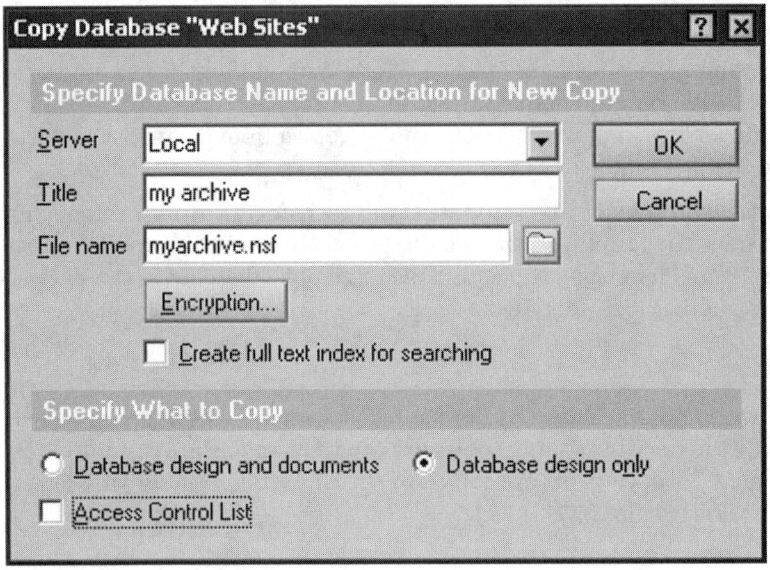

Figure 18.8   Copy Database dialog

When prompted, give the database a new title and file name. Select **Design only** to move just the Domino design elements. This enables you to copy or migrate a select number of documents. Otherwise, select **Database design and documents** to make a copy of all documents in the database.

Select **Access Control List** to keep the existing ACL settings, or deselect it to implement a new ACL setting. Click the **OK** button to build the new database.

Creating Tables

One of the robust features included with the Lotus Notes client is the ability to copy documents from a view and automatically create formatted tables that include document links. Using this feature, you can create and email documents quickly and easily.

How It Works

This built-in feature automatically creates a table in a document. The table mimics the column headers from the view and includes document links for reference purposes. When using this feature, always select documents from a server database as opposed to a local database. Otherwise, the table will include document links to a local database that most likely will not be accessible. If you do not need or want the document links included in the table, simply delete the column after the table is generated.

Implementation

The following instructions illustrate how to create a database table in a document or email.

Step 1. Open a database and select one or more documents (see Figure 18.9).

Language	Description
▼ Formula Language	
✓	Disable Ability To Copy, Print And Forward Documents
✓	Compare Two Lists - Static
✓	Compare Two Lists - Dynamic
	Collapse All Sections On A View
	Expand All Sections On A View

Figure 18.9 Selecting documents from a view

Step 2. Click the right mouse button and select the **Copy Selected as Table** menu option (see Figure 18.10).

Step 3. Create a new mail memo or other Lotus Notes document (see Figure 18.11). Move the cursor to any Rich Text field, such as the body of an email, and select the **Edit > Paste** menu options to create the table.

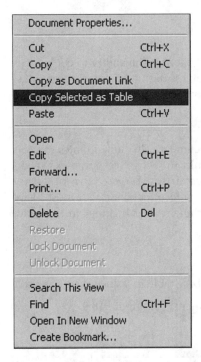

Figure 18.10   Copy Selected as Table popup menu option

Mark Elliott/Raleigh/IBM	To
04/29/2006 03:19 PM	cc
	bcc
Default custom expiration date of 07/28/2006	Subject

Here's the information you requested.

Description
Disable Ability To Copy, Print And Forward Documents
Compare Two Lists - Static
Compare Two Lists - Dynamic

Mark E. Elliott
IBM Global Services

Figure 18.11   Newly created table with document links

Modifying Data Using a LotusScript Agent

One way to modify data is through the use of agents. This section illustrates how to use LotusScript to change data stored in the database. This option provides the capability to perform much more complex logic or transactions against the data. For example, you may only want to act on documents in a particular view within a certain data range or skip documents that already have a specified value. See Chapter 16, "Sample Agents," for a simple action agent that can be used to modify data.

How It Works

When the agent is triggered, the LotusScript code loops through all documents in a specific view. Field values are checked for each document. When a field (or document) matches the specified value, field values for the document are updated or replaced. Then the looping continues with the next document in the view.

Implementation

To implement this technique, complete the following steps.

Step 1.   Create the agent. Select the **Create > Design > Agent** menu options to create the agent. When the properties dialog displays, give the agent a name. Next, set the runtime trigger parameters to **On event**, **Action menu selection**, and **None**. Close the properties dialog after these values have been defined.

Step 2.   Add the code. In the Programmer's pane, change the Language Selector from **Simple action(s)** to **LotusScript** and insert the following LotusScript code in the Initialize section. Be sure to replace **VIEW** and **FIELD** with valid design element names. Replace **VALUE1** with a text string to search and **VALUE2** with a replacement text string.

> **NOTE**
>
> This example is designed to work with a non-categorized view. Errors may occur if the field being changed is also used as the categorized column formula.

```
'--------------------------------------------------
' Define the objects
'--------------------------------------------------
Dim s As New NotesSession
Dim db As NotesDatabase
Dim doc As NotesDocument
Dim view As NotesView
Set db = s.CurrentDatabase
Set view = db.GetView( "VIEW" )
Call view.Refresh
```

```
view.AutoUpdate = False

'----------------------------------------------------
' Check all documents in the view
'----------------------------------------------------
Print "Starting data updates"
Set doc = view.GetFirstDocument
While Not(doc Is Nothing)
    If doc.FIELD(0) = "VALUE1" Then
        doc.FIELD = "VALUE2"
    End If
    Call doc.Save(True, False)
    Set doc=view.GetNextDocument(doc)
Wend
Print "Data updates complete"

End Sub
```

Archiving Data Using an Agent

In some cases, the size of the database can affect its overall responsiveness and performance. This section describes how to manage the database size and content by creating an agent that automatically moves documents older than a specific date to an archive database.

How It Works

Using a scheduled agent, all documents older than a specified date are automatically copied into a secondary database and then deleted from the primary database. This is achieved by computing the "cutoff" date and comparing it to the creation date of the document. Any document older than the cutoff date is moved to the new database. The cutoff date is calculated by using the AdjustDay method and the current date to compute a date in the past.

It's also important to understand the looping mechanism when archiving documents. To ensure that all documents in the view are checked, the routine must account for documents being removed from the view. Otherwise, the GetNextDocument method could skip documents or generate an error. This is corrected by utilizing a temporary object (tmpDoc) to store the handle to the next document object in the view or by setting the view AutoUpdate property to FALSE. For illustrative purposes, the following example includes the logic to track documents in the view (in case the AutoUpdate property is enabled).

Implementation

To implement this technique, complete the following instructions.

Step 1.   Create the archive database. To make the archive database, make a copy of the existing database. Select the **File > Database > New Copy** menu options. When prompted, change the title and file name. Consider including "archive" in the database title and file name to help to distinguish between the two databases.

Also select the **Database design only** option. This will create a new copy of the database with no documents. Be aware that if database design relies on select documents for configuration purposes, you will need to manually copy these documents into the new database. Click **OK** to create the copy.

> **NOTE**
>
> Be sure to disable any agents in the "archive" database that no longer need to run.

Step 2. Create the archive agent. Open the original database in the Designer client. Select the **Create > Design > Agent** menu options to create the agent. After it is created, give the agent a name such as **Archive** (see Figure 18.12).

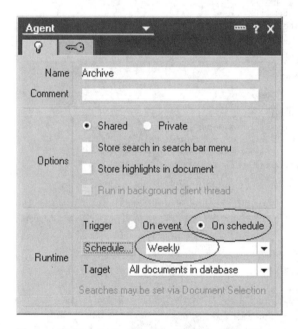

Figure 18.12 Scheduled agent property settings

Step 3. (Optional) Specify the server to run the agent. If the database replicates to multiple Domino servers, you should designate which server will manage the database archiving. Click the **Schedule** button and designate the default server in the **Run On** field. Click **OK** to accept the settings.

Close the agent properties dialog after these configuration settings are defined.

Step 4. Insert the code. In the Programmer's pane, change the Language Selector from **Simple action(s)** to **LotusScript** and add the following LotusScript in the `Initialize` section. Be sure to replace **VIEW**, **SERVER**, and **DATABASE** with valid values.

```
Sub Initialize

    '-------------------------------------------------------
    ' Define the objects
    '-------------------------------------------------------
    Dim s As New NotesSession
    Dim db As NotesDatabase
    Dim dbArchive As NotesDatabase
    Dim view As NotesView
    Dim doc As NotesDocument
    Dim tmpDoc As NotesDocument
    Dim docArchive As NotesDocument
    Dim archiveDate As NotesDateTime
    Dim createDate As NotesDateTime
    Dim count As Integer
    Dim serverName As String
    Dim archiveName As String
    Set db = s.CurrentDatabase

    '-------------------------------------------------------
    ' Set Cutoff date.  This should be a negative number.
    ' For example, set to -90 to archive documents that
    ' are over 3 months old based on the creation date.
    '-------------------------------------------------------
    Set archiveDate = New NotesDateTime( "Today" )
    Call archiveDate.AdjustDay( -90 )

    '-------------------------------------------------------
    ' Specify the view that contains documents that
    ' might be archived.
    '-------------------------------------------------------
    Set view = db.GetView("VIEW")
    view.AutoUpdate = False

    '-------------------------------------------------------
    ' Specify the server and database name to be
    ' used to store the archived documents.
    '-------------------------------------------------------
    serverName = "SERVER"
    archiveName = "DATABASE.NSF"
    Set dbArchive = New NotesDatabase( serverName, archiveName )

    '-------------------------------------------------------
    ' Begin processing
    '-------------------------------------------------------
    If dbArchive Is Nothing Then
        Print "Warning: unable to access archive database."
    Else
        '---------------------------------------------------
        ' Start archive process
        '---------------------------------------------------
```

```
            count = 0
            Set doc = view.GetFirstDocument
            While Not(doc Is Nothing)
               Set tmpDoc = view.GetNextDocument( doc )
               Set createDate = New NotesDateTime( "" )
               createDate.LocalTime = doc.Created

               If archiveDate.TimeDifference( createDate ) > 0  Then
                  Set docArchive = New NotesDocument( dbArchive )
                  Call doc.CopyAllItems( docArchive, True )
                  Call docArchive.Save( True, True )
                  Call doc.Remove( True )
                  count = count + 1
               End If
               Set doc = tmpDoc
            Wend

            Print "Complete: "+Cstr( count )+" document(s) archived."
         End If

      End Sub
```

NOTE

The archive cutoff date must be set to a negative number. In this example, the value is set to –90, which equates to three months. Increase the number of days to retain documents for a longer duration or decrease the number to retain them for a shorter period.

TIP

To test the agent, comment out the statement `Call doc.`
`Remove(True)` by prefixing this statement with a single quote or the word REM. This will keep the documents in the originating database. When you are sure the agent is working as intended, uncomment the statement, and documents will be copied to the new database and removed from the original database. Using this approach will prevent documents from being deleted in the primary database but will create documents in the archive database. After the agent has been tested and verified to be working as designed, remember to uncomment the statement.

Step 5. (Optional) Sign the agent or database. Signing the database or agent ensures that the agent will run with the appropriate authority level when executed. This step can be skipped if the person who last updated the agent has the authority to run scheduled agents on the target server. See Chapter 19, "Security," for additional information pertaining to database security.

Refreshing All Documents

Depending on database design changes, you may need to refresh all documents stored in the database for the change to be applied. For example, say a new computed field is added to the form. For the change to be visible, each document in the database needs to be opened and saved. This routine illustrates how to create an agent that automatically refreshes all documents in the database.

How It Works

Using the `ToolsRefreshAllDocs` command, every document in the database can be refreshed and saved.

Implementation

To implement this solution, perform the following steps.

Step 1. From the Domino Designer, open the database and select the **Create > Design > Agent** menu options. Name the agent **Refresh all data** (see Figure 18.13). Because this agent will affect every document in the database, consider changing the agent from **Shared** to **Private**. When this option is selected, only the author of the agent will have the ability to see the agent from the Actions menu.

Step 2. Change the Language Selector from **Simple action** to **Formula** and insert the following in the Programmer's pane.

```
@Command([ToolsRefreshAllDocs]); @All
```

Figure 18.13   Property settings for a private agent

Chapter 19

Security

Chapter Overview

This chapter provides a variety of information pertaining to database security, access permissions, and roles. Although the majority of the chapter covers various aspects of the Access Control List, it also explains how to protect LotusScript source code, sign a database, and implement digital cross certificates to allow users to access Domino servers that reside in another Domino domain.

By the end of the chapter you will have learned

- Fundamentals of the Access Control List
- Access authority levels
- How to manage database access
- How to manage form-level access
- How to manage field-level access
- How to enforce consistent ACL settings across replicas
- How to "sign" a database
- How to "cross certify" servers

Access Control List Fundamentals

The Access Control List, commonly referred to as the ACL, is used to manage database access for users. The ACL is incorporated into all Lotus Notes databases and is an integral part of its operation. It controls not only who can access the database but also what functions they

A.19.1

perform and what data they can see (or access). At the most rudimentary level, the ACL consists of the following main components:

- Person, group, or server
- User type
- Access level definition
- Access role

Although the ACL dialog contains many additional settings, these areas are used to determine what functions and data are available for all users and other Domino servers (see Figure 19.1).

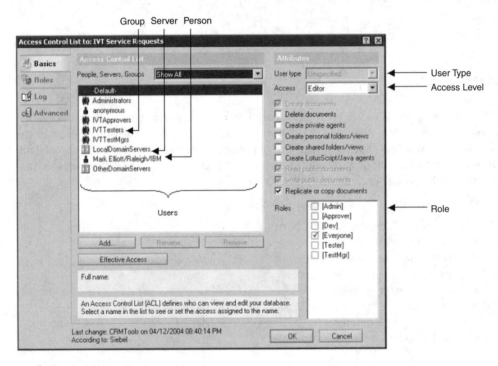

Figure 19.1   Components of the ACL

Person, Group, and Server

A.19.2

A database user can be characterized as a Person, Group, or Server (see Figure 19.2). A *Person* is defined as a single Lotus Notes userID (such as Mark Elliott/Raleigh/IBM). Individual users are typically added to the ACL when few in number or when a person needs a specific security setting. However, best practices recommend that individual user names not be added to the ACL directly. Instead, all users should be included in one or more groups that are included in the ACL.

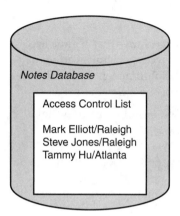

Figure 19.2 Persons explicitly defined in the ACL

A *Group* contains one or more persons (or servers) where all members in the group have the same access permission or role in the database. When working with groups, only the group name is placed in the ACL. All persons or servers associated with the group are actually managed via the Domino Directory (see Figure 19.3). This approach should be utilized when managing users that require similar access levels and permissions. A group can be created for persons, servers or a combination of both.

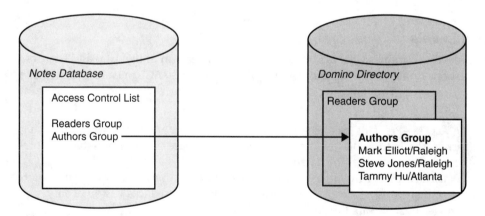

Figure 19.3 Groups reference names stored in the Domino Directory

A *Server*, as the name implies, is defined as a single Domino server. This third type permits other Domino servers to access the database. Again, consider using groups to manage ACL settings for multiple database servers.

User Type

The *user type* value indicates to the Domino server the category of user that will be accessing the database. This is an additional layer of security that prevents or limits certain database functions when the user and user type values in the ACL fail to match that of the user accessing the database. All users must be associated with one of the following values:

Unspecified—Signifies that the user's type is unknown or not defined in the ACL.

Person—Signifies that the user is a single person.

Server—Signifies that the user is a single server.

Mixed Group—Signifies that the user is a group that potentially contains one or more persons and/or servers.

Person Group—Signifies that the user is a group that contains one or more persons (and does not contain any servers).

Server Group—Signifies that the user is a group that contains one or more servers (and does not contain any persons).

> **NOTE**
>
> Always be sure to associate the user with the correct user type. For example, the user type for groups should be Mixed Group, Person Group, or Server Group. If the user is not correctly associated with the correct user type, access to the entire database may (or may not) be available to the user(s).

Access Levels

The access level determines what actions a given user can perform in the database. There are seven access levels that can be assigned. All users in the database ACL must be assigned one of these access levels. The following describes each level in order from the least to greatest level of authority.

No Access—Prevents user access to the database. Users are unable to add the database to the Lotus Notes workspace, open the database, view information, or perform any actions with the database.

Depositor—Users can only compose or create new documents. However, no data is visible in any of the views. This access level might be used in a customer survey or feedback database application.

Reader—Users can view existing documents and information but cannot create new documents in the database.

Author—Users can create new documents and modify/delete their own existing documents. Users cannot modify documents composed by another user. However, it's important to understand that security settings on the form can override the database access level settings. If the form contains a "Readers" or "Authors" field, these settings will supercede those set in the database ACL. Note that controlled access sections and encrypted fields may be used to further refine access.

Editor—Users can create new documents as well as modify or delete any document (both their own and others') in the database. However, it's important to understand that security settings on the form can override the database access level settings. If the form contains a "Readers" field, these settings will supercede those set in the database ACL. Note that controlled access sections and encrypted fields may be used to further refine access.

Designer—Users can perform all of the same transactions available to lower access levels, plus they have the ability to modify the database design and create a full-text search index.

Manager—Users can perform all of the same transactions available to lower access levels, plus they have the ability to modify the ACL, encrypt the database design, modify replication settings, and delete the database.

Access Role

Another method to refine access to data and design elements is through the use of roles. A role is a special security setting that is defined in the ACL and referenced by the database design. Using roles, you can further refine database functionality, display of information, and ability to edit content. For example, with roles, you can manage

- What views are displayed
- What data is displayed
- What forms can be used to create new documents
- What action buttons are displayed
- Who can modify documents and when
- Who can edit a particular section of data

Each person, group, or server in the ACL can be assigned one or more roles in the database. However, it's important to recognize that the creation of roles in the ACL is only half of the equation. The role subsequently needs to be married to functions in the database design. In other words, simply creating and assigning a role to a person has no effect unless the role is utilized and integrated into the database design.

Let's take, for example, a procurement request database where each request requires three distinct approvals before the item can be ordered. Each request must be approved by the person's immediate business manager, finance manager, and an executive manager. Each of these approvals could equate to a role. These roles could then be utilized in the database design.

As in Figure 19.4, you could create a separate set of "Approve" and "Decline" buttons for each of the three roles. Only persons assigned that role could click one of the associated buttons. When a person with the given role clicks the button, fields on the database can be updated and the buttons can be hidden.

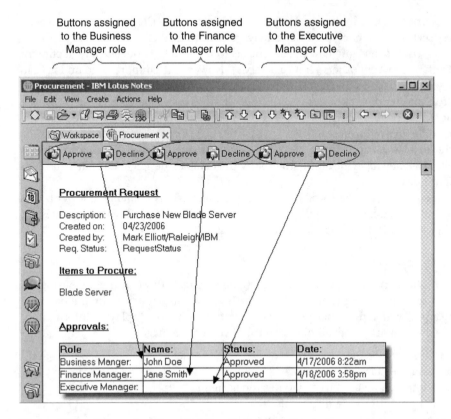

Figure 19.4   Using roles to control the display of action buttons

In many cases, the role is utilized in the "Hide When" formula for an action button, controlled section, paragraph, or field. They can even be used to control the display of forms, views, and other design elements for the database. You'll learn more about how to create roles later in this chapter.

After one or more roles have been created, they can be integrated into the database design. For example, roles can be used to control the display of the action button through the **Hide action if formula is true** property. Including a formula similar to the following will allow only users with the "ProcureMgr" role to see and use the button.

```
@IsMember("[ProcureMgr]";@UserRoles)
```

Managing Database Access

Database access is managed through the ACL. For a user to access the database, one of the following conditions must be true.

- The -**Default**- access level is set to Reader, Author, Editor, Designer, or Manager.
- The user is explicitly included in the ACL.
- The user is a member of a group in the ACL.

Based on these rules, the user will either be permitted to utilize the database or denied access altogether. The following explains how to add users to the database. After they are added, you can specify the user type, access level, and (optionally) the roles associated with the users.

> **NOTE**
>
> Only users assigned "Manager" access can modify the ACL. Alternatively, depending on the setup of the Domino Directory, you may also have the authority to add and remove users from various access groups.

Setting the Default Access

All databases automatically incorporate a special user called -**Default**- in the ACL. The access permissions associated with this user are, by default, applied to any user not explicitly specified in the ACL or included in an access group. Follow these steps to modify the default access settings for a database application.

Step 1. Locate and highlight the database in the Lotus Notes client workspace.

Step 2. Open the ACL. Select the database and choose the **File > Database > Access Control** menu options. This will display the ACL dialog.

Step 3. Modify the default access settings for the database. Locate and click on the -**Default**- user. Modify the database permissions and change the access level, user type, and roles as desired (see Figure 19.5).

> **CAUTION**
>
> Depending on the version, Lotus Notes automatically assigns "Manager" access to the -**Default**- user when a new database is created. As a best practice, you should immediately change this value to something other than Manager or Designer after creating a new database. Otherwise, literally anyone will have the ability to modify the design, delete documents, and/or change the ACL settings.

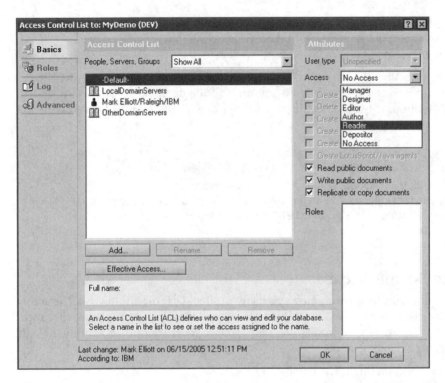

Figure 19.5   Access type attribute associated with Person, Group, or Server

Adding Users to the ACL

This section outlines the steps to add an individual user to the ACL. In general, this process should be used to manage a limited number of users. Where possible, consider using access groups (described in the next section) to manage a large number of users with similar attributes. To add users to the access list, you must have "Manager" authority. Follow these steps:

Step 1.   Locate and highlight the database in the Lotus Notes client workspace.

Step 2.   Open the ACL. Select the database and choose the **File > Database > Access Control** menu options. This will display the ACL dialog.

Step 3.   Add users. When the ACL dialog window displays, select the **Add** button. This will display the Add User dialog prompt (see Figure 19.6). At this point, you can either manually enter the user's fully qualified Lotus Notes ID or click the icon (located to the right of the field) to select a user from the Domino Directory.

Figure 19.6   Add User dialog

Step 4.   After the user has been added to the ACL, set the **User Type** and **Access** level to be associated with the user.

Step 5.   Optionally, set any additional permissions such as the ability to **Delete documents**, **Create private agents**, **Create personal folders/views**, **Create shared folders/views**, or **Create LotusScript/JavaScript agents**.

Step 6.   Repeat this process for each new user that needs to be incorporated into the ACL. Click **OK** to apply all security changes to the database.

> **TIP**
>
> If you need to add a user to the ACL who happens to require similar security settings as another user, you can use the quick add function. First, click on the existing user in the ACL and then select the **Add** button. The new user will then have the same security properties as the existing user in the ACL.

> **NOTE**
>
> Some organizations restrict the ability to assign "Manager" access to users in the database ACL. If this is true for your organization, consider utilizing groups to manage database access. After the administrator has established a group in the ACL, users can be added and removed by editing the group stored in the Notes Address Book.

Adding Groups to the ACL

Start by creating the group name in the Domino Directory. After it is created, users can be added and removed from the group without having to modify the Notes database ACL. Next, add the group name. You add groups much as you would add a person by either manually typing the group name or selecting it from the Domino Directory and assigning permissions.

Step 1. Locate and open the Domino Directory on the server where the database resides. The Domino Directory is the server address book (which is different from your Personal Address Book that is associated with your Lotus Notes client). Typically, the database title includes the server name followed by "directory". For instance, if the server name were MYSERVER, then the database title would be "MYSERVER's Directory".

Step 2. Create the Group. Expand the **Groups** category in the left navigation pane and select a view (such as **by Organization**). The view displayed may vary based on the database design (see Figure 19.7).

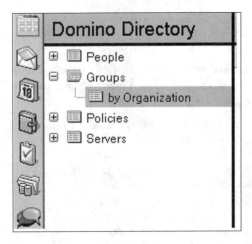

Figure 19.7   Location of the Groups view in the Domino Directory

To create a group, select the **Add Group** button located at the top of the view and complete the form. Specify a group name and a brief description of the group and list all members associated with the group (see Figure 19.8).

> **NOTE**
>
> Consider including the access level in the group name so that you can easily determine what group is assigned to a particular access level. For example, say you have a database that tracks business financials. You might have a group for users with Reader, Author, and Editor access. The group name for users with Editor access might be "FinanceDB-Editors". Using this approach, you can quickly determine the purpose of the group, database, and access level from the Domino Directory.

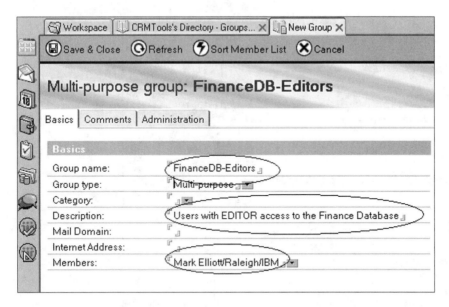

Figure 19.8 Form used to create Groups in the Domino Directory

After these values are set, save and close the document. This will add the group to the Domino Directory, and it can now be used by the Lotus Notes client (such as for an email distribution list) or a Notes database (to assign database access to the users in the ACL).

Step 3. Define access permissions for the group. Select the database and choose the **File > Database > Access Control** menu options. This will display the ACL dialog. Select the **Add** button from the ACL dialog window. This will display the Add User prompt (see Figure 19.9).

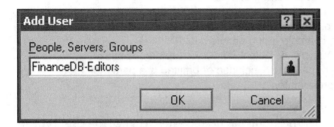

Figure 19.9 Specifying a group name in the Add User dialog

Manually enter the group name or click the icon (located to the right of the field) to select a group from the Domino Directory (see Figure 19.10).

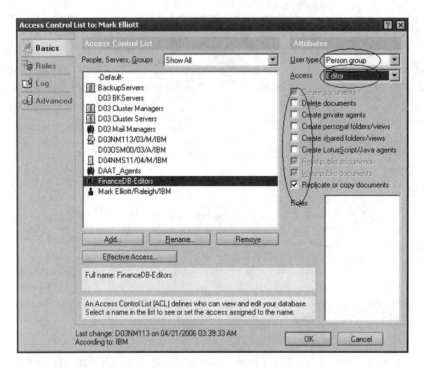

Figure 19.10   Setting the user type and database attributes for a Group

Click **OK** to add the entry to the ACL.

> **TIP**
>
> When adding several different types of groups to the ACL, consider
> incorporating the access level in the group name. Let's say, for exam-
> ple, there are three unique groups associated with the "Defect" data-
> base—users with read-only access, author access, and editor access.
> Based on this scenario, example group names could include
> DefectReaders, DefectAuthors, or DefectEditors. Group names can
> include spaces. Whether spaces are included or omitted is a personal
> style or organizational preference.

Step 4.   Set access permissions. After the group has been created, change the **User type** to
Person Group, **Server Group**, or **Mixed Group** and then set the **Access** level
(such as **Editor**).

Step 5.   (Optional) Set any additional permission such as the ability to **Delete documents**, **Create private agents**, **Create personal folders/views**, **Create shared
folders/views**, or **Create LotusScript/JavaScript agents**.

Step 6. Repeat this process for each new group and click **OK** to apply all security changes to the database.

Configuration of the ACL group is now complete. Users can be added or removed from the database access list using the group stored in the Domino Directory.

> **TIP**
>
> Domino server administrators sometimes create special groups in the Domino Directory, such as "Administrators" and "DenyAccess", which are also included in the ACL for all databases. The "Administrators" group might contain a list of all Domino developers or server administrators. The access level for this group might be "Designer" or "Manager". The "DenyAccess" group, on the other hand, might contain a list of users that should not have access to the database. By adding this group to all databases, a user name can be inserted in the group and instantly denied access to all databases on the server. This might be used for a terminated or disgruntled employee. Work with your Domino server administrator regarding implementation of these groups and understanding the business policies in place for your server.

Creating Access Roles

To create a role, select the **File** > **Database** > **Access Control** menu options to open the ACL dialog. By default, the Basics tab should be active. Next, click on the Roles tab (left side) and select the **Add** button (located at the bottom of the dialog window). This will display a new popup window called Add Role. Specify the name of the role and click **OK** to apply the change. Repeat this process for each role associated with the database.

With roles in place, switch back to the Basics tab. To assign the role to a user, server, or group, click on the entry and then select one or more roles. After all roles have been created and assigned, click **OK** to complete the ACL settings. Finally, incorporate the roles into the design of the database.

How to Enforce Consistent ACL Settings Across Replicas

The ACL includes a key setting called **Enforce a consistent Access Control List across all replicas**. This setting is found on the Advanced tab and ensures that the ACL for the replica database always matches that of the server. When implemented, the ACL settings across all database replicas are synchronized. This ensures that all settings are identical across the various database instances and, depending on the ACL settings, can prevent users from making changes to the data as well as the ACL on a local copy.

To implement this feature, locate the database on the server and select the **File > Database > Access Control** menu options. Switch to the Advanced tab (see Figure 19.11). Select the option located in the middle of the dialog and click **OK** to implement the feature.

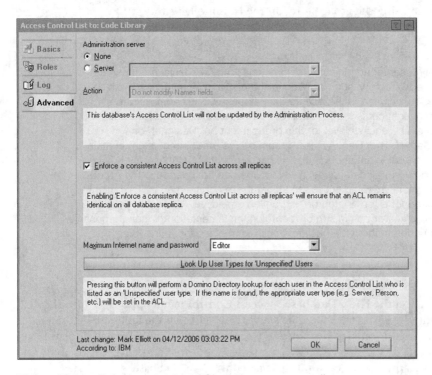

Figure 19.11   Enforce consistent ACL settings across replicas

---

NOTE

The **Enforce a consistent Access Control List across all replicas** feature can be enabled or disabled at any time by a person with Manager level authority to the database. Also note this feature *must* be enabled in order for roles to work on local replicas.

Encrypt the Database

Database encryption is used to prevent unauthorized access to databases stored on the local workstation. This provides an additional layer of security for local databases or replica databases. When implemented, it prevents unauthorized access to the database. Without encryption, it is possible for a Notes-savvy person to access data on the local workstation.

Encryption works by associating a random public key with a specific user ID and appending the resulting value to the database. When implemented, only those users listed in the ACL that can also decrypt the key will be able to access the database. Database encryption has no effect on the server instance, only the local database. This process is ideal for computers that are shared with other users.

A.19.2

Although this sounds technically complex, the implementation and subsequent usage is simple. After the database is encrypted, the decryption occurs seamlessly on the local workstation. For example, if mail is replicated to a local database, you should encrypt the database to prevent unauthorized users from accessing your mail. After the database is encrypted, however, you will still be able to open and access mail with no additional steps required.

Three levels of encryption can be implemented—Simple, Medium, and Strong. In most cases, Simple or Medium encryption is sufficient. It's important to note that the higher the encryption level, the longer it will take to open the database. Follow these steps to encrypt a database:

Step 1. Locate and highlight the database in the Lotus Notes client workspace. Then select the **File > Database > Properties** menu options to display the database properties dialog for the local database.

Step 2. Select the **Encryption Settings** button to configure the encryption for the database (see Figure 19.12).

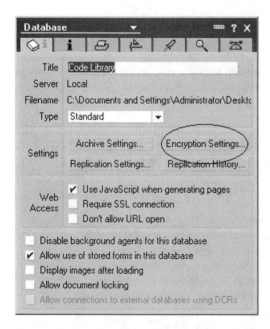

Figure 19.12   Encryption Settings button located on the Database properties dialog

Step 3. To enable encryption, select the option to **Locally encrypt this database** and pick an encryption level—Simple, Medium, or Strong (see Figure 19.13).

Click **OK** to complete the configuration. Depending on the size of the database, it will take anywhere from a few seconds to a couple minutes to initially encrypt the database. This is a one-time pass. All future encryption will be applied as documents are created and updated.

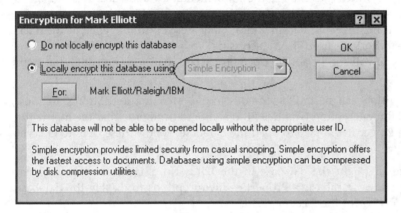

Figure 19.13   Encryption properties for the database

Managing Access to Views

Access to views can be managed based on the person, access group, or by role. Although you can explicitly include or exclude access based on individual persons, by far the most effective management approach is through the use of groups and roles.

Using this approach, you can manage the visibility of the view. This is accomplished by modifying the view design to establish which roles can access the view. Then anyone assigned the role can access the view with no additional modifications required to the design, whereas managing access at the view level for individuals will require changes to the design should you need to change access to the view.

> **WARNING**
>
> Be aware that if you restrict access to a view from the Designer client, the view will only copy to the new database if you have that role assigned to you. To ensure that all design elements and documents are copied, make sure you have all created roles assigned to you.

As previously outlined in this chapter, roles are created in the ACL. After a role has been created, it can be assigned to a person or group of users. The following illustrates how to restrict access to a view based on a role. This process can be used to control access based on the person, role, or group.

Step 1. Update the database ACL. Select the **File > Database > Access Control** menu options. Create the role and assign it to one or more persons (or groups) as describe previously in this chapter.

Step 2. Modify the view design. Open the database in the Domino Designer client. Locate and open the view. Select the **Design > View Properties** menu options to display the properties dialog. Switch to tab 6 (security) to modify the access level for the view (see Figure 19.14).

Figure 19.14 Persons, Groups, or Roles that may access the view

By default, **Who may use this view** will be set to **All readers and above**. Uncheck this option and select the roles (such as [**Administrator**]) permitted to access the view. Note that you can also assign users and groups, but this is not considered a best practice.

Step 3. Save and close the view.

NOTE

Remember to update the group stored in the Domino Directory with the user names or update the role assignments in the ACL to manage access to the view. In other words, if access to the view has been restricted based on a particular role, but no one has been assigned the role in the ACL, then the view will be hidden from everyone. Similarly, if visibility has been restricted based on a group, but the user has not been included in the group, they will not be able to see the view in the database.

Managing Access to Forms and Documents

There are numerous techniques to control access to a form. Access can be managed through the security settings located on the Form properties dialog. This approach restricts who can create new documents using the form. Access is granted based on the person, group, or role at the overall form level. (Refer to "Managing Access to Views" earlier in this chapter for additional information.)

Alternatively, access can be managed through the document. Using this approach, access is granted based on the content of the document, as opposed to the overall form design. Here, access is managed through fields on the form, which arbitrarily may be called Readers, DocReaders, Authors, or DocAuthors.

Using these fields, you can manage access to the database at the individual document level. One or both fields can be included in the form design. The Readers field determines who can see the document in the view, whereas the Authors field determines who is authorized to make changes to the view.

NOTE

The Readers and Authors fields refine the ACL permissions associated with the person. For instance, if a person has been granted "Author" authority in the database ACL but is not included in the Authors field, they will not be able to modify the document.

TIP

If the Readers field has been implemented and the user makes a new copy or replica of the database, only those documents that the user has authority to access will be migrated to the database replica or copy.

> **WARNING**
>
> If the document includes one or more Readers fields and these fields are blank, then no one will be able to see the documents, which can present a significant challenge to resolve.

Restrict Visibility of a Document

Perform the following steps to restrict the ability to view a document.

Step 1. Open the database using the Domino Designer client. Next, create or edit an existing form in the database.

Step 2. To restrict document visibility, select the **Create > Field** menu options. By default, the field properties dialog will display. Name the field **Readers** and change the file type to **Readers**. Keep the field as **Editable** to allow users to modify who can view the document or, optionally, change the value to **Computed** to prevent the changes to the document visibility.

Step 3. Set the default value for the field. This could be set to the author or users with a particular role. To allow only the author to view the document, add the following formula to the Programmer's pane.

```
@UserName
```

To allow only the users with a particular role to view the document, add the following formula to the Programmer's pane. Be sure to replace **ROLENAME** with a valid role specified in the database ACL.

```
@IsMember("[ROLENAME]"; @UserRoles)
```

Restrict the Ability to Edit a Document

Perform the following steps to restrict who has the ability to modify a document.

Step 1. Create or edit an existing form in the database.

Step 2. To restrict the ability to edit the document, select the **Create > Field** menu options. By default, the field properties dialog will display. Name the field **Authors** and change the field type to **Authors**. Keep the field as **Editable** to allow users to modify who can edit the document or, optionally, change the value to **Computed** to rely on the field formula regarding who can edit the document.

Step 3. Set the default value for the field. This could be set to the author or users with a particular role. To allow only the author to edit the document, add the following formula to the Programmer's pane.

```
@UserName
```

To allow only the users with a particular role to view the document, add the following formula to the Programmer's pane. Be sure to replace **ROLENAME** with a
valid role specified in the database ACL.

```
@IsMember("[ROLENAME]"; @UserRoles)
```

To permit the author and users with a particular role to modify the document,
insert the following formula. Be sure to replace **ROLENAME** with a valid role
specified in the database ACL.

```
@UserName : "[ROLENAME]"
```

Managing Access to Fields

A number of different methods can be used to restrict access to a single field or group of
fields on a form. One method is to restrict access based on a role created in the ACL. After
the role is created, it can be integrated into the design of the database and used to manage
access to a field or group of fields. In other words, you can selectively permit access to the
design element based on the user's name or, more importantly, the role assigned to the user.

Restricting Access to a Single Field

A.19.3

One way to manage the display of or ability to edit content at an individual field level is
through the use of "Hide When" formulas. Using this approach, you can set "Hide When"
formulas for each field to determine if the field is visible or editable.

Step 1.   Select the **File > Database > Access Control** menu options. Add the user or user
group to the ACL.

Step 2.   With the ACL window still open, select the Roles tab. Click **Add** to create one or
more roles.

Step 3.   Return to the Basics tab and assign the role to the user and user groups. First,
highlight the user's name or group and then select the role located in the lower-
right corner of the dialog to enable the role. Select **OK** to save the ACL settings.

Step 4.   Create the form and associated fields.

> **TIP**
>
> Use a table if multiple fields are stored on a single line in the form.
> Create a separate cell for each field or text label. This will enable you
> to set a unique display formula for each field on the form without affect-
> ing the other fields on the same line.

Step 5.   Select or highlight the field that should be hidden (or non-editable) and select
the **Design > Field Properties** menu options. With the properties dialog

displayed, select tab 6 to set the display formula. Select the **Hide paragraph if formula is true** option and insert the following formula (see Figure 19.15). Be sure to replace the role with a valid role name in the ACL. The role must be enclosed in brackets [].

```
@Contains (@UserRoles; "[ROLENAME]");
```

Figure 19.15   Using roles to hide a specific field

Step 6.   This is an optional step. At this point, the field settings are in place and will hide the field from users that do not have the associated role (see Figure 19.16). However, you may want the field to be displayed but not editable. This can be achieved by creating a secondary "Computed for Display" field and by adding a logical "not" to **Hide paragraph if formula is true**. Using this approach, the field will be editable for those people assigned the role and display-only for all other users.

```
! @Contains (@UserRoles; "[ROLENAME]");
```

> **NOTE**
>
> Hiding a field should not be considered a "security" feature. A proficient Lotus Notes user will still be able to view the field value by using the document properties dialog. He or she may also be able to modify the content via a local database or by using agents depending on the ACL settings or if **Enforce a consistent ACL across all replicas** is disabled. If you are looking for a more secure implementation, consider a controlled section or the inclusion of an Authors field.

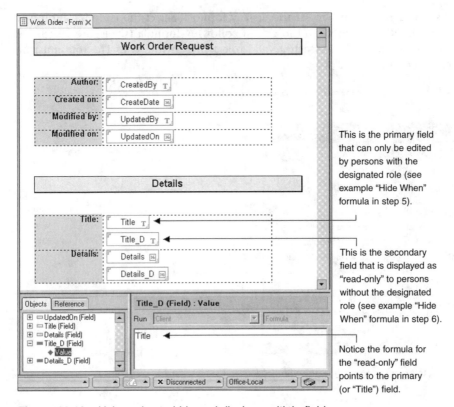

This is the primary field that can only be edited by persons with the designated role (see example "Hide When" formula in step 5).

This is the secondary field that is displayed as "read-only" to persons without the designated role (see example "Hide When" formula in step 6).

Notice the formula for the "read-only" field points to the primary (or "Title") field.

Figure 19.16   Using roles to hide and display multiple fields

Restricting Access to a Group of Fields

The following illustrates how to create a controlled section on a form. With controlled sections, only select IDs, groups, or roles can edit or access content in the section.

Step 1. Update the ACL. Select the **File** > **Database** > **Access Control** menu options. Add the user (or group) and the associated roles to the ACL. Refer to earlier material in this chapter for more detailed information.

Step 2. Manage the form layout. Open the database in the Domino Designer client and edit a form. Next, group all related fields in the same general proximity on the form. Move fields that you do not want included in the controlled section either above or below these fields.

Step 3. Create the controlled section. Using your mouse, highlight all text and design elements to be included in the controlled section. Now select the **Create** > **Section** > **Controlled Access** menu options. This creates the controlled section and displays the Section properties dialog.

Step 4.   Set the access permissions for the section. With the controlled section created, next define who can edit the fields in the section. This is accomplished by inserting a formula or role into the controlled access section.

For example, let's say you created a role called "Admin". By adding this to the section access formula, only users with this role will be permitted to edit fields in this section. In the properties dialog, switch to tab 3 and set the access formula type to **Computed** (see Figure 19.17).

Next, add the following formula in the Access Formula window of the properties dialog (or replace the formula with any valid role as defined in the ACL). Be sure that the role includes opening and closing brackets [ ].

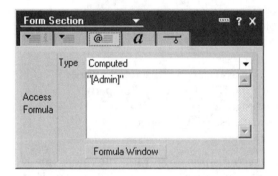

Figure 19.17   Using roles to control access to a section

Alternatively, the controlled section formula could be dynamically set based on a field on the form. Let's say the form has a Status field. Different sets of people can be permitted to change the section dynamically based on the document status.

```
@If (Status = "Draft"; @UserName;
     Status = "Submitted"; "[TeamLead]";
     Status = "Approved"; "[Procurement]";
     Status = "In Process"; "[Admin]";
     "" )
```

In this example, the people authorized to edit the fields in the section are managed in the following sequence.

1. The document author can edit the initial document when the status is "Draft".

2. The team lead can edit it when the document is "Submitted".

3. The procurement person can edit it when the document is "Approved".

4. The administrator can edit it when the document is "In Process".

5. No one is allowed to edit the document after the document is complete.

Managing Access to Source Code

Intellectual property is an important aspect of any business or application developer. As such, you can disable access to the entire database design as well as the LotusScript libraries. This can be achieved by "hiding" the database design (which is different from encrypting the data content) and by extracting the LotusScript libraries.

When hiding the database design, all design elements are compiled and can no longer be viewed or directly changed. To update the design, you must create, manage, and deploy changes through the use of templates. After the database design has been hidden, you cannot

- View the database design
- Create, modify, or delete forms, subforms, fields, etc.
- Create, modify, or delete views
- Create, modify, or delete agents
- Modify LotusScript or Formula Language associated with action buttons
- Modify the parameters associated with the "Database Open" property
- Display the synopsis of the database design
- Access the database design via a new database copy or replica
- View fields via the Document Properties box

Alternatively, people and organizations concerned primarily with the protection of LotusScript source code can export the code and still include it in the database design. Using this approach, the LotusScript library is managed externally to the Domino Designer client and incorporated (or "included") in the design when the database is compiled. This means the LotusScript source code is integrated into the design of the database, but the library cannot be viewed using the Domino Designer client or traced using the "Debug LotusScript" feature.

Hiding a Database Design

This section steps you through the process to hide the database design. Be sure you thoroughly understand how to create and use database templates to manage design changes before proceeding with this approach.

> **WARNING**
>
> After a database design has been hidden, it cannot be unhidden. All Formula Language statements are encrypted. All LotusScript is compiled and removed from the databases. So be sure to create a template of the database before hiding the design. This will enable you to make changes to the code at a later point in time. Otherwise, there is no way to change or see the code associated with the database.

Step 1. Create a database template for the current database. See "Creating a Database Template" in Chapter 20, "Application Deployment and Maintenance," for additional information.

Step 2. After the database template has been created, select the **File** > **Database** > **Replace Design** menu options for the existing database.

Step 3. Select the design template created in the previous step and choose the **Hide formulas and LotusScript** option from the dialog window (see Figure 19.18).

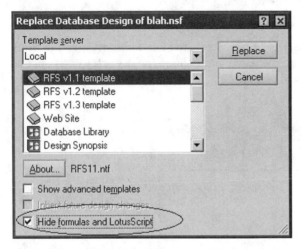

Figure 19.18   Database property to hide formulas and LotusScript

Step 4. Click the **Replace** button to continue with the process. When prompted, click **Yes** to confirm the transaction. This will hide the code. Going forward, all changes should be made in the database template and applied to this database.

Hiding a LotusScript Library

This section illustrates how to hide a LotusScript library from a database design. This is sometimes done to protect proprietary or sensitive code. When implemented, the library is no longer visible or accessible in the database design. All code is stored externally to the database in an ASCII text file that is referenced at compile time. Code that is managed in this fashion cannot be viewed in the Designer client or traced from the Lotus Notes client.

It's important to note that because the code is stored and managed externally to the Designer client, this means that the syntax checking, colors for LotusScript keywords, and the "type-ahead" features incorporated into the Designer client will not be available. Using this approach, the source code will be managed in a text editor such as Microsoft Notepad.

> **WARNING**
>
> Be sure to back up and store the LotusScript source code in a secure
> place when exporting it from the database design. If it becomes lost or
> corrupt, you will have to rewrite it from scratch. Depending on the com-
> plexity of the source code, this could prove to be a virtually impossible
> task and may also prevent future support for the database design.

To implement this technique, complete the following steps.

Step 1. Open the database in the Domino Designer client.

Step 2. Locate and open the LotusScript library. Select the **File > Export** menu options.
When prompted, provide the file name and include the **.lss** extension—such as
LotusScriptWebLibrary.lss (see Figure 19.19). Click **Export** to continue with the
process.

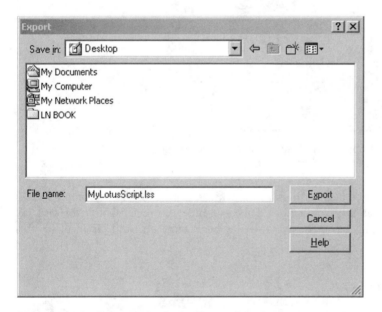

Figure 19.19   Export LotusScript library dialog

Step 3. Select the scope of the export—such as **All objects**—and click **OK** to export the
source code to an ASCII text file (see Figure 19.20).

Step 4. Confirm that the text file was created and that it contains the desired source
code.

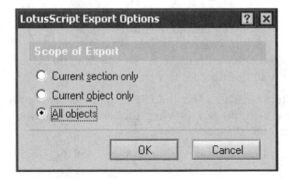

Figure 19.20   LotusScript Export Options dialog

Step 5.   After you have confirmed that the library was exported and that the text file contains all source code, remove all LotusScript from the library, but do not delete it from the database design. Remove all functions, subroutines, and associated code from the `Initialize`, `Declare`, and other events. Although the code has been removed from the Designer client, you must retain the library for those design elements (forms, views, etc.) that reference the library through the `Use` `Library` directive.

Step 6.   Add the following statement to the `Declare` event in the LotusScript library. This should be the only statement in the section where **PATH** represents the directory location and **FILENAME** represents the name of the LotusScript export file from Step 2.

```
%Include "C:\PATH\FILENAME.LSS"
```

Step 7.   Select the **Tools > Recompile All LotusScript** menu options to compile the database and incorporate the source code back into the design.

How to "Sign" a Database

Signing a database is a process whereby the design of the database is updated with the digital keys associated with a server or the person doing the signing. You can also sign a database with a special Notes ID. This usually ensures that all executable instructions—such as LotusScript, Formula Language statements, and agents—have the permission to run on the user's workstation and on the server. This also helps to reduce the number of "Execution Security Alert" messages that are displayed to the user community. In many cases, the server administrator is responsible for signing the database or providing a special ID that can be used to sign the database. In either case, you should work with the Domino administrator to have the database signed.

The instructions provided in this section are provided for reference purposes, in case you happen to be the administrator as well as the developer, and to illustrate how to sign the database from the Domino Administrator client. In order to sign the database, you'll need the Domino Administrator software installed and authority to access the Domino server. With these two items in place, complete the following steps to sign the database.

Step 1.   Launch the Domino Administrator client. Select the **File > Open Server** menu options to connect to the host Domino server. When the server is displayed, switch to the Files tab and locate the database.

Step 2.   Using the mouse, right-click on the database and select **Sign** from the popup menu (see Figure 19.21).

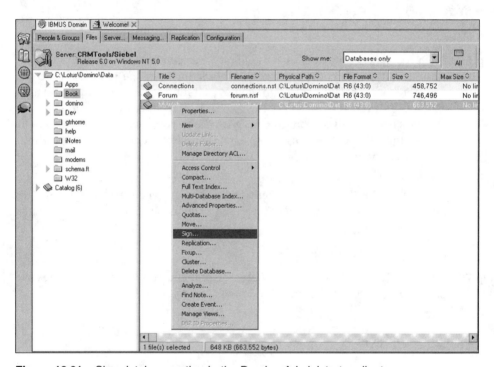

Figure 19.21   Sign database option in the Domino Administrator client

Step 3.   This will display the Sign Database dialog window. Select **Active Server's ID** and **OK** to sign the database (see Figure 19.22).

Depending on the size of the database and other activities on the server, it may take a few minutes for the process to complete. You will need to re-sign the database each time the design of the database is changed or prior to inheriting a database design using a master design and database templates.

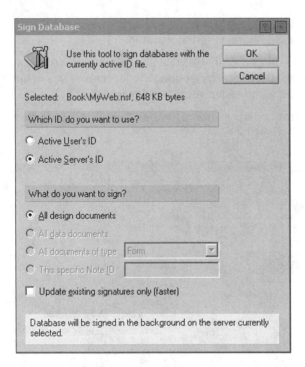

Figure 19.22 Sign Database dialog

How to Cross Certify Domino Servers

Cross certifying servers enables users (and Domino servers) in one domain—for example, "/IBM"—to communicate, connect, and exchange information with a Domino server in a different domain—like "/Lotus". Cross certifying is essentially a fancy name for swapping digital encryption keys and thus granting users in one domain access to data in another domain.

Two files are associated with the cross certification process—CERT.ID and SAFE.ID. The CERT file contains key information for the current user's domain, "/IBM", whereas the SAFE file contains key information pertaining to the other server's domain, "/Lotus". After this information is exchanged, users in the IBM domain will be able to access servers in the Lotus domain.

This process also requires access to the server configuration and the appropriate Domino Server Administrator software installed on a workstation (or server). Implementation requires access to server passwords, which most administrators will not provide or be able to share because of corporate security guidelines. You will need to work closely with the Domino server administrator to perform these tasks. However, the steps are outlined here if you happen to be the server administrator in addition to the database designer. Although the process only takes a couple minutes, navigating Domino Administrator and under-standing the terminology can be a bit tricky for novice administrators.

Step 1. Create a "safe copy" of an existing user ID file. Open your Lotus Notes client. From the **File** menu, locate the **User Security** option. The location of this menu option will vary depending on the installed version of Lotus Notes.

Step 2. Select the Your Certificates tab and **Export Notes ID (Safe Copy)** from the **Other Actions** dropdown list (see Figure 19.23).

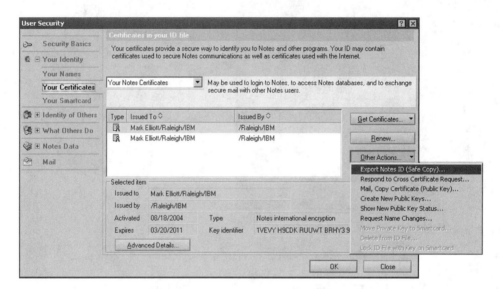

Figure 19.23   Create a safe copy ID file

Step 3. When prompted, click **Save** to create the SAFE.ID file. Based on the earlier exam-ple, this will create a safe copy of the ID file for a person in the "/IBM" domain (see Figure 19.24).

Step 4. After it is created, transfer the file to the destination Domino server (e.g., a server located in the "/Lotus" domain). Copy the file to diskette, shared directory folder, CD-ROM, or otherwise transfer the file to the server.

Step 5. Launch the Domino Administrator client. Select the **File > Open Server** menu options to connect to the Domino server.

Step 6. From the main navigation window, select the Configuration tab. Then click **Certification** and **Cross-Certify** from the right-most side. If the options are not displayed, click on the **Tools** button to expand the list configuration options.

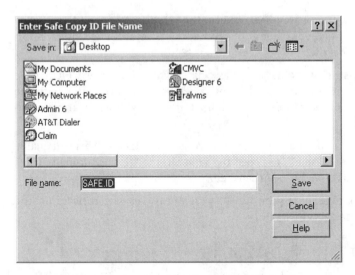

Figure 19.24   Enter a safe copy ID file name

Step 7.   From the Choose a Certifier dialog window, choose the **Certifier ID** button and select the **CERT.ID** file associated with the Domino server (see Figure 19.25). This is a special ID file that was automatically created when the Domino server was installed.

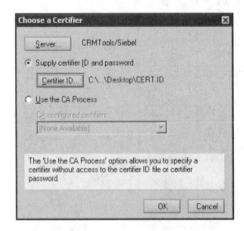

Figure 19.25   Choose a Certifier ID

A copy of the file will probably be stored on the server. Select the file and click **OK** to continue. Contact your Domino server administrator for additional information regarding this file.

Step 8. When prompted, specify the password associated with the server CERT.ID file and click **OK** to continue. You must know this password to continue with the process. Contact your Domino server administrator for additional information regarding this file.

Step 9. Next, you will be prompted to select the safe copy of the ID file. This will enable all users in the "/IBM" domain to access the server in the "/Lotus" domain. Click **OK** after the **SAFE.ID** file has been selected.

Step 10. Finally, click the **Cross Certify** button to generate the cross-certificate for the destination Domino Server Directory.

NOTE

The first time that users connect to the destination Domino server, they will be prompted to create a digital certification for the destination server. This is a one-time event. Users should click the **Yes** button when a message similar to Figure 19.26 is displayed.

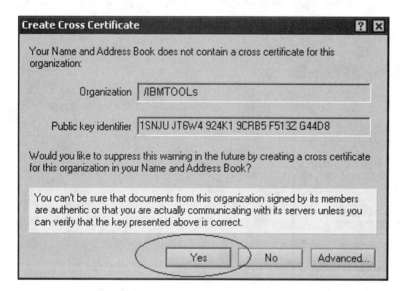

Figure 19.26   Create Cross Certificate dialog

Links to developerWorks

A.19.1 John Bergland. Frederic Dahm. Paul Ryan. Richard Schwartz. Amy Smith. Dieter Stalder. *Security Considerations in Notes and Domino 7: Making Great Security Easier to Implement*, Redbooks, March 2006. http://www.redbooks.ibm.com/Redbooks.nsf/ RedbookAbstracts/sg247256.html?Open.

A.19.2 Bryant, Susan and Spanbauer, Katherine. *Overview of Notes/Domino security*. IBM developerWorks, September 2001. http://www.ibm.com/developerworks/lotus/library/ ls-security_overview/.

A.19.3 Schwartz, Richard. *Using field encryption in applications*. IBM developerWorks, September 2001. http://www.ibm.com/developerworks/lotus/library/ls-field_encryption/ index.html.

A.19.4 Loher, Phillipe. *Security APIs in Notes/Domino 7.0*. IBM developerWorks, July 2005. http://www.ibm.com/developerworks/lotus/library/nd7-security-api/index.html.

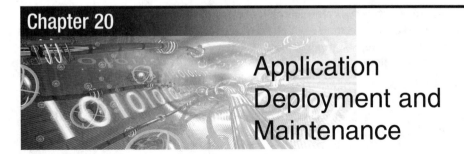

Chapter 20

Application Deployment and Maintenance

Chapter Overview

This chapter outlines how to set up a Lotus Notes development environment and deploy an application. The chapter is intended for readers who are already familiar with Domino application development and who are preparing to deploy and maintain a database.

By the end of the chapter you will have learned

- What database templates are
- What master design templates are
- How to create both database and master design templates
- How to establish a development environment
- How to deploy design changes across environments
- How to manage multiple instances of a database
- How to create application install buttons
- General system and database backup recommendations

What Are Templates?

Templates are used to manage the distribution of database designs. There are essentially two types of templates—database templates and master design templates. Database templates are used to create or replace the design of a database application. Master design templates, on the other hand, can be used to refresh the design of the database and can be configured to automatically propagate (through a process called "Inherit Design") database design changes. As a Notes database developer, you'll probably utilize both template types and distribution approaches to control changes to database applications. Let's take a look at each template in greater detail.

Database Templates

The first type of template is typically referred to as a database template and can be readily identified by the **.NTF** file extension—which stands for Notes Template Facility. This type of template allows users to create a new database or replace the design of an existing database using the Lotus Notes client.

For example, when creating a new database, a list of available design templates is displayed in the New Database dialog window. These templates can be used as the basis for a new database—a starting point, in other words. The list of available templates is displayed in the Template section of the window (see Figure 20.1).

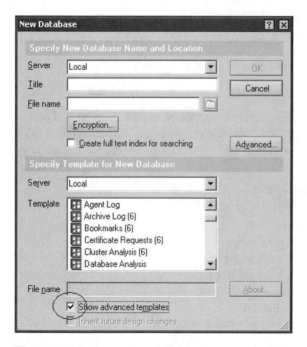

Figure 20.1   Using a template to create a new database

The Lotus Notes client application includes a number of standard design templates that can be used to create new database applications. A standard set of design templates automatically displays in the New Database dialog box. They include

- Discussion
- Document Library
- Lotus Smartsuite Library
- Microsoft Office Library
- Personal Address Book
- Personal Journal

Additional templates are also available by selecting the **Show advance templates** option. This will expand the list of templates to include other database design templates.

Creating a Database Template

Database templates can be created both from scratch (just like creating a database) and by copying the design of an existing one and changing the file extension from .NSF to .NTF. Both approaches are described in the next two sections.

WARNING

When creating a template based on an existing database or template, always copy the database using one of the Lotus Notes clients. Do not copy and rename database applications at the operating system level. Each database contains a unique database identifier called a Replica ID. Copying the database from the operating system environment will cause undesirable effects on the design of the existing database and the documents in that database. Because both databases have the same Replica ID, changes made to one database will be replicated to the other database.

Create a New Template

To create a new database template, perform the following steps.

Step 1. Open the Domino Designer client and select the **File > Database > New** menu options (or click the **Create a new database** button from the default workspace screen).

Step 2. Specify the server location and title of the database (see Figure 20.2).

TIP

Consider adding a version number to the title. This will enable you and other users to easily determine the level of code associated with a particular template design. You may want to make a new template when major changes are applied to the database. This way you can replace the database with a prior version if needed.

Step 3. Next, change the file name extension. Replace the **.nsf** file extension with **.ntf** to establish the database as a template and click **OK** to generate the database.

Step 4. Modify the design as needed. When the updates are complete, it can be used as the basis for a new database or to refresh or replace the design of an existing database (as described later in this chapter).

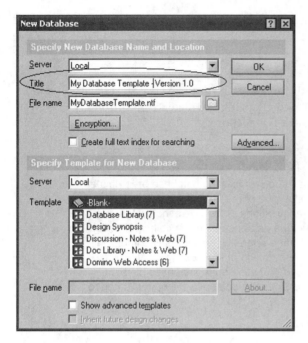

Figure 20.2   New Database dialog

Create a Template from an Existing Database

To create a template based on an existing database, complete the following steps.

Step 1.   Locate the database in the Lotus Notes client and select the **File** > **Database** > **New copy** menu options. This will display the Copy Database dialog window.

Step 2.   Similar to the previous approach, specify a title and file name for the template. Consider including a software version number in the title name for reference purposes.

Step 3.   Change the file name extension by removing the **.nsf** tag and appending the **.ntf** extension to the file name. This will signify to Lotus Notes that the database is a template.

Step 4.   Select a copy parameter. In most cases, you'll want to change the **What to Copy** parameter to **Database design only**. This will copy only the database design elements and no documents. However, if the database design depends on specific documents to manage the functionality of the database, you will need to manually copy those documents over. Alternatively, you could select the **Database design and documents** option and remove the extraneous documents afterward. Be aware that this second approach could result in a very large database.

Also note that any document that is stored in the template will be copied into the design when the template is used to create a new database. This is beneficial for databases that depend on certain documents for configuration and functionality.

Step 5. Uncheck the **Access Control List** option. By deselecting this option, the ACL for the template will be reset, and you will be assigned Manager access to the database. Select this option only if you want to keep existing ACL settings for the database. Just be aware that the ACL settings for the template database will match those set in the original database and could affect your ability to change design elements and database documents.

Step 6. Click the **OK** button to generate the template.

After the database has been created, be sure to review and disable scheduled agents. The template is now ready for use. If the template was created on the "Local" workstation, only people who use that workstation (probably just yourself) will be able to see and utilize the template. If the template was created on a Domino server, be sure to set the ACL such that users can access the template. In most cases, you'll probably want to set the default access level to Reader.

Master Design Templates

The second type of templates, master design templates, are used to manage incremental enhancements to the database and automatic propagation of design changes across one or more database applications. Using a master design template, you can make changes to a database, verify that the enhancements work as intended, and have them reviewed by the customer prior to applying them to the live production database application.

This approach is easy to implement and offers tremendous benefits for managing changes to the production database. In fact, master templates can be considered the foundation for a Domino application development environment. This approach can be used to isolate changes, track software versions, and roll back changes should you need to revert to a previous version.

So what is a master template? In the simplest terms, it is a database property that enables Domino design elements from one Notes database to be transferred to another Notes database, which is accomplished in two steps. First, you define one database as the master design, and then you associate one or more databases to inherit the design (see Figure 20.3).

Virtually any database at any point in time can be established as a master design template. As with many configuration settings, the master template is defined through the database properties dialog window. This is accomplished by setting the **Database is a master template** property on the source database and the **Inherit design from master template** property on the target database.

After these two database properties are set, design changes can be initiated manually or transferred automatically by the Domino server on a scheduled time interval.

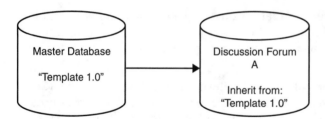

Figure 20.3   Inherit database design from a master template database

Another advantage to this approach, as implied previously, is that it allows multiple databases to be updated from a common (or central) design. Let's say you have multiple discussion forums. Although each forum is used for a separate discussion thread, the underlying design of the database remains the same. Using the master design template, you can change the design once and apply the changes to all related databases (see Figure 20.4).

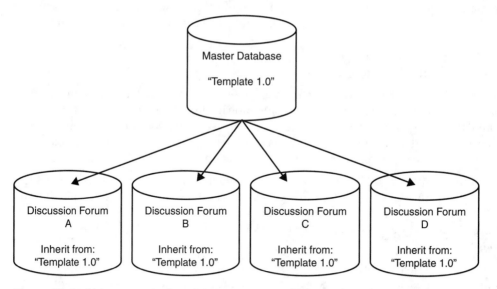

Figure 20.4   Using a master template to manage multiple database instances

> **NOTE**
>
> By default, the Domino server automatically updates (or distributes) design changes at 1:00 a.m. each morning. Ensure that all design changes are complete by the end of day to ensure that partial design changes are not prematurely distributed. Alternatively, deselect **Inherit design from master database** for all databases. This will prevent unfinished designs from being rolled into production.

> **NOTE**
>
> To ensure that changes to the master template are automatically
> applied to the target databases, be sure that all databases are located
> on the same Domino server as the master template database.

The following outlines the two-part process for creating and using master design templates.

Part I: Creating the Master Design Template

To create a master design template, perform the following steps.

Step 1.   Locate the database to be used as the master design in the Lotus Notes client.

Step 2.   Select the **File > Database Properties** menu options. Switch to tab 4 to set the
property values as illustrated in Figure 20.5.

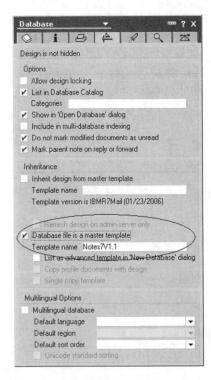

Figure 20.5   Set the master database template name for a database

Step 3.   Select the option **Database file is a master template** and specify a unique
Template name text tag.

> **TIP**
>
> In general, the master template name, as set in the database proper-
> ties dialog, should be a unique value for each database. Using the
> same value as the master template name can cause unpredictable
> results. Lotus Notes will also display warning messages when attempting
> to refresh the database design because more than one database is con-
> sidered to be the master design. To reduce potential problems and confu-
> sion, ensure that each master template has a unique template name.

Part II: Using the Master Design Template

After a master design template has been established, it can be associated with one or more
databases. Complete the following steps to associate the design with a database.

Step 1. Locate the database to be used as the master design in the Lotus Notes client.

Step 2. Select the **File > Database Properties** menu options and switch to tab 4 to set
the property values.

Step 3. Select the **Inherit design from master template** option and set the template
name in the database properties dialog (see Figure 20.6). Be sure that the template
name exactly matches the master template (as outlined in the previous section).

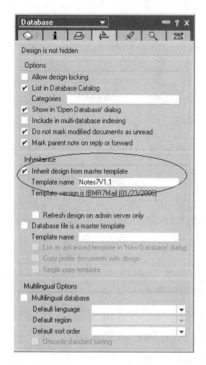

Figure 20.6   Setting the master template name that the database should inherit from

Configuration is now complete. Design changes will be applied as defined by the Domino server configuration settings. Alternatively, you can manually force a database design refresh by selecting either the **File** > **Database** > **Refresh Design** or **Replace Design** menu options.

Establishing a Development Environment

A Lotus Notes development environment is easy to establish. One approach is to have three separate databases—one for development, one for quality assurance, and one for production—and to utilize the master design templates to propagate or move database changes from one staging area to the next (see Figure 20.7).

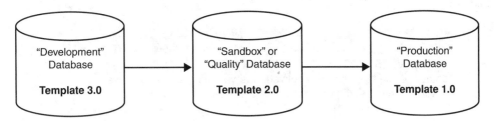

Figure 20.7   Progression of database designs across environments

Development Database

The first database provides a development area where code and design elements can be changed without affecting the production database or any system tests in the quality assurance (or sandbox) database. All database design changes originate in the development database and migrate in stages to the next database. Only those people who actually design and implement changes to the development database should have access to it.

Quality Database

The second database, sometimes referred to as a "Sandbox" or "Quality" database, provides an intermediate point where changes can be function-tested, system-tested, and reviewed by the customer prior to deployment into the production environment. The data stored in this database is typically a full copy or subset of documents from the production database.

As a general rule of thumb, no design changes should be made to this database. If changes are applied here, say for alpha-test purposes, be sure that they are also integrated back into the development database so that the changes are not lost when the next release is moved into the sandbox database. The Quality (or sandbox) database is also the ideal location to verify data imports and to make sure an agent functions properly, especially if it affects a substantial number of documents in the database.

The Access Control List for this database should be identical to the production database. This ensures that the test infrastructure matches the production environment. If the ACL is different between environments, there is the risk that the database will function differently when implemented in production. Although the ACL settings should match, you can still limit access by managing the users assigned to a particular group.

Production Database

The third database contains real production data and is currently "in use" by the Lotus Notes user community. Because this database contains live data, no design changes should ever be made to this database using the Domino Designer client. Data imports and new agents should only be performed after testing the changes in the sandbox using the current template design.

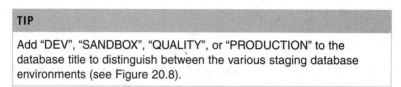

> **TIP**
>
> Add "DEV", "SANDBOX", "QUALITY", or "PRODUCTION" to the database title to distinguish between the various staging database environments (see Figure 20.8).

Figure 20.8   Including the environment name in the database title

Establishing a Multistage Development Environment

A development environment can be established at any time—for both new and existing Lotus Notes database applications. Complete the following steps to create a three-tiered development environment.

Step 1.   Create the development database. There are two approaches to this step. The first approach is to make a new database from scratch. If no database is currently in use, develop the database as you normally would, set the ACL permissions, and continue to step 2.

The second approach is to make a copy of the existing database to be used as the basis for the development environment. If a database already exists, locate the database in the Lotus Notes client and select the **File > Database > New Copy** menu options.

When prompted, give the database a unique title and file name. Because this will be the development database, consider appending "DEV" to the title. In the **What to Copy** section, select **Database design only** and uncheck the **Access Control List** option. Select **OK** to create the database.

Manually copy over any additional configuration documents. Be sure to review and disable any scheduled agents (as applicable) in the newly created database. You should now consider the original database to be the "Production" database and the copy to be the "Development" instance. If database changes or enhancements are needed, apply them to the development database.

WARNING

Use caution when making a "new copy" of any Lotus Notes database. Be sure you understand the design of the database and pay particular attention to the scheduled agents. As a general practice, you should disable scheduled agents in the new copy of the database until each can be reviewed. For example, the database may have an agent that archives data from the current database to a secondary database. If the newly created database is a "sandbox" for testing, then you probably do not want the scheduled agent to automatically copy test data into the archive database. This could cause test data and production data to merge in the archive database.

Step 2. Set the template properties for the development database. With the development database established, next set the master template properties for this database. Select the **File > Database > Properties** menu options and switch to tab 4. Select **Database file is a master template** and specify a template name such as **MyDatabaseDevTemplate**.

Step 3. Create the Quality database. The Quality database is created by making a copy of the development database. Repeat the process outlined in step 1 to make a new database copy. After the copy has been created, changes from the development environment will be migrated into the Quality database using the master template property. Also remember to set the ACL permissions for this database.

Step 4. Set the template properties for the Quality database. Select the **File > Database > Properties** menu options and switch to tab 4. Select **Database file is a master template** and specify a template name such as **MyDatabaseQualityTemplate**.

Step 5. Create the Production database. Unless the database is already established, make a new copy of the Quality database to be used as the production database.

> **TIP**
>
> Consider setting the access level for the production database to **No Access** for all users to ensure that the user community does not start using the application until it has been officially implemented or sanctioned. This will prevent users from accessing the database until it is completely ready.

The Development, Quality, and Production database environments are now set up. To review, a separate database has been established for each stage. The master template name has also been set for the Development and Quality databases. The next section will discuss how design changes are migrated between databases. In this case, changes will migrate from Development to Quality to be tested. After the changes have been validated, the design changes will then migrate from Quality to Production.

Migrating a Database Design

There are three primary methods used to migrate design changes between databases—Refresh Design, Replace Design, and Inherit Design (from an .NTF database). Database changes are often implemented in one database and then migrated to a second database. Any one of these methods can be used to propagate design changes between the development, sandbox, or production database applications. This section describes each of the three migration techniques. You should be familiar with database templates and master design templates (discussed earlier in this chapter) before proceeding.

Refreshing a Database Design

Refresh Design works by copying only design elements that have changed from one database to another. This function compares the time stamp for design objects in the source database with the target database. Any object that contains a newer time stamp in the source database is subsequently updated in the target database. No updates occur for design elements for which the dates match.

The database refresh typically works in conjunction with master design templates where the source database is marked as the master and the target database is marked as the recipient database to inherit design changes. To implement this technique, perform the following steps.

Step 1. Set the master database properties. Locate the source database and open the database properties. Switch to tab 4, select **Database file is a master template**, and specify the template name.

Step 2. Set the target database properties. Locate the database to update and open the database properties. Switch to tab 4, select **Inherit design from master template**, and specify the exact same template name used from step 1.

Step 3.   Refresh the template. Select the **File > Database > Refresh Design** menu options. A dialog window will display (see Figure 20.9). Select the Domino server where both the source and target databases reside. Click **OK** to continue with the process.

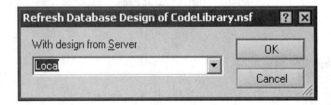

Figure 20.9   Refresh a database design

Step 4.   A warning message will be displayed. The message should read

"Refreshing a database design updates views, forms, agents, fields and roles that have been modified in the design template. Do you wish to continue?"

Select **Yes** to proceed with the design refresh. Lotus Notes will then proceed with the design refresh and update design elements where a newer object resides in the source database to the target database. Alternatively, select **No** to cancel the design refresh. After the refresh is complete, a status message will be displayed in the message bar of the Lotus Notes client.

Step 5.   Reset the inherit database properties for the target database. To prevent automatic inheritance of design changes (described later in the chapter), open the database properties, switch to tab 4, and uncheck **Inherit design from master template**.

Replacing a Database Design

When utilizing the Replace Design function, the entire database design is replaced in the target database. Using this approach, all existing design elements in the target database are removed and replaced by the design objects from the source database. This technique can be used to migrate changes between environments or to revert to a previous database version. Reverting to a prior database design is sometimes performed as a means to recover database stability when there are problems with the current database design.

The replace database function is designed to work with database templates. If you recall, database templates are essentially databases that have the .NTF file extension. The design objects associated with this type of file are used as the basis for new or existing databases. To replace a database design, perform the following steps.

Step 1.   Create the database template. Create or make a copy of the database where the file extension is set to .NTF. This database will contain the source design elements to be migrated to the target database.

Step 2.   Make a backup of the current database design. Ensure that a copy of the current database design is available in case you need to revert to the previous design. Use the **File** > **Database** > **New Copy** function and copy only the design.

Step 3.   Select the target database and replace the design. From the Lotus Notes client, select the target database and choose the **File** > **Database** > **Replace Design** menu options. This will display the Replace Database Design dialog box as illustrated in Figure 20.10.

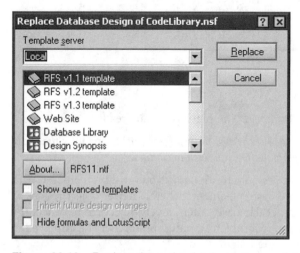

Figure 20.10   Replace the entire database design dialog

Step 4.   Specify the **Template Server**, which can be either the local workstation or a Domino server, and the corresponding database template (created in step 1).

Step 5.   Click the **Replace** button to start the process. At this point, a warning message will be displayed. The message should read

"Replacing a database design changes the database's views (except for private ones), forms, agents, fields and roles to match those in the template. Do you wish to proceed?"

Select **Yes** to proceed with the design replacement. Lotus Notes will then proceed with the design updates by removing all design elements from the target database (with the exception of private views) and applying all design elements from the source database. Alternatively, select **No** to cancel the design replacement.

Step 6.   After the design replacement is complete, a status message will be displayed in the message bar of the Lotus Notes client.

> **NOTE**
>
> Changes to the database design generally do not change the data that's already stored in the database. Although design changes may affect how the application works (e.g., the new design may have additional fields, utilize field validation, or include changes to view columns), the underlying data remains unchanged. To revert to a previous database design, simply replace the design with the prior database version.

Automatically Inherit a Database Design

Automatic inheritance of database design changes can be implemented in conjunction with master design templates. Using this approach, design changes from the source database are automatically inherited by the target database each night at 1:00 a.m. (based on the default Domino server configuration setting). Using this approach, the **Database file is a master template** property is set on the source database, whereas the **Inherit design from master template** property is set on one or more target databases. Provided that both databases reside on the same server, changes are automatically inherited each night.

> **WARNING**
>
> Use caution when setting the **Inherit design from master template** setting for a database application where the master template and the database application both reside on a Domino server. Typically, design changes will automatically be applied (or inherited) to all database applications at 1:00 a.m. each morning. If you are making changes to the master template but have not completed them before heading home for the day, the changes will automatically be incorporated into the database overnight. Subsequently, this could cause undesirable results in the production database. If changes to the master template are complete, enabling the **Inherit design from master template** setting will enable the changes to be rolled into the production database overnight and be available to users at the start of the next business day.

To implement this technique, perform the following steps.

Step 1. Set the master database properties. Locate the source database and open the database properties. Switch to tab 4, select **Database file is a master template**, and specify the template name.

Step 2. Set the target database properties. Locate the database to update and open the database properties. Switch to tab 4, select **Inherit design from master template**, and specify the exact same template name used in step 1.

After they are established, design changes between the source database and the target database(s) will be inherited based on the established time in the Domino server configuration.

> **NOTE**
>
> Both the master database template (source) and the destination (target) databases must reside on the same Domino server for automatic design inheritance to function. The databases can, however, reside in different folders on the Domino server.

> **NOTE**
>
> The 1:00 a.m. automatic propagation of changes is the default Domino server setting. The actual time and implementation may vary. Consult your Domino server administrator for more information regarding your server.

Preserve a Copy of the Database Design

Best practices recommend that you preserve a copy of each "finalized" or official database design. This should be performed as part of the deployment process and can be achieved through a variety of means. The motto "It's better to be safe than sorry" definitely applies here. So consider making multiple backup copies and storing them in separate locations.

- Create a database template on the server. Include a software version or release number in the title and file name of the database.
- Burn multiple copies of the database file to CD-ROM. Store a copy of the CD-ROM both onsite and offsite.
- Store a copy of the database file in a source code library system.
- Create a local copy of the database.
- Store a copy of the database template on other Domino servers.

Consider these options when looking to preserve a copy of a database design. This will enable quick access to the database design should you need to revert to a previous version, create an entirely new instance of the database, or copy it to use as the basis for a new release. Be sure to preserve a copy of each release deployed into the production environment.

Deploying the Production Database

With the multistage development environment in place and design templates established, it's time to discuss deployment of the database. This is typically a process whereby the database is announced and users begin to use the database. There are several key steps to consider when deploying a database application. This section outlines the general process. It also includes instructions for creating an "install" button and a "connection document" button. These buttons can be created in an email and included in an announcement message. Let's start by reviewing the process and then proceed to the instructions for creating the two buttons.

Step 1. Ensure that the correct database design has been tested and applied to the production database environment. Consider using rudimentary checks to verify that all of the required configuration files are in place and that the production database generally appears to be working as intended.

Step 2. Import data into the database (if applicable). Be sure to test this process and verify that the data imports correctly in the Sandbox prior to importing data into the production database. See Chapter 18, "Data Management," for additional information pertaining to data imports.

Step 3. Enable access to the database through the ACL. Ensure that all the appropriate users have been included in the access groups and give the correct permissions in the ACL.

Step 4. Create and distribute the "application install" and "server connection document" buttons (as described next). Announce the new application and include both buttons to enable quick and easy access to the application.

Create the Install Database Button

This routine illustrates how to create a button that adds the database icon to the user's workspace and launches the application. The button can then be added to an email and sent to anyone who is authorized to access the database. This method provides a user-friendly alternative to a database link.

> **TIP**
>
> If you manage or distribute a large number of database applications, consider storing a copy of each database install button in a document or saving them in a "stationary note" in your Lotus Notes mail database. This will enable you to copy and paste the buttons into an email for quick distribution as needed or requested.

To implement this solution, complete the following steps.

Step 1. Create the button. Using your Lotus Notes client, create a new memo. Place the cursor in the body of the memo and select the **Create > Hotspot > Button** menu options.

Step 2. Configure the button. Give the button an informative title (e.g., **Install My Database**). Next, add the following formula in the Programmer's pane. Be sure to replace **SERVER**, **PATH**, and **DATABASE** with valid values that reference the database to be announced. Be sure to separate the path and database with double backslashes because the initial backslash is treated as an escape character.

```
server := "SERVER";
dbpath := "PATH\\DATABASE.nsf";
@If (@Command([FileOpenDatabase]; server : dbpath; ""; ""; "1" );
@Success;
@Prompt([Ok];"Warning.";"An error was encountered. Please contact the
administrator."));
```

There are two primary error messages that can be produced when using this routine. The most common message is the "Unable to find path to server" message (see Figure 20.11). This usually occurs when the Lotus Notes client is unable to locate the destination server.

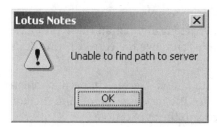

Figure 20.11 Typical error when unable to connect to Domino server

This message is most likely not related to the formula provided in this section and can also occur when a user clicks on a database link. In most cases, creating a server connection document will correct the problem. We'll talk more about the server connection document in the next section.

The second error message covers all other error messages and is produced by a routine (see Figure 20.12). The message provides an opportunity to deliver a customized error message to the user when an error is encountered. If you have a help desk phone number or email, you may want to include it in the message.

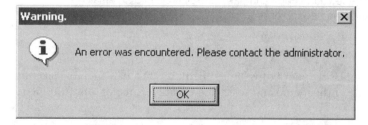

Figure 20.12 Warning message produced by the install button

The install button is now complete. Consider including a **Connection Document** button (as described in the next section) before sending the announcement. Otherwise, the button is ready to be sent.

Create a Server Connection Document Button

Connection documents are used to store connection information for Domino servers on the network. Creating a connection document will often resolve the "Unable to find path to server" error message. To help users connect to or locate Lotus databases, you can create a button that automatically adds a connection document to the user's Personal Address Book.

When the user clicks the button, the code first opens the user's local address book and searches for the server name in the Connections view. If the document is found, the user is asked whether he or she would like to continue with the update. If the user selects no, the transaction terminates. Otherwise, the existing document is updated. If no existing document is located, then a new document is established and saved.

To implement this solution, perform the following steps.

Step 1. Create the action button. From your Lotus Notes client, select the **Create > Hotspot > Button** menu options to add a button to a memo.

Step 2. Configure the button. Give the button an informative title (e.g., **Connect to Server**). Next, change the Language Selector from **Simple action(s)** to **LotusScript** and insert the following in the Click event. Be sure to replace **SERVER** with the Domino server name and **IPADDR** with the Internet Protocol address (or fully qualified domain name) assigned to the Domino server.

```
Sub Click(Source As Button)

    Dim w As New NotesUIWorkspace
    Dim s As New NotesSession
    Dim db As NotesDatabase
    Dim doc As NotesDocument
    Dim continue As Boolean
    Dim server As String
    Dim address As String
    Dim view As NotesView


    '--------------------------
    ' Specify the server name and IP address
    '--------------------------
    server =  "SERVER"   ' Domino server name e.g. NOTES123
    address = "IPADDR"   ' IP address e.g. 9.67.1.100


    '--------------------------
    ' Set object values to connect to the PAB
    '--------------------------
    Set s = New NotesSession
    Set db = s.GetDatabase( "", "names.nsf" )
    Set view = db.GetView("Connections")
    Set doc = view.GetDocumentByKey( server, True )
```

```
'----------------------------
' Determine action if existing doc is found
'----------------------------
Continue = True
If Not(doc Is Nothing) Then
   If Msgbox ("Update existing connection?", 4, "Continue?")= 7 Then
      continue = False
      Msgbox "Transaction cancelled"
   End If
Else
   Set doc = New NotesDocument( db )
End If


'----------------------------
' Create the connection document
'----------------------------
If continue Then
   doc.Form = "Local"
   doc.Type = "Connection"
   doc.ConnectionType = "0"
   doc.ConnectionLocation = "*"
   doc.Source = "*"
   doc.LanPortName = "TCPIP"
   doc.PortName = "TCPIP"
   doc.Destination = server
   doc.OptionalNetworkAddress = address
   doc.PhoneNumber  = address
   doc.Save True, True
   Msgbox "Connection doc created for " + server, ,"Success"
End If

End Sub
```

The Importance of Database Backups

All Domino server files and databases should be backed up for disaster recovery purposes. This ensures that the system can be quickly (and hopefully easily) recovered in the event that a problem occurs. Problems can arise from an assortment of natural and human errors or other reasons. Either way, users simply want things "back to normal" and as quickly as possible. The solution is to back up the server and all database files on a regular basis. Considerations should include

- Frequency of full system backups
- Frequency of incremental "delta" backups
- Number of tapes or CD-ROMs in rotation (if used)
- Documented "Backup Process"
- Documented "Restore Process"
- Documented "Escalation Process" regarding disaster recovery
- Contact names and phone numbers responsible for backup/restore
- Periodic verification of both the backup and restore process

Work with your local Domino server administrator and IT support team to define, implement, and verify disaster recovery procedures.

> **TIP**
>
> If you cannot determine the disaster recovery process for the Domino server and database, consider periodically burning a local copy of the database to CD or DVD media.

Process Synopsis

This chapter covered a lot of information pertaining to application deployment. Let's briefly review the process and steps covered in the chapter.

Step 1. Create the development database and set the ACL permissions.

Step 2. Make a copy of the development database to create the sandbox database. Set the ACL permissions and create any required application configuration documents.

Step 3. Make a copy of the sandbox database to create the production database.

Step 4. Set the "development database" as the master design template.

Step 5. Optionally, "sign" the database. (Refer to Chapter 19, "Security," for additional information pertaining to database security and how to "sign" a database.)

Step 6. Use the refresh design, replace design, and inherit design to migrate the database changes from the source database to the target database. Be sure to set the "inherit design" properties in the target environment.

Step 7. After the design has been updated, disable the "inherit design" properties so that changes are not automatically replicated by the Domino server each morning.

Step 8. Preserve the current database design by creating a new database template on the server and CD-ROM backup image.

Step 9. Deploy the production application. Enable the ACL for users. Send the application install and connection buttons to users for the initial release.

Step 10. Ensure that the database and server files are backed up on a regular basis. Work with your Domino server administrator and IT support team to establish a process. Be sure to document and know the backup/restore process and primary contacts for disaster recovery.

Links to developerWorks

A.20.1 Byrd, David and Speed, Timothy. *The trouble with templates, Part 1.* IBM developerWorks, September 2003. http://www.ibm.com/developerworks/lotus/library/ls-Templates1/index.html.

A.20.2 Byrd, David and Speed, Timothy. *The trouble with templates, Part 2.* IBM developerWorks, September 2003. http://www.ibm.com/developerworks/lotus/library/ls-Templates2/index.html.

Chapter 21

Troubleshooting

Chapter Overview

This chapter provides some tips and strategies for troubleshooting Formula Language, LotusScript, agents, and general application development problems or errors.

As with any software development language, understanding "what happened" when a function fails or produces an unexpected result can be challenging. Even experienced developers encounter problems and have to troubleshoot errors in the database design. However, given some rudimentary tools and armed with a couple problem-solving approaches, you too will be able to correct any problem that may arise.

By the end of the chapter you will have learned

- How to troubleshoot LotusScript
- How to troubleshoot agents
- Common problems and resolutions
- Where to find additional assistance

Troubleshooting LotusScript

In general, LotusScript problems can be divided into three distinct classifications—compile-time, run-time, and logic errors. There are numerous strategies and approaches for managing these types of problems. This section will review techniques to help manage each of these problem types. Let's start by defining the error classifications and then review strategies for managing them.

The Domino Designer client automatically compiles LotusScript code each time a design element is saved. As part of this built-in compile process, all code is checked for syntax errors and flagged. Errors flagged during this process are considered to be *compile-time errors*. Statements that fail to pass the syntax checks are subsequently highlighted in red. A short description of the problem is also displayed in the message bar. The message offers a clue for resolving the problem. All compile-time errors must be resolved for the design element to be saved. In addition to syntax checks during the compile, some very rudimentary syntax checks occur as statements are typed, such as checking for an incomplete statement.

The second type of problem, *run-time errors*, involves statements that pass the initial compile-time checks but that still contain invalid statements. This type of error can occur when the statements are structured correctly but are implemented or used incorrectly. Let's say, for example, you create an agent that runs when manually executed from the application interface but that fails when the same agent is changed to run on a scheduled basis. In this scenario, it's possible that the agent contains references to the user interface (UI)—also known as the front-end. Because scheduled agents interface with the application from the back-end (meaning there is no user interface to interact with), the agent fails.

The third type of problem, *logic errors*, occurs when the code compiles and runs but fails to produce the correct result. This type of error is related to the code logic. Perhaps, for example, an incorrect object is being referenced or the logical order in which statements are executed is incorrect. In any case, the net result differs from the expected result when the LotusScript code executes.

With the primary error classifications defined, the remainder of this chapter will focus on strategies to help resolve these issues.

Managing Compile-Time Errors

Compile-time errors are displayed in the Designer client as the design element is compiled or saved. When a syntax error is identified, a descriptive message is displayed in the message bar of the Designer client, and the associated statement lines are highlighted in red. These error messages are specifically related to the syntax of the LotusScript language.

For example, Figure 21.1 illustrates an error when displayed in the Designer client. In this example, the second code line is incomplete. Notice that a message is displayed in the message bar at the bottom of the screen.

Interpreting the error message is usually a good place to start when this type of error is encountered. The error message provides a number of clues intended to help resolve the problem. In this case, the error message states the following:

```
CheckValue: Click: 3: Unexpected: End-of-line; Expected: Data Type; NEW
```

This message provides a host of information pertaining to the LotusScript error. Start by breaking down the information associated with the message. In this particular example, the message references the design object, event, statement number, and description of the syntax error encountered followed by a description of the expected syntax (see Figure 21.2).

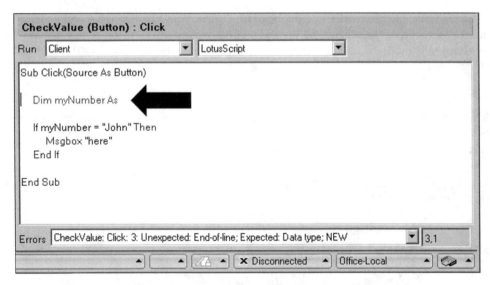

Figure 21.1 Example syntax error "Unexpected End-of-line"

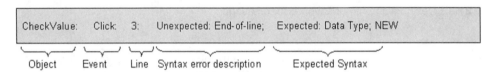

Figure 21.2 Breakdown of LotusScript error message content

The first element in the message, **CheckValue**, references the Domino design that contains the syntax error, such as a form name, subroutine name, or agent name. In this particular example, the object happens to be an action button.

The next two message elements reference the event and statement line number associated with the error. In this case, the error occurs in the **Click** event on line number **3**. These items enable you to locate the statement that has been flagged by the compiler. This line is typically highlighted in red. To locate the statement in the Designer client, place the cursor inside the Programmer's pane. As you move the cursor up, down, left, and right within the window, the cursor position will be updated in the lower-right corner of the Designer client. Notice the **3,1** displayed in Figure 21.1. This represents the vertical and horizontal position: line 3, cursor position 1.

Following the line number indicator is a short description of the syntax error that was encountered—**Unexpected: End-of-line**. This message indicates that the compiler expected to find additional syntax statements but unexpectedly found the end of the statement line. In other words, something is missing from the code line.

The last message element briefly describes the syntax that the compiler expected to encounter—**Expected: Data Type; NEW**. Upon closer examination of the code line, you'll notice that the compiler was expecting to encounter a data type and possibly the keyword NEW for the myNumber variable. The corrected statement should read as follows:

```
Dim myNumber as Integer
```

At this point, all code now appears to pass the preliminary syntax checks, which occur as code is typed in the Programmer's pane. However, a new error is generated when attempting to save the design element. First, a message is displayed (see Figure 21.3).

Figure 21.3 Design element not saved error message

This is accompanied by the following error message in the Designer message bar. These messages are specifically produced because compile-time errors were encountered.

```
CheckValue: Click: 5: Type mismatch
```

You'll notice that this new message follows the same basic format and, for the most part, includes similar information. The compiler is still encountering difficulties with the CheckValue design element in the Click event. However, the statement that contains the compile error has moved to line number **5**, and the problem encountered is a **Type mismatch**. In other words, the compiler is unable to proceed due to conflicting data types. In this example, line 5 is attempting to compare an Integer with a text string. To correct this problem, either the comparison value needs to be changed to a number or the declaration needs to be changed to a string.

```
Sub Click(Source As Button)

Dim myNumber As Integer

If myNumber = 1 Then
    Msgbox "here"
End If

End Sub
```

This illustrates a typical approach to solving compile-time errors. These are just two of the many error messages that can be produced by the compiler. There are many other syntax errors and related messages (too many to cover or explain in this publication) that could be produced. The key lesson here is to understand the process by which the compiler identifies errors and to understand how to interpret the associated error messages that are produced. Armed with this information, you can research LotusScript statement syntax or error messages using the Domino Designer Help or online support Web sites (described later in the chapter).

> **TIP**
>
> To open the Domino Designer help database, press F1 from the Designer client. Information can be sorted by the table of contents or by keyword index or searched based on a specified phrase. Click on the TIPS button to learn more about how to use the help database. Alternatively, select the **File > Database > Open** menu options. Locate and open the "Help" folder. Select and open the "Lotus Domino Designer Help" database.

Managing Run-time Errors

Run-time errors are generated when problems are encountered as the code executes from the Lotus Notes client. Here the code passes all preliminary syntax checks and compiles without error. However, as the code is executed, an error is encountered. This can occur when objects are referenced incorrectly or used in a manner other than their intended use.

As with compile-time errors, an error message is usually displayed when a run-time error is encountered. In most cases, the popup message is displayed with a brief description of the error. For example, Figure 21.4 illustrates a run-time error message. You'll notice that this error message provides no additional information pertaining to the potential source of the problem.

Figure 21.4   LotusScript variant error message

As a developer, there are three main steps you can take to troubleshoot run-time errors—declare all objects, incorporate error handling, and trace the code execution.

First, best practices suggest that you should explicitly declare all LotusScript objects. One way to ensure that all objects are properly declared is to have the following statement in the "Options" section for all LotusScript routines. When added, the Domino Designer client will verify that all LotusScript objects are appropriately declared.

```
Option Declare
```

Second, incorporate error handling in the LotusScript routine. Through the use of the On Error statement, you can trap and subsequently display the error number, error text string, line number, and module name associated with the error. This not only helps the developer troubleshoot the run-time error but also provides an opportunity to display a more user-friendly message. For example, in addition to run-time error information, the error handler could also include a message such as "A system error has occurred. Please report the following run-time error information to the help desk."

The On Error statement is used to manage errors encountered during run-time. When an error is encountered, program execution switches to the On Error section where additional code statements can be run. For example, you could branch to a block of code that manages error conditions and then resume program execution. Let's take a look at the following code to see how to implement conditional branching to manage errors.

```
Sub Click(Source As Button)

    '--------------------
    ' Set the "on error" condition
    '--------------------
    On Error Goto Oops
    Dim ErrorMsg As String

    '--------------------
    ' Normal program stuff
    '--------------------
    Dim Value1 As Integer
    Dim Value2 As Integer
    Value1 = 100
    Value2 = 0
    Msgbox "The answer is: " &  Value1 / Value2

    '--------------------
    ' Exit subroutine statement
    '--------------------
Finished:
    Exit Sub

Oops:
    '--------------------
    ' Build and display the error message
    '--------------------
    ErrorMsg = "Error #" & Err & Chr$(10) &_
```

```
|"| & Error$ & |"| & Chr$(10) & Chr$(10) & "Line " &_
Erl &   | in object: "| & Lsi_info(2) & |"|

Msgbox ErrorMsg, 16, "Unexpected Error"
Resume Finished
```

End Sub

There are four main components associated with this routine to manage run-time errors (as highlighted in bold). When a run-time error is encountered, the On Error statement is executed. In this case, a GoTo command branches execution to the Oops: section of code. Next, a message string is created using a variety of built-in functions and displayed to the user. This is followed by a Resume statement that branches execution to the Finished section to exit the subroutine.

It's important to understand that this implementation approach requires the Exit Sub statement. When an error is encountered, the message is displayed, and execution branches to this statement to halt further processing in the subroutine. However, under normal execution when no run-time error is encountered, this statement stops the execution of the Oops code. Without this statement, execution would continue, and a message would be displayed.

Finally, if still unable to resolve the error, or if you need additional information pertaining to object values, use the built-in LotusScript debugger. The debugger is a development tool that's incorporated into the Lotus Notes client. Using this tool, you can trace through the statements as they execute. Debugger benefits include the ability to

- Determine the code execution path
- Step through statements line-by-line
- Review object values during execution
- Skip or "step over" statements to manage the execution
- Terminate the execution
- Locate potential problem statements

To enable the debugger, select the **File > Tools > Debug LotusScript** menu options and open the database in the Lotus Notes client. An informational message will be displayed after the Debugger has been enabled (see Figure 21.5).

Figure 21.5 LotusScript debugger enabled message

> **NOTE**
>
> The debug tool can be enabled with the database open; however, some elements of the database design cannot be traced until after the database is closed and reopened.

With the debug tool enabled, repeat the steps necessary to reproduce the error message. The interactive debug interface will automatically launch and present information as soon as events are encountered in the application. There are several key areas of the Script Debugger that can be used to debug a LotusScript problem. Understanding how to navigate and use this tool can expedite the problem-solving process (see Figure 21.6).

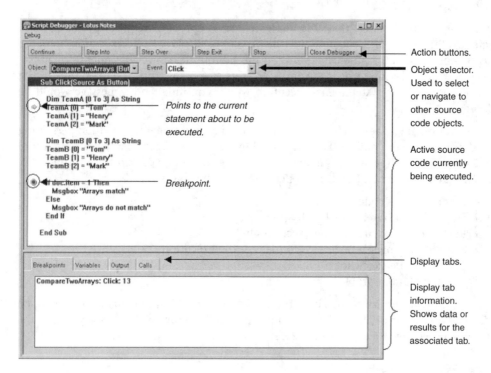

Figure 21.6 Elements of the Debugger Interface

Action Buttons. There are six action buttons used to navigate the debug environment. After the tool is launched, select one of these actions in order to continue with the debug process. Depending on the button selected you can step line-by-line through the code or have the code automatically continue executing.

- **Continue**—This button resumes normal execution. If breakpoints are set, execution will temporarily halt at the next specified point; otherwise, execution will resume without the debugger window displayed (but still active). However, the debugger window will relaunch if an error is encountered. When this occurs, the debug tool will open, and the statement in error will be highlighted.
- **Step Into**—This button executes the current statement as indicated by the yellow pointer in the source code display pane.
- **Step Over**—This button skips the current statement as indicated by the yellow pointer in the source code display pane and goes to the next statement in the source code.
- **Step Exit**—This button terminates or exits the current block of code and continues with the next statement immediately following the code block.
- **Stop**—This button halts the debugger environment but does not disable the feature. When clicked, control is returned to the Lotus Notes client. However, the debugger environment will relaunch as soon as the next action or event occurs within the database application.
- **Close Debugger**—This button halts and deactivates the LotusScript debug environment. This is essentially the same as stopping the debugger and then deselecting the option by selecting the **File > Tools > Debug LotusScript** menu options.

Object and Event Selector. The Object and Event dropdowns are used to navigate to various source code routines. These options are handy when you want to set a breakpoint for a downstream location in code and then click the Continue button.

Source Code. This window automatically shows the active code-stream being executed. A yellow pointer will display to the left of the statement that is about to be executed. A red stop sign will display next to statements containing a breakpoint.

Display Tabs. The display tabs are used to sort the various types of display information. "Breakpoints" displays all defined breakpoints for the associated code. "Variables" displays the contents of various LotusScript objects that are in scope to the code being executed. In many cases, you will find this tab to be invaluable for debugging and understanding both run-time and logic errors. "Output" displays a history of all information text messages (such as those generated by a print statement) that are posted to the Lotus Notes client. "Calls" displays a history of the function or subroutine branches.

Information Display. This window shows information associated with the selected display tab. As statements are executed, additional information will be displayed in this section.

Breakpoints. Breakpoints are used to temporarily halt or pause the execution of a routine. This feature can be particularly handy when tracing an exceptionally large block of code. By setting a breakpoint, you can click the Continue button, and execution will continue until reaching the breakpoint. A breakpoint can be set by double-clicking on a particular statement or by selecting the option from the Debug menu. You can also clear the various breakpoints by selecting either Clear Breakpoint or Clear All Breakpoints from the Debug menu.

> **TIP**
>
> Remember to disable the debug environment when you're finished with
> it. Otherwise, the tool will relaunch with the next database you open—
> including your mail database. If this happens, simply click the Close
> Debugger button to exit the tool. You may need to do this a couple
> times to exit from the tool. Leaving the debugger active will not affect
> the design or the database but can be a general annoyance.

> **NOTE**
>
> Lotus Notes also includes a Remote LotusScript Debugger for debug-
> ging LotusScript running on the server and an option to **Show Java
> Debug Console** for debugging Java code.

Managing Logic Errors

Logic errors are often the most difficult and challenging problems to resolve because no specific error message is produced at either compile-time or run-time. Resolution to functional
or logical problems often requires a step-by-step trace of the program to thoroughly understand where things went askew. This can be achieved by enabling the LotusScript debugger
and carefully observing the execution path and object values line-by-line. See the previous
section, "Managing Run-time Errors," for additional information pertaining to the
LotusScript debug tool.

In addition to the debug tool, a variety of supplemental approaches and techniques can help
identify the potential problem areas and manage information as the code executes.

Messagebox Statement. The `messagebox` command is used to display a popup message via
the user interface. This statement can be used to periodically display the contents of an
object or particular location in the LotusScript routine—say, the entrance and exit points for
the event.

```
Messagebox "Begin QUERYSAVE event"
Messagebox "The current field value is: " + doc.FIELD(0)
Messagebox "Exit QUERYSAVE event"
```

Print Statement. The `print` statement is another way to communicate messages and trace
the application execution. However, instead of displaying messages in a popup window, the
text string is displayed in the message bar located at the bottom of the Lotus Notes client.
Similar to the `messagebox` statement, `print` statements could be inserted at the start, periodically within, and at the end of the subroutine or function. For databases stored on a
Domino server, the `print` message is also displayed on the server console. For agents running on a server, the `print` message is also appended to the server log file.

```
Print "Begin COMPAREARRAY subroutine"
Print "The current field value is: " + doc.FIELD(0)
Print "Exit COMPAREARRAY subroutine"
```

Stop Statement. The `stop` statement is used to temporarily halt the LotusScript execution at the current statement, provided that the debugger is enabled. In other words, the statement acts as a breakpoint when encountered. This statement gives you the opportunity to review object values or continue the execution by manually stepping through statements. This statement can be added as a standalone statement or incorporated with other LotusScript statements. For example, if a field contains a null value, stop execution.

```
If doc.FIELD(0) = "" then Stop
```

It's important to note that this statement only executes if the debugging has been enabled. The statement is also ignored when incorporated in scheduled agents or agents called from the menu that run in the server background.

Continue Variable. Specific events, such as `QuerySave` on a form, include a `Continue` variable. This is a Boolean value that can be used to manage the completion of the event. A `TRUE` value indicates that the event can complete, whereas a `FALSE` value indicates that the event cannot complete. For example, setting this variable to `FALSE` in the form `QuerySave` event will prevent documents from being saved. This variable could be used in conjunction with data validation. If all field values are valid, the variable is set to `TRUE`, and the document can be saved. If field validation fails, set the variable to `FALSE`, and the document is not saved.

```
Continue = False
```

Troubleshooting Agents

A.21.2

This section provides techniques that can be used to troubleshoot agents. As you know, agents can be written to utilize "Simple Actions," Formula Language, LotusScript, and a variety of other languages. Given this variety, numerous tools and approaches can be used to debug problems. The tools used to debug the agent will, in part, depend on the design and implementation of the agent. The following outlines approaches that will be covered:

1. Review the agent log
2. Use the Debugger for LotusScript agents
3. Incorporate message prompts
4. Monitor the Domino Server Log (requires special access)
5. Monitor the Domino Server Console (requires special access)

As with most application development, you'll find there's no substitute for experience, and as you gain experience, you'll find one technique to be preferred over others. You'll also find there is no easy method to troubleshoot agents that utilize "Simple Actions" or Formula Language.

A.21.

Working with the Agent Log

The Domino Designer client includes a feature to test the agent. When utilized, the client performs a trial run of the agent and displays the Agent Log. The Agent Log is usually a good place to start when looking to test or troubleshoot an agent. The Agent Log contains information pertaining to the agent execution and can often help to diagnose common agent problems.

The Agent Log is produced by testing the agent. This is accomplished by selecting the agent in the Domino Designer client and choosing the **Agent > Test** menu options. The software subsequently returns the expected results along with potential errors in a dialog. Figure 21.7 illustrates a sample Agent Log.

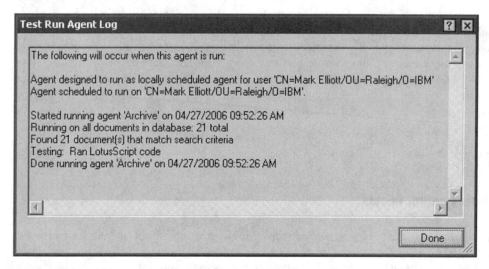

Figure 21.7   Sample of the Test Run Agent Log

In this example, statement 2 indicates that this is a scheduled agent that has been signed by "Mark Elliott". Statement 4 shows the agent name "Archive" and a timestamp when the trial run started. This is followed by the total number of documents as well as the number of documents affected by the agent. The log ends with a completion time for the agent test.

> **NOTE**
>
> The Agent Log can only be displayed for specific types of agents. For instance, agents that are developed to parse or utilize the user interface cannot utilize the "Agent Test" function. In this scenario, the Designer client will display an error message as illustrated in Figure 21.8. If you encounter this message, consider running the LotusScript Debugger and tracing the agent as it is executed in the database from the Lotus Notes client.

Figure 21.8   Some agents can only be run from the Lotus Notes client

Working with the Debugger

For agents that utilize LotusScript, the debugger can be used to trace the code and review object values as the agent executes. As described earlier in the chapter, the debugger can step through the agent execution, halt execution, and display detailed information pertaining to all LotusScript objects. Unfortunately, this feature only applies to LotusScript. There is no comparable function that can be used to trace agents that are written in "Simple Actions" or Formula Language.

Working with Message Prompts

Message prompts can be used to display data values or status points in the execution of the agent from the user interface. This approach can be used for manually triggered agents. Using Formula Language commands (such as @Prompt) or LotusScript commands (like Print, Messagebox, and Prompt), you can periodically display information in the Lotus Notes client. The resulting information can sometimes identify problems with the agent.

Other avenues include the LotusScript NotesLog class, which can be incorporated into agents that utilize LotusScript. This class offers methods to log actions, events, and errors and determine agent properties including the number of errors, program name, total actions, and parent object name. Refer to the Domino Designer help for additional information pertaining to this class.

Working with the Domino Server Log

The Domino server log contains a running history of events and informational text messages associated with the server's operation. This database resides on the server and is updated as events occur. It also tracks messages issued by the LotusScript print statement for all agents run by the server. It's important to understand that this a restricted database. Based on the default ACL settings, you probably will not have access to this database. Consult your Domino server administrator to request "Read" access to the database.

After you have appropriate access, select the **File > Database > Open** menu options to open the server. Specify the Domino server name in the Server field and locate the database. The database will most likely be named "*Server* Log" (where "Server" represents the actual name of the Domino server). The log database contains a wide variety of information associated with the Domino server's operation. For debugging purposes, select the Miscellaneous Events view. The most current document containing server log information will be located at the bottom of the view (see Figure 21.9). Open this document and review the statements for potential clues to help diagnose the problem.

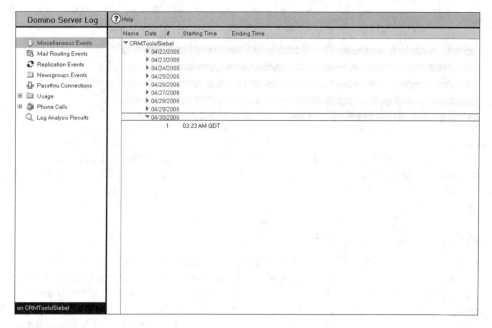

Figure 21.9   Domino Server Log

Working with the Domino Server Console

The Domino Server Console displays information pertaining to the operation of the server. This can include informational messages during agent execution, similar to those appended to the server's log file. Additionally, you can issue a variety of the commands to retrieve status information for a given agent. However, to run these commands, you must have access to the server's console window or the authority to establish a remote console connection using the Domino Administrator client. For many, these options will not be feasible. A summary of server commands has been included for those who manage both database development and server administration.

- **Tell amgr schedule**—Displays the current list of scheduled agents. The console information includes the agent work queue, trigger type, target run time, agent name, and affected database name.

- **Tell amgr status**—Displays the current status of the various agent work queues and run-time control parameters. This command is helpful to determine the control parameters as well as to obtain a general snapshot of the agent status.
- **Load amgr -?**—Displays help information for the agent manager command.
- **Show agents *DatabaseName***—Displays all agents for the specified Notes database (where *DatabaseName* represents a valid Lotus Notes database).
- **Tell amgr cancel *DatabaseName AgentName***—Terminates a scheduled agent that is currently running (where *DatabaseName* represents a valid Lotus Notes database and *AgentName* represents a valid agent). The command only applies to scheduled agents. Be sure to specify a valid database name and agent name when issuing this command.
- **Tell amgr run *DatabaseName AgentName***—This command starts a specified agent for a given database (where *DatabaseName* represents a valid Lotus Notes database and *AgentName* represents a valid agent). Be sure to specify a valid database name and agent name when issuing this command.

Common Database Problems

The following are just a few of the common error messages that may be encountered when developing a database. This section is not intended to be an exhaustive list of problems but rather a couple of the more common problems that tend to be encountered. Obviously, implementation of corrective actions will vary depending on the database design. The code examples offered in this section are intended to be a general reference point for possible solutions.

See "Where to Find Additional Assistance" at the end of this chapter for more resources to help identify and diagnose database, Lotus Notes, or Domino server–related problems.

Variant Does Not Contain an Object

Typically encountered when a LotusScript object is improperly referenced. Utilize the LotusScript Debugger to identify the statement in error. The vast majority of the time, the object is missing the reference identifier. For example, the following illustrates an invalid statement (in bold).

```
If doc.Item = 1 Then
    Messagebox "This is a sample message."
End If
```

The following illustrates the corrected statement (in bold).

```
If doc.Item(0) = 1 Then
    Messagebox "This is a sample message."
End If
```

Illegal Circular Use

The "illegal circular use" error is often encountered two different ways—when developing a database using LotusScript libraries or when copying a design element between database designs. In any case, this problem is often related to LotusScript library references. The following are a few actions to take to help with problem solving.

1. Verify that a Use *Library* statement is included in all design elements that utilize a LotusScript function or subroutine. The Use statement should always reside in the "Options" section for either the individual item (such as an action button) or the top-level design element (such as the form, view, or agent).

2. Verify that all LotusScript libraries referenced in the design elements actually exist. Check the Use statement in each design element and verify that a corresponding library exists in the **Shared Code > Script Libraries** section of the Designer client.

3. Verify that all functions and subroutines are uniquely named if multiple LotusScript libraries are associated with the database design.

4. If a design element has been copied from one database to another, comment out all the LotusScript statements for the design element. Then gradually add in the statements to determine the potential problem.

Unable to Find Path to Server

This problem occurs when the Lotus Notes client is unable to locate the destination Domino server. This can occur when the Domain Name Server (DNS) is unable to resolve the server name, which the Lotus Notes client uses to establish a connection to the server. The following are three actions that may help solve the problem.

Solution 1: Connection document

Create a connection document in the user's Lotus Notes client. Creating a connection document will often resolve the "Unable to find path to server" error message. Follow these steps to manually create a connection document in the user's Personal Address Book.

Step 1.   Locate and open the "Personal Address Book (on local)" for the user.

Step 2.   Click on the **Advanced** category (at the left side of the screen).

Step 3.   Click on the **Connections** view.

Step 4.   Click the **New** button and select **Server Connection**.

Step 5.   Set the following fields on the Basics tab of the form:

- Set **Connect type** to **Local Area Network**
- Set **Use Port** to **TCPIP**
- Specify the server name (e.g., **SERVER01**)

Step 6. Switch to the Advanced tab and add the IP address (9.56.7.100) or the fully qualified host name (e.g., D01nm100.raleigh.ibm.com) to the Destination Server Address field. You can ping the server from a DOS prompt to get the IP address. (Note that "ping" may be viewed as a Denial of Service Attack by some corporations, and servers may not return an IP address.)

Solution 2: Check Location

Verify that the Lotus Notes client location is not set to "Island" mode. Within the Lotus Notes client, users can define one or more location documents. These documents manage connectivity and other settings associated with connectivity. The "Island" location is a default location included with the installation of the Notes client. When selected, this document tells the client that there is no network connection (even when there is one). The location setting is located in the lower-right-most corner of the Lotus Notes client. To change the setting, click on the triangle and selected a valid location, such as "Office (Network)."

> **NOTE**
>
> "Location" documents are stored in the Personal Address Book for each individual's Lotus Notes client.

Solution 3: Check network connectivity

Verify that general network connectivity is available. Open a supported Web browser and connect to an Internet Web site such as CNN, Yahoo, or Google. If the Web page displays, this illustrates general network connectivity. Otherwise, a network problem exists and needs to be resolved. Work with your local network administrator or workstation support team to address the problem.

Document or Database Link Does Not Work

Although there may be a wide variety of causes, problems with document and database links can usually be attributed to either network connectivity or ACL settings. The following are a few actions to try.

1. Verify connectivity to the destination server. Review the actions list in the previous "Unable to find path to server" section.

2. One method to create a document link is through the **Edit > Copy as link** menu options. Another method to create a document link is through the Formula or LotusScript languages. Either way, the database must reside on a server for users to access the document.

3. Verify that the user has permission to access the database. Check the ACL settings to ensure that the user has a minimum of "Reader" access to the database. Otherwise, the document or database link will not work for the given user.

Database Design Does Not Update

The Domino Designer client includes a feature to lock the design of a particular element. This "No Refresh" setting prohibits design template refreshes when selected. Figure 21.10 shows several design elements that have the "No Refresh" value enabled.

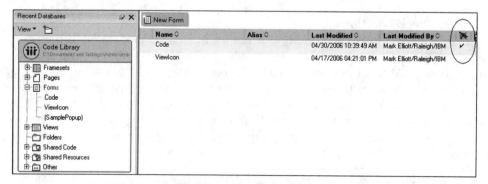

Figure 21.10   "No Refresh" setting for design elements

To disable (or enable) the "No Refresh" setting, select the design element. Then choose the **Design > Design Properties** menu options. Switch to tab 3 and toggle the value for the **Prohibit design refresh or replace to modify** setting (see Figure 21.11).

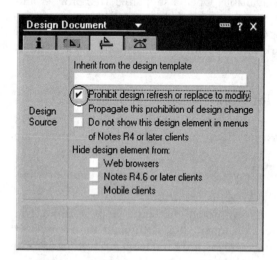

Figure 21.11   Changing the "No Refresh" property for a design element

Where to Find Additional Assistance

There are several additional resources that can be used to help with problem resolution. They include the database Synopsis, Internet discussion forums, and Web sites. The database Synopsis, a feature of the Domino Designer client, is a powerful feature that provides summary information for the database design.

A.21.4

This feature is built into the Designer client and enables users to view and search design information for key text phrases, reviewing formulas or objects throughout the entire design of the database. Information can also be found on Internet discussion forums and Web sites. Using the Internet, you can search for sample code, research error messages, post questions, and discuss problem resolutions.

Using the Database Synopsis

To use the Synopsis feature, open the Designer client and select **Synopsis** from the Designer left-side navigation pane (see Figure 21.12). It will be the last item listed in the "Other" section.

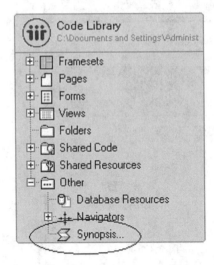

Figure 21.12   Location of the Synopsis feature

Click on **Synopsis** to launch the Design Synopsis dialog window. When launched, the dialog window will display, as shown in Figure 21.13.

This dialog is used to select design elements to be included in the detailed design synopsis. This is achieved by selecting a design element type (such as form, outline, or view) and clicking the **Add** or **Add All** button. The design elements are then appended to the Selected Elements field and included in the report. After design elements have been selected, click

OK to generate the synopsis report. You can then scroll through the information or use the **FIND** menu option to search for key text strings within the synopsis report. Figure 21.14 illustrates a sample report.

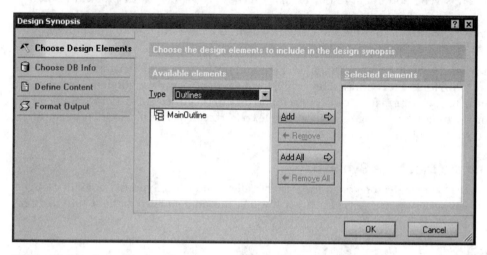

Figure 21.13   Select design elements to include in the Synopsis

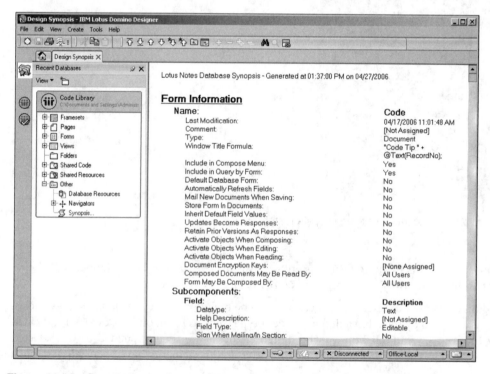

Figure 21.14   Sample Synopsis report

Discussion Forums and Web Sites

One of the best sources for information is the Lotus Web site. This site includes a wealth of information pertaining to Lotus products, software maintenance patches, known problems, technical notes, white papers, and discussion forums, among others (see Figure 21.15).

> http://www.ibm.com/developerworks/lotus
> http://www.redbooks.ibm.com/Redbooks.nsf/RedbookAbstracts/
> redp4102.html?Open

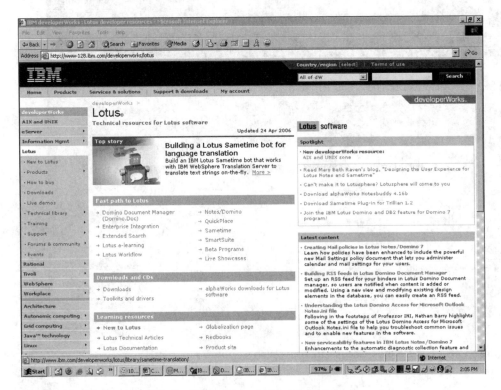

Figure 21.15   DeveloperWorks Web site for Lotus products

Given the sheer volume of information available from the Web site, let's focus on a couple key aspects of particular benefit to Domino database developers—forums, support, and downloads.

Forums. Lotus currently offers numerous public discussion forums. These discussion forums allow people to post questions regarding any product in the Lotus product family. Responses are posted by Lotus professionals, subject matter experts, and other members of the community. Using the discussion forum, you can search for error messages, pose a question, request assistance debugging a piece of code, and reuse solutions posted by other forum members.

At the time this publication was printed, you can navigate to the forums by selecting the **Forums & community** link located on the left navigation menu (see Figure 21.16). This will display all available discussion topics including the "Notes/Domino 6 & 7 Forum" and "Notes/Domino 4 & 5 Forum." These forums are specifically geared toward the Domino products, database development, and administration. Clicking on one of these links will open the discussion forum.

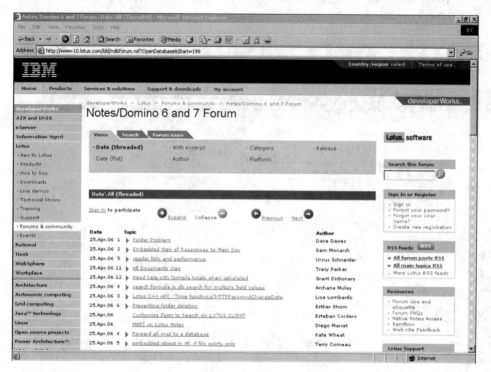

Figure 21.16   Lotus Notes discussion forum Web site

To search the discussion forum, specify search criteria in the **Search this forum** field (in the upper-right corner of the Web page). When searching for information, a good place to start is with keywords that pertain to Domino database development. Many times you can find information by searching on command, function, subroutine, or error (e.g., @Prompt or QuerySave). It's also possible to find different solutions to the same problem between the discussion forums. So be sure to search both forums when looking for answers.

To post a discussion forum topic or response, you will need to create a profile and then "sign in" to the forum using the newly created user ID and password. Registration is simple. Click on the **Create new registration** link and complete the registration (see Figure 21.17).

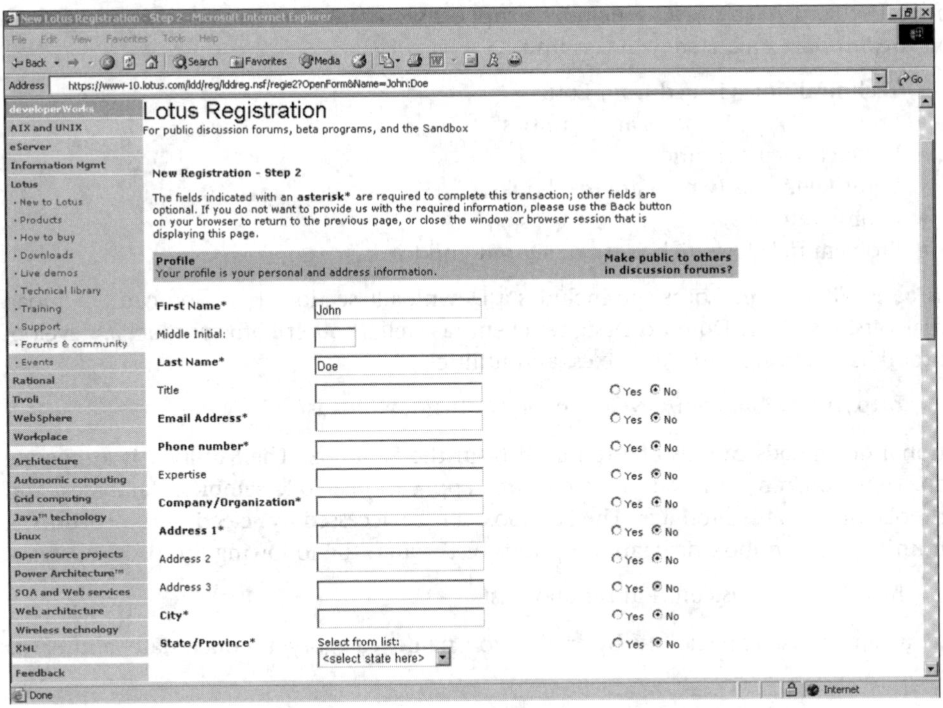

Figure 21.17   Registration form for new discussion forum users

There are several steps to the registration process. During this process, you'll need to specify your name, contact information, and email address. You're also given the opportunity to set email preferences. Additional information can also be found in the privacy statement, which is also available from the Web page. After the registration is complete and you sign in to the database, you can post new topics or responses.

> **NOTE**
>
> Be sure to search the database for solutions before posting new discussion threads. Also be concise and to the point when posting or responding to topics. Clearly stating the problem or information request generally results in more favorable and timely responses from the forum community. If no one responds to a new topic, consider restating the request.

Support. The Lotus Web site also includes a support section, which can be accessed by clicking on the **Support** link. Here you can find

- Technical notes issued from Lotus
- Product "Fixes, Updates and Utilities"
- Product documentation
- Lotus Redbooks (which are free books)
- Online tutorials
- Problem tickets, which you can submit and track

Downloads. Finally, the Lotus site includes a Downloads section. Here you can download free trial versions of the Domino Designer client (as well as other Lotus products), development toolkits, smart upgrade kits, fixes, and utilities.

> http://www.ibm.com/developerworks/lotus/downloads/

Additional downloads can also be retrieved from the Sandbox. The Sandbox is a separate section. Here you can post and download free applications, code samples, databases, and other tools for all Lotus products. The Sandbox can be accessed by selecting the **Forums & community** and **Sandbox** navigation options or through the following link:

> http://www.lotus.com/ldd/sandbox.nsf

Here you can browse applications by application name, category, product, date, author, or audience.

Links to developerWorks

A.21.1 Guirard, Andre. *Debugging LotusScript Part 1*. IBM developerWorks, July 2003. http://www.ibm.com/developerworks/lotus/library/ls-DebuggingLotusScript_1/index.html.

A.21.2 Kadashevich, Julie. *Troubleshooting agents in Notes/Domino 5 and 6*. IBM developerWorks, January 2003. http://www.ibm.com/developerworks/lotus/library/ls-Troubleshooting_agents_ND5_6/index.html.

A.21.3 Albritton, Robert and Lordan, Craig. *Create your own formula debugger*. IBM developerWorks, December 1999. http://www.ibm.com/developerworks/lotus/library/ls-Create_Formula_Debugger/index.html.

A.21.4 Product Information. Lotus Notes Product Information, August 2006. http://www-128.ibm.com/developerworks/lotus/products/notesdomino/.

A.21.5 Free Publications. Lotus Redbooks, August 2006. http://www.redbooks.ibm.com/portals/Lotus.

Online Project Files and Sample Applications

About the Online Materials

Registered readers can access from the companion Web site ready-to-use sample databases and a variety of development tools, files, and source code designed to help you rapidly build Domino database applications. The files included on the Web site are

- A Project Library containing source code for all projects in the book.
- A Developer's toolbox database filled with ready-to-use Formula Language and LotusScript source code
- Completed sample databases for each chapter project
- Enhanced versions of the project databases
- A sample database and spreadsheet file to practice data imports
- Ready-to-use LotusScript source code import files
- Sample graphics to enhance the database interface
- Sample project plans

By the end of this appendix, you will have learned

- How to access the companion Web site
- How to download and unpack the various developer toolbox files
- What is included in the developer's toolbox
- How to install one of the ready-to-use Notes databases
- How to use the Project Library database to build the various chapter projects

About the Companion Web Site

This publication includes a developer's toolbox. The toolbox contains ready-to-use software, source code, and other development-related materials. These files complement the publication and aid in the teaching process. The materials will be used to build the various projects in the book and can also serve as a model for new development projects. To receive this free supplemental content, you need to become a member of "IBM Press" Web site and register your book. After you've joined as a member, enter the book's ISBN to complete the registration process. The supplemental content can then be retrieved from the "My Registered Books" page.

Become a Member of the Companion Web Site

Access to the Web site is simple. You need to join as member and register your purchased book in order to download the files. You also need an Internet connection in order to access the supplemental files.

Step 1. Access the IBM Press Web site. You must join the Web site as a member in order to continue with the process. If you are already a member, log in and continue with the next section, "Downloading and Unpacking the Developer's Toolbox." Otherwise, proceed to Step 2.

http://www.ibmpressbooks.com/my_account/login.asp

Step 2. Start the membership process. Specify your email address and click the **Sign Up Now** button located in the "New to IBM Press" section. A confirmation email will be sent to you. To continue with the membership account setup, open the email and click the continuation link.

Step 3. Complete the membership process. Specify your first and last name, user name, password, and other required information. Next, read the privacy policy and select "I have read and understand the IBM Press privacy policy." Click the **Submit** button to complete the membership process.

Register the Book and Download the Developer's Toolbox

As a member of the Web site, you can download and unpack the developer's toolbox. All toolbox files are bundled into a single, compressed data file. This enables all sample databases, project files, and ready-to-use source code to be downloaded at one time. The file can then be unpacked into any directory that's accessible to the Lotus Notes client. This section describes how to download and unpack the toolbox onto your computer workstation.

Step 1. After you are registered, log in to display the home page. Use the login userID and password created in the previous section.

Step 2. Register the publication. Go to:

http://www.ibmpressbooks.com/bookstore/register.asp.

Step 3. Enter and submit the ISBN: **0132214482**

Step 4. Update your member profile information and click the **Submit** button.

Step 5. To complete the book registration process, you will be prompted to answer a question pertaining to the publication. Enter the response and click **Submit**. The "Lotus Notes Developer's Toolbox" should now display in the list of registered books.

Step 6. Next, locate and download the developer's toolbox. In the registration area, go to "My Registered Books". Next to the book, click on the link "**Access to protected content for this book**" to access the file downloads and save it to a local directory.

Step 7. After being retrieved, unpack the file into a local directory using Microsoft Windows Explorer, WinZip, or similar tool. The directory must be accessible to your Lotus Notes client.

About the Developer's Toolbox

All project materials and sample code presented in this publication's chapters are also available on the companion Web site in the developer's toolbox. These files are grouped by chapter for easy reference. A completed sample database is also included for all projects in the book. Both project files and sample Domino databases are organized by corresponding chapter. In addition to completed projects, there's a database for all project code. This can be copied from the Project Library into the Domino Designer client as you follow the project instructions. The intent here is to focus learning on the task and the process without having to re-type code from pages in the book.

When looking at the toolbox directories, you'll notice that each folder also includes a chapter reference, such as "Chapter 10." This indicates where to find additional information within the book for the files stored in the folder. However, not all chapters have related materials, which explains the gaps between the chapter numbers for the various toolbox folder names. Additional development utilities are stored in the "Development Tools and Files" folder. Here you will find the Project Library and Code Library databases, among other files.

Before reviewing the toolbox contents, let's spend a moment reviewing the types of files. There are several different file types included in the bundle:

.NSF—Represents a Lotus Notes database. From an application development perspective, you will need to install the Lotus Notes and Lotus Domino Designer client software to access or modify these applications. The .NSF file must be copied to a local workstation folder (see "Installing a Notes Database" later) to use, experiment with, or modify the sample database.

.TXT—Represents a text file. A number of the chapter projects require a significant amount of LotusScript or Formula Language code to be manually entered or created in order to create the database. A copy of the source code (as listed in the chapter) is also contained in the text file. This provides you with the choice of either manually entering the code (as illustrated in the chapters) or copying the code from the text file directly into the associated Domino design element. All text files can be accessed by using the Notepad application (a standard application included with Microsoft Windows) or any text editor that you prefer.

.DOC—Represents a Microsoft Word file.

.XLS—Represents a Microsoft Excel spreadsheet file.

.JPG—Represents a graphic image file.

.GIF—Represents a graphic image file.

.MPP—Represents a Microsoft Project file.

A ready-to-use version of each project can be found in the chapter folder. In some cases, an enhanced version of the database is also provided to illustrate formatting techniques. The following sections describe each file, based on the corresponding folder name.

About the "Chapter 07 Fundamentals Project" Folder

Websites.nsf—A sample database used to track and launch Web site addresses in your default Internet browser (see Figure A.1). The database can also track Web site user IDs and passwords. This database illustrates the core design elements associated with the Lotus Domino Designer client.

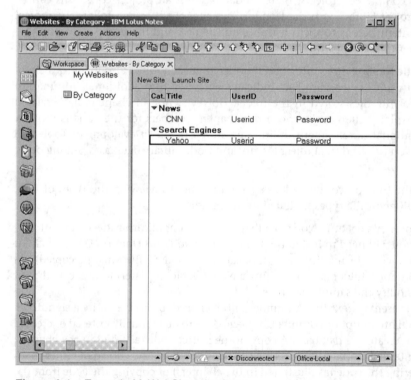

Figure A.1   Example MyWebSites database

ProjectPlanTemplate.doc—A sample project plan in Microsoft Word format. This document is intended to be a template that can be used to manage and track project-related activities.

ProjectPlanTemplate.xls—A sample project plan in Microsoft Excel format. This document is intended to be a template that can be used to manage and track project-related activities.

ProjectPlanTemplate.mpp—A sample project plan in Microsoft Project version 98 format. This document is intended to be a template that can be used to manage and track project-related activities.

LaunchWeb.txt—Contains the LotusScript library routines associated with the MyWebsites.nsf application. The source code can be entered manually based on the chapter descriptions or copied from the text file directly into the Domino design element.

About the "Chapter 08 Calendar Project" Folder

Calendar1.nsf—A sample calendar database that includes the ability to generate simple recurring events (see Figure A.2). This database illustrates the concepts for building a calendar and for creating a simple calendar document. Calendar appointments can be created for a single date or multiple consecutive dates for a given event.

Calendar2.nsf—A sample calendar database that includes the ability to create complex recurring calendar events. Events can be scheduled to repeat daily, weekly, monthly by day, monthly by date, or based on specific user-defined dates. The database illustrates how to create a custom popup dialog and LotusScript library. Figure A.3 illustrates the "recurring event" dialog box for this project database.

Calendar3.nsf—An enhanced version of the "simple" calendar database application.

Calendar4.nsf—An enhanced version of the "complex" calendar database application.

RepeatLibrary.txt—Contains the LotusScript library routines associated with the complex recurring calendar events. The source code can be entered manually based on the chapter descriptions or copied from the text file directly into the Domino design element.

RepeatChoices.txt—Contains the default field values associated with complex recurring calendar events. The source code can be entered manually based on the chapter descriptions or copied from the text file directly into the Domino design element.

CalendarArt.gif—A sample graphic image to be added to the complex recurring event dialog window (refer to Figure A.4).

ApptFormEvents.txt—Contains the LotusScript code used in the "Form" design element for calendar database.

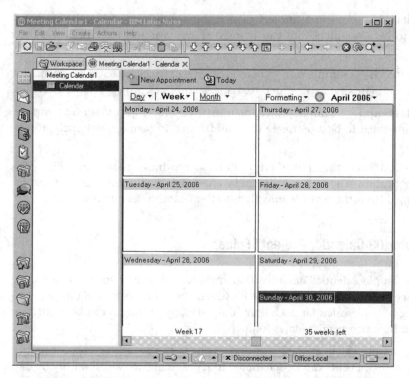

Figure A.2   Example "Simple Calendar" database

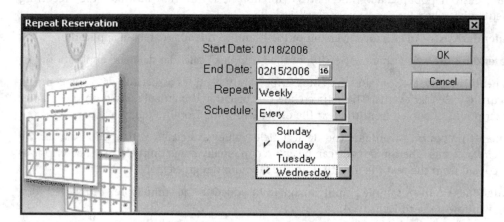

Figure A.3   Example of the "Repeat Reservation" popup in the "Complex Calendar" database

About the "Chapter 09 Collaboration Project" Folder

Forum.nsf—A sample discussion forum database (see Figure A.4). This database illustrates the concept of main "Documents," "Response," and "Response-to-Response" documents. The application includes the ability to receive email notifications (using the "Subscribe" feature) as new topics are posted. The project demonstrates several methods for generating emails and the ability to monitor the email work queue. A counter is displayed in the view to show the total number of sub-documents associated with the main discussion topic.

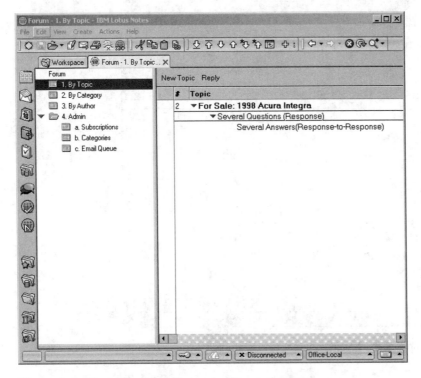

Figure A.4   Example of the Discussion Forum database

Forum2.nsf—An enhanced version of the discussion forum database application. This version includes additional graphics, formatted fonts, and enhanced forms.

ForumLibrary.txt—Contains the LotusScript library routines associated with the complex recurring calendar events. Source code can be entered manually based on the chapter or copied from the text file directly into the Domino design element.

Notebook.nsf—A sample database used to track project-related activities (see Figure A.5). This database illustrates the ability to create and implement categorized views and field inheritance and to track the last modified date and person. It's designed to be used for Project Management purposes. It can be used to track meeting agendas, minutes, action items, project documents, and team members. It provides a single online repository of information for all team members.

Notebook2.nsf—An enhanced version of the project control book database application. This version includes additional graphics, formatted fonts, and enhanced forms.

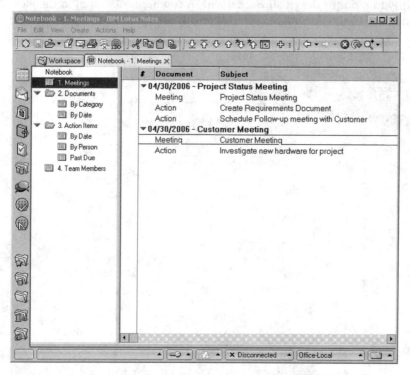

Figure A.5   Example of the "Project Notebook" database

About the "Chapter 10 Reference Library Project" Folder

ReportGenerator.nsf—This database illustrates how to dynamically create a Microsoft Excel spreadsheet for a Lotus Notes database (see Figure A.6). When the user clicks the Generate Report button, he or she is prompted to select a view from the database. The LotusScript library includes the ability to scan all views and columns in the database. After a view is selected, the spreadsheet is generated based on the column headers and data presented in the view. The "generate report" feature can be incorporated into virtually any database application.

> **NOTE**
>
> A working version of Microsoft Excel must be installed on the user's workstation for the report to generate.

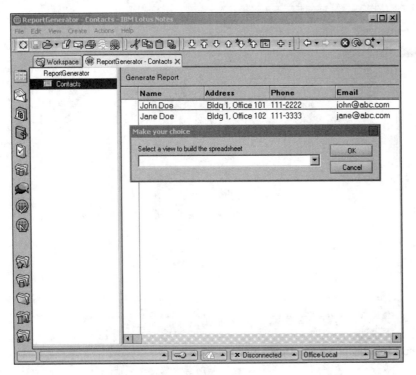

Figure A.6   Example of the Generate Report library

ReportLibrary.txt—Contains the LotusScript source code library routines used to dynamically generate a spreadsheet. The source code can be entered manually based on the chapter descriptions or copied from the text file directly into the Domino design element. This library can be incorporated into practically any database application.

Connections.nsf—A sample database that can be used to track and distribute Lotus Notes connection documents. Connection documents store information that enables the Notes client to locate and connect to a particular Domino server. Creating a connection document will often resolve the error message "Unable to find path to server." This database illustrates how to create documents in another database, create a button to allow users to import connection documents, and generate an email to send a connection document.

Connections2.nsf—An enhanced version of the connection document database application (see Figure A.7). This version includes additional graphics, formatted fonts, and enhanced forms.

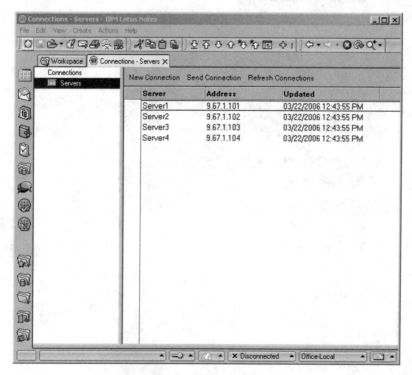

Figure A.7 Example of the Connection Document database

About the "Chapter 11 Workflow Project" Folder

Workflow.nsf—A sample workflow database (see Figure A.8). This database illustrates how to route documents electronically for approval. It illustrates the concepts associated with workflow, document routing, roles, and multiple layers of application security. The database also includes a "system profile" document used to control the configuration of the database and numerous views to track the documents, work queues, and message routing queues. Using this database, you could implement a procurement request, work order, or help desk requests database application.

Workflow2.nsf—An enhanced version of the workflow database application. This version includes additional graphics, formatted fonts, and enhanced forms.

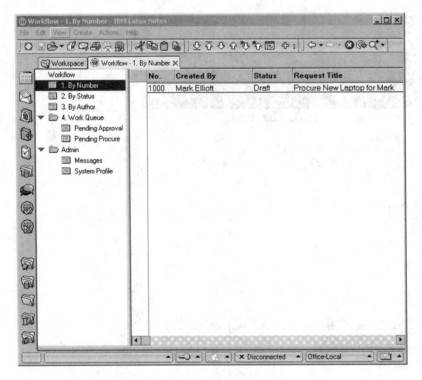

Figure A.8 Example of the Workflow database

WorkflowLibrary.txt—Contains the LotusScript library routines used to dynamically generate a spreadsheet. The source code can be entered manually based on the chapter descriptions or copied from the text file directly into the Domino design element.

About the "Chapter 12 Web Site Project" Folder

Background.gif—A sample graphic image that can be incorporated into the navigation menu for the Web site database.

MyWeb.nsf—A sample Web site database application. This database illustrates how to create a Lotus Notes database that can be accessed via the Notes client as well as a Web browser. The Domino server automatically generates the HTML used to display documents. All source code and associated HTML required for the database design is included in this example. This example also illustrates how to create a Navigation menu for the database using outlines, pages, and framesets.

MyWeb2.nsf—An enhanced version of the Web site database application (see Figure A.9). This version includes additional graphics, formatted fonts, and enhanced forms.

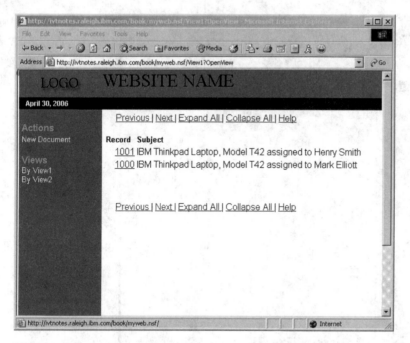

Figure A.9   Example of the Website.nsf database accessed from a Web browser

WebsiteLibrary.txt—Contains the LotusScript library routines used to support the Web site database application. The source code can be entered manually based on the chapter descriptions or copied from the text file directly into the Domino design element.

WebsiteHTML.txt—Contains the HTML used to support the Web site design. The source code can be entered manually based on the chapter descriptions or copied from the text file directly into the Domino design element.

WebsiteAgent.txt—Contains the LotusScript code library for the agent in the Web site database. This agent is used to process and save document updates made through the Internet browser. The source code can be entered manually based on the chapter instructions or copied from the text file directly into the Domino design element.

About the "Chapter 18 Data Management" Folder

DataLoad.nsf—A sample database used to illustrate the process for importing data into a Lotus Notes database application.

DataLoad.xls—A sample spreadsheet containing import data. This Microsoft Excel file is used to illustrate how to import data into a Lotus Notes database.

DataLoad.wk4—A sample spreadsheet containing import data. This Lotus 1-2-3 file is used to illustrate how to import data into a Lotus Notes database.

About the "Development Tools and Files" Folder

BookCodeLibrary.nsf—The database includes a comprehensive set of code examples to manage LotusScript, Formula Language, agent, and view customizations (see Figure A.10). Each example includes a brief description, an explanation of how the code works, and detailed step-by-step instructions to implement the code.

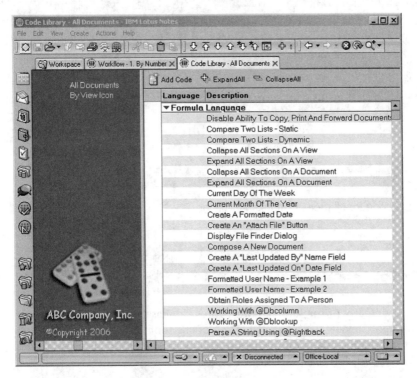

Figure A.10 The developer's code library filled with working examples of all code and customizations in this publication

ProjectSourceCode.nsf—This database contains all source code for the chapter projects (see Figure A.11). This is an alternative place to locate materials to complete the projects.

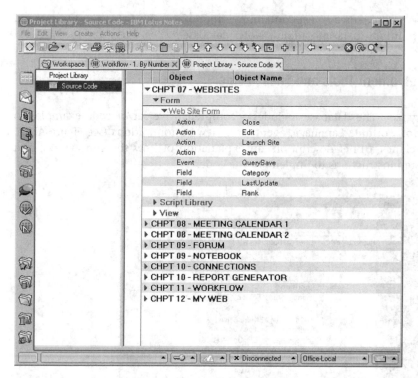

Figure A.11   Source code for all projects in this publication

Installing a Notes Database

Before installing or trying any of the sample Lotus Notes database applications, we recommend that you thoroughly review the "About the Developer's Toolbox" section in this chapter as well as the corresponding chapter information. Follow these steps to install one of the Lotus Notes database applications:

Step 1. Open the database. Locate the developer's toolbox folder and double-click on the desired database.

Step 2. Create a cross certificate. The first time you open a database, you will be prompted to create a cross certificate. This is a digital certificate that enables Lotus Notes applications created in one domain to be accessed from another domain. Click **Yes** when a message similar to the one in Figure A.12 is displayed.

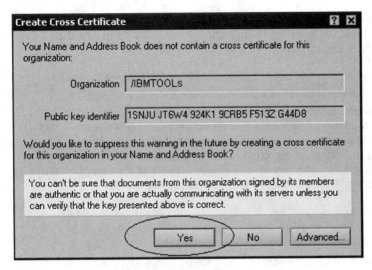

Figure A.12   Example of the "Create Cross Certificate" message

After clicking **Yes**, a digital certificate will be added to your Lotus Notes address book in the "Certificates" section and can be deleted at any time without impacting your Lotus Notes client. See Chapter 19, "Security," for additional information relating to cross certification.

Step 3.   When the database is open, you can create a new copy of the database by selecting the **File > Database > New Copy** menu options. This will enable you to play with or modify the design of the database. A dialog box similar to Figure A.13 will display.

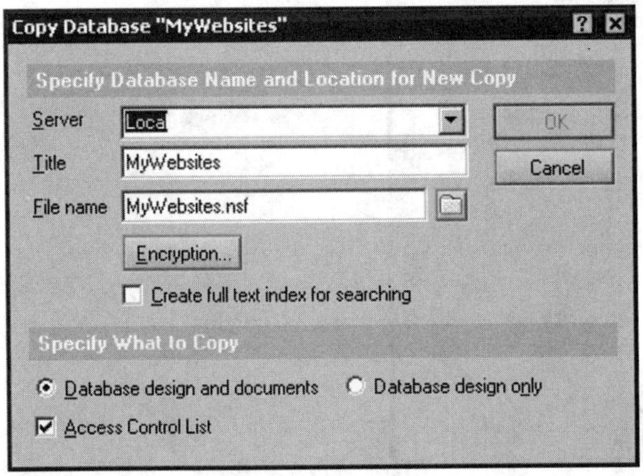

Figure A.13   Example of the "New Copy" dialog for copying databases

Step 4. Optionally, set the server location, database title, and filename values. If you prefer to create the database on a server, change the **Server** value from **Local** to a valid Domino server. Click **OK** to create a new copy of the database.

> **NOTE**
>
> It's important to understand that the default access level for the database is set to "Manager." This means that anyone may add or delete documents. It also allows anyone with access to the Domino Designer client to modify the database design. Be sure to update the ACL settings to control who can add, delete, and modify aspects of the database. See Chapter 19 for additional information regarding the ACL.

> **NOTE**
>
> You may receive "Execution Security Alert" statements the first time you run some of the database applications (see Figure A.14). When received, you can review who "signed" the database and the "action" to be performed. Select the **Start trusting the signer to execute this action** option and **OK** to continue.

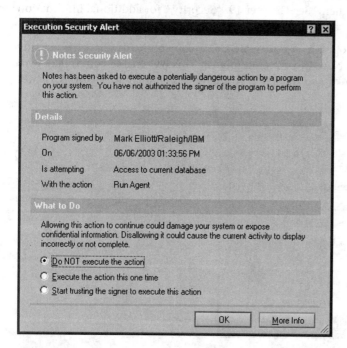

Figure A.14   Example Execution Security Alert message

Appendix B

IBM® Lotus® Notes® and Domino® —What's Next?

Every release of Lotus Notes and Domino has included improvements that enable IBM customers to increase their organizational productivity while preserving forward compatibility. This long-standing tradition of product enhancement and commitment to customers continues in the next major release of Lotus Notes and Domino.

Slated for early 2007, the next major release of Lotus Notes and Domino continues the tradition of added value and incremental improvement—a tradition that helps you get the most out of this release while preserving your significant investment in your Lotus Notes and Domino enterprise resources.

This appendix describes many of the features you can expect to see in this next release and provides Lotus developers with a look at the expanded developmental potential provided in Lotus Notes and Domino 8.[1] Version 8 extends Lotus Notes capabilities with its support of new programming options and techniques. It enables developers and organizations to innovate by building powerful composite applications and cross-platform solutions. Best of all, developers can continue to use their Lotus Notes and Domino skills and organizational assets while enjoying the option of extending those skills and assets to the realm of composite applications.

Composite applications can surface in the Lotus Notes client (also referred to as the rich client), as Lotus Notes 8 supports both the Lotus Domino and Eclipse platforms. Lotus Notes and Domino 8 also contains major improvements to mail, calendar, and contact management functions. Lotus Notes and Domino 8 also introduces activity-centric computing.

Major themes of the Lotus Notes and Domino 8 release include:

- **Improved user experience**—A major goal of Lotus Notes and Domino 8 is a simplified and more intuitive user model. For example, the redesigned mail UI supports increased use of topic threading to simplify mail management and combat the flood of incoming mail. Lotus Notes and Domino 8 also includes major improvements in contact management that make finding and managing personal contacts easier.

- **Activity-centric computing**—Based on an idea developed in IBM Research laboratories, activity-centric computing is based on the premise of moving artifacts out of email, file systems, and other repositories, and associating them with an "activity." An activity is thus a heterogeneous collection of project artifacts that might include Lotus Notes documents, word processing files, spreadsheets, chat transcripts, screenshots, purchase orders, and so on. These artifacts are collected hierarchically into a thread with access control.

  You can create an Activity that represents an *ad hoc* process. For example, people involved in a project such as a product rollout, an RFP, or other collaborative effort can manage the varied information related to the project by viewing the project as an activity. Email threads, chat logs, documents, meeting minutes, Web content, and voice messages can be collected, managed, and accessed in one place: the activity. By placing the focus on completing a task or process, activity-centric computing provides a logical and more natural way for a group to collaborate.

- **Composite application support by Lotus Notes**—A composite application is a collection of business-process-targeted components that are loosely coupled and aggregated into a unified application. Individual components can be Lotus Notes applications, Java™-based Eclipse components, HTML Web page components, IBM WebSphere® Portal portlets, as well as other types. The ability to concisely display information derived from a variety of such sources is a hallmark of a composite application.

- **Open Document Format (ODF) support**—Lotus Notes and Domino 8 users can create, manage, edit, and import documents in ODF. Supporting ODF provides the ability to access, use, and maintain documents over the long term, without concern about end-of-life uncertainties or perpetual licensing and royalty fees. IBM productivity tools can also import and edit Microsoft® Office documents and export those documents to ODF for sharing with other ODF-compliant applications and solutions.

- **Server-managed client**—This technology allows an administrator to lock down the Lotus Notes 8 client so that only plug-ins (code) pushed from the server can be run on the client, promoting a highly controlled and security-rich environment. This level of manageability allows the administrator to control what is on the desktop and not worry about client configuration inconsistencies, Java Virtual Machine (JVM) versioning issues, DLLs availability, and so forth. Additionally, this fine-grained control enables the administrator to apply bug fixes and patches without physically accessing the desktop. The administrator can now roll out changes to clients in an efficient, low-cost, and speedy manner.

Developer-Specific Enhancements

Of most interest to the developer, however, are Lotus Notes and Domino 8 enhancements related to building applications. And here the story is rich. Lotus Notes and Domino 8 tools support the building of composite applications for both Lotus Notes client software and for WebSphere Portal (browser) delivery. Using these tools in conjunction with other IBM Workplace™ tools, you can craft a Lotus Notes application, a portlet, an Eclipse component, and a composite application to help improve your organizational productivity. These tools include:

- **Lotus Domino Designer**—Lotus Notes and Domino 8 updates Lotus Domino Designer to support user-defined component interaction (loose coupling), when a Lotus Notes application is used as a component in composite application. You can enable this functionality through the familiar Lotus Domino Designer user interface and also with new LotusScript APIs.

  Lotus Domino Designer also provides new design elements to let you easily create Web service consumers in a Lotus Notes application using LotusScript or Java. These Web service consumers can run on the Lotus Domino server and Lotus Notes client, and they support the move to Service Oriented Architecture (SOA) prevalent in modern application design.

  The third major addition to Lotus Domino Designer is the refined application support for the optional IBM DB2® software integration. This functionality allows you to expose Lotus Notes data to be used relationally. It also makes access to relational data possible from a Lotus Notes client or a from a Web browser.

- **Composite Application Editor**—This Lotus Notes and Domino 8 feature enables you to assemble and edit composite applications, and to specify wiring among the components in the composite application to supply loose coupling. You can use this editor to build and modify composite applications stored on a Lotus Domino server or on WebSphere Portal.

These tools and others are discussed in greater detail later in this appendix.

What Is a Composite Application?

Most users require access to multiple applications in order to achieve their business objectives. Until recently, sequentially accessing applications to complete a business process has been the norm. Now, however, there is a better way. A new breed of application—the composite application—enables individual applications to work together in ways that support business objectives.

Figure B.1 illustrates what a typical composite application might look like. Here a Lotus Notes Corporate Customer application is "wired" to an Account Manager application that accesses data from a Web server as well as a Sales History application that surfaces information from the company ERP system.

Figure B.1   Composite application accessed through Lotus Notes 8[2]

Selecting an alternate customer in the Corporate Customer component forces the other application components to update and display documents that correspond to the newly selected customer. In essence, components in this composite communicate with each other based on user input. The net result is a more holistic approach to the business process of managing a customer base.

To make the assembly of this new breed of business applications easy, IBM has included composite application features in Lotus Notes and Domino 8. A number of business capabilities, surfaced as "components," can be brought together in one visual composition. These components are wired together so that information and data can flow between the components and run within an environment that defines and captures the business context.

This approach is unique because it not only combines the business components but does so with respect to user identity, business context, and the user's role with respect to that business context.

Benefits for Lotus Notes and Domino Customers

Productivity of workers is a top concern among all businesses today. Lotus Notes and Domino has been instrumental in defining the concepts of collaborative applications that drive improved productivity in teams of people. This capability is further enhanced with the introduction of composite applications. With composite applications, IT organizations are able to quickly capture and reuse (as components) the investments they have already made in Lotus Notes and Domino applications. In addition, the composite application framework is based on open standards, making it possible to integrate Lotus Notes and Domino applications with other line-of-business or enterprise applications systems (SAP, PeopleSoft, and so on). The ability to capture existing applications as components and to combine and recombine their capabilities means that composite applications can now directly target specific business challenges in a way that is much more effective than any "off the shelf" software solution.

Benefits for Lotus Notes and Domino Programmers

Getting started with composite applications will be quite natural for IBM Lotus Domino developers. Using what they already know about building Lotus Domino applications, developers can create composites that exhibit synergistic behavior and add important value to their organization.

New attributes have been added to form fields and to view columns in Lotus Domino Designer. These attributes allow data from one Lotus Notes application to be exposed to the interconnection mechanism called "property broker." In addition, you can define "actions" with arguments (like lookup customer) that expose the operations of the component. By wiring exposed data elements of one application to the actions of another application, the Lotus Domino application designer can create comprehensive business applications from a multiplicity of Domino databases.

Composite Application Development Tools

IBM provides several tools to help you build composite application components and to aggregate those components into a composite application. These tools include:

- **Lotus Domino Designer**—WYSIWYG script-based tool for building Lotus Domino applications. Scripting language is LotusScript. (Included in Lotus Notes and Domino 8.)
- **Application Program Interfaces (APIs)**—For greater flexibility and power, developers can make use of the rich and well-documented APIs of Lotus Notes and Domino 8. These APIs allow you to work directly in languages such as Java, C, or C++. (Included in Lotus Notes and Domino 8.)
- **IBM Workplace Designer**—WYSIWYG script-based tool for building Workplace applications. Scripting language is JavaScript. Uses data models and paradigms similar to Lotus Domino Designer to allow non-J2EE developers to create J2EE components for use with IBM Workplace and WebSphere Portal products, plus the Lotus Notes rich client. Based on Eclipse 3.0, this tool is integrated with WebSphere Portal, IBM Workplace Collaboration Services, and IBM Workplace Services Express.

For assembling a composite application, developers have two choices:

- **Composite Application Editor**—A Lotus Notes and Domino 8 rich client feature that allows developers and line-of-business users to assemble components into a composite application and to set up inter-component communication via wires. This feature can be used to build and edit composite applications stored on the Lotus Domino server and to build and edit composite applications plus composite application templates on WebSphere Portal.
- **IBM Application Editor**—Browser-based feature available in WebSphere Portal and Workplace Collaboration Services. This feature allows developers and line-of-business users to build and modify composite applications and composite application templates. Also provides role-based portlet and page access and permission management functions.

The following section takes a closer look at several of these tools, how they are used, and the skills required to use them.

IBM Lotus Domino Designer

In the Lotus Notes and Domino 8 release, Lotus Domino Designer maintains the familiar user interface but has been enhanced to provide developer support for composite applications. While your current Lotus Notes applications can be used unchanged in composite applications for the Lotus Notes client, you can also use new features of Lotus Domino Designer to enhance your current Lotus Notes applications to take advantage of the component interaction functionality of composite applications.

Component interaction for the specific composite application is defined when the composite application is assembled and wired, but it depends on properties and actions previously defined when the individual components were developed. As Lotus Domino Designer continues as the primary development tool for Lotus Notes and Domino applications, you use Lotus Domino Designer to specify the properties and actions for Lotus Notes components.

In Lotus Notes and Domino 8, Lotus Domino Designer provides new property box options plus new LotusScript classes, methods, and properties to allow the Lotus Notes developer to easily define the properties and actions for a Lotus Notes component.

IBM Workplace Designer

If your background is in Lotus Domino programming, think of Workplace Designer as a tool for providing Lotus Domino Designer-type application development functionality to the IBM Workplace family of products.

In fact, those familiar with Lotus Domino Designer will notice similarities with many IBM Workplace Designer features and concepts. This is not coincidental; Workplace Designer was created with the Lotus Domino Designer in mind. This allows experienced Lotus Domino developers to leverage existing skills to quickly create new applications for IBM Workplace products.

Workplace Designer is a scripting tool based on JavaScript, but because Lotus Domino Designer shares the same views, data connections, and logic, Lotus Domino developers are able to build components for the Workplace family of products using methods with which they are familiar. Figure B.2 illustrates the Lotus Domino Designer-like Workplace Designer user interface.

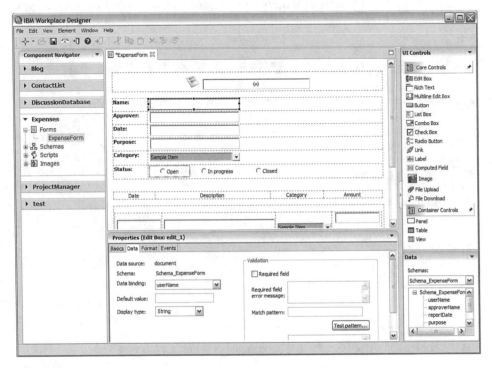

Figure B.2   User interface of IBM Workplace Designer 2.6[3]

Workplace Designer is based on Eclipse and has many of the features usually associated with Eclipse-based products, including a central page designer surrounded by palettes and navigators. This is a fully functional component development environment, with drag-and-drop support of controls onto the page, and an events editor, with which you can create JavaScript event handlers and specify whether they are to be executed on the client or on the server.

IBM Application Editor Tool

Every WebSphere Portal composite application is derived initially from a composite application template. Composite application templates allow users with proper permissions to create composite applications easily in a self-serve model. A composite application template includes the aggregation of components, pages, page layouts, application roles, role mapping, and points of variability to be applied when a new composite application is created from the template. Composite application templates can also be edited by users with proper permissions.

Figure B.3 illustrates how components are placed on a page through the IBM Application Editor. You use this editor to create or modify a composite application or a composite application template.

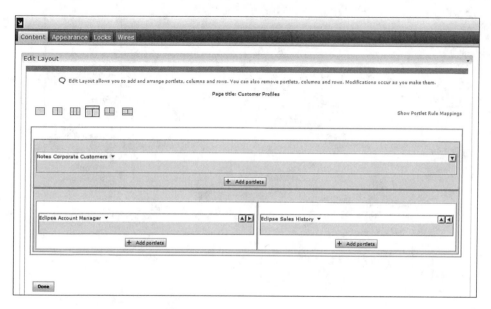

Figure B.3   Application Editor feature that is accessed through a Web browser[3]

Application Editor is the tool of choice for the less technical line-of-business user. These folks need to create applications quickly and simply, and they need an application development tool that is intuitive, easy to use, and requires no programming.

For example, assuming they have access rights to the application template, users can modify the template by selecting it. The Application Editor feature then lets the user add, delete, or relocate components on the page.

Under the covers, an application template is a representation of the application in XML and is used to provide an instance of the application. Each WebSphere Portal composite application template has roles that map to the various pages and components. Each composite application instance inherits these initial roles from the template, and these roles can then be assigned to groups or individuals by the application owner, thereby defining the access to the composite application and permissions of the users.

The Application Editor feature also allows you to modify the roles for a composite application instance and the role mapping to pages, components, and other composite application permissions.

IBM Workplace Collaboration Services includes a set of preconfigured application templates targeted at specific business processes, including discussion, document library, chat room, and team project. The templates are managed through a template catalog available on WebSphere Portal. You can modify these templates to suit user requirements, or you can create new templates.

Benefits provided by the Application Editor tool include:

- **Opportunity for cost reduction**—Costs associated with the development of collaborative applications are typically reduced because applications can be built by a line-of-business user via a browser. Costs can be further reduced by encouraging reuse of existing applications, such as SAP, Siebel, Lotus Notes and Domino, and so on.
- **Speed**—Time-to-value is reduced by reuse and modification of templates.
- **Standardization**—Best practices are promoted by encapsulation of known processes and patterns in templates.
- **Self-Service**—IT costs can be reduced by the self-service administration of applications by the business user.
- **Fast Adoption**—The learning curve is easier because the tools are similar to those available in WebSphere Portal.

Composite Application Editor

The Composite Application Editor available in Lotus Notes and Domino 8 is a rich client feature that allows you to assemble and edit composite applications. Composite application components can include Lotus Notes databases, portlets from IBM WebSphere Portal, or Eclipse components for rich clients designed using a tool such as IBM Workplace Designer. The integration of information from multiple business components provides application users with content specifically geared to their business roles and tasks.

Figure B.4 illustrates the Composite Application Editor rich client feature used to edit a composite application.

In this figure, the Composite Application Editor feature has been used to place three components into the composite. The components are selected from the component palette on the right-hand side and placed on the page through drag and drop. You can also modify the properties of the components on the selected page.

Components can be reused in different composite applications for flexible quick starts to projects without reliance on administrator support. A composite application can be hosted on either a Lotus Domino server or on WebSphere Portal. No matter where it resides, you can edit the application using the Composite Application Editor.

Figure B.4   Composite Application Editor user interface[2]

WebSphere Portal-based composite applications are listed in the Applications Catalog. Composite application templates reside in the Template Library and, using the Composite Application Editor, you can see the composite applications and application templates that you can access and edit.

Wiring Components Together

Application components interact with each other via wires. Lotus Notes and Domino supports the wiring technology used by WebSphere Portal. Wires provide a means for passing values among the components in a composite application. A single component can have multiple wires attached to it, and components can be wired together in a one-to-one or one-to-many fashion.

The wiring interface allows you to configure connections, or wires, between components at design time. At run time, property broker functionality allows properties to be exchanged automatically using the preconfigured wires. As a result, components on the page can react in an integrated and unified manner to the user's actions.

The wiring interface is a visual representation that shows you the existing connections between components in an application. It also shows you the properties from one component that can connect to another component. If a match is available between two components, you can create a wire between the two components.

Using the wiring interface, you can:

- Create a new wire between components. A wire can link components in a one-to-one or one-to-many relationship.
- Edit an existing wire.
- Delete a wire.

Components can also be wired so that they exchange properties across pages in a multi-page composite application.

The Template Library

The Template Library available in WebSphere Portal and Workplace Collaboration Services is where you manage application templates, create a new template, or import a template. You can start to work initially with the Blank Template. Application templates define the properties, page layout, roles, and parameters of composite applications belonging to a particular category. The template also defines the components that are deployed on the pages of an application. From templates, you can create multiple applications that share a common definition and customize them for different teams and communities of users. Available templates are listed in the Application Template Library (see Figure B.5).

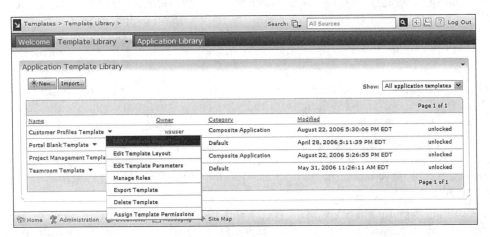

Figure B.5 Application Template Library in WebSphere Portal version 6[3]

The Template Library is where you and other users can view all templates that are available for assembling applications along with their locked/unlocked status (a template is locked if another user is editing it). Modifying a template does not alter composite applications that already exist. Template changes affect only the applications that you create after you save template changes.

For each template displayed in the Template Library, you can display its drop-down menu to see the choices available to you for editing it. Your access rights to work with application templates determine which of these actions are available to you. Possible actions include:

- Edit Template Properties
- Edit Template Layout
- Edit Template Parameters
- Manage Roles
- Export Template
- Delete Template
- Assign Template Permissions

While you edit an application template, the template file is automatically locked so that no one else can make changes to it. The locked status of the application template displays as plain text in the status column for the Application Template Library. You can unlock the template if you are the template owner or an administrator; otherwise, the lock is released when the editing session ends.

The Application Library

The Application Library (see Figure B.6) available in WebSphere Portal and Workplace Collaboration Services is the page where you see the composite application catalog. The application catalog is where you can view and open composite applications and create new ones from application templates. You open an application by clicking its name in the catalog.

If the composite application has been built using the Lotus Notes client and rich client standards, it will be accessible for editing from the WebSphere Portal Catalog using the Lotus Notes File—Open command.

Three applications are displayed in this figure. In addition, the template on which the application is based, the owner of the application, and the date of the last update to the application are also displayed. You open an application for editing by clicking its name in the leftmost column.

Composite applications on WebSphere Portal and Workplace Collaboration Services are assembled from templates that define the properties, page layout, and roles of each application instance. The membership portlet of a composite application lists the members of the application by their assigned roles, and the components of the application are deployed on one or more application pages. After you open an application, you can customize it and the current application page. Your access rights to work with the application and its pages determine the actions available to you.

In summary, components are the building blocks of a composite application and work in concert to address a business need. Components in a composite application can be portlets from WebSphere Portal, Eclipse components, and Lotus Notes components. All components in an application must reside on a page.

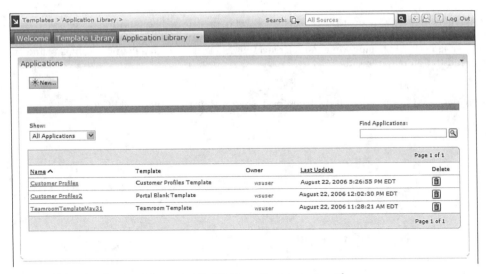

Figure B.6 Application Library in WebSphere Portal version 6[3]

Adding Value into the Future

With its release of Lotus Notes and Domino 8, IBM validates the importance, value, and widespread acceptance of the Lotus Notes client experience. IBM's approach to Lotus Notes with the version 8 release is truly evolutionary in nature. By refining and enhancing existing Lotus Notes UIs and functions, version 8 adds value for existing customers while preserving their ongoing investment in their Lotus Domino infrastructure and applications.

At the same time, Lotus Notes and Domino 8 extends Lotus Notes capabilities with its support of new programming options and techniques. It enables developers to innovate by building powerful composite applications and cross-platform solutions through existing Lotus Notes applications and other emerging technologies. And, from the developer's perspective, Lotus Notes and Domino 8 represents a potential opportunity to extend skills into new arenas (Web, WebSphere Portal, and so on) while working in a familiar and friendly environment.

Endnotes

[1] As of the time of publication, Lotus Notes and Domino 8 have not been released and, accordingly, this appendix reflects IBM's then-current product plans and strategy, which are subject to change by IBM at any time.

Index